Learning and Soft Computing

Learning and Soft Computing
Support Vector Machines, Neural Networks, and Fuzzy Logic Models

Vojislav Kecman

A Bradford Book
The MIT Press
Cambridge, Massachusetts
London, England

This book was set in Times New Roman on a 3B2 system by Asco Typesetters, Hong Kong.

Library of Congress Cataloging-in-Publication Data

Kecman, V. (Vojislav), 1948–
  Learning and soft computing: support vector machines, neural networks,
and fuzzy logic models / Vojislav Kecman.
    p.   cm. — (Complex adaptive systems)
  "A Bradford book."
  Includes bibliographical references and index.
  ISBN 978-0-262-11255-0 (hc: alk. paper) – 978-0-262-52790-3 (pb: alk. paper)
  1. Soft computing. I. Title. II. Series.
QA76.9.S63 K43   2001
006.3—dc21   00-027506

The MIT Press is pleased to keep this title available in print by manufacturing single copies, on demand, via digital printing technology.

Мојим чєститим, плємєнитим и храьрим Крајишницима.
To my honest, noble, and heroic Krayina people.

Contents

Preface

This is a book about learning from experimental data and about transferring human knowledge into analytical models. Performing such tasks belongs to soft computing. Neural networks (NNs) and support vector machines (SVMs) are the mathematical structures (models) that stand behind the idea of learning, and fuzzy logic (FL) systems are aimed at embedding structured human knowledge into workable algorithms. However, there is no clear boundary between these two modeling approaches. The notions, basic ideas, fundamental approaches, and concepts common to these two fields, as well as the differences between them, are discussed in some detail. The sources of this book are course material presented by the author in undergraduate and graduate lectures and seminars, and the research of the author and his graduate students. The text is therefore both class- and practice-tested.

The primary idea of the book is that not only is it useful to treat support vector machines, neural networks, and fuzzy logic systems as parts of a connected whole but it is in fact necessary. Thus, a systematic and unified presentation is given of these seemingly different fields—learning from experimental data and transferring human knowledge into mathematical models.

Each chapter is arranged so that the basic theory and algorithms are illustrated by practical examples and followed by a set of problems and simulation experiments. In the author's experience, this approach is the most accessible, pleasant, and useful way to master this material, which contains many new (and potentially difficult) concepts. To some extent, the problems are intended to help the reader acquire technique, but most of them serve to illustrate and develop further the basic subject matter of the chapter. The author feels that this structure is suitable both for a textbook used in a formal course and for self-study.

How should one read this book? A kind of newspaper reading, starting with the back pages, is potentially viable but not a good idea. However, there are useful sections at the back. There is an armory of mathematical weaponry and tools containing a lot of useful and necessary concepts, equations, and methods. More or less frequent trips to the back pages (chapters 8 and 9) are probably unavoidable. But in the usual way of books, one should most likely begin with this preface and continue reading to the end of chapter 1. This first chapter provides a pathway to the learning and soft computing field, and after that, readers may continue with any chapters they feel will be useful. Note, however, that chapters 3 and 4 are connected and should be read in that order. (See the figure, which represents the connections between the chapters.)

In senior undergraduate classes, the order followed was chapters 1, 3, 4, 5, and 6, and chapters 8 and 9 when needed. For graduate classes, chapter 2 on support vector machines is not omitted, and the order is regular, working directly through chapters 1–6.

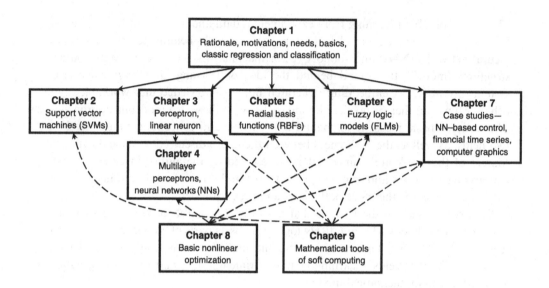

There is some redundancy in this book for several reasons. The whole subject of this book is a blend of different areas. The various fields bound together here used to be separate, and today they are amalgamated in the broad area of learning and soft computing. Therefore, in order to present each particular segment of the learning and soft computing field, one must follow the approaches, tools, and terminology in each specific area. Each area was developed separately by researchers, scientists, and enthusiasts with different backgrounds, so many things were repeated. Thus, in this presentation there are some echoes but, the author believes, not too many. He agrees with the old Latin saying, *Repetio est mater studiorum*—Repetition is the mother of learning. This provides the second explanation of "redundancy" in this volume.

This book is divided into nine chapters. Chapter 1 gives examples of applications, presents the basic tools of soft computing (neural networks, support vector machines, and fuzzy logic models), reviews the classical problems of approximation of multivariate functions, and introduces the standard statistical approaches to regression and classification that are based on the knowledge of probability-density functions.

Chapter 2 presents the basics of statistical learning theory when there is no information about the probability distribution but only experimental data. The VC dimension and structural risk minimization are introduced. A description is given of the SVM learning algorithm based on quadratic programming that leads to parsimonious SVMs, that is, NNs or SVMs having a small number of hidden layer neurons. This parsimony results from sophisticated learning that matches model capacity to data complexity. In this way, good generalization, meaning the performance of the SVM on previously unseen data, is assured.

Chapter 3 deals with two early learning units—the perceptron and the linear neuron (adaline)—as well as with single-layer networks. Five different learning algorithms for the linear activation function are presented. Despite the fact that the linear neuron appears to be very simple, it is the constitutive part of almost all models treated here and therefore is a very important processing unit. The linear neuron can be looked upon as a graphical (network) representation of classical linear regression and linear classification (discriminant analysis) schemes.

A genuine neural network (a multilayer perceptron)—one that comprises at least one hidden layer having neurons with nonlinear activation functions—is introduced in chapter 4. The error-correction type of learning, introduced for single-layer networks in chapter 3, is generalized, and the gradient-based learning method known as error backpropagation is discussed in detail here. Also shown are some of the generally accepted heuristics while training multilayer perceptrons.

Chapter 5 is concerned with regularization networks, which are better known as radial basis function (RBF) networks. The notion of ill-posed problems is discussed as well as how regularization leads to networks whose activation functions are radially symmetric. Details are provided on how to find a parsimonious radial basis network by applying the orthogonal least squares approach. Also explored is a linear programming approach to subset (basis function or support vector) selection that, similar to the QP based algorithm for SVMs training, leads to parsimonious NNs and SVMs.

Fuzzy logic modeling is the subject of chapter 6. Basic notions of fuzzy modeling are introduced—fuzzy sets, relations, compositions of fuzzy relations, fuzzy inference, and defuzzification. The union, intersection, and Cartesian product of a family of sets are described, and various properties are established. The similarity between, and sometimes even the equivalence of, RBF networks and fuzzy models is noted in detail. Finally, fuzzy additive models (FAMs) are presented as a simple yet powerful fuzzy modeling technique. FAMs are the most popular type of fuzzy models in applications today.

Chapter 7 presents three case studies that show the beauty and strength of these modeling tools. Neural networks–based control systems, financial time series prediction, and computer graphics by applying neural networks or fuzzy models are discussed at length.

Chapter 8 focuses on the most popular classical approaches to nonlinear optimization, which is the crucial part of learning from data. It also describes the novel massive search algorithms known as genetic algorithms or evolutionary computing.

Chapter 9 contains specific mathematical topics and tools that might be helpful for understanding the theoretical aspects of soft models, although these concepts and tools are not covered in great detail. It is supposed that the reader has some knowledge of probability theory, linear algebra, and vector calculus. Chapter 9 is designed only for easy reference of properties and notation.

A few words about the accompanying software are in order. All the software is based on MATLAB. All programs run in versions 5 and 6. The author designed and created the complete `aproxim` directory, the entire SVM toolbox for classification and regression, the multilayer perceptron routine that includes the error backpropagation learning, all first versions of core programs for RBF models for n-dimensional inputs, and some of the core fuzzy logic models. Some programs date back as far as 1992, so they may be not very elegant. However, all are effective and perform their allotted tasks as well as needed.

The author's students took an important part in creating user-friendly programs with attractive pop-up menus and boxes. At the same time, those students were from different parts of the world, and the software was developed in different countries— Yugoslavia, the United States, Germany, and New Zealand. Most of the software was developed in New Zealand. These facts are mentioned to explain why readers may find program notes and comments in English, Serbian,[1] and German. (However, all the basic comments are written in English.) We deliberately left these lines in various languages as nice traces of the small modern world. Without the work of these multilingual, ingenious, diligent students and colleagues, many of the programs would be less user-friendly and, consequently, less adequate for learning purposes.

As mentioned earlier, most of the core programs were developed by the author. Around them, many pieces of user-friendly software were developed as follows. In writing several versions of a program based on n-dimensional radial basis Gaussian functions Srboljub Jovanović and Lothar Niemetz took part. Oliver Wohlfarth and Kirčo Popčanovski wrote the first appealing lines of the genetic algorithm for learning in neural networks. This program was further developed by Volker Müller for static problems and by Joachim Löchner for dynamic ones. Löchner based some parts of his pop-up menus on Matthias Schanzenbach's and Herbert Vollert's program. These programs are not supplied at present. We wait to see the response to the basic routines first. Paulo Jorge Furtado Correia developed the first versions of the neural networks in C, but these had to be omitted from the MATLAB-based software. Weihong Wang wrote parts of modular networks. However, modular networks are not covered in this book, so a few software pieces on this topic are being held for a future edition. Thorsten Rommel modified and created original programs for neural networks–based control. He wrote software for recursive least squares for on-line learning of the output layer weights. Many results in section 7.1 are obtained by applying his programs. Dieter Reusing developed a few user-friendly routines for the application of five methods on the linear neuron in section 3.2.2. Chang Bing Wang was took a crucial part in developing routines for computer graphics. The graphs and animations in section 7.3 are results of his curiosity. Faimeen Shah developed appealing pieces of software for financial time series analysis. He based parts of his program on routines from Löchner but made large steps in designing user-friendly software aimed specifically at financial time series analysis. All graphs in section 7.2 are obtained by using his routines. David Simunic and Geoffrey Taylor developed a user-friendly fuzzy logic environment as a part of their final-year project. The reader will enjoy taking the first steps in fuzzy modeling using this software with good-looking frames and windows. The author took part in mathematical solutions during the design of relational matrices. Routines for fuzzy logic control of mobile robots were developed by Wei Ming Chen and Gary Chua. Zoran Vojinović is developing applications of neural networks in company resources management, and Jonathan Robinson is using SVM for image compression. Finally, Tim Wu and Ivana Hadžić just became members of the learning and soft modeling group in the Department of Mechanical Engineering, University of Auckland. Wu's part is on chunking algorithms in SVM learning, and Hadžić is investigating the linear programming approach in designing sparse NNs or SVMs. All the software that corresponds to this book is for fair use only and free for all educational purposes. It is not for use in any kind of commercial activity.

The *Solutions Manual*, which contains the solutions to the problems in this book, has been prepared for instructors who wish to refer to the author's methods of solution. It is available from the publisher (The MIT Press, Computer Science, 5 Cambridge Center, Cambridge, MA 02142-1493, U.S.A.). The MATLAB programs needed for the simulation experiments can be retrieved at ftp://mitpress.mit.edu/kecman/software. This files can also be retrieved from the book's site, www.support-vector.ws. The password is `learnscvk`.

The author is very grateful to his students, colleagues, and friends for their unceasing enthusiasm and support in the pursuit of knowledge in this tough and challenging field of learning and soft computing. A preliminary draft of this book was used in the author's senior undergraduate and graduate courses at various universities in Germany and New Zealand. The valuable feedback from the curious students who took these courses made many parts of this book easier to read. He thanks them for that. The author also warmly acknowledges the suggestions of all six unknown reviewers. He hopes that some parts of the book are more comprehensible because of their contributions.

The author thanks the University of Auckland's Research Committee for its support. As is always the case, he could have used much more money than was allotted to him, but he warmly acknowledges the tender support. The friendly atmosphere at the Department of Mechanical Engineering made the writing of this book easier than is typically the case with such an endeavor. The credit for the author's sentences being more understandable to English-speaking readers belongs partly to Emil Melnichenko, and the author thanks him. The author also thanks Douglas Sery and Deborah Cantor-Adams of The MIT Press for making the whole publishing process as smooth as possible. Their support and care in developing the manuscript, and in reviewing and editing it, are highly appreciated.

In one way or another, many people have been supportive during the author's work in the fascinating and challenging field of learning and soft computing. It is impossible to acknowledge by name all these friends, and he gives sincere thanks to them all. He is, however, particularly indebted to James H. Williams, Petar V. Kokotović, Zoran Gajić, Rolf Isermann, Peter Blessing, Heinz-Werner Röder, Stanoje Bingulac, and Dobrivoje Popović.

And, Ana was always around.

Introduction

In this book no suppositions are made about preexisting analytical models. There are, however, no limits to human curiosity and the need for mathematical models. Thus, when devising algebraic, differential, discrete, or any other models from first principles is not feasible, one seeks other avenues to obtain analytical models. Such models are devised by solving two cardinal problems in modern science and engineering:

• Learning from experimental data (examples, samples, measurements, records, patterns, or observations) by neural networks (NNs) and support vector machines (SVMs)
• Embedding existing structured human knowledge (experience, expertise, heuristics) into workable mathematics by fuzzy logic models (FLMs).

These problems seem to be very different, and in practice that may well be the case. However, after NN or SVM modeling from experimental data is complete, and after the knowledge transfer into an FLM is finished, these two models are mathematically very similar or even equivalent. This equivalence, discussed in section 6.2, is a very attractive property, and it may well be used to the benefit of both fields.

The need for a book about these topics is clear. Recently, many new "intelligent" products (theoretical approaches, software and hardware solutions, concepts, devices, systems, and so on) have been launched on the market. Much effort has been made at universities and R&D departments around the world, and numerous papers have been written on how to apply NNs, FLMs, and SVMs, and the related ideas of learning from data and embedding structured human knowledge. These two concepts and associated algorithms form the new field of soft computing. They have been recognized as attractive alternatives to the standard, well-established "hard comput-ing" paradigms. Traditional hard computing methods are often too cumbersome for today's problems. They always require a precisely stated analytical model and often a lot of computation time. Soft computing techniques, which emphasize gains in understanding system behavior in exchange for unnecessary precision, have proved to be important practical tools for many contemporary problems. Because they are universal approximators of any multivariate function, NNs, FLMs, and SVMs are of particular interest for modeling highly nonlinear, unknown, or partially known complex systems, plants, or processes. Many promising results have been reported. The whole field is developing rapidly, and it is still in its initial, exciting phase.

At the very beginning, it should be stated clearly that there are times when there is no need for these two novel model-building techniques. Whenever there is an ana-lytical closed-form model, using a reasonable number of equations, that can solve the given problem in a reasonable time, at reasonable cost, and with reasonable accuracy, there is no need to resort to learning from experimental data or fuzzy logic modeling. Today, however, these two approaches are vital tools when at least one of those criteria is not fulfilled. There are many such instances in contemporary science and engineering.

The title of the book gives only a partial description of the subject, mainly because the meaning of *learning* is variable and indeterminate. Similarly, the meaning of *soft computing* can change quickly and unpredictably. Usually, *learning* means acquiring knowledge about a previously unknown or little known system or concept. Adding that the knowledge will be acquired from experimental data yields the phrase *statistical learning*. Very often, the devices and algorithms that can learn from data are characterized as intelligent. The author wants to be cautious by stating that learning is only a part of intelligence, and no definition of intelligence is given here. This issue used to be, and still is, addressed by many other disciplines (notably neuroscience, biology, psychology, and philosophy). However, staying firmly in the engineering and science domain, a few comments on the terms *intelligent systems* or *smart machines* are now in order.

Without any doubt the human mental faculties of learning, generalizing, memorizing, and predicting should be the foundation of any intelligent artificial device or smart system. Many products incorporating NNs, SVMs, and FLMs already exhibit these properties. Yet we are still far away from achieving anything similar to human intelligence. Part of a machine's intelligence in the future should be an ability to cope with a large amount of noisy data coming simultaneously from different sensors. Intelligent devices and systems will also have to be able to plan under large uncertainties, to set the hierarchy of priorities, and to coordinate many different tasks simultaneously. In addition, the duties of smart machines will include the detection or early diagnosis of faults, in order to leave enough time for reconfiguration of strategies, maintenance, or repair. These tasks will be only a small part of the smart decision-making capabilities of the next generation of intelligent machines. It is certain that the techniques presented here will be an integral part of these future intelligent systems.

On Soft Computing

Soft computing is not a closed and clearly defined discipline at present. It includes an emerging and more or less established family of problem-stating and problem-solving methods that attempt to mimic the intelligence found in nature. Learning from experimental data (statistical learning) and fuzzy logic methods are two of the most important constituents of soft computing. In addition, there are, for example, genetic or evolutionary algorithms, probabilistic reasoning, fractals and chaos theories, and belief networks, but this book does not treat these methods in detail. Rather, it focuses on NNs and SVMs, which incorporate the ideas of learning from data, and FLMs, which are a tool for embedding structured human knowledge into an analytical model.

It was stated earlier that soft computing should mimic the intelligence found in nature. Then, what is the character of natural intelligence? Is it precise, quantitative, rigorous, and computational? Looking just at human beings, the most intelligent species, the answer is negative. We are very bad at calculations or at any kind of computing. A negligible percentage of human beings can multiply two three-digit numbers in their heads. The basic function of human intelligence is to ensure survival in nature, not to perform precise calculations. The human brain can process millions of visual, acoustic, olfactory, tactile, and motor data, and it shows astonishing abilities to learn from experience, generalize from learned rules, recognize patterns, and make decisions. It is in effect a very good engineering tool that performs these tasks as well as it can using ad hoc solutions (heuristics), approximations, low precision, or less generality, depending on the problem to be solved. We want to transfer some of these abilities into our models, algorithms, smart machines, and intelligent artificial systems in order to enable them to survive in highly technological environment, that is, to solve given tasks, based on previous experience, with reasonable accuracy at reasonable cost in a reasonable amount of time. Here is the important notion of trading off precision for costs.

The world around us is imprecise, uncertain, and randomly changing. However, we can cope with such an environment. The desire to mimic such coping leads to the basic premises and the guiding principles of soft computing. According to Zadeh (1994), the basic premises of soft computing are

- The real world is pervasively imprecise and uncertain.
- Precision and certainty carry a cost.

and the guiding principle of soft computing, which follows from these premises, is

Exploit tolerance for imprecision, uncertainty, and partial truth to achieve tractability, robustness, and low solution costs.

Both the premises and the guiding principle differ strongly from those in classical hard computing, which require precision, certainty, and rigor. However, since precision and certainty carry a cost, the soft computing approach to computation, reasoning, and decision making should exploit the tolerance for imprecision (inherent in human reasoning) when necessary. A long-standing tradition in science gives more respect to theories that are quantitative, formal, and precise than to those that are qualitative, informal, and approximate. Recently, however, the validity of this tradition has been challenged by the emergence of new desires (problems, needs) and efficient soft computing techniques to satisfy them. Many contemporary problems do not lend themselves to precise solutions within the framework of classical hard computing, for instance, recognition problems of all sorts (handwriting, speech, objects, images), computer graphics, mobile robot coordination, forecasting (weather, financial, or any other time series), and data compression, and combinatorial problems like "traveling salesman."

This last problem, which is concerned with finding an optimal route for a sales representative visiting thousands of cities, clearly shows a trade-off between precision and computing costs. For 100,000 cities and an accuracy within 0.75%, computing time amounts to seven months. Reducing the accuracy to within 1.0% lowers the computing time to just two days. An extreme reduction can be achieved for 1 million cities and an accuracy within 3.5%: the time needed to calculate the optimal route is just 3.5 hours (Zadeh 1994, paraphrasing *New York Times*, March 12, 1991).

Yet, another novel problem (Ho 1999) that replaces "the best for sure" with "good enough with high probability" belongs to the field of ordinal optimization. This "softening of the goal" considerably eases the computational burden in this problem; it is much easier to obtain a value within the top 5% than to get the best. Consider a search space of size $|\mathbf{w}| = 1$ billion, and take $N = 1000$ random samples. What is the probability that at least one sample will be in the top n? The answer is $1 - (1 - n/|\mathbf{w}|)^N$, which for the values chosen is equal to 0.01 for $n = 10,000$, or the top 0.001%, but decreases to 10^{-6} for $n = 1$. Thus, with a success probability of 0.01, approximately 100 trials are required to guarantee success, but an insistence on the best increases the number of trials by four orders of magnitude.

To be able to deal with such problems, there is often no choice but to accept solutions that are suboptimal and inexact. In addition, even when precise solutions can be obtained, their cost is generally much higher than that of solutions that are imprecise and yet yield results within the range of acceptability. Soft computing is not a mixture of NNs, SVMs, and FLMs but a discipline in which each of these constituents contributes a distinct methodology for addressing problems in its own domain, in a complementary rather than a competitive way. The common element of these three models is generalization, through nonlinear approximation and interpolation, in (usually) high-dimensional spaces. All three core soft computing techniques derive their power of generalization from approximating or interpolating to produce outputs from previously unseen inputs by using outputs from familiar (previously learned) inputs. This issue is presented and discussed at length throughout the book.

On Learning from Experimental Data

Attempting to incorporate humanlike abilities into software solutions is not an easy task. Only recently, after an attempt to analyze an ocean of data obtained by various sensors, it became clear how complex are the problems our senses routinely solve, and how difficult it is to replicate in software even the simplest aspects of human information processing. How, for example, can one make machines "see," where "see" means to recognize different objects and classify them into different classes. For smart machines to recognize or to make decisions, they must be trained first on a set of training examples. Each new smart machine (software) should be able to learn the problem in its areas of operations.

The whole learning part of this book (the first five chapters) shows how the two real-life problems of primary interest (classification and regression) can be reduced to approximation of a multivariate function. However, before considering the most relevant issues in statistical learning from experimental data, let us analyze a few ways in which human beings learn. (The following example paraphrases an example from Poggio and Girosi 1993.)

Consider the case of Jovo (pronounced "Yovo"), who leaves his homeland and moves to a country where everybody speaks some strange language (say, English). For the sake of generality, let us call the foreign country Foreignia. The first thing Jovo realizes is that he has to learn how to pronounce Foreignian words. His learning problem can be stated as follows: given a Foreignian word, find its pronunciation. Unlike in English, the problem is well defined in the Foreignian language in the sense that there is a unique map $f: X \rightarrow Y$ that maps every Foreignian word x to its Foreignian pronunciation $y = f(x)$, where X is the space of Foreignian words and Y is the space of Foreignian pronunciation. X and Y are also known, respectively, as the input and output spaces.

There are five options, or standard learning methods, for Jovo to solve this learning problem (the reader may want to compare her own experience in learning a foreign language):

1. Learn nothing.
2. Learn all the pronunciation rules.

3. Memorize all the word-pronunciation pairs in the Foreignian language.

4. Pick at random or choose the most frequent word-pronunciation pairs P, and learn (memorize) them.

5. Pick at random a set of P word-pronunciation pairs, and develop a theory (a good theory, a model) of the underlying mapping $y = f(x)$ in the Foreignian language.

Neither Jovo nor anyone else would be pleased with the first option. This is a trivial zero-learning solution, and since this is not a no-learning book, this alternative is of no further interest.

The second learning method means that Jovo should learn a complete set of pronunciation rules in the Foreignian language. This set of rules is almost completely described in Foreignian grammar books, and when applied to any word x it produces a pronunciation $f(x)$. Regrettably, the set of rules is extremely complicated and parts of the rules are hard to understand. There are also a number of exceptions, and very often applying some rule to a word x differs from the correct rule-based mapping $f(x)$. Learning the known underlying rules, meaning the ones described in grammar books $y_i = f(x_i)$, corresponds to first-principle model building. (This was not how the author learned foreign languages.)

The third alternative is to memorize the pronunciation of every single Foreignian word. However, there are two basic problems with such a look-up table approach. First, there are 800,000 words in the Foreignian language, and only about 150,000 of them are commonly used. Second, memory fades, and Jovo in common with everyone else keeps forgetting (unless he goes through the learning stage again) and cannot recover the forgotten word, not even approximately.

The fourth option is much closer to the standard problem in this book. Jovo builds a training data set $\mathcal{D} = \{(x_i, y_i) \in X \times Y\}$, $i = 1, P$, with the property that $y_i = f(x_i)$, and he is about to develop some theory (model) of the Foreignian language pronunciation rules. (P stands for the number of the training data pairs, i.e., the size of the training data set $\mathcal{D}$.) The simplest learning alternative or theory corresponds to the memorizing (the look-up table) of all provided training data pairs. It is an interpolative model or theory, which, however, does not learn the underlying mapping $y = f(x)$, and it fails whenever the new word is not from the training data set $\mathcal{D}$. In one way or another, this learning method resembles the classical artificial intelligence (AI) models.

In the fifth method, as in the fourth option, Jovo builds a training data set $\mathcal{D} = \{(x_i, y_i) \in X \times Y\}$, $i = 1, P$, that is, he knows how to pronounce a subset of the Foreignian words, but he wants to develop a good theory based upon the training pairs provided. He postulates, for example, that similar words should have similar pronunciations. In this way, when a new word appears, he finds pronunciations of similar words in the training data set and produces a pronunciation for the new word that is similar to the training data. Hence, Jovo builds a new approximate map (model) $f^*: X \to Y$, such that $f^*(x) \sim f(x)$ for $x \notin \mathcal{D}$, and $f^*(x) = f(x)$ for $x \in \mathcal{D}$. The last learning alternative (combined with some memorizing) is the one Jovo should apply to learn fluent Foreignian.

Note that each of the learning options would have a different implementation in software. The second one, where there is no training data set, would probably be a long list of IF-THEN rules. The third method is simple and not aesthetically appealing, and it does not allow for any noise in data. It requires a huge noiseless data set as well as an efficient structure for data retrieval. Currently, however, with compact and fast storage devices of high capacity, it does represent a feasible modeling process in this problem. Nevertheless, no human being is known to learn languages in this way.

The last learning option is close to the kind of learning from examples problem discussed in this book. Recall, however, that the important constituents required for this model to be a good one are as follows:

1. The size P of training data set $\mathcal{D}$ has to be sufficiently large. Having only a few hundred word-pronunciation pairs would be not enough. It is clear that the more training data pairs, the fewer will be the pronunciation mistakes. In other words, the number of errors is inversely proportional to the size of $\mathcal{D}$.

2. The assumption that similar words have similar pronunciations must hold. Stated differently, the mapping $f(x)$ and the model $f^*(x)$ are both assumed to be smooth.

3. The set of functions that models assumptions (1) and (2) has to be sufficiently powerful, that is, it should have enough modeling capacity to realistically represent the unknown mapping $f(x)$.

Learning from examples, as presented in this book, is similar to Jovo's problem in the fifth learning alternative.

In introducing the basic ideas of learning from experimental data, the author follows a theoretically sound approach as developed by Vapnik and Chervonenkis in their statistical learning theory and implemented by SVMs. NNs had a more heuristic origin. Paradigms of NN learning are discussed in detail in chapters 3, 4, and 5. This does not mean that NNs are of lesser value for not being developed from clear theoretical considerations. It just happens that their progress followed an experimental path, with a theory being evolved in the course of time. SVMs had a reverse development: from theory to implementation and experiments. It is interesting to note that the very strong theoretical underpinnings of SVMs did not make them widely appreciated at first. The publication of the first paper on SVMs by Vapnik and co-workers went largely unnoticed in 1992 because of a widespread belief in the statistical or machine learning community that, despite being theoretically appealing, SVMs were irrelevant for practical applications. SVMs were taken seriously only when very good results on practical learning benchmarks were achieved (in digit recognition, computer vision, and text categorization). Today, both data modeling tools (NNs and SVMs) show comparable results on the most popular benchmark problems. However, it happened that the theoretical status of SVMs made them an attractive and promising area of research. In its most reduced variant, the learning algorithm used in an SVM can be thought of as a new learning procedure for an RBF neural network or a fuzzy logic model. However, SVMs have many other highly esteemed properties, some of which are discussed in this book.

Thus, the learning problem setting is as follows: there is some unknown nonlinear dependency (mapping, function) $y = f(\mathbf{x})$ between some high-dimensional input vector $\mathbf{x}$ and scalar y or vector output $\mathbf{y}$. There is no information about the underlying joint probability functions. Thus, one must perform distribution-free learning. The only information available is a training data set $\mathcal{D} = \{(\mathbf{x}_i, y_i) \in X \times Y\}$, $i = 1, P$, where P stands for the number of the training data pairs and is therefore equal to the size of the training data set $\mathcal{D}$.

This problem is similar to classical statistical inference. However, there are several very important differences between the kinds of problems to be solved here and the kinds of problems that are the subject of investigation in classical statistics.

Classical statistical inference is based on three fundamental assumptions:

1. Data can be modeled by a set of linear in parameters functions; this is a foundation of a parametric paradigm in learning from experimental data.

2. In the most real-life problems, a stochastic component of data is the normal probability distribution law, that is, the underlying joint probability distribution is a Gaussian.

3. Because of the second assumption, the induction paradigm for parameter estimation is the maximum likelihood method, which is reduced to the minimization of the sum-of-error-squares cost function in most engineering applications.

All three assumptions on which the classical statistical paradigm relies turned out to be inappropriate for many contemporary real-life problems (Vapnik 1998) because of the following facts:

1. Modern problems are high-dimensional, and if the underlying mapping is not very smooth, the linear paradigm needs an exponentially increasing number of terms with

an increasing dimensionality of the input space X (an increasing number of independent variables). This is known as "the curse of dimensionality."

2. The underlying real-life data generation laws may typically be very far from the normal distribution, and a model builder must consider this difference in order to construct an effective learning algorithm,

3. From the first two points it follows that the maximum likelihood estimator (and consequently the sum-of-error-squares cost function) should be replaced by a new induction paradigm that is uniformly better, in order to model non-Gaussian distributions.

In addition, the new problem setting and inductive principle should be developed for sparse data sets containing a small number of training data pairs.

This book concentrates on nonlinear and nonparametric models as exemplified by NNs and SVMs. Here, *nonlinear* means two things. First, the model class will not be restricted to linear input-output maps, and second, the dependence of the cost function that measures the goodness of the model will be nonlinear with respect to the unknown parameters. This second nonlinearity is the part of modeling that causes most of the problems dealt within this book. *Nonparametric* does not mean that the models do not have parameters at all. On the contrary, their learning (selection, identification, estimation, or tuning) is the crucial issue here. However, unlike in classical statistical inference, the parameters are not predefined and their number depends on the training data used. In other words, parameters that define the capacity of the model are data-driven in such a way as to match the model capacity to the data complexity. This is a basic paradigm of structural risk minimization (SRM), introduced by Vapnik and Chervonenkis and their co-workers. The introductory explanations of SRM here closely follow Vapnik (1998).

Trying to accommodate methods for learning from experimental data to contemporary needs, Vapnik and Chervonenkis first improved the theory of empirical risk minimization (ERM) for pattern recognition problems. This included the general qualitative theory of generalization, with the necessary and sufficient conditions for consistency of the ERM induction principle, and the general quantitative theory that describes the bounds on the probability of the (future) test error for the function minimizing the empirical risk. However, the application of ERM does not necessarily guarantee consistency, that is, convergence to the best possible solution with an increasing number of training data. In order to ensure the consistency of learning from data, Vapnik and Chervonenkis developed the uniform law of large numbers (Vapnik and Chervonenkis 1968; 1971; Vapnik 1998) for pattern recognition problems. (These results can be extended to regression problems.) The cornerstones in their theory are the new capacity concepts for a set of indicator functions. The most popular is the Vapnik-Chervonenkis (VC) dimension of the set of indicator functions implemented by the learning machine (see chapter 2). They proved that for the distribution-free consistency of the ERM principle, it is necessary and sufficient that the set of functions implemented by the learning machine (SVM, NN, or FLM) have a finite VC dimension. The most important result, which led to the new induction principle of SRM, was that distribution-free bounds on the rate of uniform convergence depend on

- The VC dimension
- The number of training errors (or the empirical error, say sum of error squares)
- The number of training data (size P of a training data set)

Based on this, they postulated the crucial idea for controlling the generalization ability of a learning machine:

To achieve the smallest bound on the test error by minimizing the number of training errors, the learning machine (the set of predefined functions) with the smallest VC dimension should be used.

However, the two requirements, namely, to minimize the number of training errors and to use a machine with a small VC dimension, are mutually contradictory. Thus, one is destined to trade off accuracy of approximation for capacity (VC dimension) of the machine, that is, of the set of functions used to model the data. The new induction principle of SRM is introduced in order to minimize the test error by controlling these two contradictory factors—accuracy on the training data and the capacity of the learning machine.

Note that generalization (performance on previously unseen test data) depends on the capacity of the set of functions implemented by the learning machine, not on the number of free parameters. This is one of the most important results of the statistical learning theory (SLT), which is also known as the VC theory. Capacity differs from the complexity of the machine, which is typically proportional to the number of free parameters. A simple function having a single parameter with an infinite VC dimension (capacity) is shown later. The opposite may also be true. Recall that a set of functions (a learning machine implementing it) with a high capacity typically leads to the very undesirable effect of overfitting. On the other hand, if the capacity is too small, the learning machine will also model the data very badly. These issues are discussed at length later.

This book treats primarily the application aspects of NNs and SVMs. Many of their theoretical subtleties are left out here. This particularly concerns the SVMs that originated from SLT. Here, much more attention is given to the construction of SVMs than to their underlying theory. The reader interested in a deeper understanding of the theory of SLT and SRM should consult Vapnik (1995; 1998).

Furthermore, the whole field of unsupervised learning is not taken up here. This book models only causal relations between input and output variables. Such kinds of problems belong to the two large groups of contemporary tasks: pattern recognition (classification) and multivariate function approximation (regression). This means that the third standard problem in statistics, density estimation, is not dealt with here. Also, many other situations, for instance, when for given inputs the specific correct outputs are not defined, are omitted. Thus, the reader is deprived of a discussion of, two very useful unsupervised algorithms, principal component analysis and clustering. The author feels that introducing the unsupervised techniques would distract from the important topics of learning from data and fuzzy logic (the two modeling tools at the opposite poles of "not first principles" model building), and from the important property of the similarity or equivalence of NNs/SVMs and FLMs.

On Fuzzy Logic Modeling

From among the many possible topics in fuzzy logic (FL), this book chooses to focus on its applied aspects, or FL in a narrow sense. The reader interested in other facets of fuzzy (multivalued) logic theory should consult more theoretically oriented books. However, an understanding of the applied elements and properties of the FL approach will ease understanding of potentially difficult ideas in FL theory. Fuzzy logic arose from the desire to emulate human thought processes that are imprecise, deliberate, uncertain, and usually expressed in linguistic terms. In addition, human ways of reasoning are approximate, nonquantitative, linguistic, and dispositional (usually qualified).

Why is it that way? It is a consequence of the fact that the world we live in is not a binary world. There are many states between old and young, good and bad, ill and healthy, sad and happy, zero and one, no and yes, short and tall, black and white, and so on. Changes between these different extremes are gradual and have a great deal of ambiguity. This state of affairs, all our knowledge and understanding of such a world, we express in words. Language is a tool for expressing human knowledge. Words serve as a way of expressing and exploiting the tolerance for imprecision; they serve for expressing imprecise knowledge about the vague environment we live in. We use numbers only when words are not sufficiently precise. Thus, most human knowledge is fuzzy and expressed in vague terms that are usually without quantitative meaning. So, for example, temperature is typically expressed as cold, warm, or hot and usually not with numbers. FL is a tool for transforming such linguistically expressed knowledge into a workable algorithm called a fuzzy logic model. In its newest incarnation, FL is called computing with words.

The point of departure in fuzzy logic is the existence of a human solution to a problem. If there is no human solution, there will be no knowledge to model and consequently no sense in applying FL. However, the existence of a human solution is not sufficient. One must be able to articulate, to structure, the human solution in the language of fuzzy rules. These are typically IF-THEN rules. Almost all structured human knowledge can be expressed in the form of IF-THEN rules. This includes rules not only for practical skills but also for social and cultural behavior.

The criteria, in order of relevance, as to when and where to apply FL are as follows:

1. Human (structured) knowledge is available.

2. A mathematical model is unknown or impossible to obtain.

3. The process is substantially nonlinear.

4. There is a lack of precise sensor information.

5. It is applied at the higher levels of hierarchical control systems.

6. It is applied in generic decision-making processes.

Possible difficulties in applying FL arise from the following:

· Knowledge is a very subjective.

· For high dimensional inputs, the increase in the required number of rules is exponential (the curse of dimensionality).

· Knowledge must be structured, but experts bounce between a few extreme poles: they have trouble structuring the knowledge; they are too aware of their "expertise"; they tend to hide knowledge; and there may be some other subjective factors working against the whole process of human knowledge transfer.

Note that the basic premise of FL is that a human solution is good. When applied, for example, in control systems, this premise means that a human being is a good controller. Some (distrustful) scientists question this premise, calling it the basic fallacy of FL. Human beings are very poor controllers, they say, especially for complex, multivariable, and marginally stable systems. Even today, after more than 30 years and several thousands of successful applications, many similar objections are still voiced about FL techniques. The author does not intend to argue about the advantages or failures of FL. Instead, he will try to equip readers with basic FL knowledge and leave it up to them to take a side in such disputes.

Two relevant concepts within FL are

• Linguistic variables are defined as variables whose values are words or sentences.

• Fuzzy IF-THEN rules, comprising the input (antecedent) and the output (consequent), are propositions containing linguistic variables.

Chapter 6 introduces all the basic notions of FL and, together with the accompanying software, provides a reliable basis for further study of FL and its application to real-life problems. There is a remarkable ability in natural intelligence to improve existing knowledge by learning from examples. In the soft computing field, this property is covered by neurofuzzy models, where the initial FL model is first built and then improved using the available data. This is achieved by learning, that is, by applying some of the established techniques from the domains of NNs or SVMs. During this learning stage one typically crafts (changes the shapes and positions of) the input and output membership functions of the FL model. The former corresponds to updating the hidden layer weights and the latter to the learning of the output layer weights in NNs or SVMs. This is only one out of many similarities between NN SVMs and FLMs.

Particularly interesting among the FL modeling tools are fuzzy additive models (FAMs), which share with NNs and SVMs the property of being universal approximators. After transforming human knowledge by a FAM, one can obtain the nonlinear curve, surface, or hypersurface for one-, two-, or multidimensional inputs. Here, such multidimensional manifolds are called hypersurfaces of knowledge, expressing the fact that such multivariate functions are obtained after transforming human knowledge into an operational algorithm. FAMs are discussed in section 6.3. There is an interesting design problem in building FAMs. To achieve higher accuracy one typically uses more input variables or more membership functions or both. However, this leads to a rule explosion that was already mentioned as the curse of dimensionality. The rule explosion limits the further application of the fuzzy system. In order to overcome this problem when there are many input variables, fuzzy practitioners use the "patch the bumps" learning technique (Kosko 1997). The basic idea in this approach is to get a sparse (and therefore possibly the optimal) number of rules that cover the turning points or extrema of the function describing the surface of knowledge. This "patch the bumps" heuristic corresponds to optimal subset selection or support vectors learned in RBF NNs or SVMs. This book does not present the "patch the bumps" algorithm in detail. The thought is that learning can be better resolved within the neurofuzzy approach by applying well-developed methods from NNs and SVMs, in particular, subset selection techniques based on quadratic and linear programming (see chapter 2 and section 5.3.4).

In conclusion, there is nothing fuzzy about fuzzy logic. That FL is fuzzy or intrinsically imprecise might have been one of the most erroneous statements about this modeling tool. Today, the view of FL has changed, primarily for two reasons. First, FL is firmly based on multivalued logic theory and does not violate any well-proven laws of logic. Second, FL systems produce answers to any required degree of accuracy. This means that these models can be very precise if needed. However, they are aimed at handling imprecise and approximate concepts that cannot be processed by any other known modeling tool. In this sense, FL models are invaluable supplements to classical hard computing techniques. In addition, when given vague variables they go far beyond the power of classical AI approaches.

Fuzzy sets are not vague concepts either. They are aimed only at modeling such concepts. They differ from classic, or crisp, sets in that they allow partial or gradual degrees of belonging (membership) of some element to a given set. FL theory and computing are both very precise at the set level, at the inference phase, and in the defuzzification stage, or rather, as precise as needed. There is a trade-off between precision and a cost in FL modeling. This is one of the basic postulates in the soft computing field, making FL models a true component of it. Such precision control permits the writing of fuzzy rules at a rather high level of abstraction.

Fuzzy logic is a tool for representing imprecise, ambiguous, and vague information. Its power lies in its ability to perform meaningful and reasonable operations on concepts that are outside the definitions of conventional Boolean or crisp logic. FL techniques make vague concepts acceptable to computers and have therefore received widespread attention since they first appeared. At the same time as FL acquired a large number of admirers, it secured many fierce opponents. However, it survived them. In summary, fuzzy logic is a powerful and versatile modeling tool, but it is not the tool for, or the solution to, all problems. Nevertheless, by introducing elasticity to numbers and meanings, which is so natural to our minds, FL opens the door to the modeling of problems that have generally been extremely difficult or intractable for the hard computing approaches of the past.

On Terminology

Terminology in the field of learning machines and soft computing, because of its roots in the different areas of approximation theory, nonlinear optimization, and statistics, is exceptionally diverse, and very often similar concepts are variously named. In this book different terms for similar concepts are used deliberately to equip readers with the terminology and skills to readily associate similar concepts in different areas. Here, just a few typical uses of diverse names for the same or very similar notions are mentioned.

Approximating functions are models that are also known as networks or machines. The name *network* was chosen because the graphical presentation of these models resembles a kind of a network. The use of the name *machine* is more peculiar. Apparently, the very first use of it was partly commercial, in applying a Boltzmann algorithm in learning. Once in use, *machine* was added to a support vector algorithm. Today, SV machine, or SVM, is a "trademark" for application of statistical learning theory in learning from experimental data. *Machine* is actually the correct name for its use today. The soft computing machine (meaning a set of functions implemented in a piece of software or a program), when some number is supplied, does what all machines do: it processes the number and manufactures the product that is another number.

Similarly, *learning* denotes an approach to finding parameters (here typically called weights) of a model by using training data pairs. In various scientific and engineering fields the same procedure for learning from data is called training, parameter adaptation, parameter estimation, weights updating, identification, neurofuzzy learning, and tuning or adjusting of the weights. The learning can be performed in two ways, which have various names, too. The off-line method (when all the available data pairs are used at once) is also called explicit, one-shot, or batch procedure, while the on-line method (when the weights are updated after each data pair becomes available) is also called implicit, sequential, recursive, or iterative.

The weights of soft computing models represent the parameters that define the shapes and positions of the activation functions, which are usually called either basis functions or kernel functions in NNs, or membership functions, degrees of belonging, or possibility degrees in FLMs. All these differently named functions perform similar nonlinear transformations of incoming signals into neurons, processing elements, processing units, or nodes. Next—and this is another similarity between the various soft computing tools—the number of hidden layer units (neurons) in NNs turns out to be equivalent to the number of support vectors in SVMs and to the number of fuzzy logic rules in FLMs.

Training data pairs are also called samples, patterns, measurements, observations, records, and examples. The measure of goodness of approximating functions is known as cost function, norm, error function, objective function, fitness function, merit function, performance index, risk, and loss function. The author does not claim that all these terms denote exactly the same concepts, but all of them measure in one way or another the distance between training data points and the approximations.

In addition, a major topic of this book is solving regression and classification problems. The same or similar procedures in regression are called curve (surface) fittings and (multivariate) function approximations, and classification is also called pattern recognition, discriminant function analysis, and decision making.

It's time to start reading the book. It will tell the rest of the learning and soft computing story. To patient readers many intriguing secrets of modeling data or embedding human knowledge will be revealed.

Learning and Soft Computing

1 Learning and Soft Computing: Rationale, Motivations, Needs, Basics

Since the late 1980s there has been an explosion in research activity in neural networks (NNs), support vector machines (SVMs), and fuzzy logic (FL) systems. Together with new algorithms and statements of fundamental principles there has been an increase in real-world applications. Today, these areas are mature to the point where successful applications are reported across a range of fields. Examples of applications in diverse fields are given in section 1.1.

These three modeling tools complement one other. NNs and SVMs are paradigms of learning tools. They recover underlying dependencies between the given inputs and outputs by using training data sets. After training, both NNs and SVMs represent high-dimensional nonlinear functions. They are mathematical models obtained in an experimental way. If there are no data (examples, patterns, observations, or measurements), there will be no learning, and consequently no modeling by NNs and SVMs can take place.

However, one can still model the causal relations (also known as functions) between some variables provided one has an understanding about the system or process under investigation. This is the purpose of fuzzy logic. It is a tool for embedding existing structured human knowledge into mathematical models. If one has neither prior knowledge nor measurements, it may be difficult to believe that the problem at hand may be solved easily. This is by all accounts a very hopeless situation indeed. This book does not cover cases where both measurements and prior knowledge are lacking. However, even when faced with a modeling problem without either experimental data or knowledge, one is not entirely lost because there is an old scientific solution: if one cannot solve the problem posed, one poses another problem. In this book, problems are not reformulated. Rather, the text demonstrates how various real-world (conceptual or practical) tasks can be solved by learning from experimental data or by embedding structured human knowledge into mathematical models.

This chapter describes some typical nonlinear and high-dimensional problems from various fields in which soft models have been successfully applied. The range of problems that can be solved by using soft modeling approaches is wide, but all the problems belong to two major groups: pattern recognition (classification) tasks or functional approximation (regression) tasks. In this way, soft models can be looked at as being nonlinear extensions to classic linear regression and classification. This is how these standard statistical problems are introduced in section 1.4. Having a sound understanding of the concepts, performance, and limitations of linear statistical models is good preparation for understanding nonlinear modeling tools.

NNs and SVMs solve regression and classification problems by changing parameters that control how they learn as they cycle through training data. These parameters, usually called weights, influence how well the trained model performs. In order to measure the model's performance one must define some measure of goodness of the model. In mathematical terms, one should define some suitable norm. Here the cost or error (or risk) functional E is used, which expresses a dependency between an error measure and the weights, $E = E(\mathbf{w})$.

Unfortunately, as mentioned in section 1.3, genuine soft models are nonlinear approximators in the sense that an error functional $E = E(\mathbf{w})$ (the norm or measure of model goodness) depends nonlinearly upon weights that are the very subjects of learning. This means that the error hypersurface is generally not a convex function with guaranteed minimum. Therefore, a search after the best set of parameters (weights) that will ensure the best performance of the model falls into the category of nonlinear optimization problems.

As is well known, there is no general optimization method for nonlinear learning tasks. Section 1.3 introduces possibly the simplest to understand and the easiest to use: the gradient method. Despite being simple, the first-order gradient learning algorithm (also known as the error backpropagation algorithm) was the first learning procedure that made a key breakthrough in training multilayer neural networks. But this simplicity has a price: the learning procedure is too long and does not guarantee finding the best set of weights for a given NN structure. (Some improvements are discussed in chapter 8). It should be stressed that the only difference between NNs and SVMs is in how these models learn. After the learning phase, NNs and SVMs are essentially the same.

1.1 Examples of Applications in Diverse Fields

Soft computing, which comprises fuzzy logic modeling and the theory and application of the (statistical) learning techniques embedded in SVMs and NNs, is still in an early stage of development. Nevertheless, many research institutions, industries, and commercial firms have already started to apply these novel tools successfully to many diverse types of real-world problems. Practically no area of human activity is left untouched by NNs, SVMs, or fuzzy logic models. The most important applications include

- Pattern (visual, sound, olfactory, tactile) recognition (i.e., classification)
- Time series forecasting (financial, weather, engineering time series)
- Diagnostics (e.g., in medicine or engineering)
- Robotics (control, navigation, coordination, object recognition)
- Process control (nonlinear and multivariable control of chemical plants, power stations, vehicles or missiles)

- Optimization (combinatorial problems like resource scheduling, routing)
- Signal processing, speech and word recognition
- Machine vision (inspection in manufacturing, check reader, face recognition, target recognition)
- Financial forecasting (interest rates, stock indices, currencies)
- Financial services (credit worthiness, forecasting, data mining, data segmentation), services for trade (segmentation of customer data)

In certain application areas, such as speech and word recognition, NNs, FL models, or SVMs outperform conventional statistical methods. In other fields, such as specific areas in robotics and financial services, they show promising application in real-world situations.

Because of various shortcomings of both neural networks and fuzzy logic models and the advantages of combining them with other technologies, hybrid and modular solutions are becoming popular. In addition, complex real-world problems require more complex solutions than a single network (or a one-sided approach) can provide. The generic soft computing approach also supports the design of solutions to a wide range of complex problems. They include satellite image classification, advanced data analysis, optical character recognition, sales forecasting, traffic forecasting, and credit approval prediction.

The theoretical foundations, mathematics, and software techniques applied are common for all these different areas. This book describes the common fundamental principles and underlying concepts of statistical learning, neural networks, and fuzzy logic modeling as well as some of the differences between them.

A natural and direct connection exists between soft computing models (NNs, SVMs, and FL models) and classical statistics. The models presented here can be viewed as nonlinear extensions of linear regression and classification methods, tools, and approaches. However, introducing nonlinearities (i.e., nonlinear dependence of the approximating models upon model parameters) increases the complexity of the learning tools dramatically. Learning usually means nonlinear optimization, which becomes the most important task to solve in machine learning theory. This book deals with the various nonlinear optimization techniques in the framework of learning from experimental data.

Before considering some popular and successful applications of NN models, it may be interesting to look at the wide range of problems that classical (linear) statistics attempted to solve. More details on these and many others, may be found in the standard statistical literature (e.g., Anderson 1958; Johnson and Wichern 1982).

- Effects of drugs on sleeping time
- Pulmonary function modeling by measuring oxygen consumption
- Comparison of head lengths and breadths of brothers
- Classification of the Brahman, Artisan, and Korwa groups based on physical measurements
- Classification of two species of flies using data on biting flies
- Battery-failure data dependence and regression
- Financial and market analyses (bankruptcy, stock market prediction, bonds, goods transportation cost data, production cost data)
- Study of love and marriage using data on the relationships and feelings of couples
- Air pollution data classification, college test scores classification and prediction, crude oil consumption modeling, degree of relation among 11 languages.

This is only a short list, but it shows the wide diversity of problems to which linear statistics has been successfully applied. In many instances, linear models perform well. In fact, whenever there are linear (or slightly nonlinear) dependencies in regression problems or when separation functions between the classes are (closely) linear, one can obtain very good results by applying conventional statistical tools.

Today, equipped with powerful computing techniques and high-performance sensors and actuators, we want to solve much more complex (highly nonlinear and high-dimensional) problems. However, this is even more risky endeavor than solving a variety of classical linear problems; this book introduces the reader to the very challenging and promising field of nonlinear classification and regression based on learning from experimental data. In addition, it presents, as a third constituent of soft computing, fuzzy logic modeling as a tool for embedding structured human knowledge into workable algorithms.

To begin, it may be helpful to look at a few successful developments and applications of neural networks and fuzzy logic paradigms. The success of these applications spurred widespread acceptance of these novel and powerful nonlinear modeling techniques. This short review is far from conclusive. It discusses only a few of the important supervised learning NN models as well as some early pioneering applications of FL models in solving practical problems.

The construction of the first learning machine, called the perceptron, by F. Rosenblatt in late 1960s is certainly a milestone in the history of NNs (see chapter 3). This was the first model of a machine that learns from experimental data, and this is when mathematical analysis of learning from data began. The early perceptron was designed for solving pattern recognition problems, that is, classification tasks.

At the same time, a philosophy of statistical learning theory was being developed by V. Vapnik and A. Chervonenkis (1968). Unlike the experimental approach of Rosenblatt, their work formulated essential theoretical concepts: Vapnik-Chervonenkis entropy and the Vapnik-Chervonenkis dimension, which in 1974 resulted in a novel inductive principle called structural risk minimization. At this early stage, these tools were also applied to classification problems (see chapter 2).

Concurrently, B. Widrow and M. Hoff developed the first adaptive learning rule for solving linear regression problems: the least mean square (LMS) learning rule, also known as the delta learning rule (see chapter 3). It was a rule for training a (neural) processing unit called the adaline (adaptive linear neuron) for adaptive signal filtering and adaptive equalization. Hence, this linear neuron was performing linear regression tasks.

By the mid-1980s a lot of progress had been made in developing specialized hardware and software for solving real-life problems without the relevant theoretical concepts being applied to the (mostly experimental) supervised learning machines. (Many unsupervised learning algorithms and approaches were also developed during that period.) Then, about that time, a breakthrough in learning from data and in neural network development came when several authors (Le Cun 1985; Parker 1985; Rumelhart, Hinton, and Williams 1986) independently proposed a gradient method, called error backpropagation, for training hidden layer weights (see section 4.1).

Independently, continuing their research in the field of statistical learning theory, Vapnik and Chervonenkis found the necessary and sufficient conditions for consistency of the empirical risk minimization inductive principle in 1989. In this way, all the theory needed for powerful learning networks was established, and in the early 1990s Vapnik and his coworkers developed support vector machines aimed at solving nonlinear classification and regression problems (see chapter 2).

A lot of effort was devoted in the late 1980s to developing so-called regularization networks, also known as radial basis function networks (Powell 1987; Broomhead and Lowe 1988; Poggio and Girosi 1989 and later). These networks have firm theoretical roots in Tikhonov's regularization theory (see chapter 5). A few well-known and successful applications are described here. The common feature of all the models (functions or machines) in these applications is that they learn complex, high-dimensional, nonlinear functional dependencies between given input and output variables from training data.

One of the first successful applications was the NETtalk project (Sejnowski and Rosenberg 1987), aimed at training a neural network to pronounce English text consisting of seven consecutive characters from written text, presented in a moving window that gradually scanned the text. Seven letters were chosen because linguistic studies have shown that the influence of the fourth and fifth distant letters on the pronunciation of the middle character is statistically small. To simplify the problem of speech synthesis, the NETtalk network recognized only 29 valid characters: the 26 alphabetic characters from A to Z and the comma, period, and space. No distinction was made between upper and lower case, and all characters that were not one of these 29 were ignored. Thus, the input was a $7 \times 29 = 203$-dimensional vector. The desired output was a phoneme code to be directed to a speech generator giving the pronunciation of the letter at the center of the input window. The network had 26 output units, each forming one of the 26 codes for the phoneme sound generation commands. The NETtalk network is an error backpropagation model having one hidden layer with 80 processing units (neurons). For the approach taken in this book, it is important to realize that such a structure represents a highly nonlinear mapping from a 203-dimensional space into a 26-dimensional space (i.e., NETtalk is an $\Re^{203} \rightarrow \Re^{26}$ mapping). The neural network was trained on 1,024 words and achieved intelligible speech after 10 training epochs and 95% accuracy after 50 epochs. (An epoch is a sweep through all the training data.)

Gorman and Sejnowski (1988) trained the same kind of multilayer perceptron to distinguish between reflected sonar signals from two kinds of objects lying at the bottom of the sea: rocks and metal cylinders. The input signal was the frequency spectrum (Fourier transform) of the reflected sonar signal. The network had 60 input units and 2 output neurons—one for rocks and one for cylinders. Note that this is a one-out-of-two classification (pattern recognition) problem. They varied the number of hidden layer (HL) neurons from zero (when an NN is without a hidden layer) to 24. Without any HL unit, the network achieved about 80% correct performance on training data. With two HL units, the network reached almost 100% accuracy on every training trial. There was no visible improvement in the results on increasing the number of HL units from 12 to 24. After training, the network was tested on new, previously unseen, data; with 12 HL neurons, it achieved about 85% correct classification. We are here particularly interested in mathematical side of the problem being solved. Therefore, note that the sonar signals recognition network performed a highly nonlinear mapping from a 60-dimensional space into a 2-dimensional space (an $\Re^{60} \rightarrow \Re^2$ mapping).

Pomerlau (1989) reported results on designing an NN-based car driver within the framework of the ALVINN (autonomous land vehicle in a neural network) project. The ALVINN network took road images from a camera (30×32 pixel image) and a laser range finder (8×32 pixel image) as inputs. Its output was a direction of the vehicle in order to follow the road. There were 29 neurons in a single hidden layer and 46 neurons in the output layer. Thus, the input vector was 1216-dimensional, and ALVINN represented a nonlinear functional mapping from a 1216-dimensional space into a 46-dimensional space (an $\Re^{1216} \rightarrow \Re^{46}$ mapping).

Handwritten character recognition is certainly one of the most interesting areas in which NNs have found wide application. One of the first reported applications is due to Le Cun and his colleagues (1989). The network input was a 16×16 array (i.e., a 256-dimensional vector) that received a pixel image of a particular handwritten digit scaled to a standard size. This signal was fed forward through three hidden layers to the output layer, which comprised ten output units, each signifying one of the digits 0–9. There were 64 neurons in the first HL, 16 in the second, and 30 in the third. The network used 9,300 ZIP codes (numerical postal codes). Approximately one quarter (2,000) was used for the test, and it was not seen during the training. This network, named LeNet1, was trained by error backpropagation. The error on the test set was 5.1%. It is interesting that this handwritten character recognition problem became a benchmark for various NN and SVM models. Recently, competitive results were reported by applying SVM with polynomial kernel functions, which achieved accuracy of 4% on test data. In the meantime, Le Cun and his colleagues developed LeNet5, which performed better than both of the previous models. Details of comparative results with other models can be found in Vapnik (1998). From the mathematical point of view, LeNet1 represented a nonlinear functional mapping from a 256-dimensional space into a 10-dimensional space (an $\Re^{256} \rightarrow \Re^{10}$ mapping).

These four early applications are only a few of the thousands now existing in many fields of human endeavor. An important point to note about all these applications is that the models all learn high-dimensional nonlinear mappings from training data that are usually sparse. This is the world of learning from data networks (models, functions, and machines), where, at the moment, no better alternatives exist.

A brief history of fuzzy logic and its applications follows. Fuzzy logic was first proposed by L. A. Zadeh in 1965. He elaborated on his ideas in a 1973 paper, which introduced the concept of linguistic variables, or fuzzy sets. Assilian and Mamdani were the first to implement fuzzy logic rules, for controlling a steam generator, in 1974. The first industrial application followed soon after: implementing fuzzy control in a cement kiln built in Denmark in 1975. Interestingly, at this early stage fuzzy systems were ignored in the country of their theoretical origins, the United States. One explanation is that people associated FL models and approaches with artificial intelligence, expert systems, and knowledge-based engineering, which at that point had not lived up to expectations. Such early (and erroneous) associations resulted in a lack of credibility for FL in U.S. industrial firms.

In Japan, without such prejudice, interest in fuzzy systems was much stronger. This might have been part of the so-called "invented here" syndrome, in which innovative ideas supposedly get more attention if they come from far away. In any case, Hitachi's first simulations, in 1985, demonstrated the superiority of fuzzy control systems for the Sendai railway. Within two years, fuzzy systems had been adopted to control accelerating, braking, and stopping of Sendai trains.

Another event helped promote interest in fuzzy systems in Japan. During an international meeting in 1987 in Tokyo, T. Yamakawa demonstrated the use of fuzzy control in an "inverted pendulum" experiment. This is a classic benchmark problem in controlling a nonlinear unstable system. He implemented a set of simple dedicated fuzzy logic chips for solving this nonlinear control task.

Following such demonstrations of FL models' capabilities, fuzzy systems were built into many Japanese consumer goods. Matsushita vacuum cleaners used four-bit FL controllers to adjust suction power according to dust sensor information. Hitachi washing machines implemented fuzzy controllers in load-weight, fabric-mix, and dirt sensors to automatically set the wash cycle for the best use of power, water, and detergent. Canon developed an auto-focusing camera that used a charge-coupled device to measure the clarity of the image in six regions of its field of view and with the information provided to determine if the image was in focus. The dedicated FL chip also tracked the rate of change of lens movement during focusing and controlled its speed to prevent overshoot. The camera's fuzzy control system used 12 inputs: six to obtain the current clarity data provided by the charge-coupled device and six to measure the rate of change of lens movement. The output was the position of the lens. The fuzzy control system used 13 rules and required 1.1 kilobytes of memory. However, for obvious reasons, the camera was not advertised as a "fuzzy" camera. Instead, the adjective "smart" was used, which (because of the application of smart fuzzy rules) this camera certainly was.

Another example of a consumer product incorporating fuzzy controllers is an industrial air conditioner designed by Mitsubishi that used 25 heating rules and 25 cooling rules. A temperature sensor provided input, and fuzzy controller outputs were fed to an inverter, a compressor valve, and a fan motor. According to Mitsubishi, compared to the previous design, the fuzzy controller heated and cooled five times faster, reduced power consumption by one quarter, increased temperature stability by a factor of two, and used fewer sensors.

Following the first successful applications, many others were reported in fields like character and handwriting recognition, optical fuzzy systems, robotics, voice-controlled helicopter flight, control of flow of powders in film manufacture, and elevator systems.

Work on fuzzy systems also proceeded in Europe and the United States, although not with the same enthusiasm as in Japan. In Europe, at the same time as FL was introduced for control purposes, H. Zimmermann and his coworkers found it useful in modeling human decision processes. However, they realized that the classical FL proposed by Zadeh was insufficient for modeling complex human decision processes, and they developed extensions, such as compensatory aggregation operators. As an immediate result of this, INFORM Corporation introduced a decision support system for banks in 1986.

The list of large European companies that started fuzzy logic task forces includes SGS-Thompson of France and Italy as well as Klöckner-Moeler, Siemens, and Daimler-Benz of Germany. SGS-Thompson invested $20 million in a fuzzy logic task force in Catania, Italy. This project primarily targeted FL hardware. Siemens started an FL task force at its central R&D facility in Munich. This task force emphasized expanding FL theory as well as supporting applications. The Siemens applications included washing machines, vacuum cleaners, automatic transmission systems, engine idle-speed controllers, traffic controllers, paper-processing systems, and H2-leakage diagnosis systems. A survey done in 1994 identified a total of 684 applications of fuzzy logic in Europe that were classified into four categories: industrial automation (44%), decision support and data analysis (30%), embedded control (19%), and process control (7%).

The Environmental Protection Agency in the United States has investigated fuzzy control for energy-efficient motors, and NASA has studied fuzzy control for automated space docking: simulations show that a fuzzy control system can greatly reduce fuel consumption. Firms such as Boeing, General Motors, Allen-Bradley, Chrysler, Eaton, and Whirlpool have worked on fuzzy logic for use in low-power refrigerators, improved automotive transmissions, and energy-efficient electric motors.

Research and development is continuing apace in fuzzy software design, fuzzy expert systems, and integration of fuzzy logic with neural networks in so-called neurofuzzy or fuzzyneuro systems. These issues are discussed in more detail later in the book.

1.2   Basic Tools of Soft Computing: Neural Networks, Fuzzy Logic Systems, and Support Vector Machines

In recent years, neural networks, fuzzy logic models, and support vector machines have been used in many different fields. This section primarily discusses NNs and FL models. SVMs are discussed in depth in chapter 2. However, because of a very high degree of resemblance between NNs and SVMs, almost all comments about the representational properties of NNs can also be applied to SVMs. Unlike their representational capabilities, the learning stages of these two modeling tools are different. Chapters 2, 3, and 4 clarify the differences.

NNs and FL models are modeling tools. They perform in the same way after the learning stage of NNs or the embedding of human knowledge about some specific task of FL is finished. They are two sides of the same coin.[1] Whether the more appropriate tool for solving a given problem is an NN or an FL model depends upon the availability of previous knowledge about the system to be modeled and the amount of measured process data.

The classical NN and FL system paradigms lie at the two extreme poles of system modeling (see table 1.1). At the NN pole there is a black box design situation in which the process is entirely unknown but there are examples (measurements, records, observations, samples, data pairs). At the other pole (the FL model) the solution to the problem is known, that is, structured human knowledge (experience, expertise, heuristics) about the process exists. Then there is a white box situation. In short, the less previous knowledge exists, the more likely it is that an NN, not an FL, approach will be used to attempt a solution. The more knowledge available, the more suitable the problem will be for the application of fuzzy logic modeling. On the whole, both tools are aimed at solving pattern recognition (classification) and regression (multivariate function approximation) tasks.

For example, when they are applied in a system control area or the digital signal processing field, neural networks can be regarded as a nonlinear identification tool. This is the closest connection with a standard and well-developed field of estimation or identification of linear control systems. In fact, if the problem at hand is a linear one, an NN would degenerate into a single linear neuron, and in this case the weights of the neuron would correspond to the parameters of the plant's discrete transfer function $G(z)$ (see example 3.6). When applied to stock market predictions (see section 7.2) the approach will be the same as for linear dynamics identification, but the network will become a more complex structure. The underlying dependencies (if there are any) are usually far from being linear, and linear assumptions can no longer stand. A new, hidden layer of neurons will have to be added. In this way, the network can model nonlinear functions. This design step leads to a tremendous increase in modeling capacity, but there is a price: a nonlinear kind of learning will have to be performed, and this is generally not an easy task. However, this is the point where the world of neural networks and support vector machines begins.

In order to avoid too high (or too low) expectations for these new concepts of computing, particularly after they have been connected with intelligence, it might be useful to list some advantages and disadvantages that have been claimed for NNs and FL models (see tables 1.2 and 1.3). Because of the wide range of applications of

Table 1.1
Neural Networks, Support Vector Machines, and Fuzzy Logic Modeling as Examples of Modeling Approaches at Extreme Poles

Neural Networks and Support Vector Machines	Fuzzy Logic Models

Black Box

No previous knowledge, but there are measurements, observations, records, i.e., data pairs $\{x_i, d_i\}$ are known. Weights V and W are unknown.

White Box

Structured knowledge (experience, expertise, or heuristics). No data required. IF-THEN rules are the most typical examples of structured knowledge.

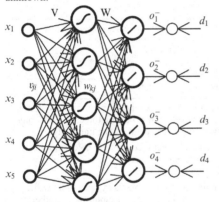

Example: Controlling the distance between two cars:
R1: IF the speed is *low* AND the distance is *small*, THEN the force on brake should be *small*.
R2: IF the speed is *medium* AND the distance is *small*, THEN the force on brake should be *big*.
R3: IF the speed is *high* AND the distance is *small*, THEN the force on brake should be *very big*.

Behind NNs and SVMs stands the idea of learning from the training data.

Behind FL stands the idea of embedding human knowledge into workable algorithms.

In many instances, we do have both *some knowledge* and *some data*.

This is the most common *gray box* situation covered by the paradigm of neuro-fuzzy or fuzzy-neuro models.

If we do not have any prior knowledge *and* we do not have any measurements (by all accounts, a very hopeless situation indeed), it may be hard to expect or believe that the problem at hand may be approached and solved easily. This is a *no-color box* situation.

Table 1.2
Some Advantages of Neural Networks and Fuzzy Logic Models

Neural Networks	Fuzzy Logic Models
Have the property of learning from the data, mimicking human learning ability	Are an efficient tool for embedding human (structured) knowledge into useful algorithms
Can approximate any multivariate nonlinear function	Can approximate any multivariate nonlinear function
Do not require deep understanding of the process or the problem being studied	Are applicable when mathematical model is unknown or impossible to obtain
Are robust to the presence of noisy data	Operate successfully under a lack of precise sensor information
Have parallel structure and can be easily implemented in hardware	Are useful at the higher levels of hierarchical control systems
Same NN can cover broad and different classes of tasks	Are appropriate tool in generic decision-making process

Table 1.3
Some Disadvantages of Neural Networks and Fuzzy Logic Models

Neural Networks	Fuzzy Logic Models
Need extremely long training or learning time (problems with local minima or multiple solutions) with little hope for many real-time applications.	Human solutions to the problem must exist, and this knowledge must be structured. Experts may have problems structuring the knowledge.
Do not uncover basic internal relations of physical variables, and do not increase our knowledge about the process.	Experts sway between extreme poles: too much aware in field of expertise, or tending to hide their knowledge.
Are prone to bad generalizations (with large number of weights, tendency to overfit the data; poor performance on previously unseen data during the test phase).	Number of rules increases exponentially with increase in the number of inputs and number of fuzzy subsets per input variable.
Little or no guidance is offered about NN structure or optimization procedure, or the type of NN to use for a particular problem.	Learning (changing membership functions' shapes and positions, or rules) is highly constrained; typically more complex than with NN.

these modeling tools, it is hard to prove or disprove these claims and counterclaims. Only a part of the answers will be found in this book. It is certain that everyone working with NNs, SVMs, and FL models will form their own opinions about these claims. However, the growing number of companies and products employing NNs and FL models and the increasing number of new neural network and fuzzy computing theories and paradigms show that despite the still many open questions NNs, SVMs, and FL models are already well-established engineering tools and are becoming a common computational means for solving many real-life tasks and problems.

1.2.1 Basics of Neural Networks

Artificial neural networks are software or hardware models inspired by the structure and behavior of biological neurons and the nervous system, but after this point of inspiration all resemblance to biologyical systems ceases.

There are about 50 different types of neural networks in use today. This book describes and discusses *feedforward* NNs with *supervised learning*. This section deals with the *representational capabilities* of NNs. It shows what NNs can model and how they can represent some specific underlying functions that generated training data. Chapters 3, 4, and 5 describe the *problem of learning*—how the best set of weights, which enables an NN to be a universal approximator, can be calculated (learned) by using these training data. Chapter 2 discusses much broader issues of statistical learning theory and in that framework presents support vector machines as approximating models with a powerful modeling capacity.

Feedforward neural networks are the models used most often for solving nonlinear classification and regression tasks by learning from data. In addition, feedforward NNs are mathematically very close, and sometimes even equivalent, to fuzzy logic models. Both NN and FL approximation techniques can be given graphical representation, which can be called a neural network or a fuzzy logic model. With such a representation of NN or FL tools, nothing new is added to approximation theory, but from the point of view of implementation (primarily in the sense of parallel and massive computing) this graphical representation is a desirable property.

There is a strong mathematical basis for developing NNs in the form of the famous Kolmogorov theorem (1957). This theorem encouraged many researchers but is still a source of controversy (see Girosi and Poggio 1989; Kurkova 1991). The Kolmogorov theorem states,

Given any continuous function $f: [0, 1]^n \rightarrow \Re^m, f(\mathbf{x}) = \mathbf{y}, f$ can be implemented exactly by a network with n neurons (fan-out nodes) in an input layer, $(2n + 1)$ neurons in the hidden layer, and m processing units (neurons) in the output layer.

However, the proof of this important theorem is not constructive in the sense that it cannot be used for network design. This is the reason this book pursues the standard constructive approaches developed in the framework of NNs or SVMs.

Artificial neural networks are composed of many computing units popularly (but perhaps misleadingly) called neurons. The strength of the connection, or link, between two neurons is called the weight. The values of the weights are true network parameters and the subjects of the learning procedure in NNs. Depending upon the problem, they have different physical meanings, and sometimes it is hard to find any physical meaning at all. Their geometrical meaning is much clearer. The weights define the positions and shapes of basis functions in neural network and fuzzy logic models.

The neurons are typically organized into layers in which all the neurons usually possess the same activation functions (AFs). The genuine neural networks are those with an input layer and at least two layers of neurons—a hidden layer (HL), and an output layer (OL)—provided that the HL neurons have nonlinear and differentiable AFs. Note that such an NN has two layers of adjustable weights that are typically organized as the elements of the weights matrices $\mathbf{V}$ and $\mathbf{W}$. The matrix $\mathbf{V}$ is the matrix of the hidden layer weights and the matrix $\mathbf{W}$ comprises the output layer weights. For a single OL neuron, $\mathbf{W}$ degenerates into a weights vector $\mathbf{w}$.

The nonlinear activation functions in the hidden layer neurons enable the neural network to be a universal approximator. Thus the nonlinearity of the AFs solves the problems of representation. The differentiability of the HL neurons' AFs makes possible the solution of nonlinear learning. (Today, using random optimization algorithms like the genetic algorithm, one may also think of learning HL weights in cases where the AFs of the hidden layer neurons are not differentiable. Fuzzy logic models are the most typical networks having nondifferentiable activation functions.)

Here, the input layer is not treated as a layer of neural processing units. The input units are merely fan-out nodes. Generally, there will not be any processing in the input layer, and although in its graphical representation it looks like a layer, the input layer is not a layer of neurons. Rather, it is an input vector, eventually augmented with a bias term, whose components will be fed to the next (hidden or output) layer of neural processing units. The OL neurons may be linear ones (for regression types of problems), or they can have sigmoidal activation functions (for classification or pattern recognition tasks). For NN-based adaptive control schemes or for (financial) times series analyses, OL neurons are typically linear units. An elementary (but powerful) feedforward neural network is shown in figure 1.1. This is a graphical representation of the approximation scheme (1.1):

$$o(\mathbf{x}, \mathbf{V}, \mathbf{w}, \mathbf{b}) = F(\mathbf{x}, \mathbf{V}, \mathbf{w}, \mathbf{b}) = \sum_{j=1}^{J} w_j \sigma_j(\mathbf{v}_j^T \mathbf{x} + b_j), \qquad (1.1)$$

where σ_j stands for sigmoidal activation functions. This network is called a multilayer perceptron (see chapters 3 and 4). J corresponds to the number of HL neurons. By explicitly writing $o = o(\mathbf{x}, \mathbf{V}, \mathbf{w}, \mathbf{b})$ we deliberately stress the fact that the output from an NN depends upon the weights (unknown before learning) contained in $\mathbf{V}$, $\mathbf{w}$, and $\mathbf{b}$. Input vector $\mathbf{x}$, bias weights vector $\mathbf{b}$, HL weights matrix $\mathbf{V}$, and OL weights vector $\mathbf{w}$ are as follows:

$$\mathbf{x} = \begin{bmatrix} x_1 & x_2 & \ldots & x_n \end{bmatrix}^T. \tag{1.2}$$

$$\mathbf{V} = \begin{bmatrix} v_{11} & \ldots & v_{1i} & \ldots & v_{1n} \\ \vdots & & \vdots & & \vdots \\ v_{j1} & \ldots & v_{ji} & \ldots & v_{jn} \\ \vdots & & \vdots & & \vdots \\ v_{J1} & \ldots & v_{Ji} & \ldots & v_{Jn} \end{bmatrix}. \tag{1.3}$$

$$\mathbf{b} = \begin{bmatrix} b_1 & b_2 & \ldots & b_J \end{bmatrix}^T. \tag{1.4}$$

$$\mathbf{w} = \begin{bmatrix} w_1 & w_2 & \ldots & w_J & w_{J+1} \end{bmatrix}^T. \tag{1.5}$$

At this point, a few comments may be needed. Figure 1.1 represents a general structure of multilayer perceptrons, radial basis function (RBF) networks, and SVMs. In the case of a multilayer perceptron, x_{n+1} will be the constant term equal to 1, called *bias*. The bias weights vector $\mathbf{b}$ can simply be integrated into an HL weights matrix $\mathbf{V}$ as its last column. After such concatenation, (1.1) can be simplified to $o = \mathbf{w}^T \sigma(\mathbf{Vx})$.[2] For RBF networks, $x_{n+1} = 0$, meaning that there is no bias input. However, it can be used in an OL (see chapter 5).

For both multilayer perceptrons and RBF networks, the HL bias term may be used but is not generally needed. The HL activation functions shown in figure 1.1 are sigmoidal, indicating that this particular network represents a multilayer perceptron. However, the structures of multilayer perceptrons, RBF networks, and fuzzy logic models are the same or very similar. The basic distinction between sigmoidal and radial basis function networks is how the input to each particular neuron is calculated (see (1.6) and (1.7) and fig. 1.2).

The basic computation that takes place in an NN is very simple. After a specific input vector is presented to the network, the input signals to all HL neurons u_j are computed either as scalar (dot or inner) products between the weights vectors $\mathbf{v}_j$ and $\mathbf{x}$ (for a linear or sigmoidal AF) or as Euclidean distances between the centers $\mathbf{c}_j$ of the RBF and $\mathbf{x}$ (for RBF activation functions). A radial basis AF is typically parameterized by two sets of parameters: the center $\mathbf{c}$, which defines its position, and a second set of parameters that determines the shape (width or form) of an RBF. In the

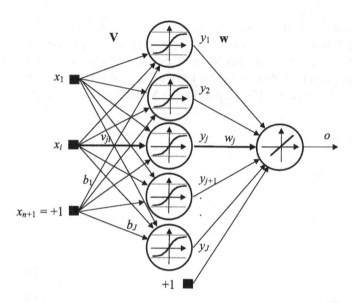

Figure 1.1
Feedforward neural network that can approximate any $\Re^n \to \Re^1$ nonlinear mapping.

case of a one-dimensional Gaussian function this second set of parameters is the standard deviation σ. (Do not confuse the standard deviation σ with the sigmoidal activation function σ given in (1.1) and shown in HL neurons in fig. 1.1.) In the case of a multivariate input vector $\mathbf{x}$ the parameters that define the shape of the hyper-Gaussian function are elements of a covariance matrix Σ. To put it simply, the ratios of HL bias weights and other HL weights of sigmoidal activation functions loosely correspond to the centers of RBF functions, whereas weights v_{ji}, which define the slope of sigmoidal functions with respect to each input variable, correspond to the width parameter of the RBF. Thus, the inputs to the HL neurons for sigmoidal AFs are given as

$$u_j = \mathbf{v}_j^T \mathbf{x}, \qquad j = 1, \ldots, J, \tag{1.6}$$

and for RBF activation functions the distances are calculated as

$$r_j = \sqrt{(\mathbf{x} - \mathbf{c}_j)^T (\mathbf{x} - \mathbf{c}_j)}, \qquad u = f(r, \sigma). \tag{1.7}$$

In the case of three-dimensional input, when $\mathbf{x} = [x_1, x_2, x_3]^T$ and $\mathbf{c} = [c_1, c_2, c_3]^T$, the Euclidean distance r_j can be readily calculated as

$$r_j = \sqrt{(\mathbf{x} - \mathbf{c}_j)^T (\mathbf{x} - \mathbf{c}_j)} = \sqrt{(x_1 - c_1)^2 + (x_2 - c_2)^2 + (x_3 - c_3)^2}. \tag{1.8}$$

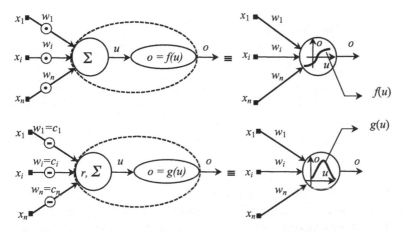

Figure 1.2
Formation of the input signal u to the neuron's activation function. *Top*, sigmoidal type activation function; input to the neuron is a scalar product $u = \mathbf{w}^T\mathbf{x}$. *Bottom*, RBF type activation function; input to the neuron is a distance r between $\mathbf{x}$ and the RBF center $\mathbf{c}$ ($r = \|\mathbf{x} - \mathbf{c}\|$), r depending on parameters of the shape or width of the RBF. For a Gaussian function, the covariance matrix Σ contains the shape parameters.

The output from each HL neuron depends on the type of activation function used. The most common activation functions in multilayer perceptrons are the squashing sigmoidal functions: the unipolar logistic function (1.9) and the bipolar sigmoidal, or tangent hyperbolic, function (1.10). These two AFs and their corresponding derivatives are presented in figure 4.3.

$$o = \frac{1}{1 + e^{-u}} \tag{1.9}$$

$$o = \tanh\left(\frac{u}{2}\right) = \frac{2}{1 + e^{-u}} - 1 \tag{1.10}$$

Figure 1.2 shows the basic difference in forming the input signals u to the AFs of the multilayer perceptron and an RBF neuron.

All three powerful nonlinear modeling tools—a multilayer perceptron, an RBF network, and an SVM—have the same structure. Thus, their representational capabilities are the same or very similar after successful training. All three models learn from a set of training data and try to be as good as possible in modeling typically sparse and noisy data pairs in high-dimensional space. (Note that none of the three adjectives used eases our learning from data task.) The output from these models is a hypersurface[3] in an $\Re^n \times \Re^m$ space, where n is the dimension of the input space and

Table 1.4
Basic Models and Their Error (Risk) Functions

Multilayer Perceptron	Radial Basis Function Network	Support Vector Machine
$E = \sum_{i=1}^{P} \underbrace{(d_i - f(\mathbf{x}_i, \mathbf{w}))^2}_{Closeness\ to\ data}$	$E = \sum_{i=1}^{P} \underbrace{(d_i - f(\mathbf{x}_i, \mathbf{w}))^2}_{Closeness\ to\ data} + \lambda \underbrace{\|\mathbf{P}f\|^2}_{Smoothness}$	$E = \sum_{i=1}^{P} \underbrace{(d_i - f(\mathbf{x}_i, \mathbf{w}))^2}_{Closeness\ to\ data} + \underbrace{\Omega(l, h, \eta)}_{Capacity\ of\ a\ machine}$

m is the dimension of the output space. In trying to find the best model, one should be able to measure the accuracy or performance of the model. To do that one typically uses some measure of goodness, performance, or quality (see section 1.3).

This is where the basic difference between the three models lies. Each uses a different norm (error, risk, or cost function) that measures the goodness of the model, and the optimization of the different measures results in different models. The application of different norms also leads to different learning (optimization) procedures. This is one of the core issues in this book. Table 1.4 tabulates the basic norms (risk or error functionals) applied in developing the three basic networks.

1.2.2 Basics of Fuzzy Logic Modeling

Fuzzy logic lies at the opposite pole of system modeling with respect to the NN and SVM methods. It is a white box approach (see table 1.1) in the sense that it is assumed that there is already human knowledge about a solution. Therefore, the modeled system is known (i.e., white). On the application level, FL can be considered an efficient tool for embedding structured human knowledge into useful algorithms. It is a precious engineering tool developed to do a good job of trading off precision and significance. In this respect, FL models do what human beings have been doing for a very long time. As in human reasoning and inference, the truth of any statement, measurement, or observation is a matter of degree. This degree is expressed through the membership functions that quantify (measure) a degree of belonging of some (crisp) input to given fuzzy subsets.

The field of fuzzy logic is very broad and covers many mathematical and logical concepts underlying the applications in various fields. The basics of these conceptual foundations are described in chapter 6. In particular, the chapter presents the fundamental concepts of crisp and fuzzy sets, introduces basic logical operators of conjunction (AND), disjunction (OR), and implication (IF-THEN) within the realm of fuzzy logic (namely, T-norms and T-conorms), and discusses the equivalence of NNs and FL models. (However, a deep systematic exposition of the theoretical issues is outside the scope of this book.) Furthermore, fuzzy additive models (FAMs) are introduced, which are universal approximators in the sense that they can approxi-

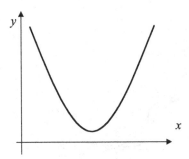 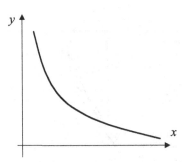

Figure 1.3
Two different nonlinear $\Re^1 \times \Re^1$ functions (mappings) to be modeled by a fuzzy additive model.

mate any multivariate nonlinear function on a compact domain to any degree of accuracy. This means that FAMs are dense in the space of continuous functions, and they share this very powerful property with NNs and SVMs.

This section discusses how FAMs approximate any (not analytically but verbally or linguistically) known functional dependency. A FAM is composed of a set of rules in the form of IF-THEN statements that express human knowledge about functional behavior. Suppose we want to model the two functions shown in figure 1.3. It is easy to model verbally the functional dependencies shown in figure 1.3. Both models would contain at least three IF-THEN rules. Using fewer rules would decrease the approximation accuracy, and using more rules would increase precision at the cost of more required computation time. This is the classical soft computing dilemma—a trade-off between imprecision and uncertainty on the one hand and low solution cost, tractability, and robustness on the other. The appropriate rules for the functions in figure 1.3 are as follows:

Left Graph	Right Graph
IF x is *low*, THEN y is *high*.	IF x is *low*, THEN y is *high*.
IF x is *medium*, THEN y is *low*.	IF x is *medium*, THEN y is *medium*.
IF x is *high*, THEN y is *high*.	IF x is *high*, THEN y is *low*.

These rules define three large rectangular patches that cover the functions. They are shown in figure 1.4 together with two possible approximators for each function.

Note that human beings do not (or only rarely) think in terms of nonlinear functions. We do not try to "draw these functions in our mind" or try to "see" them as geometrical artifacts. In general, we do not process geometrical figures, curves, surfaces, or hypersurfaces while performing tasks or expressing our knowledge. In addition, our expertise in or understanding of some functional dependencies is very

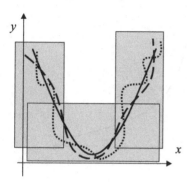 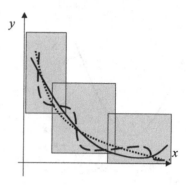

Figure 1.4
Two different functions (solid lines in both graphs) covered by three patches produced by IF-THEN rules
and modeled by two possible approximators (dashed and dotted curves).

often not a structured piece of knowledge at all. We typically perform very complex
tasks without being able to express how are we executing them. The curious reader
should try, for example, to explain to a colleague in the form of IF-THEN rules how
he is riding a bike, recognizing numerals, or surfing.

There are many steps, both heuristic and mathematical, between knowledge or
expertise and a final fuzzy model. After all the design steps and computation have
been completed, this final model is a very precisely defined nonlinear function. By
choosing the complexity of the rule basis, one can control the precision of the fuzzy
model and trade that off against solution costs. Thus, one first defines the most relevant input and output variables for a problem. In fuzzy logic terms, one must define
the universes of discourse, i.e., the domains and the ranges of relevant variables.
Then one specifies what is *low, medium, high, positive, zero, hot, cold,* and so on, in a
given task. In fuzzy logic terms, one defines the fuzzy membership functions (fuzzy
subsets or attributes) for the chosen input and output variables. Then one structures
the knowledge in the form of IF-THEN rules, that is, fuzzy rules (one establishes the
rule basis). The final stage is to perform the numerical part—applying some inference algorithm (e.g., SUM-PROD, MAX-MIN, SUM-MIN)—and to defuzzify the
resulting (usually not-normal) fuzzy subsets. The last two steps are crisp and precise
mathematical operations. *A* soft part in these calculations is the choice of membership functions as well as appropriate inference and defuzzification mechanisms.
Again, there is a trade-off between simple and fast algorithms having low computational costs and the desired accuracy. Thus, the final approximating function depends
upon many design decisions (only two out of many possible fuzzy approximators are
shown in fig. 1.4). The design decisions include the number, shapes, and placements

of the input and output membership functions, the inference mechanism applied, and the defuzzification method used.

Let us demonstrate the fuzzy modeling of a simple one-dimensional mapping $y = x^2$, $-3 < x < 0$. Choose four fuzzy *membership functions* (fuzzy subsets or attributes) for input and output variables as follows:

Input Variables	Output Variables
For $-3 < x < -2$, x is *very negative*.	For $4 < y < 10$, y is *large*.
For $-3 < x < -1$, x is *slightly negative*.	For $1 < y < 9$, y is *medium*.
For $-2 < x < 0$, x is *nearly zero*.	For $0 < y < 4$, y is *small*.
For $-1 < x < 0$, x is *very nearly zero*.	For $0 < y < 1$, y is *very small*.

These fuzzy membership functions are shown in figure 1.5. The *rule basis* for a fuzzy inference in the form of four IF-THEN rules is

R_1: IF x is *very negative* (VN),   THEN y is *large* (L).

R_2: IF x is *slightly negative* (SN),   THEN y is *medium* (M).

R_3: IF x is *nearly zero* (NZ),   THEN y is *small* (S).

R_4: IF x is *very nearly zero* (VNZ),   THEN y is *very small* (VS).

If one is not satisfied with the precision achieved, one should define more rules. This will be accomplished by a finer granulation (applying smaller patches) that can be realized by defining more membership functions. The fuzzy approximation that follows from a model with seven rules is shown in figure 1.6. The seven fuzzy membership functions (fuzzy subsets or attributes) for inputs and outputs, as well as the corresponding rule basis, are defined as follows:

Input Variables	Output Variables
For $-3.0 < x < -2.5$, x is *extremely far from zero*.	For $6.25 < y < 9$, y is *very large*.
For $-3.0 < x < -2.0$, x is *very far from zero*.	For $4 < y < 9$, y is *quite large*.
For $-2.5 < x < -1.5$, x is *quite far from zero*.	For $2.25 < y < 6.25$, y is *large*.
For $-2.0 < x < -1.0$, x is *far from zero*.	For $1 < y < 4$, y is *medium*.
For $-1.5 < x < -0.5$, x is *nearly zero*.	For $0.25 < y < 2.25$, y is *small*.
For $-1.0 < x < 0$, x is *very nearly zero*.	For $0 < y < 1$, y is *quite small*.
For $-0.5 < x < 0$, x is *extremely close to zero*.	For $0 < y < 0.25$, y is *very small*.

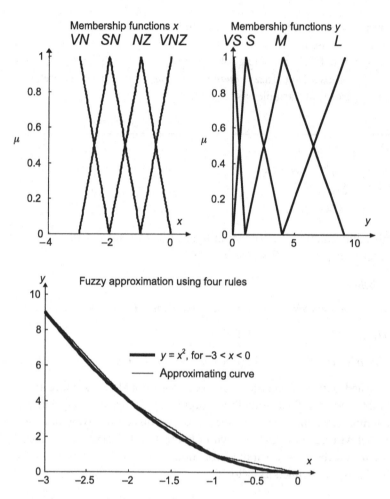

Figure 1.5
Modeling a one-dimensional mapping $y = x^2$ by a fuzzy model with four rules.

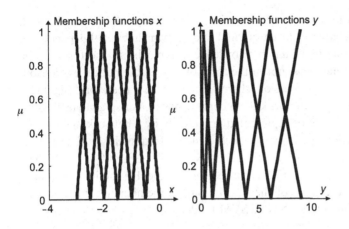

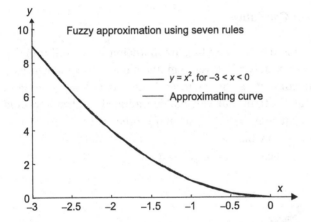

Figure 1.6
Modeling a one-dimensional mapping $y = x^2$ by a fuzzy model with seven rules.

R_1:   IF x is *extremely far from zero*,   THEN y is *very large*.

R_2:   IF x is *very far from zero*,   THEN y is *quite large*.

R_3:   IF x is *quite far from zero*,   THEN y is *large*.

R_4:   IF x is *far from zero*,   THEN y is *medium*.

R_5:   IF x is *nearly zero*,   THEN y is *small*.

R_6:   IF x is *very nearly zero*,   THEN y is *quite small*.

R_7:   IF x is *extremely close to zero*,   THEN y is *very small*

The fuzzy approximating function that results from a fuzzy additive model with seven rules is indistinguishable from an original and known functional dependency. Recall, however, that structured human knowledge is typically in the form of the (linguistically expressed) rule basis, not in the form of any mathematical expression. If one knew the mathematical expression, there would not be a need for designing a fuzzy model. One could simply use this known dependency in a crisp analytical form.

The fuzzy additive model can be represented graphically by a network like the one shown in figure 1.1. Section 6.2 discusses such structural equivalence. The resemblance, which follows from mild assumptions, can be readily seen in figure 6.25. The input membership functions of a FAM correspond to the HL activation (basis) functions in NNs, and the centers of the FAM's output membership functions are equivalent to the OL weights in an NN or SVM model.

1.3   Basic Mathematics of Soft Computing

The fields of learning from data and soft computing are mathematically well-founded disciplines. They are composed of several classical mathematics areas, shown as a "flower of learning and soft computing" in figure 1.7. One could say that both learning and soft computing are nothing but value-added applied mathematics and statistics, although this statement may be valid for many other fields as well. This book arose from a desire to show how the different areas depicted in figure 1.7, nicely connected, compose the powerful fields of learning from data and soft computing.

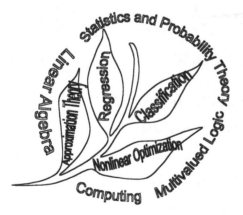

Figure 1.7
A "flower of learning and soft computing" and its basic mathematical constituents.

Here, *value-added* primarily means modern computer-based applications of standard and novel mathematical and statistical techniques. The statistical learning theory is presented in chapter 2, and fuzzy logic is the subject of chapter 6.

Two aspects of models (networks, machines, or mathematical functions) are analyzed here: what can these models represent, and how do we make them represent what we want them to? The first is *the problem of representation*, discussed in section 1.3.1. The second is *the problem of learning*, which boils down to some standard or novel nonlinear optimization techniques. Learning is the basic subject of this book, and it is analyzed in detail throughout. However, an elementary presentation of the need for, and the origins of, nonlinear optimization (learning or training) tools is given in section 1.3.2.

More specifically, section 1.3.1 presents the basics of classical and modern approaches to the approximation of multivariate functions, and section 1.3.2 introduces nonlinear optimization. Section 1.4 discusses the basics of classical statistical theory of regression and classification. Chapter 2 is devoted to the theoretically challenging area of support vector machines, which implement structural risk minimization, which is in turn developed within the framework of a new statistical learning theory. SVMs are also aimed at solving classification and regression problems, but unlike the theoretical approaches mentioned in section 1.4, which are based on known probability distributions, SVMs are the first mathematical models that do not assume any specific probability distributions and that learn from experimental data. Thus, sections 1.3 and 1.4 and chapter 2 roughly cover the basic theoretical constituents of the "learning from data" paradigm.

1.3.1 Approximation of Multivariate Functions

This section provides an elementary introduction to approximation theory. It also presents the basics of the theoretical interpolation/approximation[4] abilities of soft computing models: neural networks, support vector machines, and fuzzy logic models.

The classic one-dimensional problem is the approximation of a real continuous function $f(x)$ by an approximating function $f_a(x, \mathbf{w})$ having a fixed finite number of parameters w_i that are entries of a weights vector $\mathbf{w}$. (Later, $\mathbf{V}$ and $\mathbf{W}$ are used to denote matrices of hidden layer weights and output layer weights, respectively.) The basic problems in this book are somewhat different. One rarely tries to approximate some continuous univariate $f(x)$ or multivariate $f(\mathbf{x})$ function. The typical engineering problem to be solved is the interpolation or approximation of a set of P sparse and noisy training data points. However, to clarify the standard learning from data problem, classical issues from approximation theory are considered first. This section roughly follows Rice (1964) and Mason and Parks (1995).

Two major items in an approximation problem are the type of approximating function applied and the measure of goodness[5] of an approximation. This is also known as the question of choosing *form* and *norm*.

The choice of approximating function (form) is more important than the choice of a measure of goodness, that is, a distance function or norm that measures the distance between f and f_a. Unfortunately, there is no theoretical method of determining which out of many possible approximating functions will yield the best approximation. On the other hand, there are fortunately only a few feasible candidate functions in use or under investigation today. The most popular functions are tangent hyperbolic, a few radial basis functions (notably Gaussians and multiquadrics), polynomial functions, and three standard membership functions applied in fuzzy models (triangle, trapezoidal, and singleton). These functions are called activation, basis, and membership functions in multilayer perceptrons; radial basis function (RBF) or regularization networks, and fuzzy logic models. These models are, together with support vector machines, the most popular soft modeling and learning functions. Their mathematical forms follow.

A *multilayer perceptron* is a representative of nonlinear basis function expansion (approximation):

$$o = f_a(\mathbf{x}, \mathbf{w}, \mathbf{v}) = \sum_{i=1}^{N} w_i \varphi_i(\mathbf{x}, \mathbf{v}_i), \qquad (1.11)$$

where $\varphi_i(\mathbf{x}, \mathbf{v}_i)$ is a set of given functions (usually sigmoidal functions such as the logistic function or tangent hyperbolic—see (2.6) and chapter 3), o is the output from a model, and N is the number of hidden layer neurons. Both the output layer's weights w_i and the entries of the hidden layer weights vector $\mathbf{v}$ are free parameters that are subjects of learning.

An *RBF network* is a representative of a linear basis function expansion:

$$o = f_a(\mathbf{x}, \mathbf{w}) = \sum_{i=1}^{N} w_i \varphi_i(\mathbf{x}), \qquad (1.12)$$

where $\varphi_i(\mathbf{x})$ is a fixed (chosen in advance) set of radial basis functions (e.g., Gaussians, splines, multiquadrics). Note that when the basis functions $\varphi_i(\mathbf{x})$ are not fixed, that is, when their positions $\mathbf{c}_i$ and shape parameters $\boldsymbol{\Sigma}$ are also subjects of learning ($\varphi_i = \varphi_i(\mathbf{x}, \mathbf{c}_i, \boldsymbol{\Sigma}_i)$), RBF networks become nonlinear approximation schemes. (See chapter 5 for a more detailed discussion of RBF networks.)

A *fuzzy logic model*, like an **RBF** network, can be a representative of a linear or nonlinear basis function expansion:

$$o = y = f_a(\mathbf{x}, \mathbf{c}, \mathbf{r}) = \frac{\sum_{i=1}^{N} G(\mathbf{x}, \mathbf{c}_i) r_i}{\sum_{i=1}^{N} G(\mathbf{x}, \mathbf{c}_i)}, \tag{1.13}$$

where N is the number of rules, r is the rules, and basis functions $G(\mathbf{x}, \mathbf{c}_i)$ are the input membership functions (attributes or fuzzy subsets) centered at $\mathbf{c}_i$ (see (2.7) and section 6.1).

In addition to these models, two classic one-dimensional approximation schemes are considered: a set of *algebraic polynomials*

$$f_a(x) = \sum_{i=0}^{n} w_i x^i = w_0 + w_1 x + w_2 x^2 + w_3 x^3 + \cdots + w_{n-1} x^{n-1} + w_n x^n \tag{1.14}$$

and a *truncated Fourier series*

$$f_a(x) = a_0 + a_1 \sin(x) + b_1 \cos(x) + a_2 \sin(2x) + b_2 \cos(2x) + \cdots$$
$$+ a_n \sin(nx) + b_n \cos(nx). \tag{1.15}$$

All but the first approximation scheme here are linear approximations. However, all given models are aimed at creating nonlinear approximating functions. Thus, the adjective *linear* is used because the parameters ($\mathbf{w}$, a_i, b_i, and r_i) that are subjects of learning enter linearly into the approximating functions. In other words, the approximation depends linearly upon weights that are the subjects of learning. This very important property of linear models leads to quadratic (convex) optimization problems with guaranteed global minimums when the L_2 norm is used.

The second major question to be answered is the choice of norm (the distance between the data and the approximating function $f_a(x, \mathbf{w})$). This choice is less important than the choice of form $f_a(x, \mathbf{w})$. If $f_a(x, \mathbf{w})$ is compatible with an underlying function $f(\mathbf{x})$ that produced the training data points, then almost any reasonable measure will lead to an acceptable approximation to $f(\mathbf{x})$. If $f_a(x, \mathbf{w})$ is not compatible with $f(\mathbf{x})$, none of the norms can improve bad approximations to $f(\mathbf{x})$. However, in many practical situations one norm of approximation is naturally preferred over another.

The norm of approximation is a measure of how well a specific approximation $f_a(\mathbf{x})$ of the given form matches the given set of noisy data. Norms are (positive) scalars used as measures of error, length, size, distance, and so on, depending on context. Here a norm usually represents an error. The most common mathematical class of norms in the case of a measured discrete data set is the L_p (Hölder) norm. The L_p norm is a p-norm of an error vector $\mathbf{e}$ given as

$$\|\mathbf{e}\|_p = \|\mathbf{d} - \mathbf{f}_a(\mathbf{x}, \mathbf{w})\|_p = \|\mathbf{d} - \mathbf{o}\|_p = \left(\sum_{i=1}^{p} |d_i - o_i|^p \right)^{1/p}, \tag{1.16}$$

where P indicates the size of the training data set, that is, the number of training data pairs, and $\mathbf{d}$ and $\mathbf{o}$ stand for P-dimensional vectors of desired and actual outputs of the neural network. Note that (1.16) is strictly valid for an $\Re^d \to \Re^1$ mapping, or for an NN with a single output layer neuron. For more OL neurons, a norm would be defined as a proper matrix norm. Assuming that the unknown underlying function $f(\mathbf{x})$ is given on a discrete data set containing P measurements $f(\mathbf{x}_1), f(\mathbf{x}_2), \ldots, f(\mathbf{x}_P)$, the standard L_p norms in use are defined as

$$L_1: \quad \|f - f_a\|_1 = \sum_{i}^{P} |f(\mathbf{x}_i) - f_a(\mathbf{x}_i)| \qquad \text{(absolute value)} \tag{1.17}$$

$$L_2: \quad \|f - f_a\|_2 = \sum_{i}^{P} (|f(\mathbf{x}_i) - f_a(\mathbf{x}_i)|^2)^{1/2} \quad \text{(Euclidean norm)} \tag{1.18}$$

$$L_\infty: \quad \|f - f_a\|_\infty = \max_{i} |f(\mathbf{x}_i) - f_a(\mathbf{x}_i)| \qquad \begin{array}{l} \text{(Chebyshev, uniform, or} \\ \text{infinity norm)} \end{array} \tag{1.19}$$

The norms used during an optimization of the models are not only standard L_p norms. Usually rather more complex mathematical structures are applied in the form of cost or error functions that enforce the closeness to training data (most typically measured by an L_2 or L_1 norm) and that measure some other property of an approximating function (e.g., smoothness, model complexity, weights magnitude). These norms (actually variously defined functionals that do not possess the strict mathematical properties required for norms) are typically composed of two parts. The first component is usually a standard L_2 (or L_1) norm, and the second is some penalization term (see table 1.4 and equations (2.26)–(2.28)). Vapnik's ε-insensitive loss function (norm), which is particularly useful for regression problems, is introduced in chapter 2.

The Chebyshev (or uniform) norm is an L_p norm called an infinity norm by virtue of the identity

$$\lim_{p \to \infty} (|x_1|^p + |x_2|^p + \cdots + |x_p|^p)^{1/p} = \max_{1 \le i \le P} |x_i|. \tag{1.20}$$

The choice of the appropriate norm or a measure of the approximation's goodness depends primarily on the data and on the simplicity of approximation and optimization algorithms available. The L_2 norm is the best one for data corrupted with normally distributed (Gaussian) noise. In this case, it is known that the estimated parameters or weights obtained in L_2 norm correspond to the maximum-likelihood estimates. The L_1 norm is much better than the Euclidean norm for data that have outliers because the L_1 norm tends to ignore such data. The Chebyshev norm is ideal in the case of exact data with errors in a uniform distribution.

In many fields, particularly in signal processing and system identification and control, the L_2 or Euclidean norm is almost universally used, for two reasons. First, the assumption about the Gaussian character of the noise in a control systems environment is an acceptable and reasonable one. Second, the L_2 norm is mathematically simple and tractable.

Very often, a measure of goodness or closeness of approximation used during a learning stage does not satisfy (1.17)–(1.19) or other known properties of norms, and hence is not a norm. For example, the most common deviation from a "pure" L_2 norm is the use of the sum of error squares as a standard cost function in NN learning. The sum of error squares is the measure derived from the norm (it is a slightly changed version of a Euclidean norm without square root operation), but its minimization is equivalent to the minimization of the L_2 norm from which it is derived.

Now that the concepts of form (type of function used to approximate data) and norm (measure of closeness of approximation) have been introduced, a natural question is, what is the best approximation? Of course, in order to achieve better approximations, the approximants will generally have to be of higher and higher degree. An increase in degree, usually leads to overfitting, however. This problem is discussed in detail throughout the book.

Given the set S_n of approximating functions (say, polynomials of sixth order, or NNs with six HL neurons, or fuzzy models with six rules, $n = 6$), is there among the elements of S_n (among all possible polynomials of sixth order, or NNs with six HL neurons, or fuzzy models with six rules) one that is closer to given data points $f(\mathbf{x}_i)$, $i = 1, P$, than any other element (function, model, network) of S_n? If there is, it is known as the *best approximation* to $f(\mathbf{x})$.

Note, however, that the best approximation property depends upon the norm applied. Change the norm (the criterion of closeness of approximation) and the best approximation will change. Generally, the best approximation in the L_p norm is not the same as the best approximation in the L_q norm $(p \neq q)$. This is shown in the following one-dimensional continuous example (see also problems 1.8 and 1.9).

Example 1.1   Approximate $y = x^4$ over $[0, 1]$ by a straight line $f_a(x)$ so that

$$\int_0^1 (x^4 - f_a(x))^2 \, dx \text{ is minimum,}$$

$$\int_0^1 (x^4 - f_a(x))^2 \, dx + \int_0^1 \left(\frac{d(x^4 - f_a(x))}{dx} \right)^2 dx \text{ is minimum,}$$

$$\max_{0 \le x \le 1} |x^4 - f_a(x)| \text{ is minimum.}$$

Note that $y = x^4$ is given as a continuous function, not as a set of discrete points. Therefore, it is appropriate here to use norms defined over an interval that apply an integral operator instead of equations (1.17)–(1.19), which comprise a summing operator. Three different best approximations (solutions) corresponding to the given cost functions (norms) are

$$f_a(x) = \frac{4x}{5} - \frac{1}{5} \qquad \text{(solid line in fig. 1.8),}$$

$$f_a(x) = \frac{54x}{55} - \frac{16}{55} \qquad \text{(dashed line in fig. 1.8),}$$

$$f_a(x) = x - 0.236 \qquad \text{(dotted line in fig. 1.8).} \qquad\qquad ■[6]$$

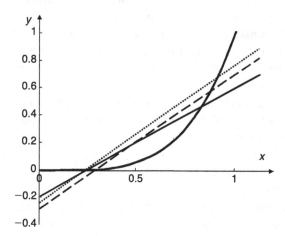

Figure 1.8
Best least square (solid), penalized least square (dashed), and uniform (dotted) linear approximations to x^4 on $[0, 1]$.

The best approximation is unique for all strict norms, that is, for $1 < p < \infty$. Thus, the best approximation with an L_2 norm is unique, but this property is not, for example, shared with L_1 and L_∞ norms. For more on the problem of a norm's uniqueness, see the related problems in the problems section of this chapter.

Before examining the approximation properties of models used in this book, one can consider some basic shortcomings of classical approximation schemes. Historically, there are two standard approximators: algebraic and trigonometric polynomials. The interested reader should consult the vast literature on the theory of approximation to find discussions on the existence and uniqueness of a solution, the best approximation calculation and its asymptotic properties, and the like. Here we start with polynomial approximators of a one-dimensional function given by discrete data. In trying to learn about the underlying dependency between inputs and outputs we are concerned with the error at all points in the range, not only at the sampled training data. Example 1.2 shows the deficiency of polynomial approximations. They behave badly in the proximity of domain boundaries even though they are perfect interpolators of given training data points.

Example 1.2   Approximate function $f(x) = 1/(1 + 25x^2)$ defined over the range $[-1, +1]$ and sampled at 21 equidistant points x_i, $i = 1, 21$, (i.e., $P = 21$) by polynomials of twelfth, sixteenth, and twentieth orders.

For this particular function (see fig. 1.9) it is found that for any point $x \neq x_i$, where $|x| > 0.75$, the error $|f_a(x) - f(x)|$ of the approximation increases without bound as

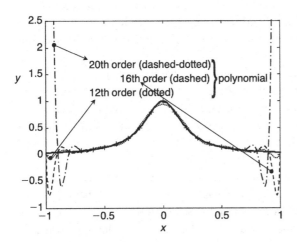

Figure 1.9
Polynomial approximations of a function $1/(1 + 25x^2)$.

the order of the approximating polynomials n increases. This is true even though $f_a(x_i) = f(x_i)$ when the order of polynomial $n = P - 1$, where P is the number of training data. In this example $f_a(x_i) = f(x_i)$ for a twentieth-order polynomial, which means that both L_1 and L_2 norms are equal to zero, wrongly suggesting perfect errorless approximation over the whole domain of input variable x.   ∎

When considering an error over a whole range, a more satisfactory objective is to make the maximum error as small as possible. This is the *minimax* or Chebyshev type of approximation where the error is defined by (1.19) and the function $f_a(x)$ is chosen so that L_∞ is minimized. It is in this context that the Chebyshev polynomials have found wide application.

There are also many other polynomials, notably a class of orthogonal polynomials, that can be used for approximations. All of them have similar deficiencies in the sense that as the number of training points P increases, the approximation improves near the center of the interval but shows pronounced oscillatory behavior at the ends of the interval.

Another popular classical approximation scheme involves rational functions (the ratio of two polynomials) given as

$$f_a(x, \mathbf{w}, \mathbf{v}) = \frac{\sum_{i=0}^{n} w_i x^i}{\sum_{i=0}^{m} v_i x^i}. \tag{1.21}$$

These functions are much more flexible, but they are nonlinear approximators (with respect to the denominator weights v_i) and learning of the weights v_i is not an easy task. They are of historical significance but are not used as basis functions in this book.

Both the polynomials and trigonometric sums have similar disadvantages in that they cannot take sharp bends followed by relatively flat behavior. Both functions are defined over the whole domain (i.e., they are globally acting activation functions), and they generally vary gently. Such characteristics can be circumvented by increasing the degree of these functions, but this has as a consequence wild behavior of the approximator close to boundaries (see fig. 1.9).

The best candidates for approximating functions that naturally originate from polynomials are the *piecewise polynomial functions*, the most popular being various *spline functions*. The spline functions are special cases of RBF functions; they are derived in chapter 5. They are defined by dividing the domain of the input variable into several intervals by a set of points called *joints* or *knots*. The approximating function is then a polynomial of specified degree between the knots. The approximation is linear for prespecified and fixed knots. However, the whole approximating scheme is nonlinear when the positions of knots are subjects of learning. The learning of knot positions, being a nonlinear optimization problem, is complex and generally not an easy task.

It is interesting to note that in the univariate case (for one-dimensional inputs) algebraic polynomials, trigonometric polynomials, and splines all have the property of providing a unique interpolation on a set of distinct points equal in number to the number of approximation parameters (weights). However, in the multivariate case it is not usually possible to guarantee a unique interpolant for these basis functions, and hence a best approximation is not necessarily unique. Problem 1.11 deals with the uniqueness of a polynomial approximation in a bivariate case. However, it deliberately emphasizes a kind of pathological case. It is important to be aware of possible pitfalls, but there are some very nice results in applying polynomials in support vector machines (see chapter 2) that exploit their properties. At the same time, RBFs uniquely interpolate any set of data on a distinct input set of training data points. This is but one of nice properties of RBF networks (RBF approximation models).

Figure 1.10 shows an interpolation of six ($P = 6$) random data points using a polynomial of fifth order. A perfect interpolation is achieved because the Vandermonde matrix $\mathbf{X}$ in (1.22) is nonsingular. (These matrices often occur in polynomial approximations, signal processing, and error-correcting codes.) However, this matrix

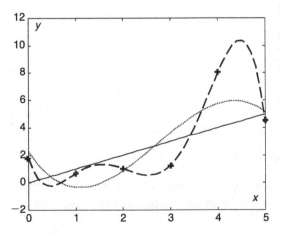

Figure 1.10
Interpolation and approximation polynomials of fifth order (dashed) and third order (dotted) to six highly noise-contaminated data points obtained by sampling the straight line (solid).

is notorious. Even for modest sizes of P, it is very ill conditioned (its determinant is very small), and solutions may be subject to severe numerical difficulties. The inter-polation curve (dashed) is a solution of a linear system of equations, and it is a (unique) least-squares solution, as is the approximation curve (dotted). The latter is, however, a third-order polynomial approximation curve. It is also the best approxi-mation in the least-squares sense but no longer passes through the training data points.

An *interpolating solution* results from solving the following system of linear equa-tions:

$$w_0 + w_1 x_i^1 + w_2 x_i^2 + w_3 x_i^3 + w_4 x_i^4 + w_5 x_i^5 = y_i, \qquad i = 1, 6,$$

which can be expressed in a matrix form as

$$\mathbf{Xw} = \mathbf{y} \Rightarrow
\begin{bmatrix}
1 & x_1 & x_1^2 & x_1^3 & x_1^4 & x_1^5 \\
1 & x_2 & x_2^2 & x_2^3 & x_2^4 & x_2^5 \\
1 & x_3 & x_3^2 & x_3^3 & x_3^4 & x_3^5 \\
1 & x_4 & x_4^2 & x_4^3 & x_4^4 & x_4^5 \\
1 & x_5 & x_5^2 & x_5^3 & x_5^4 & x_5^5 \\
1 & x_6 & x_6^2 & x_6^3 & x_6^4 & x_6^5
\end{bmatrix}
\begin{bmatrix}
w_0 \\ w_1 \\ w_2 \\ w_3 \\ w_4 \\ w_5
\end{bmatrix}
=
\begin{bmatrix}
y_1 \\ y_2 \\ y_3 \\ y_4 \\ y_5 \\ y_6
\end{bmatrix}. \tag{1.22}$$

In this case, input vector $\mathbf{x} = \begin{bmatrix} 0 & 1 & 2 & 3 & 4 & 5 \end{bmatrix}^T$ and output vector $\mathbf{y} = \begin{bmatrix} 1.83 & 0.69 & 1.03 & 1.26 & 8.03 & 4.45 \end{bmatrix}^T$. A nonsingular Vandermonde matrix $\mathbf{X}$ is

$$\mathbf{X} =
\begin{bmatrix}
1 & 0 & 0 & 0 & 0 & 0 \\
1 & 1 & 1 & 1 & 1 & 1 \\
1 & 2 & 4 & 8 & 16 & 32 \\
1 & 3 & 9 & 27 & 81 & 243 \\
1 & 4 & 16 & 64 & 256 & 1024 \\
1 & 5 & 25 & 125 & 625 & 3125
\end{bmatrix}$$

The solution vector $\mathbf{w}$ to (1.22) that ensures an interpolation is

$$\mathbf{w} = \mathbf{X}^{-1}\mathbf{y} = \begin{bmatrix} -10.84 & 18.57 & -11.60 & 2.99 & -0.26 & 1.83 \end{bmatrix}^T.$$

An *approximating solution* using a polynomial of third order (shown in fig. 1.10 as a dotted curve) is obtained by solving the following overdetermined system of six equations in four unknowns:

$$w_0 + w_1 x_i^1 + w_2 x_i^2 + w_3 x_i^3 = y_i, \qquad i = 1, 6,$$

or in matrix form,

$$
\begin{bmatrix}
1 & 0 & 0 & 0 \\
1 & 1 & 1 & 1 \\
1 & 2 & 4 & 8 \\
1 & 3 & 9 & 27 \\
1 & 4 & 16 & 64 \\
1 & 5 & 25 & 125
\end{bmatrix}
\begin{bmatrix}
w_0 \\
w_1 \\
w_2 \\
w_3
\end{bmatrix}
=
\begin{bmatrix}
1.83 \\
0.69 \\
1.03 \\
1.26 \\
8.03 \\
4.45
\end{bmatrix}
\tag{1.23}
$$

The best solution, a weights vector $\mathbf{w}$, that results from an approximation in the least squares sense is obtained as follows:

$$\mathbf{w} = \mathbf{X}^{+}\mathbf{y} = [-5.17 \quad 2.96 \quad -0.36 \quad 2.25]^{T},$$

where $\mathbf{X}^{+}$ denotes the pseudoinversion of a rectangular matrix $\mathbf{X}$.

The same set of training data points is interpolated by using *linear splines* and *cubic splines*; the interpolating curves are shown in figure 1.11.

The fifth column in a matrix $\mathbf{X}$ belonging to linear splines in (1.24) corresponds to the linear spline centered at $x = 4$ (thick dotted spline). Matrix $\mathbf{X}$ is also called a *design matrix*. The interpolation functions that are obtained by using spline functions as shown in figure 1.11 belong to radial basis functions network models. Chapter 5

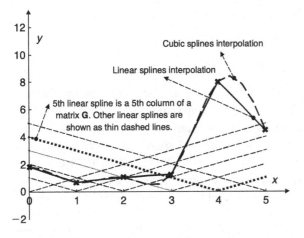

Figure 1.11
Interpolation by linear and cubic splines. Training data set is the same as in figure 1.10. Fifth linear spline corresponds to fifth column of a matrix $\mathbf{X}$ given in (1.24).

discusses these networks, also known as regularization networks. Chapter 5 also presents the origins of the linear and cubic splines applied here.

Corresponding systems of linear equations for both interpolations in matrix form and solution vectors **w** are as follows.

For linear splines,

$$\mathbf{Xw}_L = \mathbf{y} \Rightarrow \begin{bmatrix} 0 & 1 & 2 & 3 & 4 & 5 \\ 1 & 0 & 1 & 2 & 3 & 4 \\ 2 & 1 & 0 & 1 & 2 & 3 \\ 3 & 2 & 1 & 0 & 1 & 2 \\ 4 & 3 & 2 & 1 & 0 & 1 \\ 5 & 4 & 3 & 2 & 1 & 0 \end{bmatrix} \begin{bmatrix} w_1 \\ w_2 \\ w_3 \\ w_4 \\ w_5 \\ w_6 \end{bmatrix} = \begin{bmatrix} 1.83 \\ 0.69 \\ 1.03 \\ 1.26 \\ 8.03 \\ 4.45 \end{bmatrix}. \tag{1.24}$$

For cubic splines,

$$\mathbf{Xw}_C = \mathbf{y} \Rightarrow \begin{bmatrix} 0 & 1 & 8 & 27 & 64 & 125 \\ 1 & 0 & 1 & 8 & 27 & 64 \\ 8 & 1 & 0 & 1 & 8 & 27 \\ 27 & 8 & 1 & 0 & 1 & 8 \\ 64 & 27 & 8 & 1 & 0 & 1 \\ 125 & 64 & 27 & 8 & 1 & 0 \end{bmatrix} \begin{bmatrix} w_1 \\ w_2 \\ w_3 \\ w_4 \\ w_5 \\ w_6 \end{bmatrix} = \begin{bmatrix} 1.83 \\ 0.69 \\ 1.03 \\ 1.26 \\ 8.03 \\ 4.45 \end{bmatrix}. \tag{1.25}$$

The solution vectors are

$$\mathbf{w}_L = [0.06 \quad 0.74 \quad -0.057 \quad 3.27 \quad -5.17 \quad 2.4163]^T.$$

$$\mathbf{w}_C = [0.59 \quad -1.66 \quad 2.55 \quad -4.43 \quad 3.39 \quad -0.9165]^T.$$

As long as the dimensionality of input vectors is not too high, many classical approximation tools may be appropriate for modeling training data points. However, in modern soft computing, the dimensionality of input vectors is very high; it may go to dozens of thousands. In such high-dimensional spaces, data are sparse, and modeling underlying dependencies is a formidable task. NNs, SVMs, and FL models are appropriate tools for such tasks. Their theoretical interpolation and approximation capacities are briefly discussed here. Chapters 2–6 treat these issues in more detail.

Both NNs and FL models are *universal approximators* in the sense that they can approximate any function to any degree of accuracy provided that there are enough hidden layer neurons or rules. The same can also be stated for SVMs. Without any doubt, such powerful approximating faculties are the foundation of, and theoretical justification for, the wide application of NNs and FL models.

Following are the classic Weierstrass theorem for the approximation by polynomials; the Cybenko-Hornik-Funahashi theorem (Cybenko 1989; Hornik, Stinchcombe, and White 1989; Funahashi 1989), which states identical abilities of sigmoidal functions; and the theorem for universal approximation properties using the Gaussian (radial basis) activation functions.

CLASSICAL WEIERSTRASS THEOREM   The set $P_{[a,b]}$ of all polynomials

$$p(x) = \sum_{j=0}^{n} w_j x^j \tag{1.26}$$

is dense in $C[a,b]$. In other words, given $f \in C[a,b]$ and $\varepsilon > 0$, there is a polynomial p for which

$$|p(x) - f(x)| < \varepsilon, \quad \text{for all } x \in [a,b].$$

CYBENKO-HORNIK-FUNAHASHI THEOREM   Let σ be any sigmoidal function and I_d the d-dimensional cube $[0,1]^d$. Then the finite sum of the form

$$f_a(\mathbf{x}) = \sum_{j=1}^{n} w_j \sigma_j(\mathbf{v}_j^T \mathbf{x} + b_j) \tag{1.27}$$

is dense in $C[I_d]$. In other words, given $f \in C[I_d]$ and $\varepsilon > 0$, there is a sum $f_a(\mathbf{x})$ for which

$$|f_a(\mathbf{x}) - f(\mathbf{x})| < \varepsilon, \quad \text{for all } \mathbf{x} \in I_d,$$

where w_j, $\mathbf{v}$, and b_j represent OL weights, HL weights, and bias weights of the hidden layer, respectively.

THEOREM FOR THE DENSITY OF GAUSSIAN FUNCTIONS   Let G be a Gaussian function and I_d the d-dimensional cube $[0,1]^d$. Then the finite sum of the form

$$f_a(\mathbf{x}) = \sum_{j=1}^{n} w_j G(\|\mathbf{x} - \mathbf{c}_j\|) \tag{1.28}$$

is dense in $C[I_d]$. In other words, given $f \in C[I_d]$ and $\varepsilon > 0$, there is a sum $f_a(\mathbf{x})$ for which

$$|f_a(\mathbf{x}) - f(\mathbf{x})| < \varepsilon, \quad \text{for all } \mathbf{x} \in I_d,$$

where w_i and $\mathbf{c}_i$ represent OL weights and centers of HL multivariate Gaussian functions, respectively.[7]

The same results of universal approximation properties exist for fuzzy models, too. Results of this type can also be stated for many other different functions (notably trigonometric polynomials and various kernel functions). They are very common in approximation theory and hold under very weak assumptions. Density in the space of continuous functions is a necessary condition that every approximation scheme should satisfy.

However, the types of problems in this book are slightly different. In diverse tasks where NNs and SVMs are successfully applied, the problem is usually not one of approximating some continuous univariate $f(x)$ or multivariate $f(\mathbf{x})$ function over some interval. The typical engineering problem involves the interpolation or approximation of sets of P sparse and noisy training data points.

The NNs or SVMs will have to model the mapping of a finite training data set of P n-dimensional input training patterns $\mathbf{x}$ to the corresponding P m-dimensional output (desired or target) patterns $\mathbf{y}$. (These $\mathbf{y}$ are denoted by $\mathbf{d}$ during the training, where $\mathbf{d}$ stands for *desired*.) In other words, these models should model the dependency (or the underlying function, i.e., the hypersurface) $f: \Re^n \to \Re^m$. In the case of classification, the problem is to find the discriminant hyperfunctions that separate m classes in an n-dimensional space. The learning (adaptation, training phase) of our models corresponds to the linear or nonlinear optimization of a fitting procedure based on knowledge of the training data pairs. This is a task of hypersurface fitting in the generally high-dimensional space $\Re^n \otimes \Re^m$. RBF networks have a nice property that they can interpolate any set of P data points. The same is also true for fuzzy logic models, support vector machines, or multilayer perceptrons, and this powerful property is the basis for the existence of these novel modeling tools.

To *interpolate* the data means that the interpolating function $f_a(\mathbf{x}_p)$ must pass through each particular point in $\Re^n \otimes \Re^m$ space. Thus, an interpolating problem is stated as follows:

Given is a set of P measured (observed) data: $X = \{\mathbf{x}_p, \mathbf{d}_p, p = 1, \ldots, P\}$ consisting of the input pattern vectors $\mathbf{x} \in \Re^n$ and output desired responses or targets $\mathbf{d} \in \Re^m$. An interpolating function is such that

$$f_a(\mathbf{x}_p) = \mathbf{d}_p, \qquad p = 1, \ldots, P. \tag{1.29}$$

Note that an interpolating function is required to pass through each desired point $\mathbf{d}_p$. Thus, the cost or error function (norm) E that measures the quality of modeling (at this point, we use the sum of error squares) in the case of interpolation must be equal to zero

$$E = \sum_{p=1}^{P} \mathbf{e}_p^2 = \sum_{p=1}^{P} [\mathbf{d}_p - f_a(\mathbf{x}_p)]^2 = 0. \tag{1.30}$$

Strictly speaking, an interpolating function $f_a(\mathbf{x}_p)$ and therefore the error function E, are parameterized by approximation coefficients here called weights, and a more proper notation for these two functions would be $f_a(\mathbf{x}, \mathbf{w}, \mathbf{v})$ and $E(\mathbf{x}, \mathbf{w}, \mathbf{v})$. Weights $\mathbf{w}$ and $\mathbf{v}$ are typically a network's output layer weights and hidden layer weights, respectively. Writing this dependency explicitly stresses the fact that the weights will be subjected to an optimization procedure that should result in a good f_a and a small E. (Generally, weights are organized in matrices $\mathbf{W}$ and $\mathbf{V}$.)

Note that in order to interpolate data set X, the RBF network, for example, should have exactly P neurons in a hidden layer. Work with NNs typically involves sets of hundreds of thousands of patterns (measurements), which means that the size of such an interpolating network would have to be large. The numerical processing of matrices of such high order is very intractable. There is another important reason why the idea of data interpolation is usually not a good one. Real data are corrupted by noise, and interpolation of noisy data leads to the problem of overfitting. What we basically want NNs to do is to model the underlying function (dependency) and to filter out the noise contained in the training data. There are many different techniques for doing this, and some of these approaches are presented later. Chapter 2 is devoted to this problem of matching the complexity of a training data set to the capacity of an approximating model. The approach presented there also results in models with fewer processing units (HL neurons) than there are training patterns.

The number of neurons in a hidden layer and the parameters that define the shapes of these HL activation (basis) functions are the most important design parameters with respect to the approximation abilities of neural networks. Recall that both the number of input components (features) and the number of output neurons are in general determined by the very nature of the problem. At the same time, the number of HL neurons, which primarily determines the real representation power of a neural network and its generalization capacity, is a free parameter. In the case of general nonlinear regression performed by an NN, the main task is to model the underlying function between the given inputs and outputs and to filter out the disturbances contained in the noisy training data set. Similar statements can be made for pattern recognition (classification) problems. In the SVM field, one can say that the model complexity (capacity) should match the data complexity during training. Model capacity is most often controlled by the number of neurons in the hidden layer. In changing the number of HL nodes, two extreme solutions should be avoided: filtering out the underlying function (not enough HL neurons) and modeling the noise or overfitting the data (too many HL neurons). Therefore, there is a need to comment on appropriate measures of model quality.

In the theory of learning from data, the problems of measuring the model's performance are solved by using different approaches and inductive principles. Applying some simple norm, for instance, any L_p norm, is usually not good enough. Perfect performance on training data does not guarantee good performance on previously unseen inputs (see example 1.3). Various techniques aimed at resolving the trade-off between performance on training data and performance on previously unseen data are in use today. The concept of simultaneous minimization of a bias and a variance, known as the *bias-variance dilemma*, originated from the field of mathematical statistics (see chapter 4). Girosi analyzed the concepts of an approximation error and an estimation error (see section 2.3). Finally, in the field of SVMs one applies the structural risk minimization principle, which controls both the empirical risk and a confidence interval at the same time. In all three approaches, one tries to keep both components of an overall error or risk as low as possible. All these measures of the approximation performance of a model are similar in spirit but originate from different inductive principles, and they cannot be made equivalent.

One more classical statistical tool for resolving the trade-off between the performance on training data and the complexity of a model is the cross-validation technique. The basic idea of the cross-validation is founded on the fact that good results on the training data do not ensure good generalization capability. Generalization refers to the capacity of a neural network to give correct answers on previously unseen data. This set of previously unseen data is called a *test set* or *validation set* of patterns. The standard procedure to obtain this particular data set is to take out a part (say, one quarter) of all measured data, which will not be used during training but in the validation or test phase only. The higher the noise level in the data and the more complex the underlying function to be modeled, the larger the test set should be. Thus, in the cross-validation procedure the performance of the network is measured on the test or validation data set, ensuring the good generalization property of a neural network.

Example 1.3 demonstrates some basic phenomena during modeling of a noisy data set. It clearly shows why the idea of interpolation is not very sound.

Example 1.3 The dependency (plant or system to be identified) between two variables is given by $y = x + \sin(2x)$. Interpolate and approximate these data by an RBF network having Gaussian basis functions by using a highly corrupted training data set (25% Gaussian noise with zero mean) containing 36 measured patterns (x, d).

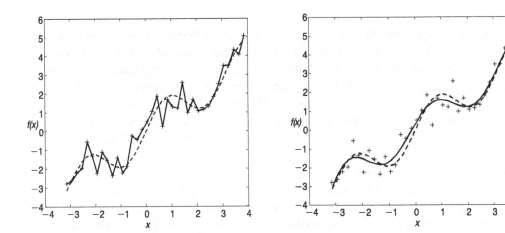

Figure 1.12
Modeling of noisy data by an RBF (regularization) network with Gaussian basis functions. *Left*, interpolation and overfitting of noisy data (36 hidden layer neurons). *Right*, approximation and smoothing of noisy data (8 hidden layer neurons). Underlying function (dashed) is $y = x + \sin(2x)$. Number of training patterns (crosses) $P = 36$.

Figure 1.12 shows the interpolation and the approximation solutions. Clearly, during the optimization of the network's size, one of the smoothing parameters is the number of HL neurons that should be small enough to filter out the noise and large enough to model the underlying function. This simple example of a one-dimensional mapping may serve as a good illustration of overfitting. It is clear that perfect performance on a training data set does not guarantee a good model (see left graph, where the interpolating function passes through the training data). The same phenomena will be observed while fitting multivariate hypersurfaces. ∎

In order to avoid overfitting, one must relax an interpolation requirement like (1.29) while fitting noisy data and instead do an *approximation* of the training data set that can be expressed as

$$f_a(\mathbf{x}_p) \approx \mathbf{d}_p, \qquad p = 1, \ldots, P. \tag{1.31}$$

In the case of approximation, the error or cost function is not required as $E = 0$. The requirement is only that the error function

$$E = \sum_{p=1}^{P} \mathbf{e}_p^2 = \sum_{p=1}^{P} [\mathbf{d}_p - f_a(\mathbf{x}_p)]^2$$

be small and the noise be filtered out as much as possible. Thus, approximation is related to interpolation but with the relaxed condition that an approximant $f_a(\mathbf{x}_p)$ does not have to go through all the training data points. Instead, it should approach the data set points as closely as possible, trying to minimize some measure of the error or disagreement between the approximated point $f_a(\mathbf{x}_p)$ and the desired value $\mathbf{d}$. These two concepts of curve fitting are readily seen in figure 1.12. In real technical applications the data set is usually colored or polluted with noise, and it is better to use approximation because it is a kind of smooth fit of noisy data. If one forces an approximating function to pass each noisy data point, one will easily get a model with high variance and poor generalization.

The interpolation and the approximation in example 1.3 were done by an RBF neural network as given in (1.28), with 36 and 8 neurons in the hidden layer, respectively. Gaussian functions (HL activation functions here) were placed symmetrically along the x-axis, each having the same standard deviation σ equal to double the distance between two adjacent centers. With such a choice of σ, a nice overlapping of the basis (activation) functions was obtained. Note that both parameters (centers c_i and standard deviations σ_i) of Gaussian bells were fixed during the calculation of the best output layer weights w_i. (In terms of NNs and FL models, the hidden layer weights and parameters that define positions and shapes of membership functions, respectively, were fixed or frozen during the fitting procedure.) In this way, such learning was the problem of linear approximation because the parameters w_i enter linearly into the expression for the approximating function $f_a(\mathbf{x})$. In other words, approximation error $e(\mathbf{w})$ depends linearly upon the parameters (here the OL weights w_i). Note that in this example the approximation function $f_a(\mathbf{x})$ represents physically the output from the single OL neuron, and the approximation error for a pth data pair (x_p, d_p) can be written as

$$e_p = e_p(\mathbf{w}) = d_p - f_a(x_p, \mathbf{w}) = d_p - o(x_p, \mathbf{w}). \tag{1.32}$$

Generally, x will be the $(n+1)$-dimensional vector $\mathbf{x}$. When approximation error e depends linearly upon the weights, the error function $E(\mathbf{w})$, defined as the sum of error squares, is a hyperparaboloidal bowl with a guaranteed single (global) minimum. The weights vector $\mathbf{w}^*$, which gives the minimal point $E_{min} = E(\mathbf{w}^*)$, is the required solution, and in this case the approximating function $f_a(\mathbf{x})$ from (1.28) or (1.33) has a property of best approximation. Note that despite the fact that this approximation problem is linear, the approximating function $f_a(\mathbf{x})$ is nonlinear, resulting from the summation of weighted nonlinear basis function φ_i.

A variety of basis functions for approximation are available for use in NNs or FL models. (In the NN area, basis functions are typically called activation functions, and in the field of FL models, the most common names are membership functions, possibility distributions, attributes, fuzzy subsets, or degree-of-belonging functions.) The basic linear approximation scheme, as given by (1.12)–(1.15), can be rewritten as

$$f_a(\mathbf{x}) = \sum_{i=1}^{N} w_i \varphi_i(\mathbf{x}), \tag{1.33}$$

where N is the number of HL neurons, and $\mathbf{x}$ is an n-dimensional input vector. Equation (1.33) represents an $\Re^n \rightarrow \Re^1$ mapping, and $f_a(\mathbf{x})$ is a hypersurface in an $(n+1)$-dimensional space.

In the learning stage of a linear parameters model the weights w_i are calculated knowing training patterns $\{\mathbf{x}_i, d_i\}$, $i = 1, P$, and equation (1.33) is rewritten in the following matrix form for learning purposes:

$$\mathbf{d} = \mathbf{X}\mathbf{w} \Rightarrow \begin{bmatrix} d_1 \\ d_2 \\ \vdots \\ d_P \end{bmatrix} = \begin{bmatrix} \varphi_1(\mathbf{x}_1) & \varphi_2(\mathbf{x}_1) & \cdots & \varphi_N(\mathbf{x}_1) \\ \varphi_1(\mathbf{x}_2) & \varphi_2(\mathbf{x}_2) & \cdots & \varphi_N(\mathbf{x}_2) \\ \vdots & \vdots & \vdots & \vdots \\ \varphi_1(\mathbf{x}_P) & \varphi_2(\mathbf{x}_P) & \cdots & \varphi_N(\mathbf{x}_P) \end{bmatrix} \begin{bmatrix} w_1 \\ w_2 \\ \vdots \\ w_N \end{bmatrix}, \tag{1.34}$$

where P is the number of training data pairs, and N is the number of neurons. Typically, $P > N$, meaning that $\mathbf{X}$ is a rectangular matrix and the solution vector $\mathbf{w}$ substituted in (1.33) produces an approximating hypersurface. When $P = N$, matrix $\mathbf{X}$ is square and $f_a(\mathbf{x})$ is an interpolating function passing through each training data point. It is assumed that none of the training data points coincide, i.e., $\mathbf{x}_i \neq \mathbf{x}_j$, $i = 1, P$, $j = 1, P$, $i \neq j$. In this case, and when $P = N$, a design matrix $\mathbf{X}$ is nonsingular.

The solution weights vector $\mathbf{w}$ is obtained from

$$\mathbf{w} = \mathbf{X}^+ \mathbf{d}, \tag{1.35}$$

where $\mathbf{X}^+$ denotes pseudoinversion of a design matrix $\mathbf{X}$. The solution (1.35) is the least-squares solution. For $P = N$, $\mathbf{X}^+ = \mathbf{X}^{-1}$. Elements of a design matrix $\mathbf{X}$ are the values (scalars) of a basis function $\varphi_i(\mathbf{x})$ evaluated at the measured values $\mathbf{x}_i$ of the independent variable. The measured values of the dependent variable y, i.e., an unknown function $f(\mathbf{x})$, are the elements of a desired vector $\mathbf{d}$. Note that for an $\Re^n \rightarrow \Re^1$ mapping, a design matrix $\mathbf{X}$ is always a $(P \times N)$ array, independently of the dimensionality n of an input vector $\mathbf{x}$. When $P > N$, the system of linear equations (1.33) has more equations than unknowns (it is *overdetermined*). Equation (1.23) is an example of such an overdetermined system. An important and widely used method for solving overdetermined linear equation systems is the *method of least squares* (see a solution to (1.23) and (1.34)). Its application leads to relatively simple computations, and in many applications it can be motivated by statistical arguments.

Unlike the previous linear approximations, the one given in (1.27) represents a nonlinear multivariate approximation (now **x** is a vector and not a scalar):

$$f_a(\mathbf{x}) = \sum_{i=1}^{n} w_i \sigma_i(\mathbf{v}_i^T \mathbf{x} + b_i), \tag{1.36}$$

where σ_i typically denotes sigmoidal, (S-shaped) functions. (Note that biases b_i can be substituted into the corresponding weights vector $\mathbf{v}_i$ as the last or the first entries and are not necessarily expressed separately. Thus, bias b is meant whenever weights vector **v** is used). As before, $f_a(\mathbf{x})$ is a nonlinear function, and its characteristic as a nonlinear approximation results from the fact that $f_a(\mathbf{x})$ is no longer the weighted sum of *fixed* basis functions. The positions and the shapes of basis functions σ_i, defined as HL weights vectors $\mathbf{v}_i$ (and biases b_i), are also the subjects of the optimization procedure. The approximating function $f_a(\mathbf{x})$ and the error function E depend now on two sets of weights: linearly upon the OL weights vector **w** and nonlinearly upon the HL weights matrix **V**, where the rows of **V** are weights vectors $\mathbf{v}_i$. If one wants to stress this fact, one may write these dependencies explicitly $f_a(\mathbf{x}, \mathbf{w}, \mathbf{V})$ and $E(\mathbf{w}, \mathbf{V})$. Now, the problem of finding the best set of weights is a nonlinear optimization problem, which is much more complex than the linear one. Basically, the optimization, or searching for the weights that result in the smallest error function $E(\mathbf{w}, \mathbf{V})$, will now be a lengthy iterative procedure that does not guarantee finding the global minimum. This problem is discussed in section 1.3.2 to show the need for, and the origins of, nonlinear optimization. Chapter 8 is devoted to the methods of nonlinear optimization, and these questions are discussed in detail there.

1.3.2   Nonlinear Error Surface and Optimization

Most of the complex, very sophisticated art of learning from data is the art of optimization. It is the second stage in building soft computing models, after decisions have been made about what form—approximating function, model, network type, or machine—to use. In this second stage, one first decides what is to be optimized, i.e. what norm should be used. There are many possible cost or error (risk) functionals that can be applied (see (2.26)–(2.28)). Then optimization aimed at finding the best weights to minimize the chosen norm or function can begin.

The previous section is devoted mostly to the problem of representation of our models. Here we present the origin of, and need for, a classic nonlinear optimization that is a basic learning tool. Nonlinear optimization is not the only tool currently used for training (learning, adapting, adjusting, or tuning) parameters of soft computing models. Several versions of massive search techniques are also in use, the most popular being genetic algorithms and evolutionary computing. But nonlinear optimization is still an important tool. From the material in this section the reader can understand why it was needed in the field of learning from data and how it came to be adopted for this purpose. Here a classic gradient algorithm is introduced without technicalities or detailed analysis. Chapter 8 is devoted to various nonlinear optimization techniques and discusses a few relevant algorithms in detail.

There are two, in general high-dimensional, spaces analyzed in the representational and learning parts of a model. Broadly speaking, the representational problem analyzes differences between two hypersurfaces in a $(\mathbf{x}, y)$ hyperspace, one being the approximated unknown function $f(\mathbf{x})$ given by sampled data pairs, and the other the approximating function $f_a(\mathbf{x})$. Both $f(\mathbf{x})$ and $f_a(\mathbf{x})$ lie over an n-dimensional space of input variable $\mathbf{x}$. During learning phase, however, it is more important to analyze an error hypersurface $E(\mathbf{w})$ that, unlike $f_a(\mathbf{x})$, lies over the weight space. Specifically, we follow how $E(\mathbf{w})$ changes (typically, how it decreases) with a change of weights vector $\mathbf{w}$. Both representational and learning space are introduced in example 1.4.

Example 1.4 The functional dependency between two variables is given by $y = 2x$. A training data set contains 21 measured patterns (x, d) sampled without noise. Approximate these data pairs by a linear model $y_a = w_1 x$ and show three different approximations for $w_1 = 0, 2$, and 4 as well as the dependency $E(w_1)$ graphically.

This example is a very simple one-dimensional learning problem that allows visualization of both a modeled function $y(x)$ and a cost function $E(w_1)$. Here $E(w_1)$ is derived from an L_2 norm. It is a sum of error squares. (Note that the graphical presentation of $E(\mathbf{w})$ would not have been possible with a simple quadratic function $y(x) = w_0 + w_1 x + w_2 x^2$ for approximation. $E(\mathbf{w})$ in this case would be a hypersurface lying over a three-dimensional weight space, i.e., it would have been a hypersurface in a four-dimensional space.) The right graph in figure 1.13, showing functional dependency $E(w_1)$, is relevant for a learning phase. All learning is about finding the optimal weight w_1^* where the minimum[8] of a function $E(w_1)$ occurs. Even in this simple one-dimensional problem, the character of a quadratic curve $E(w)$ is the same for all linear in parameters models. Hence, this low-dimensional

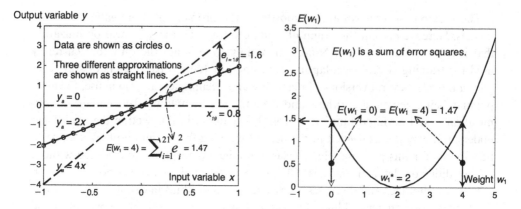

Figure 1.13
Modeling 21 data points obtained by sampling a straight line $y = 2x$ without noise. Three models are shown: a perfect interpolant when $w_1 = 2$, and two (bad) approximating lines with $w_1 = 0$ and $w_1 = 4$ that have the same sum of error squares. Number of training patterns $P = 21$.

example is an appropriate representative of all sum of error squares cost functions $E(w_1) = \sum_{i=1}^{P} e_i^2$. ∎

$E(w_1, w_2)$ is a paraboloidal bowl when there are two weights to be learned and a paraboloidal hyperbowl for more than two weights. (See equations (3.45)–(3.48) of a quadratic hyperbowl that are obtained for a general linear neuron with n-dimensional input vector.) However, in all three cases, that is, for $n = 1, 2$ and $n > 2$, an important and desirable fact related to the learning task is that there is a single guaranteed global minimum $E_{\min}(\mathbf{w})$. Therefore, there is no risk of ending the learning in some local minimum, which is always a suboptimal solution.

In example 1.4, there is an interpolation for $w_1 = 2$, and the minimum $E(w_1 = 2) = 0$. It is always like that for all interpolating hypersurfaces $f_a(\mathbf{x})$. However, as already mentioned, the goal is not to interpolate data points. Thus, in the case of an approximating hypersurface $f_a(\mathbf{x})$ this minimal error $E_{\min}(\mathbf{w}) > 0$. Usually one is more interested in finding an optimal $\mathbf{w}^*$ that produces a minimum $E_{\min} = E(\mathbf{w}^*)$ than in knowing the exact value of this minimum.

Unfortunately, genuine soft models are nonlinear approximators in the sense that an error function (a norm or measure of model goodness) depends nonlinearly upon weights that are the subjects of learning. Thus, the error hypersurface is no longer a convex function, and a search for the best set of parameters (weights) that will ensure the best performance of the model is now a much harder and uncertain task than the search for a quadratic (convex) error function like the one in the right graph of figure 1.13.

Example 1.5 introduces a nonlinear nonconvex error surface. Again, for the sake of visualization, the example is low-dimensional. In fact, there are two weights only. It is clear that an error surface $E(w_1, w_2)$ depending on two weights is the last one that can be seen. No others of higher order can be visualized.

Example 1.5 Find a Fourier series model of the underlying functional dependency $y = 2.5 \sin(1.5x)$. That the function is a sine is known, but its frequency and amplitude are unknown. Hence, using a training data set $\{\mathbf{x}, d\}$, system can be modeled with an NN model consisting of a single HL neuron (with a sine as an activation function) and a single linear OL neuron as given in figure 1.14.

Note that the NN shown in figure 1.14 is actually a graphical representation of a standard sine function $y = w_2 \sin(w_1 x)$. This figure could also be seen as a truncated Fourier series with a single term only.

There is a very important difference between classic Fourier series modeling and the NN modeling here, even when the activation functions are trigonometric. When sine and cosine functions are applied as basis functions in NN models, the goal is to learn both frequencies and amplitudes. Unlike in this nonlinear learning task, in classical Fourier series modeling one seeks to calculate amplitudes only. The frequencies are preselected as integer multiples of some user-selected base frequency. Therefore, because the frequencies are known, classical Fourier series learning is a linear problem.

The problem in this example is complex primarily because the error surface is nonconvex (see fig. 1.15). This is also a nice example of why and how the concepts of function, model, network, or machine are equivalent. A function $y = w_2 \sin(w_1 x)$ is shown as a network in figure 1.14, which is actually a model of this function. At the same time, this artifact is a machine that, as all machines do, processes (transforms) a

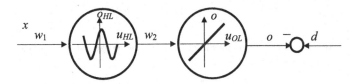

Figure 1.14
Neural network for modeling a data set obtained by sampling a function $y = 2.5 \sin(1.5x)$ without noise. Amplitude $A = 2.5$ and frequency $\omega = 1.5$ are unknown to the model. The weights w_1 and w_2 that represent these two parameters should be learned from a training data set.

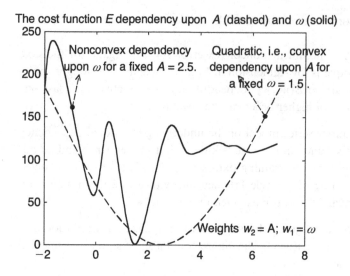

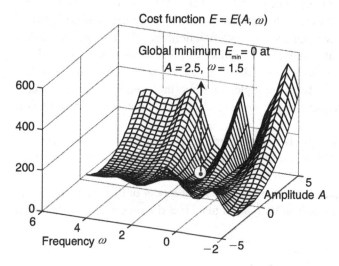

Figure 1.15
Dependence of an error function $E(w_1, w_2)$ upon weights while learning from training data sampled from a function $y = 2.5 \sin(1.5x)$.

given input into some desirable product. Here, a given input is x, and a product is an output of the network o that "equals" (models) an underlying function y for correct values of the weights w_1 and w_2. Here, after a successful learning stage, the weights have very definite meanings: w_1 is a frequency ω, and w_2 corresponds to amplitude A. In this particular case, they are not just numbers.

Now, the error e can readily be expressed in terms of the weights as

$$e(\mathbf{w}) = d - o = d - w_2 \sin(w_1 x). \tag{1.37}$$

There is an obvious linear dependence upon weight w_2 and a nonlinear relation with respect to weight w_1. This nonlinear relation comes from the fact that error e "sees" the weight w_1 through the nonlinear sine function. The dependence of the cost function $E(w_1, w_2) = \frac{1}{2}\sum_{i=1}^{P} e_i^2$ on the weights is shown in figure 1.15. Note that an error function $E(w_1, w_2)$ is not an explicit function of input variable x. $E(w_1, w_2)$ is a scalar value calculated for given weights w_1 and w_2 over all training data points, that is, for all values of input variable x.

Note in figure 1.15 a detail relevant to learning: the error surface is no longer a convex function and with a standard gradient method for optimization, the training outcome is very uncertain. This means that besides ending in a global minimum the learning can get stuck at some local minima. In the top graph of figure 1.15, there are five local minima and one global minimum for a fixed value of amplitude $A = 2.5$, and a learning outcome is highly uncertain. Thus, even for known amplitude, learning of unknown frequency from a given training data set may have a very unsatisfactory outcome. Note that in a general high-dimensional $(N > 2)$ case, $E(\mathbf{w})$ is a hilly hypersurface that cannot be visualized. There are many valleys (local minima), and it is difficult to control the optimization process. ∎

One of the first, simplest, and most popular methods for finding the optimal weights vector $\mathbf{w}^*$ where either the global or local minimum of an error function $E(\mathbf{w})$ occurs is an iterative method based on the principle of going downhill to the lowest point of an error surface. This is the idea of the *method of steepest descent*, or *gradient method*. This basic method is introduced after example 1.6, which sheds more light on the origins of the nonlinear characteristics of an error cost function.

However, in considering the gradient-based learning algorithm, one should keep in mind the weakness of going downhill to find the lowest point of the error surface. Unless by chance one starts on the slope over the global minimum, one is unlikely to find the lowest point of a given hypersurface. All that can be done in the general case with plenty of local minima is to start at a number of random (or somehow well-chosen) initial places, then go downhill until there is no lower place to go, each time finding a local minimum. Then, from all the found local minima, one selects the lowest and takes the corresponding weights vector **w** as the best one, knowing that better local minima or the global minimum may have been missed.

Example 1.6 Consider a simple neural network having one neuron with a bipolar sigmoidal activation function as shown in figure 1.16. The activation function is

$$o = \frac{2}{1 + e^{-(w_1 x + w_2)}} - 1. \tag{1.38}$$

Assume the following learning task: using a training data set $\{\mathbf{x}, d\}$, learn the weights so that the network models the underlying unknown bipolar sigmoidal function

$$y = \frac{2}{1 + e^{-(ax+b)}} - 1. \tag{1.39}$$

Note that (1.38) is a standard representative of S-shaped functions σ_i given in (1.36). The solution is clear because the underlying function between the input x and the output y is known. However, for this network, the underlying function (1.39) is unknown, and the optimal weights of the neuron $w_{1\text{opt}} = a$, and $w_{2\text{opt}} = b$ should be found by using the training data set.

At this point, however, we are more interested in an error function whose minimum should evidently be at the point (a, b) in the weights' plane. Again use as an error function the sum of error squares

$$E(w_1, w_2) = \sum_{p=1}^{P} e_p^2 = \sum_{p=1}^{P} \left[d_p - \left(\frac{2}{1 + e^{-(w_1 x_p + w_2)}} - 1 \right) \right]^2, \tag{1.40}$$

where P is the number of patterns or data pairs used in training. As in (1.37), an error at some training data pair e_p is nonlinear. Here, it is nonlinear in terms of both unknown weights.

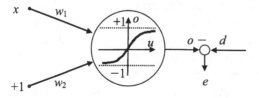

Figure 1.16
Simple neural network with a single neuron.

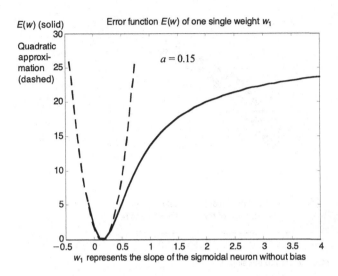

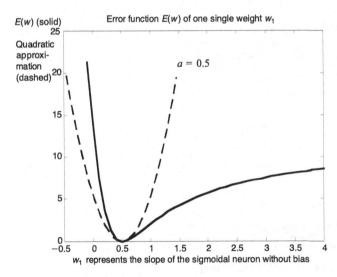

Figure 1.17
Nonlinear error curve and its quadratic approximation.

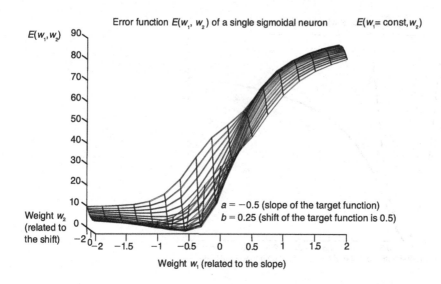

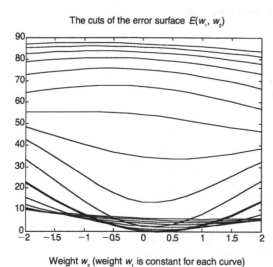

Figure 1.18
Nonlinear error surface and its cuts as the error curves for constant w_1.

It is easy to see in figure 1.17 that even in this simple example the actual shape of a nonlinear error curve $E(w_1, w_2)$ is both nonquadratic and nonconvex. To make the analysis even simpler, model the sigmoidal function with $b = 0$ first. Then $w_2 = 0$, and $E = E(w_1)$. This one-dimensional function shows the nonlinear character of E as well as the character of the quadratic approximation of E in the neighborhood of its minimum. (The quadratic approximation of an error function is a common assumption in proximity to a minimum. This can readily be seen in fig. 1.17). The figure also shows that the shape of E depends on the value of a (slope of the sigmoidal function to be approximated).

In this particular case, the error function E is a curve over the weight w_1 that has a single minimum exactly at $w_1 = a$. There is no saddle point, and all convergent iterative schemes for optimization, starting from any initial random weight w_{10}, will end up at this stationary point $w_1 = a$. Note that the shape of E, as well as its quadratic approximation, depends on the slope a of an approximated function. The smaller the slope a, the steeper the quadratic approximation will be. Expressed in mathematical terms, the curvature at $w_1 = a$, represented in a Hessian matrix[9] of second derivatives of E with respect to the weight, increases with the decrease of a. In this special case, when an error depends on a single weight only, that is, $E = E(w_1)$, the Hessian matrix is a $(1, 1)$ matrix, or a scalar. The same is true for the gradient of this one-dimensional error function. It is a scalar at any given point. Also note that a quadratic approximation to an error function $E(w_1)$ in proximity to an optimal weight value $w_{\text{opt}} = a$ may be seen as a good one.

Now, consider the case where the single neuron is to model the same sigmoidal function y, but with $b \neq 0$. This enables the function y from (1.39) to shift along the x-axis. The complexity of the problem increases dramatically. The error function $E = E(w_1, w_2)$ becomes a surface over the (w_1, w_2) plane. The gradient and the Hessian of E are no longer scalars but a $(2, 1)$ column vector and a $(2, 2)$ matrix, respectively.

Let us analyze the error surface $E(w_1, w_2)$ of the single neuron trying to model function (1.39), as shown in figure 1.18. The error surface in fig 1.18 has the form of a nicely designed driver's seat, and from the viewpoint of optimization is still a very desirable shape in the sense that there is only one minimum, which can be easily reached starting from almost any initial random point. ■

Now, we take up the oldest, and possibly the most utilized, nonlinear optimization algorithm: the gradient-based learning method. It is this method that is a foundation of the most popular learning method in the neural networks field, the error back-propagation method, which is discussed in detail in section 4.1.

A gradient of an error function $E(\mathbf{w})$ is a column vector of partial derivatives with respect to each of the n parameters in $\mathbf{w}$:

$$\mathbf{g} = \nabla E(\mathbf{w}) = \frac{\partial E}{\partial \mathbf{w}} = \left[\frac{\partial E}{\partial w_1} \quad \frac{\partial E}{\partial w_2} \quad \cdots \quad \frac{\partial E}{\partial w_n} \right]^T. \tag{1.41}$$

An important property of a gradient vector is that its local direction is always the direction of steepest ascent. Therefore, the negative gradient shows the direction of steepest descent. The gradient changes its direction locally (from point to point) on the error hypersurface because the slope of this surface changes. Hence, if one is able to follow the direction of the local negative gradient, one should be led to a local minimum. Since all the nearby negative gradient paths lead to the same local minimum, it is not necessary to follow the negative gradient exactly.

The method of steepest descent exploits the negative gradient direction. It is an iterative method. Given the current point $\mathbf{w}_i$, the next point $\mathbf{w}_{i+1}$ is obtained by a one-dimensional search in the direction of $-\mathbf{g}(\mathbf{w}_i)$ (the gradient vector is evaluated at the current point $\mathbf{w}_i$):

$$\mathbf{w}_{i+1} = \mathbf{w}_i - \eta_i \mathbf{g}(\mathbf{w}_i). \tag{1.42}$$

The initial point $\mathbf{w}_1$ is (randomly or more or less cleverly) chosen, and the learning rate η_i is determined by a linear search procedure or experimentally defined. The gradient method is very popular, but there are many ways it can be improved (see section 4.1 and chapter 8). The basic difficulties in applying it are, first, that it will always find a local minimum only, and second, that even though a one-dimensional search begins in the best direction, the direction of steepest descent is a local rather than a global property. Hence, frequent changes (calculations) of direction are often necessary, making the gradient method very inefficient for many problems.

Both these difficulties are readily seen in figure 1.19. Starting from a point A it is unlikely that an optimization, following gradient directions, can end up in the global minimum. Negative gradient vectors evaluated at points A, B, C, D, and E are along the gradient directions AA^*, BB^*, CC^*, DD^* and EE^*. Thus the error function $E(\mathbf{w})$ decreases at the fastest rate in direction AA^* at point A but not at point B. The direction of the fastest decrease at point B is BB^*, but this is not a steepest descent at point C, and so on.

In applying the first-order gradient method, convergence can be very slow, and many modifications have been proposed over the years to improve its speed. In the first-order methods only the first derivative of the error function, namely, the gradient $\nabla E(\mathbf{w})$, is used. The most common improvement is including in the algorithm the

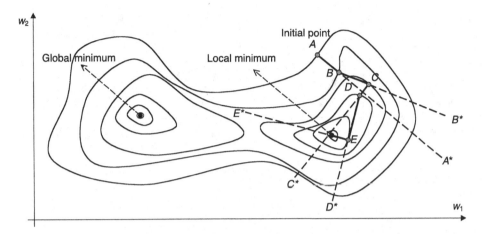

Figure 1.19
Contours of a nonlinear error surface $E(w_1, w_2)$ and steepest descent minimization.

second derivatives (i.e., Hessian matrix) that define the curvature of the function. This leads to a second-order Newton-Raphson method and to various quasi-Newton procedures (see section 4.1 and chapter 8).

The most troublesome parts of an error hypersurface are long, thin, curving valleys. In such valleys, the successive steps oscillate back and forth across the valley. For such elongated valleys the eigenvalues ratio $\lambda_{max}/\lambda_{min}$ of the corresponding Hessian matrix is much larger than 1. For such an area, using a Hessian matrix may greatly improve the convergence.

In applying the steepest descent method given by (1.42), the following question immediately arises: How large a step should be taken in the direction $-\mathbf{g}(\mathbf{w}_i)$ from one current point to the next. From (1.42) it is clear that a learning rate η_i determines the length of a step. A more important question is whether the choice of a learning rate η_i can make the whole gradient descent procedure an unstable process. On a one-dimensional quadratic error surface as shown in figure 1.20, the graphs clearly indicate that training diverges for learning rates $\eta > 2\eta_{opt}$.

For a quadratic one-dimensional error curve $E(w_1)$ the optimal learning rate can readily be calculated, and one can follow this calculation in figure 1.21. From (1.42), and when a learning rate is fixed ($\eta_i = \eta$), it follows that the weight change at the ith iteration step is

$$\Delta w_{1i} = \eta \frac{\partial E}{\partial w_1}\bigg|_i. \tag{1.43}$$

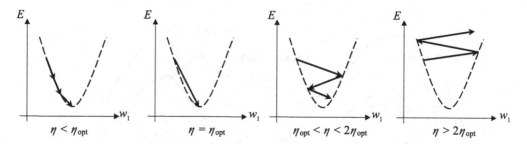

Figure 1.20
Gradient descent for a one-dimensional quadratic error surface $E(w_1)$ and the influence of learning rate η size on the convergence of a steepest descent approach.

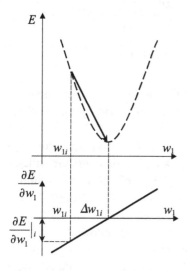

Figure 1.21
Scheme for the calculation of an optimal learning rate η_{opt} for a one-dimensional quadratic error surface $E(w_1)$.

For a quadratic error surface one can exploit that

$$
\frac{\partial^2 E}{\partial w_1^2}\bigg|_i \Delta w_{1i} = \frac{\partial E}{\partial w_1}\bigg|_i , \tag{1.44}
$$

and combining (1.43) and (1.44), one obtains

$$
\eta_{\text{opt}} = \left(\frac{\partial^2 E}{\partial w_{1i}^2}\right)^{-1} . \tag{1.45}
$$

One reaches a minimum in a single step using this learning rate, but one must calculate a second derivative that is a scalar for an error function $E(w_1)$. When there are two or more (say, N) unknown weights, an error function is a hypersurface $E(\mathbf{w})$, and one must calculate the corresponding (N, N) symmetric Hessian matrix, defined as

$$
\mathbf{H}(\mathbf{w}) = \begin{bmatrix}
\dfrac{\partial^2 E(\mathbf{w})}{\partial w_1^2} & \dfrac{\partial^2 E(\mathbf{w})}{\partial w_1 \partial w_2} & \cdots & \dfrac{\partial^2 E(\mathbf{w})}{\partial w_1 \partial w_N} \\[2ex]
\dfrac{\partial^2 E(\mathbf{w})}{\partial w_2 \partial w_1} & \dfrac{\partial^2 E(\mathbf{w})}{\partial w_2^2} & \cdots & \dfrac{\partial^2 E(\mathbf{w})}{\partial w_2 \partial w_N} \\[2ex]
\vdots & \vdots & \vdots & \vdots \\[2ex]
\dfrac{\partial^2 E(\mathbf{w})}{\partial w_N \partial w_1} & \dfrac{\partial^2 E(\mathbf{w})}{\partial w_N \partial w_2} & \cdots & \dfrac{\partial^2 E(\mathbf{w})}{\partial w_N^2}
\end{bmatrix} \tag{1.46}
$$

The symmetry of $\mathbf{H}(\mathbf{w})$ follows from the fact that cross partial derivatives are independent of the order of differentiation:

$$
\frac{\partial^2 E(\mathbf{w})}{\partial w_i \partial w_j} = \frac{\partial^2 E(\mathbf{w})}{\partial w_j \partial w_i}, \qquad i, j = 1, 2, \ldots, N.
$$

Note that $E(\mathbf{w})$ is a scalar and that on a general hypersurface both gradient $\mathbf{g} = \mathbf{g}(\mathbf{w})$ and Hessian matrix $\mathbf{H} = \mathbf{H}(\mathbf{w})$, that is, they depend on $\mathbf{w}$ (they are local properties) and do change over the domain space $\Re^N$.

Gradient descent in N dimensions can be viewed as N independent one-dimensional gradient descents along the eigenvectors of the Hessian. Convergence is obtained for $\eta < 2/\lambda_{\max}$, where $\lambda_{\max}$ is the largest eigenvalue of the Hessian. The optimal learning rate in N dimensions η_{opt} that yields the fastest convergence in the direction of highest curvature is $\eta_{\text{opt}} = 1/\lambda_{\max}$.

Note that in a one-dimensional case the optimal learning rate is inversely proportional to a second derivative of an error function. It is known that this derivative is a

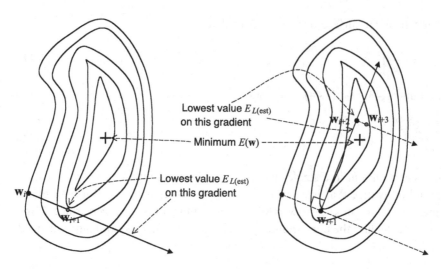

Figure 1.22
Gradient descent on a two-dimensional nonquadratic error surface $E(w_1, w_2)$. An optimal learning rate η_{opt} defines a minimum along the current negative gradient line.

measure of a curvature of a function. Equation (1.45) points to an interesting rule: the closer to a minimum, the higher the curvature and the smaller the learning rate must be. The maximum allowable learning rate for a one-dimensional quadratic error curve is

$$\eta_{max} = 2\eta_{opt}. \tag{1.47}$$

For learning rates higher than η_{max}, training does not converge (see fig. 1.20). In a general case, the error surface is not quadratic, and the previous considerations only indicate that there are constraints on the learning rate. They also show why η should decrease while approaching a (usually local) minimum of an error surface.

For a nonquadratic error surface (see figure 1.22), calculation of a Hessian at each step may be very time-consuming, and an optimal learning rate is found by a one-dimensional search as follows. The negative gradient at the ith step is perpendicular to the local contour curve and points in the direction of steepest descent. The best strategy is then to search along this direction for a local minimum. To do this, step forward applying equal-sized steps until three points are found, and calculate the corresponding values of the error functions. (A stricter presentation of Powell's quadratic interpolation method can be found in the literature.) Now use a quadratic approximation and estimate the minimum along a current gradient direction $E_{L(est)}$.

For a quadratic surface, this minimum estimate $E_{L(\text{est})}$ is exact. For a nonquadratic error surface, it is an approximation of a minimum E_L only, but there is a little point in being very accurate because on a given slope above some (local) minimum of $E_{\min}(\mathbf{w})$, gradients at all points are nearly all directed toward this particular minimum. (Note the differences between the minimum of a nonconvex error surface $E_{\min}(\mathbf{w})$, the minimum along a current gradient direction E_L, and the minimum estimate along a current gradient direction $E_{L(\text{est})}$.)

At this minimum estimate point $E_{L(\text{est})}$, the current gradient line is tangent to the local level curve. Hence, at this point the new gradient is perpendicular to the current gradient, and the next search direction is orthogonal to the present one (see right graph in fig. 1.22). Repeating this search pattern obtains a local or, more desirable, a global minimum $E_{\min}(\mathbf{w})$ of the error function surface. Note that this procedure evaluates the error function $E(\mathbf{w})$ frequently but avoids frequent evaluation of the gradient.

Such gradient descent learning stops when a given stopping criterion is met. There are many different rules for stopping (see section 4.3.5).

The algorithm of a steepest descent is as follows:

1. Initialize some suitable starting point $\mathbf{w}_1$ (chosen at random or based on previous knowledge) and perform gradient descent at the ith iteration step ($i = 2, K$, where K denotes the iteration step when the stopping criterion is met; K is not known in advance) as in the following steps.

2. Compute the negative gradient in each j direction ($j = 1, N$, where N denotes the number of weights)

$$-g_{ji} = \nabla E(w_j)_i = \left. \frac{\partial E}{\partial w_j} \right|_i .$$

3. Step forward (applying equal-sized steps) until three points (a current point w_j, a middle point $w_j - bg_{ji}$, and a last point $w_j - cg_{ji}$) are found. Evaluate the error function for these three points. (For a nonquadratic surface, the middle point should have the lowest of the three values of the error function.)

4. Use quadratic approximation in each j direction with Powell's quadratic interpolation method to find the optimal learning rate

$$\eta_{\text{opt}} = \frac{1}{2} \left(\frac{(b^2 - c^2)E_a + (c^2 - a^2)E_b + (a^2 - b^2)E_c}{(b - c)E_a + (c - a)E_b + (a - b)E_c} \right)$$

where s is a step length, $a = 0$, $b = s$, $c = 2s$, $E_a = E(w_j - ag_{ji})$, $E_b = E(w_j - bg_{ji})$, and $E_c = E(w_j - cg_{ji})$. (See fig. 1.23.)

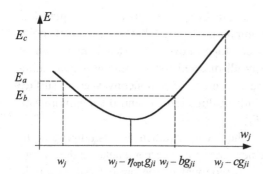

Figure 1.23
Quadratic interpolation about the middle point for a calculation of an optimal learning rate η_{opt} that
defines a minimum $E(w_j)$ along the current negative gradient line.

5. Estimate the minimum along the current gradient direction for each j

$$w_{j_{i+1}} = w_{j_i} - \eta_{\text{opt}} \frac{\partial E}{\partial w_{j_i}}.$$

6. Evaluate error function $E(\mathbf{w}_{i+1})$, and if the stopping criterion is met, stop optimization; if not, return to step 2. In virtue of (1.45) as the iterations progress, we are
closer to some local minimum, and it will usually be necessary to decrease the search
step s, which will result in a smaller optimal learning rate η_{opt}.

Note that the steepest descent shown in figure 1.19 was not performed by applying
the optimal learning rate. Had η_{opt} been used, the first descent would have ended up
near point D. All sliding along the nonquadratic surface shown in figure 1.19 was
done using $\eta < \eta_{\text{opt}}$.

A major shortcoming of the gradient method is that no account is taken of the
second derivatives of $E(\mathbf{w})$, and yet the curvature of the function (which determines
its behavior near the minimum) depends on these derivatives. There are many methods
that partly overcome this disadvantage (see section 4.1 and chapter 8). At the same
time, despite these shortcomings, the gradient descent method made a breakthrough
in learning in neural networks in the late 1980s, and as mentioned, it is the foundation of the popular error backpropagation algorithm.

This concludes the basic introduction to approximation problems and the description of the need for nonlinear optimization tools in learning from data. Section 1.4
introduces the basics of classical regression and classification approaches that are
based on known probability distributions. In this way, the reader will more easily be
able to follow the learning from data methods when nothing or very little is known
about the underlying dependency.

1.4 Learning and Statistical Approaches to Regression and Classification

There are many theories and definitions of what learning is, but the objective here is to consider how artificial systems, mathematical models, or generally, machines learn. Thus, in the framework of this book, a sound view may be that *learning is inferring functional dependencies* (regularities) *from a set of training examples* (data pairs, patterns, samples, measurements, observations, records).

In *supervised learning*, a set of training data pairs typically contains the inputs $\mathbf{x}_i$ and the desired outputs $y_i = d_i$. (A system's outputs y_i that are used in the training phase are also called desired values. Therefore, when referring to the training stage, this book alternatively uses both notations, y_i and d_i, where d_i stands for *desired*.) There are many different ways and various learning algorithms to extract underlying regularities between inputs and outputs. Successful learning ends in the values of some parameters of a learning machine[10] that capture these inherent dependencies. For a multilayer perceptron NN, these parameters are usually called the hidden and output layer weights. For a fuzzy logic model, they are the rules, as well as the parameters that describe the positions and shapes of the fuzzy subsets. And for a polynomial classifier, these parameters are the coefficients of a polynomial.

The choice of a particular type of learning machine depends on the kind of problem to be solved. They can be machines that learn system dependencies in order to predict future outcomes from observed data. For example, in control applications, signal processing, and financial markets, learning machines are used to predict various signals and stock prices based on past performance. In the case of optical character recognition and for other recognition tasks, learning machines are used to recognize (predict) particular alphabetic, numeric, or symbolic characters based on the data obtained by scanning a piece of paper. These examples involve predictions of two different types of outcome: *continuous variables* in control applications, signal processing, and stock markets, and *categorical variables* (class labels) in optical character or pattern recognition.

The prediction of continuous variables is known as *regression*, and the prediction of categorical variables is known as *classification*. Because of their utmost practical importance, this book takes up only regression and classification models. The third important problem in statistics, density estimation, is not the subject of investigation here. The basics of standard statistical techniques of regression and classification are presented first to aid in the understanding of inferring by using data. Traditionally, by using training patterns, mechanical fitting of the prespecified line, curve, plane, surface, or hypersurface solved these kinds of learning tasks. Here, these estimation problems are approached by using neural networks, fuzzy logic models, or support

vector machines. Thus, sections 1.4.1 and 1.4.2, about the basic and classical theories
of regression and classification, may give sound insights on learning from data
problems.

1.4.1 Regression

The elementary presentation of regression is given using a two-dimensional case. In
this way, vital concepts can be shown graphically, which should ease understanding
of the true nature of the problem. Conceptually nothing changes in multivariate cases
with higher dimensional inputs and outputs, but they cannot be visualized with the
relevant hypercurves or hypersurfaces. First, a theoretical regression curve is defined
that will later serve as a model for understanding the empirical regression curve.[11]
The short definition for this curve states that *the theoretical regression curve is (a
graph of) the mean of a conditional probability-density function $P(y \mid x)$.*

A geometrical insight into the theory of regression may be the easiest way to introduce the concepts that follow. In the two-dimensional case (where only two random
variables are involved) the general joint probability-density function[12] $P(x, y)$ can be
thought of as a surface $z = P(x, y)$ over the (x, y) plane. If this surface is intersected
by a plane $x = x_i$, we obtain a curve $z = P(x_i, y)$ over the line $x = x_i$ in the (x, y)
plane. The ordinates z of this curve are proportional to the conditional probability-
density of y given $x = x_i$. If x has the fixed value x_i, then along the line $x = x_i$ in the
(x, y) plane the mean (expected or average) value of y will determine a point whose
ordinate is denoted by $\mu_{y|x_i}$. As different values of x are selected, different mean
points along the corresponding vertical lines will be obtained. Hence, the ordinate
$\mu_{y|x_i}$ of the mean point in the (x, y) plane is a function of the value of x_i selected. In
other words, μ depends upon x, $\mu = \mu(x)$. The locus of all mean points will be the
graph of $\mu_{y|x}$. This curve is called the *regression curve* of y on x. Figure 1.24 indicates
the geometry of the typically nonlinear regression curve for a general density distribution (i.e., for the general joint probability-density function $P(x, y)$). Note that the
surface $P(x, y)$ is not shown in this figure. Also, the meaning of the graph in figure
1.24 is that the peak of the conditional probability-density function $P(y \mid x)$ indicates
that the most likely value of y given x_i is $\mu_{y|x_i}$. Analytically, the derivation of the
regression curve is presented as follows.

Let x and y be random variables with a joint probability-density function $P(x, y)$.
If this function is continuous in y, then the *conditional probability-density function* of
y with respect to fixed x can be written as

$$P(y \mid x) = \frac{P(x, y)}{P(x)} = \frac{P(x, y)}{\int_{-\infty}^{+\infty} P(x, y)\, dy},$$

(1.48)

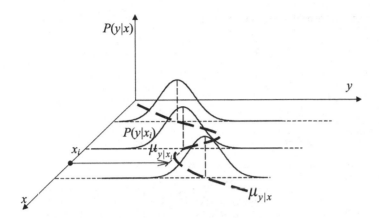

Figure 1.24
Geometry of the typical regression curve for a general density distribution.

where $P(x)$ represents the *marginal probability-density function* $P(x) = \int_{-\infty}^{+\infty} P(x,y)\,dy$. By using this function the regression curve is defined as the expectation of y for any value of x

$$\mu_{y|x} = \mathbb{E}(y\,|\,x) = \int_{-\infty}^{+\infty} yP(y\,|\,x)\,dy = \int_{-\infty}^{+\infty} y\frac{P(x,y)}{P(x)}\,dy = \frac{\int_{-\infty}^{+\infty} yP(x,y)\,dy}{P(x)}. \qquad (1.49)$$

This function (1.49) is the regression curve of y on x. It can be easily shown that this regression curve gives the best estimation of y in the mean squared error sense. Note that there is no restriction on function $\mu_{y|x}$. Depending upon the joint probability-density function $P(x,y)$, this function belongs to a certain class, for example, the class of all linear functions or the class of all functions of a given algebraic or trigonometric polynomial form, and so on. Example 1.7 gives a simple illustration of how (1.49) applies.

Example 1.7 The joint probability-density function $P(x,y)$ is given as

$$P(x,y) = \begin{cases} 2 - x - y, & 0 < x < 1, 0 < y < 1 \\ 0 & \text{elsewhere} \end{cases}.$$

Find the regression curve of y on x.

In order to find $\mu_{y|x}$, first find the marginal probability-density function

$$P(x) = \int_{-\infty}^{+\infty} P(x,y)\,dy = \int_{0}^{1} (2 - x - y)\,dy = \frac{3}{2} - x.$$

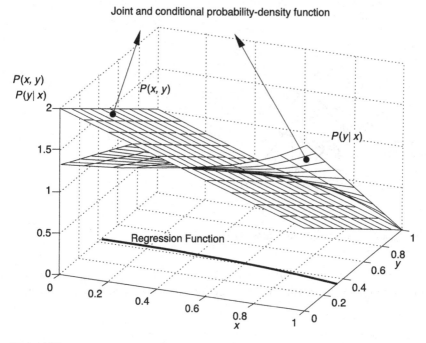

Figure 1.25
The joint probability-density function $P(x, y) = 2 - x - y$, the corresponding conditional probability-density function $P(y \mid x) = (2 - x - y)/(1.5 - x)$, and the regression function (curve) $\mu_{y\mid x}$.

From (1.49),

$$\mu_{y\mid x} = \mathbb{E}(y \mid x)$$

$$= \frac{\int_{-\infty}^{+\infty} y P(x, y) \, dy}{P(x)} = \int_{0}^{1} y \, \frac{2 - x - y}{(3/2) - x} \, dy$$

$$= \frac{1}{(3/2) - x} \int_{0}^{1} [(2 - x) y - y^2] \, dy = \frac{3x - 4}{6x - 9}.$$

Thus, the regression curve is the hyperbola. The joint probability-density function $P(x, y)$, the conditional probability-density function $P(y \mid x)$, and the regression curve $\mu_{y\mid x}$ are shown in figure 1.25. ∎

Example 1.8 shows that the regression function for jointly normally distributed variables is linear, that is, a straight line. This is an interesting property that was heavily exploited in statistics. Linear regression and correlation analysis, which are closely related, are both very developed and widely used in diverse fields. The explanation for such broad application of these theories lies in the remarkable fact that under certain circumstances the probability distribution of the sum of independent random variables, each having an arbitrary (not necessarily normal) distribution, tends toward a normal probability distribution as the number of variables in the sum tends toward infinity. In statistics, this statement, together with the conditions under which the result can be proved, is known as the *central limit theorem*. These conditions are rarely tested in practice, but the empirically observed facts are that a joint probability-density function of a great many random variables closely approximates a normal distribution. The reason for the widespread occurrence of normal joint probability-density functions for random variables is certainly stated in the central limit theorem and in the fact that superposition may be common in nature.

Before proceeding to the next example remember that the joint probability-density function for two independent variables is $P(x, y) = P(x)P(y)$. If both variables are normally distributed, it follows that the normal bivariate (two-dimensional) joint probability-density function for independent random variables x and y is

$$P(x,y) = P(x)P(y) = \frac{1}{2\pi\sigma_x\sigma_y} \exp\left(-\frac{1}{2}\left[\left(\frac{x-\mu_x}{\sigma_x}\right)^2 + \left(\frac{y-\mu_y}{\sigma_y}\right)^2\right]\right). \tag{1.50}$$

If the variables x and y are not independently distributed, it is necessary to modify (1.50) to take into account the relationship between x and y. This is done in (1.51) by introducing a cross-product term in the exponent of (1.50). The *linear correlation coefficient* ρ of this term is defined as $\rho = \sigma_{xy}/\sigma_x\sigma_y$, where σ_{xy}, σ_x, and σ_y are the covariance and variances in directions x and y, respectively. ρ is equal to zero when x and y are independent, and equal to $+1$ or -1 when these two variables are deterministically connected. Equation (1.51) is defined for $-1 < \rho < +1$. For $\rho = \pm 1$, (1.51) does not have any sense. Note that the correlation coefficient ρ is defined for the linear dependence between two random variables, and it is a measure of the strength of this linear relationship. Thus, $\rho = 0$ does not imply that two variables are not closely related. It implies only that these variables are not linearly related. For nonlinearly depending variables, the linear correlation coefficient ρ as previously defined is equal to zero ($\rho = 0$).

Note also that the statistical functional relationships between two (or more) variables in general, and the correlation coefficient ρ in particular, are completely devoid of any cause-and-effect implications. For example, if one regresses (correlates) the size of a person's left hand (dependent variable y) to the size of her right hand (independent variable x), one will find that these two variables are highly correlated. But this does not mean that the size of a person's right hand *causes* a person's left hand to be large or small. Similarly, one can try to find the correlation between the death rate due to heart attack (infarction) and the kind of sports activity of a player at the moment of death. One will eventually find that the death rate while playing bowls or chess (low physical activity) is much higher than while taking part in boxing, soccer, or a triathlon (high physical activity). Despite this correlation, the conclusion that one is more likely to suffer heart attack while playing bowls, cards, or chess is wrong, for there is no direct cause-effect relationship between the correlated events of suffering an infarction and taking part in certain sports activities. It is far more likely that, typically, senior citizens are more involved in playing bowls and the cause of death is their age in the first instance. In short, note that two or more variables can be highly correlated without causation being implied.

Example 1.8 Consider two random variables that possess a bivariate normal joint probability-density function

$$P(x,y) = \frac{\exp\left(-\dfrac{1}{2(1-\rho^2)}\left[\left(\dfrac{x-\mu_x}{\sigma_x}\right)^2 - 2\rho\left(\dfrac{x-\mu_x}{\sigma_x}\right)\left(\dfrac{y-\mu_y}{\sigma_y}\right) + \left(\dfrac{y-\mu_y}{\sigma_y}\right)^2\right]\right)}{2\pi\sigma_x\sigma_y\sqrt{(1-\rho^2)}}.$$

$$(1.51)$$

Show that both the marginal $(P(x), P(y))$ and the conditional $(P(y\,|\,x), P(x\,|\,y))$ probability-density functions are normal distributions. Show that the curve of regression is linear.

The marginal probability-density function is defined as $P(x) = \int_{-\infty}^{+\infty} P(x,y)\,dy$, where $P(x,y)$ is defined in (1.51). Simplify this integration by changing the variables to $u = (x - \mu_x)/\sigma_x$ and $v = (y - \mu_y/\sigma_y)$. Then $dy = \sigma_y\,dv$ and

$$P(x) = \frac{1}{2\pi\sigma_x\sqrt{(1-\rho^2)}}\int_{-\infty}^{+\infty}\exp\left(-\frac{1}{2(1-\rho^2)}(u^2 - 2\rho uv + v^2)\right)dv.$$

Adding and subtracting $\rho^2 u^2$ to the exponent in order to complete the square in v gives

$$P(x) = \frac{\exp(-(u^2/2))}{2\pi\sigma_x\sqrt{1-\rho^2}}\int_{-\infty}^{+\infty}\exp\left(-\frac{1}{2(1-\rho^2)}(v - \rho u)^2\right)dv$$

$$= \frac{\exp(-(u^2/2))}{2\pi\sigma_x}\int_{-\infty}^{+\infty}\exp(-(z^2/2))\,dz,$$

where

$$z = \frac{v - \rho u}{\sqrt{1 - \rho^2}} \quad \text{and} \quad dv = \sqrt{1 - \rho^2}\, dz.$$

Substituting back the value of u in terms of x and inserting the value $\sqrt{2\pi}$ for this familiar integral, $P(x)$ finally reduces to

$$P(x) = \frac{\exp\left(-\frac{1}{2}\left(\frac{x - \mu_x}{\sigma_x}\right)^2\right)}{\sqrt{2\pi}\sigma_x}. \tag{1.52}$$

The corresponding result for $P(y)$ follows from symmetry, and (1.52) shows that the marginal distributions (probability-density functions) of a joint normal distribution are normal. Note that if one sets ρ equal to zero in (1.51), this equation reduces to (1.50), which is the joint normal distribution for two independent normal variables. Thus, if two normal variables are uncorrelated, they are independently distributed. Note, however, that from the preceding discussion of correlation, it should be clear that the lack of a linear correlation does not imply a lack of dependence (relationship) of every (notably nonlinear) kind between two, or more, variables.

For regression problems, the conditional probability distribution is of utmost importance, and in the case of the joint normal distribution it possesses interesting properties. In order to find $P(y \mid x)$, use the definition (1.48) as well as the substitutions u and v given previously, which yields

$$P(y \mid x) = \frac{\dfrac{\exp\left(-\dfrac{1}{2(1 - \rho^2)}(u^2 - 2\rho uv + v^2)\right)}{2\pi\sigma_x\sigma_y\sqrt{(1 - \rho^2)}}}{\dfrac{\exp(-(u^2/2))}{\sqrt{2\pi}\sigma_x}}$$

$$= \frac{\exp\left(-\dfrac{1}{2(1 - \rho^2)}(v^2 - 2\rho uv + \rho^2 u^2)\right)}{\sqrt{2\pi}\sigma_y\sqrt{(1 - \rho^2)}}$$

$$= \frac{\exp\left(-\dfrac{1}{2}\left(\dfrac{v - \rho u}{\sqrt{(1 - \rho^2)}}\right)^2\right)}{\sqrt{2\pi}\sigma_y\sqrt{(1 - \rho^2)}}.$$

Expressing u and v in terms of the original variables x and y and, in order to stress a dependence of y on the selected value of x, denoting y as y_x, the last expression reduces to

$$P(y\,|\,x) = \frac{\exp\left(-\frac{1}{2}\left(\frac{y_x - \mu_y - \rho\frac{\sigma_y}{\sigma_x}(x-\mu_x)}{\sqrt{(1-\rho^2)}}\right)^2\right)}{\sqrt{2\pi}\sigma_y\sqrt{(1-\rho^2)}}. \tag{1.53}$$

In order to find the regression curve $\mu_{y|x}$ defined in (1.49) as the expectation $\mu_{y|x} = E(y\,|\,x)$, note that x is the fixed variable in (1.53), and that this equation represents the normal density function for y_x. Hence, for given x, the mean of (1.53) is the sum of the second and third terms in the numerator of the exponent in (1.53). According to the definition of the regression curve, being the locus of the means of a conditional probability-density, the regression curve of y on x when x and y are jointly normally distributed is the straight line whose equation is

$$\mu_{y|x} = \mu_y + \rho\frac{\sigma_y}{\sigma_x}(x - \mu_x). \tag{1.54}$$

By symmetry a similar result holds for x and y interchanged, that is, for the curve of regression of x on y. The fact that the regression curve of two normally distributed variables is a straight line helps to justify the frequent use of linear regression models because variables that are approximately normally distributed are encountered frequently.   ∎

1.4.2 Classification

The standard statistical techniques for solving classification tasks cover the broad fields of pattern recognition and decision-making problems. Many artificial systems perform classification tasks: speech or character recognition systems, fault detection systems, readers of magnetic-strip codes on credit cards, readers of UPC bar codes, various alarm systems, and so on. In all these different systems the classifier is faced with different observations (measurements, records, patterns) that should be assigned meaning (class or category). *Classification* or *pattern recognition* is inferring meaning (category, class) from observations.

There are two basic stages in designing a classifier: the training phase and the test (generalization or application) phase. The most general schemes of these two stages are shown in figure 1.26.

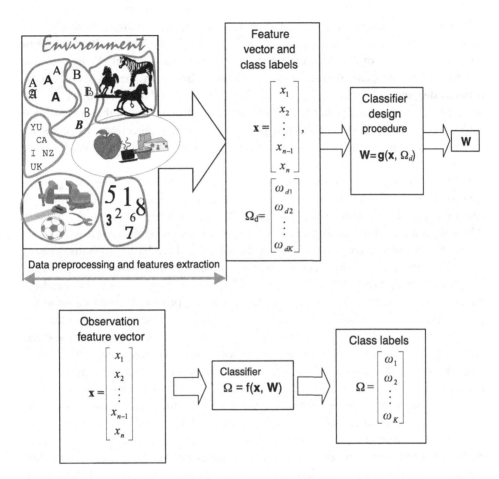

Figure 1.26
Classification's training phase (*top*) and test (application) phase (*bottom*). The training phase, or classifier design, ends up in a set of parameters **W** that define the disjoint class regions.

During the training phase the classifier is given training patterns comprised of selected *training feature vectors* **x** and *desired class labels* Ω_d. The result of the training phase is the set of classifier's parameters that are called weights **W** here. These weights define the general discriminant functions that form the class boundaries between disjoint class or category regions. These class boundaries are points, curves, surfaces, and hypersurfaces in the case of one-, two-, three-, and higher-dimensional feature space, respectively. In the test phase, or later in applications, the classifier recognizes (classifies) the inputs in the form of (previously unseen) measured feature vectors **x**.

Figure 1.26 indicates that classification is a very broad field. Human beings typically process visual, sound, tactile, olfactory, and taste signals. In science and engineering the goal is to understand and classify these and many other signals, notably different geometrical (shape and size) and temporal (time-dependent) signals. In order to do this the pattern recognition system should solve three basic problems: sensing desired variables, extracting relevant features, and based on these features, performing classification. While the first and second parts are highly problem-dependent, the classification procedure is a more or less general approach. Depending upon the specific problem to be solved, measurement (recording, observation) and features extraction would be done by different sensing devices: thermocouples, manometers, accelerometers, cameras, microphones, or other sensors. Today, using A/D converters, all these different signals would be transformed into digital form, and the relevant features would be extracted. It is clear that this preprocessing part is highly problem-dependent. A good features extractor for geometrical shape recognition would be of no use for speech recognition tasks or for fingerprint identification.

At the same time, the classification part is a more general tool. A pattern classifier deals with features and partitions (tessellates, carves up) the feature space into line segments, areas, volumes, and hypervolumes, called *decision regions*, in the case of one-, two-, three-, or higher-dimensional features, respectively. All feature vectors belonging to the same class are ideally assigned to the same category in a decision region. Decision regions are often single nonoverlapping volumes or hypervolumes. However, decision regions of the same class may also be disjoint, consisting of two or more nontouching regions.

Only the basics of the statistical approach to the problem of feature pattern classification are presented here. The objects are feature vectors x_i and class labels ω_i. The features extraction procedure is taken for granted in the hope that the ideal features extractor would produce the same feature vector **x** for each pattern in the same class and different feature vectors for patterns in different classes. In practice, because of the probabilistic nature of the recognition tasks, one must deal with stochastic (noisy) signals. Therefore, even in the case of pattern signals belonging to the same category, there will be different inputs to the features extractor that will always produce different feature vectors $\mathbf{x}$, but, one hopes that the within-class variability is small relative to the between-class variability. In this section, the fundamentals of the Bayesian approach for classifying the handwritten numerals 1 and 0 are presented first. This is a simple yet important task of two-class (binary) classification (or dichotomization). This procedure is then generalized for multifeature and multiclass pattern classification. Despite being simple, these binary decision problems illustrate most of the concepts that underlie all decision theory.

There are many different but related criteria for designing classification decision rules. The six most frequently used decision criteria are maximum likelihood, Neyman-Pearson, probability-of-(classification)error, min-max, *maximum-a-posteriori (MAP)*, known also as the *Bayes' decision criterion*, and finally, the *Bayes' risk decision criterion*. This book cannot cover all these approaches, and it concentrates on the Bayes' rule-based criteria only. We start with a seventh criterion, maximum-a-priori, in order to gradually introduce the reader to the MAP or Bayes' classification rule. The interested reader can check the following claims regarding the relationships among these criteria:

• The probability-of-(classification)-error decision criterion is equivalent to the MAP (Bayes') decision criterion; this is shown later in detail.

• For the same prior probabilities, $P(\omega_1) = P(\omega_2)$, the maximum likelihood decision criterion is equivalent to the probability-of-(classification)-error decision criterion, that is, to the MAP (Bayes') decision criterion.

• For the same conditional probability-densities, $P(x \mid \omega_1) = P(x \mid \omega_2)$, the maximum-a-priori criterion is equivalent to the MAP (Bayes') decision criterion.

• The Neyman-Pearson criterion is identical in form (which is actually a test of likelihood ratio against a threshold) to the maximum likelihood criterion. They differ in the values of thresholds and, when the threshold is equal to unity, the N-P criterion is equivalent to the maximum likelihood criterion.

• The Bayes' risk decision criterion represents a generalization of the probability-of-(classification)-error decision criterion, and for a 0-1 loss function these two classification methods are equivalent. This is shown later.

After the Bayes' (MAP) classification rule has been introduced, the subsequent sections examine an important concept in decision making: a *cost* or *loss* regarding a given classification. This leads to the classification schemes that minimize some *risk* function. This approach is important in all applications where misclassification of some classes is very costly (e.g., in medical or fault diagnosis and in investment decisions, but also in regression and standard classification problems where the risk would measure some error or discrepancy regarding desired values or misclassification of data).

Finally, the concepts of discriminant functions are introduced and an important class of problems is analyzed: classification of normally distributed classes that generally have quadratic decision boundaries. A more detailed treatment of these topics may be found in Cios, Pedrycz, and Swiniarski (1998, ch. 4) and in Schürmann (1996) as well as in classical volumes on decision and estimation (Melsa and Cohn 1978) or on classification (Duda and Hart 1973). The development here roughly follows Cios et al. and Melsa and Cohn.

Bayesian Classification in the Case of Two Classes   The Bayesian approach to classification assumes that the problem of pattern classification can be expressed in probabilistic terms and that the a priori probabilities $P(\omega_i)$ and the conditional probability-density functions $P(x \mid \omega_i)$, $i = 1, 2$, of feature pattern vectors are known. As is the case in regression, this initial assumption will generally not be fulfilled in practice. Nevertheless, a sound understanding of the classical Bayesian approach is fundamental to grasping basic concepts about learning from training data sets without knowledge of any probability distribution.

Assume recognition of two handwritten numerals (or any characters): 1 and 0. In the experiment, the optical device is supplied with typical samples (on, say, a 16×16 grid), as shown in figure 1.27. The 0's generally cover a larger total area of the grid than do the 1's, and the total area covered by the numeral is chosen as a suitable feature in this example.

The task here is to devise an algorithm for the classification of handwritten characters into two distinct classes: 1's and 0's. Assume that the characters emerge in

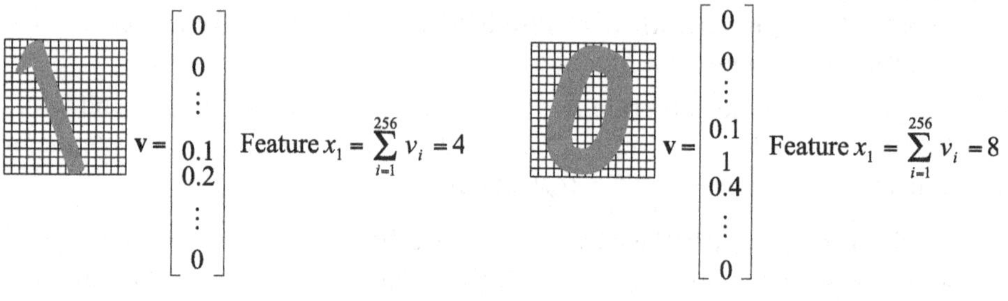

$$\mathbf{v} = \begin{bmatrix} 0 \\ 0 \\ \vdots \\ 0.1 \\ 0.2 \\ \vdots \\ 0 \end{bmatrix} \quad \text{Feature } x_1 = \sum_{i=1}^{256} v_i = 4 \qquad \mathbf{v} = \begin{bmatrix} 0 \\ 0 \\ \vdots \\ 0.1 \\ 1 \\ 0.4 \\ \vdots \\ 0 \end{bmatrix} \quad \text{Feature } x_1 = \sum_{i=1}^{256} v_i = 8$$

Figure 1.27
Typical samples for a two-class recognition with pattern vectors v_i and features x_i.

random sequence but that each can be only a 1 or a 0. In statistical terms, a *state of nature* (or class space) Ω, an emerged character, has only two distinct states—either it is "a 1" or "a 0":

$$\Omega = \{\omega_1, \omega_2\} = \{\text{"a 1", "a 0"}\}. \tag{1.55}$$

Ω is a random variable taking two distinct values, ω_1 for a 1 and ω_2 for a 0. ω_i can be assigned a numerical coding, for example, $\omega_1 = 1$ (or 0, or -1, or any), and $\omega_2 = 0$ (or -1, or 1, or any). Note that a numeral is perceived as an object, an image, or a pattern. This pattern will then be analyzed considering its features. (There is a single feature, x_1, for this two-class task at the moment. In the next section, on multiclass classification, a second feature is introduced and the feature space becomes two-dimensional.) Since characters emerge in a random way, Ω is a random variable. So are the features, and the whole task is described in probabilistic terms.

The goal of the Bayesian method is to classify objects statistically in such a way as to minimize the probability of their misclassification. The classification ability of new patterns will depend on prior statistical information gathered from previously seen randomly appearing objects. In particular, such classification depends upon *prior* (a priori) *probabilities* $P(\omega_i)$ and on *conditional probability-density functions* $P(x \mid \omega_i)$, $i = 1, 2$. The prior probability $P(\omega_1)$ corresponds to the fraction n_{ω_1} of 1's in the total number of characters N. Therefore, the prior probabilities can be defined as

$$P(\omega_i) = \frac{n_{\omega_i}}{N}, \qquad i = 1, 2. \tag{1.56}$$

Thus, $P(\omega_i)$ denotes the *unconditional probability function* that an object belongs to class ω_i, without the help of any other information about this object in the form of feature measurements. A prior probability $P(\omega_i)$ represents prior knowledge (in probabilistic terms) of how likely it is that the pattern belonging to class i may appear even before its actual materialization. Thus, for example, if one knew from prior experiments that there are four times more 1's than 0's in the strings of numerals under observation, one would have $P(\omega_1) = 0.8$ and $P(\omega_2) = 0.2$. Note that the sum of prior probabilities is equal to 1:

$$\sum_{i=1}^{N} P(\omega_i) = 1. \tag{1.57}$$

Bayesian Classification Based on Prior Probabilities Only Let us start classifying under the most restricted assumption first. Suppose that the optical device is out of order and there is no information about feature x of a materialized numeral. Thus, the only available statistical knowledge of the character strings to be classified is the prior probabilities $P(\omega_1) = 0.8$ and $P(\omega_2) = 0.2$. It is difficult to believe that the classification will be very good with so little knowledge, but let us try to establish a decision strategy that should lead to the smallest misclassification error. The best and natural decision now is to assign the next character to the class having the higher prior probability. Therefore, with only the prior probabilities $P(\omega_1)$ and $P(\omega_2)$ known, the decision rule would be

Assign a character to

class ω_1 if $P(\omega_1) > P(\omega_2)$,   or to   (1.58)

class ω_2 if $P(\omega_2) > P(\omega_1)$.

If $P(\omega_1) = P(\omega_2)$, both classes are equally likely, and either decision would be correct.

The task is to minimize the probability of a classification error, which can be expressed as

$$P(\text{classification error}) = \begin{cases} P(\omega_2) & \text{if we decide } \Omega = \omega_1, \\ P(\omega_1) & \text{if we decide } \Omega = \omega_2. \end{cases}$$ (1.59)

Thus, selecting a class with a bigger prior probability gives a smaller probability of classification error. If one chooses class ω_1 in this example without seeing any features, the probability of misclassification is $P(\omega_2) = 0.2$. This is the best classification strategy with so little information—$P(\omega_i)$ only—about the objects to be classified.

Frankly, one would never attempt to solve real-life classification problems with so little knowledge, and typical problems are those with available features.

Bayesian Classification Based on Prior Probabilities and Features   It is clear that by including information on the total area covered by a numeral in the problem of classifying 1's and 0's, one can increase classification accuracy and consequently minimize the number of misclassified characters. Note that characters are stochastic images. Each person writes differently and writes the same characters differently each time. Thus, a feature x (the total area of a grid covered by a character) takes random values. This is a continuous variable over a given range, and experimentally by extracting features from 500 samples of each character, *discrete class-conditional probability-density functions* in the form of two histograms are obtained, as shown in figure 1.28. If the number of samples is increased to infinity, these discrete distribution densities converge into two *continuous class-conditional probability-density functions* $P(x\,|\,\omega_i)$, as shown in figure 1.28. $P(x\,|\,\omega_i)$ can also be called the *data*

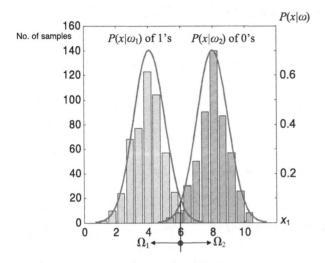

Figure 1.28
Typical histograms (*left ordinate*) and class-conditional probability-density functions $P(x \mid \omega_i)$ (*right ordinate*) for two-class recognition with a single feature x_1. The decision boundary, shown as a point $x_1 = 6$, is valid for equal prior probabilities $P(\omega_1) = P(\omega_2) = 0.5$.

generator's conditional probability-density functions or *the likelihood of class* ω_i with respect to the value x of a feature variable.

The probability distributions presented in figure 1.28 are fairly similar, but depending on the state of nature (the specific data generation mechanism), they can be rather different. The probability-density

$$P(x \mid \omega_i), \qquad i = 1, 2, \tag{1.60}$$

is the probability-density function for a value of a random feature variable x given that the pattern belongs to a class ω_i. The conditional probability-density functions $P(x \mid \omega_1)$ and $P(x \mid \omega_2)$ represent distributions of variability of a total area of the image covered by a 1 and a 0. These areas are thought to be different, and $P(x \mid \omega_1)$ and $P(x \mid \omega_2)$ may capture this difference in the case of 1's and 0's. Thus, information about this particular feature will presumably help in classifying these two numerals.

Remember that the joint probability-density function $P(\omega_i, x)$ is the probability-density that a pattern is in a class ω_i and has a feature variable value x. Recall also that the conditional probability function $P(\omega_i \mid x)$ denotes the probability (and not probability-density) that the pattern class is ω_i given that the measured value of the feature variable is x. The probability $P(\omega_i \mid x)$ is also called the *posterior* (a posteriori) *probability*, and its value depends on the a posteriori fact that a feature variable has a concrete value x. Because $P(\omega_i \mid x)$ is the probability function,

$$\sum_{i=1}^{2} P(\omega_i \mid x) = 1. \tag{1.61}$$

Now, use the relations

$$P(\omega_i, x) = P(\omega_i \mid x)P(x), \qquad i = 1, 2,$$
$$P(\omega_i, x) = P(x \mid \omega_i)P(\omega_i), \qquad i = 1, 2, \tag{1.62}$$

where $P(x)$ denotes the *unconditional probability-density function* for a feature variable x

$$P(x) = \sum_{i=1}^{2} P(x \mid \omega_i)P(\omega_i) = P(x \mid \omega_1)P(\omega_1) + P(x \mid \omega_2)P(\omega_2). \tag{1.63}$$

The posterior probability $P(\omega_i \mid x)$ is sought for classifying the handwritten characters into corresponding classes. From equations (1.62) this probability can be expressed in the form of a Bayes' rule

$$P(\omega_i \mid x) = \frac{P(x \mid \omega_i)P(\omega_i)}{P(x)}, \qquad i = 1, 2, \tag{1.64}$$

or

$$P(\omega_i \mid x) = \frac{P(x \mid \omega_i)P(\omega_i)}{\sum_{i=1}^{2} P(x \mid \omega_i)P(\omega_i)} = \frac{P(x \mid \omega_i)P(\omega_i)}{P(x \mid \omega_1)P(\omega_1) + P(x \mid \omega_2)P(\omega_2)}. \tag{1.65}$$

The probability-density function $P(x)$ only scales the previous expressions, ensuring in this way that the sum of posterior probabilities is 1 ($P(\omega_1 \mid x) + P(\omega_2 \mid x) = 1$). The practicability of these Bayes' rules lies in the fact that the conditional probability function $P(\omega_i \mid x)$ can be calculated using $P(x \mid \omega_i)$ and $P(\omega_i)$, which can be estimated from data much more easily than $P(\omega_i \mid x)$ itself. Equipped with (1.65) and having the feature measurement x while knowing probabilities $P(\omega_i)$ and $P(x \mid \omega_i)$, one can calculate $P(\omega_i \mid x)$. Having the posterior probabilities $P(\omega_i \mid x)$, one can formulate the following classification decision rule based on both prior probability and observed features:

Assign a character to a class ω_i having the larger value of the posterior conditional probability $P(\omega_i \mid x)$ for a given feature x.

This is called the Bayes' classification rule, and it is the best classification rule for minimizing the probability of misclassification. In other words, this rule is the best one for minimizing the probability of classification error. In the case of two-class handwritten character recognition, for a given numeral with observed feature x, the conditional probability of the classification error is

$$P(\text{classification error} \,|\, x) = \begin{cases} P(\omega_2 \,|\, x) & \text{if we decide } \Omega = \omega_1, \\ P(\omega_1 \,|\, x) & \text{if we decide } \Omega = \omega_2. \end{cases} \tag{1.66}$$

Note that for equal prior probabilities $P(\omega_1) = P(\omega_2)$, the decision depends solely on the class-conditional probability-density functions $P(x \,|\, \omega_i)$, and the character is assigned to the class having the bigger $P(x \,|\, \omega_i)$. Thus, in this classification task, having $P(\omega_1) = P(\omega_2) = 0.5$, the decision boundary in figure 1.28 is at the intersecting point ($x = 6$) of the two class-conditional probability-density functions. (In the case of a one-dimensional feature, the decision regions are line segments, and the decision boundary is a point.)

Analyzing many differently written 1's and 0's will yield different feature values x, and it is important to see whether the Bayes' classification rule minimizes the *average probability of error*, because it should perform well for all possible patterns. This averaging is given by

$$P(\text{classification error}) = \int_{-\infty}^{+\infty} P(\text{classification error}, x) \, dx$$

$$= \int_{-\infty}^{+\infty} P(\text{classification error} \,|\, x) P(x) \, dx \tag{1.67}$$

Clearly, if the classification rule as given by (1.66) minimizes the probability of misclassification for each x, then the average probability of error given by (1.67) will also be minimized. Thus, the Bayes' rule minimizes the *average* probability of a classification error. In the case of two-class classification,

$$P(\text{classification error} \,|\, x) = \min(P(\omega_1 \,|\, x), P(\omega_2 \,|\, x)). \tag{1.68}$$

Using Bayes' rule (1.64),

$$P(\text{classification error} \,|\, x) = \min\left(\frac{P(x \,|\, \omega_1)P(\omega_1)}{P(x)}, \frac{P(x \,|\, \omega_2)P(\omega_2)}{P(x)}\right). \tag{1.69}$$

Note that $P(x)$ is not relevant for the final decision. It is a scaling only, and in the case of two-class decisions the Bayes' classification rule becomes

Decide

class ω_1 if $P(x|\omega_1)P(\omega_1) > P(x|\omega_2)P(\omega_2)$,

class ω_2 if $P(x|\omega_2)P(\omega_2) > P(x|\omega_1)P(\omega_1)$. (1.70a)

By making such a decision the probability of a classification error and consequently the *average* probability of a classification error will be minimized. One obtains another common form of this rule by using the *likelihood ratio* $\Lambda(x) = P(x|\omega_1)/P(x|\omega_2)$:

Decide

class ω_1 if $\Lambda(x) = \dfrac{P(x|\omega_1)}{P(x|\omega_2)} > \dfrac{P(\omega_2)}{P(\omega_1)}$,

class ω_2 if $\Lambda(x) = \dfrac{P(x|\omega_1)}{P(x|\omega_2)} < \dfrac{P(\omega_2)}{P(\omega_1)}$. (1.70b)

The decision rule given by (1.70b) can also be rewritten as

$$\Lambda(x) \underset{\omega_2}{\overset{\omega_1}{\gtrless}} \frac{P(\omega_2)}{P(\omega_1)}.$$ (1.70c)

For equal prior probabilities, a threshold of likelihood ratio is equal to 1, and this rule becomes identical to the maximum likelihood decision criterion.

A good practical point about this rule is that both the prior probabilities $P(\omega_i)$ and the class-conditional probability-density functions $P(x|\omega_i)$ can be more easily estimated from data than the posterior probability $P(\omega_i|x)$ on which the whole rule is based.

General Bayesian Classification Real pattern recognition problems today often involve patterns belonging to more than two classes and high-dimensional feature vectors. In the case of handwritten numerals there are ten different classes, and using a single feature as in the previous case of two-class classification, it would be relatively difficult to separate all ten numbers reliably. Suppose that in addition to the 1's and 0's, one wants to classify the handwritten number 8, as shown in figure 1.29.

Now, the single feature x_1 (the total area covered by the character) is insufficient to classify all three numbers, since the 0's and the 8's seem to cover almost the same total grid area. Defining another feature x_2 as the sum of the areas of the character on the diagonal grid cells and combining these two features in the two-dimensional feature vector may suffice for the classification of all three numerals.

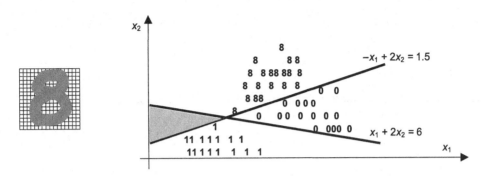

Figure 1.29
Left, typical sample of a handwritten number 8 on a 16 × 16 grid. *Right*, the decision regions and decision boundaries for a three-class character (1, 0, and 8) recognition problem.

Figure 1.29 depicts the positions of the training patterns in two-dimensional feature space. Despite its simplicity, this problem involves all the relevant concepts for solving problems with higher-dimensional feature vectors and more than three classes. By means of this introductory multifeature and multiclass example, the theory of classification is developed in general terms and later applied to cases involving normal or Gaussian distributions.

The two straight lines shown in figure 1.29 are the *decision boundary functions* that divide the feature space into disjoint decision regions. The latter can be readily associated with three given classes. The shaded area is a so-called indecision region in this problem, and the patterns falling in this region would be not assigned to any class.

When objects belong to more classes (say k, and for numerals $k = 10$), we have

$$\Omega = \{\omega_1, \omega_2, \ldots, \omega_k\}. \tag{1.71}$$

Now, Bayes' classification rule will be similar to the rule for two classes. In the case of multiclass and multifeature tasks, $P(\omega_i)$ denotes the prior probability that the given pattern belongs to a class ω_i, and it corresponds to the fraction of characters in an ith class. The class-conditional probability-density function is denoted for all k classes by $P(\mathbf{x}|\omega_i)$ and the joint probability-density function by $P(\omega_i, \mathbf{x})$, $i = 1, \ldots, k$. $P(\omega_i, \mathbf{x})$ is the probability-density that a pattern is in class ω_i and has a feature vector value $\mathbf{x}$. The conditional probability function $P(\omega_i|\mathbf{x})$ is the posterior probability that a pattern belongs to a class ω_i given that the observed value of a feature is $\mathbf{x}$, and

$$\sum_{i=1}^{k} P(\omega_i | \mathbf{x}) = 1. \tag{1.72}$$

As in the two-class case the prior and posterior probabilities are connected by

$$P(\omega_i, \mathbf{x}) = P(\omega_i \mid \mathbf{x})P(\mathbf{x}), \qquad i = 1, 2, \ldots, k,$$

$$P(\omega_i, \mathbf{x}) = P(\mathbf{x} \mid \omega_i)P(\omega_i), \qquad i = 1, 2, \ldots, k, \tag{1.73}$$

where $P(\mathbf{x})$ is the unconditional probability-density function for a feature vector $\mathbf{x}$:

$$P(\mathbf{x}) = \sum_{i=1}^{k} P(\mathbf{x} \mid \omega_i)P(\omega_i)$$

$$= P(\mathbf{x} \mid \omega_1)P(\omega_1) + P(\mathbf{x} \mid \omega_2)P(\omega_2) + \cdots + P(\mathbf{x} \mid \omega_k)P(\omega_k). \tag{1.74}$$

From (1.73) follows Bayes' theorem for a multifeature and multiclass case

$$P(\omega_i \mid \mathbf{x}) = \frac{P(\mathbf{x} \mid \omega_i)P(\omega_i)}{P(\mathbf{x})}, \qquad i = 1, 2, \ldots, k, \tag{1.75}$$

or

$$P(\omega_i \mid \mathbf{x}) = \frac{P(\mathbf{x} \mid \omega_i)P(\omega_i)}{\sum\limits_{i=1}^{k} P(\mathbf{x} \mid \omega_i)P(\omega_i)} = \frac{P(\mathbf{x} \mid \omega_i)P(\omega_i)}{P(\mathbf{x} \mid \omega_1)P(\omega_1) + \cdots + P(\mathbf{x} \mid \omega_k)P(\omega_k)}. \tag{1.76}$$

Now, for a multifeature and multiclass case, Bayes' classification rule can be generalized as follows:

Assign a pattern to a class ω_i having the largest value of the posterior conditional probability $P(\omega_i \mid \mathbf{x})$ for a given feature $\mathbf{x}$.

In other words, assign a given pattern with an observed feature vector $\mathbf{x}$ to a class ω_i when

$$P(\omega_i \mid \mathbf{x}) > P(\omega_j \mid \mathbf{x}), \qquad j = 1, 2, \ldots, k, \ i \neq j. \tag{1.77}$$

Within the framework of learning from data it is much easier to estimate prior probability and class-conditional probability-density functions than the posterior probability itself. Therefore, a Bayes' classification rule (1.77) for a multifeature and multiclass case should be expressed as follows:

For a given feature vector $\mathbf{x}$, decide class ω_i if

$$P(\mathbf{x} \mid \omega_i)P(\omega_i) > P(\mathbf{x} \mid \omega_j)P(\omega_j), \qquad j = 1, 2, \ldots, k, \ i \neq j. \tag{1.78}$$

This final expression was obtained by using (1.75) after neglecting a scaling factor $P(\mathbf{x})$. Again, Bayes' classification rule is best for minimizing classification error.

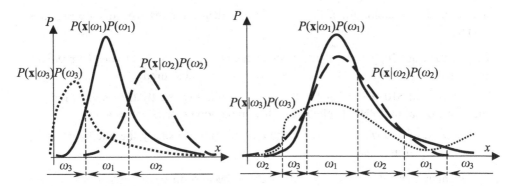

Figure 1.30
Bayes' classification rule for three classes may result in three single nonoverlapping decision regions (*left*) or in three nonoverlapping disjoint decision regions consisting of two (or generally more) nontouching regions (*right*). Other configurations of decision regions are possible, too.

Figure 1.30 illustrates (1.78) for three classes and, for the sake of clarity, only a single feature.

Statistical Classification Minimizing Risk   For problems containing uncertainties, decisions are seldom based on probabilities alone. In most cases, one must be aware of the consequences (namely, the errors, potential profits or losses, penalties, or rewards involved). Thus, there is a need for combining probabilities and consequences, and for this reason, the concepts of *cost* or *loss*, and of *risk* (defined as expected loss) are introduced here. This is important in all decision-making processes. Introducing the minimization criterion involving potential loss into a classification decision made for a given true state of nature (for a given feature vector **x**) acknowledges the fact that misclassification of classes in some areas may be more costly than in others. The loss function can be very different in various applications, and its form depends upon the nature of the problem. Before considering the theory involving loss and risk functions, let us first study them inductively in example 1.9.

Example 1.9   Eleven boiler units in a plant are operating at different pressures. Three are operating at 101 bar, two at 102 bar, and others at 103, 105, 107, 110, 111, and 112 bar. A single process computer is, with the help of specific boiler pressure sensors (manometers), randomly reading the corresponding pressures, and the last eleven recorded samples are (101, 112, 101, 102, 107, 103, 105, 110, 102, 101, 111 bar). The pressures in the various boilers are mutually independent. In order to check a young engineer's understanding of this process and its random characteristics, his superior asks him to predict the next manometer reading under three different decision scenarios (*l* stands for a loss (function), *r* denotes a reward, and *f* designates a fine):

1. A reward of \$10 ($l = r = +10$) if the next reading is exactly the one he predicts, and a fine of \$1 ($l = f = -1$) if a different pressure is measured

2. A reward of \$10 ($l = r = +10$) if the next reading is exactly the one he predicts, and a fine equal in dollars to the size of his prediction error ($l = f = -|e|$)

3. A reward of \$10 ($l = r = +10$) if the next reading is exactly the one he predicts, and a fine equal in dollars to the square of his prediction error ($l = f = -(e^2)$)

The engineer needs to make a good decision because there are penalties for being wrong. His boss knows that if there were no penalty for being wrong or rewards for being right or close, nothing would be at stake and the engineer might just as well predict manometer readings of 50, 103.4, or 210.5 even though he knows that there will be no such readings. Therefore, in each case, the engineer should select the best possible decision to maximize expected profit (or to minimize expected loss).

Note that the different character of the loss functions in this example will lead to different decisions. In case 1, there is no reward for coming close to the correct manometer reading, so the size of the decision error does not matter. In case 2, the loss is proportional to the size of the error, and in case 3, the loss increases with the square of the error. (Note that the last fine resembles the sum-of-error-squares cost function.) What should the engineer decide in order to maximize expected profit?

In the first case, if he predicts a manometer reading of 101 (the mode, or most frequent observation, of the eleven samples), he stands to make \$10 with a probability of 3/11 and to lose \$1 with a probability of 8/11. Now, his expected profit (EP)[13] is

$$EP = \sum_{i=1}^{11} l_i p_i = 10\frac{3}{11} + (-1)\frac{8}{11} = \$2.$$

It can be easily verified that this is the best possible prediction given the loss functions $l = 10$ and $l = -1$ for a right and a wrong decision, respectively. Checking, for example, the prediction of 103 bar, one finds that $EP = \$0$. Note in this example that regardless of the value of the specific loss, the prediction of 101 bar will always be the best one, ensuring maximal profit or minimal loss. So, for example, if a correct prediction were rewarded by \$1 and a bad one fined by \$10, the expected profit would be negative:

$$EP = \sum_{i=1}^{11} l_i p_i = 1\frac{3}{11} + (-10)\frac{8}{11} = -\$7,$$

denoting the expected loss of $7. Now, if the engineer predicts a reading of 103, the expected loss (or risk) is $1/11 - 10(10/11) = \$9$, and for a predicted reading of 102 the expected loss is $8. Hence, the expected loss is again the smallest when 101 bar is predicted, given that the fine does not depend on the size of the estimation error. Note also that other predictions like 102.5 or 108 bar would now entail a *certain* loss of $10. (Recall that the manometers can display only the integer values of the operating boiler pressures, and none is operating at these two pressures.) Thus, when there is no reward for coming close to some characteristics of the sample, the best decision is to use the *mode*, or the most frequent measurement.

In the second case, when the fine is proportional to the possible error, $l = f = -|e|$, it is the *median* (103 bar here) that maximizes the expected profit. Thus, if the engineer predicts that the next displayed reading will be 103, the fine will be $2, $1, $2, $4, $7, $8, or $9, depending on whether the reading is 101, 102, 105, 107, 110, 111, or 112, and the expected profit is

$$EP = \sum_{i=1}^{11} l_i p_i = -2\frac{3}{11} - 1\frac{2}{11} + 10\frac{1}{11} - 2\frac{1}{11} - 4\frac{1}{11} - 7\frac{1}{11} - 8\frac{1}{11} - 9\frac{1}{11} = -\$2.55.$$

In other words, in this second case, the best decision cannot make any profit but would only entail the least possible loss of $2.55. If the reward were $38, the maximal expected profit would be $0. Again, regardless of the reward assigned to the decision, the best possible prediction, given that the fine is proportional to the size of the prediction error, is a median (103 bar).

The expected fine or loss would be greater for any number other than the median. For instance, if the engineer predicts that the next reading will be 105, the *mean* of the eleven possible readings, the fine will be $4, $3, $2, $2, $5, $6, or $7, depending on whether the reading is 101, 102, 103, 107, 110, 111, or 112, and the expected profit is

$$EP = \sum_{i=1}^{11} l_i p_i = -4\frac{3}{11} - 3\frac{2}{11} - 2\frac{1}{11} + 10\frac{1}{11} - 2\frac{1}{11} - 5\frac{1}{11} - 6\frac{1}{11} - 7\frac{1}{11} = -\$2.73.$$

Case 3 describes the scenario when the fine increases quadratically (rapidly) with the size of the error. This leads naturally to the *method of least squares*, which plays a very important role in statistical theory. It is easy to verify that for such a loss function the best possible prediction is the mean, 105, of the eleven sample manometer readings. The engineer finds that the fine will be $16, $9, $4, $4, $25, $36, or $49, depending on whether the reading is 101, 102, 103, 107, 110, 111, or 112, and the expected profit is

$$EP = \sum_{i=1}^{11} l_i p_i = -16\frac{3}{11} - 9\frac{2}{11} - 4\frac{1}{11} + 10\frac{1}{11} - 4\frac{1}{11} - 25\frac{1}{11} - 36\frac{1}{11} - 49\frac{1}{11} = -\$12.10.$$

Again, in this third predicted scenario the best decision, to predict the mean, cannot make any profit but would only entail the least expected loss of \$12.10, given the reward of only \$10 for the correct prediction. It is left to the reader to verify this claim by calculating the expected profit (or loss) for any other possible decision. Note that, in the case when the fine increases quadratically with the size of the error, the expected profit is \$0 only if the reward is \$143.

The final decision (or simply a result) depends on the loss function used. As mentioned in section 1.3, the best solution depends upon the norm applied. Problems 1.8 and 1.9 illustrate this important observation in a nice graphical way.

The last two scenarios indicate that the reward defined by the engineer's superior is not very generous. But one can hope that using the correct prediction strategy—mode, median, and mean are the best decisions to maximize expected profit given various loss functions—will benefit the engineer more in his future professional life than his superior's present financial offer.   ■

Now, these questions of the best decisions in classification tasks while minimizing risk (expected loss) can be set into a more general framework. First, define a loss function

$$L_{ji} = L(\text{decision class}_j \mid \text{true class}_i) \tag{1.79}$$

as a cost or penalty for assigning a pattern to a class ω_j when a true class is ω_i. In the case of an l-class classification problem, define an $l \times l$ loss matrix $\mathbf{L}$ as

$$\mathbf{L} = \begin{bmatrix} L_{11} & L_{12} & \cdots & L_{1l} \\ L_{21} & L_{22} & \cdots & L_{2l} \\ \vdots & \vdots & \vdots & \vdots \\ L_{l1} & L_{l2} & \cdots & L_{ll} \end{bmatrix}. \tag{1.80}$$

A loss matrix $\mathbf{L}$, or the selection of the L_{ij}, is highly problem-dependent. At this point, selecting specific penalties or rewards is less important than understanding the concept of risk that originates from decision theory while combining probabilities with consequences (penalties or rewards). Recall that until now the best decision strategy was based only on the posterior probability $P(\omega_i \mid \mathbf{x})$, and using Bayes' rule,

$P(\omega_i \,|\, \mathbf{x})$ was expressed in terms of the prior probability $P(\omega_i)$ and a class-conditional probability-density $P(\mathbf{x} \,|\, \omega_i)$. Now, using the posterior probability $P(\omega_i \,|\, \mathbf{x})$ in a similar way as previously, one can define the *conditional risk*, or *expected (average) conditional loss*, associated with a decision that the observed pattern belongs to class ω_j when in fact it belongs to a class ω_i, $i = 1, 2, \ldots, l; i \neq j$:

$$R(\omega_j \,|\, \mathbf{x}) = \sum_{i=1}^{l} L(\text{decision class}_j \,|\, \text{true class}_i) P(\omega_i \,|\, \mathbf{x}) = \sum_{i=1}^{l} L_{ji} P(\omega_i \,|\, \mathbf{x}). \qquad (1.81)$$

Thus, the conditional risk of making a decision ω_j, $R_j = R(\omega_j \,|\, \mathbf{x})$, is defined as the expectation of loss that is, through the use of $P(\omega_l \,|\, \mathbf{x})$, conditioned on the realization $\mathbf{x}$ of a feature vector. Hence, the best decision now should be a classification decision ω_j that minimizes the conditional risk R_j, $j = 1, 2, \ldots, l$. The *overall risk* is defined as the *expected loss* associated with a given classification decision and is considered for all possible realizations $\mathbf{x}$ of an n-dimensional feature vector from a feature vector space $\mathfrak{R}_{\mathbf{x}}$:

$$R = \int_{\mathfrak{R}_{\mathbf{x}}} R_j \, d\mathbf{x} = \int_{\mathfrak{R}_{\mathbf{x}}} R(\omega_j \,|\, \mathbf{x}) \, d\mathbf{x} = \int_{\mathfrak{R}_{\mathbf{x}}} \sum_{i=1}^{l} L_{ji} P(\omega_i \,|\, \mathbf{x}) \, d\mathbf{x}, \qquad (1.82)$$

where the integral is calculated over an entire feature vector space $\mathfrak{R}_{\mathbf{x}}$.

The overall risk R is used as a classification criterion for the risk minimization while making a classification decision. The integral in (1.82) will be minimized if a classification decision ω_j minimizes the conditional risk $R(\omega_j \,|\, \mathbf{x})$ for each realization $\mathbf{x}$ of a feature vector.

This is a generalization of the Bayes' rule for minimization of a classification error (1.67), but here the minimization is of an overall risk R, or an expected loss. For this general classification problem we have the following Bayes' procedure and classification rule:

For a given feature vector $\mathbf{x}$ evaluate all conditional risks

$$R(\omega_j \,|\, \mathbf{x}) = \sum_{i=1}^{l} L_{ji} P(\omega_i \,|\, \mathbf{x})$$

for all possible classes ω_j, and choose a class (make a decision) ω_j for which the conditional risk $R(\omega_j \,|\, \mathbf{x})$ is minimal:

$$R(\omega_j \,|\, \mathbf{x}) < R(\omega_k \,|\, \mathbf{x}), \qquad k = 1, 2, \ldots, l, \ k \neq j. \qquad (1.83)$$

Such classification decisions guarantee that the overall risk R will be minimal. This *minimal overall risk* is called *Bayes' risk*.

The last equation can be rewritten as

$$\sum_{i=1}^{l} L_{ji} P(\omega_i \mid \mathbf{x}) < \sum_{i=1}^{l} L_{ki} P(\omega_i \mid \mathbf{x}), \qquad k = 1, 2, \ldots, l, \ k \neq j, \tag{1.84}$$

and using Bayes' rule, (1.64),

$$P(\omega_i \mid \mathbf{x}) = \frac{P(\mathbf{x} \mid \omega_i) P(\omega_i)}{P(\mathbf{x})},$$

can be written as

$$\sum_{i=1}^{l} L_{ji} \frac{P(\mathbf{x} \mid \omega_i) P(\omega_i)}{P(\mathbf{x})} < \sum_{i=1}^{l} L_{ki} \frac{P(\mathbf{x} \mid \omega_i) P(\omega_i)}{P(\mathbf{x})}, \qquad k = 1, 2, \ldots, l, \ k \neq j. \tag{1.85}$$

Canceling the positive scaling factor $P(\mathbf{x})$ on both sides of this inequality yields the final practical form of Bayes' classification rule, which minimizes overall (Bayes') risk.

Choose a class (make a decision) ω_j for which

$$\sum_{i=1}^{l} L_{ji} P(\mathbf{x} \mid \omega_i) P(\omega_i) < \sum_{i=1}^{l} L_{ki} P(\mathbf{x} \mid \omega_i) P(\omega_i), \qquad k = 1, 2, \ldots, l, \ k \neq j. \tag{1.86}$$

For binary classification decision problems, Bayes' risk criterion (1.86) is given as follows. Let L_{ij} be the loss (cost) of making decision ω_i when ω_j is true. Then for the binary classification problem there are four possible losses:

L_{11} = loss (cost) of deciding ω_1 when, given $\mathbf{x}$, ω_1 is true,

L_{12} = loss (cost) of deciding ω_1 when, given $\mathbf{x}$, ω_2 is true,

L_{21} = loss (cost) of deciding ω_2 when, given $\mathbf{x}$, ω_1 is true,

L_{22} = loss (cost) of deciding ω_2 when, given $\mathbf{x}$, ω_2 is true,

or

$$\mathbf{L} = \begin{bmatrix} L_{11} & L_{12} \\ L_{21} & L_{22} \end{bmatrix}.$$

Note that there is nothing strange in associating a loss or cost with a correct decision. One can often set $L_{11} = L_{22} = 0$, but there will also be very common problems when both the correct and the wrong decisions are associated with certain costs. The Bayes' risk criterion will result in a (classification) decision when the expected loss or risk is minimal.

The risk (expected or average loss) that should be minimized is

$$R(\omega_1 \,|\, \mathbf{x}) = \sum_{i=1}^{2} L_{1i} P(\omega_i \,|\, \mathbf{x}) = L_{11} P(\omega_1 \,|\, \mathbf{x}) + L_{12} P(\omega_2 \,|\, \mathbf{x}),$$

$$R(\omega_2 \,|\, \mathbf{x}) = \sum_{i=1}^{2} L_{2i} P(\omega_i \,|\, \mathbf{x}) = L_{21} P(\omega_1 \,|\, \mathbf{x}) + L_{22} P(\omega_2 \,|\, \mathbf{x}),$$

or

$$R = R(\omega_1 \,|\, \mathbf{x}) + R(\omega_2 \,|\, \mathbf{x})$$

$$= L_{11} P(\omega_1 \,|\, \mathbf{x}) + L_{12} P(\omega_2 \,|\, \mathbf{x}) + L_{21} P(\omega_1 \,|\, \mathbf{x}) + L_{22} P(\omega_2 \,|\, \mathbf{x}). \tag{1.87}$$

The Bayes' risk formulation can be viewed as a generalization of a maximum-a-posteriori (MAP), or probability-of-error, decision criterion as given by (1.67). To show that, (1.67) can be rewritten as

$$P(\text{classification error}) = \int_{-\infty}^{+\infty} P(\text{classification error} \,|\, x) P(x) \, dx$$

$$= \int_{-\infty}^{+\infty} (P(\omega_1 \,|\, \mathbf{x}) + P(\omega_2 \,|\, \mathbf{x})) P(\mathbf{x}) \, d\mathbf{x}.$$

Clearly, by minimizing the probability of misclassification for each $\mathbf{x}$ (as the classification rule given by (1.66) requires), the average probability of error given by (1.67) (and by the preceding equation) will also be minimized.

At the same time, by assigning the losses $L_{11} = L_{22} = 0$ and $L_{12} = L_{21} = 1$, the risk (1.87) becomes

$$R = 0 \cdot P(\omega_1 \,|\, \mathbf{x}) + 1 \cdot P(\omega_2 \,|\, \mathbf{x}) + 1 \cdot P(\omega_1 \,|\, \mathbf{x}) + 0 \cdot P(\omega_2 \,|\, \mathbf{x}) = P(\omega_1 \,|\, \mathbf{x}) + P(\omega_2 \,|\, \mathbf{x}),$$

and this is exactly the argument of the preceding integral. In other words, by minimizing a risk, given a *zero-one loss function*, the average probability of classification error is also minimized.

Thus, for a zero-one loss function, a classification (decision) by minimizing risk is identical to the Bayes' (maximum-a-posteriori) classification decision criterion that minimizes the average (expected) probability of classification error. Note that in dichotomization (two classes only or binary) tasks, as long as $L_{ii} = 0$, that is, $L_{11} = L_{22} = 0$, the risk minimization criterion can be nicely expressed in a known form of a likelihood ratio

$$\Lambda(x) \underset{\omega_2}{\overset{\omega_1}{\gtrless}} \frac{L_{12}}{L_{21}} \frac{P(\omega_2)}{P(\omega_1)}. \tag{1.88}$$

Hence, whenever the likelihood ratio $\Lambda(x) = P(x \mid \omega_1)/P(x \mid \omega_2)$ is larger than the product of the two ratios on the right-hand side of (1.88), the decision will be class 1. The last expression follows from (1.86), or after applying Bayes' theorem (1.64) in (1.87). Note that the costs L_{12} and L_{21} do not necessarily have to be equal to 1 now. Also, both the MAP (Bayes' decision criterion) and the maximum likelihood criterion are just special cases of the risk minimization criterion (1.88). Namely, the MAP rule follows when $L_{12} = L_{21} = 1$, and the maximum likelihood criterion results when $L_{12} = L_{21} = 1$ and $P(\omega_1) = P(\omega_2)$.

Finally, note that in more general multiclass problems, the zero-one loss matrix $\mathbf{L}$ (1.80) is given as

$$\mathbf{L} = \begin{bmatrix} 0 & 1 & \cdots & 1 \\ 1 & 0 & \cdots & 1 \\ \vdots & \vdots & \vdots & \vdots \\ 1 & 1 & \cdots & 0 \end{bmatrix}. \tag{1.89}$$

Decision Regions and Discriminant Functions   Pattern recognition systems perform multiclass, multifeature classification regardless of the type of decision rule applied. Recall that there are various decision rules that, depending on information about the patterns available, may be applied. Six different rules were listed at the beginning of section 1.4.2, and both the Bayes' rule for minimizing the average probability of error and the Bayes' rule for minimizing risk have been studied in more detail.

A pattern classifier assigns the feature vectors **x** to one of a number of possible classes ω_i, $i \in \{1, 2, \dots, l\}$, and in this way partitions feature space into line segments, areas, volumes, and hypervolumes, which are decision regions $R_1, R_2, \dots, R_l$, in the case of one-, two-, three-, or higher-dimensional features, respectively. All feature vectors belonging to the same class are ideally assigned to the same category in a decision region. The decision regions R_i are often single nonoverlapping volumes or hypervolumes, and decision regions of the same class may also be disjoint, consisting of two or more nontouching regions (see fig. 1.30). The boundaries between adjacent regions are called decision boundaries because classification decisions change

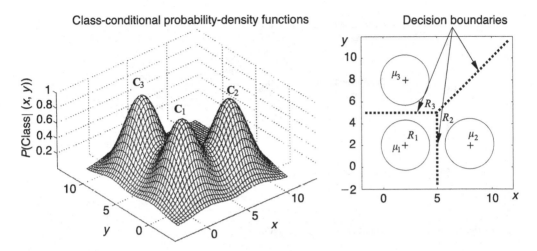

Figure 1.31
Class-conditional probability-density functions (*left*) and decision regions R_i and decision boundaries (*right*) for three classes result in three single nonoverlapping decision regions.

across boundaries. These class boundaries are points, straight lines or curves, planes or surfaces, and hyperplanes or hypersurfaces in the case of one-, two-, three- and higher-dimensional feature space, respectively. In the case of straight lines, planes, and hyperplanes, the decision boundaries are linear.

Figure 1.31 shows three class-conditional probability-density functions (likelihood functions) as well as the partitioning of two-dimensional feature space into three separated decision areas. The likelihood functions are three normal distributions with equal covariance matrices and centers at (2, 2), (8, 2) and (2, 8). Because of the equal covariance matrices, the three decision boundaries are straight lines (why this is so is explained later). In the case of three- and higher-dimensional feature space, the decision regions are volumes and hypervolumes, respectively, and visualization is no longer possible. Nevertheless, the classification decision procedures and the underlying theories are the same. The optimal classification strategy will most typically be the one that minimizes the probability of classification error, and the latter will be minimized if, for $P(\mathbf{x}\,|\,\omega_1)P(\omega_1) > P(\mathbf{x}\,|\,\omega_2)P(\omega_2)$, $\mathbf{x}$ is chosen to be in the region R_1.

More generally, classification decisions based on feature vector $\mathbf{x}$ may be stated using a set of explicitly defined *discriminant functions*

$$d_i(\mathbf{x}), \qquad i = 1, 2, \ldots, l, \tag{1.90}$$

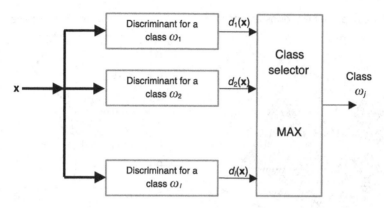

Figure 1.32
Discriminant classifier for multiclass pattern recognition.

where each discriminant is associated with a particular recognized class ω_i, $i = 1, 2, \ldots, l$.

The discriminant type of classifier (i.e., the classifier designed using the discriminant functions) assigns a pattern with feature vector $\mathbf{x}$ to a class ω_j for which the corresponding discriminant value d_j is the largest:

$$d_j(\mathbf{x}) > d_i(\mathbf{x}), \quad \text{for all } i = 1, 2, \ldots, l, \ i \neq j. \tag{1.91}$$

Such a discriminant classifier can be designed as a system comprising a set of l discriminants $d_i(\mathbf{x})$, $i = 1, 2, \ldots, l$, associated with each class ω_i, $i = 1, 2, \ldots, l$, along with a module that selects the largest-value discriminant as a recognized class (see fig. 1.32).

Note that the classification is based on the largest discriminant function $d_j(\mathbf{x})$ regardless how the corresponding discriminant functions are defined. Therefore, any monotonic function of a discriminant function $f(d(\mathbf{x}))$ will provide identical classification because of the fact that for the monotonic function $f(\cdot)$, the maximal $d_j(\mathbf{x})$ gives rise to the maximal $f(d_j(\mathbf{x}))$. It may be useful to understand this basic property of discriminant functions. If some $d_i(\mathbf{x})$, $i = 1, \ldots, l$, are the discriminant functions for a given classifier, so also are the functions $\ln d_i(\mathbf{x})$, $d_i(\mathbf{x}) + C$, or $Cd_i(\mathbf{x})$ for any class-independent constant C. This is widely explored in classification theory by using the natural logarithmic function $\ln d(\mathbf{x})$ as a discriminant function. Thus, in the case of a Bayes' classifier, instead of

$$d_i(\mathbf{x}) = P(\omega_i \mid \mathbf{x}) = P(\mathbf{x} \mid \omega_i)P(\omega_i)$$

the natural logarithm of $P(\omega_i \,|\, \mathbf{x})$ is used as a discriminant function, that is, the discriminant function is defined as

$$d_i(\mathbf{x}) = \ln P(\omega_i \,|\, \mathbf{x}) = \ln(P(\mathbf{x} \,|\, \omega_i)P(\omega_i))$$

$$= \ln P(\mathbf{x} \,|\, \omega_i) + \ln P(\omega_i), \qquad i = 1, 2, \ldots, l. \tag{1.92}$$

Discriminant functions define the decision boundaries that separate decision regions. Decision boundaries between neighboring regions R_j and R_i are obtained by equalizing the corresponding discriminant functions:

$$d_j(\mathbf{x}) = d_i(\mathbf{x}). \tag{1.93}$$

These boundaries between the decision regions are the points, lines or curves, planes or surfaces, and hyperplanes or hypersurfaces in the case of one-, two-, three-, and higher-dimensional feature vectors, respectively.

Depending upon the criteria for choosing which classification decision rule to apply, the discriminant function may be

$$d_i(\mathbf{x}) = P(\omega_i \,|\, \mathbf{x}) \qquad \text{in the case of Bayes' (MAP) classification,} \tag{1.94a}$$

$$d_i(\mathbf{x}) = P(\mathbf{x} \,|\, \omega_1) \qquad \text{in the case of maximum likelihood classification,} \tag{1.94b}$$

$$d_i(\mathbf{x}) = P(\omega_i) \qquad \text{in the case of maximum-a-priori classification,} \tag{1.94c}$$

$$d_i(\mathbf{x}) = -R(\omega_i \,|\, \mathbf{x}) \qquad \text{in the case of Bayes' minimal risk classification,} \tag{1.94d}$$

$$i = 1, 2, \ldots, l.$$

Many other (not necessarily probabilistic) discriminant functions may also be defined. Note the minus sign in the last definition of the discriminant function, which denotes that the maximal value of the discriminant function $d_i(\mathbf{x})$ corresponds to the minimal conditional risk $R(\omega_i \,|\, \mathbf{x})$.

In the case of two-class or binary classification (dichotomization), instead of two discriminants $d_1(\mathbf{x})$ and $d_2(\mathbf{x})$ applied separately, typically a *dichotomizer* is applied, defined as

$$d(\mathbf{x}) = d_1(\mathbf{x}) - d_2(\mathbf{x}). \tag{1.95}$$

A dichotomizer (1.95) calculates a value of a single discriminant function $d(\mathbf{x})$ and assigns a class according to the *sign* of this value. When $d_1(\mathbf{x})$ is larger than $d_2(\mathbf{x})$, $d(\mathbf{x}) > 0$ and a pattern $\mathbf{x}$ will be assigned to class 1, otherwise it is assigned to class 2. Thus, for Bayes' rule–based discriminant functions (1.94a), the dichotomizer for a binary classification is given as

$$d(\mathbf{x}) = P(\omega_1 \mid \mathbf{x}) - P(\omega_2 \mid \mathbf{x}) = P(\mathbf{x} \mid \omega_1)P(\omega_1) - P(\mathbf{x} \mid \omega_2)P(\omega_2).$$

Accordingly, the decision boundary between two classes is defined by

$$d_1(\mathbf{x}) = d_2(\mathbf{x}) \quad \text{or by} \quad d(\mathbf{x}) = 0. \tag{1.96}$$

Checking the geometrical meaning of (1.96) in the right graph in figure 1.33 for two-dimensional features, one sees that the separating function, or the decision boundary, is the intersecting curve (surface or hypersurface for three- and higher-dimensional features, respectively) between the dichotomizer $d(\mathbf{x})$ and the feature plane. Another useful form of the dichotomizer that uses a Bayes' (MAP) classification decision criterion can be obtained from (1.92) as follows:

$$d(\mathbf{x}) = \ln P(\omega_1 \mid \mathbf{x}) - \ln P(\omega_2 \mid \mathbf{x}) = \ln(P(\mathbf{x} \mid \omega_1)P(\omega_1)) - \ln(P(\mathbf{x} \mid \omega_2)P(\omega_2))$$

$$= (\ln P(\mathbf{x} \mid \omega_1) + \ln P(\omega_1)) - (\ln P(\mathbf{x} \mid \omega_2) + \ln P(\omega_2)),$$

or

$$d(\mathbf{x}) = \ln \frac{P(\mathbf{x} \mid \omega_1)}{P(\mathbf{x} \mid \omega_2)} + \ln \frac{P(\omega_1)}{P(\omega_2)}. \tag{1.97}$$

For a given feature vector $\mathbf{x}$, a dichotomizer $d(\mathbf{x})$ calculates a single value and assigns a class based on the sign of this value. In other words, because $d(\mathbf{x})$ is calculated as the difference $d_1(\mathbf{x}) - d_2(\mathbf{x})$, when $d(\mathbf{x}) > 0$ the pattern is assigned to class ω_1 and when $d(\mathbf{x}) < 0$ the pattern is assigned to class ω_2.

The next section takes up discriminant functions for normally distributed classes, which are very common. Solving classification tasks involving Gaussian examples can yield very useful closed-form expressions for calculating decision boundaries.

Discriminant Functions for Classification of Normally Distributed Classes   In the case of normally distributed classes (Gaussian classes) discriminant functions are quadratic. These become linear (straight lines, planes, and hyperplanes for two-, three- and n-dimensional feature vectors, respectively) when the covariance matrices of corresponding classes are equal. The quadratic and linear classifiers belong to the group of *parametric classifiers* because they are defined in terms of Gaussian distribution parameters—mean vectors $\boldsymbol{\mu}_i$ and covariance matrices $\boldsymbol{\Sigma}_i$.

Let us start with the simplest case of a binary classification problem in a one-dimensional feature space when two classes are generated by two Gaussian probability functions having the same variances $\sigma_1^2 = \sigma_2^2 = \sigma^2$ but different means $\mu_1 \neq \mu_2$ (see fig. 1.28, a classification of 1's and 0's). In this case, the class-conditional probability-density functions $P(x \mid \omega_i)$ are given as

$$P(x \mid \omega_1) = \frac{\exp\left(-\frac{1}{2}\left(\frac{x-\mu_1}{\sigma_1}\right)^2\right)}{\sqrt{2\pi}\sigma_1}, \qquad P(x \mid \omega_2) = \frac{\exp\left(-\frac{1}{2}\left(\frac{x-\mu_2}{\sigma_2}\right)^2\right)}{\sqrt{2\pi}\sigma_2},$$

and applying (1.97) results in

$$d(x) = \ln\frac{P(x \mid \omega_1)}{P(x \mid \omega_2)} + \ln\frac{P(\omega_1)}{P(\omega_2)} = \ln\frac{\exp\left(-\frac{1}{2}\left(\frac{x-\mu_1}{\sigma}\right)^2\right)}{\exp\left(-\frac{1}{2}\left(\frac{x-\mu_2}{\sigma}\right)^2\right)} + \ln\frac{P(\omega_1)}{P(\omega_2)},$$

or

$$d(x) = \frac{\mu_1 - \mu_2}{\sigma^2}x + \frac{\mu_2^2 - \mu_1^2}{2\sigma^2} + \ln\frac{P(\omega_1)}{P(\omega_2)}. \qquad (1.98)$$

Hence, for a one-dimensional feature vector, given equal variances of normal class-conditional probability-density functions $P(x \mid \omega_i)$, the dichotomizer is linear (straight line). The decision boundary as defined by (1.96) or by $d(x) = 0$, is the point

$$x = \frac{\mu_1 + \mu_2}{2} + \frac{\sigma^2}{\mu_2 - \mu_1}\ln\frac{P(\omega_1)}{P(\omega_2)}. \qquad (1.99)$$

Note that in the equiprobable case when $P(\omega_1) = P(\omega_2)$, the decision boundary is a point x_{DB} in the middle of the class centers $x_{DB} = (\mu_1 + \mu_2)/2$. Otherwise, the decision boundary point x_{DB} is closer to the center of the less probable class. So, for example, if $P(\omega_1) > P(\omega_2)$, then $|\mu_2 - x_{DB}| < |\mu_1 - x_{DB}|$.

In the case of the multiclass classification problem in an n-dimensional feature space[14] when classes are generated according to Gaussian distributions with different covariance matrices $\Sigma_1 \neq \Sigma_2 \neq \cdots \neq \Sigma_i$ and different means $\mu_1 \neq \mu_2 \neq \cdots \neq \mu_i$, the class-conditional probability-density function $P(\mathbf{x} \mid \omega_i)$ is described by

$$P(\mathbf{x} \mid \omega_i) = \frac{1}{(2\pi)^{n/2}|\Sigma_i|^{1/2}}\exp\left(-\frac{1}{2}(\mathbf{x}-\mu_i)^T\Sigma_i^{-1}(\mathbf{x}-\mu_i)\right), \qquad i = 1, 2. \qquad (1.100)$$

Now $\mathbf{x}$ and μ_i are $(n, 1)$ vectors and the covariance matrices Σ_i are square and symmetric (n, n) matrices. $|\Sigma|$ denotes the determinant of the covariance matrix. In the most general case for normally distributed classes, the discriminant function defined as $d(\mathbf{x}) = \ln P(\omega \mid \mathbf{x}) = \ln P(\mathbf{x} \mid \omega)P(\omega)$ becomes

$$d_i(\mathbf{x}) = \ln \frac{1}{(2\pi)^{n/2}|\mathbf{\Sigma}_i|^{1/2}} \exp\left(-\frac{1}{2}(\mathbf{x} - \mathbf{\mu}_i)^T \mathbf{\Sigma}_i^{-1}(\mathbf{x} - \mathbf{\mu}_i)\right) + \ln P(\omega_i), \quad i = 1, 2, \ldots, l,$$

or after expanding the logarithm,

$$d_i(\mathbf{x}) = -\frac{1}{2}\ln|\mathbf{\Sigma}_i| - \frac{1}{2}(\mathbf{x} - \mathbf{\mu}_i)^T \mathbf{\Sigma}_i^{-1}(\mathbf{x} - \mathbf{\mu}_i) - \frac{n}{2}\ln(2\pi) + \ln P(\omega_i), \qquad i = 1, 2, \ldots, l.$$
$$(1.101)$$

The constant term $n\ln(2\pi)/2$ is equal for all classes (i.e., it cannot change the classification), and consequently it can be eliminated in what results as a *quadratic discriminant function*,

$$d_i(\mathbf{x}) = -\frac{1}{2}\ln|\mathbf{\Sigma}_i| - \frac{1}{2}(\mathbf{x} - \mathbf{\mu}_i)^T \mathbf{\Sigma}_i^{-1}(\mathbf{x} - \mathbf{\mu}_i) + \ln P(\omega_i), \qquad i = 1, 2, \ldots, l. \quad (1.102)$$

Decision boundaries (separation hypersurfaces) between classes i and j are the hyperquadratic functions in n-dimensional feature space (e.g., hyperspheres, hyperellipsoids, hyperparaboloids) for which $d_i(\mathbf{x}) = d_j(\mathbf{x})$. The specific form of discriminant functions and of decision boundaries is determined by the characteristics of covariance matrices.

The second term in (1.102) is the *Mahalanobis distance*, which calculates the distance between the feature vector $\mathbf{x}$ and the mean vector $\mathbf{\mu}_i$. Recall that for correlated features, covariance matrices $\mathbf{\Sigma}_i$ are nondiagonal symmetric matrices for which off-diagonal elements $\sigma_{ij}^2 \neq 0$, $i = 1, \ldots, l$, $j = 1, \ldots, l$, $i \neq j$.

The quadratic discriminant function is the most general discriminant in the case of normally distributed classes, and decisions are based on the Bayes' decision rule that minimizes the probability of error or the probability of misclassification. This is also known as the *minimum error rate classifier*.

The classification decision algorithm based on the quadratic Bayes' discriminants is now the following:

1. For given classes (feature vectors $\mathbf{x}$), calculate the mean vectors and the covariance matrices.

2. Compute the values of the quadratic discriminant functions (1.102) for each class.

3. Select a class ω_j for which $d_j(\mathbf{x}) = \max(d_i(\mathbf{x}))$, $i = 1, 2, \ldots, l$.

Example 1.10 illustrates how equation (1.102) applies to the calculation of quadratic discriminant functions. The computation of decision boundaries between two classes in the case of the two-dimensional feature vector $\mathbf{x}$ is also shown.

Example 1.10 Feature vectors **x** of two classes are generated by Gaussian distributions having parameters (covariance matrices Σ_i and means $\boldsymbol{\mu}_i$) as follows:

$$\Sigma_1 = \begin{bmatrix} 1 & 0 \\ 0 & 0.25 \end{bmatrix}, \quad \boldsymbol{\mu}_1 = \begin{bmatrix} 0 \\ 0 \end{bmatrix}.$$

$$\Sigma_2 = \begin{bmatrix} 0.25 & 0 \\ 0 & 1 \end{bmatrix}, \quad \boldsymbol{\mu}_2 = \begin{bmatrix} 0 \\ 2 \end{bmatrix}.$$

Find the discriminant functions and decision boundaries. Classes are equiprobable $(P(\omega_i) = P(\omega) = P)$. (Recall that the covariance matrices are diagonal when the features are statistically independent. The geometrical consequence of this fact can be seen in figure 1.34, where the principal axes of the contours of the Gaussian class densities are parallel to the feature axes.)

Quadratic discriminant functions for two given classes are defined by (1.102). The constant and the class-independent term $\ln P(\omega_i)$ can be ignored, and the two discriminants are obtained as

$$d_1(\mathbf{x}) = -\frac{1}{2}\ln|\Sigma_1| - \frac{1}{2}\left(\begin{bmatrix} x_1 \\ x_2 \end{bmatrix} - \begin{bmatrix} 0 \\ 0 \end{bmatrix}\right)^T \begin{bmatrix} 1 & 0 \\ 0 & 0.25 \end{bmatrix}^{-1}\left(\begin{bmatrix} x_1 \\ x_2 \end{bmatrix} - \begin{bmatrix} 0 \\ 0 \end{bmatrix}\right)$$

$$= 0.693 - \frac{1}{2}[x_1 \quad x_2]\begin{bmatrix} 1 & 0 \\ 0 & 4 \end{bmatrix}\begin{bmatrix} x_1 \\ x_2 \end{bmatrix} = 0.693 - 0.5(x_1^2 + 4x_2^2),$$

$$d_2(\mathbf{x}) = -\frac{1}{2}\ln|\Sigma_2| - \frac{1}{2}\left(\begin{bmatrix} x_1 \\ x_2 \end{bmatrix} - \begin{bmatrix} 0 \\ 2 \end{bmatrix}\right)^T \begin{bmatrix} 0.25 & 0 \\ 0 & 1 \end{bmatrix}^{-1}\left(\begin{bmatrix} x_1 \\ x_2 \end{bmatrix} - \begin{bmatrix} 0 \\ 2 \end{bmatrix}\right)$$

$$= 0.693 - \frac{1}{2}[x_1 \quad (x_2-2)]\begin{bmatrix} 4 & 0 \\ 0 & 1 \end{bmatrix}\begin{bmatrix} x_1 \\ x_2-2 \end{bmatrix} = 0.693 - 0.5(4x_1^2 + (x_2-2)^2).$$

Both discriminant functions and the dichotomizing discriminant function are shown in figure 1.33.

The decision boundary, or separation line, in the feature plane follows from $d(\mathbf{x}) = d_1(\mathbf{x}) - d_2(\mathbf{x}) = 0$ as

$$d(\mathbf{x}) = d_1(\mathbf{x}) - d_2(\mathbf{x}) = 1.5x_1^2 - 1.5x_2^2 - 2x_2 + 2 = 0.$$

Note that the decision regions in the feature plane, shown in figure 1.34, are non-overlapping patches. The decision region for class 2 comprises two disjoint areas. It is not surprising that region R_2 is disjoint. This can be seen in figure 1.33, and it also

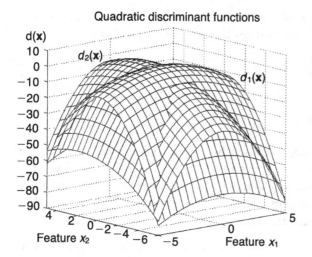

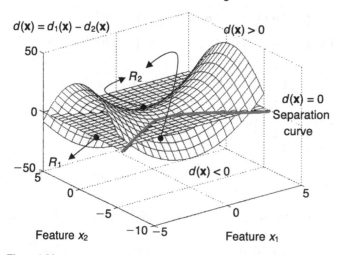

Figure 1.33
Classification of two Gaussian classes with different covariance matrices $\Sigma_1 \neq \Sigma_2$. *Top*, quadratic discriminant functions $d_1(\mathbf{x})$ and $d_2(\mathbf{x})$. *Bottom*, quadratic dichotomizing discriminant function $d(\mathbf{x}) = d_1(\mathbf{x}) - d_2(\mathbf{x})$. The decision boundary (separation curve) $d(\mathbf{x}) = d_1(\mathbf{x}) - d_2(\mathbf{x}) = 0$ in the right graph is the intersection curve between the dichotomizer $d(\mathbf{x})$ and the feature plane. Note that the decision regions in the feature plane are nonoverlapping parts of the feature plane, but the decision region for class 2 comprises two disjoint areas.

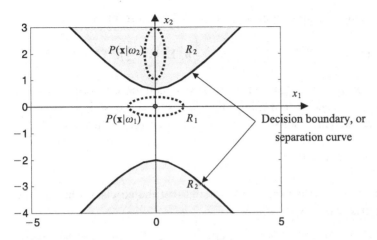

Figure 1.34
Quadratic decision boundary (separation curve) $d(\mathbf{x}) = d_1(\mathbf{x}) - d_2(\mathbf{x}) = 0$ for two Gaussian classes with different covariance matrices $\mathbf{\Sigma}_1 \neq \mathbf{\Sigma}_2$. This decision boundary is obtained by the intersection of the dichotomizing discriminant function $d(\mathbf{x})$ and the feature plane. Note that the decision region for class 2 comprises two disjoint areas.

follows from these considerations: the prior probabilities are equal, and the decision rule, being the minimum error rate classifier, chooses the class whose likelihood function $P(\mathbf{x}\,|\,\omega)$ is larger. Since the variance in the x_2 direction is larger for class 2 than for class 1, the class-conditional probability-density function (likelihood) $P(\mathbf{x}\,|\,\omega_2)$ is actually larger than $P(\mathbf{x}\,|\,\omega_1)$ for most of the lower half-plane in figure 1.34, despite the fact that all these points are closer (in the sense of the Euclidean distance) to the mean of class 1. The quadratic separation function shown in figure 1.34 is obtained from $d(\mathbf{x}) = 0$. All points in the feature plane for which $d(\mathbf{x}) < 0$ belong to class 1, and when $d(\mathbf{x}) > 0$ the specific pattern belongs to class 2. This can be readily checked analytically as well as in figures 1.33 and 1.34.

There are two simpler, widely used discriminant functions, or decision rules, that under certain assumptions follow from the quadratic discriminant function (1.102).

∎

Linear Discriminant Function for Equal Covariance Matrices   When the covariance matrices for all classes are equal ($\mathbf{\Sigma}_i = \mathbf{\Sigma}$, $i = 1, 2, \ldots, l$) so is the first term in (1.102) equal for all classes, and being class-independent, it can be dropped from (1.102), yielding a discriminant of the form

$$d_i(\mathbf{x}) = -\frac{1}{2}(\mathbf{x} - \boldsymbol{\mu}_i)^T \mathbf{\Sigma}_i^{-1}(\mathbf{x} - \boldsymbol{\mu}_i) + \ln P(\omega_i), \qquad i = 1, 2, \ldots, l. \tag{1.103}$$

This discriminant function is linear, which can be readily seen from the expansion

$$\frac{1}{2}(\mathbf{x} - \boldsymbol{\mu}_i)^T \boldsymbol{\Sigma}^{-1}(\mathbf{x} - \boldsymbol{\mu}_i) = \frac{1}{2}\mathbf{x}^T \boldsymbol{\Sigma}^{-1}\mathbf{x} - \frac{1}{2}\mathbf{x}^T \boldsymbol{\Sigma}^{-1}\boldsymbol{\mu}_i - \frac{1}{2}\boldsymbol{\mu}_i^T \boldsymbol{\Sigma}^{-1}\mathbf{x} + \frac{1}{2}\boldsymbol{\mu}_i^T \boldsymbol{\Sigma}^{-1}\boldsymbol{\mu}_i.$$

The quadratic term $\mathbf{x}^T \boldsymbol{\Sigma}^{-1}\mathbf{x}$ is class-independent and can be dropped from this expansion. Furthermore, since the covariance matrix is symmetric, so is its inversion and, $\mathbf{x}^T \boldsymbol{\Sigma}^{-1}\boldsymbol{\mu}_i = \boldsymbol{\mu}_i^T \boldsymbol{\Sigma}^{-1}\mathbf{x}$. This results in a set of linear discriminant functions

$$d_i(\mathbf{x}) = \boldsymbol{\mu}_i^T \boldsymbol{\Sigma}^{-1}\mathbf{x} - \frac{1}{2}\boldsymbol{\mu}_i^T \boldsymbol{\Sigma}^{-1}\boldsymbol{\mu}_i + \ln P(\omega_i), \qquad i = 1, 2, \ldots, l. \tag{1.104}$$

The classification decision algorithm for normally distributed classes having the same covariance matrix $\boldsymbol{\Sigma}$ is now the following:

1. For given classes (feature vectors $\mathbf{x}$), calculate the mean vectors and the covariance matrix $\boldsymbol{\Sigma}$.

2. Compute the values of the linear discriminant functions (1.104) for each class.

3. Select a class ω_j for which $d_j(\mathbf{x}) = \max(d_i(\mathbf{x}))$, $i = 1, 2, \ldots, l$.

Decision boundaries corresponding to $d_i(\mathbf{x}) = d_j(\mathbf{x})$ are hyperplanes. In the case of a two-dimensional feature vector $\mathbf{x}$, these boundaries are straight lines in a feature plane. Linear discriminant functions and linear boundaries are closely related to neural network models (see chapter 3). Here the linear discriminant functions are presented in the "neural" form

$$d_i(\mathbf{x}) = \mathbf{w}_i^T \mathbf{x} + w_{i0}, \tag{1.105}$$

where

$$\mathbf{w}_i^T = \boldsymbol{\mu}_i^T \boldsymbol{\Sigma}^{-1} \quad \text{and} \quad w_{i0} = -\frac{1}{2}\boldsymbol{\mu}_i^T \boldsymbol{\Sigma}^{-1}\boldsymbol{\mu}_i + \ln P(\omega_i).$$

The decision boundary between classes Ω_i and Ω_j in neural form is given as a hyperplane,

$$d_i(\mathbf{x}) - d_j(\mathbf{x}) = \mathbf{w}\mathbf{x} + w_{ij0} = 0, \tag{1.106}$$

where

$$\mathbf{w} = (\boldsymbol{\mu}_i^T - \boldsymbol{\mu}_j^T)\boldsymbol{\Sigma}^{-1} \quad \text{and} \quad w_{ij0} = -\frac{1}{2}(\boldsymbol{\mu}_i^T \boldsymbol{\Sigma}^{-1}\boldsymbol{\mu}_i - \boldsymbol{\mu}_j^T \boldsymbol{\Sigma}^{-1}\boldsymbol{\mu}_j) + \ln \frac{P(\omega_i)}{P(\omega_j)}.$$

It is straightforward to show that in the case of a one-dimensional feature vector x, equation (1.99), which defines the separation point, follows from (1.106). In the case of two feature patterns, (1.106) represents straight lines. Example 1.11 shows this.

Example 1.11   Figure 1.31 depicts the classification of three normally distributed classes that result in three linear separation lines and in the tessellation (partition) of a two-dimensional feature space (plane) into three separated decision regions. The likelihood functions of the three normal distributions have equal covariance matrices $\Sigma = I_2$ and centers (means) at $(2, 2)$, $(8, 2)$, and $(2, 8)$. Check the validity of the right graph in figure 1.31 by applying (1.105) and (1.106) for the equiprobable classes.

Having identity covariance matrices and equiprobable classes (meaning that the last terms $\ln P(\omega_i)$ in (1.105) can be eliminated), three linear discriminant functions (planes) that follow from (1.105) are

$$d_i(\mathbf{x}) = \mathbf{w}_i^T \mathbf{x} + w_{i0} = \boldsymbol{\mu}_i^T \mathbf{x} - \tfrac{1}{2}\boldsymbol{\mu}_i^T \boldsymbol{\mu}_i, \qquad i = 1, 2, 3,$$

or

$$d_1(\mathbf{x}) = 2x_1 + 2x_2 - 4, \qquad d_2(\mathbf{x}) = 8x_1 + 2x_2 - 34, \qquad d_3(\mathbf{x}) = 2x_1 + 8x_2 - 34.$$

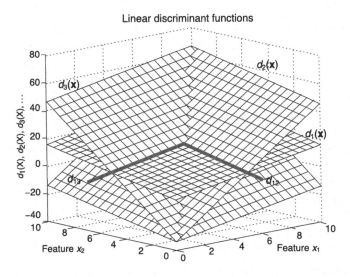

Figure 1.35
Linear discriminant functions (decision planes $d_i(\mathbf{x})$ in the case of two-dimensional features) for three Gaussian classes with the same covariance matrix $\Sigma = I_2$ as in figure 1.31. Three corresponding decision boundaries obtained as the planes' intersections divide the feature plane into three single nonoverlapping decision regions. (The two visible separation lines, d_{12} and d_{13}, are depicted as solid straight lines.

Similarly, the decision boundaries or the separation lines that follow from (1.106) are

$$d_{12}(\mathbf{x}) = d_1(\mathbf{x}) - d_2(\mathbf{x}) = -6x_1 + 30 = 0, \quad \text{or} \quad x_1 = 5,$$

$$d_{13}(\mathbf{x}) = d_1(\mathbf{x}) - d_3(\mathbf{x}) = -6x_2 + 30 = 0, \quad \text{or} \quad x_2 = 5,$$

$$d_{23}(\mathbf{x}) = d_2(\mathbf{x}) - d_3(\mathbf{x}) = 6x_1 - 6x_2 = 0, \quad \text{or} \quad x_2 = x_1.$$

Three discriminant planes $d_i(\mathbf{x})$, $i = 1, 2, 3$, together with the two visible decision boundary lines that separate given classes, are shown in figure 1.35. (All three separation lines are shown in the right graph in figure 1.31.) ∎

Minimum Mahalanobis Distance and Euclidean Distance Classifiers   Two particular cases for the classification of normally distributed (Gaussian) classes follow after applying several additional assumptions regarding their class distribution properties. If there are equal covariance matrices for all classes ($\mathbf{\Sigma}_i = \mathbf{\Sigma}$, $i = 1, 2, \ldots, l$) and also equal prior probabilities for all classes ($P(\omega_i) = P(\omega) = P$), then the second term on the right-hand side of (1.103) can be eliminated. Additionally, being class-independent, the constant $1/2$ can be neglected, and this results in the following discriminant functions:

$$d_i(\mathbf{x}) = -(\mathbf{x} - \mathbf{\mu}_i)^T \mathbf{\Sigma}^{-1} (\mathbf{x} - \mathbf{\mu}_i), \qquad i = 1, 2, \ldots, l. \tag{1.107}$$

Thus, classification based on the maximization of these discriminants will assign a given pattern with a feature vector $\mathbf{x}$ to a class ω_k, for which the Mahalanobis distance $(\mathbf{x} - \mathbf{\mu}_k)^T \mathbf{\Sigma}^{-1} (\mathbf{x} - \mathbf{\mu}_k)$ of $\mathbf{x}$ to the mean vector $\mathbf{\mu}_k$ is the smallest. Note that because of the minus sign in (1.107), minimization of the Mahalanobis distance corresponds to maximization of the discriminant function $d(\mathbf{x})$. In other words, a pattern will be assigned to the closest class center $\mathbf{\mu}_k$ in the Mahalanobis sense. Note also that the Mahalanobis distance is relevant for correlated features, or when the off-diagonal elements of the covariance matrix $\mathbf{\Sigma}$ are not equal to zero (or when $\mathbf{\Sigma}$ is not a diagonal matrix, i.e., when $\sigma_{ij}^2 \neq 0$, $i = 1, \ldots, l$, $j = 1, \ldots, l$, $i \neq j$).

The classifier (1.107) is called a *minimum Mahalanobis distance classifier*. In the same way as (1.104), the Mahalanobis distance classifier can be given in linear form as

$$d_i(\mathbf{x}) = \mathbf{\mu}_i^T \mathbf{\Sigma}^{-1} \mathbf{x} - \tfrac{1}{2} \mathbf{\mu}_i^T \mathbf{\Sigma}^{-1} \mathbf{\mu}_i, \qquad i = 1, 2, \ldots, l. \tag{1.108}$$

Applying an even more restrictive assumption for the equiprobable classes ($P(\omega_i) = P(\omega) = P$), namely, assuming that the covariance matrices for all classes are not only equal but are also diagonal matrices, meaning that the features are statistically independent ($\mathbf{\Sigma}_i = \mathbf{\Sigma} = \sigma^2 \mathbf{I}_n$, $i = 1, 2, \ldots, l$), one obtains the simple discriminant functions

$$d_i(\mathbf{x}) = -\frac{(\mathbf{x} - \boldsymbol{\mu}_i)^T (\mathbf{x} - \boldsymbol{\mu}_i)}{\sigma^2} = -\frac{\|\mathbf{x} - \boldsymbol{\mu}_i\|^2}{\sigma^2} = -\|\mathbf{x} - \boldsymbol{\mu}_i\|^2, \qquad i = 1, 2, \ldots, l. \quad (1.109)$$

The class-independent coefficient variance σ^2 is neglected in the final stage of the classifier design.

Thus (1.109) represents the *minimum Euclidean distance classifier* because the discriminants (1.109) will assign a given pattern with a feature vector $\mathbf{x}$ to a class ω_k for which the *Euclidean distance* $\|\mathbf{x} - \boldsymbol{\mu}_k\|$ of $\mathbf{x}$ to the mean vector $\boldsymbol{\mu}_k$ is the smallest. As in the preceding case of a nondiagonal covariance matrix, and because of the minus sign, the minimal Euclidean distance will result in a maximal value for the discriminant function $d_i(\mathbf{x})$, as given in (1.109). In other words, a minimum (Euclidean) distance classifier assigns a pattern with feature $\mathbf{x}$ to the closest class center $\boldsymbol{\mu}_k$.

A linear form of the minimum distance classifier (neglecting a class-independent variance σ^2) is given as

$$d_i(\mathbf{x}) = \boldsymbol{\mu}_i^T \mathbf{x} - \tfrac{1}{2} \boldsymbol{\mu}_i^T \boldsymbol{\mu}_i, \qquad i = 1, 2, \ldots, l. \quad (1.110)$$

The algorithm for both the Mahalanobis and the Euclidean distance classifiers is the following. The mean vectors for all classes $\boldsymbol{\mu}_i$, $i = 1, 2, \ldots, l$, a feature vector $\mathbf{x}$, and a covariance matrix Σ are given.

1. Calculate the values of the corresponding distances between $\mathbf{x}$ and means $\boldsymbol{\mu}_i$ for all classes. The Mahalanobis distance for correlated classes is

$$D = (\mathbf{x} - \boldsymbol{\mu}_k)^T \Sigma^{-1} (\mathbf{x} - \boldsymbol{\mu}_k), \qquad \Sigma \text{ nondiagonal.}$$

The Euclidean distance for statistically independent classes is

$$D = \|\mathbf{x} - \boldsymbol{\mu}_k\|, \qquad \Sigma \text{ diagonal.}$$

2. Assign the pattern to the class ω_k for which the distance D is minimal.

Both of these minimum distance classifiers are minimum error rate classifiers. In other words, for given assumptions, they are the Bayes' minimal probability of an error classifier. Furthermore, for both classifiers the mean vectors $\boldsymbol{\mu}_i$, $i = 1, \ldots, l$, act as *templates* or *prototypes* for l classes. By measuring the distances between each new pattern $\mathbf{x}$ and these centers, each new feature vector $\mathbf{x}$ is matched to these templates. Hence, both the Mahalanobis and the Euclidean distance classifiers belong to the group of *template matching classifiers*.

Template matching is a classic, natural approach to pattern classification. Typically, noise-free versions of patterns are used as templates or as the means of the corresponding classes. To classify a previously unseen and noisy pattern, simply compare it to given templates (means) and assign the pattern to the closest template (mean, center). Template matching works well when the variations within a class are due to additive noise. But there are many other possible noises in classification and decision-making problems. For instance, regarding geometrically distorted patterns, some common distortions of feature vectors are translation, rotation, shearing, warping, expansion, contraction, and occlusion. For such patterns, more sophisticated techniques must be used. However, these are outside the scope of this book.

Limitations and Deficiencies of the Classical Bayesian Approach Almost all the methods and techniques presented in the preceding sections have a serious practical limitation. In order to apply the most general Bayes' minimum cost or minimum risk procedure (and related approaches) practically everything about the underlying analyzed process must be known. This includes the priors $P(\omega_i)$ and the class-conditional probability-densities (or likelihoods) $P(\mathbf{x} \mid \omega_i)$ as well as the costs of making errors $L(\omega_j \mid \omega_i)$. The fact that pattern recognition and regression problems are of random character and therefore expressed in probabilistic terms does not make the task simpler.

Suppose one wants to perform fault detection in engineering or in medical diagnosis. One must know how probable the different faults or symptoms (classes) are a priori ($P(\omega_i)$ are required). In other words, the prior probability of a system under investigation to experience different faults must be known. This is an intricate problem because very often it is difficult to distinguish priors $P(\omega_i)$ from class-conditional probability-densities $P(\mathbf{x} \mid \omega_i)$. One remedy is to use decision rules that do not contain priors (or to ignore them). The maximum likelihood classification rule is such a rule. Similarly, in regression, other approaches that require fewer assumptions can be tried, such as Markov estimators or the method of least squares.

The amount of assumed initial knowledge available on the process under investigation decreases in the following order: for the Bayes' procedure one should know everything; for the maximum likelihood approach one should know the class-conditional probability-density functions (likelihoods); for the Markov techniques in regression problems one should know the covariance matrix of noise; and for the least squares method one need only assume that random processes can be approximated sufficiently by the model chosen. But even in such a series of simplifications one must either know some distribution characteristics in advance or estimate the means, covariance matrices, or likelihoods (class-conditional probability densities) by using training patterns.

However, there are practical problems with density estimation approaches. To implement even the simplest Euclidean minimum distance classifier, one must know the mean vectors (centers or templates) $\boldsymbol{\mu}_i$, $i = 1, \ldots, l$, for all the classes. For this approach it is assumed that the underlying data-generating distribution is a Gaussian one, that the features are not correlated, and that the covariance matrices are equal. (This is too many assumptions for the simplest possible method.) To take into account eventually correlated features, or in considering the effects of scaling and linear transformation of data for which the Euclidean metric is not appropriate, the Mahalanobis metric should be used. However, in order to implement a minimum Mahalanobis distance classifier, both the mean vectors and the covariance matrices must be known. Recall that all that is typically available is training data and eventually some previous knowledge. Usually, this means estimating all these parameters from examples of patterns to be classified or regressed.

Yet this is exactly what both statistical learning theory (represented by support vector machines) and neural networks are trying to avoid. This book follows the approach of bypassing or dodging density estimation methods. Therefore, there is no explicit presentation of how to learn means, covariance matrices, or any other statistics from training data patterns. Instead, the discussion concerns SVM and NN tools that provide novel techniques for acquiring knowledge from training data (patterns, records, measurements, observations, examples, samples).

However, it should be stressed that the preceding approaches (which in pattern recognition problems most often result in quadratic or linear discriminant functions, decision boundaries and regions, and in regression problems result in linear approximating functions) still are and will remain very good theoretical and practical tools if the mentioned assumptions are valid. Very often, in modern real-world applications, many of these postulates are satisfied only approximately. However, even when these assumptions are not totally sound, quadratic and linear discriminants have shown acceptable performance as classifiers, as have linear approximators in regression problems. Because of their simple (linear or quadratic) structure, these techniques do not overfit the training data set, and for many regression tasks they may be good starting points or good first estimates of regression hyperplanes. In classification, they may indicate the structure of complex decision regions that are typically hyper-volumes in n-dimensional space of features.

Problems

1.1. Let $\mathbf{x} = [-2 \quad 1]^T$, $\mathbf{y} = [-3 \quad 1]^T$, $\mathbf{v} = [4 \quad -3 \quad 2]^T$, $\mathbf{w} = [5 \quad 6 \quad -1]^T$.

a. Compute $\dfrac{\mathbf{x}^T\mathbf{y}}{\mathbf{x}^T\mathbf{x}}$ and $\dfrac{\mathbf{x}^T\mathbf{y}}{\mathbf{x}^T\mathbf{x}}\mathbf{x}$.

b. Calculate a unit vector $\mathbf{u}$ in the direction of $\mathbf{v}$.

c. Are vectors $\mathbf{v}$ and $\mathbf{w}$ orthogonal?

1.2. Calculate the L_1, L_2, and L_∞ norms of the following vectors:

a. $\mathbf{x} = \begin{bmatrix} -2 & 1 & 3 & 2 \end{bmatrix}^T$.

b. $\mathbf{y} = \begin{bmatrix} -3 & 1 \end{bmatrix}^T$.

c. $\mathbf{v} = \begin{bmatrix} 4 & -3 & 2 \end{bmatrix}^T$.

d. $\mathbf{w} = \begin{bmatrix} -5 & -6 & -1 & -3 & -5 \end{bmatrix}^T$.

1.3. Let $x_1, x_2, \ldots, x_n$ be fixed numbers. The Vandermonde matrix $\mathbf{X}$ is

$$
\mathbf{X} = \begin{bmatrix}
1 & x_1 & x_1^2 & \cdots & x_1^{n-2} & x_1^{n-1} \\
1 & x_2 & x_2^2 & \cdots & x_2^{n-2} & x_2^{n-1} \\
\vdots & \vdots & \vdots & \cdots & \vdots & \vdots \\
\vdots & \vdots & \vdots & \cdots & \vdots & \vdots \\
1 & x_{n-1} & x_{n-1}^2 & \cdots & x_{n-1}^{n-2} & x_{n-1}^{n-1} \\
1 & x_n & x_n^2 & \cdots & x_n^{n-2} & x_n^{n-1}
\end{bmatrix}.
$$

Given $\mathbf{d} = \begin{bmatrix} d_1 & d_2 & \cdots & d_n \end{bmatrix}^T$, suppose that $\mathbf{w} \in \mathfrak{R}^n$ satisfies $\mathbf{Xw} = \mathbf{d}$, and define the polynomial

$$ y(x) = w_0 + w_1 x + w_2 x^2 + \cdots + w_{n-1} x^{n-1}. $$

a. Show that $y(x_1) = d_1, \ldots, y(x_n) = d_n$ (i.e., that the polynomial $y(x)$ passes through each training data point).

b. Show that when $x_1, x_2, \ldots, x_n$ are distinct, the columns of $\mathbf{X}$ are linearly independent.

c. Prove that if $x_1, x_2, \ldots, x_n$ are distinct numbers and $\mathbf{d}$ is an arbitrary vector, then there is an interpolating polynomial of degree $\leq n-1$ for all pairs (x_1, d_1), $(x_2, d_2), \ldots, (x_n, d_n)$.

1.4. For the training data pairs $(1, 2)$, $(2, 1)$, $(5, 10)$ find

a. the interpolating polynomial of second order,

b. the best least squares approximating straight line.

1.5. Compute L_∞ and L_2 norms for the function $f(x) = (1 + x)^{-1}$ on the interval $[0, 1]$. (See hint in problem 1.6b.)

1.6. Find the best approximating straight lines to the curve $y = e^x$ such that

a. the L_2 (Euclidean) norm of the error function on the discrete set $x = \begin{bmatrix} -1 & -0.5 & 0 & 0.5 & 1 \end{bmatrix}$ is as small as possible,

b. the L_2 (Euclidean) norm of the error function on the interval $[-1, \quad 1]$ is as small as possible. (*Hint:* Use $\int_a^b |E(w)|^2 \, dw$ for the L_2 (Euclidean) norm of the continuous error function on the interval $[a, b]$.)

1.7. Figure P1.1 shows the unit sphere of the L_2 norm in $\mathfrak{R}^2$.

a. Draw unit spheres of L_p norms for $p = 0.5, 1, 10$, and ∞. Comment on the geometrical meaning of these spheres.

b. Draw unit spheres of L_p norms for $p = 1, 2$, and ∞ in $\mathfrak{R}^3$.

1.8. Consider vector $\mathbf{x}$ in $\mathfrak{R}^2$ shown in figures P1.2a and P1.2b. Find the best approximation to $\mathbf{x}$ in a subspace SL (a straight line) in

a. L_1 norm,

b. L_2 norm,

c. L_∞ norm.

Draw your result and comment on the equality or difference of the best approximations in given norms.

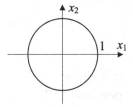

Figure P1.1
Graph for problem 1.7.

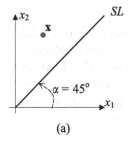
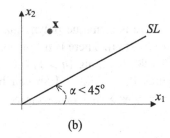

(a)   (b)

Figure P1.2
Graphs for problem 1.8.

Figure P1.3
Graph for problem 1.9.

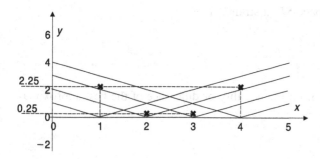

Figure P1.4
Graph for problem 1.10.

1.9. For a given vector $\mathbf{x}$ find a subspace (a straight line SL) of $\Re^2$ for which the best approximations to $\mathbf{x}$ in SL, in L_1 and L_2 norms, are equal. Comment on the best approximation in L_∞ norm in this straight line. (See figure P1.3.)

1.10. Consider four measurement points given in figure P1.4. Find the weights corresponding to four linear splines that ensure an interpolating (piecewise linear) curve $y_a(x)$.

1.11. It was shown that there is a unique polynomial interpolant for a one-dimensional input x (i.e., when $y = y(x)$). There is no theorem about a unique polynomial interpolation for an $\Re^n \rightarrow \Re^1$ mapping ($n > 1$) (i.e., for $y = y(\mathbf{x})$). Check whether four given points in figures P1.5a and P 1.5b can be uniquely interpolated by a bilinear polynomial $y_a = w_1 + w_2 x_1 + w_3 x_2 + w_4 x_1 x_2$. Training data pairs are given as

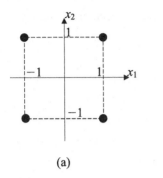

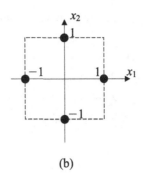

(a)   (b)

Figure P1.5
Graphs for problem 1.11.

Figure 1.5a				Figure 1.5b			
d_1	d_2	d_3	d_4	d_1	d_2	d_3	d_4
1	−1	−1	1	1	0	−1	0
1	1	−1	−1	0	1	0	−1

(*Hint:* For both problems write down a system of four equations in four unknowns and check whether there is a unique solution.)

1.12. Many phenomena are subject to seasonal fluctuations (e.g., plant growth, monthly sales of products, airline ticket sales). To model such periodic problems, the preferred approximating scheme is

$$y_a = w_0 + w_1 x + w_2 \sin \frac{2\pi x}{12}.$$

a. Show this model graphically as a network.

b. Give the design matrix $\mathbf{X}$.

c. Is the approximation problem linear?

1.13. (a) Expand a function $f(\mathbf{x})$ about $\mathbf{x}_0$ in a Taylor series, and show this expansion graphically as a ("neural") network, retaining the first three terms only. An input to the network is $\Delta \mathbf{x}$, and the output is Δf.

(b) Show as a network a Taylor expansion of a function e^{kx}, retaining the first four terms only.

1.14. Determine the gradient vector and the Hessian matrix for each error function $E(\mathbf{w})$:

(a) $E(\mathbf{w}) = 3w_1 w_2^2 + 4e^{w_1 w_2}$.

(b) $E(\mathbf{w}) = w_1^{w_2} + \ln w_1 w_2$.

(c) $E(\mathbf{w}) = w_1^2 + w_2^2 + w_3^2$.

(d) $E(\mathbf{w}) = \ln(w_1^2 + w_1 w_2 + w_2^2)$.

1.15. The gradient path for minimizing the elliptic paraboloid $E(\mathbf{w}) = w_1^2 + 2w_2^2$ is $w_2 = e^c w_1^2$. Both the level curves (contours) and the gradient path are shown in figure P1.6. Show that the gradient path is orthogonal to the level curves. (*Hint:* Use the fact that if the curves are orthogonal, then their normal vectors are also orthogonal.)

1.16. Show that the optimal learning rate η_{opt} for minimizing the quadratic error function

$$E(\mathbf{w}) = 0.5\mathbf{w}^T \mathbf{Q} \mathbf{w} \text{ is } \eta_{\text{opt}} = -\frac{\mathbf{w}^T \mathbf{Q}^2 \mathbf{w}}{\mathbf{w}^T \mathbf{Q}^3 \mathbf{w}}\bigg|_i.$$

(*Hint:* Express the value of the error function at step $i+1$, and minimize this expression with respect to learning rate η. Use that for quadratic forms $\mathbf{Q} = \mathbf{Q}^T$.)

1.17. Perform two iterations of the optimal gradient algorithm to find the minimum of $E(\mathbf{w}) = 2w_1^2 + 2w_1 w_2 + 5w_2^2$. The starting point is $\mathbf{w}_0 = [2-2]^T$. Draw the contours, and show your learning path graphically. Check the orthogonality of gradient vectors at the initial point and at the next one. (*Hint:* Express $E(\mathbf{w})$ in matrix form, and use the expression for η_{opt} from problem 1.16.)

1.18. Which of the four given functions in figure P1.7 are probability-density functions? (*Hint:* Use that $\int_{-\infty}^{+\infty} P(x)\, dx = 1$.)

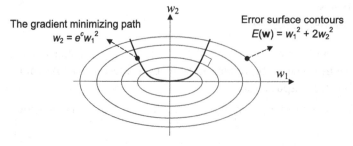

Figure P1.6
Graph for problem 1.15.

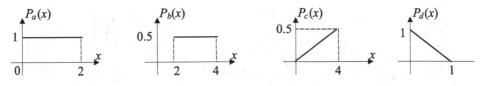

Figure P1.7
Graphs for problem 1.18.

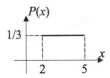

Figure P1.8
Graph for problem 1.19.

1.19. Consider a continuous variable that can take on values on the interval from 2 to 5. Its probability-density function is shown in figure P1.8. (This is called the uniform density.) What is the probability that the random variable will take on a value

a) between 3 and 4,

b) less than 2.8,

c) greater than 4.3,

d) between 2.6 and 4.4?

1.20. The three graphs in figures P1.9a, P1.9b, and P1.9c show uniform, normal, and triangular probability-density functions, respectively. Find the constants C_i for each function.

1.21. A random variable x is defined by its probability-density function

$$P(x) = \begin{cases} \dfrac{C}{8} e^{-x/(C+2)} & x \geq 0, \\[2mm] 0 & \text{otherwise.} \end{cases}$$

a) Calculate constant C and comment on the results.

b) Find a mean μ_x and a variance σ_x^2.

c) Calculate the probability $P(-1 \leq x < 2)$.

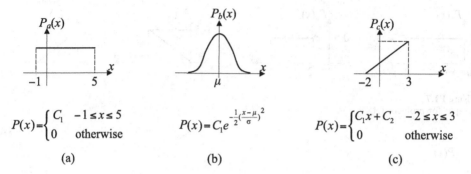

$$P(x)=\begin{cases} C_1 & -1\le x\le 5 \\ 0 & \text{otherwise} \end{cases}$$

(a)

$$P(x)=C_1e^{-\frac{1}{2}(\frac{x-\mu}{\sigma})^2}$$

(b)

$$P(x)=\begin{cases} C_1x+C_2 & -2\le x\le 3 \\ 0 & \text{otherwise} \end{cases}$$

(c)

Figure P1.9
Graphs for problem 1.20.

1.22. Let x and y have the joint probability-density function

$$P(x,y) = \begin{cases} 5 & 0 < x < y < 1, \\ 0 & \text{otherwise.} \end{cases}$$

a) Find the marginal and conditional probability-density functions $P(x)$, $P(y)$, and $P(x,y)$.

b) Find the regression function $x = f(y)$ (i.e., find the conditional mean of x given $y = y_0$).

1.23. Consider two random variables defined as $|x| \le 4$ and $0 \le y \le 2 - 0.5|x|$. Let them have a joint probability-density function

$$P(x,y) = \begin{cases} C & \text{over the sample space,} \\ 0 & \text{elsewhere.} \end{cases}$$

a) Draw the joint probability-density function.

b) Find C.

c) Are random variables x and y independent?

d) Calculate a correlation coefficient ρ.

1.24. The joint probability-density function of two variables is given as

$$P(x,y) = \begin{cases} q & x \ge 0, y \ge 0, x^2 + y^2 \le 1, \\ 0 & \text{elsewhere.} \end{cases}$$

a) Draw the sample space.

b) Find q.

c) Calculate the marginal probability-density function $P(x)$.

d) Find a mean μ_x and a variance σ_x^2.

Hint:

$$\int \sqrt{a^2 - x^2} \, dx = \frac{1}{2}\left(x\sqrt{a^2 - x^2} + a^2 \arcsin\frac{x}{a}\right)$$

$$\int x\sqrt{a^2 - x^2} \, dx = -\frac{1}{3}\sqrt{(a^2 - x^2)^3}$$

$$\int x^2 \sqrt{a^2 - x^2} \, dx = -\frac{x}{4}\sqrt{(a^2 - x^2)^3} + \frac{a^2}{8}\left(x\sqrt{a^2 - x^2} + a^2 \arcsin\frac{x}{a}\right)$$

1.25. Let two random variables be defined by the joint probability-density function

$$P(x,y) = \begin{cases} k & 0 \le x \le 1,\ 1 \le x+y \le 2, \\ 0 & \text{otherwise.} \end{cases}$$

a) Draw the graph of $P(x,y)$.

b) Calculate k, $P(x)$, and $P(y)$.

c) Find μ_x, μ_y, $\sigma_{xy} = E\{xy\}$, σ_x^2, and σ_y^2.

d) Are x and y dependent variables? Are they correlated?

1.26. Consider two random variables having the joint probability-density function

$$P(x,y) = \begin{cases} x+y & 0 < x < 1,\ 0 < y < 1, \\ 0 & \text{elsewhere.} \end{cases}$$

Find the correlation coefficient ρ of x and y.

1.27. The joint probability-density function $P(x,y)$ is given as

$$P(x,y) = \begin{cases} \frac{1}{2}xy & 0 < x < 2,\ 0 < y < x, \\ 0 & \text{otherwise.} \end{cases}$$

a) Draw the sample space in an (x,y) plane.

b) Find the marginal probability-density functions $P(x)$ and $P(y)$.

1.28. Find the equation of a regression curve $\mu_{y|x} = y = f(x)$ in problem 1.27.

1.29. A theoretical correlation coefficient is defined as $\rho = \sigma_{xy}/\sigma_x\sigma_y$. Apply this expression to example 1.7 and find ρ.

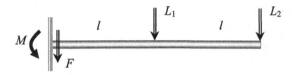

Figure P1.10
Graph for problem 1.30.

1.30. A beam in figure P1.10 is subjected to two random loads L_1 and L_2, which are statistically independent with means and standard deviations μ_1, σ_1, and μ_2, σ_2, respectively. Are the shear force F and bending moment M correlated? Find the correlation coefficient. For $\sigma_1 = \sigma_2$, is there no correlation at all? Are F and M just correlated, or are they highly correlated? Are they causally related? (*Hint:* $F = L_1 + L_2$, $M = lL_1 + 2lL_2$. Find the means and standard deviations of force and moment, calculate the correlation coefficient, and discuss your result.)

1.31. The probability-density function $P(\mathbf{x})$ of a multivariate n-dimensional Gaussian distribution is given by

$$P(\mathbf{x}) = \frac{1}{(2\pi)^{n/2}|\mathbf{\Sigma}|^{1/2}} \exp(-0.5(\mathbf{x} - \boldsymbol{\mu})^T \mathbf{\Sigma}^{-1}(\mathbf{x} - \boldsymbol{\mu}))$$

that is, it is parameterized by the mean vector $\boldsymbol{\mu}$ and covariance matrix $\mathbf{\Sigma}$. For a two-dimensional vector $\mathbf{x}$, $\boldsymbol{\mu} = [\mu_1 \quad \mu_2]^T$ and $\mathbf{\Sigma} = \begin{bmatrix} \sigma_1^2 & \sigma_{12}^2 \\ \sigma_{21}^2 & \sigma_2^2 \end{bmatrix}$. Sketch the contours of $P(\mathbf{x})$ in an (x_1, x_2) plane for the following four distributions:
a) $\boldsymbol{\mu} = [2 \quad 3]^T$, $\sigma_{12} = \sigma_{21} = 0$, $\sigma_{11} = \sigma_{22} = \sigma$.
b) $\boldsymbol{\mu} = [-2 \quad 2]^T$, $\sigma_{12} = \sigma_{21} = 0$, $\sigma_{11} > \sigma_{22}$.
c) $\boldsymbol{\mu} = [-3 \quad -3]^T$, $\sigma_{12} = \sigma_{21} = 0$, $\sigma_{11} < \sigma_{22}$.
d) $\boldsymbol{\mu} = [3 \quad -2]^T$, $\sigma_{12} = \sigma_{21} > 0$.

1.32. Find the equations of $P(\mathbf{x})$, and of the contours for which $P(\mathbf{x}) = 0.5$, for the following three two-dimensional Gaussian distributions:

a) $\boldsymbol{\mu} = [2 \quad 2]^T$, $\mathbf{\Sigma} = \begin{bmatrix} 1 & 0 \\ 0 & 1 \end{bmatrix}$.

b) $\boldsymbol{\mu} = [2 \quad 2]^T$, $\mathbf{\Sigma} = \begin{bmatrix} 2 & 0 \\ 0 & 1 \end{bmatrix}$.

c) $\boldsymbol{\mu} = [2 \quad 2]^T$, $\boldsymbol{\Sigma} = \begin{bmatrix} 3 & 1 \\ 1 & 2 \end{bmatrix}$.

1.33. Given the covariance matrix and mean vector of a four-dimensional normal distribution

$$\boldsymbol{\Sigma} = \begin{bmatrix} 15 & 3 & 1 & 0 \\ 3 & 16 & 6 & -2 \\ 1 & 6 & 4 & 1 \\ 0 & -2 & 1 & 3 \end{bmatrix}, \quad \boldsymbol{\mu} = [10 \quad 0 \quad -10 \quad 1]^T$$

determine the probability-density function $P(\mathbf{x})$. (*Hint:* Calculate $\boldsymbol{\Sigma}^{-1}$ and $|\boldsymbol{\Sigma}|$. Do not leave the exponent of $P(\mathbf{x})$ in matrix form.)

1.34. Consider a three-dimensional Gaussian probability-density function

$$P(\mathbf{x}) = \frac{\sqrt{3}}{16\pi^{3/2}} \exp\left(-\frac{1}{8}(2x_1^2 + 4x_2^2 - 2x_2(x_3 + 5) + (x_3 + 5)^2)\right).$$

a) Find the covariance matrix $\boldsymbol{\Sigma}$. (*Hint:* Note that in this problem $P = P_1(x_1) \cdot P_2(x_2, x_3)$, meaning that $\sigma_{12} = \sigma_{13} = 0$).

b) Determine the locus of points for which the probability-density is 0.01.

1.35. Consider the multivariate n-dimensional Gaussian probability-density function $P(\mathbf{x})$ for which the covariance matrix $\boldsymbol{\Sigma}$ is diagonal (i.e., $\sigma_{ij} = 0$, $i \neq j$).

a) Show that $P(\mathbf{x})$ can be expressed as

$$P(\mathbf{x}) = \frac{1}{\prod_{i=1}^{n} \sigma_i \sqrt{(2\pi)}} \exp\left(-\frac{1}{2}\sum_{i=1}^{n}\left(\frac{x_i - \mu_i}{\sigma_i}\right)^2\right).$$

b) What are the contours of constant probability-density? Show graphically the contours for $\mathbf{x} = [x_1 \quad x_2]^T$, $\boldsymbol{\mu} = [-2 \quad 3]^T$, and $\sigma_2 = 2\sigma_1$.

c) Show that the expression in the exponent of $P(\mathbf{x})$ in (a) is a Mahalanobis distance.

1.36. Consider three classes with Gaussian class-conditional probability-density functions having the same covariance matrix $\boldsymbol{\Sigma}_i = \boldsymbol{\Sigma} = \begin{bmatrix} 1 & 0 \\ 0 & 0.5 \end{bmatrix}$, $i = 1, 2, 3$, and with means $\boldsymbol{\mu}_1 = [0 \quad 2]^T$, $\boldsymbol{\mu}_2 = [4 \quad 1]^T$, $\boldsymbol{\mu}_3 = [1 \quad 0]^T$.

a) Draw the contours of $P_i(\mathbf{x})$ in an (x_1, x_2) plane.

b) Find both the decision (discriminant) functions and the equations of decision boundaries. Draw the boundaries in the graph in (a).

1.37. The calculation of a Bayes's classifier requires knowledge of means and covariance matrices. However, typically only training data are known. The following two feature patterns $(\mathbf{x} \in \mathfrak{R}^2)$ from the two equiprobable normally (Gaussian) distributed classes (class 1 = 0, and class 2 = 1) have been drawn:

Class 1			Class 2		
x_1	x_2	d	x_1	x_2	d
1	2	0	6	8	1
2	2	0	7	8	1
2	3	0	8	7	1
3	1	0	8	8	1
3	2	0	7	9	1

a) Find discriminant (decision) functions for both classes.

b) Calculate the dichotomizing function. Draw (in an (x_1, x_2) plane) the training data pairs, the dichotomizing function, and the intersections of the two discriminant functions with an (x_1, x_2) plane.

c) Test the performance of your dichotomizer by classifying the previously unseen pattern $\mathbf{x}_1 = \begin{bmatrix} 4 & 1 \end{bmatrix}^T$, $\mathbf{x}_1 = \begin{bmatrix} 6 & 7 \end{bmatrix}^T$. (*Hint:* Calculate the empirical means and covariance matrices from the data first, and then apply appropriate equations for calculation of discriminant functions. Use

$$\mathbf{\Sigma}_{i(\text{est})} = \frac{\sum_{p=1}^{P} (\mathbf{x}_p^{\text{class } i} - \mathbf{\mu}^{\text{class } i})(\mathbf{x}_p^{\text{class } i} - \mathbf{\mu}^{\text{class } i})^T}{(P-1)}$$

for a covariance matrix calculation. Subscript (est) denotes an estimate.)

1.38. A two-dimensional random vector $\mathbf{y}$ has the probability-density function

$$P(\mathbf{y}) = \begin{cases} \dfrac{1}{a^2} & 0 \le y_1, y_2 \le a, \\ 0 & \text{otherwise.} \end{cases}$$

Another two-dimensional random vector $\mathbf{x}$ related to $\mathbf{y}$ has the conditional density function

$$P(\mathbf{x}\,|\,\mathbf{y}) = \frac{1}{2\pi\sigma_1\sigma_2}\exp\left(-\left(\frac{(x_1-y_1)^2}{2\sigma_1^2}+\frac{(x_2-y_2)^2}{2\sigma_2^2}\right)\right).$$

Find the posterior probability-density function $P(\mathbf{y}\,|\,\mathbf{x})$. Is there a closed form solution? (*Hint:* Find the joint probability-density function $P(\mathbf{x},\mathbf{y})$ first, and use it for computing $P(\mathbf{y}\,|\,\mathbf{x})$. If this problem seems to be too difficult, go to the next problem and return to this one later.)

1.39. Assign the feature $x = 0.6$ to the one of two equiprobable classes by using the maximum likelihood decision rule associated with classes that are given by the following class-conditional probability-density functions:

$$P(x\,|\,\omega_1) = \left(\frac{1}{2\pi}\right)^{0.5}\exp\left(-\frac{x^2}{2}\right) \quad\text{and}\quad P(x\,|\,\omega_2) = \left(\frac{1}{2\pi}\right)^{0.5}\exp\left(-\frac{(x-1)^2}{2}\right).$$

Draw the class-conditional probability-density functions, and show the decision boundary. (*Hint:* Assuming equal prior probability-densities $(P(\omega_1) = P(\omega_2))$, the maximum likelihood decision rule is equivalent to the MAP (Bayes') decision criterion.)

1.40. Determine the maximum likelihood decision rule associated with the two equiprobable classes given by the following class-conditional probability-density functions:

$$P(x\,|\,\omega_1) = \left(\frac{1}{2\pi}\right)^{0.5}\exp\left(-\frac{x^2}{2}\right) \quad\text{and}\quad P(x\,|\,\omega_2) = \left(\frac{1}{8\pi}\right)^{0.5}\exp\left(-\frac{x^2}{8}\right).$$

Draw the class-conditional probability-density functions and show the decision boundaries. (*Hint:* Note that the means are equal.)

1.41. The class-conditional probability-density functions of two classes are given by

$$P(x\,|\,\omega_1) = \left(\frac{1}{2\pi}\right)^{0.5}\exp\left(-\frac{x^2}{2}\right) \quad\text{and}\quad P(x\,|\,\omega_2) = \left(\frac{1}{2\pi}\right)^{0.5}\exp\left(-\frac{(x-1)^2}{2}\right).$$

Prior probability for a class 1 is $P(\omega_1) = 0.25$. Find the decision boundary by minimizing a probability of classification error, that is, use the MAP (Bayes') decision criterion. (*Hint:* Use (1.70b).)

1.42. The class-conditional probability-density functions of two classes are given by

$$P(x\,|\,\omega_1) = \frac{1}{2}\exp(-|x|) \quad \text{and} \quad P(x\,|\,\omega_2) = \exp(-2|x|).$$

Prior probability for a class 1 is $P(\omega_1) = 0.25$, and the losses are given as $L_{11} = L_{22} = 0$, $L_{12} = 1$, and $L_{21} = 2$. Find the decision boundaries by minimizing Bayes' risk. (*Hint:* Use (1.86).)

1.43. The class-conditional probability-density functions of two classes are given by

$$P(x\,|\,\omega_1) = 2\exp(-2x) \quad \text{and} \quad P(x\,|\,\omega_2) = \exp(-x),$$

both for $x \geq 0$; otherwise both are equal to zero).

a) Find the maximum likelihood decision rule.

b) Find the minimal probability of error decision rule. Prior probability for a class 1 is $P(\omega_1) = 2/3$.

c) Find the minimal risk decision rule for equally probable classes and with the losses $L_{11} = 0$, $L_{22} = 1$, $L_{12} = 2$, and $L_{21} = 3$.

(Solving this problem, you will confirm that here (as in the case of function approximation tasks), the best solution depends upon the norm applied. Note that in (a) the best means maximization, and in (b) and (c) the best is the minimizing solution.)

1.44. Find the posterior probability-density functions $P(\omega_1\,|\,x)$ and $P(\omega_2\,|\,x)$ for the two equiprobable one-dimensional normally distributed classes given by likelihood functions (class-conditional probability-density functions that are also known as data generation mechanisms)

$$P(x\,|\,\omega_1) = \frac{1}{\sqrt{2\pi}\sigma}\exp\left[-\frac{1}{2}\left(\frac{x-\mu_1}{\sigma}\right)^2\right],$$

$$P(x\,|\,\omega_2) = \frac{1}{\sqrt{2\pi}\sigma}\exp\left[-\frac{1}{2}\left(\frac{x-\mu_2}{\sigma}\right)^2\right].$$

(*Hint:* Start with Bayes' rule, plug in the given likelihoods, and find the desired posterior probability-density functions in terms of distribution means and standard deviation.)

1.45. Derive the posterior probability-density function $P(\omega_1\,|\,x)$ for the likelihood functions defined in problem 1.44 but having different variances ($\sigma_1 \neq \sigma_2$).

1.46. Find the posterior probability-density function $P(\omega_1 \,|\, \mathbf{x})$ for a binary (two classes only) classification problem when $\mathbf{x}$ is an n-dimensional vector. The two Gaussian multivariate class-conditional probability-densities have arbitrary mean vectors $\boldsymbol{\mu}_i$, $i = 1, 2$, equal prior probabilities, and the same covariance matrix $\boldsymbol{\Sigma}$. Sketch the classification problem in an (x_1, x_2) plane, and explain your graph for the case of an identity covariance matrix ($\boldsymbol{\Sigma} = \mathbf{I}$). (*Hint:* Start by plugging the multivariate Gaussian likelihood functions into Bayes' rule. At the end of the derivation, similar to the previous one-dimensional case, the posterior probability-density function $P(\omega_1 \,|\, \mathbf{x})$ should have a form of logistic function and should be expressed in terms of vector quantities comprising means and covariance matrix.)

Simulation Experiments

The simulation experiments in chapter 1 have the purpose of familiarizing the reader with interpolation/approximation, that is, nonlinear regression. (Nonlinear regression and classification are the core problems of soft computing.) The programs used in chapter 2 on support vector machines cover both classification and regression by applying the SVM technique. There is no need for a manual here because all routines are simple (if anything is simple about programming). The experiments are aimed at reviewing many basic facets of regression (notably problems of over- and underfitting, the influence of noise, and the smoothness of approximation). The first two approximators are classic ones, namely, one-dimensional algebraic polynomials and Chebyshev polynomials. The last three are radial basis function approximators: linear splines, cubic splines, and Gaussian radial basis functions. In addition, there is a fuzzy model that applies five different membership functions.

Be aware of the following facts about the program `aproxim`:

1. It is developed for interpolation/approximation problems.

2. It is designed for one-dimensional input data ($y = f(x)$).

3. It is user-friendly, even for beginners in using MATLAB, but you must cooperate. It prompts you to select, to define, or to choose different things.

Experiment with the program `aproxim` as follows:

1. Launch MATLAB.

2. Connect to directory `learnsc` (at the `matlab` prompt, type `cd learnsc` ⟨RETURN⟩). `learnsc` is a subdirectory of `matlab`, as `bin`, `toolbox`, and `uitools` are. While typing `cd learnsc`, make sure that your working directory is `matlab`, not `matlab/bin`, for example.

3. Type `start` ⟨RETURN⟩.

4. The pop-up menu will prompt you to choose between several models. Choose 1D Approximation.

5. The pop-up box offers five approximators (networks, models, or machines). Click on one.

6. Follow the prompting pop-up menus to make some modeling choices. Note that if you want to have your function polluted by 15% noise, type `0.15`.

Now perform the following experiments (start with the `demo` function):

1. Look at the difference between the interpolation and approximation. Add 25% noise (noise = 0.25), and in order to do interpolation, choose the model order for polynomials to be $n = P - 1$, where P equals the number of training data. (The number will be printed on the screen.) For radial basis functions, interpolation will take place when you choose $t = 1$. Choosing $t = 1$ means that you are placing one radial basis function at each training data point. If you want to approximate the given function, you select $n < P - 1$ and $t > 1$ for polynomials and RBFs, respectively. It is clear that $t < P$.

Experiment type 1   Start with any `demo` function with 25% noise. Interpolate it first. Reduce the order of the polynomial gradually, and observe the changes in modeling quality. Always check the final error of models. Note that if there is a lot of noise, lower-order models do filter the noise out. But don't overdo it. At some stage, further decreasing the model's order (or the capacity of the model) leads to underfitting. This means that you are starting to filter out both the noise and the underlying function.

Experiment type 2   Now repeat experiment 1 with an RBF model. Controlling the capacity of your model to avoid overfitting noisy data is different for polynomials than for RBFs. The order of the model controls the polynomial capacity, and the number of basis functions is the smoothing parameter (the parameter for capacity control) for RBFs. It is not the only parameter, however. This is one of the topics in chapter 5.

Compare the smoothness of linear splines approximators and cubic splines approximators. When using Gaussian basis functions, you will have to choose k_σ. Choosing, for example, the value for this coefficient $k_\sigma = 2$, you define a standard deviation of Gaussian bells $\sigma = 2\Delta c$. This means that σ of all bells is equal to two distances between the Gaussian bell centers. For good (smooth) approximations, $0.75 < \sigma < 10$. This is both a broad and an approximate span for σ values. σ is typically the subject of learning. However, you may try experimenting with various values for the standard deviation σ. You will be also prompted to choose an RBF with bias or without it. Choose both, and compare the results. Many graphs will be displayed, but they are not that complicated to read. Try to understand them. More is explained in chapter 5.

2. Look at the effects of different noise levels on various interpolators or approximators. Note that noise = 1.0 means that there is 100% noise. For many practical situations, this is too high a noise level. On the other hand, in many recognition tasks, pollution by noise may be even higher. Repeat all experiments from (1) with a different noise level.

3. You are now ready to define your own functions and to perform experiments that you like or are interested in.

2 Support Vector Machines

The classical regression and Bayesian classification statistical techniques presented in chapter 1 were based on the very strict assumption that probability distribution models or probability-density functions are known. Unfortunately, in many practical situations, there is not enough information about the underlying distribution laws, and *distribution-free regression* or *classification* is needed that does not require knowledge of probability distributions. This is a very serious restriction but very common in real-world applications. Mostly, all we have are recorded training patterns, which are usually high-dimensional and scarce in present-day applications. High-dimensional spaces seem terrifyingly empty, and our learning algorithms (machines) must be able to operate in such spaces and to learn from sparse data. It is said that redundancy provides knowledge, so the more data pairs are available, the better the results will be. These essentials are depicted in figure 2.1.

Basic performance of classical statistical techniques is only roughly sketched in figure 2.1. Very small sample size is exceptionally unreliable and in practical terms little better than a random data set. It usually results in high error. In section 2.2 sample size is defined more precisely as the ratio of the number of training patterns l to the VC (Vapnik-Chervonenkis) dimension h of functions of a learning machine (neural network, polynomial approximator, radial basis function (RBF) neural network, fuzzy model). When this ratio is larger than 20, the data set is considered to be of medium size. The higher the noise level, or the more complex the underlying function, the more data are needed in order to make good approximations or classifications. The same is valid for the dimensionality of input vector space. A large data set is the one that comprises enough training data pairs to yield optimal results. By increasing the number of training data patterns, the best that can be achieved

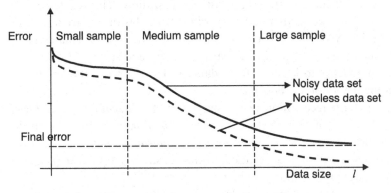

Figure 2.1
Dependence of modeling error on training data set size.

is an error that converges to Bayes' minimal error. To be on the safe side, one must develop worst-case techniques and approaches. Here, *worst-case* refers to techniques that are expected to perform in an acceptable manner in high-dimensional spaces and with sparse training patterns. The presentation of methods that promise acceptable performance under such conditions is the main point of interest in this section.

A relatively new promising method for learning separating functions in pattern recognition (classification) tasks or for performing functional estimation in regression problems is the support vector machine (SVM). This originated from the *statistical learning theory* (SLT) developed by Vapnik and Chervonenkis.[1]

SVMs can also be seen as a new method for training polynomial models, neural networks (NNs), fuzzy models, or RBF classifiers/regressors. Here the practical, constructive aspects of this new tool are of chief interest.

SVMs represent novel learning techniques that have been introduced in the framework of *structural risk minimization* (SRM) and in the theory of *VC bounds*. More precisely, unlike classical adaptation algorithms that work in an L_1 or L_2 norm and minimize the absolute value of an error or of an error square, the SVM performs SRM. In this way, it creates a model with a minimized VC dimension. The developed theory (Vapnik 1995; 1998) shows that when the VC dimension of the model is low, the expected probability of error is low as well, which means good performance on unseen data, (good generalization). This property is of particular interest to the whole soft computing field because the model that generalizes well is a good model and not the model that performs well on training data pairs. Good performance on training data is a necessary but insufficient condition for a good model.

It is interesting to note that Girosi (1997b) has shown that under some constraints the SVM can also be derived in the framework of regularization theory rather than the statistical learning theory or structural risk minimization. The regularization approach and the RBF networks that naturally follow from this theory are discussed in chapter 5. Here, the SVM is presented as a learning technique that originated from the theoretical foundations of the statistical learning theory and structural risk minimization. These approaches to learning from data are based on the new induction principle and on the theory of VC bounds.

In the simplest pattern recognition tasks, support vector machines use a linear separating hyperplane to create a *classifier with a maximal margin*. In order to do that, the learning problem is cast as a *constrained nonlinear optimization problem*. In this setting the cost function is quadratic and the constraints are linear (i.e., one has to solve a quadratic programming problem).

In cases when given classes cannot be linearly separated in the original input space, the SVM first nonlinearly transforms the original input space into a higher-dimensional feature space. This transformation can be achieved by using various nonlinear mappings: polynomial, sigmoidal as in multilayer perceptrons, RBF mappings having as basis functions radially symmetric functions such as Gaussians, different spline functions, or multiquadrics. After this nonlinear transformation step, the task of an SVM in finding the linear optimal separating hyperplane in this feature space is relatively trivial. Namely, the optimization problem to solve will be of the same kind as the calculation of a separating hyperplane in original input space for linearly separable classes. The resulting hyperplane in feature space will be optimal in the sense of being a maximal margin classifier with respect to training data. How nonlinearly separable problems in input space can become linearly separable problems in feature space after specific nonlinear transformation is shown in this chapter and in chapter 3 (see section 2.4.3 and figs. 3.9 and 3.10).

Sections 2.1–2.3 present the basic theory and approach of SRM and SVMs as developed by Vapnik, Chervonenkis, and their co-workers: Vapnik (1995; 1998), Cherkassky (1997), Cherkassky and Mulier (1998), Schölkopf (1998), Burges (1998), Gunn (1997), Niyogi and Girosi (1994), Poggio and Girosi (1998), and Smola and Schölkopf (1997). The reader interested primarily in the application of SVMs may skip directly to section 2.4, which describes how SVMs learn from data.

The standard learning stage can be set graphically as in figure 2.2. From this point on, the book deals with distribution-free learning from data methods that can be applied to both regression and classification problems.

By its very nature, learning is a stochastic process. The training data set is formed of two (random) sets of variables—the input variable $\mathbf{x}_i$, which is randomly, with probability $P(\mathbf{x}_i)$, drawn from the input set X, and the system's response y_i, which belongs to the output set Y. y_i is observed with probability $P(y_i \mid \mathbf{x}_i)$. This measured,

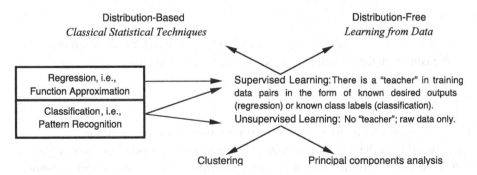

Figure 2.2
Standard categorization of learning from data tasks.

or observed, response y_i is denoted by d_i (for *desired*) during the training phase. Thus, $P(d_i \,|\, \mathbf{x}_i) = P(y_i \,|\, \mathbf{x}_i)$. The scalar value of the output variable y is used here only for simplicity. All derivations remain basically the same in the case of vector output $\mathbf{y}$.

The probability of collecting a training data point $(\mathbf{x}, d)$ is therefore[2]

$$P(\mathbf{x}, d) = P(\mathbf{x})P(y \,|\, \mathbf{x}). \tag{2.1}$$

The observed response of a system is probabilistic, and this is described by the conditional probability $P(y \,|\, \mathbf{x})$, which states that the same input $\mathbf{x}$ generates a different output y each time. In other words, there is no guaranteed response y for the same input $\mathbf{x}$. Four reasons that the same input $\mathbf{x}$ would produce different outputs y are as follows:

1. There is deterministic underlying dependence but there is noise in measurements.

2. There is deterministic underlying dependence but there are uncontrollable inputs (input noise).

3. The underlying process is stochastic.

4. The underlying process is deterministic, but incomplete information is available.

The handwritten character recognition problem, for example, belongs to the case of stochastically generated data (reason 3). It is a typical example of random patterns: we each write differently, and we write the same characters differently each time.

The randomness due to additive measurement noise (reason 1) is typically described as follows. Suppose the actual value of the temperature measured in a room at location $\mathbf{x}$ is $\vartheta(\mathbf{x})$. (Vector $\mathbf{x}$ that describes a point in three-dimensional space is a $(3, 1)$ vector; it has three rows and one column here.) Under the assumption of Gaussian (normally distributed) noise, one will actually measure

$$y = \vartheta(\mathbf{x}) + \varepsilon, \tag{2.2}$$

where additive noise ε has a Gaussian distribution with standard deviation σ. In this case, the conditional probability $P(y \,|\, \mathbf{x})$ will be proportional to

$$\exp\left(-\frac{1}{2}\left(\frac{y - \vartheta(\mathbf{x})}{\sigma}\right)^2\right).$$

This assumption about the Gaussian distribution of ε is most common while sampling a function in the presence of noise. The dashed circle around the output $y(\mathbf{x})$ in figure 2.3 denotes both the area of the most probable values of the system's response and the probabilistic nature of data set D.

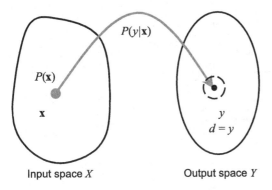

Input space X Output space Y

Figure 2.3
Stochastic character of learning while collecting a training data set.

In such a probabilistic setting, there are three basic components in learning from data: a *generator* of random inputs $\mathbf{x}$, a *system* whose training responses y are used for training the learning machine, and a *learning machine* that, using inputs $\mathbf{x}$ and the system's responses y, should learn (estimate, model) the unknown dependency between these two sets of variables (see fig. 2.4). This figure shows the most common learning setting in various fields, notably control system identification and signal processing.

During the (successful) training phase a learning machine should be able to find the relationship between X and Y using data D in regression tasks or find a function that separates data in classification tasks. The result of a learning process is an approximating function $f_a(\mathbf{x}, \mathbf{w})$, which in statistical literature is also known as a *hypothesis* $f_a(x, \mathbf{w})$. (This function approximates the underlying (or true) dependency between the input and output in regression or the decision boundary, or separation function, in classification.) The chosen hypothesis $f_a(\mathbf{x}, \mathbf{w})$ belongs to a *hypothesis space of functions* H ($f_a \in H$), and it is a function that minimizes some *risk function* $R(\mathbf{w})$. A risk $R(\mathbf{w})$ is also called the average (expected) loss or the expectation of a loss, and it is calculated as

$$R(\mathbf{w}) = \int L(y, o)\, dP(\mathbf{x}, y) = \int L(y, f_a(\mathbf{x}, \mathbf{w}))\, dP(\mathbf{x}, y), \tag{2.3}$$

where the specific *loss function* $L(y, f_a(\mathbf{x}, \mathbf{w}))$ is calculated on the training set $D(\mathbf{x}_i, y_i)$. Note that this is the continuous version of the risk function (1.81) that was used in the case of a (discrete) classification problem comprising a finite number of classes.

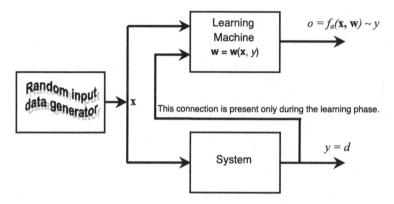

Figure 2.4
Model of a learning machine $\mathbf{w} = \mathbf{w}(\mathbf{x}, y)$ that during the training phase (by observing inputs $\mathbf{x}$ to, and outputs y from, the system) estimates (learns, adjusts) its parameters $\mathbf{w}$ thus learns mapping $y = f(\mathbf{x})$ performed by the system. $f_a(\mathbf{x}, \mathbf{w}) \sim y$ denotes that one will rarely try to interpolate training data pairs but would rather seek an approximating function that can generalize well. After training, at the generalization or test phase, the output from a machine $o = f_a(\mathbf{x}, \mathbf{w})$ is expected to be a good estimate of a system's true response y.

The loss function $L(y, o) = L(y, f_a(\mathbf{x}, \mathbf{w}))$ typically represents some classical or standard cost (error, objective, merit) function. Depending upon the character of the problem, different loss functions are used.

In regression, two functions in use are the square error (L_2 norm),

$$L(y, o) = L(y, f_a(\mathbf{x}, \mathbf{w})) = (y - f_a)^2, \tag{2.4a}$$

and the absolute error (L_1 norm),

$$L(y, o) = L(y, f_a(\mathbf{x}, \mathbf{w})) = |y - f_a|. \tag{2.4b}$$

In a two-class classification, a 0-1 error (loss) function is

$$L(y, o) = 0 \quad \text{if} \quad o = y,$$

$$L(y, o) = 1 \quad \text{if} \quad o \neq y. \tag{2.4c}$$

o denotes a learning machine's output, or $o = f_a(\mathbf{x}, \mathbf{w})$. Later in this section, in designing an SVM for regression, a loss function more appropriate for regression tasks is introduced: Vapnik's ε-insensitive loss function.

Under the general name "approximating function" we understand any mathematical structure that maps inputs $\mathbf{x}$ into outputs y. Thus, in this book, "approximating function" can mean a multilayer perceptron, a neural network, an RBF network, an

SVM, a fuzzy model, a Fourier truncated series, a polynomial approximating function, or a hypothesis. A set of parameters $\mathbf{w}$ is the subject of learning, and generally these parameters are called *weights*. As mentioned, these parameters have different geometrical or physical meanings. Depending upon the hypothesis space of functions H, the parameters $\mathbf{w}$ are usually

- The hidden layer and output layer weights in multilayer perceptrons
- The rules and the parameters describing the positions and shapes of fuzzy subsets
- The coefficients of a polynomial or Fourier series
- The centers and variances or covariances of Gaussian basis functions as well as the output layer weights of this RBF network

Some typical hypothesis spaces H (mathematical models, classification/regression schemes, or computing machines) are summarized here.

An *RBF network* is a representative of a linear basis function expansion

$$o = y = f_a(\mathbf{x}, \mathbf{w}) = \sum_{i=1}^{N} w_i \varphi_i(\mathbf{x}), \tag{2.5}$$

where $\varphi_i(\mathbf{x})$ is a *fixed* set of radial basis functions (Gaussians, splines, multiquadric —see chapter 5). When the basis functions $\varphi_i(\mathbf{x})$ are *not fixed* (when their positions $\mathbf{c}_i$ and shape parameters Σ are also subjects of learning—when $\varphi_i = \varphi_i(\mathbf{x}, \mathbf{c}_i, \Sigma_i)$, an RBF network becomes a nonlinear approximation scheme.

A *multilayer perceptron* is a representative of a nonlinear basis function expansion

$$o = y = f_a(\mathbf{x}, \mathbf{w}, \mathbf{v}) = \sum_{i=1}^{N} w_i \varphi_i(\mathbf{x}, \mathbf{v}_i), \tag{2.6}$$

where $\varphi_i(\mathbf{x}, \mathbf{v}_i)$ is a set of given functions (usually sigmoidal functions such as the logistic function or tangent hyperbolic—see chapter 3). Both the output layer's weights w_i and the entries of the hidden layer weights vector $\mathbf{v}$ are free parameters that are subjects of learning.

A *fuzzy logic model*, like an RBF network, can be a representative of linear or nonlinear basis function expansion):[3]

$$o = y = f_a(\mathbf{x}, \mathbf{c}, \mathbf{r}) = \frac{\sum_{i=1}^{N} G(\mathbf{x}, \mathbf{c}_i) r_i}{\sum_{i=1}^{N} G(\mathbf{x}, \mathbf{c}_i)}, \tag{2.7}$$

where N is the number of rules. The model given by (2.7) corresponds to the case where

· The input membership functions are, for example, Gaussians $G(\mathbf{x}, \mathbf{c}_i)$ centered at $\mathbf{c}_i$.

· The output membership functions are singletons.

· The algebraic product was used for the AND operator.

· The defuzzification was performed by applying the "center-of-area for singletons" algorithm (see section 6.1.7).

Other hypothesis spaces are a set of *algebraic polynomials*

$$f(x) = a_0 + a_1 x + a_2 x^2 + a_3 x^3 + \cdots + a_{n-1} x^{n-1} + a_n x^n \tag{2.8}$$

and a *truncated Fourier series*

$$f(x) = a_0 + a_1 \sin(x) + b_1 \cos(x) + a_2 \sin(2x) + b_2 \cos(2x) + \cdots$$
$$+ a_n \sin(nx) + b_n \cos(nx) \tag{2.9}$$

There is another important class of functions in learning from examples tasks. A learning machine tries to capture an unknown *target function* $f_o(\mathbf{x})$ that is believed to belong to some target space T, or class T, also called a *concept class*. The target space T is rarely known, and the learning machine generally does not belong to the same class of functions as the unknown target function $f_o(\mathbf{x})$. Typical examples of target spaces are continuous functions with s continuous derivatives in n variables, Sobolev spaces (comprising square integrable functions in n variables with s square integrable derivatives), band-limited functions, functions with integrable Fourier transforms, Boolean functions, and so on. In what follows, it is assumed that the target space T is a space of differentiable functions. The main problem is that very little is known about the possible underlying function between the input and the output variables. All that is available is a training data set of labeled examples drawn by independently sampling a $(X \times Y)$ space according to some unknown probability distribution.

The following sections present the basic ideas and techniques of the statistical learning theory developed by Vapnik and Chervonenkis, which is the first comprehensive theory of learning developed for learning with small samples. In particular, the following are discussed:

· Concepts describing the conditions for consistency of the empirical risk minimization principle

· Bounds of the generalization ability of a learning machine

- Inductive principles for small training data sets
- Constructive design methods for implementing this novel inductive principle

2.1   Risk Minimization Principles and the Concept of Uniform Convergence

Learning can be considered a problem of finding the best estimator f using available data. In order to measure the goodness of an estimator f, one must define an appropriate measure. The most common measures, or norms, are given by (2.4). Following a presentation of the theoretical concepts of risk minimization for regression problems, for which the most common norm is the L_2 norm (2.4a),[4] an explanation is given of why and how results change when all information is contained only in training data.

The average error or expected risk of the estimator f given by (2.3) is now

$$R[f] = \mathbb{E}[(y - f(\mathbf{x}))^2] = \int (y - f(\mathbf{x}))^2 P(\mathbf{x}, y)\, d\mathbf{x}\, dy. \tag{2.10}$$

The domain of the estimator f is the target space T, and using the preceding, criterion the objective is to find the best element f of T that minimizes $R[f]$. At this point, no explicit dependency of the estimating function $f(\mathbf{x})$ upon weight parameters $\mathbf{w}$ that define the relevant approximating features of $f(\mathbf{x})$ is stated. These relevant features are primarily the geometrical properties of the estimator $f(\mathbf{x})$—the shape and position of these multivariate functions. Hence, for the time being, the best estimator $f(\mathbf{x}) \in T$ is sought, and subsequently the estimating function is defined and analyzed as the *parameterized function* $f = f(\mathbf{x}, \mathbf{w})$ that actually depends upon the weight parameter $\mathbf{w}$.

The expected risk (2.10) can now be decomposed as

$$R[f] = \mathbb{E}[(f_o(\mathbf{x}) - f(\mathbf{x}))^2] + \mathbb{E}[(y - f_o(\mathbf{x}))^2], \tag{2.11}$$

where $(\mathbf{x}, y)$ are data pairs and $f_o(\mathbf{x})$ is the (theoretical) regression function that in section 1.4.1 (see equation (1.49)) was defined as the mean of a conditional probability-density function $P(y \mid \mathbf{x})$. Equation (2.11) indicates that the regression function minimizes the expected risk in T, and it is therefore the best possible estimator. Thus,

$$f_o(\mathbf{x}) = \arg \min_{f \in T} R[f]. \tag{2.12}$$

Equation (2.12) states that the regression function $f_o(\mathbf{x})$ is the argument (here, a function) that belongs to the target space T and that minimizes the risk $R[f]$. It is easy to follow this assertion. Note that there are two summands in (2.11). The first one depends on the choice of the estimator f and does not depend upon a system's outputs y. The second does depend on a noisy system's output y, and it is this term that limits the quality of the estimation. In noise-free, or deterministic, situations $y = f_o(\mathbf{x})$, that is, the mean of a conditional probability-density function $P(y \mid \mathbf{x})$ is measured exactly and the second term is equal to zero. Hence, this second stochastic term on the right side of (2.11) acts as an intrinsic limitation and vanishes only when $y = f_o(\mathbf{x})$. The conclusion that the best estimator is the regression function $f_o(\mathbf{x})$ is obvious because for $f = f_o(\mathbf{x})$ the first term on the right side of (2.11) is equal to zero. Therefore, in a general probabilistic setting, when input and output variables are random variables, even the regression function makes an error. Namely, for $f = f_o(\mathbf{x})$, the remaining part $\mathbb{E}[(y - f_o(\mathbf{x}))^2]$ is error due to noise and is equal to the noise variance. Hence, the bigger the noise-to-signal ratio, the larger the error.

However, there is a problem in applying (2.10). The joint probability function $P(\mathbf{x}, y)$ is unknown, and distribution-free learning must be performed based only on the training data pairs.

The supervised learning algorithm embedded in a learning machine attempts to learn the input-output relationship (dependency or function) $f_o(\mathbf{x})$ by using a training data set $D = \{[\mathbf{x}(i), y(i)] \in \Re^n \times \Re, i = 1, \ldots, l\}$ consisting of l pairs[5] $(\mathbf{x}_1, y_1)$, $(\mathbf{x}_2, y_2), \ldots, (\mathbf{x}_l, y_l)$, where the inputs $\mathbf{x}$ are n-dimensional vectors $\mathbf{x} \in \Re^n$ and the labels (or system responses) $y \in \Re$ are continuous values for regression tasks and discrete (e.g., Boolean) for classification problems. With the only source of information a data set, the expected risk $R[f]$ must be approximated by the *empirical risk* $R_{\mathrm{emp}}[f]$:

$$R_{\mathrm{emp}}[f] = \frac{\sum\limits_{i=1}^{l} (y_i - f(\mathbf{x}_i, \mathbf{w}))^2}{l}. \tag{2.13}$$

Hence, because $P(\mathbf{x}, y)$ is unknown, an *induction principle* of *empirical risk minimization* (ERM) replaces the average over $P(\mathbf{x}, y)$ by an average over the training sample. Note that the estimating function f is now expressed explicitly as the parameterized function that depends upon the weight parameter $\mathbf{w}$—$f = f(\mathbf{x}, \mathbf{w})$. A discussion of the relevance of the weights $\mathbf{w}$ in defining the concept of the uniform convergence of the empirical risk R_{emp} to the expected risk R follows. To start with, recall that the classical law of large numbers ensures that the empirical risk R_{emp} converges to the expected risk R as the number of data points tends toward infinity $(l \to \infty)$:

$$\lim_{l \to \infty} \left(|R[f] - R_{\mathrm{emp}}[f]| \right) = 0. \tag{2.14}$$

This law is a theoretical basis for widespread and often successful application of the least-squares estimation approaches provided that the training data set is large enough.

However, (2.14) does not guarantee that the function f_{emp} that minimizes the empirical risk R_{emp} converges to the true (or best) function f that minimizes the expected risk R. The previous statement applies as well for the parameters $\mathbf{w}_{emp}$ and $\mathbf{w}_o$, which define functions f_{emp} and f, respectively. What is needed now is *asymptotic consistency* or *uniform convergence*. This property of consistency is defined in the key learning theorem for bounded loss functions (Vapnik and Chervonenkis 1989; Vapnik 1995; 1998), for bounded loss functions which states that the *ERM principle is consistent if and only if empirical risk converges uniformly* to true risk in the following probabilistic sense:

$$\lim_{l \to \infty} P\left[\left\{ \sup_{\mathbf{w}} |R[\mathbf{w}] - R_{emp}[\mathbf{w}]| > \varepsilon \right\}\right] = 0, \qquad \forall \varepsilon > 0. \tag{2.15}$$

P denotes the probability, and (2.15) states the convergence "in probability". R_{emp} and R denote the empirical and the expected (true) risk for the same parameter $\mathbf{w}$. (The supremum of some nonempty set S designated by sup S is defined by the smallest element s such that $s \geq x$ for all $x \in S$. If no such s exists, sup $S = \infty$). Equation (2.15) and the underlying VC theory assert that the consistency is determined by the worst-case function from the set of approximating functions that provides the largest error between the empirical risk and the true expected risk. This theory provides bounds valid for any learning machine, expressed in terms of the size of the training set l and the VC dimension h of the learning machine.

The condition of consistency (2.15) has many interesting theoretical properties. One of the most important results is that the necessary and sufficient condition for a fast rate of convergence and for distribution-independent consistency of ERM learning is that the VC dimension of a set of approximating functions be finite. The VC dimension is discussed in section 2.2. A detailed, in-depth presentation of the consistency of the ERM principle can be found in Vapnik (1995) and in Cherkassky and Mulier (1998). Following the presentation of Vapnik (1995), it can be stated that with the probability $(1 - \eta)$, the following two inequalities are satisfied simultaneously:

$$R(\mathbf{w}_{emp}) - R_{emp}(\mathbf{w}_{emp}) < \varepsilon, \tag{2.16}$$

$$R_{emp}(\mathbf{w}_o) - R(\mathbf{w}_o) < \varepsilon, \tag{2.17}$$

where the weight $\mathbf{w}_{emp}$ minimizes the empirical risk R_{emp} (2.13), and $\mathbf{w}_o$ minimizes the true expected risk R (2.11). From the last two equations it follows that

$$R_{\text{emp}}(\mathbf{w}_{\text{emp}}) \leq R_{\text{emp}}(\mathbf{w}_o), \tag{2.18}$$

because $\mathbf{w}_{\text{emp}}$ and $\mathbf{w}_o$ are optimal values for corresponding risks (meaning that they define minimal points). By adding (2.16) and (2.17), and using (2.18), the following is obtained with probability $(1 - \eta)$:

$$R(\mathbf{w}_{\text{emp}}) - R(\mathbf{w}_o) < 2\varepsilon. \tag{2.19}$$

In other words, the uniform convergence theorem states that the weights vector $\mathbf{w}_{\text{emp}}$ obtained by minimizing the empirical risk will minimize the true expected risk as the number of data increases. Note this important consistency property, which ensures that the set of parameters minimizing the empirical risk will also minimize the true risk when $l \to \infty$.

However, the principle of ERM consistency (2.15) does not suggest how to find a constructive procedure for model design. First, this problem of finding the minimum of the empirical risk is an ill-posed problem. (See section 5.1). Here, the "ill-posed" characteristic of the problem is due to the infinite number of possible solutions to the ERM problem. At this point, just for the sake of illustration, remember that all functions that interpolate data points will result in a zero value for R_{emp}. Figure 2.5 shows a simple example of three out of infinitely many different interpolating functions of training data pairs sampled from a noiseless function $y = \sin(x)$. Each

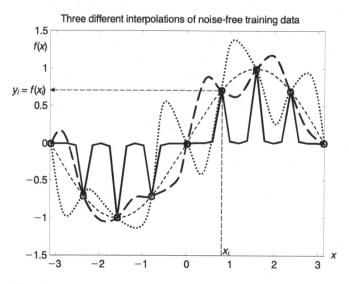

Figure 2.5
Three out of infinitely many interpolating functions resulting in $R_{\text{emp}} = 0$ (thick solid, dashed, and dotted curves) are bad models of a true function $y = \sin(x)$ (thin dashed lines).

interpolant results in $R_{emp} = 0$, but at the same time, each one is a very bad model of the true underlying dependency between x and y, because all three functions perform very poorly outside the training inputs. In other words, none of these three particular interpolants can generalize well. However, not only interpolating functions can mislead. There are many other approximating functions (learning machines) that will minimize the empirical risk (approximation or training error) but not necessarily the generalization error (true, expected or guaranteed risk).[6] This follows from the fact that a learning machine is trained by using some particular sample of the true underlying function, and consequently it always produces biased approximating functions. These approximants depend necessarily on the specific training data pairs (the training sample) used.

A solution to this problem proposed in the framework of the statistical learning theory is restricting the hypothesis space H of approximating functions to a set smaller than that of the target function T while simultaneously controlling the flexibility (complexity) of these approximating functions. The models used are parameterized, and with an increased number of parameters, they form a nested structure in the following sense

$$H_1 \subset H_2 \subset H_3 \subset \cdots \subset H_{n-1} \subset H_n \subset \cdots \subset H.$$

Thus, in the nested set of functions, every function always contains the previous, less complex, function (see fig. 2.6). Typically, H_n may be the set of polynomials in one variable of degree $n - 1$; a fuzzy logic model having n rules; multilayer perceptrons; or an RBF network having n hidden layer neurons. Minimizing R_{emp} over the set H_n approximates the regression function f_o by the function

$$\hat{f}_{n,l} \equiv \arg \min_{f \in H_n} R_{emp}|f|. \tag{2.20}$$

Typically, NN models and SVMs can be represented as the linear combination of fixed basis functions $f_a(\mathbf{x}, \mathbf{w}) = \sum_{\alpha=1}^{n} w_\alpha \varphi_\alpha(\mathbf{x})$, or more generally, as the linear combination of moving and shape-adjusting functions $f_a(\mathbf{x}, \mathbf{w}, \mathbf{v}) = \sum_{\alpha=1}^{n} w_\alpha \varphi_\alpha(\mathbf{x}, \mathbf{v}_\alpha)$. The first scheme is linear in parameter and consequently easier to optimize; in the second scheme the approximation function depends nonlinearly upon the hidden layer weights $\mathbf{v}$. Multilayer perceptrons are the most typical examples of the latter models. For linear in parameters models, the VC dimension h, which defines the complexity and capacity of approximating functions, is equal to $n + 1$. This is an attractive property of linear in parameters models.

For these typical models, equation (2.20) can be rewritten as given in Niyogi and Girosi (1994):

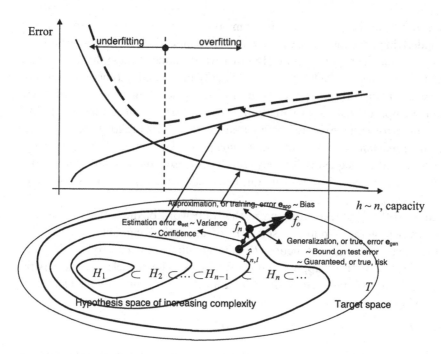

Figure 2.6
Structure of nested hypothesis functions and different errors that depend on the number of basis functions n for fixed sample size l. h denotes the VC dimension, which is equal to $n + 1$, for the linear combination of n fixed basis functions. Confidence is a confidence interval on the training error.

$$\hat{f}_{n,l} \equiv \arg \min_{w_\alpha, v_\alpha} R_{\text{emp}}|f|. \tag{2.21}$$

Instead of minimizing the expected risk by estimating the regression function f_o over the large target space T, the function $\hat{f}_{n,l}$ is obtained by minimizing the empirical risk over the smaller set of functions H_n. Consequently, there will always be a *generalization error* $\mathbf{e}_{\text{gen}}$, which can be decomposed into two components:

$$\mathbf{e}_{\text{gen}} = \mathbf{e}_{\text{app}} + \mathbf{e}_{\text{est}}. \tag{2.22}$$

This is shown in figure 2.6 as the vector sum of the two sources of possible errors in learning from data tasks.

The first source of error is trying to approximate the regression function f_o, which is an infinite dimensional structure in T, with a function $f_n \in H_n$, which is parameterized with a finite number of parameters. This is an *approximation error*, which can be measured as the $L_2(P)$ distance between the best function f_n in H_n and the regression function f_o. The $L_2(P)$ distance, where P stands for "in probability," is defined as the expected value of the Euclidean distance

$$\mathbf{e}_{\text{app}} = \mathbb{E}[(f_o - f_n)^2] = R[f_n] - R[f_o]. \tag{2.23}$$

The approximation error depends only on the approximating power of the chosen hypothesis class H_n, not on the training data set. Assume that the hypothesis space H_n is dense in the sense that one can always approximate any regression (or discriminant) function in T, to any degree of accuracy, by taking a sufficiently rich hypothesis space of the approximating functions H_n. Corresponding theorems about the universal approximation capability of different modeling schemes are given in section 1.3.1.

The second source of error stems from not minimizing the expected risk that would result in f_n, which is the best approximant in the set H_n. Instead, the empirical risk is minimized using a finite and usually sparse training data set. Such learning results in $\hat{f}_{n,l} \in H_n$, which is the best approximation function given the particular training data set. The approximating function $\hat{f}_{n,l}$ will perform better and better as the number of training data l increases. In accordance with the theorem of uniform convergence, when l increases, an estimate of the expected risk, the function $\hat{f}_{n,l}$, improves, and the empirical risk R_{emp} converges to the expected risk R.

The measure of the discrepancy between these two risks is defined as the *estimation error* $\mathbf{e}_{\text{est}}$

$$\mathbf{e}_{\text{est}} = |R_{\text{emp}}[f] - R[f]|. \tag{2.24}$$

Vapnik and Chervonenkis have shown that a bound on the estimation error in the following form is valid with probability $1 - \eta$:

$$\mathbf{e}_{\text{est}} = |R_{\text{emp}}[f] - R[f]| \leq \Omega(l, n, \eta), \qquad \forall f \in H_n. \tag{2.25}$$

The particular form of $\Omega(l, n, \eta)$ depends upon the problem setting, but it is generally a decreasing function of sample size l and an increasing function of the number of free approximating function parameters n. The relationship between the goodness of the approximating function $\hat{f}_{n,l}$ and n is not that simple. As the capacity of $\hat{f}_{n,l}$ increases (by using higher-order terms in polynomial expansion or by applying more fuzzy rules or taking more hidden layer neurons), the approximation capability of the learning machine increases by using additional adjustable parameters. At the same time, however, this larger set of parameter values must be optimized by using the same amount of training data, which in turn worsens the estimate of the expected risk. Therefore, an increase in n requires an increase in l in order to ensure uniform convergence. At what rate and under what conditions the estimator $\hat{f}_{n,l}$ will improve depends on the properties of the regression function (target space T) and on the particular approximation scheme used (H_n). A detailed analysis of this relationship between generalization error, hypothesis complexity, and sample complexity for RBF networks is given in Niyogi and Girosi (1994). In the case of binary classification, a particular $\Omega(l, n, \eta)$ is shown in figure 2.13.

Figure 2.6 illustrates the relationships between model complexity, expressed by n, and two differently named measures of model performance. The use of the "approximately equal" sign, $\sim$, suggests the similarity in spirit, or the analogy, between various ways of formulating the trade-off between the approximation error and the estimation error. (A similar concept, known as the bias-variance dilemma, is presented in section 4.3.2.) The following suggest the similarities between the different nomenclatures:

Approximation, or training, error $\mathbf{e}_{app}$ $\sim$ empirical risk $\sim$ bias.

Estimation error $\mathbf{e}_{est}$ $\sim$ variance $\sim$ confidence on the training error $\sim$ VC confidence interval.

Generalization (true, expected) error $\mathbf{e}_{gen}$ $\sim$ bound on test error $\sim$ guaranteed, or true, risk.

At this point, it is worthwhile to consider some general characteristics of the problem of learning from training data. Regarding model complexity, one can choose between two extremes in modeling a data set: a very simple model and a very complex model. Simple models do not have enough representational power (there are too few adjustable parameters—small n), and they typically result in high approximation (training) error. These are the models with a high bias. However, they are rather robust—data-insensitive—in that they do not depend heavily on the particular training data set used. Thus, they have low estimation error (low variance). On the other hand, the application of complex, higher-order models, for which n is large, results in low training error because more parameters can be adjusted, resulting in very good modeling of training data points. When a complex model interpolates data points, the training error (empirical risk) is equal to zero. Stated differently, complex models can model not only the data originating from the underlying function but also the noise contained in data. Having a lot of approximation power, complex models are able to model any data set provided for training. Complex models overfit the data. Therefore, each particular training data set will give rise to a different model, meaning that the estimation error (variance) of these complex structures will be high.

Proposed concepts of errors (or of various risks as their measures) suggest that there is always a trade-off between n and l for a certain generalization error. For a fixed sample size l, an increase in n results in a decrease of the approximation error, but an increase in the estimation error. Therefore, it is desirable to determine an n that defines an optimal model complexity, which in turn is the best match for given training data complexity. This question of matching the model capacity to the training sample complexity is optimally resolved in the framework of the statistical learning theory and structural risk minimization.

Before considering the basics of these theories and their constructive realization in the form of SVMs, recall that there are many other methods (or inductive principles) that try to resolve this trade-off. The regularization approach, presented in chapter 5, tries to minimize the cost function

$$R[f] = \sum_{i=1}^{l}(d_i - f(\mathbf{x}_i))^2 + \lambda \Phi[f] = \sum_{i=1}^{l}\underbrace{(d_i - f(\mathbf{x}_i))^2}_{Closeness\ to\ data} + \lambda\underbrace{\|\mathbf{P}f\|^2}_{Smoothness}, \tag{2.26}$$

where λ is a small, positive number (the Lagrange multiplier) also called the *regularization parameter*. The function in (2.26), that is, the error or cost function, or risk $R[f]$, is composed of two parts. The first part minimizes the empirical risk (approximation or training error, or discrepancy between the data d and the approximating function $f(\mathbf{x})$), and the second part enforces the smoothness of this function.

The simplest form of regularization is known as *ridge regression* (also called *weight decay* in the NNs field), which is useful for linear in parameters models (notably for RBF networks). Ridge regression restricts model flexibility by minimizing a cost function containing a (regularization) term that penalizes large weights:

$$R[f] = \sum_{i=1}^{l}(d_i - f(\mathbf{x}_i))^2 + \lambda \sum_{i=1}^{n} w_i^2. \tag{2.27}$$

Another, more heuristic but not necessarily inefficient, method for designing a learning machine with the smallest possible generalization error is the *cross-validation* technique. A cross-validation can be applied, and it is particularly efficient, when data are not scarce and can therefore be divided into two parts: one part for training and one for testing. In this way, using the training data set, several learning machines of different complexity are designed. They are then compared using the test set and controlling the trade-off between bias and variance. This approach is discussed in section 4.3.2.

The goal of these three inductive principles—minimization of cost function, ridge regression, and cross-validation—is to select the best model from a large (theoretically, infinite) number of possible models using only available training data. In addition to these, three other well-known inductive principles are structural risk minimization (SRM), Bayesian inference, and minimum descriptive length (MDL). All the previously mentioned inductive principles differ (Cherkassky 1997) in terms of

- Embedding (representation) of a priori knowledge
- The mechanism for combining a priori knowledge with data
- Applicability when the true model does not belong to the set of approximating functions
- Availability of constructive learning methods

The remainder of this chapter analyzes the SRM principle and its algorithmic realization through SVMs. SRM also tries to minimize the cost function, now called the *generalization bound R*, comprising two terms:

$$R[f] \leq R_{\text{emp}}[f] + \Omega(l, h, \eta). \tag{2.28}$$

In (2.28) the VC dimension h (defining model complexity) is a controlling parameter for minimizing the generalization bound R. This expression is similar to (2.25) with the difference that instead of parameter n, which defines model complexity, it uses the VC dimension h, which is usually but not always related to n. The statistical learning theory controls the generalization ability of learning machines by minimizing the risk function (2.28); it is specifically designed for a small training sample. The sample size l is considered to be small if the ratio l/h is small, say, $l/h \sim < 20$. l/h is the ratio of the number of training patterns l to the VC dimension h of learning machine functions (i.e., of an NN, a polynomial approximator, an RBF NN, a fuzzy model). The analysis of the term $\Omega(l, h, \eta)$ is deferred until later, after the important concept of the VC dimension h has been discussed.

2.2   The VC Dimension

The VC (Vapnik-Chervonenkis) dimension h is a property of a set of approximating functions of a learning machine that is used in all important results in the statistical learning theory. Despite the fact that the VC dimension is very important, the unfortunate reality is that its analytic estimations can be used only for the simplest sets of functions. The basic concept of the VC dimension is presented first for a two-class pattern recognition case and then generalized for some sets of real approximating functions.

Let us first introduce the notion of an *indicator function* $i_F(\mathbf{x}, \mathbf{w})$, defined as the function that can assume only two values, say, $i_F(\mathbf{x}, \mathbf{w}) \in \{0, 1\}$ or $i_F(\mathbf{x}, \mathbf{w}) \in \{-1, 1\}$, $\forall \mathbf{x}, \mathbf{w}$. (A standard example of an indicator function is the hard limiting threshold

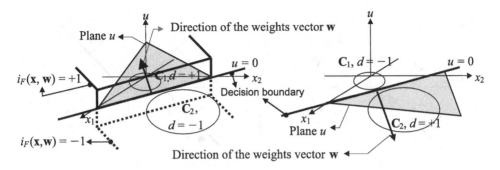

Figure 2.7
The indicator function $i_F(\mathbf{x}, \mathbf{w}) = \text{sign}(u)$ is the stairwise function shown in the left graph. In the input plane (x_1, x_2), $i_F(\mathbf{x}, \mathbf{w})$ is specified by the oriented straight line $u = 0$, also called a decision boundary or a separating function. The direction of the weights vector $\mathbf{w}$ points to the half-plane (x_1, x_2), giving positive values for the indicator function.

function given as $i_F(\mathbf{x}, \mathbf{w}) = \text{sign}(\mathbf{x}^T\mathbf{w})$; see fig. 2.7 and section 3.1.) In the case of two-class classification tasks, the *VC dimension of a set of indicator functions* $i_F(\mathbf{x}, \mathbf{w})$ is defined as the *largest number h of points that can be separated (shattered) in all possible ways.* For two-class pattern recognition, a set of l points can be labeled in 2^l possible ways. According to the definition of the VC dimension, given some set of indicator functions $i_F(\mathbf{x}, \mathbf{w})$, if there are members of the set that are able to assign all labels correctly, the VC dimension of this set of functions $h = l$.

Let us analyze the concept of shattering in the case of a two-dimensional input vector $[x_1 \quad x_2]^T$. The set of planes in $\mathfrak{R}^3$ is defined as $u = w_1x_1 + w_2x_2 + w_0$, or $u = (\mathbf{x}^T\mathbf{w})$, where $\mathbf{x}^T = [x_1 \quad x_2 \quad 1]$ and $\mathbf{w}^T = [w_1 \quad w_2 \quad w_0]$. A particular set of indicator functions in $\mathfrak{R}^3$ is defined as

$$i_F(\mathbf{x}, \mathbf{w}) = \text{sign}(u) = \text{sign}(w_1x_1 + w_2x_2 + w_0) = \text{sign}\left(\sum_{i=1}^{2} w_ix_i + w_0\right). \qquad (2.29)$$

This set can be graphically presented as the oriented straight line in the space of features $\mathfrak{R}^2(x_1, x_2)$, so that all points on one side are assigned the value $+1$ (class 1) and all points on the other side are assigned the value -1 (class 2) (see fig. 2.7). An arrow line of the weights vector $\mathbf{w}$ indicates the positive side of the indicator function. Note that the indicator function is not shown in the right graph in figure 2.7. Comparing the left and right graphs in the figure, note how the orientation of the indicator function changes if the assignments of the two classes change. Figure 2.8 shows all $2^3 = 8$ possible variations of the three labeled points shattered by an indicator func-

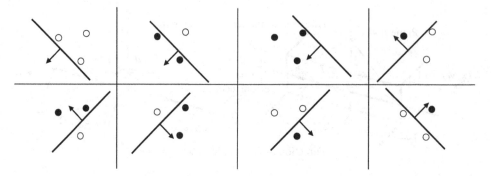

Figure 2.8
Three points in $\Re^2$ shattered in all possible $2^3 = 8$ ways by an indicator function $i_F(\mathbf{x}, \mathbf{w}) = \text{sign}(u)$ represented by the oriented straight line $u = 0$. For this $i_F(\mathbf{x}, \mathbf{w})$, $h = 3$. The direction of the weights vector $\mathbf{w}$ points to the half-plane (x_1, x_2), giving positive values for the indicator function.

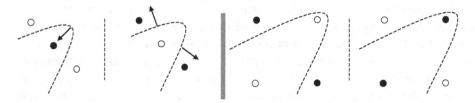

Figure 2.9
Left, an indicator function $i_F(\mathbf{x}, \mathbf{w}) = \text{sign}(u)$ cannot shatter all possible labelings of the three co-linear points; two labelings that cannot be shattered are shown. *Right*, $i_F(\mathbf{x}, \mathbf{w}) = \text{sign}(u)$ cannot shatter the depicted two out of sixteen labelings of four points. A quadratic indicator function (dashed line) can easily shatter both sets of points.

tion $i_F(\mathbf{x}, \mathbf{w}) = \text{sign}(u)$. Note that if the VC dimension is h, then there exists at least one set of h points in input space that can be shattered. This does not mean that every set of h points can be shattered by a given set of indicator functions (see left side of fig. 2.9).

The left side of figure 2.9 shows two out of eight possible labelings of the three co-linear points that cannot be shattered by an indicator function $i_F(\mathbf{x}, \mathbf{w}) = \text{sign}(u)$. (The reader should try to show that the remaining six possible labelings can be shattered by this function.) The right side of figure 2.9 shows the set of four points that cannot be separated by $i_F(\mathbf{x}, \mathbf{w}) = \text{sign}(u)$. In fact, there is no arrangement of four points in a two-dimensional input space (x_1, x_2) all of whose possible labelings can be separated by this indicator function. In other words, the VC dimension of the indicator function $i_F(\mathbf{x}, \mathbf{w}) = \text{sign}(u)$ in a two-dimensional space of inputs is 3. In an n-dimensional input space, the VC dimension of the oriented hyperplane indicator function, $i_F(\mathbf{x}, \mathbf{w}) = \text{sign}(u)$, is equal to $n + 1$, that is, $h = n + 1$.

Note that in an n-dimensional space of features the oriented straight line indicator function $i_F(\mathbf{x}, \mathbf{w}) = \text{sign}(u)$ has exactly $h = n + 1$ unknown parameters that are elements of the weights vector $\mathbf{w} = [w_0 \quad w_1 \quad w_2 \quad \ldots \quad w_{n-1} \quad w_n]^T$. This conclusion suggests that the VC dimension increases as the number of weights vector parameters increases. In other words, one could expect that a learning machine with many parameters will have a high VC dimension, whereas a machine with few parameters will have a low VC dimension. This statement is far from true. The following example shows that a simple learning machine with just one parameter can have an infinite VC dimension. (A set of indicator functions is said to have infinite VC dimension if it can shatter (separate) a deliberately large number of l points.) So, for example, the set of indicator functions $i_F(\mathbf{x}, \mathbf{w}) = \text{sign}(\sin(wx))$, $x, w \in \Re$, has an infinite VC dimension. Recall that the definition of a VC dimension requires that there be just one set of l points that can be shattered by a set of indicator functions. Thus, if one chooses l points placed at $x_i = 10^{-i}$, $i = 1, \ldots, l$, and if one assigns random (any) labelings $y_1, y_2, \ldots, y_l$, and $y_i \in \{-1, +1\}$, then an indicator function $i_F(\mathbf{x}, \mathbf{w}) = \text{sign}(\sin(wx))$ with

$$w = \pi \left(1 + \sum_{i=1}^{l} \frac{(1 - y_i) 10^i}{2} \right)$$

will be able to separate all l points. This is shown in figure 2.10. Note that the parameter (frequency) w is chosen as the function of random y labelings. The example is due to Denker and Levine (see Vapnik 1995).

The VC dimension of the specific loss function $L[y, f_a(\mathbf{x}, \mathbf{w})]$ is equal to the VC dimension of the approximating function $f_a(\mathbf{x}, \mathbf{w})$ for both classification and regression tasks (Cherkassky and Mulier 1998). It is interesting to note that for regression the VC dimension of a set of RBFs as given by (2.5):

$$f_a(\mathbf{x}, \mathbf{w}) = \sum_{i=1}^{N} w_i \varphi_i(\mathbf{x}) + w_0, \tag{2.30}$$

is equal to $N + 1$, where N is the number of hidden layer neurons. Equation (2.30) is given to separately show the bias term (in this way it is similar to (2.29)). In an N-dimensional space spanned by RBFs $\varphi_i(\mathbf{x}) = \{\varphi_1(\mathbf{x}), \varphi_2(\mathbf{x}), \ldots, \varphi_N(\mathbf{x})\}$, equation (2.30) is equivalent to linear functions (2.29). Hence, for a linear basis function

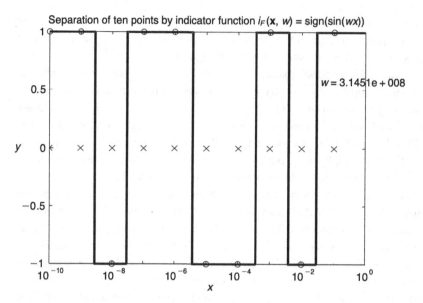

Figure 2.10
Shattering of ten points, $l = 10$. An indicator function $i_F(\mathbf{x}, \mathbf{w}) = \mathrm{sign}(\sin(wx))$ has only one parameter, but it can separate any number l of randomly labeled points, i.e., its VC dimension is infinite. The figure shows one random labeling only: $y = +1$ (solid circles), $y = -1$ (void circles). However, by an appropriately calculated parameter w any set of randomly labeled y's will be correctly separated.

expansion the VC dimension $h = N + 1$, where N stands for the number of hidden layer neurons.

The VC dimension of an RBF network increases proportionally to the number of neurons. This means that theoretically an RBF network can have an infinitely large VC dimension or that for a binary classification problem an RBF network can shatter any possible labeling of l training data. This is easy to show. Design an RBF network having l neurons in the hidden layer, place RB functions into training data—$\mathbf{c}_i = \mathbf{x}_i$, $i = 1, l$—and take the shape parameter (standard deviation σ in the case of Gaussian basis functions) to be smaller than the distance between adjacent centers. Figure 2.11 shows two different random labelings of 21 data pairs (top) and 41 data pairs (bottom) in the case of one-dimensional input x. Basis functions are Gaussians placed at the corresponding inputs x_i. Note that the graphs do not represent indicator functions. They can be easily redrawn by sketching the indicator functions

$$i_F(\mathbf{x}, \mathbf{w}) = \mathrm{sign}\left(\sum_{i=1}^{l} w_i G_i(x, c_i)\right)$$

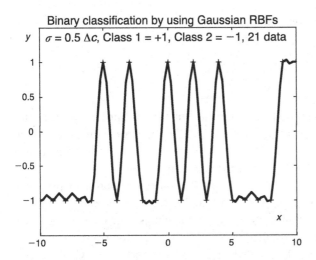

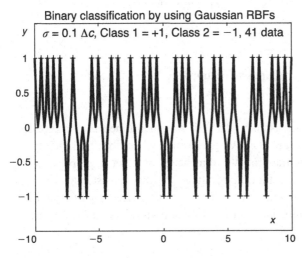

Figure 2.11
Shattering of 21 points (*top*) and 41 points (*bottom*) by using an RBF network having Gaussian basis functions. The RBF network has 21 parameters (*top*) and 41 parameters (*bottom*). These are the output layer weights. Thus, its VC dimension is 21 (*top*) and 41 (*bottom*). The figure shows two different random labelings: $y = +1$ for class 1, and $y = -1$ for class 2. Any set of l randomly labeled y's will be always separated (shattered) correctly by an RBF network having l neurons.

instead of the interpolating functions shown as

$$f_i(\mathbf{x}, \mathbf{w}) = \sum_{i=1}^{l} w_i G_i(x, c_i),$$

where $l = 21$ (top) and $l = 41$ (bottom).

The calculation of a VC dimension for nonlinear function expansions, such as the one exemplified by multilayer perceptrons given by (2.6), is a very difficult task, if possible at all. Even, in the simple case of the sum of two basis functions, each having a finite VC dimension, the VC dimension of the sum can be infinite.

In the statistical learning theory, the concept of *growth function* also plays an important role. Consider l points $(\mathbf{x}_1, \mathbf{x}_2, \ldots, \mathbf{x}_l)$ and a set S of indicator functions $i_F(\mathbf{x}, \mathbf{w})$. Let $N_d(\mathbf{x})$ denote the number of different labelings that can be classified binarily (shattered, dichotomized) by the set S. Then (because for two-class pattern recognition a set of l points can be labeled in 2^l possible ways), $N_d(\mathbf{x}) \leq 2^l$. The (distribution-independent) growth function $G(l)$ is now defined as

$$G(l) = \ln\left(\max_x(N_d(\mathbf{x}))\right),\tag{2.31}$$

where the maximum is taken over all possible samples of size l. Therefore,

$$G(l) \leq l \ln 2.\tag{2.32}$$

In presenting the condition of consistency (2.15), it was mentioned that a necessary and sufficient condition for a fast rate of convergence and for distribution-independent consistency of ERM learning is that the VC dimension of a set of approximating functions be finite. In fact, this definition results from the consistency condition expressed in terms of the growth function, stating that the necessary and sufficient condition for a fast rate of convergence and for distribution-independent consistency of ERM learning is that

$$\lim_{l \to \infty} \frac{G(l)}{l} = 0.\tag{2.33}$$

Vapnik and Chervonenkis (1968) proved that for a set of indicator functions, the growth function can be either linear or bounded by a logarithmic function of the number of training samples l. Nothing in between linear growth and logarithmic growth is possible. In other words, $G(l)$ can only change as the two solid lines in figure 2.12 do but cannot behave like the dashed line. For $G(l) = l \ln 2$, a learning machine is able to separate (shatter) l chosen points in all possible 2^l ways. If there exists some maximal l for which this shattering is possible, this number is called the

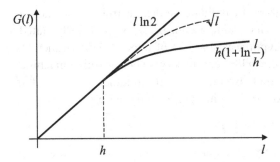

Figure 2.12
The growth function can either change linearly as the straight line $l \ln 2$ or be bounded by a logarithmic function $h(1 + \ln(l/h))$. When $G(l)$ changes linearly, the VC dimension for the corresponding indicator functions is infinite.

VC dimension and is denoted by h. From this point on, or for $l \geq h$, the growth function $G(l)$ starts to slow down, and the bounding logarithmic function is

$$G(l) = h\left(1 + \ln\frac{1}{h}\right). \tag{2.34}$$

The growth function of the indicator function $i_F(\mathbf{x}, \mathbf{w}) = \text{sign}(\sin(wx))$ shown in figure 2.10 is equal to $G(l) = l \ln 2$, or it increases linearly with regard to the number of samples l. This is a consequence of the already stated fact that this indicator function can shatter any number of training data pairs. Hence, the growth function $G(l)$ is unbounded, or the VC dimension is infinite. The practical consequence is that $i_F(\mathbf{x}, \mathbf{w}) = \text{sign}(\sin(wx))$ is not a good candidate for this dichotomization task because this particular indicator function is able to shatter (to separate or to overfit) any training data set.

Because all results in the statistical learning theory use the VC dimension, it is important to be able to calculate this learning parameter. Unfortunately, this is very often not an easy task. This quantity depends on both the set of specific approximating functions $f_a(\mathbf{x}, \mathbf{w})$ and the particular type of learning problem (classification or regression) to be solved. But even when the VC dimension cannot be calculated directly, results from the statistical learning theory are relevant for an introduction of structure on the class of approximating functions.

2.3 Structural Risk Minimization

Structural risk minimization is a novel inductive principle for learning from finite training data sets. It is very useful when dealing with small samples. The basic idea of

SRM is to choose, from a large number of candidate models (learning machines), a model of the right complexity to describe training data pairs. As previously stated, this can be done by restricting the hypothesis space H of approximating functions and simultaneously controlling their flexibility (complexity). Thus, learning machines will be those parameterized models that, by increasing the number of parameters (called weights $\mathbf{w}$ here), form a nested structure in the following sense:

$$H_1 \subset H_2 \subset H_3 \subset \cdots \subset H_{n-1} \subset H_n \subset \cdots \subset H. \tag{2.35}$$

In such a nested set of functions, every function always contains a previous, less complex, function (for a sketch of this nested set idea, see fig. 2.6). Typically, H_n may be a set of polynomials in one variable of degree n; a fuzzy logic (FL) model having n rules; multilayer perceptrons; or an RBF network having n hidden layer neurons. The definition of nested sets (2.35) is satisfied for all these models because, for example, an NN with n neurons is a subset of an NN with $n + 1$ neurons, an FL model comprising n rules is a subset of an FL model comprising $n + 1$ rules, and so on. The goal of learning is one of *subset selection*, which matches training data complexity with approximating model capacity. In other words, a learning algorithm chooses an optimal polynomial degree or an optimal number of hidden layer neurons or an optimal number of FL model rules.

For learning machines linear in parameters, this capacity, expressed by the VC dimension, is given by the number of weights (the number of free parameters). For approximating models nonlinear in parameters, the calculation of the VC dimension is perhaps feasible. Even for these networks, by using simulation experiments, one can find a model of appropriate capacity.

The optimal choice of model capacity ensures the minimization of expected risk (generalization error) in the following way. There are various generalization bounds for a learning machine implementing ERM that analytically connect generalization error $R(\mathbf{w}_n)$, approximating error $R_{\text{emp}}(\mathbf{w}_n)$, VC dimension h, number of training samples l, and probability (or, level of confidence) $1 - \eta$ for all approximating functions for both binary classification and regression. The minimization of these bounds is the essence of structural risk minimization.

The generalization bound for binary classification given by (2.36) holds with the probability of at least $1 - \eta$ for all approximating functions (weights $\mathbf{w}_n$ that define these functions) including the function (a weight $\mathbf{w}_n^*$) that minimizes empirical risk:

$$R(\mathbf{w}_n) \leq R_{\text{emp}}(\mathbf{w}_n) + \Omega\left(\frac{h}{l}, \frac{\ln \eta}{l}\right), \tag{2.36a}$$

where the second term on the right-hand side is called a *VC confidence* (confidence term or confidence interval) defined as

$$\Omega\left(\frac{h}{l}, \frac{\ln \eta}{l}\right) = \sqrt{\frac{h[(\ln(2l/h) + 1) - \ln(\eta/4)]}{l}}. \tag{2.36b}$$

The notation for risks given previously using $R(\mathbf{w}_n)$ says that risk is calculated over a set of functions $f_n(\mathbf{x}, \mathbf{w}_n)$ of increasing complexity. Different bounds can also be formulated in terms of other concepts, such as *growth function* or *annealed VC entropy*. Bounds also differ for classification and regression tasks and according to the character of approximating functions. More details can be found in Vapnik (1995) and Cherkassky and Mulier (1998). However, the general characteristics of the dependence of the confidence interval on the number of training data l and on the VC dimension h are similar (see fig. 2.13).

Equations (2.36) show that when the number of training data increases, that is, for $l \rightarrow \infty$ (with other parameters fixed), true risk $R(\mathbf{w}_n)$ is very close to empirical risk $R_{\text{emp}}(\mathbf{w}_n)$ because $\Omega \rightarrow 0$. On the other hand, when the probability $1 - \eta$ (also called a *confidence level*)[7] approaches 1, the generalization bound grows large, because in the case when $\eta \rightarrow 0$ (meaning that the confidence level $1 - \eta \rightarrow 1$), the value of

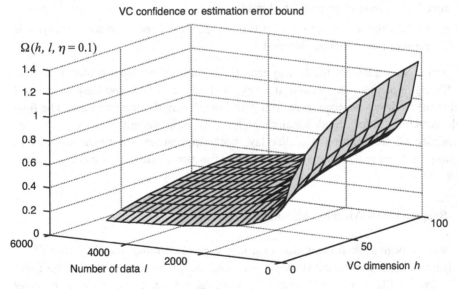

Figure 2.13
Dependence of VC confidence $\Omega(h, l, \eta)$ on the number of training data l and on the VC dimension h, $h < l$, for a fixed confidence level $1 - \eta = 1 - 0.1 = 0.9$.

$\Omega \to \infty$. This has an intuitive interpretation (Cherkassky and Mulier 1998) in that any learning machine (model, estimates) obtained from a finite number of training data cannot have an arbitrarily high confidence level. There is always a trade-off between the accuracy provided by bounds and the degree of confidence (in these bounds). Figure 2.13 also shows that the VC confidence interval increases with an increase in a VC dimension h for a fixed number of the training data pairs l.

Now, almost all the basic ideas and tools needed in the statistical learning theory and in structural risk minimization have been introduced. At this point, it should be clearer how an SRM works—it uses the VC dimension as a controlling parameter (through a determination of confidence interval) for minimizing the generalization bound $R(\mathbf{w}_n)$ given in (2.36). However, some information about how an SVM implements the SRM principle is still missing. One needs to show that SVM learning actually minimizes both the VC dimension (confidence interval, estimation error) and the approximation error (empirical risk) at the same time. This proof is given later. Meanwhile, it is useful to summarize two basic approaches to designing statistical learning from data models, that is, two ways to minimize the right-hand side of (2.36a) (Vapnik 1995):

• Choose an appropriate structure (order of polynomials, number of hidden layer neurons, number of fuzzy logic rules), and keeping the confidence interval fixed, minimize the training error (empirical risk).

• Keeping the value of the training error fixed (equal to zero or to some acceptable level), minimize the confidence interval.

Classical NNs implement the first approach (or some of its sophisticated variants), and SVMs implement the second strategy. In both cases, the resulting model will resolve the trade-off between underfitting and overfitting the training data. The final model structure (order) should ideally match the learning machine's capacity with the complexity of the training data. Today, both approaches are generalizations of learning machines with a set of linear indicator functions that were constructed in the 1960s.

2.4 Support Vector Machine Algorithms

This section begins the presentation of a new type of learning machine—the SVM, which implements the second strategy—keeping the training error fixed while minimizing the confidence interval. First, an example is presented of linear decision rules (i.e., the separating functions will be hyperplanes) for binary classification (dichotomization) of linearly separable data. In such a problem, data pairs can be perfectly classified, that is, an empirical risk can be set to zero. It is the easiest classification problem and yet an excellent introduction to all the important ideas underlying the statistical learning theory, structural risk minimization, and SVMs.

The presentation gradually increases in complexity. It begins in section 2.4.1 with a linear maximal margin classifier for linearly separable data, where there is no sample overlapping. Then, in section 2.4.2, some degree of overlapping of training data pairs is allowed while classes are separated using linear hyperplanes: a linear soft margin classifier for overlapping classes. In problems when linear decision hyperplanes are no longer feasible (section 2.4.3), an input space is mapped into a feature space (the hidden layer in NN models), resulting in a nonlinear classifier. Finally, in section 2.4.4, the same techniques are considered for solving regression (function approximation) problems.

2.4.1 Linear Maximal Margin Classifier for Linearly Separable Data

Consider the problem of binary classification, or dichotomization. Training data are given as

$$(\mathbf{x}_1, y_1), (\mathbf{x}_2, y_2), \dots, (\mathbf{x}_l, y_l), \qquad \mathbf{x} \in \Re^n, \qquad y \in \{+1, -1\}. \tag{2.37}$$

For the purpose of visualization, the case of a two-dimensional input space, $\mathbf{x} \in \Re^2$, is considered. Data are linearly separable, and there are many different hyperplanes[8] that can perform separation (see fig. 2.14). How can one find the best one?

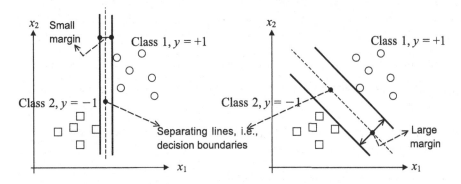

Figure 2.14
Two out of many separating lines: *right*, a good one with a large margin, and *left*, a less acceptable one with a small margin.

Remember only sparse training data are available. Thus, the optimal separating function must be found without knowing the underlying probability distribution $P(\mathbf{x}, y)$. There are many functions that can solve given pattern recognition (or functional approximation) tasks. In such a problem setting, the statistical learning theory shows that it is crucial to restrict the class of functions implemented by a learning machine to one with a complexity suitable for the amount of available training data.

In the case of classification of linearly separable data, this idea is transformed into the following approach: among all the hyperplanes that minimize the training error (empirical risk), find the one with the largest margin. This is an intuitively acceptable approach. Just by looking at figure 2.14, one can see that the dashed separation line shown in the right graph seems to promise a good classification with previously unseen data (in the generalization phase). Or, at least, it seems to promise better performance in generalization than the dashed decision boundary having a smaller margin, shown in the left graph. This can also be expressed as the idea that a classifier with a smaller margin will have a higher expected risk.

Using the given training examples during the learning stage, the machine finds parameters $\mathbf{w} = [w_1 \quad w_2 \quad \ldots \quad w_n]^T$ and b of a discriminant or decision function $d(\mathbf{x}, \mathbf{w}, b)$ given as

$$d(\mathbf{x}, \mathbf{w}, b) = \mathbf{w}^T \mathbf{x} + b = \sum_{i=1}^{n} w_i x_i + b, \tag{2.38}$$

where $\mathbf{x}, \mathbf{w}, \in \Re^n,$[9] and the scalar b is (possibly wrongly) called *a bias*. (Note that the dashed lines in fig. 2.14 represent lines that follow from $d(\mathbf{x}, \mathbf{w}, b) = 0$ (see explanation later). After the successful training stage, using the weights obtained, the learning machine, given a previously unseen pattern $\mathbf{x}$, produces output o according to an indicator function given as

$$i_F = o = \text{sign}(d(\mathbf{x}, \mathbf{w}, b)), \tag{2.39}$$

where o is the standard notation for the output from a learning machine. In other words, the decision rule is

If $d(\mathbf{x}_p, \mathbf{w}, b) > 0$, pattern $\mathbf{x}_p$ belongs to a class 1 (i.e., $o = y_1 = +1$), and if $d(\mathbf{x}_p, \mathbf{w}, b) < 0$, it belongs to a class 2 (i.e., $o = y_2 = -1$).

Note that the indicator function o given by (2.39) is a stepwise function (see figs. 2.15 and 2.16). At the same time, the decision (or discriminant) function $d(\mathbf{x}, \mathbf{w}, b)$ is a hyperplane. Also, a decision hyperplane d "lives in" $(n + 1)$-dimensional space or it lies "over" a training pattern's n-dimensional space of features. There is another

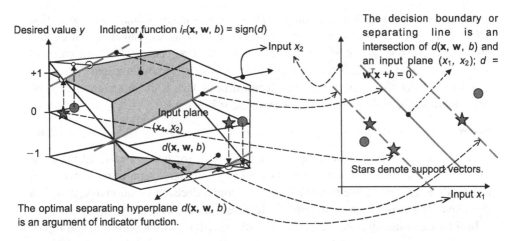

Figure 2.15
Definition of a decision (discriminant) function or hyperplane $d(\mathbf{x}, \mathbf{w}, b)$, decision (separating) boundary $d(\mathbf{x}, \mathbf{w}, b) = 0$, and indicator function $i_F = \text{sign}(d(\mathbf{x}, \mathbf{w}, b))$ whose value represents a learning, or support vector, machine's output o.

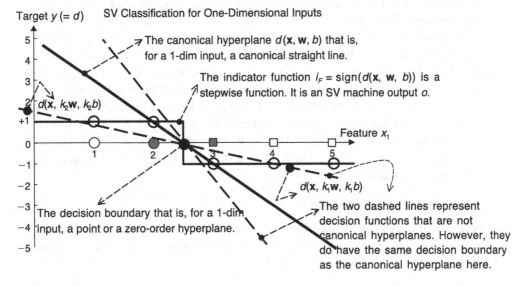

Figure 2.16
Graphical presentation of a canonical hyperplane. For one-dimensional inputs, it is actually a canonical straight line (solid) that passes through points $(+2, +1)$ and $(+3, -1)$ defined by support vectors (solid circle and solid square for class 1 and class 2, respectively). The dashed lines are two other separating hyperplanes, i.e., straight lines. The training input patterns $\{x_1 = 1, x_2 = 2\} \in$ class 1 have a desired or target value (label) $y_1 = +1$. The inputs $\{x_3 = 3, x_4 = 4, x_5 = 5\} \in$ class 2 have the label $y_1 = -1$. The two support vectors are filled training data, namely, $x_2 = 2$ is SV_1, and $x_3 = 3$ is SV_2.

mathematical object in classification problems, called a *decision boundary* (see section 1.4.2), that "lives in" the same n-dimensional space of features, that is, it is in a space of input vectors $\mathbf{x}$, and it separates vectors $\mathbf{x}$ into two classes. Here, in cases of linearly separable data, this decision boundary is also a (separating) hyperplane but of a lower order than $d(\mathbf{x}, \mathbf{w}, b)$. This decision boundary is an intersection of decision function $d(\mathbf{x}, \mathbf{w}, b)$ and a space of features. It is given by

$$d(\mathbf{x}, \mathbf{w}, b) = 0. \tag{2.40}$$

All these functions and relationships can be followed, for two-dimensional inputs $\mathbf{x}$, in figure 2.15. In this particular case, the decision boundary (separating hyperplane) is actually a separating line in a (x_1, x_2) plane, and a decision function $d(\mathbf{x}, \mathbf{w}, b)$ is a plane over this two-dimensional space of features, that is, over an (x_1, x_2) plane.

In the case of one-dimensional training patterns x (i.e., for one-dimensional inputs x to a learning machine), the decision function $d(x, w, b)$ is a line in an (x, y) plane. An intersection of this line with the x-axis defines a point that is a decision boundary between two classes. This can be followed in figure 2.16.

Before seeking an optimal separating hyperplane having the largest margin, consider the concept of the *canonical hyperplane*. This concept is depicted with the help of the one-dimensional example shown in figure 2.16. Not quite incidentally, the decision plane $d(\mathbf{x}, \mathbf{w}, b)$ shown in figure 2.15 is also a canonical plane. Namely, the values of d and of i_F are the same, and both are equal to $|1|$ for the support vectors depicted by stars. At the same time, for all other training patterns $|d| > |i_F|$. To understand the concept of the canonical plane, first note that there are many hyperplanes that can correctly separate data. In figure 2.16 three different separating functions $d(\mathbf{x}, \mathbf{w}, b)$ are shown. There are infinitely many more. In fact, if $d(\mathbf{x}, \mathbf{w}, b)$ is a separating function, then all functions $d(\mathbf{x}, k\mathbf{w}, kb)$, where k is a positive scalar, are correct decision functions, too. Also, for any $k \neq 0$, the hyperplanes given in (2.41) are the same hyperplanes

$$\{\mathbf{x} \mid \mathbf{w}^T \mathbf{x} + b = 0\} \equiv \{\mathbf{x} \mid k\mathbf{w}^T \mathbf{x} + kb = 0\}. \tag{2.41}$$

Because parameters $(\mathbf{w}, b)$ describe the same hyperplane as parameters $(k\mathbf{w}, kb)$, there is a need for the notion of a *canonical hyperplane*. A hyperplane is in canonical form with respect to training data $\mathbf{x} \in X$ if

$$\min_{x_i \in X} |\mathbf{w}^T \mathbf{x}_i + b| = 1. \tag{2.42}$$

The solid line $d(\mathbf{x}, \mathbf{w}, b) = -2x + 5$ in figure 2.16 fulfills (2.42) because its minimal absolute value for the given five training patterns belonging to two classes is 1. It achieves this value for two patterns, namely for $x_2 = 2$, and $x_3 = 3$. For all other patterns, $|d| > 1$.

Note an interesting detail regarding canonical hyperplanes that is easily checked. There are many different hyperplanes (planes and straight lines in figs. 2.15 and 2.16) that have the same decision boundary (solid line and in figs. 2.15 (right) and dot in figure 2.16). At the same time, there are far fewer hyperplanes that can be defined as canonical ones fulfilling (2.42). In figure 2.16, for a one-dimensional input vector x, the canonical hyperplane is unique. This is not the case for training patterns of higher dimension. Depending upon the configuration of a class's elements, various canonical hyperplanes are possible.

Therefore, there is a need to define an *optimal canonical hyperplane* as a canonical hyperplane having a *maximal margin*. This search for a separating, maximal margin, canonical hyperplane is the ultimate learning goal in statistical learning theory underlying SVMs. Carefully note the adjectives in the previous sentence. This hyperplane obtained from limited training data must have a *maximal margin* because, it will probably better classify new data. It must be in *canonical* form because this will ease the quest for significant patterns, here called support vectors. The canonical form of the hyperplane will also simplify the calculations. Finally, the resulting hyperplane must ultimately *separate* training patterns.

In order to introduce the concepts of a margin and optimal canonical hyperplane, some basics of analytical geometry are presented. The notion of distance between a point and a hyperplane is very useful and important. In $\Re^n$ let there be a given point $P(x_{1p}, x_{2p}, \ldots, x_{np})$ and a hyperplane $d(\mathbf{x}, \mathbf{w}, b) = 0$ defined by $w_1 x_1 + w_2 x_2 + \cdots + w_n x_n \pm b = 0$. The distance D from point P to hyperplane d is given as

$$D = \frac{|(\mathbf{w}\mathbf{x}_p) \pm b|}{\|\mathbf{w}\|} = \frac{|w_1 x_{1p} + w_2 x_{2p} + \cdots + w_n x_{np} \pm b|}{\sqrt{w_1^2 + w_2^2 + \cdots + w_n^2}}. \tag{2.43}$$

Thus, for example, the distance between the point $(1, 1, 1, 1)$ and a hyperplane $x_1 + 2x_2 + 3x_3 + 4x_4 - 2 = 0$ is

$$D = \frac{|[1 \quad 2 \quad 3 \quad 4][1 \quad 1 \quad 1 \quad 1]^T - 2|}{\sqrt{30}} = \frac{8}{\sqrt{30}}.$$

At this point, we can consider an optimal canonical hyperplane, that is, a canonical hyperplane having a maximal margin. Among all separating canonical hyperplanes there is a unique one having a maximal margin. The geometry needed for this presentation is shown in figure 2.17.

The margin M that is to be maximized during the training stage is a projection, onto the separating hyperplane's normal (weights) vector direction, of a distance

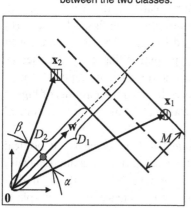
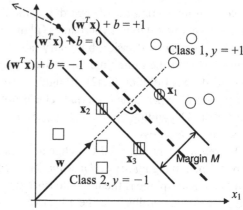

Optimal separating hyperplane with the largest margin intersects halfway x_2 between the two classes.

Figure 2.17
Optimal canonical separating hyperplane (OCSH) with the largest margin intersects halfway between the two classes. The points closest to it (satisfying $y_j|\mathbf{w}^T\mathbf{x}_j + b| = 1, j = 1, N_{SV}$) are support vectors, and the OCSH satisfies $y_i(\mathbf{w}^T\mathbf{x}_i + b) \geq 1, i = 1, l$ (where l denotes the number of training data and N_{SV} stands for the number of support vectors). Three support vectors (x_1 from class 1, and x_2 and x_3 from class 2) are training data shown textured by vertical bars. The margin M calculation is framed at left.

between any two support vectors belonging to different classes. In the example shown in the framed picture in figure 2.17, this margin M is equal to

$$M = (\mathbf{x}_1 - \mathbf{x}_2)_\mathbf{w} = (\mathbf{x}_1 - \mathbf{x}_3)_\mathbf{w}, \tag{2.44}$$

where the subscript $\mathbf{w}$ denotes the projection onto the weights vector $\mathbf{w}$ direction. The margin M can now be found using support vectors $\mathbf{x}_1$ and $\mathbf{x}_2$ as follows:

$$D_1 = \|\mathbf{x}_1\| \cos(\alpha), \qquad D_2 = \|\mathbf{x}_2\| \cos(\beta), \qquad M = D_1 - D_2, \tag{2.45}$$

where α and β are the angles between $\mathbf{w}$ and $\mathbf{x}_1$ and between $\mathbf{w}$ and $\mathbf{x}_2$, respectively as given by

$$\cos(\alpha) = \frac{\mathbf{x}_1^T\mathbf{w}}{\|\mathbf{x}_1\| \|\mathbf{w}\|} \quad \text{and} \quad \cos(\beta) = \frac{\mathbf{x}_2^T\mathbf{w}}{\|\mathbf{x}_2\| \|\mathbf{w}\|}. \tag{2.46}$$

Substituting (2.46) into (2.45) results in

$$M = \frac{\mathbf{x}_1^T\mathbf{w} - \mathbf{x}_2^T\mathbf{w}}{\|\mathbf{w}\|}, \tag{2.47}$$

and by using the fact that $\mathbf{x}_1$ and $\mathbf{x}_2$ are support vectors satisfying $y_j|\mathbf{w}^T\mathbf{x}_j + b| = 1$, $j = 1, 2$, that is, $\mathbf{w}^T\mathbf{x}_1 + b = 1$ and $\mathbf{w}^T\mathbf{x}_2 + b = -1$, we finally obtain

$$M = \frac{2}{\|\mathbf{w}\|}. \tag{2.48}$$

In deriving this important result, a geometric and graphical approach was taken. Alternatively, a shorter, algebraic approach could have been employed to show the relationship between a weights vector norm $\|\mathbf{w}\|$ and a margin M: (2.43) expresses the distance D between any support vector and a canonical separating plane. Thus, for example, for the two-dimensional inputs shown in figure 2.17, the distance D between a support vector $\mathbf{x}_2$ and a canonical separating line is equal to half of a margin M, and from (2.43) it follows that

$$D = \frac{M}{2} = \frac{|\mathbf{w}^T\mathbf{x}_2 + b|}{\|\mathbf{w}\|} = \frac{1}{\|\mathbf{w}\|}.$$

This again gives $M = 2/\|\mathbf{w}\|$, using (2.42), that is, the fact that $\mathbf{x}_2$ is a support vector. In this case, the numerator in the preceding expression for D is equal to 1.

Equation (2.48) represents a very interesting result, showing that minimization of a norm of a hyperplane normal weights vector $\|\mathbf{w}\| = \sqrt{(\mathbf{w}\mathbf{w})} = \sqrt{w_1^2 + w_2^2 + \cdots + w_n^2}$ leads to a maximization of a margin M. Because $\sqrt{f}$ is a monotonic function, minimization of $\sqrt{f}$ is equivalent to minimization of f. Consequently, minimization of norm $\|\mathbf{w}\|$ is equal to minimization of $\mathbf{w}^T\mathbf{w} = (\mathbf{w}\mathbf{w}) = \sum_{i=1}^{n} w_i^2 = w_1^2 + w_2^2 + \cdots + w_n^2$, and this leads to a maximization of a margin M.

Therefore, the optimal canonical separating hyperplane (OCSH), that is, a separating hyperplane with the largest margin defined by $M = 2/\|\mathbf{w}\|$, specifies support vectors (training data points closest to it) that satisfy $y_j[\mathbf{w}^T\mathbf{x}_j + b] \equiv 1$, $j = 1, N_{SV}$. At the same time, the OCSH satisfies inequalities

$$y_i[\mathbf{w}^T\mathbf{x}_i + b] \geq 1, \qquad i = 1, l, \tag{2.49}$$

where l denotes the number of training data and N_{SV} stands for the number of support vectors. The last equation can be checked visually in figures 2.15 and 2.16 for two-dimensional and one-dimensional input vectors $\mathbf{x}$, respectively.

Thus, in order to find the optimal separating hyperplane having a maximal margin, a learning machine should minimize $\|\mathbf{w}\|^2$ subject to inequality constraints (2.49). This is a classic *nonlinear optimization problem with inequality constraints*. Such an optimization problem is solved by the *saddle point* of the Lagrange function (Lagrangian)[10]

$$L(\mathbf{w}, b, a) = \frac{1}{2}\mathbf{w}^T\mathbf{w} - \sum_{i=1}^{l} \alpha_i\{y_i[\mathbf{w}^T\mathbf{x}_i + b] - 1\}, \tag{2.50}$$

where the α_i are Lagrange multipliers. The search for an optimal saddle point $(\mathbf{w}_o, b_o, \alpha_0)$ is necessary because Lagrangian L must be *minimized* with respect to $\mathbf{w}$ and b and *maximized* with respect to non-negative α_i (i.e., maximal $\alpha_i \geq 0$ should be found). This problem can be solved either in a *primal space* (which is the space of parameters $\mathbf{w}$ and b) or in a *dual space* (which is the space of Lagrange multipliers α_i). The second approach gives insightful results, and the solution is considered in a dual space. The Karush-Kuhn-Tucker (KKT) conditions for the optimum of a constrained function are used. In this case, both the objective function (2.50) and constraints (2.49) are convex, and the KKT conditions are necessary and sufficient for a maximum of (2.50). These conditions are as follows. At the saddle point $(\mathbf{w}_o, b_o, \alpha_o)$, derivatives of Lagrangian L with respect to primal variables will vanish, which leads to,

$$\frac{\partial L}{\partial \mathbf{w}_o} = 0, \quad \text{or} \quad \mathbf{w}_o = \sum_{i=1}^{l} \alpha_i y_i \mathbf{x}_i, \tag{2.51}$$

$$\frac{\partial L}{\partial b_o} = 0, \quad \text{or} \quad \sum_{i=1}^{l} \alpha_i y_i = 0. \tag{2.52}$$

Also, the complementarity conditions must be satisfied:

$$\alpha_i\{y_i[\mathbf{w}^T\mathbf{x}_i + b] - 1\} = 0, \qquad i = 1, l. \tag{2.53}$$

Substituting (2.51) and (2.52) into a *primal variables Lagrangian* $L(\mathbf{w}, b, \alpha)$ (2.50), we obtain the *dual variables Lagrangian* $L_d(\alpha)$:

$$L_d(\alpha) = \sum_{i=1}^{l} \alpha_i - \frac{1}{2}\sum_{i,j=1}^{l} y_i y_j \alpha_i \alpha_j \mathbf{x}_i^T\mathbf{x}_j. \tag{2.54}$$

In order to find the optimal hyperplane, a dual Lagrangian $L_d(\alpha)$ must be maximized with respect to non-negative α_i (i.e., α_i in the non-negative quadrant)

$$\alpha_i \geq 0, \qquad i = 1, l, \tag{2.55}$$

under constraints (2.52). Note that the dual Lagrangian $L_d(\alpha)$ is expressed in terms of training data and depends only on the scalar products of input patterns $(\mathbf{x}_i\mathbf{x}_j)$. This property of $L_d(\alpha)$ will be very handy later when analyzing nonlinear decision boundaries and for general nonlinear regression. Note also that the number of unknown variables is equal to the number of training data l. After learning, the number of free parameters is equal to the number of SVs but does not depend on the dimensionality of input space.

This is a standard quadratic optimization problem that can be expressed in matrix notation and formulated as follows:

Maximize

$$L_d(\alpha) = -0.5\alpha^T \mathbf{H}\alpha + \mathbf{f}^T \alpha, \tag{2.56a}$$

subject to

$$\mathbf{y}^T \mathbf{\alpha} = 0, \tag{2.56b}$$

$$\alpha \geq \mathbf{0}, \tag{2.56c}$$

where $(\alpha)_i = \alpha_i$, $\mathbf{H}$ denotes the Hessian matrix $(H_{ij} = y_i y_j(\mathbf{x}_i \mathbf{x}_j) = y_i y_j \mathbf{x}_i^T \mathbf{x}_j)$ of this problem, and $\mathbf{f}$ is a unit vector $\mathbf{f} = \mathbf{1} = [1 \quad 1 \quad \dots \quad 1]^T$. (Some standard optimization programs typically *minimize* the given objective function, but such programs can be applied, and the same solution would be obtained if $L_d(\alpha) = 0.5\alpha^T \mathbf{H}\alpha - \mathbf{f}^T \alpha$ were minimized, subject to the same constraints.)

Solutions α_{oi} of this dual optimization problem determine the parameters $\mathbf{w}_o$ and b_o of the optimal hyperplane according to (2.51) and (2.53) as follows:

$$\mathbf{w}_o = \sum_{i=1}^{l} \alpha_{oi} y_i \mathbf{x}_i, \qquad i = 1, l, \tag{2.57a}$$

$$b_o = \frac{1}{N_{SV}} \left(\sum_{s=1}^{N_{SV}} \left(\frac{1}{y_s} - \mathbf{x}_s^T \mathbf{w}_o \right) \right), \qquad s = 1, N_{SV}. \tag{2.57b}$$

N_{SV} denotes the number of support vectors. Note that an optimal weights vector $\mathbf{w}_o$, the same as the bias term b_o, is calculated using support vectors only (despite the fact that the summations in (2.57a) go over all training data patterns). This is because Lagrange multipliers for all non–support vectors are equal to zero $(\alpha_{oi} = 0, i = N_{SV} + 1, l)$. There are also other ways to find b_o. Finally, having calculated $\mathbf{w}_o$ and b_o, we obtain a decision hyperplane $d(\mathbf{x})$ and an indicator function $i_F = o = \text{sign}(d(\mathbf{x}))$:

$$d(\mathbf{x}) = \sum_{i=1}^{l} w_{oi} x_i + b_o = \sum_{i=1}^{l} y_i \alpha_i \mathbf{x}^T \mathbf{x}_i + b_o,$$

$$i_F = o = \text{sign}(d(\mathbf{x})). \tag{2.58}$$

Training data patterns having nonzero Lagrange multipliers are called *support vectors*. For linearly separable training data, all support vectors lie on the margin, and they are generally just a small portion of all training data (typically, $N_{SV} \ll l$). Figure 2.18 shows standard results for nonoverlapping classes. The dashed line is the separation line obtained by the least mean square (LMS) algorithm (see chapter 3). The LMS line is the best approximation in the L_2 norm of a theoretical decision boundary for these two Gaussian classes that can be obtained from available data. A theoretical decision boundary can be calculated using (1.106). The top graph of figure 2.18 shows that with a large number of training data points, the decision boundaries obtained by the two methods approach each other. However, in the case of an SVM, the corresponding separation line (solid) is determined by only the three support vectors closest to the class boundaries. Training samples in both graphs originate from two Gaussian classes having the same covariance matrices but different means $(\mu_1 = [0 \quad 0]^T, \mu_2 = [5 \quad 5]^T)$. For small data sets, decision boundaries obtained by an SVM and a linear neuron implementing an LMS learning rule disagree a lot (see fig. 2.18, bottom).

Interestingly, there are several specific constellations of training data sets for which separation lines obtained by LMS and SVM algorithms coincide. Generally, whenever all the training data are chosen as support vectors, the SVM and LMS solutions are equivalent. This can be seen in the top graph in figure 2.19. In the bottom graph of figure 2.19, not all the training examples are support vectors (there are only two support vectors, one belonging to each class). However, because of the symmetrical configuration of training data, the decision boundaries obtained by the two methods (SVM and LMS) coincide in the bottom graph, too.

The Hessian matrix $\mathbf{H}$ of a dual Lagrangian functional, belonging to the problem shown in the right graph of fig. 2.19, is

$$\mathbf{H} = \begin{bmatrix} 0 & 0 & 0 & 0 & 0 & 0 \\ 0 & 2 & 4 & -6 & -8 & -10 \\ 0 & 4 & 8 & -12 & -16 & -20 \\ 0 & -6 & -12 & 18 & 24 & 30 \\ 0 & -8 & -16 & 24 & 32 & 40 \\ 0 & -10 & -20 & 30 & 40 & 50 \end{bmatrix}.$$

Note that $\mathbf{H}$ is badly conditioned. In fact, in this particular example, its conditional number is equal to infinity, and before solving a quadratic programming problem, $\mathbf{H}$ must be regularized by some standard numerical technique. This is typically accomplished by adding a very small (random) number to the diagonal elements of $\mathbf{H}$.

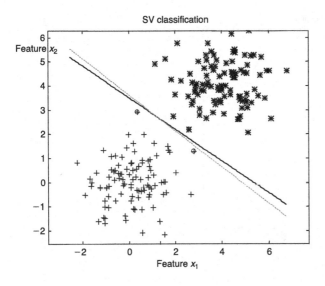

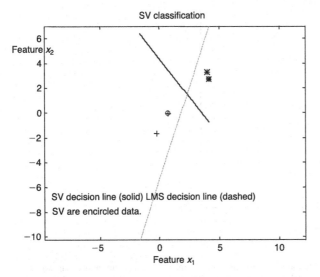

Figure 2.18
Decision boundaries for a dichotomization problem with (*top*) plenty of data and (*bottom*) a sparse data set. The solid separation line is obtained by the SVM algorithm, and the dashed line is the LMS solution. Support vectors are encircled training data points. *Top*, 100 data in each class, $\mathbf{w}_o = [-1.76 \quad -2.68]^T$, $b_o = 9.41$. *Bottom*, two examples in each class, $\mathbf{w}_o = [-0.3506 \quad -0.2859]^T$, $b_o = 1.2457$.

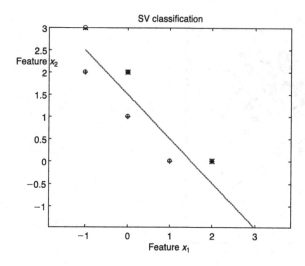

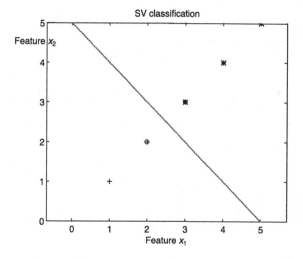

Figure 2.19
Decision boundaries for a dichotomization problem for two specific configurations of training patterns. Separation lines obtained by the SVM algorithm and the LMS method coincide. Support vectors are encircled training data points. *Top*, $\mathbf{w}_o = [-2 \quad -2]^T$, $b_o = 3$. *Bottom*, $\mathbf{w}_o = [-1 \quad -1]^T$, $b_o = 5$.

Before applications of OCSH for both overlapping classes and classes having nonlinear decision boundaries are presented, it must be shown that SV-based linear classifiers actually implement the SRM principle. In other words, we must prove that SV machine training actually minimizes both the VC dimension and a generalization error at the same time. In section 2.2, it was stated that the VC dimension of the oriented hyperplane indicator function, in an n-dimensional space of features, is equal to $n + 1$ (i.e., $h = n + 1$). It was also demonstrated that the RBF neural network (or the SVM having RBF kernels) can shatter infinitely many points (its VC dimension can be infinitely large, $h = \infty$). Thus, an SVM could have a very high VC dimension. At the same time, in order to keep the generalization error (bound on the test error) low, the confidence interval (the second term on the right-hand side of (2.36a)) was minimized by imposing a structure on the set of approximating functions (see fig. 2.13).

Therefore, to perform SRM, one must introduce a structure on the set of canonical hyperplanes and then, during training, choose the one with a minimal VC dimension.

A structure on the set of canonical hyperplanes is introduced by considering various hyperplanes having different $\|\mathbf{w}\|$. In other words, sets S_A are analyzed such that

$$\|\mathbf{w}\| \le A. \tag{2.59}$$

Then, if $A_1 \le A_2 \le A_3 \le \cdots \le A_n$, a nested set $S_{A1} \subset S_{A2} \subset S_{A3} \subset \cdots \subset S_{An}$ results. Equation (2.43) states that in $\Re^n$ the distance D from a point $P(x_{1p}, x_{2p}, \ldots, x_{np})$ to a hyperplane $d(\mathbf{x}, \mathbf{w}, b) = 0$ defined by $w_1 x_1 + w_2 x_2 + \cdots + w_n x_n \pm b = 0$ is given as $D = (|\mathbf{w}^T \mathbf{x}_p \pm b|)/\|\mathbf{w}\|$. Thus, imposing the constraint $\|\mathbf{w}\| \le A$, the canonical hyperplane cannot be closer than $1/A$ to any of the training points $\mathbf{x}_i$. This follows from the definitions of both a canonical hyperplane (2.42) and a margin (2.48). Specifically, the distance of the closest point to a canonical hyperplane is equal to $1/\|\mathbf{w}\|$. The influence of A on the capacity of the classifier is shown in figure 2.20.

Vapnik (1995) states that the VC dimension h of a set of canonical hyperplanes in $\Re^n$ such that $\|\mathbf{w}\| \le A$ is

$$h \le \min[R^2 A^2, n] + 1, \tag{2.60}$$

where all the training data points (vectors) are enclosed by a sphere of the smallest radius R. Therefore, a small $\|\mathbf{w}\|$ results in a small h, and minimization of $\|\mathbf{w}\|$ is an implementation of the SRM principle. In other words, during training, a minimization of the canonical hyperplane weight norm $\|\mathbf{w}\|$ maximizes the margin given by (2.48) and minimizes the VC dimension according to (2.60) at the same time. More on this can be found in Vapnik (1995; 1998) and Burges (1998).

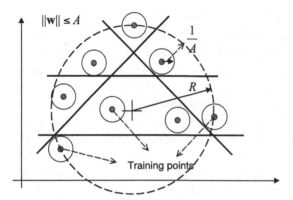

Figure 2.20
Constraining hyperplanes to remain outside spheres of radius $1/A$ around each training data point.

There is a simple and powerful result (Vapnik 1995) connecting the generalization ability of learning machines and the number of support vectors. Once the support vectors have been found, the bound on the expected probability of committing an error on a test example can be calculated as follows:

$$E_l[P(\text{error})] \leq \frac{E[\text{number of support vectors}]}{l}, \tag{2.61}$$

where E_l denotes expectation over all training data sets of size l. Note how easy it is to estimate this bound, which is independent of the dimensionality of the input space. Therefore, an SVM having a small number of support vectors will have good generalization ability even in very high-dimensional space.

2.4.2 Linear Soft Margin Classifier for Overlapping Classes

The learning procedure presented in the preceding section is valid for linearly separable data, that is, for training data sets without overlapping. Such problems are rare in practice. At the same time, there are many instances when linear separating hyperplanes can be good solutions even when data are overlapped. (Recall, for example, from section 1.4.2, normally distributed classes having the same covariance matrices.) However, the quadratic programming solutions presented previously cannot be used in the case of overlapping because the constraints $y_i[\mathbf{w}^T\mathbf{x}_i + b] \geq 1$, $i = 1$, l, given by (2.49) cannot be satisfied. Lagrangian multipliers α_i are highest for support vectors. For overlapping, some data points cannot be correctly classified, and for any misclassified training data point $\mathbf{x}_i$, the corresponding α_i will be at the upper bound. This particular data point (by increasing the corresponding α_i value) attempts to exert a stronger influence on the decision boundary in order to be classified correctly. When the α_i value reaches the maximal bound, it can no longer increase its effect, and this point will stay misclassified. In such a situation, the algorithm introduced in the previous section chooses (almost) all training data points as support vectors. To find a classifier with a maximal margin, this algorithm must be changed, allowing some data to be unclassified, or on the "wrong" side of a decision boundary. In practice, we allow a *soft margin*, and all data inside this margin (whether on the correct or wrong side of the separating line) are neglected (see fig. 2.21). The width of a soft margin can be controlled by a corresponding penalty parameter C that determines the trade-off between the training error and the VC dimension of the model.

The optimal margin algorithm is generalized (Cortes 1995; Cortes and Vapnik 1995) to nonseparable problems by the introduction of non-negative *slack variables* ξ_i $(i = 1, l)$ in the statement of the optimization problem. Now, instead of fulfilling (2.49), the separating hyperplane must satisfy

$$y_i[\mathbf{w}^T\mathbf{x}_i + b] \geq 1 - \xi_i, \qquad i = 1, l, \; \xi_i \geq 0, \tag{2.62}$$

or

$$\mathbf{w}^T\mathbf{x}_i + b \geq +1 - \xi_i, \quad \text{for } y_i = +1, \tag{2.63a}$$

$$\mathbf{w}^T\mathbf{x}_i + b \leq -1 + \xi_i, \quad \text{for } y_i = -1. \tag{2.63b}$$

For such a generalized optimal separating hyperplane, the function to be minimized comprises an extra term accounting the cost of overlapping errors. The changed objective functional with penalty parameter C is

$$J(\mathbf{w}, \xi) = \frac{1}{2}\mathbf{w}^T\mathbf{w} + C\left(\sum_{i=1}^{l} \xi_i\right)^k, \tag{2.64}$$

subject to inequality constraints (2.61). C is a design weighting parameter chosen by the user. Increasing C corresponds to assigning a higher penalty to errors, simultaneously resulting in larger weights. This is a convex programming problem, and by choosing exponent $k = 1$, neither slack variables ξ_i nor their Lagrange multipliers β_i appear in a dual Lagrangian L_d. As for a linearly separable problem, the solution to a quadratic programming problem (2.64), subject to inequality constraints (2.62), is given by the saddle point of the primal Lagrangian $L_p(\mathbf{w}, b, \xi, \alpha, \beta)$:

$$L_p(\mathbf{w}, b, \xi, \alpha, \beta) = \frac{1}{2}\mathbf{w}^T\mathbf{w} + C\left(\sum_{i=1}^{l} \xi_i\right) - \sum_{i=1}^{l} \alpha_i\{y_i[\mathbf{w}^T\mathbf{x}_i + b] - 1 + \xi_i\} - \sum_{i=1}^{l} \beta_i\xi_i,$$

$$\tag{2.65}$$

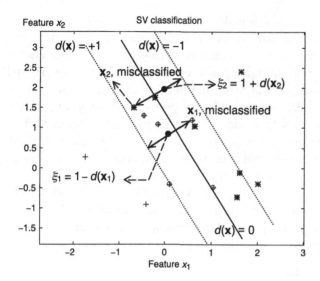

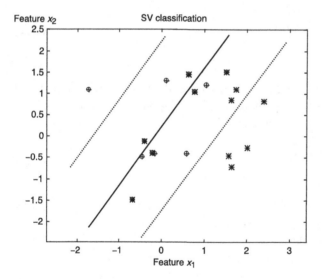

Figure 2.21
Soft decision boundaries for dichotomization problems with data overlapping, for two different configurations of training patterns. Separation lines (solid), margins (dashed), and support vectors (encircled training data points) are obtained by an SVM algorithm. *Top*, seven examples in each class; $C = 1$, $\mathbf{w}_o = [-1.19 \quad -0.64]^T$, $b_o = 0.88$; two misclassifications in each class. *Bottom*, six examples in class 1 ($+$) and twelve examples in class 2 ($*$); $C = 10$, $\mathbf{w}_o = [-0.68 \quad 0.5]^T$, $b_o = -0.12$; four misclassifications in class 1 and two in class 2.

where α_i and β_i are the Lagrange multipliers. Again, one should find an *optimal* saddle point $(\mathbf{w}_o, b_o, \xi_o, \mathbf{\alpha}_o, \mathbf{\beta}_o)$ because the Lagrangian L_p must be *minimized* with respect to $\mathbf{w}$, b, and ξ, and *maximized* with respect to non-negative α_i and β_i. This problem can also be solved in either a primal space or dual space (which is the space of Lagrange multipliers α_i and β_i). As before, a solution in dual space is found using standard conditions for an optimum of a constrained function

$$\frac{\partial L}{\partial \mathbf{w}_o} = 0, \quad \text{or} \quad \mathbf{w}_o = \sum_{i=1}^{l} \alpha_i y_i \mathbf{x}_i, \tag{2.66}$$

$$\frac{\partial L}{\partial b_o} = 0, \quad \text{or} \quad \sum_{i=1}^{l} \alpha_i y_i = 0, \tag{2.67}$$

$$\frac{\partial L}{\partial \xi_{io}} = 0, \quad \text{or} \quad \alpha_i + \beta_i = C, \tag{2.68}$$

and the KKT complementarity conditions

$$\alpha_i \{ y_i [\mathbf{w}^T \mathbf{x}_i + b] - 1 + \xi_i \} = 0, \qquad i = 1, l. \tag{2.69}$$

The dual variables Lagrangian $L_d(\alpha)$ is now not a function of β_i and is the same as before:

$$L_d(\alpha) = \sum_{i=1}^{l} \alpha_i - \frac{1}{2} \sum_{i,j=1}^{l} y_i y_j \alpha_i \alpha_j \mathbf{x}_i^T \mathbf{x}_j. \tag{2.70}$$

In order to find the optimal hyperplane, a dual Lagrangian $L_d(\alpha)$ must be maximized with respect to non-negative α_i (i.e., α_i in the non-negative quadrant)

$$C \geq \alpha_i \geq 0, \qquad i = 1, l, \tag{2.71}$$

under the constraints (2.67).

Therefore, the final quadratic optimization problem is practically the same as the separable case, the only difference being in the modified bounds of the Lagrange multipliers α_i. The penalty parameter C, which is now the upper bound on α_i, is determined by the user. Note that in the previous linearly separable case without data overlapping, this upper bound $C = \infty$. This can also be expressed in matrix notation, as in equations (2.56). Most important, the learning problem is expressed only in terms of unknown Lagrange multipliers α_i and known inputs and outputs. Furthermore, optimization does not solely depend upon inputs $\mathbf{x}_i$, which can be of a very high dimension, but it depends upon a scalar product of input vectors $\mathbf{x}_i$. This property will be very useful in section 2.4.3, which considers SVMs that can create non-linear separation boundaries.

Finally, expressions for both a decision function $d(\mathbf{x})$ and an indicator function $i_F = \text{sign}(d(\mathbf{x}))$ for a soft margin classifier, given by (2.58), are the same as for linearly separable classes.

2.4.3   The Nonlinear Classifier

The linear classifiers presented in the two previous sections are very limited. Mostly, not only are classes overlapped but the genuine separation lines are nonlinear hyper-surfaces. A nice characteristic of the preceding approach is that it can be extended in a relatively straightforward manner to create nonlinear decision boundaries. The motivation for such an extension is that an SVM that can create a nonlinear decision hypersurface will be able to classify nonlinearly separable data. This will be achieved by considering a linear classifier in feature space. A very simple example, shown in figure 2.22, is the previous linearly separable example in figure 2.19 but here with the exchanged positions of training data points chosen as support vectors. It is clear that no errorless linear separating hyperplane can now be found. The best linear hyperplane, shown as a dashed line, would make two misclassifications. Yet, using the nonlinear decision boundary line, one can separate two classes without any error. Generally, for n-dimensional input patterns, instead of nonlinear curves, an SVM must be able to create nonlinear separating hypersurfaces.

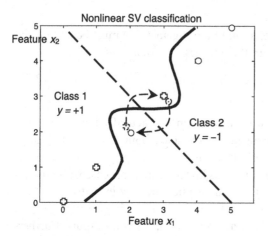

Figure 2.22
Nonlinear SV classification. A decision boundary in input space is a nonlinear separation line. Arrows show the direction of the exchange of two data points, from previously linearly separable positions (dashed) to new nonlinearly separable positions (solid).

One basic idea in designing nonlinear SVMs is to map input vectors $\mathbf{x} \in \mathfrak{R}^n$ into vectors $\mathbf{z}$ of a higher-dimensional feature space F ($\mathbf{z} = \mathbf{\Phi}(\mathbf{x})$, where $\mathbf{\Phi}$ represents a mapping $\mathfrak{R}^n \to \mathfrak{R}^f$), and to solve a linear classification problem in this feature space:

$$\mathbf{x} \in \mathfrak{R}^n \to \mathbf{z}(\mathbf{x}) = [a_1\phi_1(\mathbf{x}), a_2\phi_2(\mathbf{x}), \ldots, a_n\phi_n(\mathbf{x})]^T \in \mathfrak{R}^f. \tag{2.72}$$

A mapping $\mathbf{\Phi}(\mathbf{x})$ is chosen in advance; it is a fixed function. (For constants a_i, see (2.78)). Note that an input space (**x**-space) is spanned by components x_i of an input vector **x**, and a feature space F (**z**-space) is spanned by components $\phi_i(\mathbf{x})$ of a vector **z**. By performing such a mapping, one hopes that in a **z**-space the learning algorithm will be able to linearly separate images of **x** by applying the linear SVM formulation. This approach is also expected to lead to the solution of a quadratic optimization problem with inequality constraints in **z**-space. The solution for an indicator function $i_F(\mathbf{x}) = \text{sign}(\mathbf{w}^T\mathbf{z}(\mathbf{x}) + b)$, which is a linear classifier in a feature space F, will create a nonlinear separating hypersurface in the original input space given by (2.73). (Compare this solution with (2.58) and note the appearances of scalar products in both expressions.)

$$i_F(\mathbf{x}) = \text{sign}\left(\sum_{i=1}^{l} \alpha_i y_i \mathbf{z}^T(\mathbf{x})\mathbf{z}(\mathbf{x}_i) + b\right). \tag{2.73}$$

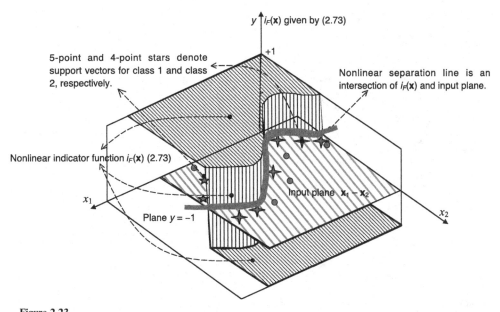

Figure 2.23
Nonlinear SV classification. The decision boundary in input space is a nonlinear separation line. The real separation line was a sine function, and the one shown was obtained by using Gaussian (RBF) kernels placed at each training data point (circles). Most SVs for class 1 are hidden behind $i_F(\mathbf{x})$.

Example 2.1 A three-dimensional input vector $\mathbf{x} = [x_1 \; x_2 \; x_3]$ is mapped into the feature vector $\mathbf{z}(\mathbf{x}) = [\phi_1(\mathbf{x}) \quad \phi_2(\mathbf{x}) \quad \ldots \quad \phi_9(\mathbf{x})]^T \in \Re^9$, where $\phi_i(\mathbf{x})$ are given as

$$\phi_1(\mathbf{x}) = x_1, \qquad \phi_2(\mathbf{x}) = x_2, \qquad \phi_3(\mathbf{x}) = x_3, \qquad \phi_4(\mathbf{x}) = (x_1)^2, \qquad \phi_5(\mathbf{x}) = (x_2)^2,$$

$$\phi_6(\mathbf{x}) = (x_3)^2, \qquad \phi_7(\mathbf{x}) = x_1 x_2, \qquad \phi_8(\mathbf{x}) = x_1 x_3, \qquad \phi_9(\mathbf{x}) = x_2 x_3.$$

Show that a linear decision hyperplane in feature space F corresponds to a nonlinear (polynomial) hypersurface in an original input space $\mathbf{x}$.

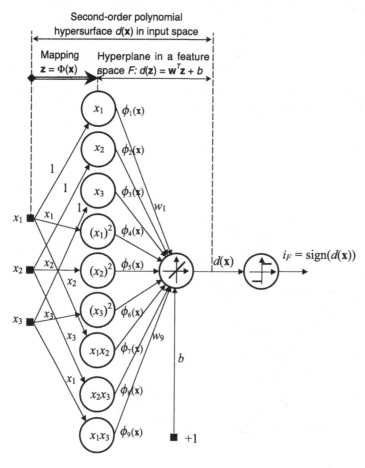

Figure 2.24
SVMs arise from mapping input vectors $\mathbf{x} = [x_1 \quad x_2 \quad \ldots \quad x_n]^T$ into feature vectors $\mathbf{z} = \Phi(\mathbf{x})$.

A decision hyperplane in a nine-dimensional feature space is given as $d(\mathbf{z}) = \mathbf{w}^T\mathbf{z} + b$. Calculating weights vector $\mathbf{w}$ and bias b in a feature space, and substituting $\mathbf{z} = \mathbf{z}(\mathbf{x})$ into the last expression for $d(\mathbf{z})$, a decision hypersurface over a three-dimensional original space ($\mathbf{x}$-space) is the second-order polynomial hypersurface

$$d(\mathbf{x}) = [w_1 \quad w_2 \quad w_3 \quad w_4 \quad w_5 \quad w_6 \quad w_7 \quad w_8 \quad w_9]$$

$$\times \left[x_1 \quad x_2 \quad x_3 \quad (x_1)^2 \quad (x_2)^2 \quad (x_3)^2 \quad x_1x_2 \quad x_1x_3 \quad x_2x_3\right]^T + b,$$

$$= w_1x_1 + w_2x_2 + w_3x_3 + w_4(x_1)^2 + w_5(x_2)^2 + w_6(x_3)^2$$

$$+ w_7x_1x_2 + w_8x_1x_3 + w_9x_2x_3 + b.$$

This transformation is presented graphically in figure 2.24.   ∎

The graphical appearance of an SV classifier in figure 2.24 is the same as the one for feedforward neural networks (notably multilayer perceptrons and RBF networks). Arrows, connecting $\mathbf{x}$-space with (feature) $\mathbf{z}$-space, denote a convolution operator here and correspond to the hidden layer weights in neural networks. The output layer connections are the weights w_i, and their meaning in SVMs and NNs is basically the same after the learning stage.

There are two basic problems in taking this approach when mapping an input $\mathbf{x}$-space into higher-order $\mathbf{z}$-space: the choice of mapping $\mathbf{\Phi}_i(\mathbf{x})$, which should result in a rich class of decision hypersurfaces; and the calculation of the scalar product $\mathbf{z}^T(\mathbf{x})\mathbf{z}(\mathbf{x})$, which can be computationally very discouraging if the number of features f (the dimensionality f of a feature space) is very large. The second problem is connected with a phenomenon called the "curse of dimensionality." For example, to construct a decision surface corresponding to a polynomial of degree 2 in an input space, a dimensionality of a feature space $f = n(n + 3)/2$. In other words, a feature space is spanned by f coordinates of the form $z_1 = x_1, \ldots, z_n = x_n$ (n coordinates), $z_{n+1} = (x_1)^2, \ldots, z_{2n} = (x_n)^2$ (next n coordinates), $z_{2n+1} = x_1x_2, \ldots, z_f = x_nx_{n-1}$ ($n(n - 1)/2$ coordinates). The separating hyperplane created in this space is a second-degree polynomial in the input space (Vapnik 1998). Thus, constructing a polynomial of degree 2 in a 256-dimensional input space leads to a dimensionality of a feature space $f = 33{,}152$. Performing a scalar product operation with vectors of such (or higher) dimensions is not an easily manageable task. (Recall that a standard grid for optical character recognition systems as given in fig. 1.29 is 16×16, resulting in a 256-dimensional input space.) The problems become serious (but fortunately solvable) if one wants to construct a polynomial of degree 4 or 5 in the same 256-dimensional space, leading to the construction of a decision hyperplane in a billion-dimensional feature space.

This explosion in dimensionality can be avoided by noticing that in the quadratic optimization problem given by (2.54) and (2.70), as well as in the final expression for a classifier (2.58), training data only appear in the form of scalar products $\mathbf{x}_i^T \mathbf{x}_j$. These products are replaced by scalar products $\mathbf{z}^T \mathbf{z}_i = [\phi_1(\mathbf{x}), \phi_2(\mathbf{x}), \dots, \phi_n(\mathbf{x})]$ $[\phi_1(\mathbf{x}_i), \phi_2(\mathbf{x}_i), \dots, \phi_n(\mathbf{x}_i)]^T$ in a feature space F, and the latter is expressed by using the *kernel function*

$$K(\mathbf{x}_i, \mathbf{x}_j) = \mathbf{z}_i^T \mathbf{z}_j = \mathbf{\Phi}^T(\mathbf{x}_i)\mathbf{\Phi}(\mathbf{x}_j). \tag{2.74}$$

Note that a kernel function $K(\mathbf{x}_i, \mathbf{x}_j)$ is a function in input space. Thus, the basic advantage in using a kernel function $K(\mathbf{x}_i, \mathbf{x}_j)$ is in avoiding having to perform a mapping $\mathbf{\Phi}(\mathbf{x})$. Instead, the required scalar products in a feature space $\mathbf{\Phi}^T(\mathbf{x}_i)\mathbf{\Phi}(\mathbf{x}_j)$ are calculated directly by computing kernels $K(\mathbf{x}_i, \mathbf{x}_j)$ for given training data vectors in an input space. In this way, one bypasses the possibility of an extremely high dimensionality of a feature space F. Thus, using the chosen kernel $K(\mathbf{x}_i, \mathbf{x}_j)$, an SVM can be constructed that operates in an infinite dimensional space. In addition, as will be shown, by applying kernels one does not even have to know what the actual mapping $\mathbf{\Phi}(\mathbf{x})$ is.

In utilizing kernel functions, the basic question is: What kinds of kernel functions are admissible? or Are there any constraints on the type of kernel functions suitable for application in SVMs?

The answer is related to the fact that any *symmetric function* $K(\mathbf{x}, \mathbf{y})$ *in input space* can represent a *scalar product in feature space* if

$$\iint K(\mathbf{x}, \mathbf{y})g(\mathbf{x})g(\mathbf{y}) \, d\mathbf{x} \, d\mathbf{y} > 0, \qquad \forall g \in L_2(R^n), \tag{2.75}$$

where $g(\cdot)$ is any function with a finite L_2 norm in input space, meaning a function for which $\int g^2(\mathbf{x}) \, d\mathbf{x} < \infty$. The corresponding features in a $\mathbf{z}$-space F are the eigenvectors of an integral operator associated with K:

$$\int K(\mathbf{x}, \mathbf{y})\phi_i(\mathbf{x}) \, d\mathbf{x} = \lambda_i \phi_i(\mathbf{x}), \tag{2.76}$$

and the kernel function K has the following expansion in terms of the ϕ_i:

$$K(\mathbf{x}, \mathbf{y}) = \sum_{i=1}^{\infty} \lambda_i \phi_i(\mathbf{x})\phi_i(\mathbf{y}). \tag{2.77}$$

Therefore, if there exists a set of functions $\{\phi_i\}_{i=1}^{\infty}$ such that

$$\int K(\mathbf{x}, \mathbf{y})\phi_i(\mathbf{x}) \, d\mathbf{x} = \lambda_i \phi_i(\mathbf{x}),$$

Table 2.1
Admissible Kernels and Standard Type of Classifiers

Kernel Functions	Type of Classifier
$K(\mathbf{x}, \mathbf{x}_i) = [(\mathbf{x}^T \mathbf{x}_i) + 1]^d$	Polynomial of degree d
$K(\mathbf{x}, \mathbf{x}_i) = e^{-1/2[(\mathbf{x} - \mathbf{x}_i)^T \Sigma^{-1} (\mathbf{x} - \mathbf{x}_i)]}$	Gaussian RBF
$K(\mathbf{x}, \mathbf{x}_i) = \tanh[(\mathbf{x}^T \mathbf{x}_i) + b]^*$	Multilayer perceptron

* Only for certain values of b.

then features

$$\mathbf{z}(\mathbf{x}) = [\sqrt{\lambda_1}\phi_1(\mathbf{x}) \quad \sqrt{\lambda_2}\phi_2(\mathbf{x}) \quad \cdots \quad \sqrt{\lambda_n}\phi_n(\mathbf{x}) \quad \cdots] \tag{2.78}$$

are admissible in the sense that the scalar product can be computed as

$$\mathbf{z}(\mathbf{x})^T \mathbf{z}(\mathbf{y}) = \sum_{i=1}^{\infty} \lambda_i \phi_i(\mathbf{x})\phi_i(\mathbf{y}) = K(\mathbf{x}, \mathbf{y}). \tag{2.79}$$

These *Mercer conditions*, according to Hilbert-Schmidt theory, characterize *admissible symmetric functions* (kernels) $K(\mathbf{x}, \mathbf{y})$. The *Mercer kernels* belong to a set of *reproducing kernels*. For further details, see Mercer (1909), Aizerman, Braverman, and Rozonoer (1964), Smola and Schölkopf (1997), and Vapnik (1998).

Many candidate functions can be applied to a convolution of an inner product (i.e., for kernel functions) $K(\mathbf{x}, \mathbf{x}_i)$ in an SVM. Each of these functions constructs a different nonlinear decision hypersurface in an input space. Interestingly, by choosing the three specific functions given in table 2.1, SVMs, after the learning stage, create the same type of decision hypersurfaces as do some well-developed and popular NN classifiers. Note that the training of these diverse models is different. However, after the successful learning stage, the resulting decision surfaces are identical. It is interesting to observe the differences in learning and the equivalence in representation. These two aspects of every learning machine are not necessarily connected, in the sense that different learning strategies do not have to lead to different models. It is not an easy task to categorize various learning approaches because increasingly mixed (blended) techniques are used in training today. However, let us trace the basic historical training approaches for three different models (multilayer perceptrons, RBF networks, and SVMs). Original learning in multilayer perceptrons is a steepest-gradient procedure (also known as error backpropagation). In RBF networks, as well as in polynomial classification and functional approximation schemes, learning is (after fixing the positions and shapes of radial basis functions, or the order of a polynomial) a linear optimization procedure. Finally, SVMs learn by solving a quadratic optimization problem. Nevertheless, after the learning phase, assuming the same kernels, these different models construct the same type of hypersurfaces.

Finally, we can consider learning in nonlinear classifiers (the ultimate object of interest). The learning algorithm for a nonlinear SVM (classifier) follows from the design of an *optimal separating hyperplane in a feature space*. This is the same procedure as the construction of a hard and a soft margin classifier in **x**-space. Now, in **z**-space, the dual Lagrangian, given in (2.54) and (2.70), is

$$L_d(\alpha) = \sum_{i=1}^{l} \alpha_i - \frac{1}{2} \sum_{i,j=1}^{l} y_i y_j \alpha_i \alpha_j \mathbf{z}_i^T \mathbf{z}_j, \tag{2.80}$$

and, according to (2.74), by using chosen kernels, one can maximize the Lagrangian

$$L_d(\alpha) = \sum_{i=1}^{l} \alpha_i - \frac{1}{2} \sum_{i,j=1}^{l} y_i y_j \alpha_i \alpha_j K(\mathbf{x}_i, \mathbf{x}_j), \tag{2.81}$$

subject to

$$\alpha_i \geq 0, \qquad i = 1, l,$$

$$\sum_{i=1}^{l} \alpha_i y_i = 0. \tag{2.82}$$

Note that in the case that one uses Gaussian kernels (i.e., basis functions) there is no need for equality constraints (2.67) because Gaussian basis functions do not necessarily require bias terms. In other words, there are no equality constraints $\sum_{i=1}^{l} \alpha_i y_i = 0$ in equations (2.82) and (2.83) while maximizing dual Lagrangian (2.80).

In a more general case, because of noise or the features of a generic class, training data points will overlap. Nothing but constraints change, as for the soft margin classifier. Thus, the nonlinear soft margin classifier will be the solution of the quadratic optimization problem given by (2.81) subject to constraints

$$C \geq \alpha_i \geq 0, \qquad i = 1, l,$$

$$\sum_{i=1}^{l} \alpha_i y_i = 0. \tag{2.83}$$

Again, the only difference from the separable nonlinear classifier is the upper bound C on the Lagrange multipliers α_i. In this way, one limits the influence of training data points that will remain on the wrong side of a separating nonlinear hypersurface. The decision hypersurface $d(\mathbf{x})$ is determined by

$$d(\mathbf{x}) = \sum_{i=1}^{l} y_i \alpha_i K(\mathbf{x}, \mathbf{x}_i) + b, \tag{2.84}$$

and the indicator function (2.85), which is generally also a hypersurface for $n > 3$, will define the nonlinear SV classifier.

$$i_F(\mathbf{x}) = \text{sign}(d(\mathbf{x})) = \text{sign}\left(\sum_{i=1}^{l} y_i \alpha_i K(\mathbf{x}, \mathbf{x}_i) + b\right). \tag{2.85}$$

Note that the summation is not actually performed over all training data but rather over the support vectors because only for them do the Lagrange multipliers differ from zero. The calculation of a bias b is now not a direct procedure as it is for a linear hyperplane. Depending upon the applied kernel, the bias b can be implicitly part of the kernel function. If, for example, Gaussian RBFs are chosen as kernels, they can use a bias term as the $(f + 1)$th feature in $\mathbf{z}$-space with a constant output $= +1$, but not necessarily (see chapter 5).

Therefore, if a bias term can be accommodated within the kernel function, the nonlinear SV classifier is

$$i_F(\mathbf{x}) = \text{sign}(d(\mathbf{x})) = \text{sign}\left(\sum_{i=1}^{l} y_i \alpha_i K(\mathbf{x}, \mathbf{x}_i)\right) = \text{sign}\left(\sum_{s=1}^{\substack{\text{number} \\ \text{of SVs}}} y_s \alpha_s K(\mathbf{x}, \mathbf{x}_s)\right). \tag{2.86}$$

The last expression in (2.86) is presented merely to stress that the summation is actually performed over the support vectors only.

Figure 2.23 shows all the important mathematical objects of a nonlinear SV classifier except the decision function $d(\mathbf{x})$. Example 2.2, by means of a classic XOR (exclusive-or) problem, graphically shows (see fig. 2.25) all the mathematical functions (objects) involved in nonlinear classification, namely, the nonlinear decision function $d(\mathbf{x})$, the indicator function $i_F(\mathbf{x})$, training data $(\mathbf{x}_i)$, support vectors $(\mathbf{x}_{SV})_i$, and separation lines.

Example 2.2 Construct an SV classifier, employing Gaussian functions as kernels, for a two-dimensional XOR problem given as

$$\mathbf{x}_1 = [0 \quad 0], \qquad \mathbf{x}_2 = [1 \quad 1], \qquad \mathbf{x}_3 = [1 \quad 0], \qquad \mathbf{x}_4 = [0 \quad 1],$$

$$\mathbf{y} = [1 \quad 1 \quad -1 \quad -1]^T.$$

The symmetric Hessian matrix required in this example for the maximization of a dual Lagrangian (2.81) is given as

$$
\mathbf{H} = \sum_{i,j=1}^{4} y_i y_j G(\mathbf{x}_i, \mathbf{x}_j) =
\begin{bmatrix}
1.0000 & 0.0183 & -0.1353 & -0.1353 \\
0.0183 & 1.0000 & -0.1353 & -0.1353 \\
-0.1353 & -0.1353 & 1.0000 & 0.0183 \\
-0.1353 & -0.1353 & 0.0183 & 1.0000
\end{bmatrix}.
$$ ∎

It is interesting to compare the solution obtained using Gaussian kernels with a solution that results after applying a polynomial kernel of second order. This polynomial decision function, the corresponding indicator function (classifier), and the Hessian matrix are shown in figure 2.26.

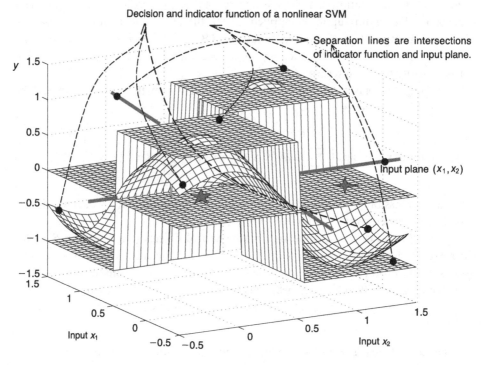

Figure 2.25
Nonlinear SVM classifier having Gaussian kernel (basis) functions $G(\mathbf{x}_i, \mathbf{x}_j)$ solving an XOR problem. The covariance matrix of kernels G: $\Sigma = \mathrm{diag}([0.25 \quad 0.25])$. All training data are selected as support vectors. One SV of each class is shown: a five-point star (class 1, $y = +1$) and a four-point star (class 2, $y = -1$); two (one belonging to each class) are hidden behind the indicator function.

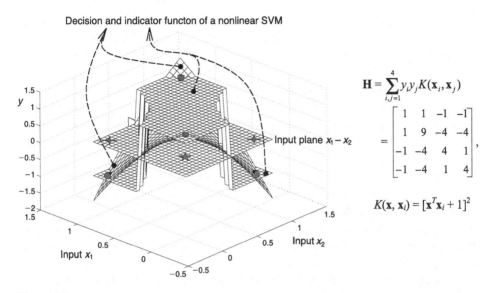

$$\mathbf{H} = \sum_{i,j=1}^{4} y_i y_j K(\mathbf{x}_i, \mathbf{x}_j)$$

$$= \begin{bmatrix} 1 & 1 & -1 & -1 \\ 1 & 9 & -4 & -4 \\ -1 & -4 & 4 & 1 \\ -1 & -4 & 1 & 4 \end{bmatrix},$$

$$K(\mathbf{x}, \mathbf{x}_i) = [\mathbf{x}^T \mathbf{x}_i + 1]^2$$

Figure 2.26
Nonlinear SVM classifier with polynomial kernel of second order solving an XOR problem. The decision function is a second-order (quadric) "saddle" surface. All four training data are selected as support vectors. One shown as a five-point star corresponds to class 1 ($y = +1$), and both SVs from class 2 ($y = -1$) are shown as four-point stars. A second SV from class 1 is hidden behind the indicator function. All training points $(\mathbf{x}, y)$ lie on both a decision function and an indicator function (dotted grid).

Thus, nonlinear classification problems can be successfully solved by applying one out of several possible kernel functions. Using *kernels in input space*, one calculates a *scalar product required in a (high-dimensional) feature space* and avoids mapping $\Phi(\mathbf{x})$. One does not have to know explicitly what mapping Φ is at all. Also, remember that the kernel "trick" applied in designing an SVM can be utilized in all other algorithms that depend on a scalar product (e.g., in principal component analysis or in the nearest-neighbor procedure).

In addition to the three admissible kernels, given in table 2.1, that can be applied in the field of learning and neural networks, there are many others, for instance, additive kernels, spline and B-spline kernels, and slightly reformulated Fourier series. The reader can find these in the specialized literature. Here, highlighting a link between SVMs and other soft computing models like fuzzy logic models, consider *multidimensional tensor product kernels* that result from tensor products of one-dimensional kernels,

$$K(\mathbf{x}_k, \mathbf{x}_i) = \prod_{j=1}^{n} k(x_{kj}, x_{ji}), \tag{2.87}$$

where n is the dimensionality of input space, and k_i are one-dimensional kernels (basis functions that in the fuzzy logic field are also known as membership or characteristic functions). These kernels k_i, located in input space, do not strictly have to be functions of the same type.

All that can be said at this point regarding the choice of a particular type of kernel function is that there *is* no clear-cut answer. No theoretical proofs yet exist supporting or suggesting applications for any particular type of kernel function. Presumably there will never be a general answer. Many factors determine a particular choice of kernel function—the class of problem, the unknown underlying functional dependency, the type and number of data, the noise-to-signal ratio, the suitability for on-line or off-line learning, the computational resources, and experience—the expertise and software already developed for some specific kernels. Very often, such sympathy factors have a decisive role. For the time being, one can only suggest that various models be tried on a given data set and that the one with the best generalization capacity be chosen.

The kernel "trick" introduced in this section is also very helpful in solving functional approximation (regression) problems.

2.4.4 Regression by Support Vector Machines

Initially developed for solving classification problems, SV techniques can also be successfully applied in regression (functional approximation) problems (Drucker et al. 1997; Vapnik, Golowich, and Smola 1997). Unlike pattern recognition problems, where the desired outputs y_i are discrete values like Booleans, here there are *real-valued* functions. The general regression learning problem is set as follows. The learning machine is given l training data, from which it attempts to learn the input-output relationship (dependency, mapping, or function) $f(\mathbf{x})$. A training data set $D = \{[\mathbf{x}(i), y(i)] \in \Re^n \times \Re, i = 1, \ldots, l\}$ consists of l pairs $(\mathbf{x}_1, y_1), (\mathbf{x}_2, y_2), \ldots,$ $(\mathbf{x}_l, y_l)$, where the inputs $\mathbf{x}$ are n-dimensional vectors $\mathbf{x} \in \Re^n$, and the system responses $y \in \Re$ are continuous values. The SVM considers approximating functions of the form

$$f(\mathbf{x}, \mathbf{w}) = \sum_{i=1}^{N} w_i \varphi_i(\mathbf{x}),$$ (2.88)

where the functions $\phi_i(\mathbf{x})$ are called features, as in nonlinear classification. Note that this, the most general model, corresponds entirely with RBF models and to some extent with fuzzy logic models, and it is close in appearance to multilayer perceptron network models. Note also that the bias term b is not shown explicitly. When there is

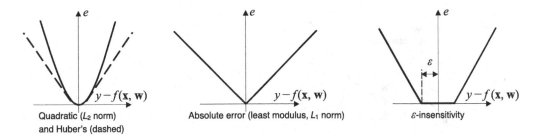

Quadratic (L_2 norm)
and Huber's (dashed)   Absolute error (least modulus, L_1 norm) ε-insensitivity

Figure 2.27
Loss (error) functions.

a bias term b, it will be incorporated in the weights vector $\mathbf{w}$. The function $f(\mathbf{x}, \mathbf{w})$ in (2.88) is explicitly written as a function of the weights $\mathbf{w}$ that are the subjects of learning. This equation is a nonlinear regression model because the resulting hypersurface is a nonlinear surface hanging over the n-dimensional $\mathbf{x}$-space.

To introduce all relevant and necessary concepts of SV regression in a gradual way, linear regression is considered first.

$$f(\mathbf{x}, \mathbf{w}) = \mathbf{w}^T \mathbf{x} + b. \tag{2.89}$$

Now, in regression, typically some measure, or *error of approximation*, is used instead of the margin between an optimal separating hyperplane and support vectors, which was used in the design of SV classifiers. Recall that there are different error (loss) functions in use and that each one results in a different final model. Two classic error functions were given in (2.4)—a square error (L_2 norm, $(y - f)^2$) and an absolute error (L_1 norm, least modulus $|y - f|$). The latter is related to Huber's error function. An application of Huber's error function results in robust regression. It is the most reliable technique if nothing specific is known about the model of noise. Huber's loss function is not presented here in analytic form, but it is shown as the dashed curve in figure 2.27a. Figure 2.27 shows the typical shapes of all mentioned error (loss) functions, including Vapnik's ε-insensitivity (fig. 2.27c).

Vapnik introduced a general type of error (loss) function, the *linear loss function with ε-insensitivity zone*:

$$|y - f(\mathbf{x}, \mathbf{w})|_\varepsilon = \begin{cases} 0 & \text{if } |y - f(\mathbf{x}, \mathbf{w})| \le \varepsilon, \\ |y - f(\mathbf{x}, \mathbf{w})| - \varepsilon & \text{otherwise.} \end{cases} \tag{2.90}$$

The loss is equal to zero if the difference between the predicted $f(\mathbf{x}, \mathbf{w})$ and the measured value is less than ε. Vapnik's ε-insensitivity loss function (2.90) defines an ε tube (see fig. 2.28). If the predicted value is within the tube, the loss (error or cost) is

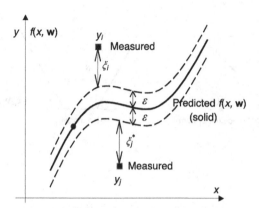

Figure 2.28
The parameters used in (one-dimensional) support vector regression.

zero. For all other predicted points outside the tube, the loss is equal to the magnitude of the difference between the predicted value and the radius ε of the tube. Note that for $\varepsilon = 0$, Vapnik's loss function is equivalent to a least modulus function. Figure 2.28 shows a typical graph of a regression problem and all relevant mathematical objects required in learning unknown coefficients w_i.

An SV algorithm for the linear case is formulated first, and then kernels are applied in constructing a nonlinear regression hypersurface. This is the same order of presentation as for classification tasks. In order to perform SVM regression, a new empirical risk is introduced:

$$R_{\text{emp}}^{\varepsilon}(\mathbf{w}, b) = \frac{1}{l} \sum_{i=1}^{l} \left| y_i - \mathbf{w}^T \mathbf{x}_i - b \right|_{\varepsilon}. \tag{2.91}$$

The ε-*insensitivity* function $|g|_{\varepsilon}$ is given by (2.90) and shown in figure 2.27c. Figure 2.29 shows two linear approximating functions having the same empirical risk $R_{\text{emp}}^{\varepsilon}$.

In formulating an SV algorithm for regression, the objective is to minimize the empirical risk $R_{\text{emp}}^{\varepsilon}$ and $\|\mathbf{w}\|^2$ simultaneously. Thus, estimate a linear regression hyperplane $f(\mathbf{x}, \mathbf{w}) = \mathbf{w}^T \mathbf{x} + b$ by minimizing

$$R = \frac{1}{2} \|\mathbf{w}\|^2 + C \left(\sum_{i=1}^{l} \left| y_i - f(\mathbf{x}_i, \mathbf{w}) \right|_{\varepsilon} \right). \tag{2.92}$$

Note that the last expression resembles the ridge regression scheme given by (2.27). However, here Vapnik's ε-insensitivity loss function replaces squared error, and

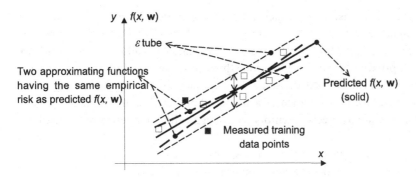

Figure 2.29
Two linear approximations inside an ε tube have the same empirical risk R_{emp}^{ε}.

$C \sim 1/\lambda$. From (2.90) and figure 2.28 it follows that for all training data outside an ε tube,

$$|y - f(\mathbf{x}, \mathbf{w})| - \varepsilon = \xi \quad \text{for data "above" an } \varepsilon \text{ tube,}$$

$$|y - f(\mathbf{x}, \mathbf{w})| - \varepsilon = \xi^* \quad \text{for data "below" an } \varepsilon \text{ tube.}$$

Thus, minimizing the risk R in (2.92) is equivalent to minimizing the risk (Vapnik 1995; 1998)

$$R_{\mathbf{w}, \xi, \xi^*} = \left[\frac{1}{2} \|\mathbf{w}\|^2 + C \left(\sum_{i=1}^{l} \xi + \sum_{i=1}^{l} \xi^* \right) \right], \tag{2.93}$$

under constraints

$$y_i - \mathbf{w}^T \mathbf{x}_i - b \leq \varepsilon + \xi, \qquad i = 1, l, \tag{2.94a}$$

$$\mathbf{w}^T \mathbf{x}_i + b - y_i \leq \varepsilon + \xi^*, \qquad i = 1, l, \tag{2.94b}$$

$$\xi \geq 0, \qquad i = 1, l, \tag{2.94c}$$

$$\xi^* \geq 0, \qquad i = 1, l, \tag{2.94d}$$

where ξ and ξ^* are slack variables, shown in figure 2.28 for measurements "above" and "below" an ε tube. Both slack variables are positive values. Lagrange multipliers α_i and α_i^*, corresponding to ξ and ξ^*, will be nonzero values for training points "above" and "below" an ε tube. Because no training data can be on both sides of the tube, either α_i or α_i^* will be nonzero. For data points inside the tube, both multipliers will be equal to zero.

Note also that the constant C, which influences a trade-off between an approximation error and the weights vector norm $\|\mathbf{w}\|$, is a design parameter chosen by the user. An increase in C penalizes larger errors (large ξ and ξ^*) and in this way leads to a decrease in approximation error. However, this can be achieved only by increasing the weights vector norm $\|\mathbf{w}\|$. At the same time, an increase in $\|\mathbf{w}\|$ does not guarantee good generalization performance of a model. Another design parameter chosen by the user is the required precision embodied in an ε value that defines the size of an ε tube.

As with procedures applied to SV classifiers, this constrained optimization problem is solved by forming a primal variables Lagrangian $L_p(\mathbf{w}, \xi, \xi^*)$:

$$L_p(\mathbf{w}, b, \xi, \xi^*, \alpha_i, \alpha_i^*, \beta_i, \beta_i^*)$$

$$= \frac{1}{2}\mathbf{w}^T\mathbf{w} + C\left(\sum_{i=1}^{l}\xi_i + \sum_{i=1}^{l}\xi_i^*\right) - \sum_{i=1}^{l}\alpha_i^*[y_i - \mathbf{w}^T\mathbf{x}_i - b + \varepsilon + \xi_i^*]$$

$$- \sum_{i=1}^{l}\alpha_i[\mathbf{w}^T\mathbf{x}_i + b - y_i + \varepsilon + \xi_i] - \sum_{i=1}^{l}(\beta_i^*\xi_i^* + \beta_i\xi_i). \qquad (2.95)$$

A primal variables Lagrangian $L_p(w_i, b, \xi, \xi^*, \boldsymbol{\alpha}, \boldsymbol{\alpha}^*, \boldsymbol{\beta}, \boldsymbol{\beta}^*)$ has to be *minimized* with respect to primal variables $\mathbf{w}$, b, ξ, and ξ^* and *maximized* with respect to non-negative Lagrange multipliers $\boldsymbol{\alpha}$, $\boldsymbol{\alpha}^*$, $\boldsymbol{\beta}$, and $\boldsymbol{\beta}^*$. Again, this problem can be solved either in a primal space or in a dual space. A solution in a dual space is chosen here. Applying the Karush-Kuhn-Tucker (KKT) conditions for regression, maximize a dual variables Lagrangian $L_d(\boldsymbol{\alpha}, \boldsymbol{\alpha}^*)$:

$$L_d(\boldsymbol{\alpha}, \boldsymbol{\alpha}^*) = -\varepsilon\sum_{i=1}^{l}(\alpha_i^* + \alpha_i) + \sum_{i=1}^{l}(\alpha_i^* - \alpha_i)y_i - \frac{1}{2}\sum_{i,j=1}^{l}(\alpha_i^* - \alpha_i)(\alpha_j^* - \alpha_j)\mathbf{x}_i^T\mathbf{x}_j, \quad (2.96)$$

subject to constraints

$$\sum_{i=1}^{l}\alpha_i^* = \sum_{i=1}^{l}\alpha_i, \qquad (2.97a)$$

$$0 \leq \alpha_i^* \leq C, \qquad i = 1, l, \qquad (2.97b)$$

$$0 \leq \alpha_i \leq C, \qquad i = 1, l. \qquad (2.97c)$$

Note that a dual variables Lagrangian $L_d(\boldsymbol{\alpha}, \boldsymbol{\alpha}^*)$ is expressed in terms of Lagrange multipliers $\boldsymbol{\alpha}$ and $\boldsymbol{\alpha}^*$ only. However, the size of the problem, with respect to the size of an SV classifier design task, is doubled now. There are $2l$ unknown multipliers for linear regression, and the Hessian matrix $\mathbf{H}$ of the quadratic optimization problem in the case of regression is a $(2l, 2l)$ matrix. This standard quadratic optimization problem can be expressed in a matrix notation and formulated as follows:

Maximize

$$L_d(\boldsymbol{\alpha}) = -0.5\boldsymbol{\alpha}^T \mathbf{H} \boldsymbol{\alpha} + \mathbf{f}^T \boldsymbol{\alpha}, \qquad (2.98)$$

subject to (2.97), where for a linear regression,

$$\mathbf{H} = [\mathbf{x}^T \mathbf{x} + 1], \quad \mathbf{f} = [\varepsilon - y_1 \quad \varepsilon - y_2 \quad \dots \quad \varepsilon - y_N \quad \varepsilon + y_1 \quad \varepsilon + y_2 \quad \dots \quad \varepsilon + y_N].$$

Again, if one uses some standard optimization routine that typically minimizes a given objective function, (2.98) should be rewritten as $L_d(\boldsymbol{\alpha}) = 0.5\boldsymbol{\alpha}^T \mathbf{H} \boldsymbol{\alpha} - \mathbf{f}^T \boldsymbol{\alpha}$, and solved subject to the same constraints.

Learning results in l Lagrange multiplier pairs $(\boldsymbol{\alpha}, \boldsymbol{\alpha}^*)$. After learning, the number of free (nonzero) parameters α_i or α_i^* is equal to the number of SVs. However, this number does not depend on the dimensionality of input space, and this is particularly important while working in high-dimensional spaces. Because at least one element of each pair (α_i, α_i^*), $i = 1, l$, is zero, the product of α_i and α_i^* is always zero.

After calculating Lagrange multipliers α_i and α_i^*, find an optimal desired weights vector of the regression hyperplane as

$$\mathbf{w}_o = \sum_{i=1}^{l} (\alpha_i^* - \alpha_i)\mathbf{x}_i, \qquad (2.99)$$

and an optimal bias b_o of the regression hyperplane as

$$b_o = \frac{1}{l} \left(\sum_{i=1}^{l} (y_i - \mathbf{x}_i^T \mathbf{w}_o) \right). \qquad (2.100)$$

The best regression hyperplane obtained is given by

$$z = f(\mathbf{x}, \mathbf{w}) = \mathbf{w}^T \mathbf{x} + b. \qquad (2.101)$$

A more challenging (and common) problem is solving a nonlinear regression task. As with nonlinear classification, this is achieved by considering a linear regression hyperplane in feature space.

Thus, in designing SV machines for creating a nonlinear regression function, map input vectors $\mathbf{x} \in \Re^n$ into vectors $\mathbf{z}$ of a higher-dimensional feature space F ($\mathbf{z} = \Phi(\mathbf{x})$, where Φ represents a mapping $\Re^n \to \Re^f$), and solve a linear regression problem in this feature space. A mapping $\Phi(\mathbf{x})$ is again chosen in advance; it is a fixed function. Note that an input space ($\mathbf{x}$-space) is spanned by components x_i of an input vector $\mathbf{x}$, and a feature space F ($\mathbf{z}$-space) is spanned by components $\phi_i(\mathbf{x})$ of a vector $\mathbf{z}$. By performing such a mapping, one hopes that in a $\mathbf{z}$-space the learning algorithm will be able to obtain a linear regression hyperplane by applying the linear regression SVM formulation. This approach is expected to lead to the solution of a quadratic optimization problem with inequality constraints in $\mathbf{z}$-space. The solution for a regression hyperplane $f = \mathbf{w}^T \mathbf{z}(\mathbf{x}) + b$, which is linear in a feature space F, will create a nonlinear regressing hypersurface in the original input space. The most popular kernel functions are polynomials and RBFs with Gaussian kernels. Both kernels are given in table 2.1.

In the case of nonlinear regression, (2.98) is used, the only change being in the Hessian matrix $\mathbf{H}$, now given as

$$\mathbf{H} = \begin{bmatrix} \mathbf{G} & -\mathbf{G} \\ -\mathbf{G} & \mathbf{G} \end{bmatrix}, \tag{2.102}$$

where $\mathbf{G}$ denotes the corresponding kernel (design) matrix $\mathbf{G}(\mathbf{x}_k, \mathbf{x}_i)$.

After calculating Lagrange multiplier vectors $\boldsymbol{\alpha}$ and $\boldsymbol{\alpha}^*$, find an optimal desired weights vector of the *kernels expansion* as

$$\mathbf{w}_o = \boldsymbol{\alpha}^* - \boldsymbol{\alpha}, \tag{2.103}$$

and an optimal bias b_o as

$$b_o = \frac{1}{l} \sum_{i=1}^{l} (y_i - g_i), \tag{2.104}$$

where $\mathbf{g} = \mathbf{G}\mathbf{w}_o$, and the matrix $\mathbf{G}$ is a corresponding design matrix of given RBF kernels. In the case of Gaussian basis (kernel) functions, one does not need a bias term b. Similarly, if one uses expression for a polynomial kernel as given in table 2.1, b is not needed.

The best nonlinear regression hyperfunction is given by

$$z = f(\mathbf{x}, \mathbf{w}) = \mathbf{G}\mathbf{w} + b. \tag{2.105}$$

There are a number of learning parameters that can be utilized in constructing SV machines for regression. The two most relevant are the insensitivity zone e and the penalty parameter C, which determines the trade-off between the training error and VC dimension of the model. Both parameters are chosen by the user. Example 2.3 and figure 2.30 show how an increase in an insensitivity zone e has smoothing effects

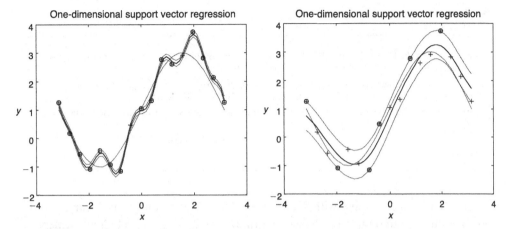

Figure 2.30
Influence of an insensitivity zone *e* on modeling quality. A nonlinear SVM creates a regression function with Gaussian kernels and models a highly polluted (25% noise) sine function (dashed). Seventeen measured training data points (plus signs) are used. *Left*, $\varepsilon = 0.1$, fifteen SV are chosen (encircled plus signs). *Right*, $\varepsilon = 0.5$, six chosen SVs produced a much better regressing function.

on modeling highly noisy polluted data. An increase in *e* means a reduction in requirements for the accuracy of approximation. It also decreases the number of SVs, leading to data compression.

Example 2.3 Construct an SV machine for modeling measured data pairs. The underlying function (known to us but not to the SVM) is a sine function corrupted by 25% of normally distributed noise with a zero mean. Analyze the influence of an insensitivity zone on modeling quality.

The application of kernel functions introduces various parameters that define them. For the polynomial kernels this is the degree *d*, and for the Gaussian RBFs it is the variance matrix Σ, whose entries define the shape of the RBFs. (Another important parameter is the mean μ, which defines the position of a Gaussian kernel. In designing SVMs, means are chosen by placing the kernels at the data points.) The choice of the design parameters *d* and Σ is experimental: train the SVM for different values of *d* and Σ, estimate the VC dimension, and select the model with the lowest VC dimension (Vapnik 1995). ∎

Box 2.1 summarizes the design steps for training an SVM. The SV training works almost perfectly for not too large data bases. However, when the number of data points is large (say $l > 2000$), the quadratic programming problem becomes

Box 2.1
Design Steps in Support Vector Machine Training

Step 1. Select the kernel function that determines the shape of the decision function in classification problems or the regression function in regression problems.

Step 2. Select the shape (the smoothing parameter) of the kernel function (e.g., the polynomial degree for polynomials or the variance of the Gaussian RBF for RBF kernels.

Step 3. Choose the penalty factor C, and select the desired accuracy by defining the insensitivity zone ε.

Step 4. Solve the quadratic programming problem in l variables (classification) or $2l$ variables (regression).

---

extremely difficult to solve with standard methods. For example, a training set of 50,000 examples amounts to a Hessian matrix $\mathbf{H}$ with 2.5×10^9 (2.5 billion) elements. Using an eight-byte floating-point representation would require $20,000 \text{ MB} = 20 \text{ GB}$ of memory (Osuna, Freund, and Girosi 1997). This cannot be easily fit into the memory of standard computers at present, and this is the single basic disadvantage of the SVM method. Three approaches resolve the quadratic programming problem for large data sets. Vapnik (1995) proposed the *chunking method*, which is a decomposition approach. Another decomposition approach was proposed by Osuna et al. (1997). The sequential minimal optimization algorithm (Platt 1998) is of a different character; it seems to be an error backpropagation algorithm for SVM learning. These various techniques are not covered in detail here. The interested reader can consult the mentioned references or investigate an alternative linear programming approach presented in section 5.3.4.

Problems

2.1. Three co-linear points are given in figure P2.1. Show graphically all possible labelings and separations by an indicator function $i_F(\mathbf{x}, \mathbf{w}) = \text{sign}(u)$ represented by an oriented straight line $u = 0$.

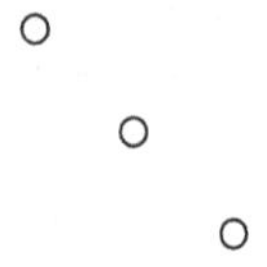

o

    o

      o

Figure P2.1
Graph for problem 2.1.

2.2. Two different sets comprising four points each are given in figure P2.2. For each set, show graphically all possible labelings and separations by an indicator function $i_F(\mathbf{x}, \mathbf{w}) = \text{sign}(u)$ represented by an oriented straight line $u = 0$.

2.3. In figure 2.10, it was shown how an indicator function $i_F(\mathbf{x}, \mathbf{w}) = \text{sign}(\sin(wx))$ having one parameter only can separate any number l of randomly labeled points. This shows that a VC dimension of this specific indicator function is infinite. However, check whether $i_F(\mathbf{x}, \mathbf{w}) = \text{sign}(\sin(wx))$ can separate the four equally spaced points given in figure P2.3.

2.4. The graphs in figure P2.4 represent three different one-dimensional classification (dichotomization) tasks. What is the lowest-order polynomial decision function that can correctly classify the given data? Black dots denote class 1 with targets $y_1 = +1$, and white dots depict class 2 with targets $y_2 = -1$. What are the decision boundaries?

Figure P2.2
Graphs for problem 2.2.

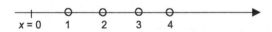

Figure P2.3
Graph for problem 2.3.

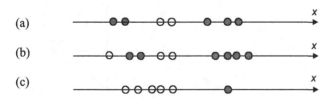

Figure P2.4
Graphs for problems 2.4 and 2.5.

2.5. If you wanted to classify the three data sets shown in figure P2.4 using SVMs with Gaussian basis functions, how many hidden layer neurons would you need for each problem?

2.6. What is the lowest-order polynomial that can classify (shatter) any possible labeling of l one-dimensional data points? Support your answer with a graph for two, three, and four data points.

2.7. The graphs in figure P2.5 show different binary classification problems when the patterns are one-, two-, and three-dimensional. Draw both decision boundaries and discriminant (decision) functions, and comment whether the given examples are linearly separable or not. Circles denote class 1 with targets $y_1 = +1$, and squares depict class 2 with targets $y_2 = -1$.

2.8. Define the VC dimension of the following two sets of functions:

a. $f(x, \mathbf{w}) = w_0 + w_1 \sin(x) + w_2 \sin(2x) + w_3 \sin(3x)$.

b. $f(x, \mathbf{w}) = w_0 + w_1 \sin(x) + w_2 \sin(2x) + w_3 \sin(w_4 x)$.

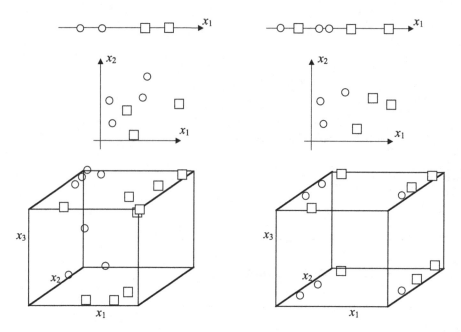

Figure P2.5
Graphs for problem 2.7.

(*Hint:* First find out whether the set is linear with respect to weights, and then use the statements made in the chapter about the VC dimension.)

2.9. Determine the VC dimension of the set of indicator functions defined by quadric functions (conics) in $\Re^2$. In particular, find it for circles, ellipses, and hyperbolas in $\Re^2$.

2.10. Find the distance from a point $\mathbf{x}$ to a (hyper)plane. Check your result in (a) graphically.

a. $\mathbf{x} = \begin{bmatrix} 0 & 1 \end{bmatrix}^T$, a plane or hyperplane is a straight line $y = x$.

b. $\mathbf{x} = \begin{bmatrix} -2 & 2 & 3 \end{bmatrix}^T$, a plane or hyperplane is a plane $z = x + y + 3$.

c. $\mathbf{x} = \begin{bmatrix} 1 & 1 & 1 & 1 & 1 \end{bmatrix}^T$, a hyperplane is $x_1 - x_2 + x_3 - x_4 + x_5 + 1 = 0$.

2.11. Two different one-dimensional classification tasks are given in the following tables. Draw the two-class data points in an (x, y) plane. (Draw two separate graphs.) Find analytically and sketch the optimal canonical hyperplanes belonging to these two classification tasks. Determine the equations for decision boundaries. (*Hint:* Identify the SVs first; the OCSH is defined by them.)

a. x	$y = d$		b. x	$y = d$
2	1		3	1
−1	−1		1	−1
−2	−1		−1	−1
1	1			

2.12. Two one-dimensional data shown in figure P2.6 should be classified by applying the first-order polynomial as given in table 2.1. Solve (2.81) for $\boldsymbol{\alpha}$, and find the decision function. (*Hint:* $K = \begin{bmatrix} 2 & 0; 0 & 2 \end{bmatrix}$. Maximize L_d.)

2.13. Solve problem P2.12 by applying B-spline functions as shown in figure P2.7. (*Hint:* Find K (the **G** matrix) and maximize L_d.)

2.14. Three different binary classification problems are given in figure P2.8. Calculate the OCSH for each problem. (*Hint:* Identify SVs. Find the maximal margin M.

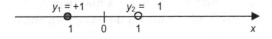

Figure P2.6
Graph for problem 2.12.

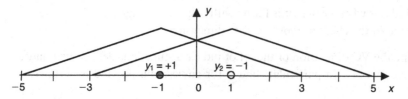

Figure P2.7
Graph for problem 2.13.

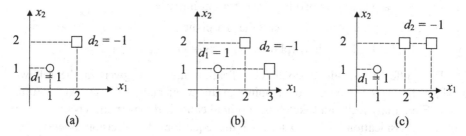

Figure P2.8
Graphs for problem 2.14.

Use (2.49) to find w_i and b. After deriving equations for the OCSHs, check their correctness by plugging in the SV coordinates.)

2.15. Calculate the Hessian matrices $\mathbf{H}$ required in problem 2.14 for the maximization of a dual Lagrangian.

2.16. Example 2.1 shows a mapping of a three-dimensional input vector $\mathbf{x}$ into second-order polynomials. Find a mapping of a two-dimensional input vector $\mathbf{x} = [x_1 \quad x_2]^T$ into third-order polynomials. Show the resulting SVM graphically.

2.17. Example 2.2 shows how the XOR problem can be solved by applying Gaussian RBF kernels and a polynomial of the second-order kernel. The XOR problem solved is given as $\mathbf{x}_1 = [0 \quad 0]^T$, $d_1 = +1$, $\mathbf{x}_2 = [1 \quad 1]^T$, $d_2 = +1$, $\mathbf{x}_3 = [1 \quad 0]^T$, $d_3 = -1$, and $\mathbf{x}_4 = [0 \quad 1]^T$, $d_4 = -1$. In calculating the Hessian matrix $\mathbf{H}$ a polynomial kernel $K(\mathbf{x}, \mathbf{x}_i) = [\mathbf{x}^T\mathbf{x}_i + 1]^2$ was applied. Find the Hessian matrix $\mathbf{H}$ for a polynomial kernel $K(\mathbf{x}, \mathbf{x}_i) = [\mathbf{x}^T\mathbf{x}_i]^2$, and explain the differences. Why is a kernel $K(\mathbf{x}, \mathbf{x}_i) = [\mathbf{x}^T\mathbf{x}_i + 1]^2$ preferred? Find the Hessian matrix applying the third-order polynomial kernel $K(\mathbf{x}, \mathbf{x}_i) = [\mathbf{x}^T\mathbf{x}_i + 1]^3$.

2.18. Find the maximum of the function $f(\mathbf{x}) = x_1^2 + 4x_2^2$ subject to the constraint $x_1 + 2x_2 = 6$. Use the technique of Lagrange multipliers.

2.19. Verify the validity of KKT theorem in finding the maximum of the function $f(\mathbf{x}) = -x_1^2 - x_2^2$ subject to the constraints

$2x_1 + x_2 \geq 2,$

$2x_1 + x_2 \leq 8, \qquad x_1 \geq 0, \qquad x_2 \geq 0,$

$x_1 + x_2 \leq 6.$

2.20. Using the KKT stationary conditions, find the minimum of the function $f(\mathbf{x}) = (x_1 - 1)^2 + (x_2 - 2)^2$, subject to the following constraints. Check your answer graphically.

$x_2 - x_1 = 1.$

$x_1 + x_2 \leq 2.$

$x_1 \geq 0, \qquad x_2 \geq 0.$

2.21. Derive equation (2.11), which describes the decomposition of the expected risk (2.10). (*Hint:* Add and subtract the regression function to the squared error on the right-hand side of (2.10), and continue devising the final decomposed expression (2.11).)

Simulation Experiments

The simulation experiments in chapter 2 have the purpose of familiarizing the reader with support vector machines. Two programs cover classification and regression (`svclass.m` and `svregress.m`) by applying the SVM technique in the MATLAB 5 or MATLAB 6 version. There is no need for a manual here because both programs are user-friendly. The experiments are aimed particularly at understanding basic concepts in the SVM field: support vectors, decision functions, decision boundaries, indicator functions, and canonical hyperplanes. One- and two-dimensional patterns (classification) and $\Re^1 \to \Re^1$ mappings (regression) are employed for ease of visualization.

You should meticulously analyze all resulting graphs, which nicely display difficult-to-understand basic concepts and terminology used in the SVM field. Be aware of the following facts about the programs `svclass.m` and `svregress.m`.

1. They are developed for classification and regression tasks, respectively.

2. They are designed for one-dimensional and two-dimensional classification and one-dimensional regression problems.

3. They are user-friendly, even for beginners in using MATLAB, but you must cooperate. They prompt you to select, to define, or to choose different things.

Experiment with the program `svclass.m` as follows:

1. Launch MATLAB.

2. Connect to directory `learnsc` (at the `matlab` prompt, type `cd learnsc` ⟨RETURN⟩). `learnsc` is a subdirectory of `matlab`, as `bin`, `toolbox`, and `uitools` are. While typing `cd learnsc`, make sure that your working directory is `matlab`, not `matlab/bin`, for example.

3. Type `start` ⟨RETURN⟩. This will start the program. Choose SVM. Choose Classification.

4. The pop-up menu will prompt you to decide about the number of training data in a class. You will be prompted to choose data with overlapping or without over-lapping in the first example only.

5. You will obtain two graphs. The first graph shows support vectors and decision boundaries obtained by an SVM and by the LMS method (dashed). The second graph shows many other important concepts such as decision functions, indicator functions, and canonical planes. For one-dimensional inputs, you will obtain a canonical straight line and your decision boundary will be a point. Rotate figure 2 to find an angle when all important concepts are shown in a three-dimensional view.

There are 12 different prepared one- and two-dimensional training data sets. You may add several more. The first seven examples are for application of linear (hard and soft) margin classifiers. Cases 10–15 are one- or two-dimensional examples of non-linear classification with polynomial kernels or RBFs with Gaussian basis functions.

Experiment with the program `svregress` as follows:

1. Launch MATLAB.

2. Connect to directory `learnsc` (at the `matlab` prompt, type `cd learnsc` ⟨RETURN⟩). `learnsc` is a subdirectory of `matlab` as `bin`, `toolbox`, and `uitools` are. While typing `cd learnsc`, make sure that your working directory is `Matlab`, not `matlab/bin`, for example.

3. Type `start` ⟨RETURN⟩. Choose SVM. Choose Regression. This will start a pop-up menu to select one out of three demo examples. The program can generate a lin-ear or a nonlinear regression model. In the case of nonlinear regression, an SVM uses Gaussian (RBF) kernels. You will be prompted to define the shape (width) of the

Gaussians by defining the coefficient ks. The standard deviation of Gaussian kernels $\sigma = ks^*\Delta c$, where Δc stands for a distance between the two adjacent centers. Using $ks < 1$ results in narrow basis functions without much overlapping and with poor results.

Now perform various experiments (start with prepared examples), changing a few design parameters. Run repeatedly the same example, experimenting with different parameters. For instance, change SV insensitivity ε, SVM margin upper bound C (default = inf), or the width of Gaussian basis functions (kernels). The general advice in performing such a multivariate choice of parameters is to change only *one* parameter at time.

Again, meticulously analyze all resulting graphs after each simulation run. Many useful geometrical objects are shown that depict intricate theoretical concepts.

You are now ready to define your own one- and two-dimensional data sets for classification or one-dimensional functions for linear or nonlinear regression by applying SVMs.

3 Single-Layer Networks

This chapter describes two classical neurons, or neural network structures—the *perceptron* and the *linear neuron*, or *adaline* (adaptive linear neuron). They differ in origin and were developed by researchers from rather different fields, namely, neurophysiology and engineering. Frank Rosenblatt's perceptron was a model aimed to solve visual perception tasks or to perform a kind of pattern recognition tasks. In mathematical terms, it resulted from the solution of the classification problem. Bernard Widrow's adaline originated from the field of signal processing or, more specifically, from the adaptive noise cancellation problem. The mathematical problem of learning was solved by finding the regression hyperplane on which the trajectories of the inputs and outputs from the adaline should lie. This hyperplane is defined by the coefficients (weights) of the noise canceller (linear filter, adaline) that should be learnt.

The roots of both the perceptron and the adaline were in the linear domain. The perceptron is the simplest yet powerful classifier providing the *linear separability* of class patterns or examples. The adaline is the best regression solution if the relationship between the input and output signals is linear or can be treated as such. It also provides the best classification solution when the decision boundary is linear.

However, in real life we are faced with nonlinear problems, and the perceptron was superseded by more sophisticated and powerful neuron and neural network structures. But traces of it can be recognized in a popular neural network used today—the multilayer perceptron with its hidden layer of neurons with sigmoidal activation functions (AFs). These AFs are nothing but softer versions of the original perceptron's hard limiting or threshold activation function.

An even more important connection between the classical and the modern perceptrons may be found in their learning algorithms. This chapter extensively discusses this important concept of learning and related algorithms. Learning is a cornerstone of the whole soft computing field, but here it results from more heuristic arguments than those presented in chapter 2. Additionally, the concepts of decision lines and decision surfaces are discussed here. Their geometrical significance and their connections with the perceptron's weights are explained. Graphical presentations and explanations of low (two)-dimensional classification problems should ensure a sound understanding of the learning process. Typical problems in the soft computing field are of much higher order, but the insights given by two-dimensional problems will be of great use because in high-dimensional patterns one can no longer visualize decision surfaces. However, the algorithms developed for the classification of two-dimensional patterns remain the same.

The adaline being a neuron with a simple linear AF, it is still in widespread use. Equipped with a simple yet powerful learning law, it is a part of both neural networks and fuzzy models. Typically, these linear neurons are the units in the output layer of the neural networks or fuzzy models. The linear AF has an important property: it is the simplest differentiable function, and thus one can construct an error function or cost function dependent on adaline weights. Learning is the name for the algorithm that adapts and changes the weights vectors in order to minimize the error function. As well known from the classical optimization field, this minimization can be achieved by using first or second derivatives of the cost function in respect to the parameters (weights) that should be optimized. This scheme is simple, given the differentiable activation function. The linear AF possesses this nice property. Although such learning is simple in idea, there are different ways to find the best weights that will minimize the error function (see section 3.2).

3.1   The Perceptron

The perceptron was one of the first processing elements that was able to learn. At the time of its invention the problem of learning was a difficult and unsolved task, and the very idea of autonomous adapting of weights using data pairs (examples, patterns, measurements, records, observations, digital images) was a very exciting one. Learning was an iterative *supervised learning* paradigm.

In such a supervised adapting scheme, the first or initial random weights vector $\mathbf{w}_1$ is chosen and the perceptron is given a randomly chosen data pair (input features vector $\mathbf{x}_1$) and desired output d_1. The perceptron learning algorithm is an *error-correction rule* that changes the weights proportional to the error $e_1 = d_1 - o_1$ between the actual output o_1 and the desired output d_1. After the new weights vector is calculated according to the simple rule $\mathbf{w}_2 = \mathbf{w}_1 + \Delta\mathbf{w}_1 = \mathbf{w}_1 + \eta(d_1 - o_1)\mathbf{x}_1$, the next data pair is drawn randomly from the data set and the whole scheme is repeated. Constant η is called the *learning rate*. It determines the magnitude of the change $\Delta\mathbf{w}$ but not its direction. Here, with the classical perceptron, η does not have a big impact on learning, but because it is an important part of the more sophisticated error-correction learning schemes, it is given explicitly. Here, with perceptron learning, it can be set to 1. The reader may investigate the influence of the learning rate η on the weight-adapting process. Some time may be saved in believing the claim that with larger η the number of training iteration steps increases.

Such a weight-adapting procedure is an iterative one and should gradually reduce the error to zero. The classical perceptron attempted to recognize and classify patterns autonomously and was very successful given that the two classes of patterns were *linearly separable*. The concept of linear separability is an important one, and it is given in detail later. Let us first analyze the mathematical model and the graphical representation of the perceptron.

The computing scheme of the perceptron is a simple one. Given the input vector $\mathbf{x}$, it computes a weighted sum of its components

$$u = \sum_{i=1}^{n+1} w_i x_i = w_1 x_1 + w_2 x_2 + \cdots + w_n x_n + w_{n+1} x_{n+1} \tag{3.1}$$

and produces an output of $+1$ if u is positive; otherwise, an output of -1 results. (The last entry of $\mathbf{x}$ is not the feature component of the input pattern but the constant input $x_{n+1} = +1$ called *bias*.

In mathematical terms, the output from a perceptron is given by

$$o = \mathrm{sign}(u) = \mathrm{sign}\left(\sum_{i=1}^{n+1} w_i x_i\right). \tag{3.2}$$

Sign stands for the signum function (known also as the Heaviside function.)

$$\mathrm{sign}(u) = \begin{cases} +1 & \text{for } u > 0, \\ -1 & \text{for } u < 0, \end{cases} \tag{3.3}$$

and its standard graphical representation is given by a hard limiting threshold function that can be seen inside the neuron in figure 3.1. (The argument $u = 0$ of the signum function is a kind of singular point in the sense that its value can be chosen. Here, if $u = 0$, the output from the perceptron is taken as $o = +1$.)

Because it is not evident, the following point deserves comment. Vector $\mathbf{x}$ comprises the features component x_i ($i = 1, \ldots, n$), and the constant input component $x_{n+1} = +1$. ($x_{n+1} = -1$ may be used, too. The sign of this constant input is not

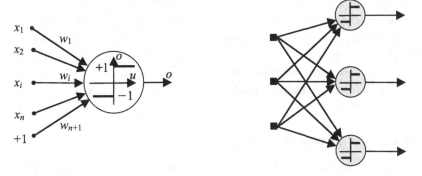

Figure 3.1
Single perceptron and single-layer perceptron network.

important. Its real impact will be taken into account in the sign of the weight w_{n+1}.) In the neural networks field this component is known as *bias, offset,* or *threshold.* These three terms may be used interchangeably. Thus, in this book (unless stated otherwise) the $(n+1)$-dimensional input vector $\mathbf{x}$ and its corresponding weights vector $\mathbf{w}$, connecting the input vector $\mathbf{x}$ with the (neural) processing unit, are defined as the following column vectors:

$$\mathbf{x} = [x_1 \quad x_2 \quad \cdots \quad x_n \quad +1]^T. \tag{3.4}$$

$$\mathbf{w} = [w_1 \quad w_2 \quad \cdots \quad w_n \quad w_{n+1}]^T. \tag{3.5}$$

Thus, both $\mathbf{x}$ and $\mathbf{w}$ will almost always be augmented by $+1$ and w_{n+1}, respectively, and the argument u of the signum function can be rewritten as

$$u = \mathbf{w}^T\mathbf{x} = \mathbf{x}^T\mathbf{w}. \tag{3.6}$$

Note that the choice of $\mathbf{x}$ and $\mathbf{w}$ as column vectors is deliberate. They could have been chosen differently. Actually, the notation will soon change so that a weights vector will be written as a row vector. Such choices of notation should be natural ones in the sense that they should ensure easier vector-matrix manipulations; and they are not of paramount importance. However, it is important to realize that (3.1), or its vector notation (3.6), represents the scalar (or dot) product of $\mathbf{x}$ and $\mathbf{w}$, that is, the result of this multiplication is a scalar.

If $\mathbf{w}$ had been defined as a row vector, (3.6) would have had the following form:

$$u = \mathbf{w}\mathbf{x} = \mathbf{x}^T\mathbf{w}^T. \tag{3.7}$$

(3.7) results in the same single scalar value for u as (3.6) does. In another words, the whole input vector $\mathbf{x}$, after being weighted by $\mathbf{w}$, is transformed into one single number that is the argument u of the activation function of a perceptron.

The activation function of a perceptron is a hard limiting threshold or signum function, and depending on whether u is positive or negative, the output of a perceptron will be $+1$ or -1, respectively. Remember that the perceptron is aimed at solving classification tasks; by prohibiting its output from having a value of 0, one basically throws out from the training data set all training patterns whose correct classification is unknown.

3.1.1 The Geometry of Perceptron Mapping

The first question at this point may be, in terms of learning, or solving classification tasks, what does this simple mathematical operation—finding the inner product and then taking the sign of the resulting single scalar—represent?

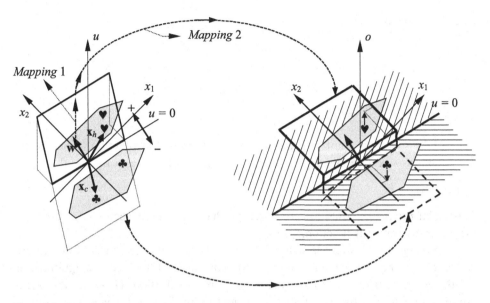

Figure 3.2
Geometry of perceptron mapping.

Let us analyze the geometry of these two operations. Suppose one wants to classify two linearly separable classes, represented in figure 3.2 as hearts (class 1) and clubs (class 2). In this case, (3.1), or (3.6), represents the plane u in a three-dimensional space (x_1, x_2, u):

$$w_1 x_1 + w_2 x_2 - u + w_3 = 0, \tag{3.8}$$

or

$$u(\mathbf{x}) = \begin{bmatrix} w_1 & w_2 \end{bmatrix} \begin{bmatrix} x_1 \\ x_2 \end{bmatrix} + w_3 = \mathbf{w}^T \mathbf{x} + w_3, \tag{3.9}$$

where $\mathbf{w}$ stands for the weights vector. The equation $u(\mathbf{x}) = 0$ defines the *decision boundary*, or *separation line*, that separates the two classes. In the case of data having only two features (x_1, x_2), the discriminant function is the straight line

$$x_2 = -\frac{w_1}{w_2} x_1 - \frac{w_3}{w_2}. \tag{3.10}$$

Note the geometry of the classification task in figure 3.2, where the plane u divides two classes passing through the origin in feature or pattern space. In this case, w_3 is equal to zero ($w_3 = 0$), and the linear discriminant function, represented in figure 3.2

by a thick line, is given by

$$x_2 = -\frac{w_1}{w_2} x_1, \tag{3.11}$$

or

$$\mathbf{w}^T \mathbf{x} = 0. \tag{3.12}$$

Let us take two data points, $\mathbf{x}_1$ and $\mathbf{x}_2$, on the discriminant function. (The vectors $\mathbf{x}_1$, $\mathbf{x}_2$ and $(\mathbf{x}_1 - \mathbf{x}_2)$ are not represented in fig. 3.2.) From (3.12) it follows that

$$\mathbf{w}^T(\mathbf{x}_1 - \mathbf{x}_2) = 0. \tag{3.13}$$

This scalar product is equal to zero, meaning that the weights vector $\mathbf{w}$ is normal to the linear discriminant function.

Some things are apparent in figure 3.2. First, the weights vector $\mathbf{w}$ and the feature vector $\mathbf{x}$ lie in the very same feature (x_1, x_2) plane. Second, the actual magnitude (or length) of vector $\mathbf{w}$ does not have any impact on classification. However, the orientation or direction of this weights vector is important. The vector $\mathbf{w}$ is normal (perpendicular) to the discriminant line and always points to the *positive side* of the u plane. Thus, the scalar product of $\mathbf{w}$ and any vector $\mathbf{x}$ belonging to hearts, or class 1, will always be positive, $u > 0$. The resulting output from the perceptron $o = \mathrm{sign}(u)$ will be $+1$. (On the right-hand side of fig. 3.2 this is shown by the small upward arrow above the heart.) Note, too, that the magnitude of u (and u is an argument of the activation function of the perceptron) is not relevant. This is the most significant feature of the signum function. It maps the whole positive semiplane u (or the positive part of the u-axis of the perceptron's AF) into one single number, $+1$. In this way, the whole semiplane with the vertical pattern lines in figure 3.2 will be mapped into a single output value from the perceptron $o = +1$. In mathematical terms, two basic mappings for the hearts pattern are taking place inside the perceptron: (3.1) represents mapping 1, and (3.2) represents mapping 2. This can also be said for all patterns $\mathbf{x}$ belonging to clubs, or class 2. They lie in the semiplane with the horizontal pattern lines in figure 3.2. All the class 2 data vectors $\mathbf{x}$ and the weights vector $\mathbf{w}$ point in opposite directions, and their scalar (inner) product is always negative $(u < 0)$. Thus, the perceptron's output for clubs will be $o = -1$. In this way, after learning, the perceptron maps the whole (x_1, x_2) plane into a stairwise surface in three-dimensional space $\{x_1, x_2, u\}$ that can have two values only: $+1$ or -1. In the general case (see fig. 3.3) the arrangement of two classes is such that, after learning, the linear discriminant function will be shifted out of origin. This shift will be enabled by the constant input term $x_{n+1} = +1$ (offset, bias) in input vector $\mathbf{x}$, and it will be

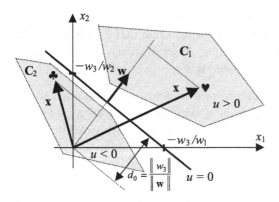

Figure 3.3
Linear decision boundary between two classes.

represented in the weights vector's component w_{n+1}. The distance of the separation line from the origin is

$$d_0 = \frac{\|w_3\|}{\|\mathbf{w}\|}. \tag{3.14}$$

It is easy to show that all hearts lie on the positive side of the u plane. The length of the projection of any pattern vector $\mathbf{x}$ (see (2.45) and (2.46)) onto the line through the origin and weights vector $\mathbf{w}$ is

$$d = \frac{\mathbf{w}^T \mathbf{x}}{\|\mathbf{w}\|}. \tag{3.15}$$

With (3.9) this results in

$$d\|\mathbf{w}\| + w_3 = u(\mathbf{x}). \tag{3.16}$$

For the decision line $u(\mathbf{x}) = 0$, $d = d_0$, $w_3 = -d_0\|\mathbf{w}\|$, and

$$u(\mathbf{x}) = \|\mathbf{w}\|(d - d_0). \tag{3.17}$$

Thus, for all data $\mathbf{x}$ from class 2, u will be always negative, and the corresponding perceptron's output $o = -1$. Similarly, all hearts will result with $o = +1$.

3.1.2 Convergence Theorem and Perceptron Learning Rule

Two questions about the perceptron (or any other neuron) are, What can this simple processing unit represent? and How can it be made to represent it? The first is the problem of representation, discussed in the previous section. The second is the problem of learning. Here, both parts are connected in the sense that a perceptron will always be able to learn what it is able to represent. More precisely, the famous Perceptron Convergence Theorem (Rosenblatt 1962) states,

Given an elementary α-perceptron, a stimulus world W, and any classification $C(W)$ for which a solution exists, let all stimuli W occur in any sequence, provided that each stimulus must reoccur in finite time. Then, beginning from an arbitrary initial state, an error-correction procedure will always yield a solution to $C(W)$ in finite time.

It might be useful to reformulate this theorem in terms used in this book:

Given a single perceptron unit, a set of training data X comprising linearly separable input pattern vectors $\mathbf{x}_i$ and desired outputs d_i, let the training pairs $(\mathbf{x}_i, d_i)$ be drawn randomly from a set X. Then, beginning from an arbitrary initial weights vector $\mathbf{w}_1$, error-correction learning (training, adapting) will always correctly classify data pairs in finite time.

The proof of this important theorem is as follows. If the classes are linearly separable, then there exists the solution weights vector $\mathbf{w}^*$. (Note that this vector is not unique.) The magnitude of this vector does not have any impact on the final classification. Thus, it is convenient to work with a normalized solution vector $\|\mathbf{w}^*\| = 1$, where the scalar product of this vector with any pattern vector $\mathbf{x}$ will be

$$\mathbf{w}^{*T}\mathbf{x} \geq \alpha > 0 \qquad \text{for each } \mathbf{x} \in \mathbf{C}_1,$$
$$\mathbf{w}^{*T}\mathbf{x} \leq -\alpha < 0 \quad \text{for each } \mathbf{x} \in \mathbf{C}_2,$$
$$\tag{3.18}$$

where α is a small positive constant. The scalar product of the solution vector $\mathbf{w}^*$ and any weights vector during learning is given as

$$\mathbf{w}^{*T}\mathbf{w} = \|\mathbf{w}^*\| \, \|\mathbf{w}\| \cos(\varphi) = \|\mathbf{w}\| \cos(\varphi). \tag{3.19}$$

After the first learning step, and starting from $\mathbf{w}_1 = \mathbf{0}$, the scalar product may also be written as

$$\mathbf{w}^{*T}\mathbf{w}_2 = \mathbf{w}^{*T}(\mathbf{w}_1 + \Delta\mathbf{w}) = \mathbf{w}^{*T}(\mathbf{w}_1 + \mathbf{x}_1) = \mathbf{w}^{*T}\mathbf{w}_1 + \mathbf{w}^{*T}\mathbf{x}_1 \geq \alpha. \tag{3.20}$$

Note that the weight increment is calculated as $\Delta\mathbf{w} = \eta\mathbf{x}$, where $\eta = 1$. This is one of a few slightly different forms in which the perceptron learning rule may appear (see box 3.1).

After the second learning step,

$$\mathbf{w}^{*T}\mathbf{w}_3 = \mathbf{w}^{*T}(\mathbf{w}_2 + \mathbf{x}_2) = \mathbf{w}^{*T}\mathbf{w}_2 + \mathbf{w}^{*T}\mathbf{x}_2 \geq 2\alpha. \tag{3.21}$$

Thus, $\mathbf{w}^{*T}\mathbf{w}_{n+1}$ can be written as

$$\mathbf{w}^{*T}\mathbf{w}_{n+1} \geq n\alpha. \tag{3.22}$$

From the Cauchy-Schwarz inequality, and taking into account $\|\mathbf{w}^*\| = 1$, it follows that

$$(\mathbf{w}^{*T}\mathbf{w}_{n+1})^2 \leq \|\mathbf{w}^*\|^2 \|\mathbf{w}_{n+1}\|^2 \leq \|\mathbf{w}_{n+1}\|^2, \tag{3.23}$$

or

$$\|\mathbf{w}_{n+1}\|^2 \geq n^2\alpha^2. \tag{3.24}$$

Note that during learning the following is true:

$$\mathbf{w}_2 = \mathbf{w}_1 + \Delta\mathbf{w} = \mathbf{w}_1 + \mathbf{x}_1 = \mathbf{x}_1 \quad \text{if } \mathbf{x}_1 \text{ was misclassified,}$$

$$\mathbf{w}_2 = \mathbf{w}_1 + \Delta\mathbf{w} = \mathbf{w}_1 + \mathbf{0} = \mathbf{0} \quad \text{if } \mathbf{x}_1 \text{ was correctly classified (recall } \mathbf{w}_1 = \mathbf{0}),$$

or

$$\|\mathbf{w}_2\|^2 \leq \|\mathbf{x}_1\|^2. \tag{3.25}$$

Similarly, it can be written that for any value of $\mathbf{w}$ during the learning process or generally,

$$\|\mathbf{w}_{n+1}\|^2 \leq \sum_{k=1}^{n} \|\mathbf{x}_k\|^2. \tag{3.26}$$

If the pattern vector $\mathbf{x}$ is defined with maximal norm

$$\beta = \max_{\mathbf{x} \in X} \|\mathbf{x}\|^2, \tag{3.27}$$

(3.26) can be rewritten as

$$\|\mathbf{w}_{n+1}\|^2 \leq n\beta. \tag{3.28}$$

Hence, the squared Euclidean norm of the weights vector increases linearly at most with the number of iterations n. Equations (3.24) and (3.28) are contradictory, and after sufficiently large values of iteration steps n, they can and will be satisfied at some N_{max}-th iteration step when the equality sign holds:

$$N_{max}^2\alpha^2 = N_{max}\beta \Rightarrow N_{max} = \frac{\beta}{\alpha^2}. \tag{3.29}$$

Thus, the number of learning steps cannot grow indefinitely, and training must converge in a finite number of steps. This maximal number of learning steps N_{max} depends on the learning rate η and the initial weights vector $\mathbf{w}_1$, and on the generally random sequence of training patterns submitted. The convergence theorem is valid for any number of classes provided that all are mutually linearly separable.

There are a few more characteristics of the perceptron's learning process to consider. Let us start with a classification task that can be solved according to the given convergence theorem.

The two classes shown in figure 3.4 are said to be linearly separable because there is no overlapping of data points and the decision boundary that separates these two classes is a straight line. In mathematical terms, this classification task is an *ill-posed problem* in the sense that the number of solutions to this problem is infinite. According to the perceptron convergence theorem, once learning is completed, the resulting decision boundary will be any line that separates these two classes. Figure 3.4 shows three out of an infinite number of possible straight lines that would solve the problem. Visual inspection would suggest that line b might eventually be the best solution.

However, the perceptron learning does not optimize a solution. The final weights vector does not result from any optimization task. During learning no attempt is

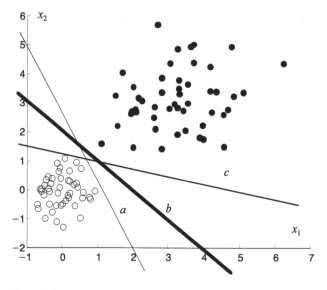

Figure 3.4
Simple data set consisting of two linearly separable classes drawn from two normal distributions: $\mathbf{C}_1$, void circles, 50 data, $\mu_1 = (0,0)$, $\sigma_1 = 0.5$; $\mathbf{C}_2$, solid circles, 50 data, $\mu_2 = (3,3)$, $\sigma_1 = 1$.

made to minimize any cost or error function. The objective is only to find the line that separates two linearly separable classes. As soon as the first solution weights vector $\mathbf{w}^*$, which separates *all the data pairs* correctly, is found, there will be no further changes of the vector $\mathbf{w}^*$. This vector will not be optimal in the sense that some predefined error function would take some minimal value for this particular $\mathbf{w}^*$. Simply, there was no predefined error function during learning.

Let us discuss the relation between class labeling and both the resulting decision boundary and the weights vector $\mathbf{w}^*$ that defines this line of separation between classes. Clearly, how labels are assigned to classes must not affect the classification results. Figure 3.5 shows two classes, hearts and clubs, that are to be classified. The resulting decision boundary between these two classes is defined by

$$u(\mathbf{x}) = 0 \tag{3.30}$$

The left graph shows the resulting decision plane u when the desired value $+1$ was assigned to class 1, and correspondingly, the desired value of class 2 was -1. The labeling in the right graph is opposite to the first one, and so is the resulting decision plane. But the labeling does not affect the decision boundary between the classes or the position of the resulting weights vector $\mathbf{w}^*$, which is always perpendicular to the decision boundary. However, the direction of $\mathbf{w}^*$ does change. This weights vector $\mathbf{w}^*$ always points in the positive direction of the plane u. Because this positive (negative) part of the u plane depends upon the labeling of the classes, so does the orientation of the weights vector $\mathbf{w}^*$.

The learning algorithm of a single perceptron is an *on-line* or *pattern-based* procedure. This recursive technique, organized in training sequences, is shown in box 3.1.

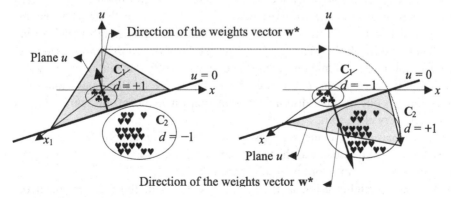

Figure 3.5
Influence of class labeling on perceptron learning results.

Box 3.1
Summary of Perceptron Learning

Given is a set of P measured data pairs that are used for training:

$X = \{\mathbf{x}_j, d_j, j = 1, \ldots, P\}$,

consisting of an input pattern vector $\mathbf{x}$ and output desired response d.

$\mathbf{x} = [x_1 \quad x_2 \quad \ldots \quad x_n \quad +1]^T$, $\quad \mathbf{w} = [w_1 \quad w_2 \quad \ldots \quad w_n \quad w_{n+1}]^T$.

Perform the following training steps for $p = 1, 2, 3, \ldots, P$:

Step 1. Choose the learning rate $\eta > 0$ and initial weights vector $\mathbf{w}_1$. ($\mathbf{w}_1$ can be random or $\mathbf{w}_1 = 0$.)

Step 2. Apply the next (the first one for $p = 1$) training pair $(\mathbf{x}_p, d_p)$ to the perceptron, and using (3.1) and (3.2), find the perceptron's output for the data pair applied and the given weights vector $\mathbf{w}$.

Step 3. Find the error, and adapt the weights vector $\mathbf{w}$ using one of the two most popular methods:

$e_p = d_p - o_p$.

Method 1: $\mathbf{w}_{p+1} = \mathbf{w}_p + \Delta \mathbf{w}_p = \mathbf{w}_p + \eta(d_p - o_p)\mathbf{x}_p$,

or

Method 2: $\mathbf{w}_{p+1} = \mathbf{w}_p + \Delta \mathbf{w}_p = \mathbf{w}_p + \eta \mathbf{x}_p$ if $o \neq d$, $\quad \mathbf{w}_{p+1} = \mathbf{w}_p$ otherwise.

Step 4. Stop the adaptation of the weights if $e = 0$ for *all* data pairs. Otherwise go back to step 2.

In this variant of learning the training data pairs, consisting of the input pattern and desired output $(\mathbf{x}_n, d_n)$, are considered in sequence or selected at random from the training data set X. Perceptron output and error as well as weight changes are reevaluated at each learning step. Learning stops at the first $\mathbf{w}^*$ that classifies *all patterns* perfectly. Here, *perfectly* means that there will be no misclassified pattern after training. In accordance with the perceptron convergence theorem, when the data are linearly separable, this $\mathbf{w}^*$ will be reached in a finite number of learning steps. Note that this solution is not unique and that the word *optimal* is not used here. In figure 3.4 all three discriminant functions perfectly classify the data from two given classes, but it is clear that line b separates classes 1 and 2 better then lines a and c do. There actually is one optimal discriminant function (in L_2 norm) in figure 3.4, and line b is very, very close to it.

One may occasionally come across slightly different expressions for the weight changes $\Delta \mathbf{w}_p$ in the literature, but the two given as methods 1 and 2 in box 3.1 are the most commonly used, and both methods work well.

Adaptation of weights using method 1 in box 3.1 is in the form of an error-correction rule that changes the weights proportional to the error $e = d - o$ between the actual output o and the desired output d. This rule is an interesting one. The

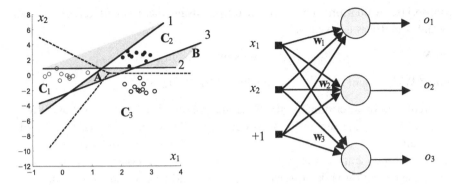

Figure 3.6
Classification of three linearly separable classes consisting of data drawn from three normal distributions (ten data in each class).

weight change $\Delta\mathbf{w}_p$ is determined by three components: learning rate η, error signal e, and actual input $\mathbf{x}$ to the perceptron. Here, for the perceptron, the error signal is equal to the *actual error e*, but in the error back propagation algorithm, presented in chapter 4, this error signal is not generally equal to the actual error and is instead called *delta*. Later, a very similar learning rule is obtained as a result of the *minimization of some predefined cost or error function*.

Note that the learning preceding rule is in a form that is exact for a single perceptron having one scalar-valued output o. Therefore the desired output d is also a scalar variable. But the algorithm is also valid for a single-layer perceptron network as given in figures 3.1 and 3.6. When perceptrons are organized and connected as a network, the only change is that the actual and desired outputs $\mathbf{o}$ and $\mathbf{d}$ are then vectors. Furthermore, with more than one perceptron unit (neuron), there will be more weights vectors $\mathbf{w}$ connecting input $\mathbf{x}$ with each neuron in an output layer. These vectors can be arranged in a weights matrix $\mathbf{W}$ consisting of row (or column) vectors $\mathbf{w}$.

To be more specific, let us analyze a single-layer perceptron network for the classification of three linearly separable classes as given in figure 3.6. A weights matrix $\mathbf{W}$ is comprised of three weights vectors. As stated earlier, they can be arranged as row vectors or as column vectors. If $\mathbf{x}$ and $\mathbf{d}$ are column vectors, the following arrangements of a weights matrix can be made:

$$\mathbf{W} = \begin{bmatrix} \mathbf{w}_1 \\ \mathbf{w}_2 \\ \mathbf{w}_3 \end{bmatrix} \qquad \text{(weights vectors are row vectors)}, \qquad (3.31)$$

$$\mathbf{W} = [\mathbf{w}_1 \quad \mathbf{w}_2 \quad \mathbf{w}_3] \quad \text{(weights vectors are column vectors)}. \qquad (3.32)$$

The appropriate evaluation of perceptron output using these two differently composed weights matrices is given as

$$\mathbf{o} = \text{sign}(\mathbf{Wx}) \qquad \text{(for weights matrix as in (3.31))}, \qquad (3.33)$$

$$\mathbf{o} = \text{sign}(\mathbf{x}^T\mathbf{W})^T = \text{sign}(\mathbf{W}^T\mathbf{x}) \quad \text{(for weights matrix as in (3.32))}. \qquad (3.34)$$

Two different sets of discriminant functions are presented in figure 3.6. Solid lines denoted as 1, 2, and 3 are separation lines determined by weights vectors $\mathbf{w}_1, \mathbf{w}_2$, and $\mathbf{w}_3$. The orientation of the dividing (hyper)planes[1] is determined by normal vectors (by the first n components of weights vectors, where n represents the number of features), and their location is determined by the threshold (offset, bias) component of these weights vectors (the $(n + 1)$th component of $\mathbf{w}$; see fig. 3.3). After training, each particular separation line separates its own class from the other two. This kind of nonoptimal splitting of a feature plane results in large areas without decision (the gray patches in the left graph of fig. 3.6). The regions where classification is undefined result from each particular neuron taking care of its class only. For example, region **A** in figure 3.6 is on the negative side of all three discriminant functions. None claims this part of the plane as belonging to any of the three classes. The undefined character of region **B** is of a different kind. In this case, separation lines 2 and 3 claim this territory as belonging to class 2 or 3, respectively. Similar conclusions can be drawn for all other regions without decision.

However, there is a set of discriminant functions in figure 3.6 (dashed lines). They are obtained as the separation lines between classes i and j using the fact that the boundary between classes i and j must be the portion of the (hyper)plane H_{ij} defined by

$$u_i(\mathbf{x}) = u_j(\mathbf{x}), \qquad (3.35)$$

or

$$\mathbf{w}_i^T\mathbf{x} + w_{3i} - \mathbf{w}_j^T\mathbf{x} - w_{3j} = 0. \qquad (3.36)$$

The dashed lines in figure 3.6 follow from (3.36).

What is the soft computing part of a perceptron and its learning algorithm? This is the very character of the problem to be solved. The classification task is an ill-posed problem. There are many (in fact, an infinite number of) solutions to this problem, and a perceptron will stop learning as soon as it finds the first weights vector $\mathbf{w}^*$ that correctly separates its particular class from the others. It should be admitted that in choosing a good or better solution there are not too many choices left. One must accept any first-obtained solution, or if not satisfied with it, repeat the learning process while remaining aware that its final outcome cannot be controlled. Later, using a differentiable activation function, some measure of the performance of the learning process will be obtained, and the solutions will become less soft. (It is possible to construct and use a perceptron's error function as well, but this is beyond the scope of this book. Details can be found in Duda and Hart (1973) and Shynk (1990). However, the reader may attempt to solve problems 3.8 and 3.9 related to this issue.)

Example 3.1 This example traces the classification of three linearly separable classes consisting of data drawn from three normal distributions (see fig. 3.7). In order for this example to be tractable, there are just two data in each class. Thus, the characteristic features of a normal distribution are unlikely to be seen. The perceptron network is structured as in figure 3.6.

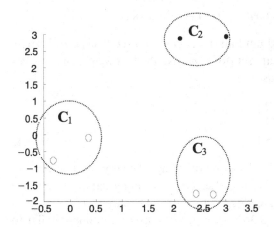

Patterns **x** from three classes, two data per class

0.3456	−0.3793	3.0154	2.1201	2.4170	2.6505
−0.0485	−0.7035	2.9371	2.8806	−1.6612	−1.6842
1.0000	1.0000	1.0000	1.0000	1.0000	1.0000

Desired target values **d**

1	1	−1	−1	−1	−1
−1	−1	1	1	−1	−1
−1	−1	−1	−1	1	1

Figure 3.7
Graph for Example 3.1.

The calculations for the training are as follows.

Initial Random Weights Matrix $\mathbf{W}_1$			Pattern $\mathbf{x}_1$	Output $\mathbf{o}_1$	Error e_1
−0.8789	0.0326	−0.0120	0.3456	1	2
0.8093	−0.3619	−0.4677	−0.0485	−1	0
0.0090	0.9733	−0.8185	1.0000	1	0

Change of Weights Matrix $\Delta\mathbf{W}_1$ after the First Pattern Presented			New Weights Matrix $\mathbf{W}_2$		
0.6912	−0.0970	2.0000	−0.1877	−0.0644	1.9880
0	0	0	0.8093	−0.3619	−0.4677
0	0	0	0.0090	0.9733	−0.8185

These calculations should be repeated until all the data are correctly classified. Here, after cycling four times through the data set (four *epochs*), the first weights matrix $\mathbf{W}^*$ that achieved perfect classification was

$$\mathbf{W}^* = \begin{bmatrix} -5.5274 & -6.0355 & 1.9880 \\ 2.0060 & 8.8347 & -0.4677 \\ 0.3295 & -5.4094 & -4.8185 \end{bmatrix}.$$

Note that further cycling through the data cannot change the very first correct $\mathbf{W}^*$. The perceptron learning rule stops adapting after all the training data are correctly separated ($\Delta\mathbf{w}(i, j) = 0$). By using weights vectors of each particular perceptron (rows of $\mathbf{W}$) in equations (3.17) and (3.36), one can draw separation lines similar to the discriminant functions (solid or dashed) in figure 3.6.

The perceptron learning rule is simple, and its appearance on the scene excited researchers, but not for long. It suffers from severe problems: it cannot separate patterns when there is an overlapping of data or when classes are not linearly separable. Minsky and Papert (1969) devoted a whole book to perceptron problems and proved mathematically that a single-layer perceptron cannot model complex logic functions. They realized that by introducing one more layer (a hidden one), a perceptron can represent the simple XOR problem, but at that point there was no method for weight adaptation (learning) in such a layered structure. Because of its inability to learn in a multilayered structure, the perceptron, having a hard limiting, not differentiable,

Table 3.1
Logic Functions of Two Variables

x_1	x_2	f_1	f_2	f_3	f_4	f_5	f_6	f_7	f_8	f_9	f_{10}	f_{11}	f_{12}	f_{13}	f_{14}	f_{15}	f_{16}
0	0	0	1	0	1	0	1	0	1	0	1	0	1	0	1	0	1
0	1	0	0	1	1	0	0	1	1	0	0	1	1	0	0	1	1
1	0	0	0	0	0	1	1	1	1	0	0	0	0	1	1	1	1
1	1	0	0	0	0	0	0	0	0	1	1	1	1	1	1	1	1

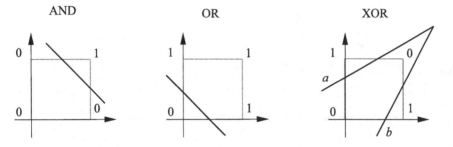

Figure 3.8
Possible partitions for three basic logic functions.

activation function, fell into obscurity, and the whole field of neural computing lost momentum as well.

Let us examine the origins of these troubles, or analyze what a perceptron can do when faced with the simplest logic functions of two variables only. Table 3.1 presents all 16 possible logic functions of two variables (e.g., f_9 is the AND, f_{15} is the OR, and f_7 is the exclusive OR, or XOR, function). Two out of these 16 functions cannot be represented by a perceptron (XOR and the identity function f_{10}). The separability is clear for the three two-dimensional examples presented in figure 3.8, and the problem does not change in higher-dimensional feature spaces. A perceptron can represent only problems that can be solved by linear partitioning a feature (hyper)space into two parts. This is not possible with a single-layer perceptron structure in the cases of functions f_7 and f_{10}. The separation lines in figure 3.8 for AND and OR problems are just two out of an infinite number of lines that can solve these problems. For the XOR problem, neither of the two lines (a or b) can separate the 0's from the 1's. There is no linear solution for this parity problem,[2] but the number of nonlinear separation lines is infinite. One out of many nonlinear discriminant functions for the XOR problem is the piecewise-linear line consisting of lines a and b taken together.

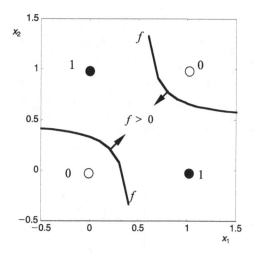

Figure 3.9
Nonlinear discriminant function for the XOR (parity) problem in (x_1, x_2) plane.

However, the XOR problem can be solved by using a perceptron *network*. This can be done by introducing one additional neuron in a special way.

Now, the structure counts. This newly introduced perceptron must be in a hidden layer. It is easy to show this by following a kind of heuristic path.

Note that XOR is a nonlinearly separable problem. Many different nonlinear discriminant functions that separate 1's from 0's can be drawn in a feature plane. Suppose the following one is chosen:

$$f(\mathbf{x}) = x_1 + x_2 - 2x_1 x_2 - \tfrac{1}{3}. \tag{3.37}$$

This separation line is shown in figure 3.9. Function f is a second-order surface with a saddle point, and the orientation of its positive part is denoted by arrows. Replacing the nonlinear part $(x_1 x_2)$ by the new variable

$$x_3 = x_1 x_2, \tag{3.38}$$

(3.37) can be written as

$$f(\mathbf{x}) = x_1 + x_2 - 2x_3 - \tfrac{1}{3}. \tag{3.39}$$

In a new, three-dimensional space (x_1, x_2, x_3), the XOR function f_7 from table 3.1 can be represented as shown in figure 3.10. Note that x_3 is equal to 1 only when both x_1 and x_2 are equal to 1. Clearly, in accordance with the perceptron convergence

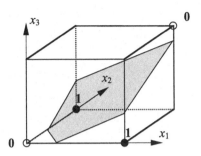

Figure 3.10
Discriminant function for the XOR problem after the introduction of a new variable x_3. Note that the separation "line" is a plane in a new (x_1, x_2, x_3) space.

theorem, a single perceptron having as input variables x_1, x_2, and x_3 will be able to model the XOR function. In three-dimensional space the 1's and the 0's are linearly separable. However, there are two problems at this point.

First, how can one ensure that, in the framework of a neural network, x_3 is permanently supplied? Second, can one learn inside this new structure? The answer to the first part is positive and to the second basically negative. (More than 30 years ago, the second answer was a negative one indeed. Today, with random optimization algorithms, e.g., with the genetic algorithm, one may think about learning in perceptron networks having hidden layers, too. However, at the moment, this is not the focus of interest.)

The signal x_3, which is equal to the nonlinearly obtained $x_3 = x_1 x_2$ from (3.39), can be produced in the following way:

$$x_3 = \text{sign}(x_1 + x_2 - 1.5). \tag{3.40}$$

For the given inputs from table 3.1, the last x_3 is equal to the one obtained in (3.38), avoiding any multiplication. Unlike equation (3.38), (3.40) can be realized by a single perceptron. The resulting perceptron network is shown in figure 3.11.

Thus trying to solve the XOR problem resulted in a perceptron network with a layered structure. It is an important and basic structure in the soft computing field. The most powerful and popular artificial neural networks and fuzzy logic models have the same structure, comprising two layers (hidden and output) of neurons. (The structure of SVMs, shown in fig. 2.24, is the same.) An important fact to notice is that the neuron in the hidden layer is nonlinear. Here, it has a hard limiting activation function, but many others can be used, too. There is no sense in having neural processing units with a linear activation function in the hidden layer because simple

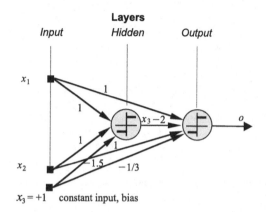

Figure 3.11
Perceptron network with a hidden layer that can solve the XOR problem.

matrix multiplication can restructure such a network into one with input and output layers only. The appearance of the hidden layer (the name is due to Hinton and is borrowed from "hidden Markov chains") is intriguing. It does not have any contact with the outside world; it receives signals from the input layer nodes and sends transformed variables to the output layer neurons. The whole power of neural networks lies in this nonlinear mapping of an $(n + 1)$-dimensional input pattern vector into an m-dimensional imaginary vector, where m denotes the number of hidden layer neurons. This number of hidden layer units is a typical design parameter in the application of neural networks. (This problem is deferred to chapter 4.)

Thus, with a hidden layer, a perceptron can solve the XOR problem. Many other (not necessarily neural or fuzzy) computing schemes can do it, too. The basic question is whether the perceptron learning rule, by using a training data set, can find the right weights. It cannot in its classic form, as presented in box 3.1. After this simple fact was proven by Minsky and Papert (1969), the perceptron and the neural networks field went off the stage. A dark age for neurocomputing had begun. Almost two decades passed before its resurrection in the late 1980s.

There was a simple yet basic reason for the insufficiency of the existing learning rule. The introduction of hidden (imaginary) space, which solves the problem of representation, brought in an even more serious problem of learning a particular set of hidden weights that connect input with the hidden layer of a perceptron. (In fig. 3.11 there are three such weights.) In both methods for adapting perceptron weights (see box 3.1) one needs information about the error at the perceptron output unit caused by a given weights set. With this information, the performance of the specific weights is easy to measure: just compare the desired (or target) output value with the actual output from the network, and in the accordance with the learning law, change the weights. The serious problem with the hidden layer units is that there is no way of knowing what the desired output values from the hidden layer should be for a given input pattern. This is a crucial issue in neurocomputing, or to be more specific, in its learning part. If the desired outputs from the hidden layer units for some particular training data set were known, the adaptation or learning problem would eventually not exist. The same perceptron learning rule for the adaptation of hidden layer weights could be used. The algorithm would remain the same, but there would be two error signals: one for the output layer weights and another for the hidden layer weights (all the weights connected to the output and hidden layer neurons, respectively). At the time of the perceptron there was no algorithm for finding the error signal for hidden layer weights.

The classical approach to this problem is to define some *performance measure* (*error* or *cost function*) for a network that depends upon the weights only, and by changing (adapting, optimizing, learning, training) the weights, try to optimize this performance measure. Depending upon what error function is chosen, optimization may be either minimization (e.g., of sum of error squares or absolute value of error) or maximization (e.g., of maximum likelihood or expectation). With the error function, the standard approach in calculus for finding the optimal weights matrix $\mathbf{W}^*$ is to use the first (and eventually the higher-order) derivatives of this function with respect to the weights w_{ij}. In the framework of neural networks weights learning, the second derivatives are the highest ones in use.

Thus, the activation function of neurons must be a differentiable one. Unfortunately, this is exactly the property that a perceptron activation function (a signum function) does not possess. The simplest one having this property is the linear activation function of Widrow-Hoff's adaline (adaptive linear neuron). The name adaline is rarely used today. What remains are the last two words of the original name: linear neuron. However, the adjective *adaptive* is a good one in this case. It describes the most essential property of this simple processing unit—the ability to learn. This ability is the core of intelligence, and *adaptive* at least deserves a place in the title of the next section.

3.2   The Adaptive Linear Neuron (Adaline) and the Least Mean Square Algorithm

The adaline in its early stage consisted of a neuron with a linear AF, a hard limiter (a thresholding device with a signum AF), and the least mean square (LMS) learning rule for adapting the weights. During its development in the 1960s, it was a great novelty with a capacity for a wide range of applications whenever the problem at hand could be treated as linear (speech and pattern recognition, weather forecasting, adaptive control tasks, adaptive noise canceling and filtering, and adaptive signal processing; all these problems are treated as nonlinear today). All its power in the linear domain is still in full service, and despite being a simple neuron, it is present (without a thresholding device) in almost all neural or fuzzy models.

This section discusses the two most important parts of the adaline—its linear activation function and the LMS learning rule. The hard limiter is omitted in the rest of the presentation, not because it is irrelevant, but for being of lesser importance to the problems to be solved here. The words *adaline* and *linear neuron* are both used here for a neural processing unit with a linear activation function and a corresponding learning rule (not necessarily LMS). More about the advanced aspects of the adaline can be found in Widrow and Walach (1996), Widrow and Stearns (1985), and Widrow and Hoff (1960).

3.2.1 Representational Capabilities of the Adaline

The processing unit with a linear activation function is the most commonly used neuron in the soft computing field. It will almost always be the only type of neuron in the output layer of neural networks and fuzzy logic models. Its mathematics is simpler than that of the perceptron. Because the signum part, or hard limiting quantizer, of the classical adaline is missing here, the linear neuron model is given by

$$o = u = \sum_{i=1}^{n+1} w_i x_i = w_1 x_1 + w_2 x_2 + \cdots + w_n x_n + w_{n+1} x_{n+1}, \tag{3.41}$$

or

$$o = \mathbf{w}^T \mathbf{x} = \mathbf{x}^T \mathbf{w}. \tag{3.42}$$

The model of a single-layer network (without hidden layers) with a linear neurons is given by

$$\mathbf{o} = \mathbf{W}\mathbf{x}, \tag{3.43}$$

where the weights vectors **w** connecting the components of the input vector **x** with each particular linear neuron in the output layer are the row vectors in the weights matrix **W**, or

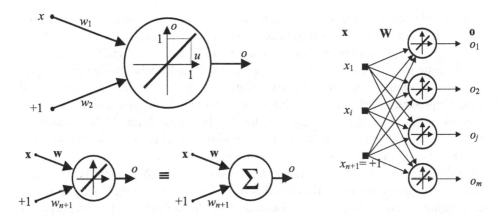

Figure 3.12
Top left, linear processing neuron. *Bottom left*, equivalency between the graphs of a linear neuron and summation. *Right*, single-layer neural network.

$$
\mathbf{W} = \begin{bmatrix} \mathbf{w}_1 \\ \mathbf{w}_2 \\ \vdots \\ \mathbf{w}_j \\ \vdots \\ \mathbf{w}_m \end{bmatrix} = [\mathbf{w}_1^T \quad \mathbf{w}_2^T \quad \cdots \quad \mathbf{w}_j^T \quad \cdots \quad \mathbf{w}_m^T]^T. \tag{3.44}
$$

The linear processing neuron in figure 3.12 (top left) has a one-dimensional or scalar input x, and the inputs in the other two parts of the figure are n-dimensional feature vectors augmented with bias $+1$. Note that $\mathbf{x}$ and $\mathbf{w}$ are n-dimensional vectors now. The neuron labeled with the summation sign is equivalent to a linear neuron. The single-layer network in figure 3.12 is a graphical (or network) representation of the standard linear transformation given by the linear matrix equation (3.43).

Despite the fact that the linear neuron is mathematically very simple, it is a very versatile and powerful processing unit. Equipped with an effective learning rule, it can successfully solve different kinds of linear problems in the presence of noise. It can be efficient in the modeling of slight nonlinearities, too. Thus it may be instructive to show different problems that the adaline can solve, deferring study of the learning rule until section 3.2.2. This will demonstrate the representational capability of a simple linear neuron. In order to better understand the results obtained, note that unlike in the case of perceptron learning, the adaline adapts weights in order to minimize the sum-of-error-squares cost function. Thus we work in L_2 norm here. The final weights vector results as a solution of an optimization task, though sometimes the optimal result does not necessarily mean a good solution (see example 3.2).

The examples in this section originate from different fields. The input (feature) vector is low-dimensional to enable visualization of the results. There is no difference in the representational power of a linear neuron when faced with high-dimensional patterns at the input layer or target vectors at the output layer. If the problem at hand can be treated as linear, the adaline will always be able to provide the solution that is the best in the least-squares sense. In other words, the errors that result will be such that the sum of error squares will be the *smallest* one. With input patterns and targets of higher dimensions, the only difference with respect to the solutions will be in computing time, and generally visualization of high-dimensional spaces will not be possible. (Some readers are eventually able to imagine hyperspaces, separation hyperplanes, or error hyperparaboloidal surfaces.) Even so, some of the problems expressed through high-dimensional input patterns can be properly visualized, such as identification of linear dynamic systems or linear filters design. Examples 3.2 and 3.3 are classification problems, and in examples 3.4–3.6 a linear neuron is performing regression tasks.

Example 3.2   Consider the classification of two linearly separable classes drawn from two normal distributions: $\mathbf{C}_1$, 25 data, $\mu_1 = (1, -1)$, $\sigma_1 = 0.5$, and $\mathbf{C}_2$, 25 data, $\mu_2 = (3, 2)$, $\sigma_2 = 0.5$. The adaline should find the separation line between these two classes for two slightly different data sets: without an outlier, and when there is a single outlier data point in class 2. The classes are linearly separable.

The classes in this example (with and without outlier in class 2) are linearly separable, and a perceptron would be able to solve this classification problem perfectly. It is not like that with adaline solutions. When there are no outliers and the data are drawn from Gaussian distributions, the adaline solution will perfectly separate two classes. This kind of solution is represented by a solid line in figure 3.13. When there is an outlier, the separation line (dashed in fig. 3.13) is not a good one. The adaline solution is always one in the least-squares sense, and its learning rule does not have the ability to reduce the effect of the outlier data points. Thus, the separation line when there is an outlier is optimal in the least-squares sense but may not be very good. This is a well-known deficiency of the L_2 norm when faced with non-Gaussian data. This norm cannot reduce the influence of outlier data points during learning. Fortunately, in many real-world problems the assumption about the Gaussian origin of the data may very often be an acceptable one.   ∎

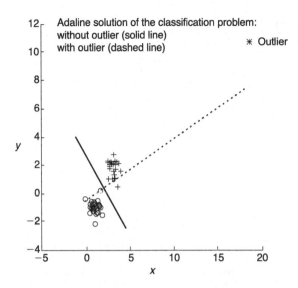

Figure 3.13
Classification of two linearly separable classes drawn from two normal distributions: C_1 (circles), 25 data, $\mu_1 = (1, -1)$, $\sigma_1 = 0.5$; C_2 (crosses), 25 data, $\mu_2 = (3, 2)$, $\sigma_2 = 0.5$.

The real advantage of using a linear neuron for the solution of classification tasks will be in cases when classes are not linearly separable. A perceptron cannot solve these problems, and the adaline provides the solution in the least-squares sense.

Example 3.3 Consider the classification of two not linearly separable classes with overlapping, drawn from two normal distributions: C_1, 100 data, $\mu_1 = (1, -1)$, $\sigma_1 = 2$, and C_2, 100 data, $\mu_2 = (3, 2)$, $\sigma_2 = 2$. The adaline should find the separation line between these two classes. (Recall that an SVM is able to solve such a problem with the soft margin classifier.)

The solid separation line shown in figure 3.14 is the one that ensures the minimal sum of error squares of misclassified data points. ∎

Linear or nonlinear regression is a prominent method for fitting data in science, statistics, or engineering. The adaline will be in charge of linear regression. Regression provides the answer to how one or more variables are related to, or affected by, other variables. The following examples present linear regression solutions obtained by an adaline. The examples are restricted to one or two features and one output variable. Consideration of high-dimensional, nonlinear regression (the basic problem in soft computing) is deferred to chapter 4. (Recall that chapter 2 discussed how

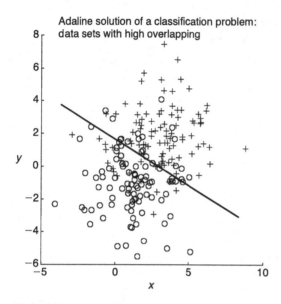

Figure 3.14
Classification of two not linearly separable classes with overlapping drawn from two normal distributions: C_1 (circles), 100 data, $\mu_1 = (1, -1)$, $\sigma_1 = 2$; C_2 (crosses), 100 data, $\mu_2 = (3, 2)$, $\sigma_2 = 2$.

SVMs solve nonlinear regression tasks.) As in the case of a perceptron or of examples 3.2 and 3.3, the end result of the learning process will be the set of weights, or the weights vector **w**, that defines the least-squares regression line, plane, or hyperplane.

Example 3.4 Consider the problem of finding the underlying function between two variables x and y. The training data consist of 200 measured data pairs and 10 measured data pairs from the process described by the linear function $y = 2.5x - 1 + n$, $x \in [0, 10]$, where n is a Gaussian random variable with a zero mean and such variance that it corrupts the desired output y with 20% noise. The structure of the adaline is the same as in figure 3.12 (top left). Using the data set, find (learn) the weights w_1 and w_2 that ensure the modeling of the unknown underlying function (known to us but not to the linear neuron).

The solutions to this one-dimensional regression problem are shown in figure 3.15. They were obtained by the adaline learning procedure using two training data sets (200 data pairs and 10 data pairs). Note that the more data used, the better will be the estimation of the adaline weights.

Redundancy in data provides knowledge. This is a standard fact in the field of estimation, that is, in learning from data tasks like the ones shown here. The prob-

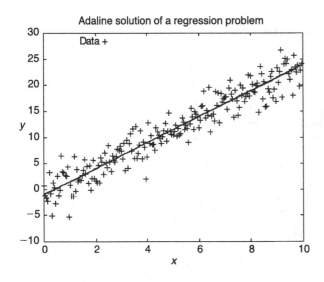

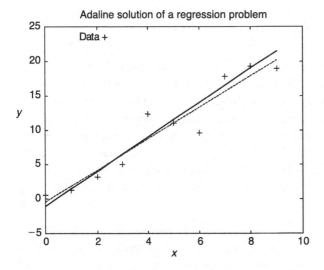

Figure 3.15
Solution of a regression task for the underlying function $y = 2.5x - 1 + n$ using (*top*) 200 data pairs, and (*bottom*) 10 data pairs. True function (solid line); regression function (dashed line).

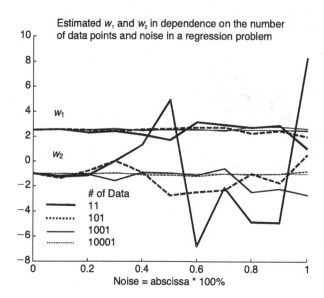

Figure 3.16
Dependence of weights estimates upon the noise level and the size of the data set.

lem in real-world applications is that the number of data required increases exponentially with problem dimensionality, but typical learning environments (usually of
a very high order) provide only sparse training data sets. This is only one of the
curses of dimensionality. (Recall that one remedy, shown in chapter 2, was applying
kernel functions.) Figure 3.16 shows how the quality of weight estimation depends
upon the noise level and the size of the data set. Clearly, the higher the noise level, the
more data are needed in order to find a good estimate. Note that the estimation of
bias weight w_2 is much more sensitive to both noise level and the number of training
data.   ■

The geometrical meaning of weight components in regression tasks is different
from that in classification problems. In figure 3.16, w_1 represents the slope and w_2
represents the intercept of the regression line. This will be similar for patterns of
higher dimension.

Let us now analyze a two-dimensional regression problem, which might provide
better understanding of what a linear neuron does in hyperspace (*hint*: it models
regression hyperplanes).

Example 3.5 Consider the problem of finding the underlying function between three
variables: x and y are the input, or independent, variables, and z is the dependent,

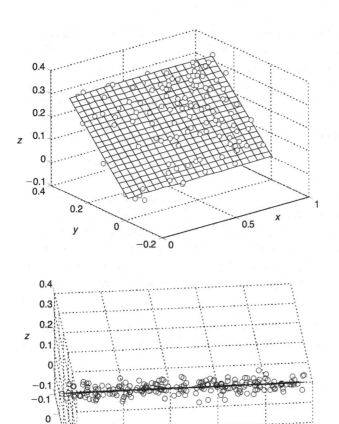

Figure 3.17
Solution of the regression task for the underlying function $z = 0.004988x + 0.995y + n$ using a training data set of 200 patterns. The picture below is a view along a plane.

output variable. The training data consist of 200 measured data pairs from the process described by linear function $z = 0.004988x + 0.995y + n$, $x \in [0, 1]$, $y \in [-0.25, +0.25]$, where n is a Gaussian random variable with a zero mean and such variance that it corrupts the desired output z with 20% noise. The structure of the adaline is the same as in figure 3.12 (bottom left), with $\mathbf{x}$ and $\mathbf{w}$ being two-dimensional (do not forget the constant input term $+1$ and its corresponding weight w_3). Using the data set, learn the weights w_1, w_2, and w_3 that ensure the modeling of the unknown underlying plane.

The optimal solution to this problem is presented with two graphs in figure 3.17. The bottom graph is given under the angle along the plane to show that the adaline drew the plane through the noisy data in the least-squares sense. The character of the solution is equivalent to the solution in a one-dimensional regression problem, and the same will be true for similar regression tasks of any dimension. Provided that there are enough training data pairs $(\mathbf{x}, y)$, where $\mathbf{x}$ is an n-dimensional input vector and y is a one-dimensional output vector, after the learning phase the resulting $(n + 1)$-dimensional hyperplane will pass through the cloud of data points in an $(n + 1)$-dimensional space.   ∎

Let us conclude the examination of the representational capability of a single linear processing unit with a standard control problem—the identification of linear plant dynamics.

Example 3.6 Linear single input—single output dynamic systems can be described by the following generic discrete equation:

$$y_k = a_1 y_{k-1} + a_2 y_{k-2} + \cdots + a_n y_{k-n} + b_1 u_{k-1} + b_2 u_{k-2} + \cdots + b_n u_{k-n} + n_k,$$

where y_{k-i} and u_{k-i} are past inputs and outputs, and n_k is additive white noise. The system identification problem of determining a's and b's can be viewed as a regression (functional approximation) problem in $\Re^{n+n+1}$. (In a more general case, the orders of the input and output delays differ and $\Re = \Re^{m+n+1}$). Now, consider the identification of the following second-order system:

$$Y(s) = \frac{3}{s^2 + s + 3} U(s).$$

With the sampling rate $\Delta T = 0.25s$, we obtain the discrete equation

$$y_k = 1.615 y_{k-1} - 0.7788 y_{k-2} + 0.08508 u_{k-1} + 0.07824 u_{k-2}.$$

Using a set of 50 input-output data pairs, a linear neuron estimates the values of the parameters a and b. The training input u was a pseudo-random-binary-signal

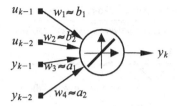

Figure 3.18
Structure of a linear neuron for the identification of a second-order system.

(PRBS), and the output of the system was corrupted by 5% white noise with a zero mean.

For this problem the input patterns are four-dimensional vectors consisting of $u_{k-1}, u_{k-2}, y_{k-1}, y_{k-2}$ for each instant k and $k \in [3, t_K]$, where the subscript K denotes the number of discrete steps. Simulation time is equal to $K\Delta T$. The output from the linear neuron is y_k. The structure of the linear neuron to be used is given in figure 3.18. Note that in this type of discrete difference equation the constant input (bias) term is missing. This expresses the fact that the hyperplane in a five-dimensional space is a homogeneous one, that is, this hyperplane passes through the origin with no shift along any axis. All possible trajectories y for the corresponding input signals u will lie on this hyperplane if there is no noise. In the presence of disturbances these trajectories will lie around it. The expressions $w_i \approx a_i$ and $w_i \approx b_i$ in figure 3.18 denote that by the end of the learning, the w_i will be the *estimates* of the parameters a_i and b_i.

Hence the physical meaning of the weights, which are the subjects of learning, is again different than it was in the previous examples. Moreover, in this particular identification problem, the weights can be thought of in two different ways: as coefficients of the hyperplane in a five-dimensional space on which all possible trajectories of the given second-order dynamics would lie, or as the constant coefficients of the given second-order difference equation. Both views are correct, and the task is to learn the weights $w_1, w_2, w_3,$ and w_4 that ensure the modeling of the unknown underlying plane by using the data set. The training results are presented in figure 3.19. Both graphs show that a linear neuron can be a reliable model of a linear dynamic system.

The same phenomena as in figure 3.16, concerning the dependence of the relative error of the estimated parameters for a second-order linear discrete dynamic system upon the size of the data set, may be seen in figure 3.20. In this example, the estimation error when using fewer than 150 data pairs may be larger than 10%. This is a considerable error, and in order to have a good model of this second-order system, a

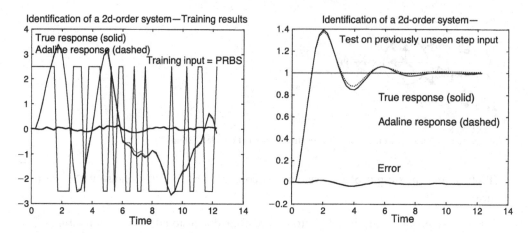

Figure 3.19
Identification of a linear second-order plant. *Left*, training results. *Right*, test results.

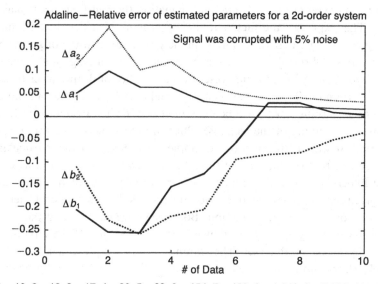

1 = 10, 2 = 12, 3 = 17, 4 = 30, 5 = 62, 6 = 154, 7 = 460, 8 = 1,648, 9 = 7,080, 10 = 36,573

Figure 3.20
Dependence of the relative error of estimated parameters for a second-order linear discrete dynamic system upon the size of a data set.

larger data set must be used. (Recall from chapter 2 the ratio l/h, which defines the size of a training data set.)   ■

3.2.2 Weights Learning for a Linear Processing Unit

The previous section discussed the representational capability of a neural processing unit with a linear activation function (the adaline). In the world of neural computing, the learning part is of the same, or even greater, importance as the representation part. Adapting weights of a linear neuron using a data set can be done in several different ways. (This is also true for other types of processing units.) How weights learning can be solved for a neuron having a linear activation function is the subject of this section. Five methods are demonstrated.

Consider the single linear neuron in figure 3.21. An input signal $\mathbf{x}$ comprising features and augmented by a constant input component (bias) is applied to the neuron, weighted, and summed to give an output signal o.

A learning problem is a problem of parameter estimation of a chosen model between the input vectors $\mathbf{x}$ and the outputs o. Using linear activation functions in a neuron the underlying function between these variables is expected to be satisfactorily modeled by a linear regression line, plane, or hyperplane.

Thus the learning task is to find the weights of the neuron (estimate the parameters of the proposed linear model) using a *finite* number of measurements, observations, or patterns. Note that the weights w_i result from an estimation procedure, and in the literature on statistics or identification in control, these estimated parameters are typically denoted as $\hat{w}_i$. For the sake of simplicity this circumflex is not used here, but

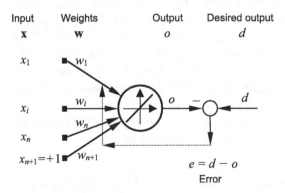

Figure 3.21
Learning scheme for a linear neuron. Dashed arrows indicate that weights adaptation usually depends on the output error.

one must not forget the statistical character of the weights. They are random values depending upon the samples or patterns used during training (see figs. 3.16 and 3.20).

The learning environment comprises a training set of measured data (patterns) $X = \{\mathbf{x}(j), \mathbf{d}(j), j = 1, \ldots, P\}$ consisting of an input vector $\mathbf{x}$ and output, or system response, vector $\mathbf{d}$, and the corresponding learning rule for the adaptation of the weights. (In what follows learning algorithms are for the case of one neuron only, and the desired output is a scalar variable d. The extensions of the algorithms for $\mathbf{d}$, a vector, are straightforward and are presented subsequently.) The choice of a performance criterion, or the measure of goodness of the estimation, may be made between a few different candidates. For example, one can minimize the sum of error squares, maximize the likelihood function, or maximize expectation. (Alternatively, as shown in chapter 2, one can minimize more complex functionals.)

In the neural networks field, the most widely used performance criterion for the estimation of model parameters (here, a vector $\mathbf{w}$) is the sum of error squares. It is relatively straightforward to show that if the data are corrupted with Gaussian noise with a zero mean, minimization of the sum of error squares results in the same parameters as maximization of the likelihood function. (To show this, solve problem 3.22.) However, in the case of maximal likelihood estimates one must know and take into account the statistical properties of noise. Nothing about the character of disturbances need be assumed when working with a sum-of-error-squares cost function, and no statistical model is assumed for the input variable $\mathbf{x}$.

Following are five different methods for adapting linear neuron weights using a training data set. The first three methods are *batch* (off-line, explicit, one-shot) *methods*, which use all the data at once, and the last two are *on-line* (implicit, sequential, recursive, iterative) *procedures*. The latter are of great interest for real-time control, signal processing, and filtering tasks, or more generally, for applications where there is a need to process measurements or observations as soon as they become available.

Note that the sum of error squares is taken as the cost function to be minimized, meaning that the derivation of the learning rule will be made through deterministic arguments only. The resulting least-squares estimates may be preferred to other estimates when there is no possibility of, or need for, assigning probability-density functions to $\mathbf{x}$ and d (or $\mathbf{d}$ in the case of a single-layer network of linear neurons—see fig. 3.12 (right)).

Method 1:   Minimal Squared Error and the Pseudoinverse   Assume that a data set of P measurements d (P must be equal or larger than the number of weight components to be estimated) can be expressed as a linear function of an $(n + 1)$-dimensional input vector $\mathbf{x}$ (n features + bias term) plus a random additive measurement error (disturbance or noise) e:

$$d = \mathbf{w}^T\mathbf{x} + e, \tag{3.45}$$

where both $\mathbf{x}$ and $\mathbf{w}$ are $(n+1,1)$ vectors. Note that assumption (3.45) is the rationale for using a linear neuron. Using $o = \mathbf{w}^T\mathbf{x}$ from (3.42), an error at the pth presented data pair may be expressed as

$$e_p = d_p - o_p = d_p - \mathbf{w}^T\mathbf{x}_p, \tag{3.46}$$

where the weights $\mathbf{w}$ are fixed during the pth epoch, or during the pth presentation of the whole set of training data pairs ($p = 1, P$). Now, the cost function is formed as

$$E = \sum_1^P e_p^2, \tag{3.47}$$

or using that $\mathbf{w}^T\mathbf{x} = \mathbf{x}^T\mathbf{w}$,

$$E = \sum_1^P (\mathbf{w}^T\mathbf{x}_p - d_p)(\mathbf{w}^T\mathbf{x}_p - d_p)$$

$$= \mathbf{w}^T\left(\sum_1^P (\mathbf{x}_p\mathbf{x}_p^T)\right)\mathbf{w} - 2\mathbf{w}^T\sum_1^P d_p\mathbf{x}_p + \sum_1^P d_p^2, \tag{3.48}$$

For the sake of simplicity and generality of the learning model, a matrix of input vectors $\mathbf{x}_p$ (known also as a data matrix $\mathbf{X}$) and vector $\mathbf{D}$ of desired outputs d_p are introduced as follows:

$$\mathbf{X} = [\mathbf{x}_1 \quad \mathbf{x}_2 \quad \cdots \quad \mathbf{x}_P], \qquad \mathbf{D} = [d_1 \quad d_2 \quad \cdots \quad d_P]^T, \tag{3.49}$$

where $\mathbf{X} \in \Re^{n+1, P}$, and $\mathbf{D} \in \Re^{P, 1}$. Note that columns of $\mathbf{X}$ are the input patterns $\mathbf{x}_p$. However, matrix $\mathbf{X}$ could have been arranged so that its rows were $\mathbf{x}_p$. This is unimportant, and matrix $\mathbf{X}$ is chosen this way only to make clear the connection between (3.48) and (3.50). The entries of $\mathbf{D}$ are class labels for classification tasks. In regression problems, they are the values of dependent variables. Now, the error function can be rewritten in matrix form as

$$E = \mathbf{w}^T[\mathbf{X}\mathbf{X}^T]\mathbf{w} - 2\mathbf{w}^T\mathbf{X}\mathbf{D} + \mathbf{D}^T\mathbf{D}. \tag{3.50}$$

In this least-squares estimation task the objective is to find the *optimal* $\mathbf{w}^*$ that minimizes E. The solution to this classic problem in calculus is found by setting the gradient of E, with respect to $\mathbf{w}$, to zero:

$$\frac{\partial E}{\partial \mathbf{w}} = 2(\mathbf{X}\mathbf{X}^T)\mathbf{w} - 2\mathbf{X}\mathbf{D} = 0. \tag{3.51}$$

In the least-squares sense, the best or optimal solution of (3.51), $\mathbf{w}^*$, results from the *normal equation* $(\mathbf{X}\mathbf{X}^T)\mathbf{w} = \mathbf{X}\mathbf{D}$:

$$\mathbf{w}^* = (\mathbf{X}\mathbf{X}^T)^{-1}\mathbf{X}\mathbf{D} = \mathbf{X}^+\mathbf{D}, \tag{3.52}$$

where the matrix $\mathbf{X}^+$ is an $(n+1, P)$ pseudoinverse matrix of the matrix $\mathbf{X}^T$ and it is assumed that the matrix $\mathbf{X}\mathbf{X}^T$ is nonsingular.[3] The optimal solution $\mathbf{w}^*$ in (3.52) is called the Wiener-Hopf solution in the signal processing field (Widrow and Walach 1996; Haykin 1991). Extended discussion of learning in a linear neuron may also be found in Widrow and Stearns (1985) and Widrow and Walach (1996).

When the number of training samples is equal to the number of weights to be determined, $\mathbf{X}$ is a square matrix and $\mathbf{X}^+ = (\mathbf{X}^T)^{-1}$. Thus, the optimal solution results as a unique solution of a set of linear equations. This is of little practical interest. Training patterns will almost always be corrupted with noise, and to reduce the influence of these disturbances, the number of training samples must be (much) larger than the number of adapted weights (see figs. 3.16 and 3.20). From a computational point of view, the calculation of optimal weights requires the pseudo-inversion of the $(P, n+1)$-dimensional matrix. With respect to computing time, the critical part is the inversion of the $(n+1, n+1)$ matrix $\mathbf{X}\mathbf{X}^T$. In the application of neural networks it is quite common for input vectors to be of a very high dimension, and in such a situation this part of the calculation may not be easy. One possible solution to this type of problem is shown in method 5 in this section.

It is useful to look at the geometry of the cost function E (hyper)surface. Recall that the objective is to find the weights vector that defines its minimum, and it may save some time to ask only two basic questions: does the error (hyper)surface E have a minimum at all, and is this minimum unique? Fortunately, in the case of a linear activation function, E is a quadratic surface[4] of the weight components with a guaranteed unique minimum. The proof is simple. From (3.46) it is clear that the error e_p for each particular data pair $(\mathbf{x}_p, d_p)$ is a linear function of the weight components. The cost function E from (3.47) is a result of squaring and summing individual errors e_p. Thus, E will contain maximally second-order terms of weights vector components. Generally, in the case of a linear neuron, E is a (hyper)paraboloidal bowl hanging over an $(n+1)$-dimensional space spanned by the weights vector components w_i, $i = 1, n+1$. The picture is much less complex for a one-dimensional weights vector when E is a parabola over the w_1 axis. When there are only two components in a weights vector, $\mathbf{w} = [w_1 \quad w_2]^T$, E is an elliptical paraboloid (bowl-shaped surface) over the plane spanned by w_1 and w_2.

The unique minimal sum of error squares $E_{\min}$ is determined by $\mathbf{w}^*$ from (3.52):

$$E_{\min} = E(\mathbf{w}^*) = \mathbf{D}^T\mathbf{D} - \mathbf{w}^{*T}\mathbf{X}\mathbf{D} = (\mathbf{D}^T - \mathbf{w}^{*T}\mathbf{X})\mathbf{D}. \tag{3.53}$$

Using (3.46) and (3.49), it is easy to show that without noise $E(\mathbf{w}^*) = 0$.

Method 2: Newton-Raphson Optimization Scheme   One of the second-order optimization methods is Newton's iterative learning scheme. It is described in chapter 8 for the general case when the error (hyper)surface depends nonlinearly on the weights vector. Here, devising this learning law is relatively straightforward for the sum-of-error-squares cost function.

First, rewrite the expression for the gradient of the error function from (3.51):

$$\frac{\partial E}{\partial \mathbf{w}} = \nabla_{\mathbf{w}} E = 2(\mathbf{X}\mathbf{X}^T)\mathbf{w} - 2\mathbf{X}\mathbf{D}. \tag{3.54}$$

The second derivative of E with respect to the weights vector $\mathbf{w}$, known also as a Hessian matrix, is

$$\frac{\partial^2 E}{\partial \mathbf{w}^2} = \mathbf{H} = 2(\mathbf{X}\mathbf{X}^T). \tag{3.55}$$

After multiplying (3.54) from the left by $\mathbf{H}^{-1} = \frac{1}{2}(\mathbf{X}\mathbf{X}^T)^{-1}$,

$$\frac{1}{2}(\mathbf{X}\mathbf{X}^T)^{-1}\frac{\partial E}{\partial \mathbf{w}} = \mathbf{w} - (\mathbf{X}\mathbf{X}^T)^{-1}\mathbf{X}\mathbf{D}, \tag{3.56}$$

where the second term on the right-hand side of (3.56) is the optimal solution $\mathbf{w}^*$ given by (3.52). Now, rewrite (3.56) as

$$\mathbf{w}^* = \mathbf{w} - \mathbf{H}^{-1}\frac{\partial E}{\partial \mathbf{w}}. \tag{3.57}$$

Equation (3.57), which results in the optimal weights vector $\mathbf{w}^*$, is exactly the Newton-Raphson optimization algorithm. It is simple in form and yet a powerful tool, particularly for quadratic cost surfaces and when the Hessian is a positive definite matrix. This is always the case with a sum-of-error-squares cost function, and (3.57) shows that starting from any initial weights vector $\mathbf{w}$, the optimal one, $\mathbf{w}^*$, will always be found in one iteration step only. (This is not true for a general nonlinear cost function, where more iteration steps are usually required. Also, using the Newton-Raphson method does not guarantee that the global minimum will be reached when the cost function depends nonlinearly upon the weights.)

Method 3: Ideal Gradient Descent Method   A classical optimization method that has become widely used in the field of soft computing is the method of steepest descent (for minimization tasks) or ascent (for maximization tasks).[5] Changes of the weights are made according to the following algorithm:

$$\mathbf{w}_{p+1} = \mathbf{w}_p - \eta_1 \left. \frac{\partial E}{\partial \mathbf{w}} \right|_p, \tag{3.58}$$

where η_1 denotes the learning rate, and p stands for the actual iteration step. Note that here the pth iteration step means the pth *epoch*, or the pth presentation of the whole training data set. Thus, the gradient is calculated across the entire set of training patterns.

There are many different strategies in the neural networks field concerning what the initial weight $\mathbf{w}_1$ to start the optimization should be. Much can be said about learning rate, too. It is a standard design parameter during learning. Moreover it is highly problem-dependent. Two alternatives are either to keep the learning rate η small and fixed, or to change it (usually to decrease it) during the iterative adaptation procedure. The smaller η is, the smoother but slower will be the approach to the optimum. Subscript $_1$ is used for the sake of notational simplification only. It will be lost in the next line while deriving this gradient learning rule.

Introducing the expression for the gradient (3.54) into equation (3.58) and changing the notation for the learning rate to $\eta = 2\eta_1$,

$$\mathbf{w}_{p+1} = \mathbf{w}_p - \eta(\mathbf{X}\mathbf{X}^T \mathbf{w}_p - \mathbf{X}\mathbf{D}) \tag{3.59a}$$

$$= \mathbf{w}_p - \eta\mathbf{X}\mathbf{X}^T \mathbf{w}_p + \eta\mathbf{X}\mathbf{D} = (\mathbf{I} - \eta\mathbf{X}\mathbf{X}^T)\mathbf{w}_p + \eta\mathbf{X}\mathbf{D}$$

$$= (\mathbf{I} - \eta\mathbf{X}\mathbf{X}^T)((\mathbf{I} - \eta\mathbf{X}\mathbf{X}^T)\mathbf{w}_{p-1} + \eta\mathbf{X}\mathbf{D}) + \eta\mathbf{X}\mathbf{D}$$

$$\vdots$$

$$= (\mathbf{I} - \eta\mathbf{X}\mathbf{X}^T)^p \mathbf{w}_1 + \sum_{m=0}^{p-1} (\mathbf{I} - \eta\mathbf{X}\mathbf{X}^T)^m \eta\mathbf{X}\mathbf{D}. \tag{3.59b}$$

Starting from the initial weight $\mathbf{w}_1 = \mathbf{0}$ and with a sufficiently small learning rate η, which ensures a convergence of (3.59),

$$\lim_{p \to \infty} \mathbf{w}_{p+1} = \mathbf{w}_\infty = \underbrace{\sum_{m=0}^{\infty} (\mathbf{I} - \eta \mathbf{X}\mathbf{X}^T)^m \eta \mathbf{X}\mathbf{D}}_{\mathbf{X}^+} = \mathbf{X}^+\mathbf{D}, \tag{3.60}$$

or

$$\mathbf{w}_\infty = \mathbf{w}^* = \mathbf{X}^+\mathbf{D}. \tag{3.61}$$

In other words, under these conditions, the ideal gradient procedure will ultimately end up with the same optimal solution vector $\mathbf{w}^*$ as methods 1 and 2 did. (The introduction of the pseudoinverse matrix $\mathbf{X}^+$ in (3.60) as well as many other interesting properties of pseudoinverse matrices are covered in the literature; see, for example, Rao, and Mitra (1971)).

The learning rate η controls the stability and rate of adaptation. The ideal gradient learning algorithm converges as long as

$$0 < \eta < \frac{2}{trace(\mathbf{X}\mathbf{X}^T)}. \tag{3.62}$$

How different learning rates affect the decrease in the error cost function is shown in example 3.7. Very similar error trajectories are found during learning in a nonlinear environment and in optimizing a much higher number of weights. The general approach in choosing η is to decrease the learning rate as soon as it is observed that adaptation does not converge. In the nonlinear case, there are other sources of trouble, such as the possibility of staying at a local minimum. Nonlinear optimization problems are discussed in more detail in chapter 8. For a detailed study of convergence while adapting the weights in a linear neuron, the reader is referred to Widrow and Stearns (1985), Widrow and Walach (1996), and Haykin (1991).

Example 3.7 Dependency (the plant or system to be identified) between two variables is given by $y = 3x - 1$. Using a highly corrupted (25% noise) training data set containing 41 measured patterns $(\mathbf{x}, d)$, estimate the weights of a linear neuron that should model this plant by using the ideal (off-line) gradient procedure. Show how the learning rate η affects the learning trajectory of the error.

The optimal solution to this problem, obtained by method 1, that is, by using a pseudoinverse of the input matrix $\mathbf{X}^T$, is $w_1 = 2.92$ $w_2 = -1.04$, and minimal squared error E_{min}, obtained from (3.53), is equal to 179.74. The trajectories presented in figure 3.22 clearly indicate that the smaller η is, the smoother but slower will be the approach to the optimum. Beyond the critical learning rate $\eta_C = 2/trace(\mathbf{X}\mathbf{X}^T)$, learning is either highly oscillatory (η being still close to η_C) or unstable. ■

Linear neuron. Trajectory of the error cost function decrease

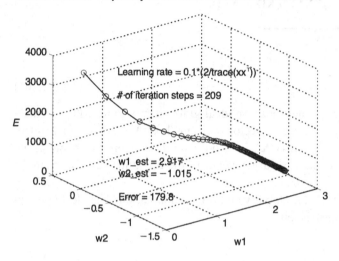

Linear neuron. Trajectory of the error cost function decrease

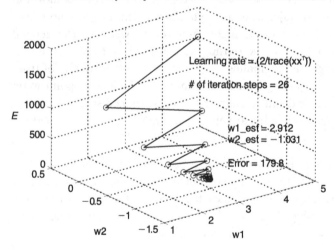

Figure 3.22
Influence of learning rate on the adaptation of weights in a linear neuron.

Linear neuron. Trajectory of the error cost function decrease

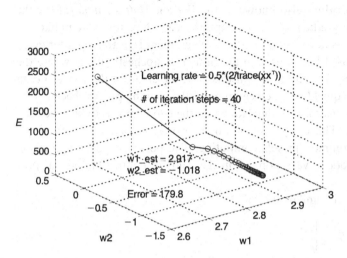

Linear neuron. Trajectory of the error cost function decrease

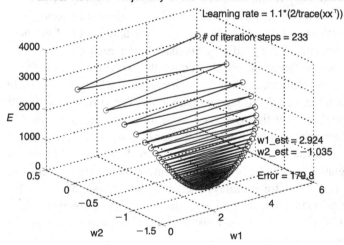

Figure 3.22 (continued)

Method 4:   Gradient Descent Method, or Least Mean Square Algorithm   The least
mean square (LMS) algorithm (also known as the *Widrow-Hoff learning rule* or the
delta learning rule), is a gradient descent adapting procedure, too, but unlike the
ideal gradient method, it is not a batch method: the gradient is evaluated after every
sample is presented. Thus, LMS is used in an on-line or stochastic mode where the
weights are updated after every iteration. In this way, the error on the training data
generally decreases more quickly at the beginning of the training process because the
network does not have to wait for all the data pairs (the entire epoch) to be processed
before it learns anything. This early reduction in error may be one explanation why
on-line techniques are common in soft computing. The possibility of adapting the
weights in an on-line mode is very popular in the fields of control and signal processing, too.

The LMS learning rule is similar to (3.58),

$$\mathbf{w}_{p+1} = \mathbf{w}_p + \Delta\mathbf{w}_p = \mathbf{w}_p - \eta \left. \frac{\partial E}{\partial \mathbf{w}} \right|_p , \tag{3.63}$$

the only difference being that the subscript p now denotes the iteration step after
single training data pairs (usually randomly drawn) are presented. Thus, the calculation of the weight change $\Delta\mathbf{w}_p$, or of the gradient needed for this, is *pattern-based*,
not *epoch-based* as in method 3. It is relatively easy to show that the ideal gradient
(method 3) is equal to the sum of the gradients calculated after each pattern is presented for fixed weights during the whole epoch. (To see this, solve problem 3.27.)

The LMS algorithm is also known as the *delta learning rule*, which was an early
powerful strategy for adapting weights using data pairs only. The variable (or signal)
δ designates an *error signal*, but not the error itself as defined in (3.46) and shown in
figure 3.21. Thus, δ will generally not be equal to the error $e_p = d_p - o_p$. Interestingly,
the equality $\delta = e$ does hold for a linear activation function. In the world of neural
computing, the error signal δ used to be of the highest importance. After a hiatus in
the development of learning rules for multilayer networks for almost 20 years, this
adaptation rule made a breakthrough in 1986 and was named the *generalized delta
learning rule*. Today, this rule is also known as the *error backpropagation* (EBP)
learning rule (see chapter 4).

It is now appropriate to present the basics of the *error-correction delta rule*, which
uses a gradient descent strategy for adapting weights in order to reduce the error
(cost) function. The EBP algorithm is demonstrated for a single neuron having *any*
differentiable activation function (see fig. 3.23). This will be just a small (nonlinear)
deviation from the derivation of adaptation rules for the linear activation function
and the corresponding hyperbowl-shaped error performance surface. Including this

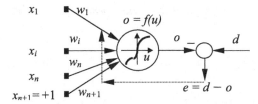

Figure 3.23
Neural unit with any differentiable activation function.

small deviation is a natural step in presenting a gradient descent–based LMS algorithm for a linear neuron. After an EBP algorithm for any activation function has been derived the LMS rule will be treated as one particular case only, when the activation function is a linear one.

Thus, the problem is to find the expression for, and to calculate, the gradient $\nabla_\mathbf{w} E|_p$, given in (3.63), using a training set of pairs of input and output patterns. Recall that learning is in an on-line mode. First, define the error function

$$E_p = \tfrac{1}{2}e_p^2 = E(\mathbf{w}_p).$$ (3.64)

The constant $\tfrac{1}{2}$ is used for computational convenience only; it will be canceled out by the required differentiation that follows. Note that $E(\mathbf{w}_p)$ is a nonlinear function of the weights vector now, and the gradient cannot be calculated using expressions similar to (3.54). Fortunately, the calculation of the gradient is straightforward in this simple case. For this purpose, the chain rule is

$$\left.\frac{\partial E}{\partial \mathbf{w}}\right|_p = \underbrace{\frac{\partial E_p}{\partial u_p}}_{-\delta} \frac{\partial u_p}{\partial \mathbf{w}_p},$$ (3.65)

where the first term on the right-hand side is called the *error signal δ*. It is a measure of an error change due to the input to the neuron u when the pth pattern is presented. The second term shows the influence of the weights vector $\mathbf{w}_p$ on that particular input u_p. Applying the chain rule again,

$$\left.\frac{\partial E}{\partial \mathbf{w}}\right|_p = \frac{\partial E_p}{\partial e_p}\frac{\partial e_p}{\partial o_p}\frac{\partial o_p}{\partial u_p}\frac{\partial u_p}{\partial \mathbf{w}_p},$$ (3.66)

or

$$\left.\frac{\partial E}{\partial \mathbf{w}}\right|_p = e_p(-1)f'(u_p)\mathbf{x}_p.$$ (3.67)

The last term follows from the fact that $u_p = \mathbf{w}_p^T \mathbf{x}_p$, and the *delta learning rule* can be written as

$$\mathbf{w}_{p+1} = \mathbf{w}_p - \eta \frac{\partial E}{\partial \mathbf{w}}\bigg|_p = \mathbf{w}_p + \Delta \mathbf{w}_p = \mathbf{w}_p + \eta(d_p - o_p)f'(u_p)\mathbf{x}_p. \qquad (3.68)$$

This is the most general learning rule that is valid for a single neuron having any nonlinear and differentiable activation function and whose input is formed as a scalar product of the pattern and weights vector. Because of its importance in the development of the general EBP algorithm for a multilayer neural network, it might be useful to separately present the expression for the error signal δ_p here:

$$\delta_p = (d_p - o_p)f'(u_p). \qquad (3.69)$$

The calculation of a particular change of a single weights vector component w_j is straightforward and follows after rewriting the vector equation (3.68) in terms of the vectors' components:

$$w_{j,p+1} = w_{j,p} + \eta(d_p - o_p)f'(u_p)x_{j,p} = w_{j,p} + \eta\delta_p x_{j,p}. \qquad (3.70)$$

Note that the error signal δ_p is the same for each particular component of the weights vector. Thus, the very change of w_j is determined by, and is proportional to, its corresponding component of the input vector x_j.

The LMS learning rule for a linear neuron, taking into account that $f'(u_p) = 1$, is given as

$$\mathbf{w}_{p+1} = \mathbf{w}_p + \Delta \mathbf{w}_p = \mathbf{w}_p + \eta(d_p - o_p)\mathbf{x}_p = \mathbf{w}_p + \eta\delta_p \mathbf{x}_p. \qquad (3.71)$$

The LMS is an error-correction type of rule in the sense that the weight change $\Delta \mathbf{w}_p$ is proportional to the error $e_p = (d_p - o_p)$. A similar learning rule was presented for a single perceptron unit (see method 1 in box 3.1). However, the origins and the derivation of these rules are different. Unlike the heuristic perceptron learning rule, the LMS results from the minimization of a predefined error function using the gradient descent procedure. (It can be shown that the perceptron learning rule can also be obtained by minimizing its error function, but that was not how this rule was originally developed.)

Concerning the learning rate η, which controls the stability and the rate of adaptation, the criterion given in (3.62) is valid here, too. The LMS algorithm converges as long as $\eta < \eta_C = 2/trace(\mathbf{X}\mathbf{X}^T)$. For $\eta < 0.1\eta_C$, the LMS results are equivalent to those obtained by method 3, the ideal gradient method. The learning process is always of a random character, and *equivalence* denotes equality in the mean.

Methods 3 and 4 in this section are iterative learning schemes that use the gradient or the first derivative of the error function with respect to weights. Thus, they belong to the group of first-order optimization algorithms. For on-line application, the LMS has been a widely used algorithm for years, and it still is. Provided that the learning rate is smaller than η_C, both methods converge to the optimal solution $\mathbf{w}^* = (\mathbf{X}\mathbf{X}^T)^{-1}\mathbf{X}\mathbf{D} = \mathbf{X}^+\mathbf{D}$ given by (3.52).

It is well known that by using the information about the curvature of the error function to be optimized, one can considerably speed up the learning procedure. Information about the curvature is contained in the second derivative of the error function with respect to the weights, or in the Hessian matrix (3.55). For the quadratic cost function, the Newton-Raphson solution (3.57) is equal to the optimal $\mathbf{w}^*$. The Newton-Raphson method is a second-order optimization scheme, but the solution given by (3.57) is an off-line solution that uses a batch containing all the training patterns. Thus, a natural question may be, is it possible to make an on-line estimation of the parameters by using second-order descent down the error surface? The answer is yes, and this method is known as the recursive least squares algorithm. This method may well be the best on-line algorithm (whenever the error depends linearly on weights) for a wide range of applications.

Method 5: Recursive Least Squares Algorithm   The recursive least squares (RLS) algorithm is the last learning method presented here for a linear processing unit. For most real-life problems it might well be the best on-line weight-adapting alternative, provided that there is a linear dependency between the sets of input and output variables.

The RLS method shares all the good on-line features of the LMS method, but its rate of convergence (in terms of iteration steps) is an order of magnitude faster. The price for this is increased computational complexity, but whenever the amount of calculation can be carried out within one sampling interval, this complexity is not important in the framework of on-line applications.

In the derivation of the RLS algorithm, a basic result in linear algebra known as the *matrix-inversion lemma* is used. Let us start with the optimal solution (3.52), which can be calculated having a set of P training data pairs

$$\mathbf{w}_p = (\mathbf{X}_p\mathbf{X}_p^T)^{-1}\mathbf{X}_p\mathbf{D}_p = \mathbf{X}_p^+\mathbf{D}_p, \tag{3.72}$$

where the subscript p denotes the fact that the training set having P patterns is used for the calculation of $\mathbf{w}_p$. In what follows, the off-line procedure (note that $\mathbf{X}$ and $\mathbf{D}$ contain a batch of P data pairs), which requires the inversion of an $(n+1, n+1)$ input data matrix, is transformed into an on-line algorithm that avoids this matrix inversion. (Recall that there are n features and that the $(n+1)$th component is a bias term. Without this constant input term the matrix $\mathbf{X}_p\mathbf{X}_p^T$ to be inverted is an (n,n) matrix; see example 3.6).

At the pth iterative step, and using $\mathbf{w}_p$ from (3.72), the desired value will be equal to the output from the linear neuron plus some error:

$$d_p = \mathbf{x}_p^T\mathbf{w}_p + e_p. \tag{3.73}$$

With the new measurement or pattern $(\mathbf{x}_{p+1}, d_{p+1})$ and using weight $\mathbf{w}_p$,

$$d_{p+1} = \mathbf{x}_{p+1}^T\mathbf{w}_p + e_{p+1}, \tag{3.74}$$

or

$$e_{p+1} = d_{p+1} - \mathbf{x}_{p+1}^T\mathbf{w}_p. \tag{3.75}$$

The critical point is when the new output and corresponding error at step $p+1$ are predicted using the weight found at step p. Fortunately, with proper initialization of the iterative procedure, the process converges to the correct weights vector in the $(n+1)$th iterative step. Rewrite (3.72) as

$$\mathbf{w}_p = (\mathbf{X}_p\mathbf{X}_p^T)^{-1}\mathbf{X}_p\mathbf{D}_p = \mathbf{P}_p\mathbf{F}_p, \tag{3.76}$$

where

$$\mathbf{P}_p = (\mathbf{X}_p\mathbf{X}_p^T)^{-1}, \tag{3.77}$$

$$\mathbf{F}_p = \mathbf{X}_p\mathbf{D}_p. \tag{3.78}$$

With $p+1$ measurements, the solution weights vector $\mathbf{w}_{p+1}$, which can be obtained by using the whole batch of $p+1$ data, would be

$$\mathbf{w}_{p+1} = (\mathbf{X}_{p+1}\mathbf{X}_{p+1}^T)^{-1}\mathbf{X}_{p+1}\mathbf{D}_{p+1} = \mathbf{P}_{p+1}\mathbf{F}_{p+1}. \tag{3.79}$$

The basic strategy from the very beginning has been to avoid the batch part, meaning the operation of matrix inversion. In order to do that, rearrange (3.79) by the separation of the new measurement from the batch of p past data:

$$\underbrace{\mathbf{X}_{p+1}\mathbf{X}_{p+1}^T}_{\mathbf{P}_{p+1}^{-1}} = [\mathbf{X}_p \quad \mathbf{x}_{p+1}]\begin{bmatrix}\mathbf{X}_p^T\\\mathbf{x}_{p+1}^T\end{bmatrix} = \underbrace{\mathbf{X}_p\mathbf{X}_p^T}_{\mathbf{P}_p^{-1}} + \mathbf{x}_{p+1}\mathbf{x}_{p+1}^T, \tag{3.80}$$

$$\underbrace{\mathbf{X}_{p+1}\mathbf{D}_{p+1}}_{\mathbf{F}_{p+1}} = [\mathbf{X}_p \quad \mathbf{x}_{p+1}]\begin{bmatrix}\mathbf{D}_p\\d_{p+1}\end{bmatrix} = \underbrace{\mathbf{X}_p\mathbf{D}_p}_{\mathbf{F}_p} + \mathbf{x}_{p+1}d_{p+1}. \tag{3.81}$$

From (3.76),

$$\mathbf{F}_p = \mathbf{P}_p^{-1}\mathbf{w}_p. \tag{3.82}$$

Combining $\mathbf{F}_p$ from (3.82) with (3.74) and (3.81),

$$\mathbf{F}_{p+1} = \mathbf{P}_{p+1}^{-1}\mathbf{w}_p + \mathbf{x}_{p+1}\mathbf{x}_{p+1}^T\mathbf{w}_p + \mathbf{x}_{p+1}e_{p+1}. \tag{3.83}$$

Now, (3.79) and (3.82) yield

$$\mathbf{w}_{p+1} = \mathbf{P}_{p+1}\big((\mathbf{P}_p^{-1} + \mathbf{x}_{p+1}\mathbf{x}_{p+1}^T)\mathbf{w}_p + \mathbf{x}_{p+1}e_{p+1}\big). \tag{3.84}$$

Using (3.80),

$$\mathbf{w}_{p+1} = \mathbf{w}_p + \mathbf{P}_{p+1}\mathbf{x}_{p+1}e_{p+1}. \tag{3.85}$$

The matrix inversion is almost done. The weights vector in step $p + 1$, $\mathbf{w}_{p+1}$, is expressed in recursive form, but the critical part, the operation of matrix inversion, is still present in the calculation of the matrix $\mathbf{P}_{p+1}$. This part is solved using the matrix inversion lemma

$$[\mathbf{A} + \mathbf{B}\mathbf{C}\mathbf{D}]^{-1} = \mathbf{A}^{-1} - \mathbf{A}^{-1}\mathbf{B}(\mathbf{C}^{-1} + \mathbf{D}\mathbf{A}^{-1}\mathbf{B})^{-1}\mathbf{D}\mathbf{A}^{-1}. \tag{3.86}$$

Rewrite (3.80) as

$$\mathbf{P}_{p+1}^{-1} = \mathbf{P}_p^{-1} + \mathbf{x}_{p+1}(1)\mathbf{x}_{p+1}^T, \tag{3.87}$$

and compare the matrices (3.86) and (3.87). Note that $\mathbf{A} = \mathbf{P}_p^{-1}$, $\mathbf{B} = \mathbf{x}_{p+1}$, $\mathbf{C} = 1$, and $\mathbf{D} = \mathbf{x}_{p+1}^T$. Also, on the right-hand side of (3.86), the only "serious" inversion required is $\mathbf{A}^{-1}$, which is equal to $\mathbf{P}_p$. Now, this yields

$$\mathbf{P}_{p+1} = (\mathbf{P}_{p+1}^{-1})^{-1} = \mathbf{P}_p - \mathbf{P}_p\mathbf{x}_{p+1}(1 + \mathbf{x}_{p+1}^T\mathbf{P}_p\mathbf{x}_{p+1})^{-1}\mathbf{x}_{p+1}^T\mathbf{P}_p. \tag{3.88}$$

Thus, starting from an initial matrix $\mathbf{P}_0$, matrix $\mathbf{P}_{p+1}$ can be calculated in a recursive manner avoiding any matrix inversion. The inversion present in (3.88) is not an inversion of the matrix because $\mathbf{x}_{p+1}^T\mathbf{P}_p\mathbf{x}_{p+1}$ is a scalar. The order in which particular variables or matrices in the RLS algorithm are calculated is important, and it may be useful to summarize the RLS algorithm (see boxes 3.2 and 3.3). Two slightly different versions of the RLS procedure are summarized. They are theoretically equivalent but possess different numerical properties. The size of the data set, the noise-to-signal ratio in data, and whether the plant to be modeled is stationary or not are the factors that influence the performance of each version.

Both versions introduce a *forgetting factor* λ. As λ approaches 1, the memory of the learning process tends to be a perfect one equaling all past measurements with

Box 3.2
Summary of the Recursive Least Squares Algorithm—Version 1

Given is a set of P measured data pairs that are used for training:

$X = \{\mathbf{x}_j, d_j, j = 1, \ldots, P\},$

consisting of the input pattern vector $\mathbf{x}$ and output desired response d.

$\mathbf{x} = [x_1 \quad x_2 \quad \ldots \quad x_n \quad +1]^T, \qquad \mathbf{w} = [w_1 \quad w_2 \quad \ldots \quad w_n \quad w_{n+1}]^T.$

Perform the following training steps for $p = 1, 2, 3, \ldots, P$:

Step 1. Initialize the weights vector $\mathbf{w}_1 = \mathbf{0}$ and the matrix $\mathbf{P}_1 = \alpha \mathbf{I}_{(n+1)}$, where α should be a very large number, say $\alpha = 10^8 - 10^{15}$.

Step 2. Apply the next (the first one for $p = 1$) training pair $(\mathbf{x}_p, d_p)$ to the linear neuron.

Step 3. By using (3.75) calculate the error for both the data pair applied and the given weights vector $\mathbf{w}_p$:

$e_{p+1} = d_{p+1} - \mathbf{x}_{p+1}^T \mathbf{w}_p.$

Step 4. Find the matrix $\mathbf{P}_{p+1}$ from (3.88):

$\mathbf{P}_{p+1} = (\mathbf{P}_p - \mathbf{P}_p \mathbf{x}_{p+1} (\lambda + \mathbf{x}_{p+1}^T \mathbf{P}_p \mathbf{x}_{p+1})^{-1} \mathbf{x}_{p+1}^T \mathbf{P}_p)/\lambda.$

Step 5. Calculate the updated weights vector $\mathbf{w}_{p+1}$ from (3.85):

$\mathbf{w}_{p+1} = \mathbf{w}_p + \mathbf{P}_{p+1} \mathbf{x}_{p+1} e_{p+1}.$

Step 6. Stop the adaptation of the weights if the error E from (3.47) is smaller than the predefined E_{des}. Otherwise go back to step 2.

---

more recent ones. If the process is known to be a stationary one (no significant changes in the process parameters), working with $\lambda = 1$ will result in good estimated weights. In a nonstationary environment, with changing system dynamics, the influence of past observations will be reduced and λ will be smaller than 1. In this way, the present measurements are given a heavier weighting and have a stronger influence on the weight estimates than the past ones. What the value of λ should be if one wants some amount of forgetting during learning is highly problem-dependent. A good rule of thumb is $\lambda = 0.92 \div 0.99$.

The two versions of the RLS algorithm are quite similar. The value γ_{p+1} (in box 3.3) is the first part of the second term on the right-hand side of (3.88) for the calculation of a matrix $\mathbf{P}_{p+1}$. However, the order of the calculation of the variables in the two versions is slightly different, resulting in their different numerical behavior. In a stationary environment the forgetting factor $\lambda = 1$.

The RLS is the best alternative for on-line applications when there is no change in system dynamics (for stationary problems). In the case of nonstationary problems

Box 3.3
Summary of the Recursive Least Squares Algorithm—Version 2

Given is a set of P measured data pairs that are used for training:

$X = \{\mathbf{x}_j, d_j, j = 1, \ldots, P\}$,

consisting of the input pattern vector $\mathbf{x}$ and output desired response d.

$\mathbf{x} = [x_1 \quad x_2 \quad \ldots \quad x_n \quad +1]^T, \qquad \mathbf{w} = [w_1 \quad w_2 \quad \ldots \quad w_n \quad w_{n+1}]^T$.

Perform the following training steps for $p = 1, 2, 3, \ldots, P$ (steps 1, 2, and 3 are the same as in version 1—see box 3.2):

Step 4. Calculate the value γ_{p+1} as follows:

$\gamma_{p+1} = \mathbf{P}_p \mathbf{x}_{p+1} (\lambda + \mathbf{x}_{p+1}^T \mathbf{P}_p \mathbf{x}_{p+1})^{-1}$.

Step 5. Calculate the updated weights vector $\mathbf{w}_{p+1}$:

$\mathbf{w}_{p+1} = \mathbf{w}_p + \gamma_{p+1} e_{p+1}$.

Step 6. Find the matrix $\mathbf{P}_{p+1}$:

$\mathbf{P}_{p+1} = (\mathbf{P}_p - \gamma_{p+1} \mathbf{x}_{p+1}^T \mathbf{P}_p)/\lambda$.

Step 7. Stop the adaptation of the weights if the error E from (3.47) is smaller than the predefined E_{des}. Otherwise go back to step 2.

---

with changing system dynamics, it is difficult to say whether the LMS or the RLS method is better—possibly the latter. Both LMS and RLS possess advantages and drawbacks. One should experiment with both methods before deciding which one is more suitable for the problem at hand. There have been claims that if the signal is highly corrupted with noise, the LMS may be more robust. These and other interesting properties and comparisons of both on-line algorithms are discussed in detail in the literature. For an in-depth study of the RLS and LMS algorithms, the reader is referred to the many books in the fields of adaptive control, identification, and signal processing, for instance, Brogan (1991), Eykhoff (1974), and Haykin (1991).

So far the discussion has concerned learning algorithms for a single linear processing unit as given in figure 3.21, which represents a mapping of the n-dimensional input vector $\mathbf{x}$ into a one-dimensional output o. In other words, assuming a linear dependency between $\mathbf{x}$ and o, the linear neuron has been modeling the (hyper)plane in $(n + 1)$-dimensional space. By augmenting $\mathbf{x}$ with a constant input (bias) the hyperplane could be shifted out of the origin. Otherwise, without a bias term, one would only be able to model a homogeneous (hyper)plane passing through the origin.

In the general case, one might want to model the mapping of an n-dimensional pattern vector $\mathbf{x}$ into an m-dimensional output vector $\mathbf{o}$. On an abstract mathematical level, a matrix is a tool that provides mapping from one vector space to another. Therefore, the required mapping may be defined by a simple linear matrix equation

$$\mathbf{o} = \mathbf{W}\mathbf{x}. \tag{3.89}$$

Equation (3.89) is the same as (3.43). At this point, it might be useful to rewrite (3.44), combine it with (3.89), and comment on the graphical representation of the resulting equation (3.90) in terms of a single layer of neurons neural network. (Because the subject of learning is weights, perhaps a more appropriate name would be a single layer of weights neural network.)

$$\mathbf{o} = \mathbf{W}\mathbf{x} \Rightarrow \begin{bmatrix} o_1 \\ o_2 \\ \vdots \\ o_j \\ \vdots \\ o_m \end{bmatrix} = \begin{bmatrix} w_{11} & w_{12} & \cdots & w_{1i} & \cdots & w_{1n} \\ w_{21} & w_{22} & \cdots & w_{2i} & \cdots & w_{2n} \\ \vdots & \vdots & \vdots & \vdots & \vdots & \vdots \\ w_{j1} & w_{j2} & \vdots & w_{ji} & \vdots & w_{jn} \\ \vdots & \vdots & \vdots & \vdots & \vdots & \vdots \\ w_{m1} & w_{m2} & \cdots & w_{mi} & \cdots & w_{mn} \end{bmatrix} \begin{bmatrix} x_1 \\ x_2 \\ \vdots \\ x_i \\ \vdots \\ x_n \end{bmatrix}. \tag{3.90}$$

Equation (3.90) is graphically represented in figure 3.24, which is equivalent to figure 3.12 (right). There is a slight difference only in that there is no bias term in figure 3.24. If the input vector $\mathbf{x}$ were augmented by a bias, there would be one more column in $\mathbf{W}$ and one more row in $\mathbf{x}$. In terms of linear algebra, the output vector $\mathbf{o}$ is

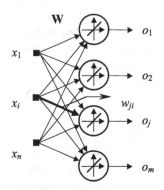

Figure 3.24
Single-layer neural network with linear activation functions.

a linear combination of the column vectors of $\mathbf{W}$ or it is in the column space of $\mathbf{W}$:

$$\mathbf{o} = x_1 \mathbf{w}_1 + x_2 \mathbf{w}_2 + \cdots + x_n \mathbf{w}_n. \tag{3.91}$$

In terms of neural networks, the weights matrix $\mathbf{W}$ can be seen in two different ways. It is formed of row and column vectors. The components w_{ji} of a jth row of $\mathbf{W}$ are the weights *coming in* to the jth output neuron and *going out* from the ith input neuron. Thus, rows of $\mathbf{W}$ are the *incoming weights vectors* to the output neurons, and columns of $\mathbf{W}$ are the *outgoing weights vectors* from the input units. Equation (3.91) can be read as "the output vector is equal to a linear combination of the outgoing weights vectors from the input units" (Jordan 1993). Here, for convenience, *weights vectors* refers to the incoming ones, or the rows of the weights matrix $\mathbf{W}$.

Equation (3.90) and its graphical representation are the best tools for modeling or solving multivariate linear regression problems. One of the important commonplaces in the neural networks field is that the multilayer neural network (meaning two layers of weights at least, with a hidden layer neuron having nonlinear activation functions) can approximate any nonlinear function to any degree of accuracy. Such a statement does not have any meaning for a network with linear activation functions, and it is easy to show that for linear problems there is no sense in using more than one layer of neurons (an output one only).

Consider the network that represents the $\Re^5 \rightarrow \Re^3$ mapping given in figure 3.25. For the sake of simplicity, only three of the five input nodes are shown. The left network in figure 3.25 is arranged in a cascade. The output $\mathbf{y}$ of the first (previously, output) layer is the input to the next layer. In this way, the first output layer becomes the hidden one. The composite system is now a two-layer system, and it is described

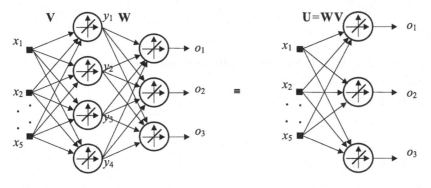

Figure 3.25
Neural network with two layers of neurons and all linear processing units is equivalent to a single-layer neural network.

by the two matrix transformations

$$\mathbf{y} = \mathbf{V}\mathbf{x} \quad \text{and} \quad \mathbf{o} = \mathbf{W}\mathbf{y}, \tag{3.92}$$

where the hidden layer weights matrix $\mathbf{V}$ is a $(4,5)$ matrix and the output layer weights matrix $\mathbf{W}$ is a $(3,4)$ matrix. Substituting $\mathbf{V}\mathbf{x}$ for $\mathbf{y}$ in the last equation,

$$\mathbf{o} = \mathbf{W}(\mathbf{V}\mathbf{x}) = \mathbf{U}\mathbf{x}, \tag{3.93}$$

where the $(3,5)$ weights matrix $\mathbf{U}$ follows from the standard multiplication of the two matrices: $\mathbf{U} = \mathbf{W}\mathbf{V}$. Equation (3.93) indicates that when all the activation functions are linear, the two-layer (or any-layer) neural network is equivalent to a single-layer neural network. This equivalency is shown in figure 3.25.

Insofar as learning is concerned, when there are more output layer neurons, all the methods presented in this section can be used either separately for each output neuron (the algorithms are repeated m times) or for all output neurons at once. If one pursues the latter path, care must be taken about the appropriate arrangements of the input $\mathbf{X}$ output $\mathbf{D}$, and weights $\mathbf{W}$ matrices.

Linear networks are limited in their computational and representational capabilities. They work well if the problem at hand may be treated as a linear one. In that case, as demonstrated, multilayer linear networks provide no increase in modeling power over a single-layer linear network. Unfortunately, the assumption about linear dependency is only valid for a subset of problems that one might wish to solve.

Real-world problems are typically highly nonlinear, and if one wants to expand a network's capability beyond that of a single-layer linear network, one must introduce at least one hidden layer with nonlinear activation functions. Chapter 4 is devoted to multilayer neural networks with at least one hidden layer of neurons having nonlinear activation functions.

Problems

3.1. Find the input u to the perceptron activation function for following input vectors $\mathbf{x}$ and weights vectors $\mathbf{w}$:

a. $\mathbf{x} = [-1 \quad 0 \quad 2]^T, \mathbf{w} = [-1 \quad 0 \quad 2]^T$.
b. $\mathbf{x} = [0 \quad 2]^T, \mathbf{w} = [1 \quad 0 \quad 2]^T$.
c. $\mathbf{x} = [-1 \quad 0 \quad 2 \quad 4]^T, \mathbf{w} = [-1 \quad -3 \quad 2 \quad -5]^T$.
d. $\mathbf{x} = [-1 \quad 0 \quad 2]^T, \mathbf{w} = [4 \quad 0 \quad 2]^T$.

3.2. Calculate the outputs of the perceptron network shown in figure P3.1. Activation functions are bipolar thresholding units ($o = -1$ for $u < 0$; $o = +1$ for $u > 0$).

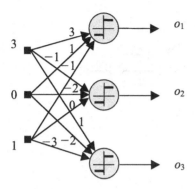

Figure P3.1
Network for problem 3.2.

3.3. For the perceptron network in problem 3.2, find the equation of the separating straight line and its normal vector, and draw all three separating lines in the (x_1, x_2) plane. Find the segments of the (x_1, x_2) plane that are assigned to each neuron. Show also the indecision regions.

3.4. Four one-dimensional data points belonging to two classes, the corresponding desired values (labelings), and the initial weights vector are given as

$$\mathbf{x} = [1 \quad -0.5 \quad 3 \quad -2]^T, \quad \mathbf{d} = [1 \quad -1 \quad 1 \quad -1]^T; \quad \mathbf{w} = [-2.5 \quad 1.75]^T.$$

Applying perceptron learning rules, find the decision line that separates the two classes. Draw the changes of both separating lines and weights vectors during the learning in two separate graphs. Use the following learning rule $\mathbf{w}_{p+1} = \mathbf{w}_p + d\mathbf{x}_p$. It will take four epochs (four times sweeping through all given data points) to obtain the first separating line that perfectly separates the classes. Check the first learning steps by applying either of the two learning rules given in box 3.1. (Note that the weight changes and results will not be the same.) What is a decision boundary in this problem?

3.5. What is the same and what is different in the two perceptrons shown in figure P3.2? Draw the separating lines (decision boundaries) for both neurons, together with the corresponding normal vectors. Draw separate graphs for each perceptron. Draw the decision functions u for each graph.

3.6. Consider the two classes shown in figure P3.3. Can they be separated by a single perceptron? Does the learning rate influence the outcome? Does the class labeling have an effect on the performance of the perceptron? Show graphically the decision

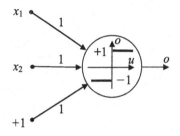

Figure P3.2
Networks for problem 3.5.

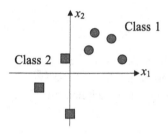

Figure P3.3
Graph for problem 3.6.

plane $u = w_1 x_1 + w_2 x_2 + w_3$ when class 1 is labeled as positive $(d_1 = +1)$ and class 2 as negative $(d_2 = -1)$. Draw the decision plane u when the labeling is opposite.

3.7. A network of perceptrons (fig. P3.4, left) should solve the XOR problem (fig. P3.4, right).

a. Show the decision lines defined by the network. (Sketch these lines in the right graph and express them analytically).

b. Can this network solve the problem successfully? Support your conclusion with the corresponding calculus, and show why it can or cannot.

c. Comment whether learning is possible.

3.8. Two adaptation methods (learning rules) are given in box 3.1 for the perceptron. Both rules are obtained from heuristic arguments. Show that the first method in box 3.1 can be derived by minimizing the following error function at the pth iteration step:

$$E(\mathbf{w})|_p = -e_p u_p = -(d_p - o_p)u_p.$$

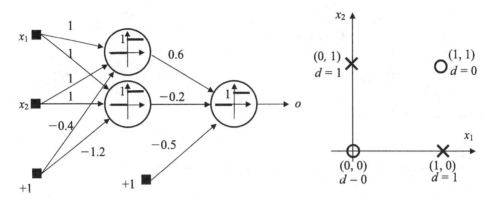

Figure P3.4
Network and graph for problem 3.7.

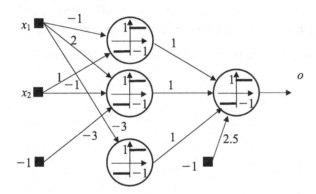

Figure P3.5
Network for problem 3.10.

3.9. Show that minimization of an error function $E(\mathbf{w})|_p = |u_p| - d_p u_p$ leads to the same learning rule as does the error function in problem 3.8.

3.10. The perceptron network shown in figure P3.5 maps the entire (x_1, x_2) plane into a binary value o. Draw the separating lines, and find the segment of the (x_1, x_2) plane for which $o = +1$.

3.11. Table 3.1 shows all 16 possible logic functions of two variables. All but two can be implemented by a perceptron. Which two logic functions cannot, and why? Design perceptrons for realizing AND, OR, and COMPLEMENT functions.

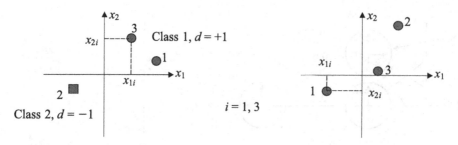

Figure P3.6
Graphs for problem 3.12. *Left*, classification task; *right*, regression problem.

3.12. A linear neuron (adaline) can solve both classification and regression problems as long as the separating hyperplanes and regression hyperplanes are acceptable. Figure P3.6 shows three data points that should be classified, or linearly separated (left), and approximated by a straight regression line (right). Give the matrix **X** and desired vector **D** for both cases. Each data point is given as a pair (x_{1i}, x_{2i}), $i = 1, 3$.

3.13. Three different experiments produced three sets of data that should be classified by using a linear neuron:

a.

x_1	x_2	d
0	0	+1
0	1	−1

b.

x_1	x_2	d
0	0	+1
1	1	−1

c.

x_1	x_2	d
0	0	+1
1	1	−1
2	2	−1

Calculate the least-squares separation line, and draw your result in an (x_1, x_2) plane.

3.14. Find the equation $y_a = w_1 + w_2 x$ of the least-squares line that best fits the following data points:

a. $(2,2)$, $(1,1)$, $(0,1)$, $(3,2)$.

b. $(0,1)$, $(-1,0)$, $(2,4)$, $(1,2)$.

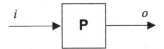

Figure P3.7
Graph for problem 3.15.

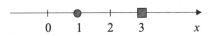

Figure P3.8
Graph for problem 3.16.

Draw the corresponding linear neurons, and denote the weights with calculated values.

3.15. It is believed that the output o of a plant, shown in figure P3.7, is linearly related to the input i, that is, $o = w_1 i + w_2$.

a. What are the values of w_1 and w_2 if the following measurements are obtained: $i = 2$, $o = 5$; $i = -2$, $o = 1$.

b. One more measurement is taken: $i = 5$, $o = 7$. Find a least-squares estimate of w_1 and w_2 using all three measurements.

c. Find the unique minimal sum of error squares in this linear fit to the three points.

3.16. Design a linear neuron for separating two one-dimensional data $x = 1$, $d = +1$; $x = 3$, $d = -1$ (see fig. P3.8).

a. Find the optimal values of the linear neuron weights, and draw the neuron with numerical weights at corresponding weight connections between input layer and neuron.

b. What is the geometrical meaning of input u to the linear neuron? (*Hint:* see fig. 2.16 and fig. 3.2).

c. Draw the u line in an (x, u) plane. What is a decision boundary in this problem? Draw it in the same graph.

d. Find the unique minimal sum of error squares in this classification task.

3.17. Design a linear neuron for separating three one-dimensional data shown in the following table and in figure P3.9. Repeat all calculations from problem 3.16, that is, find the weights and draw the u line in an (x, u) plane. Draw the decision boundary in the same graph, and find the unique minimal sum of error squares.

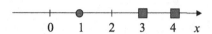

Figure P3.9
Graph for problem 3.17.

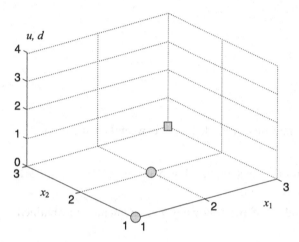

Figure P3.10
Graph for problem 3.19.

x	d
1	+1
3	−1
4	−1

3.18. What would have been the sum of error squares after successful learning in problem 3.17 had you applied a perceptron with a bipolar threshold unit? Comment on differences with respect to a linear neuron.

3.19. Design a linear neuron for separating three two-dimensional data shown in figure P3.10. The circles belong to class 1, with $d = +1$, and the square is an element of class 2, with $d = −1$. Find the optimal weights, and draw the u plane in an $(\mathbf{x}, u)$-space. Draw the decision boundary in the same graph, and calculate the unique minimal sum of error squares.

3.20. Assuming $\mathbf{H}$ is symmetric, solve for $\dfrac{\partial}{\partial \mathbf{x}} \dfrac{1}{2} \mathbf{x}^T \mathbf{H} \mathbf{x}$.

3.21. Solve for $\dfrac{\partial}{\partial \mathbf{x}} \dfrac{1}{2} (\mathbf{y} - \mathbf{Hx})^T (\mathbf{y} - \mathbf{Hx})$.

3.22. What is the difference between the probability-density function and a maximum likelihood function? Express both functions in the case of one-dimensional and n-dimensional normal (Gaussian) probability distributions, respectively. In section 3.2.1, the sum of error squares was used as a cost function. The text stated, "It is relatively straightforward to show that if the data are corrupted with Gaussian noise with a zero mean, minimization of the sum of error squares results in the same parameters as maximization of the likelihood function." Prove this statement. (*Hint:* Express the Gaussian probability-density function for P independent identically distributed data pairs, take its logarithm, and maximize it. In this way, you will arrive at the sum-of-error-squares function. Do it for both one- and n-dimensional distributions.)

3.23. The network in figure P3.11 represents an $\mathfrak{R}^m \to \mathfrak{R}^n$ mapping. What is dimension m of the input space, and what is dimension n of the output space?

a. Organize the weights vectors $\mathbf{w}_i$, $i = 1, 4$, as rows of the weights matrix $\mathbf{W}$, and write the matrix equation (model) that this networks represents.

b. Organize the weights vectors $\mathbf{w}_i$ as columns of the weights matrix $\mathbf{W}$, and write the model that this networks represents.

c. Write the matrix form of the LMS rule (3.71) for both cases.

3.24. Design perceptron networks that can separate the given classes in the two graphs of figure P3.12. (*Hint:* The number of input neurons is equal to the number of

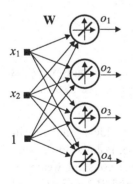

Figure P3.11
Network for problem 3.23.

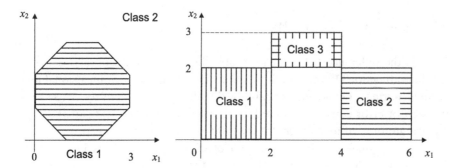

Figure P3.12
Graphs for problem 3.24.

features, but do not forget the bias term. The number of outputs is determined by the number of classes, and the number of hidden layer neurons corresponds to the number of separating lines needed to perform a classification. Thus, just find correct values for the weights.)

3.25. Both the LMS learning rule given by (3.71) and the learning rule that was presented for a single perceptron unit in box 3.1, method 1, are the error-correction types of rules in the sense that the weight change $\Delta \mathbf{w}_p$ is proportional to the error $e_p = (d_p - o_p)$. Compare these similar rules in terms of the features of input to the neuron u, output signal from neuron o, desired response d, and error (function) e at each updating step.

3.26. Learning rule (3.71), which calculates the weights vector after the pth training data pair is presented, can be rewritten in a normalized version as

$$\mathbf{w}_{p+1} = \mathbf{w}_p + \Delta \mathbf{w}_p = \mathbf{w}_p + \eta(d_p - o_p)\frac{\mathbf{x}_p}{\|\mathbf{x}_p\|^2},$$

where the learning rate $0 < \eta < 1$. Prove that if the same training data pair $(\mathbf{x}_p, d_p)$ is repeatedly applied at the iteration steps p and $p+1$, the error is reduced $(1 - \eta)$ times.

3.27. By using the expression (3.54) for a gradient, show that the ideal gradient calculated by using the batch containing the whole data training set is equal to the sum of gradients calculated after each sample is presented. Assume constant weight $\mathbf{w}$ during the whole epoch. (*Hint:* Start with (3.54), express $\mathbf{X}$ and $\mathbf{D}$ by (3.41), and perform the required multiplications.)

Simulation Experiments

No program is provided for learning and modeling using a perceptron or a linear neuron. They are the simplest possible learning paradigms, and it may be very useful if the reader writes his own routines, beginning with these.

Write the numerical implementations of the perceptron learning algorithms as given in box 3.1. Also, design your own learning code for a linear neuron. Start with method 1 in section 3.2.2. It is just about calculating the pseudoinversion of an input data matrix $\mathbf{X}^T$. Implement method 4 in that section to be closer to the spirit of iterative learning. It is an on-line, recursive, first-order gradient descent method.

Generate a data set consisting of a small number of vectors (training data pairs in one or two dimensions, each belonging to one of two classes). There are many learning issues to analyze.

1. Experiment with nonoverlapping classes and the perceptron learning rule first. Start with random initial weights vector (it can also be $\mathbf{w}_0 = \mathbf{0}$), keep it constant, and change the learning rate to see whether an initialization has any effect on the final separation of classes. Now keep a learning rate fixed, and start each learning cycle with different initial weights vectors.

2. Generate classes with overlapping, and try to separate them using a perceptron.

3. Repeat all the preceding calculations using your linear neuron code. In particular, check the influence of the learning rate on the learning process.

4. Generate data for linear regression, and experiment with linear neuron modeling capacity. Try different noise levels, learning rates, initializations of weights, and so on.

In particular, compare method 3 in section 3.2.2 (the ideal gradient learning in batch version) with method 4 (on-line version of a gradient method). Compare the differences while changing the learning rate.

Write numerical implementations of recursive least squares algorithms as given in boxes 3.2 and 3.3. Compare the performance of the RLS and the LMS algorithms in terms of number of iterations and computing times on a given data set.

5. Now, repeat all the examples from this chapter by applying your software.

The general advice in designing programs for iterative learning is that you should always control what is happening with your error function E. Start by using the sum of error squares, and always display both the number of iteration steps and the change of error E after every iteration. Store the error E, and plot its changes after learning.

While solving two-dimensional classification problems, it may also be helpful to plot both the data points and the decision boundary after every iteration.

4 Multilayer Perceptrons

Genuine neural networks are those with at least two layers of neurons—a hidden layer (HL) and an output layer (OL), provided that the hidden layer neurons have nonlinear and differentiable activation functions. The nonlinear activation functions in a hidden layer enable a neural network to be a universal approximator. Thus, the nonlinearity of the activation functions solves the problem of representation. The differentiability of the hidden layer neurons' activation functions solves the nonlinear learning task. As mentioned in chapter 3, by the use of modern random optimization algorithms like evolutionary computing, learning hidden layer weights is possible even when the hidden layer neurons' activation functions are not differentiable. The most typical networks that have nondifferentiable activation functions (membership functions) are fuzzy logic models.

Here, the input layer is not treated as a layer of neural processing units. The input units are merely fan-out nodes. Generally, no processing will occur in the input layer, and although in its graphical appearance it looks like a layer, *it is not a layer of neurons*. Rather, it is an input vector, eventually augmented with a bias term, whose components will be fed to the next (hidden or output) layer of neural processing units. The output layer neurons may be linear (for regression problems), or they can have sigmoidal activation functions (usually for classification or pattern recognition tasks).

There is a theoretically sound basis for the wide application of two-layered networks, which asserts that a network with an arbitrarily large number of nonlinear neurons in the hidden layer can approximate any continuous function $\Re^n \rightarrow \Re^m$ over a compact subset of $\Re^n$. See, for example, Cybenko (1989), Funahashi (1989), and Hornik, Stinchcombe, and White (1989) for neural networks with sigmoidal activation functions, and Hartman, Keeler, and Kowalski (1990) and Park and Sandberg (1991) for neural networks with radial basis functions.

Let us consider first a neural network's intriguing and important ability to learn, which is introduced via a most elementary gradient descent algorithm, the error backpropagation algorithm.

4.1 The Error Backpropagation Algorithm

The basic idea behind the error backpropagation (EBP) algorithm is that the error signal terms δ_{yj} (i.e., δ_h) for hidden layer neurons are calculated by backpropagating the error signal terms of the output layer neurons δ_o.

Backpropagation is still the most commonly used learning algorithm in the field of soft computing. The development of the EBP algorithm shares the destiny of many achievements in the history of science. The backpropagation of error through non-linear systems was used in the field of variational calculus more than a hundred years ago. This approach was also used in the field of optimal control long before its application in learning in neural networks (see, for example, Bryson and Ho 1969; 1975). The EBP algorithm has been independently reinvented many times by different individuals or groups of researchers (e.g., Werbos 1974; Le Cun 1985; Parker 1985; Rumelhart, Hinton, and Williams 1986). The paper by Rumelhart et al. is a popular one because it was developed within the framework of learning in neural networks. It is the core chapter of a seminal and very influential two-volume book (Rumelhart and McClelland, eds., 1986) that revived interest and research in the whole neural computing field after almost two decades of dormancy. The formulation of the EBP learning rule can be found in many books in the neural networks field. The development here is closest to Rumelhart and McClelland (1986) and to Zurada (1992).

Let us first examine the learning algorithm for a neural network (NN) without a hidden layer, that is, with only input and output layers. Starting from the output layer with nonlinear activation functions is certainly in the spirit of backpropagation. Basically this derivation is the same as the one for the least mean square (LMS) algorithm, presented as method 4 in section 3.2.2. Hence, this first step toward the most general learning procedure is a first-order method. The learning law is developed for the case when there are multiple neurons having a nonlinear activation function in the output layer. (The multiple neural processing units in an output layer typically correspond to the classes in a multiclass pattern recognition problem.)

Consider the single-layer NN presented in figure 4.1. (Now the notation y is used for the input signal to the output layer, keeping x for the input to the whole network comprising the input, hidden, and output layers). The sum-of-error-squares cost function for this neural network, having K output layer neurons and P training data pairs, or patterns, is

$$E = \frac{1}{2} \sum_{p=1}^{P} \sum_{k=1}^{K} (d_{pk} - o_{pk})^2. \tag{4.1}$$

Equation (4.1) represents the total error over all the training data patterns (the first summation sign) and all the output layer neurons (the second summation sign). Typically, the EBP algorithm adapts weights in an on-line mode, and in this case the first summation sign in (4.1) should be left out. The EBP algorithm is a first-order optimization method that uses the gradient descent technique for weights adjustment. Thus, an individual weight change will be in the direction of a negative gradient, and at each iteration step it will be calculated as

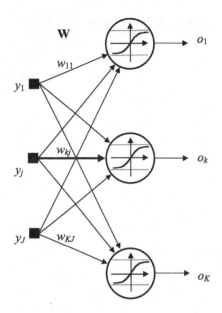

Figure 4.1
Single-layer neural network with nonlinear activation function.

$$\Delta w_{kj} = \eta \frac{\partial E}{\partial w_{kj}}. \tag{4.2}$$

The derivation here is of the learning law for the adaptation of weights in an on-line mode. Thus, for reasons of brevity, the subscript p is omitted during the derivation. The input signal u_k to each output layer neuron $(k = 1, \ldots, K)$ is given as

$$u_k = \sum_{j=1}^{J} w_{kj} y_j. \tag{4.3}$$

As in the case of the LMS algorithm, the *error signal term* for the kth *neuron* δ_{ok} is defined as

$$\delta_{ok} = -\frac{\partial E}{\partial u_k}, \tag{4.4}$$

where the subscript o stands for the output layer. The use of this subscript is necessary because the error signal terms for output layer neurons must be distinguished from those for hidden layer processing units.

Applying the chain rule, the gradient of the cost function with respect to the weight w_{kj} is

$$\frac{\partial E}{\partial w_{kj}} = \frac{\partial E}{\partial u_k} \frac{\partial u_k}{\partial w_{kj}}, \qquad\qquad\qquad\qquad (4.5)$$

and

$$\frac{\partial u_k}{\partial w_{kj}} = \frac{\partial(w_{k1}y_1 + w_{k2}y_2 + \cdots + w_{kj}y_j + \cdots + w_{kJ}y_J)}{\partial w_{kj}} = y_j. \qquad (4.6)$$

Combining the last three equations gives

$$\frac{\partial E}{\partial w_{kj}} = -\delta_{ok}y_j. \qquad\qquad\qquad\qquad (4.7)$$

The weight change from (4.2) can now be written as

$$\Delta w_{kj} = -\eta \frac{\partial E}{\partial w_{kj}} = \eta \delta_{ok} y_j, \qquad k = 1, \ldots, K, j = 1, \ldots, J. \qquad (4.8)$$

Applying the chain rule, the expression for the error signal δ_{ok} is

$$\delta_{ok} = -\frac{\partial E}{\partial u_k} = -\frac{\partial E}{\partial o_k} \frac{\partial o_k}{\partial u_k} = \underbrace{(d_k - o_k)}_{e_k} f'(u_k), \qquad k = 1, \ldots, K, \qquad (4.9)$$

where the term $f'(u_k)$ represents the slope $\partial o_k / \partial u_k$ of the kth neuron's activation function. Finally, the error adjustments can be calculated from

$$w_{kj} = w_{kj} + \Delta w_{kj} = w_{kj} + \eta(d_k - o_k)f'(u_k)y_j$$

$$= w_{kj} + \eta \delta_{ok} y, \qquad k = 1, \ldots, K, j = 1, \ldots, J. \qquad (4.10)$$

This is the most general expression for the calculation of weight changes between the hidden layer neurons and the output layer neurons. Note that (4.10) is valid provided that the cost function is the sum of error squares and that the input to the kth (output) neuron is the scalar product between the input vector $\mathbf{y}$ and the corresponding weights vector $\mathbf{w}_k$. The graphical representation of (4.10), for adapting weights connecting the jth hidden layer neuron with the kth output layer neuron, is given in figure 4.2. Note that the weight change Δw_{kj} is proportional to both the input vector component y_j and the error signal term δ_{ok}, and it does not directly depend upon the activation function of the preceding neuron.

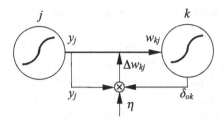

Figure 4.2
Weight w_{kj} connecting the jth hidden layer neuron with the kth output layer neuron and its adaptation Δw_{kj}.

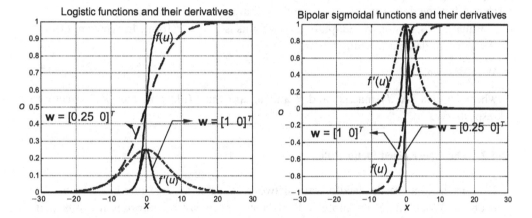

Figure 4.3
Unipolar logistic and bipolar sigmoidal activation functions and their derivatives.

The most common activation functions are the squashing sigmoidal functions: the *unipolar logistic function* (4.11) and the *bipolar sigmoidal function* (related to a tangent hyperbolic) (4.12), which together with their derivatives are presented in figure 4.3.

$$o = \frac{1}{1 + e^{-u}}. \tag{4.11}$$

$$o = \frac{2}{1 + e^{-u}} - 1. \tag{4.12}$$

The term *sigmoidal* is usually used to denote monotonically increasing and S-shaped functions. The two most famous ones are the logistic function and the tangent hyperbolic. But instead of a sigmoidal function, any nonlinear, smooth, differentiable, and preferably nondecreasing function can be used. The sine between $-\pi/2$ and $\pi/2$, the error function $erf(x)$, and the function $x/(1 + |x|)$ belong to this group, too. The requirement for the activation function to be differentiable is basic for the EBP algorithm. On the other hand, the requirement that a nonlinear activation function should monotonically increase is not so strong, and it is connected with the desirable property that its derivative does not change the sign. This is of importance with regard to the EBP algorithm when there are fewer problems getting stuck at local minima in the case of an always positive derivative of an activation function (see fig. 4.3). Note that because $w_2 = 0$, all activation functions in figure 4.3 pass through the origin. The bipolar squashing function (4.12) is in close relation to a tangent hyperbolic function. (Note that the derivative functions in fig. 4.3 are in terms of u, not x.)

Equation (4.10) for the adaptation of weights is in scalar form. In vector notation, the gradient descent learning law is

$$\mathbf{W} = \mathbf{W} + \eta \boldsymbol{\delta}_o \mathbf{y}^T, \tag{4.13}$$

where $\mathbf{W}$ is a (K, J) matrix, and $\mathbf{y}$ and $\boldsymbol{\delta}_o$ are the $(J, 1)$ and the $(K, 1)$ vectors, respectively.

4.2   The Generalized Delta Rule

Now let us analyze the feedforward network that has at least one hidden layer of neurons. When there are more hidden layers, each layer comprises neurons that receive inputs from the preceding layer and send outputs to the neurons in the succeeding layer. There are no feedback connections or connections within the layer. The simplest and most popular such structure is a network with one hidden layer (see fig. 4.4). Fuzzy logic models are basically of the same structure, but their activation functions (membership, grade of belonging, or possibility functions) are usually closer to radial basis functions than to sigmoidal ones.

The derivation of the learning rule or of the equation for the weight change Δv_{ji} of any hidden layer neuron (the same as for an output layer neuron) is the first-order gradient procedure

$$\Delta v_{ji} = -\eta \frac{\partial E}{\partial v_{ji}}, \qquad j = 1, \ldots, J-1, \, i = 1, \ldots, I. \tag{4.14}$$

(Note that the Jth node in fig. 4.4 is the augmented bias term $y_J = +1$ and that no weights go to this "neuron." That is why the index j in (4.14) terminates at $J - 1$. If

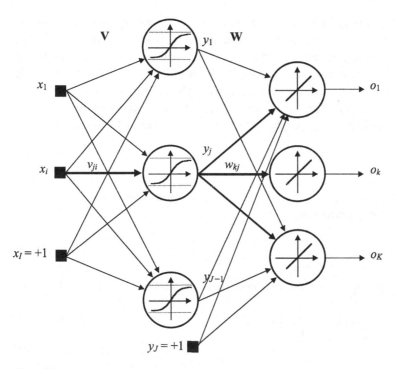

Figure 4.4
Multilayer neural network.

there is no bias term, the last, that is, the Jth neuron is a processing unit receiving signals from the preceding layer, and $j = 1, \ldots, J$.)

As in (4.5),

$$\frac{\partial E}{\partial v_{ji}} = \frac{\partial E}{\partial u_j} \frac{\partial u_j}{\partial v_{ji}}. \tag{4.15}$$

Note that the inputs to the hidden layer neurons are x_i and that the second term on the right-hand side of (4.15) is equal to x_i. Now, the weights adjustment from (4.14) looks like (4.8):

$$\Delta v_{ji} = -\eta \frac{\partial E}{\partial v_{ji}} = \eta \delta_{yj} x_i, \qquad j = 1, \ldots, J-1, i = 1, \ldots, I, \tag{4.16}$$

and the error signal term for the hidden layer weights is

$$\delta_{yj} = -\frac{\partial E}{\partial u_j}, \qquad j = 1, \ldots, J-1. \tag{4.17}$$

The problem at this point is to calculate the error signal term δ_{yj} as given in (4.17). This step is the most important one in the generalized delta rule: the derivation of the expression for δ_{yj} was a major breakthrough in the learning procedure for neural networks. Note that now u_j contributes to the errors at all output layer neurons (see the bold lines fanning out from the jth hidden layer processing unit in fig. 4.4), unlike in the case of the output layer neurons where u_k affected only the kth neuron's output and its corresponding error e_k. Applying the chain rule, from (4.17) there follows

$$\delta_{yj} = -\frac{\partial E}{\partial y_j}\frac{\partial y_j}{\partial u_j}. \tag{4.18}$$

The calculation of the derivative given in the second term on the right-hand side of (4.18) is relatively straightforward:

$$\frac{\partial y_j}{\partial u_j} = f_j'(u_j). \tag{4.19}$$

Error E is given in (4.1), and the first term on the right-hand side of (4.18) can be written as

$$\frac{\partial E}{\partial y_j} = \frac{\partial}{\partial y_j}\left\{\frac{1}{2}\sum_{k=1}^{K}[d_k - f(u_k(\mathbf{y}))]\right\}^2, \tag{4.20}$$

$$\frac{\partial E}{\partial y_j} = -\sum_{k=1}^{K}(d_k - o_k)\frac{\partial}{\partial y_j}\{f[u_k(\mathbf{y})]\}. \tag{4.21}$$

The calculation of the derivatives in brackets results in

$$\frac{\partial E}{\partial y_j} = -\sum_{k=1}^{K}\underbrace{(d_k - o_k)f'(u_k)}_{\delta_{ok}\ from\ (4.9)}\frac{\partial u_k}{\partial y_j}. \tag{4.22}$$

Using $u_k = w_{k1}y_1 + w_{k2}y_2 + \cdots + w_{kj}y_j + \cdots + w_{kJ}y_J$, the derivative term in (4.22) is equal to w_{kj}, and

$$\frac{\partial E}{\partial y_j} = -\sum_{k=1}^{K}\delta_{ok}w_{kj}. \tag{4.23}$$

Combining (4.18), (4.19), and (4.23),

$$\delta_{yj} = f_j'(u_j)\sum_{k=1}^{K}\delta_{ok}w_{kj}. \tag{4.24}$$

Finally the weight's adjustment from (4.16) is given by

$$\Delta v_{ji} = \eta f_j'(u_j) x_i \sum_{k=1}^{K} \delta_{ok} w_{kj}, \qquad j = 1, \ldots, J-1, \, i = 1, \ldots, I. \tag{4.25}$$

Equation (4.25) is the most important equation of the generalized delta learning rule. It explains how to learn (adapt, change, train, optimize) hidden layer weights. In each iteration step, the new weight v_{ji} will be adjusted by using the equation

$$v_{ji} = v_{ji} + \Delta v_{ji} = v_{ji} + \eta f_j'(u_j) x_i \sum_{k=1}^{K} \delta_{ok} w_{kj}, \qquad j = 1, \ldots, J-1, \, i = 1, \ldots, I \tag{4.26}$$

In vector notation this gradient descent learning rule for hidden layer neurons is

$$\mathbf{V} = \mathbf{V} + \eta \boldsymbol{\delta}_y \mathbf{x}^T, \tag{4.27}$$

where $\mathbf{V}$ is a $(J-1, I)$ matrix, and $\mathbf{x}$ and $\boldsymbol{\delta}_y$ are the $(I, 1)$ and the $(J-1, 1)$ vectors, respectively.

The derivatives of the activation functions in the hidden layer or output layer neurons, required in the calculation of the corresponding error signal terms δ if these activation functions are unipolar or bipolar sigmoidal functions given by (4.11) and (4.12), can be expressed in terms of the output from the neuron as follows:

$$f'(u) = (1 - o)o \qquad \text{(for the unipolar (logistic) function)}, \tag{4.28}$$

$$f'(u) = {}^1\!/_2 (1 - o^2) \quad \text{(for the bipolar sigmoidal function)}, \tag{4.29}$$

where for the hidden layer neurons $o = y$.

Box 4.1a summarizes the procedure and equations for the *on-line* EBP algorithm, in which a training pattern is presented at the input layer, and then in the back-propagation part, all weights are updated before the next pattern is presented. This is *incremental* learning. An alternative, summarized in box 4.1b, is to employ *off-line* or *batch* learning, where the weight changes are accumulated over some number (over a batch) of training data pairs before the weights are updated. Typically the batch may contain all data pairs. The weights adaptation equations and the whole EBP algorithm basically remain the same. The only difference is in the calculation of the weight changes in steps 6–9 (step 10 has no meaning if the batch contains all data pairs). The overall error function is given by (4.1).

It may be helpful to remember that δ_{yj} and δ_{ok} are the *error signal terms*, not errors of any type. (As mentioned in chapter 3, δ is equal to the error e at the corresponding neuron only when the neuron activation function is linear and with slope 1.) At the

Box 4.1a
Summary of the Error Backpropagation Algorithm—On-line Version

---

Given is a set of P measured data pairs that are used for training:

$X = \{\mathbf{x}_p, \mathbf{d}_p, p = 1, \dots, P\}$,

consisting of the input pattern vector

$\mathbf{x} = [x_1 \quad x_2 \quad \dots \quad x_n \quad +1]^T$

and the output desired responses

$\mathbf{d} = [d_1 \quad d_2 \quad \dots \quad d_K]^T$.

Feedforward Part

Step 1. Choose the learning rate η and predefine the maximally allowed, or desired, error E_{des}.

Step 2. Initialize weights matrices $\mathbf{V}_p(J-1, I)$ and $\mathbf{W}_p(K, J)$.

Step 3. Perform the on-line training (weights are adjusted after each training pattern), $p = 1, \dots, P$. Apply the new training pair $(\mathbf{x}_p, d_p)$ is sequence or randomly to the hidden layer neurons.

Step 4. Consecutively calculate the outputs from the hidden and output layer neurons:

$y_{jp} = f_h(u_{jp}), \qquad o_{kp} = f_o(u_{kp})$.

Step 5. Find the value of the sum of errors square cost function E_p for the data pair applied and the given weights matrices $\mathbf{V}_p$ and $\mathbf{W}_p$ (in the first step of an epoch initialize $E_p = [\ ]$):

$$E_p = \frac{1}{2} \sum_{k=1}^{K} (d_{kp} - o_{kp})^2 + E_p.$$

Note that the value of the cost function is accumulated over all the data pairs.

Backpropagation Part

Step 6. Calculate the output layer neurons' error signals δ_{okp}:

$\delta_{okp} = \underbrace{(d_{kp} - o_{kp})}_{e_{kp}} f'_{ok}(u_{kp}), \qquad k = 1, \dots, K$.

Step 7. Calculate the hidden layer neurons' error signal δ_{yjp}:

$$\delta_{yjp} = f'_{hj}(u_{jp}) \sum_{k=1}^{K} \delta_{okp} w_{kjp}, \qquad j = 1, \dots, J-1.$$

Step 8. Calculate the updated output layer weights $w_{kj,p+1}$:

$w_{kj,p+1} = w_{kjp} + \eta \delta_{okp} y_{jp}$.

Step 9. Calculate the updated hidden layer weights $v_{ji,p+1}$:

$v_{ji,p+1} = v_{jip} + \eta \delta_{yjp} x_{ip}$.

Step 10. If $p < P$, go to step 3. Otherwise go to step 11.

Step 11. The learning epoch (the sweep through all the training patterns) is completed: $p = P$. For $E_P < E_{\text{des}}$, terminate learning. Otherwise go to step 3 and start a new learning epoch: $p = 1$.

Box 4.1b
Summary of the Error Backpropagation Algorithm—Off-line Version

---

Backpropagation Part

Weights w_{kj} and w_{ji} are frozen, or fixed, for the whole batch of training patterns:

Step 6. Calculate the output layer weight changes Δw_{kj}:

$$\Delta w_{kj} = \sum_{p=1}^{P} \underbrace{(d_{kp} - o_{kp})}_{e_{kp}} f'_{ok}(u_{kp}) y_{jp}, \qquad k = 1, \ldots, K, \ j = 1, \ldots, J.$$

Step 7. Calculate the hidden layer weight changes Δv_{ji}:

$$\Delta v_{ji} = \sum_{p=1}^{P} x_{ip} f'_{hj}(u_{jp}) \sum_{k=1}^{K} \delta_{okp} w_{kjp}, \qquad j = 1, \ldots, J-1, \ i = 1, \ldots, I.$$

Step 8. Calculate the updated output layer weights w_{kj}:

$$w_{kj} = w_{kj} + \eta \Delta w_{kj}.$$

Step 9. Calculate the updated hidden layer weights v_{ji}:

$$v_{ji} = v_{ji} + \eta \Delta v_{ji}.$$

---

same time, as example 4.1 shows, these δ variables are extremely useful signals, and because of their utility the whole algorithm was named the generalized delta rule. This following example should elucidate the application of the EBP algorithm and the usefulness of the output layer and hidden layer neurons' delta signals.

Example 4.1 For the network shown in figure 4.5, calculate the expressions for the weight changes using the EBP algorithm in an on-line learning mode. The training data, consisting of the input pattern vectors $\mathbf{x} = [x_1 \quad x_2]^T$ and the output desired responses $\mathbf{d} = [d_1 \quad d_2]^T$, are given as $X = \{\mathbf{x}_p, \mathbf{d}_p, p = 1, \ldots, P\}$. h_j and o_k denote the HL and OL activation functions, respectively.

After presenting input vector $\mathbf{x} = [x_1 \quad x_2]^T$, the output vector $\mathbf{o} = [o_1 \quad o_2]^T$ is calculated first. Knowing the activation functions in neurons, their derivatives can be readily calculated, and using the given desired vector $\mathbf{d} = [d_1 \quad d_2]^T$, the delta signals for the OL neurons can be calculated:

$$\delta_{ok} = \underbrace{(d_k - o_k)}_{e_k} f'_{ok}(u_k), \qquad k = 1, 2.$$

Having δ_{ok}, one can find the hidden layer neurons' deltas (error signals) δ_{hj} as follows:

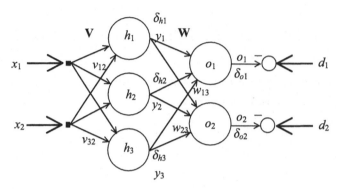

Figure 4.5
Scheme of variables for error backpropagation learning in a multilayer neural network.

$$\delta_{hj} = \delta_{yj} = f'_{hj}(u_j) \sum_{k=1}^{K} \delta_{ok} w_{kj}, \qquad j = 1, 2, 3, k = 1, 2.$$

Only now can the weight changes for specific weights be calculated. Thus, for example,

$$\Delta v_{12} = \eta \delta_{h1} x_2, \qquad \Delta v_{32} = \eta \delta_{h3} x_2, \qquad \Delta w_{23} = \eta \delta_{o2} y_3, \qquad \Delta w_{13} = \eta \delta_{o1} y_3.$$

After the first data pair has been used, the new weights obtained are

$$v_{12n} = v_{12o} + \Delta v_{12}, \quad v_{32n} = v_{32o} + \Delta v_{32}, \quad w_{23n} = w_{23o} + \Delta w_{23}, \quad w_{13n} = w_{13o} + \Delta w_{13},$$

where the subscripts n and o stand for *new* and *old*.   ∎

4.3   Heuristics or Practical Aspects of the Error Backpropagation Algorithm

Multilayer neural networks are of great interest because they have a sound theoretical basis, meaning that they are general multivariate function approximators in the sense that they can uniformly approximate any continuous function to within an arbitrary accuracy, provided that there are a sufficient number of neurons in the network.[1]

Despite this sound theoretical foundation concerning the representational capabilities of neural networks, and notwithstanding the success of the EBP learning algorithm, there are many practical drawbacks to the EBP algorithm. The most troublesome is the usually long training process, which does not ensure that the absolute minimum of the cost function (the best performance of the network) will be achieved. The algorithm may become stuck at some local minimum, and such a termination with a suboptimal solution will require repetition of the whole learning process by changing the structure or some of the learning parameters that influence the iterative scheme.

As in many other scientific and engineering disciplines, so in the field of artificial neural networks, the theory (or at least part of it) was established only after a number of practical neural network applications had been implemented. Many practical questions still remain open, and for a broad range of engineering tasks the design of neural networks, their learning procedures, and the corresponding training parameters is still an empirical art. In this respect, the EBP algorithm is a genuine representative of nonlinear optimization schemes. The discussion in the following sections concerning the structure of a network and learning parameters does not yield conclusive answers, but it does represent a useful aggregate of experience acquired during the last decade of extensive application of the EBP algorithm and many related learning techniques. The practical aspects of EBP learning considered are the number of hidden layers, the number of neurons in a hidden layer, the type of activation functions, weight initialization, choice of learning rate, choice of the error stopping function, and the momentum term.

4.3.1 One, Two, or More Hidden Layers?

One of the first decisions to be made is how many hidden layers are needed in order to have a good model. First, it should be stated that there is no need to have more than two hidden layers. This answer is supported both by the theoretical results and by many simulations in different engineering fields, although there used to be debates about networks with three and more hidden layers having better mapping properties (e.g., Huang and Lipmann 1988). The real issue at present is whether one or two hidden layers should be used. A clear description of the disagreement over this problem can be found in two papers: Chester (1990) and Hayashi, Sakata, and Gallant (1990). Both papers were published in the same year but were presented at different conferences. The title of the first one is very explicit: "Why Two Hidden Layers Are Better Than One." The second, besides claiming that for certain problems the single-layer NN gives a better performance, states, "Never try a multilayer model for fitting data until you have first tried a single-layer model." This claim was somehow softened by calling it a rule of thumb, but this is very often the case in the NN field because there is no clean-cut theoretical proof for many experimentally obtained results.

Both architectures are theoretically able to approximate any continuous function to the desired degree of accuracy. As already stated, Cybenko (1989), Funahashi et al. (1990), and Hornik et al. (1989) independently proved this approximation property for a single hidden layer network, and Kurkova (1992) gave a direct proof of the universal approximation capabilities of a feedforward neural network with two hidden layers. She also showed how to estimate the number of hidden neurons as a function of the desired accuracy and the rate of increase of the function being approximated. These proofs are reflected in many papers using networks with one or two hidden layers. There are some indications (Hush and Horne 1993) that for some problems a small network with two hidden layers can be used where a network with one hidden layer would require an infinite number of nodes. At present, there are not many sound results from networks having three or more hidden layers. However, there are exceptions (see Le Cun et al. 1989).

It is difficult to say which topology is better. A reasonable answer would specify the cost function for a neural network's performance, including size of the NN, learning time, implementability in hardware, accuracy achieved, and the like. Based on the author's experience (and intuition), the rule of thumb stating that it might be useful to try solving the problem at hand using an NN with one hidden layer first seems appropriate.

4.3.2 Number of Neurons in a Hidden Layer, or the Bias-Variance Dilemma

The number of neurons in a hidden layer[2] (HL) is the most important design parameter with respect to the approximation capabilities of a neural network. Recall that both the number of input components (features) and the number of output neurons is in general determined by the nature of the problem. Thus, the real representational power of an NN and its generalization capacity are primarily determined by the number of HL neurons. In the case of general nonlinear regression (and similar statements can be made for pattern recognition, i.e., classification problems) the main task is to model the underlying function between the given inputs and outputs by filtering out the disturbances contained in the noisy training data set. By changing the number of HL nodes, two extreme solutions should be avoided: filtering out the underlying function (not enough HL neurons) and modeling of noise or overfitting the data (too many HL neurons). In mathematical statistics, these problems are discussed under the rubric of *bias-variance dilemma*, which (strictly speaking) has been developed for the squared loss function only. Geman, Bienenstock, and Doursat (1992) discussed this issue of the error decomposition into bias and variance components at length. This section first presents the basic statistical characteristics and nature of these two components, which are related to learning procedure, and then presents the mathematics of error decomposition into bias and variance. The focus is on least-squares estimators, but the issues are generally valid for a much broader class of neural networks and fuzzy logic models).

One of the statistical tools to resolve the trade-off between bias and variance is the *cross-validation* technique. The basic idea of cross-validation is founded on the fact that good results on training data do not ensure good generalization capability. By generalization is meant the capacity of an NN to give correct solutions when using data that were not seen during training. This previously unseen data set is a *test* or *validation* set of patterns. The standard way to obtain this data set is to hold out a part (say, one third) of all the measured data and use it, not during training, but in the validation or test phase only. The higher the noise level in the data and the more complex the underlying function to be modeled, the larger the test set should be. Thus, by using the cross-validation procedure, the performance of a network is measured on the test or validation data set, ensuring in this way a good generalization capability.

The basic ideas are presented for the simplest possible nonlinear regression task—a mapping from $\Re^1 \to \Re^1$, or the modeling of the one-dimensional function $y = f(x)$ using an NN. The low dimensionality of the problem does not annul the validity of the concepts in the case of high-dimensional or multivariate functions. All relevant results are valid in the more complex mappings also, and the simple examples are useful mostly because they allow visualization of the problems.

Let us first discuss the concept of the bias-variance dilemma as given in example 4.2. The network with one HL neuron (dashed curves) and the network with 26 HL neurons (dotted curves) in figure 4.6 represent different kinds of bad models of the underlying function $f(x)$. In terms of the mathematical theory of approximation, the

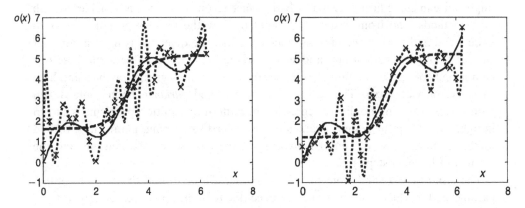

Figure 4.6
Curve fittings based on two different data sets (26 patterns represented by crosses, 25% noise). Underlying function $f(x) = x + \sin(2x)$ (solid curves); approximation by neural network with one hidden layer neuron (dashed curves)—high bias, low variance; interpolation by neural network with 26 hidden layer neurons (dotted curves)—low bias, high variance.

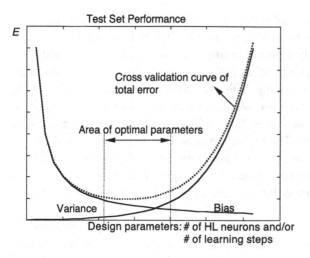

Figure 4.7
Sketch of typical dependence of bias and variance upon neural network design parameters (smoothing parameters).

dashed curves represent the *approximating* function and the dotted curves represent the *interpolating* function that passes through each training data point. Thus, the dotted curve suffers from poor generalization capability although it is a perfect interpolant.

However, whether to make an interpolation or an approximation is not of crucial importance in curve fitting. Good or bad surface reconstruction can be achieved with both methods, and from a statistical point of view the most important task is to understand and resolve the bias-variance dilemma; the objective is to fit a curve or surface having both small bias and small variance. The trade-off between these two components of approximation error arises from parameters giving low bias and high variance, or vice versa. The dependence of *bias* and *variance* upon some design parameters in solving nonlinear regression or pattern recognition problems is shown in figure 4.7. (Typical design parameters, also called smoothing, parameters, related to the learning phase of neural networks are the number of HL neurons and the number of learning steps.)

The task of cross-validation, or the test phase, will be to find the area of optimal parameters for which both bias and variance (the total error) are reasonably low.

Example 4.2   Identify (model, fit, or reconstruct) the unknown relation or process $y = f(x) = x + \sin(2x)$ between (just) two variables x and y. In other words, design a neural network such that its output $o \approx f(x)$, having a set of 26 data pairs from measurements highly corrupted by 25% white noise with zero mean. (More accurately, the problem is to fit the ensemble from which the data were drawn. In figs. 4.6 and 4.8 the data sets are represented graphically by crosses.) Model the data using 1, 8, and 26 HL neurons having tangent hyperbolic activation functions.

Using artificial NNs with different numbers of HL neurons in order to recover this particular functional dependency $f(x) = x + \sin(2x)$, two extreme results are obtained, shown in figure 4.6. The solid curves, representing the underlying function, would probably be the ideal fit and the best approximation of $f(x)$. (In the field of soft computing such a perfect fit is not a realistic goal. Moreover, closely approaching such perfect solutions is usually very costly in terms of computing time and hardware cost. However, one should try to come as close as possible to such a solution at reasonable costs.)

Fittings with dashed approximating curves would have large bias—a great error or disagreement with the data set—but small variance—the difference between the approximating functions obtained using different data sets will not be large. (Note the "closeness" of the two dashed lines in the left and right graphs in figure 4.6.) At the same time, the dotted interpolation curves are not pleasing either, because neither represents a proper fit. In this case, the function reconstruction has a very small bias. Here, with 26 HL neurons, there is no disagreement or error at all between the interpolating function and the training data for the given data points, and the error for the given data set is equal to zero. However, the variance is large because for the different data sets of the same underlying function there are always very different fitting curves. (Compare the two dotted interpolating curves in the left and right graphs in fig. 4.6.)

Generally, from the point of view of neural network design, the dashed curves in figure 4.6 correspond to NNs with a small number of neurons leading to a rough and imprecise model that has filtered out both the noise and the underlying function. The dotted curves represent NNs with an excessive number of neurons leading to the overfitting of data (noise is also modeled but not filtered out), which not only provides poor generalization after training but also, with a lot of HL weights to be trained, makes learning very slow.

In practical applications of NNs one should build and train many differently structured NNs that differ in bias-variance and then pick the best one. (This is part of the cross-validation procedure.) Figure 4.8 shows the results of fitting two different noisy data sets, originating from the same process, $f(x) = x + \sin(2x)$, using eight neurons in the HL. In this simple example, this is the network that can reconstruct

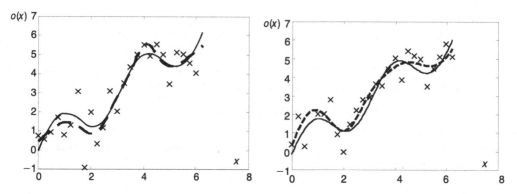

Figure 4.8
Curve fittings based on two different data sets (26 patterns represented by crosses, 25% noise). Underlying function $f(x) = x + \sin(2x)$ (solid curves); approximation by neural network with eight hidden layer neurons—reasonable bias and variance (dashed curves).

the function with a dashed approximating curve that is actually the best compromise in balancing bias and variance and keeping each as low as possible.   ■

The cross-validation technique is widely used in the neural networks field, although there is no guarantee that it will produce an optimal model. The smaller the test or validation data set and the higher the noise level, the more likely it is that cross-validation will result in a far from optimal model. Despite this, it has been and still is a popular technique. Recently, many other techniques for the determination of the optimal number of HL neurons have been developed, the most popular being different *pruning* procedures (Le Cun, Denker, and Solla 1990; Hassibi and Stork 1993). The basic idea of these algorithms is to start with a relatively large number of hidden layer neurons and gradually reduce their number. The opposite idea (called the *growing* algorithm) is to start with a few HL neurons and then add new ones (Bello 1992).

The mathematical presentation here of a classical bias-variance decomposition follows that given in Geman et al. (1992). A standard learning problem in an NN involves an input (features) vector $\mathbf{x}$, a desired output d, and a learning task to find the network's structure as well as a set of the NN's weights capable of modeling the underlying relationship between the input and output variables. The training data pairs obey some unknown joint probability distribution, *PD*. Typically, training and test data patterns $(\mathbf{x}, d)$ are independently drawn from *PD*. The fact that d is a scalar, meaning that there is a single neuron in the output layer, does not restrict the results. The conclusions and remarks that follow apply generally, and the choice of d as a scalar is for the sake of simplicity only. The neural network is solving a nonlinear regression task in which the *regression* of d on $\mathbf{x}$ is a function of $\mathbf{x}$, which gives the mean value of d conditioned on $\mathbf{x}$, $\mathbb{E}[d \mid \mathbf{x}]$, where $\mathbb{E}$ denotes the expectation operator with respect to PD. The use of the statistical expectation operator $\mathbb{E}$ states that the desired value d will be realized on average, given a particular input vector $\mathbf{x}$. Taking into account the statistical character of the learning, the cost function to be minimized for the regression task is the mean squared error

$$\text{MSE} = \mathbb{E}[(d - o(\mathbf{x}))^2], \tag{4.30}$$

where both d and o are conditional on $\mathbf{x}$, and the output from an NN o is parameterized by the network weights. (Because of the dependence on the weights, $o = o(\mathbf{x}, \mathbf{w})$, but this dependence is obvious in an NN, and $\mathbf{w}$ is omitted for the sake of brevity.)

First, it should be shown that regression is a proper tool for fitting data (actually, for modeling the underlying function or an ensemble of observations from which the data are drawn during training). In order to show the property of regression, a useful expression for the mean squared error (MSE) is derived for any function $o(\mathbf{x})$ and any fixed $\mathbf{x}$:

$$
\begin{aligned}
\text{MSE} &= \mathbb{E}[(d - o(\mathbf{x}))^2 \mid \mathbf{x}] \\
&= \mathbb{E}[((d - \mathbb{E}[d \mid \mathbf{x}]) + (\mathbb{E}[d \mid \mathbf{x}] - o(\mathbf{x})))^2 \mid \mathbf{x}] \\
&= \mathbb{E}[(d - \mathbb{E}[d \mid \mathbf{x}])^2 \mid \mathbf{x}) + (\mathbb{E}[d \mid \mathbf{x}] - o(\mathbf{x}))^2 + 2\mathbb{E}[(d - \mathbb{E}[d \mid \mathbf{x}]) \mid \mathbf{x}](\mathbb{E}[d \mid \mathbf{x}] - o(\mathbf{x})) \\
&= \mathbb{E}[(d - \mathbb{E}[d \mid \mathbf{x}])^2 \mid \mathbf{x}) + (\mathbb{E}[d \mid \mathbf{x}] - o(\mathbf{x}))^2 + 2(\mathbb{E}[d \mid \mathbf{x}] - \mathbb{E}[d \mid \mathbf{x}])(\mathbb{E}[d \mid \mathbf{x}] - o(\mathbf{x})) \\
&= \mathbb{E}[(d - \mathbb{E}[d \mid \mathbf{x}])^2 \mid \mathbf{x}] + (\mathbb{E}[d \mid \mathbf{x}] - o(\mathbf{x}))^2 \\
&\geq \mathbb{E}[(d - \mathbb{E}[d \mid \mathbf{x}])^2 \mid \mathbf{x}]. \tag{4.31}
\end{aligned}
$$

Thus, among all the functions of $\mathbf{x}$, regression is the best model of d given $\mathbf{x}$, in the mean-squared-error sense. After the learning, the solution of a regression problem will be the set of an NN's weights that models the function $o(\mathbf{x})$.

The NN output $o(\mathbf{x})$ depends upon the training data set $D = \{(\mathbf{x}_j, d_j), j = 1, \ldots, P\}$, too, and this dependence will be stressed by explicitly writing $o = o(\mathbf{x}; D)$. Given D, and given a particular $\mathbf{x}$, the cost function that measures the effectiveness of $o(\mathbf{x}; D)$ is the mean squared error

$$\text{MSE} = \mathbb{E}[(d - o(\mathbf{x}; D))^2 \mid \mathbf{x}, D]. \tag{4.32}$$

To emphasizing the dependence of the NN model on D, the penultimate line in (4.31) can be written as

$$\mathbb{E}[(d - o(\mathbf{x}; D))^2 \mid \mathbf{x}, D] = \mathbb{E}[(d - \mathbb{E}[d \mid \mathbf{x}])^2 \mid \mathbf{x}, D] + (o(\mathbf{x}; D] - \mathbb{E}[d \mid \mathbf{x}])^2, \qquad (4.33)$$

where the first term on the right-hand side in (4.33), namely, $\mathbb{E}[(d - \mathbb{E}[d \mid \mathbf{x}])^2 \mid \mathbf{x}, D]$, is the variance of the desired output d given $\mathbf{x}$, which does not depend on the data D or on the NN model $o(\mathbf{x}, D)$. Hence, the effectiveness of the NN model $o(\mathbf{x}, D)$ can be measured by the squared distance to the regression function

$$(o(\mathbf{x}; D) - \mathbb{E}[d \mid \mathbf{x}])^2, \qquad (4.34)$$

and the mean squared error of o as an estimator of the regression $\mathbb{E}[d \mid \mathbf{x}]$ is

$$\mathrm{MSE} = \mathbb{E}_D[(o(\mathbf{x}; D) - \mathbb{E}[d \mid \mathbf{x}])^2]. \qquad (4.35)$$

The subscript D denotes an expectation $\mathbb{E}$ with respect to a training set D, or in other words, $\mathbb{E}_D$ represents the average over the ensemble of possible D for a fixed sample size P. The dependence of the approximating function $o(\mathbf{x}, D)$ on different training data sets is given in figs. 4.6 and 4.8, and generally $o(\mathbf{x}, D)$ varies substantially with D. This may result in the average of $o(\mathbf{x}, D)$ (over all possible training patterns D) being rather far from the regression $\mathbb{E}[d \mid \mathbf{x}]$. These effects will be more pronounced for a high level of noise in data, and the mean squared error (4.35) can be very large, making the approximating function $o(\mathbf{x}, D)$ an unreliable NN model of d. A useful way to assess these sources of estimation error is via the bias-variance decomposition of the MSE, which can be derived similarly to (4.31):

$$\mathbb{E}_D[(o(\mathbf{x}; D) - \mathbb{E}[d \mid \mathbf{x}])^2]$$

$$= \mathbb{E}_D[((o(\mathbf{x}; D) - \mathbb{E}_D[o(\mathbf{x}; D)]) + (\mathbb{E}_D[o(\mathbf{x}; D)] - \mathbb{E}[d \mid \mathbf{x}]))^2]$$

$$= \mathbb{E}_D[(o(\mathbf{x}; D) - \mathbb{E}_D[o(\mathbf{x}; D)])^2] + \mathbb{E}_D[(\mathbb{E}_D[o(\mathbf{x}; D)] - \mathbb{E}[d \mid \mathbf{x}])^2]$$

$$+ 2\mathbb{E}_D[(o(\mathbf{x}; D) - \mathbb{E}_D[o(\mathbf{x}; D)])(\mathbb{E}_D[o(\mathbf{x}; D)] - \mathbb{E}[d \mid \mathbf{x}])$$

$$= \mathbb{E}_D[(o(\mathbf{x}; D) - \mathbb{E}_D[o(\mathbf{x}; D)])^2] + (\mathbb{E}_D[o(\mathbf{x}; D)] - \mathbb{E}[d \mid \mathbf{x}])^2]$$

$$+ 2\mathbb{E}_D[o(\mathbf{x}; D) - \mathbb{E}_D[o(\mathbf{x}; D)]](\mathbb{E}_D[o(\mathbf{x}; D)] - \mathbb{E}[d \mid \mathbf{x}])$$

$$= \underbrace{(\mathbb{E}_D[o(\mathbf{x}; D)] - \mathbb{E}[d \mid \mathbf{x}])^2}_{bias^2} + \underbrace{\mathbb{E}_D[(o(\mathbf{x}; D) - \mathbb{E}_D[o(\mathbf{x}; D)])^2]}_{variance}. \qquad (4.36)$$

Bias of the approximating function represents the difference between the expectation of the approximating function, i.e., the NN output, $o(\mathbf{x}; D)$ and the regression function $\mathbb{E}[d \mid \mathbf{x}]$. *Variance* is given by the ensemble-averaged term $\mathbb{E}_D[(o(\mathbf{x}; D) - \mathbb{E}_D[o(\mathbf{x}; D)])^2]$, where the first term represents the NN output on a given particular training data set D, and the second is the average of all training patterns used. All the preceding discussion is related to finite training data sets that are typically used in the training of an NN.

Thus, an appropriate NN should balance the bias and variance, trying to keep each as low as possible. It has been shown that for any given size of data patterns (figs. 4.6–4.8) there is some optimal balance between bias and variance. In order to reduce both bias and variance, one must use larger training data sets. Neural networks belong to the class of *consistent* estimators, meaning that they can approximate any regression function to an arbitrary accuracy in the limit as the number of data goes to infinity (White 1990).

Unfortunately, in practice the number of training data is limited and other techniques should be used to balance bias and variance. Few out of many statistical techniques aimed at resolving the bias-variance dilemma have been mentioned. The newest approaches to training (learning) are based on *small sample statistics*. By taking into account the size of the data set, which is very often small with respect to problem dimensionality, one can obtain better solutions to most pattern recognition or regression tasks. Whole new statistical learning techniques for small training data sets are being developed with promising results. This approach was introduced in chapter 2. For more details, the reader should consult, for example, Vapnik (1995; 1998) and Cherkassky and Mulier (1998).

4.3.3 Type of Activation Functions in a Hidden Layer and the Geometry of Approximation

As with many other practical questions in the neural networks field, there are no definite answers concerning the choice of activation functions (AFs) in a hidden layer. Many different nonlinear functions can be used, ensuring the universal approximation capacity of a specific network. It is not so difficult to choose AFs for output layer neurons—they are typically linear (for regression types of problems) or sigmoidal (mostly for classification or pattern recognition tasks, although linear neurons may perform well in the case of classification, too). The two most popular activation functions, the unipolar logistic and the bipolar sigmoidal functions, were introduced in section 4.1 for the multilayer perceptrons (MLPs) that learn using the EBP algorithm or related iterative algorithms. (The most famous of the bipolar sigmoidal functions is the tangent hyperbolic function.) It was also mentioned that instead of a sigmoidal function, any nonlinear, smooth, differentiable, and preferably nondecreasing function can be used, but the most serious competitors to the MLPs are the networks that use radial basis functions (RBFs) in hidden layer neurons.

Let us consider the basics of sigmoidal and radial basis activation functions. The most representative and popular RBF is a (multivariate) Gaussian function, known from courses on probability as the function of (multivariate) normal distribution. This function is representative of many other RBFs.

Whether a sigmoidal or a Gaussian activation function is preferable is difficult to say. Both types have certain advantages and shortcomings, and the final choice depends mostly on the problem (data set) being studied. A notable difference is in the way the input signal u to a neuron is calculated. The input to a sigmoidal unit is a scalar product $u = \mathbf{w}^T \mathbf{x}$, and the input to an RBF is the distance (usually a Euclidean one) between the input vector $\mathbf{x}$ and the center of the corresponding Gaussian $\mathbf{c}$.

It is commonly held that a fundamental difference between these two types of NNs that feedforward MLP NNs are representatives of global approximation schemes, whereas NNs with RBFs (typically with Gaussian activation functions) are representatives of local approximation schemes. (But note that not all RBFs are localized, e.g., multiquadric RBFs are not.) The adjectives *global* and *local* are connected with the region of input space of the network for which the NN has nonzero output. (Here, *nonzero* means a computationally relevant, not very small output.) For Gaussians, nonzero output is a small region around the centers, and for sigmoidal logistic functions it is always one half of input space. From a statistical point of view, the difference may be that global approximation schemes are likely to have high bias and low variance and local ones high variance and low bias. However, these aspects are not crucial. With different smoothing parameters (e.g., number of neurons, number of iteration cycles during training, or the regularization parameter in RBF networks) these differences may be controlled. Also, at least part of the popularity of RBF networks stems from their firm theoretical grounding in the framework of regularization theory (Tikhonov and Arsenin 1977).

From a learning perspective, sigmoidal and Gaussian activation functions differ substantially. Unlike multilayer perceptrons, RBF networks usually do not use the EBP algorithm. For example, the change of sign of the Gaussian function's derivative, which is necessary in the EBP algorithm, does not support the fast and smooth convergence of the algorithm in RBF networks. Also, for RBF networks, when the centers of Gaussian functions in neurons are fixed (one neuron, a center of the specific Gaussian bell, belongs to a single training pattern, and each center represents the connection strength, or weight, between the input and hidden layers), only the output layer weights (connections between the hidden and output layers) are learned during training. The solution (P-dimensional output layer weights vector) is obtained by solving the linear system of P equations by matrix inversion (Broomhead and Lowe 1988; Poggio and Girosi 1989a; 1989b; 1990a; 1993). P, as previously noted, corresponds to the number of data pairs or patterns in a training set. In terms of CPU time and memory needed, this method is computationally acceptable with several hundred or a maximum of a few thousand data pairs. In many applications, the number of patterns is much larger (tens or even hundreds of thousands), and it is no longer computationally tractable to perform matrix inversion with, say, 23,456 rows and columns. This is the case when there are exactly 23,456 data pairs or patterns, ($P = 23,456$). Chapter 5 presents details about appropriate learning algorithms for RBF networks.

There is a stronger connection between the feedforward MLP and RBF networks than just their similarity in architecture (both have one hidden layer of neurons) or their shared property of being general approximators of any multivariate function. Recently, Maruyama, Girosi, and Poggio (1992) showed that for *normalized* input feedforward MLPs are RBF networks with a nonstandard radial function, which is a good approximation of the Gaussian basis function for a range of values of the bias parameter. It was also shown that for normalized input a feedforward MLP with a sigmoidal activation function can always approximate arbitrarily well a given RBF and that the converse is true only for a certain range of the bias parameter in the sigmoidal neuron. The authors stated that for normalized input MLP networks are more powerful than RBF networks but noted why this property of being more powerful might not necessarily be an advantage. More about this connection can be found in the Maruyama report, but it should be stressed that the normalization of signals has been used by many researchers with good results despite the fact that a theoretically strong explanation is still lacking or is not yet well understood.

The rest of this section considers the geometry of learning—what happens with sigmoidal activation functions during learning.

First consider a problem that can be visualized, a network with a one-dimensional input vector (one feature only) and one-dimensional output (see fig. 4.9). As usual, the input vector is augmented by a bias term. The activation function is the bipolar sigmoidal function

$$o = \frac{2}{1 + e^{-u}} - 1 = \frac{1 - e^{-u}}{1 + e^{-u}} = \frac{2}{1 + e^{-(w_{11}x + w_{12})}} - 1. \tag{4.37}$$

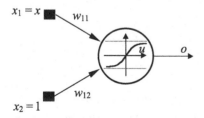

Figure 4.9
Single nonlinear neuron with a bipolar sigmoidal function.

Through linear transformation $u = 2u^*$ (4.37) becomes a tangent hyperbolic function whose weights are scaled by 0.5, or $w_{11}^* = 0.5w_{11}$ and $w_{12}^* = 0.5w_{12}$.

$$o = \frac{e^{u^*} - e^{-u^*}}{e^{u^*} + e^{-u^*}}. \qquad (4.38)$$

The subjects of learning in this simple case are the weights w_{11} and w_{12}. The geometrical meaning of these changes is interesting and important. The bipolar sigmoidal AF will change both its slope and its shift along the x-axis during the learning (Smith 1993).

The slope of the bipolar sigmoidal AF (4.37), defined as the ratio of infinitesimal change in o to a correspondingly infinitesimal change in x, is determined by the value w_{11} in the following way:

$$\text{slope} = \frac{do}{dx} = 0.5(1 - o^2)w_{11}. \qquad (4.39)$$

Note that at the shift point x^* the slope $= 0.5w_{11}$ and that the slope is proportional to w_{11} for a tangent hyperbolic having the same weights vector as a bipolar sigmoidal function. A shift x^* along the x-axis is the same for a bipolar sigmoidal function and a tangent hyperbolic (given the same weights vector) and is determined by the ratio $-w_{12}/w_{11}$ (see fig. 4.10):

$$x^* = \frac{-w_{12}}{w_{11}}. \qquad (4.40)$$

Thus, by changing a (hidden layer) weights vector, one can craft a sigmoidal (or any other) activation function to meet any need. With more neurons in the hidden layer, the corresponding AFs will change their shapes and positions to fit the data as well as possible. At the same time, they will be supported by the output layer weights vector $\mathbf{w}$ (or, for more output neurons, by the weights matrix $\mathbf{W}$).

The output o from the NN in the case of a network with a linear output neuron (usually in regression tasks; see fig. 4.11) is given as

$$o = \sum_{j=1}^{J} w_j y_j(v_{j1}x + v_{j2}) = \mathbf{w}^T \mathbf{y}, \qquad (4.41)$$

and $y_J = 1$.

As to whether the logistic or the tangent hyperbolic activation function should be chosen for HL neurons, there is plenty of evidence to suggest that the tangent hyperbolic performs much better in terms of convergence of learning, that is, in the number of iteration steps needed. It has also been shown that the tangent hyperbolic

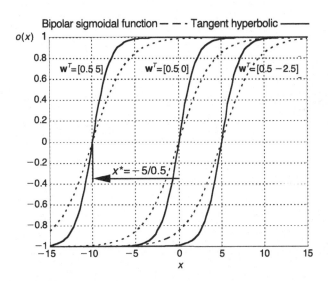

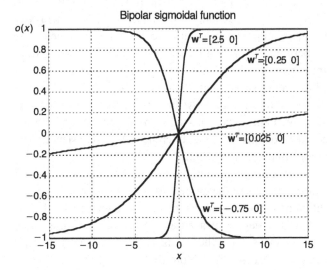

Figure 4.10
Crafting sigmoidal functions by changing weights: slopes and shifts as functions of the weights vector **w**.

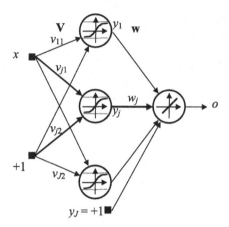

Figure 4.11
Multilayer perceptron for modeling one-dimensional mapping $\Re \rightarrow \Re$, $o = o(x)$.

has much better approximation properties than the logistic function in applying an NN for dynamic systems identification (Kecman 1993a), and similar conclusions can be found in many other papers applying NNs in different fields. It is generally recognized that the tangent hyperbolic (or its relative the bipolar sigmoidal function) always gives better approximation properties, and it is because of this better performance that practitioners tend to use it even though the logistic function was the first to make a breakthrough with the EBP algorithm. At first sight, this is a rather surprising result because it had seemed there were no substantial differences between these two functions. For theoretical details on these differences, see Bialasiewicz and Soloway (1990) and Soloway and Bialasiewicz (1992).

It was just demonstrated that by changing weights one can produce a sigmoidal function of any shape. With more neurons in the hidden layer, or by combining more sigmoidal functions having different shapes and shifts, one can design a network that models any nonlinear function to any degree of accuracy. Example 4.3 shows how HL activation functions place themselves along the x-axis, trying to model a training data set well by following changes of HL weights. Note that starting from an initial random position, almost all the AFs try to place their nonlinear parts inside the domain of the input variable x during learning (compare the positions of the AFs after initialization, shown in fig. 4.12, and after learning, shown in fig. 4.13a).

Example 4.3 Consider modeling (fitting, reconstructing) the same unknown relation or process $y = f(x) = x + \sin(2x)$ between two variables x and y as in example 4.2, with a neural network structured as in figure 4.11 (now having five HL neurons) such that its output $o \approx f(x)$. The training data set comprises 36 data pairs from mea-

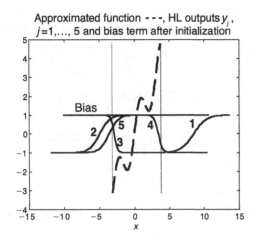

Figure 4.12
Outputs from hidden layer neurons, or the positions of activation functions, after initialization.

surements corrupted by 10% white noise with zero mean. (More accurately, the problem is to fit the ensemble from which the data were drawn. In fig. 4.13c, the data set is represented graphically by crosses.) Model the data using HL neurons with tangent hyperbolic activation functions.

Learning starts with some initial (usually random) weights. The problem of weights initialization is the subject of much research in the field. The reason for such interest can be seen in figure 4.12, where, after random initialization, the AFs of the first, second, and fifth neurons are almost lost as serious candidates for modeling the highly nonlinear dashed function $x + \sin(2x)$. Two vertical lines denote the domain of the input variable x. In this domain, these three AFs are constant values -1, $+1$, and $+1$, and they cannot model any nonlinearity. Within this initialized position, all three AFs together have a modeling power of a single bias term only. The task of learning is to shift their nonlinear parts into the area between the vertical bars, the domain of the function. In that case, these nonlinear parts could participate in modeling the training data. These shifts occured after 70 epochs, and the resulting AF curves are given in figure 4.13a.

The final placement of the HL activation functions depends on the HL weights, shown in Fig 4.13d. The components of the first column $\mathbf{v}_1$ determine the shape of the corresponding tanh. (The signs control the directions of the slopes, and the magnitudes define their steepness.) At the same time, together with the components of the second column of weights $\mathbf{v}_2$, and according to (4.40), they determine the shifts of these tanh functions, too.

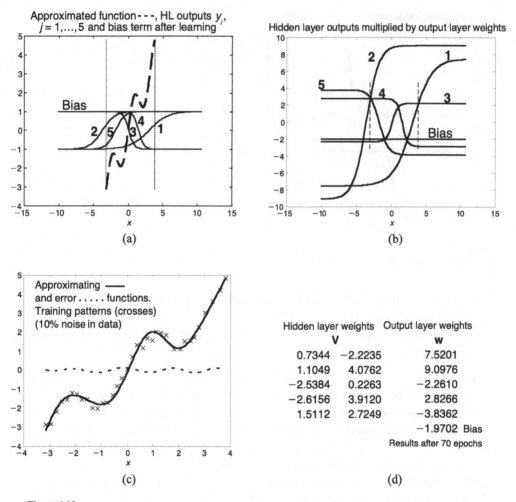

Figure 4.13
(a) Positions and shapes of hidden layer outputs y_j after learning. (b) Hidden layer outputs after multiplication by the output layer weights but before summation. (c) Approximating function after summation of the curves from (b), error, and training data. (d) The weights after training.

The direction of the slopes depends also upon the signs of the components of the output layer weight $\mathbf{w}$. Note in figure 4.13b that the directions (but not the steepness) of the third and fifth AFs are changed after being multiplied by w_3 and w_5, respectively. The amplitudes given in figure 4.13b are the result of multiplying the outputs y_j from the HL neurons, as given in figure 4.13a, by the OL weight components w_j in figure 4.13d. The resulting approximating function for the training patterns, which are represented by crosses in figure 4.13c, is obtained after all the curves from figure 4.13b are summed up. These last two steps, multiplication of the HL outputs and summation of the corresponding product functions, are carried out in the single linear OL neuron shown in figure 4.11.   ■

The basic learning scheme and the way the multilayer perceptron models any underlying nonlinear function between the input and the output data set are basically the same for RBF and fuzzy logic models. The geometrical meaning of the weights between the input and the hidden layer, and the difference between types of AF in the HL neurons, is of lesser relevance. All learning is about crafting the HL activation functions (finding their proper shapes and positions) and finding the OL weights in order to reduce the chosen cost function E below some prescribed value. However, because of the nonlinear dependence of the cost function $E(\mathbf{V}, \mathbf{w})$ on both the hidden and the output layer weights, the task is not an easy one.

The problem of learning when there are more OL neurons is the same in geometrical terms. The whole learning procedure should be done simultaneously for all the OL neurons because they share the same hidden layer neurons. The solution (the weights matrices) $\mathbf{V}$ and $\mathbf{W}$ should now minimize the cost function $E(\mathbf{V}, \mathbf{W})$. Note that in the case of the multidimensional output vector $\mathbf{o}$, one cannot train the MLP network to optimize each particular output o_k, $k = 1, \ldots, K$, separately because the optimal HL weights matrix $\mathbf{V}$ will necessarily be a different one for every output o_k. The optimal $\mathbf{V}$ for one particular output variable will rarely ever be the best one for the rest of the outputs from the NN. (This is known from classic optimization theory.) Thus, the learning (optimization) procedure must be done for all the outputs simultaneously. The resulting HL weights matrix $\mathbf{V}$, which is shared by all the OL neurons, will perform best on average.

As in the case of a one-dimensional input, an NN with a two-dimensional input vector (two-feature data set) will be able to approximate any nonlinear function of two independent variables, and the same is true for the input vectors of any dimension. The two-dimensional input and one-dimensional output, or a mapping $\Re^2 \rightarrow \Re^1$, is the highest-order mapping that can be visualized. Therefore, it may be useful to understand the geometry of the learning in the NN having two inputs and to examine the similarities to the results presented for the one-dimensional input.

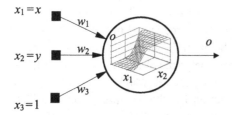

Figure 4.14
Single tanh neuron with two-dimensional input. The activation function is a surface over the (x_1, x_2) plane.

The increase in the complexity of presentation is not a linear one, but the underlying principles eventually are. This may be of help in discovering the ideas, principles, and methods that generalize to the more complex multidimensional input vectors.

Let us first examine the basic functioning of a single neuron having a two-dimensional input augmented with a bias term (see fig. 4.14). The features are designated by x_1 and x_2, and a classical mathematical notation for the two-dimensional input x and y is also used. (This should not be confused with the standard notation in this book, where y denotes the outputs from the hidden layer neurons.) The functioning of a two-dimensional neuron is the same as with a one-dimensional input. Input to the neuron is a scalar product $u = \mathbf{w}^T \mathbf{x}$, and its output is a result of the nonlinear transformation $o = f(u)$. In figure 4.14, $f(u) = \tanh(u)$.

The weights w_i determine the position and shape of this two-dimensional surface, as in the previous case. This surface will move along the x and y axes, tilting in both directions as a result of the weight changes during the learning phase. The process and the mathematics are practically the same as in the one-dimensional case. The tangent hyperbolic (or any other nonlinear activation) surfaces of all the HL neurons will try to find the best position and shape to model the data.

Figure 4.15a shows the intersections of a two-dimensional bipolar sigmoidal function with the plane $o = 0$ for three different weights vectors, and figure 4.15b represents the surface of the same function having the weights vector $\mathbf{w}^T = [2 \quad 2 \quad 2]$. The intersections show how the sigmoidal surface shifts along the x and y axes and rotates with the change of the weights. Similarly to (4.40), the points at which the intersection line crosses the axes (the intersection lines' intercepts) are given as

$$x^* = \frac{-w_3}{w_1},\tag{4.42}$$

$$y^* = \frac{-w_3}{w_2}.\tag{4.43}$$

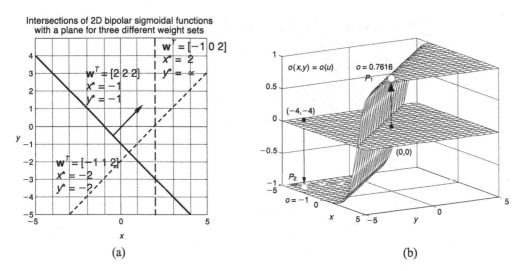

Figure 4.15
Two-dimensional bipolar sigmoidal activation function.

The arrow in figure 4.15a indicates the direction of the surface increase. This direction may be checked in figure 4.15b. The surface increases with both inputs because the weight components w_1 and w_2 are positive. The bigger the magnitude of the weight, the steeper the surface in a specific direction. The surface corresponding to the diagonal dashed intersection line in figure 4.15a decreases with x (w_1 is negative) but increases with y. The surface corresponding to the vertical dashed intersection line in fig. 4.15a does not change with y (w_2 is equal to zero) and decreases with x because $w_1 = -1$. Note that the shifting is enabled by the bias term, or the weight component w_3. For $w_3 = 0$, a sigmoidal surface cannot shift along any of the axes and always passes through the origin.

Each input vector maps into one single value $o = f(x, y)$ at the neuron output. The mappings of two input vectors $\mathbf{x}_1 = [0 \quad 0]^T$, $u_1 = 2$, and $\mathbf{x}_2 = [-4 \quad -4]^T$, $u_2 = -14$, are represented by points P_1 and P_2, respectively, on the surface in figure 4.15b.

By combining more neurons in the hidden layer, one can design an NN as in figure 4.11 that will be able to approximate any two-dimensional function to any degree of accuracy provided that it has enough HL neurons. A simple example of how four HL neurons can form a three-dimensional surface is presented in figure 4.16.

Figure 4.17 presents intersection lines with the plane $o = 0$, indicating the orientation of the corresponding sigmoidal surfaces. The signs of the weight components

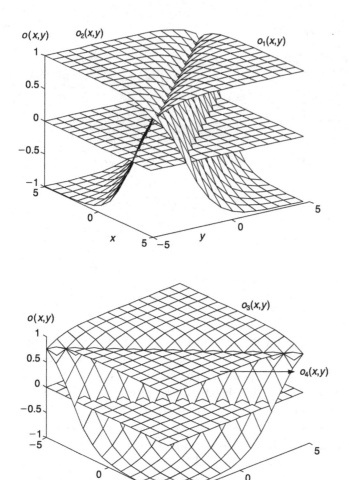

Figure 4.16
Crafting two-dimensional surfaces by using four hidden layer neurons with bipolar sigmoidal activation functions.

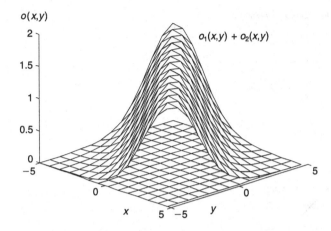

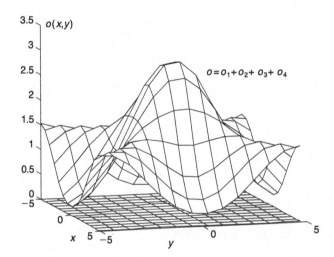

Figure 4.16 (continued)

Intersections of 2D bipolar sigmoidal functions with a plane o = 0

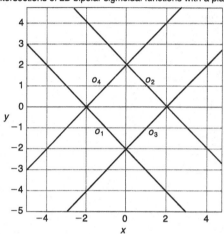

Weight vectors
$$\mathbf{v}_1 = [\,1\ \ 1\ \ 2\,]^T$$
$$\mathbf{v}_2 = [\,-1\ \ -1\ \ 2\,]^T$$
$$\mathbf{v}_3 = [\,-1\ \ 1\ \ 2\,]^T$$
$$\mathbf{v}_4 = [\,1\ \ -1\ \ 2\,]^T$$

Shift x^*	Shift y^*	
−2	−2	$\mathbf{v}_1$
2	2	$\mathbf{v}_2$
2	−2	$\mathbf{v}_3$
−2	2	$\mathbf{v}_4$

Figure 4.17
Intersection lines and weights vectors of the sigmoidal surfaces from figure 4.16.

given in figure 4.17 indicate the increases and decreases of these surfaces along the axes.

The surface shown at the bottom right in figure 4.16 merely corresponds to the sum of the outputs o_j, $j = 1, \ldots, 4$, from the HL neurons, meaning that all the OL weights are equal to 1.

Typical networks in the soft computing field have to cope with high-dimensional input vectors having hundreds or thousands of components, when visualization is no longer possible. However, the geometry of the model remains the same.

In the general case of a multidimensional input (I-dimensional input vector in figure 4.4, with the Ith component being the bias $x_I = 1$)[3] the activation functions y_j

in the HL neurons are hypersigmoidals, or the sigmoid-shaped hypersurfaces in an $(I+1)$-dimensional space. As in the one- and two-dimensional examples, the shifts along the axes, or the shifts of the intercepts of intersection hyperplanes with the hyperplane $y = 0$, are determined by

$$x_{ji} = \frac{-v_{jI}}{v_{ji}}, \qquad i = 1, \ldots, I, \ j = 1, \ldots, J-1, \tag{4.44}$$

where v_{ji} denotes the components of the jth HL weights vector. Thus, the bias weight components v_{jI} control the distances of the hypersigmoidals from the origin, and the weight components v_{ji} control their orientation and steepness, along each of the I dimensions. When all the OL neurons are linear, each output y_j of the HL hypersigmoidals (including the HL bias term) is multiplied by its corresponding OL weight w_{kj} and summed up to form the outputs o_k, $k = 1, \ldots, K$, of the network.

$$\mathbf{o} = \mathbf{W}\mathbf{y} \Rightarrow \mathbf{o} = \begin{bmatrix} o_1 \\ o_2 \\ \vdots \\ o_k \\ \vdots \\ o_K \end{bmatrix} = \begin{bmatrix} w_{11} & w_{12} & \cdots & w_{1j} & \cdots & w_{1J} \\ w_{21} & w_{22} & \cdots & w_{2j} & \cdots & w_{2J} \\ \vdots & \vdots & \vdots & \vdots & \vdots & \vdots \\ w_{k1} & w_{k2} & \vdots & w_{ki} & \vdots & w_{kJ} \\ \vdots & \vdots & \vdots & \vdots & \vdots & \vdots \\ w_{K1} & w_{K2} & \cdots & w_{Kj} & \cdots & w_{KJ} \end{bmatrix} \begin{bmatrix} y_1 \\ y_2 \\ \vdots \\ y_j \\ \vdots \\ y_J \end{bmatrix}. \tag{4.45}$$

For classification (pattern recognition) tasks, the output layer neurons are usually of the same type as the HL neurons—hypersigmoidals $f(u)$ in a $(J+1)$-dimensional space, with an input vector to the OL neurons $\mathbf{u}$ defined as in (4.45):

$$\mathbf{u} = \mathbf{W}\mathbf{y}, \tag{4.46}$$

and the Kth dimensional output vector $\mathbf{o}$ will have components given as

$$o_k = f(u_k). \tag{4.47}$$

Using matrix notation, the network output is expressed as

$$\mathbf{o} = \mathbf{\Phi}[\mathbf{u}] = \mathbf{\Phi}[\mathbf{W}\mathbf{y}], \tag{4.48}$$

where $\mathbf{\Phi}$ denotes the nonlinear diagonal operator

$$\mathbf{\Phi} = \begin{bmatrix} f(\cdot) & 0 & \cdots & 0 \\ 0 & f(\cdot) & \cdots & 0 \\ \vdots & \vdots & \cdots & \vdots \\ 0 & 0 & \cdots & f(\cdot) \end{bmatrix}. \tag{4.49}$$

Now the standard choice for the AFs will be bipolar hypersigmoidals, or the multi-dimensional tangent hyperbolic $f = \tanh(u)$.

There is no great difference with respect to lower-order mapping as far as the basic functioning of a network having high-dimensional inputs and outputs is concerned. In both cases the input signal to the hypersigmoidals is a single scalar value u, which results from the scalar product of a specific input vector and the corresponding weights vector. At the same time, the output from the neuron is neither complex nor a high-dimensional vector or function, but rather a single scalar value y_j or o_k for the HL and OL neurons, respectively. The high-dimensional, nonlinear, and unknown relation between the input and output vectors is mediated through the hidden layer, which enables the reconstruction of the underlying function (if there is a one) by creating many simpler and, more important, known functions. These functions will be the components of the approximating function to the training data. Thus, the I-dimensional input vector $\mathbf{x}$ is mapped into a hidden (internal, imaginary) J-dimensional vector $\mathbf{y}$, which is subsequently transformed into a K-dimensional output vector $\mathbf{o}$.

4.3.4 Weights Initialization

The learning procedure using the EBP algorithm begins with some initial set of weights, which is usually randomly chosen. However, the initialization is a controlled random one. This first step in choosing weights is important because with "less lucky" initial weights matrices $\mathbf{V}$ and $\mathbf{W}$, the training will last forever without any significant learning or adapting of the weights, or it will stop soon at some local minima. (The problems with local minima are not related only to initialization.) The initialization of the HL weights matrix $\mathbf{V}$ is of particular importance because the weights v_{ji} determine the positions and shapes of the corresponding activation functions, as can be seen in figure 4.18. Consequently, the initialization of the HL weights is discussed first.

The left graph in figure 4.18 shows a typical example of very bad initialization of the HL weights matrix $\mathbf{V}$. The nonlinear parts of all five HL outputs are shifted outside the domain of the approximated nonlinear function, which has the magnitudes $+1$ or -1 inside this domain, and their derivatives are almost equal to zero. (The left and right graphs in fig. 4.18 are both examples of extremely bad initializations. It is very unlikely that all the neurons would be so badly initialized simultaneously.)

Practically no learning will occur with such a bad initialization (fig. 4.18, left) because the error signal terms of both the HL neurons $\delta_{yj} = f'_{hj}(u_j)\Sigma(\delta_{ok}w_{kj})$ and the OL neurons $\delta_{ok} = (d_k - o_k)f'_{ok}(u_k)$ depend directly upon the derivatives of the acti-

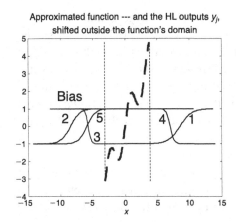
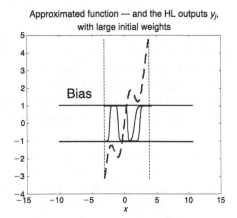

Figure 4.18
Two different bad initializations. *Left,* hidden layer outputs shifted outside the function's domain. *Right,* hidden layer outputs with large initial weights. Approximated function (dashed curve) and its domain (two vertical dashed bars).

vation function f' (see box 4.1). Restarting the weights initialization will be the best one can do in such a situation. To avoid the repetition of a similar situation it would be useful to find a suitable choice of initial weights that will lead to faster and more reliable learning. The positions of the HL activation functions after learning, as given in figure 4.13a (which will also be the case for high-dimensional mappings), suggest that the slopes, or the nonlinear parts, of the HL activation functions should be inside the domain of the approximated function. That can successfully be achieved, but care must also be given to weight magnitudes. In the right graph of figure 4.18 all five sigmoidals lie inside the function's domain, but all have large weights, resulting in steep functions. Such functions for most of the domain of the approximated function also have the derivatives almost equal to zero.

Therefore, the basic strategy would be to ensure that after initialization most of the sigmoidals are not too steep and are inside the domain of the approximated data points. In this way, one avoids extreme output values from the neurons that are connected with small activation function derivatives. All these always produce small initial weight changes and consequently very slow learning. A first guess, and a good one, is to start learning with small initial weights matrices. How small the weights must be depends on the training data set and particularly upon how large the inputs are. Learning is very often a kind of empirical art, and there are many rules of thumb about how small the weights should be. One is that the practical range of initial weights for HL neurons with an I-dimensional input vector should be $[-2/I, 2/I]$

(Gallant 1993). A similar criterion given by Russo (1991) suggests that the weights should be uniformly distributed inside the range $[-2.4/I, 2.4/I]$. These and similar rules for a large I may lead to very small HL weights, resulting in small slope linear activation functions, which again leads to slow learning. Bishop (1995) suggests that initial weights should be generated by a normal distribution with a zero mean and with a standard deviation σ that is proportional to $1/I^{-1/2}$ for the *normalized* input vectors, to ensure that the activation of the hidden neurons is determined by the nonlinear parts of the sigmoidal functions without saturation.

However, the initialization of the OL weights should not result in small weights. There are two reasons for this. If the output layer weights are small, then so is the contribution of the HL neurons to the output error, and consequently the effect of the hidden layer weights is not visible enough. Next, recall that the OL weights are used in calculating the error signal terms for the hidden layer neurons δ_{yj}. If the OL weights are too small, these deltas also become very small, which in turn leads to small initial changes in the hidden layer weights. Learning in the initial phase will again be too slow. Thus, Smith (1993) proposes that a randomly chosen half of OL weights should be initialized with $+1$, and the other half with -1. If there is an odd number of OL weights, then the bias should be initialized at zero.

Initialization by using random numbers is very important in avoiding the effects of symmetry in the network. In other words, all the HL neurons should start with guaranteed different weights. If they have similar (or, even worse, the same) weights, they will perform similarly (the same) on all data pairs by changing weights in similar (the same) directions. This makes the whole learning process unnecessarily long (or learning will be the same for all neurons, and there will practically be no learning).

The author's experience is that very small HL initial weights must also be avoided. Many iteration steps can be saved in the case of *not normalized* input vectors by controlling the initial shifts of the nonlinear parts of the activation functions and by moving these nonlinear parts into the domain of the approximated function. With a one-dimensional input vector this task is easily solvable using (4.40). First randomly initialize the HL weights v_{j1} as well as the required shifts along the x-axis x_j^*, and then calculate all the weights connecting the bias input $+1$ with all the HL neurons v_{j2} using (4.40). The same strategy is applied for high-dimensional input vectors.

4.3.5 Error Function for Stopping Criterion at Learning

In section 4.1, the EBP algorithm resulted from a combination of the sum of error squares as a cost function to be optimized and the gradient descent method for weights adaptation. If the training patterns are colored by Gaussian noise, the minimization of the sum of error squares is equivalent to the results obtained by maximizing the likelihood function. A natural cost function is cross-entropy. Problems 4.18 and 4.19 analyze it. Here, the discussion concerns the choice of function in relation to the learning phase stopping criterion in solving general nonlinear regression tasks. The sum of error squares and the resulting EBP are basic learning tools for these problems. Many different advanced algorithms can be used instead of the first-order gradient procedure, but here the focus is on a measure of a quality of approximation, i.e., a stopping criterion, not the learning procedure.

The learning process is always controlled by the prescribed maximally allowed or desired error E_{des} (step 1 in box 4.1a). Therefore, the final modeling capability of the network is assumed in the very first step. More precisely, one should have an expectation about the magnitude of the error at the end of the learning process while approximating the data points. As in all estimation tasks, one usually knows or can guess the amount of noise in data. This information is usually important in defining E_{des}. (The cross-validation technique can be used if this is unknown.) It may therefore be useful to link E_P and E_{des} with the amount of noise in data, defining E_{des} as a percentage. For instance, $E_{des} = 0.20$ denotes a modeling error of around 20%.

The sum of error squares across all the OL neurons and over all the training data pairs is accumulated in an on-line version of the EBP algorithm ($E_p = 0.5 \sum_1^K (d_{kp} - o_{kp})^2 + E_p$—step 5 in box 4.1a). After the learning epoch (the sweep through all the training patterns) is completed ($p = P$), the total error E_P is compared with the desired one, and for $E_P < E_{des}$, learning is terminated (step 11 in box 4.1a); otherwise, a new learning epoch is started. The sum of error squares is not good as a stopping criterion because E_P increases with the increase of the number of data pairs. The more data, the larger is E_P.

Henceforth, it is good to define an error function that is related to the amount of noise in data for the assessment of the network's performance. The connection between the error function and the amount of the noise will only require the scaling of the error function (4.1), and there will be no need to change the learning algorithm. Now, the relation of some possible stopping (error) functions E_P to the amount of noise in data is analyzed, and an error function that contains reliable information about noise is proposed.

The *root mean square error* (RMSE) is a widely used error function

$$E_{RMSo} = \frac{1}{2} \frac{\sqrt{\sum_{p=1}^{P} \sum_{k=1}^{K} (d_{pk} - o_{pk})^2}}{PK} = \frac{1}{2} \frac{\sqrt{\sum_{p=1}^{P} \|\mathbf{d}_p - \mathbf{o}_p\|^2}}{PK}, \tag{4.50}$$

where P is the number of patterns in the training data set and K is the number of OL neurons. It is convenient to use a slightly changed expression for the stopping criterion for the purpose of connecting the error (stopping) functions E_P with noise in a data set:

$$E_{\mathrm{RMS}} = \sqrt{\frac{\sum\limits_{p=1}^{P}\sum\limits_{k=1}^{K}(d_{pk} - o_{pk})^2}{PK}} = \sqrt{\frac{\sum\limits_{p=1}^{P}\|\mathbf{d}_p - \mathbf{o}_p\|^2}{PK}}. \tag{4.51}$$

Next, consider four more error stopping functions and their relations to the amount of noise (or noise-to-signal ratio in the control and signal processing fields) in the training data.

$$E_\sigma = \frac{\sqrt{\dfrac{\sum\limits_{p=1}^{P}\|\mathbf{d}_p - \mathbf{o}_p\|^2}{PK}}}{\sigma_d}, \tag{4.52}$$

$$E_d = \frac{\sqrt{\dfrac{\sum\limits_{p=1}^{P}\|\mathbf{d}_p - \mathbf{o}_p\|^2}{PK}}}{|\bar{d}|}, \tag{4.53}$$

$$E_{(\sigma+d)} = \frac{\sqrt{\dfrac{\sum\limits_{p=1}^{P}\|\mathbf{d}_p - \mathbf{o}_p\|^2}{PK}}}{0.5(\sigma_d + |\bar{d}|)}, \tag{4.54}$$

$$E_{(\exp d\sigma)} = \frac{\sqrt{\dfrac{\sum\limits_{p=1}^{P}\|\mathbf{d}_p - \mathbf{o}_p\|^2}{PK}}}{e^{-|\bar{d}|}\sigma_d + |\bar{d}|}, \tag{4.55}$$

where σ_d and $\bar{d}$ denote the standard deviation and the mean of the desired values, respectively.

Consider now, in figure 4.19, two noisy (25% Gaussian noise with zero mean) underlying processes: left graph, $y_a = \sin(x)$, and right graph, $y_b = x^3$, $x = [0, 2\pi]$, and analyze the performance of the given stopping criterion for the original func-

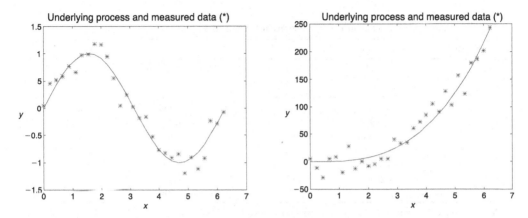

Figure 4.19
Two underlying processes and sampled training data sets (25% noise, $n = 0.25$). *Left*, $y = \sin(x)$. *Right*, $y = x^3$.

tions y and the same functions shifted along 10 and 200 units, respectively, that is, $y_{sa} = 10 + \sin(x)$, $y_{sb} = 200 + x^3$. (Analyze the influence of $\bar{d}$ on the error function using these shifts and keeping σ_d constant.)

From table 4.1 it follows that the root mean square error E_{RMS} cannot be a good measure for the amount of noise in data. It is highly dependent on both the standard deviation σ and the mean $\bar{d}$ of the desired values. Both E_σ and E_d are also dependent on the mean $\bar{d}$ of the desired values. The larger $\bar{d}$ is, the higher is E_σ. The error function E_d performs well unless $\bar{d}$ is close to zero. The closer $\bar{d}$ is to zero, the higher is E_d. $E_{(\sigma+d)}$ avoids problems for both small and high values of $\bar{d}$; it is consistent, but it reproduces scaled information about the noise. Only the error function $E_{(\exp d\sigma)}$ is consistently related to the amount of noise in the training data set, and it is the least dependent on the magnitudes of both σ and $\bar{d}$.

Therefore, the error stopping function $E_P = E_{(\exp d\sigma)}$ is calculated in step 5 of box 4.1a, the EBP algorithm, and it is used in step 11 as a stopping criterion $E_P < E_{\text{des}}$ of the learning phase.

A word of caution is needed here. The noise-to-signal ratio (noise variance) in standard learning from data problems is usually unknown. This means that, in the most elementary approach, defining E_{des} is usually a trial-and-error process in the sense that a few learning runs will be required to find an appropriate E_{des}. However, using the function $E_{(\exp d\sigma)}$ as a stopping criterion ensures a relation to noise content, provided that the approximating function is very close to a genuine regression function.

Table 4.1
The Performance of Five Different Error Functions in Estimating Noise

Noise $= 0.25$	$y = \sin(x)$	$y = 10 + \sin(x)$	$y = x^3$	$y = 200 + x^3$
E_{RMS}	0.1521 ~good	2.4544 bad	15.1136 very bad	63.5553 very bad
E_σ	0.2141 good	3.4545 bad	0.2069 good	0.8699 bad
E_d	200.8643 very bad	0.2455 good	0.2422 good	0.2422 good
$E_{(\sigma+d)}$	0.4277 not bad	0.4583 not bad	0.2231 good	0.3789 ~good
$E_{(\exp d\sigma)}$	0.2140 good	0.2455 good	0.2422 good	0.2422 good

Note: Results are the mean values of 100 random samplings for each function.

4.3.6   Learning Rate and the Momentum Term

In section 3.2 on the linear neuron the influence of the learning rate η on the learning trajectory during optimization was analyzed. The error function E, defined as a sum of error squares (when the error $e = d - o(\mathbf{w})$ depends linearly upon the weights), is a parabola, paraboloidal bowl, or paraboloidal hyperbowl for one, two, or more weights, respectively. There is a strong relationship between the curvature of the error function $E(\mathbf{w})$ and the learning rate even in the simplest case. The learning rate for the quadratic error function must be smaller than the maximally allowed learning rate $\eta_{max} = 2/\lambda_{max}$, where λ_{max} represents the maximal eigenvalue of the error function's Hessian matrix of second derivatives. (Note that in section 3.2 a stronger and more practical bound was used for the convergence $\eta_{T\,max} = 2/trace(\mathbf{XX}^T)$, which corresponds to $\eta_{T\,max} = 2/trace(\mathbf{H})$. One is on the safe side concerning the optimization convergence as long as the Hessian matrix is positive definite, meaning that the error function is a hyperbowl with a guaranteed minimum, and using $\eta_{T\,max}$ smaller than η_{max}.) The higher the curvature, the larger the eigenvalues, the smaller η must be. Obtaining information about the shape of the error function is usually time-consuming, and it can be easier and faster to run the optimization and experimentally find out the proper learning rate η.

However, there is a simple rule. The smaller η is, the smoother the convergence of the search but the higher the number of iteration steps needed. We have already seen these phenomena for the linear neuron (fig. 3.22). Descending by small η will lead to the nearest minimum when the error $E(\mathbf{w})$ is a nonlinear function of the weights. Usually that will be a local minimum of the cost function, and if this $E_{min}(\mathbf{w})$ is larger than the predefined maximally allowed (desired) error E_{des}, the whole learning process must be repeated starting from some other initial weights vector $\mathbf{w}_0$. Therefore, working with small η may be rather costly in terms of computing time. A typical rule of thumb is to start with some larger learning rate η and reduce it during optimization. (Clearly, what is considered a small or a large learning rate is highly problem-dependent, and proper η should be established in the first few runs for a given problem.)

Despite the fact that the EBP algorithm triggered a revival of the whole neural networks field, it was clear from the beginning that the standard EBP algorithm is not a serious candidate for finding the optimal weights vector (the global minimum of the cost function) for large-scale nonlinear problems. Many improved algorithms have been proposed in order to find a reliable and fast strategy for optimizing the learning rate in a reasonable amount of computing time. Details are not given here. Instead, one of the first, simple yet powerful, improvements of the standard EBP algorithm is presented here—the *momentum* term (Plaut, Nowlan, and Hinton 1986; Polyak 1987).

The use of momentum has a physical analogy in a heavy ball rolling down the inside of a bowl (Polyak 1987). The heavier the ball, the greater is its momentum, and the optimizing path does not follow the direction of the instant gradient. Thus, the oscillatory behavior of a light ball (no momentum) is avoided. The descending trajectory of a heavy ball is much smoother and results in faster convergence (a smaller number of iterative steps needed to reach the minimum) than if a light ball were used.

Formally, the modified gradient descent is given as

$$\mathbf{w}(n+1) = \mathbf{w}(n) - \eta \nabla E_{\mathbf{w}(n)} + \eta_m \underbrace{[\mathbf{w}(n) - \mathbf{w}(n-1)]}_{\Delta \mathbf{w}_{n-1}}$$

$$= \mathbf{w}(n) - \eta \nabla E_{\mathbf{w}(n)} + \eta_m [-\eta \nabla E_{\mathbf{w}(n-1)}], \tag{4.56}$$

where η_m denotes the *momentum learning rate* and $\nabla E_{\mathbf{w}} = \partial E / \partial \mathbf{w}$.

The momentum term is particularly effective with error functions that have substantially different curvatures along different weight directions. In such a situation, the error function is no longer radially symmetric, and it has the shape of an elongated bowl. The eigenvalues ratio $\lambda_{\max}/\lambda_{\min}$ of the corresponding Hessian matrix is now larger than 1. A simple gradient descent procedure progresses toward the minimum very slowly in such valleys, and with higher learning rates η this is an oscillatory descent.

Figure 4.20 shows the effect of the introduction of momentum for a second-order quadratic error function surface with an eigenvalues ratio $\lambda_{\max}/\lambda_{\min} = 3.5/0.5 = 7$.

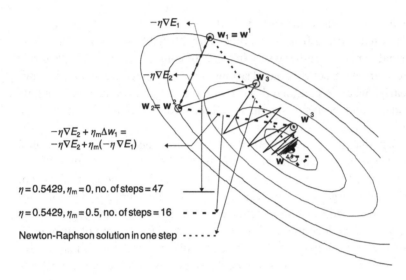

Figure 4.20
Optimization on quadratic surfaces without momentum (solid line) and with momentum (thick dashed line).

The subscripts indicate the solutions $\mathbf{w}_i$ obtained without the momentum term, and the superscripts correspond to those obtained using the momentum $\mathbf{w}^i$.

The choice of both learning rates η and η_m is highly problem-dependent and usually a trial-and-error procedure. The momentum learning rate is typically $0 < \eta_m < 1$. There is a relatively strong relationship between the symmetry of the error function and the momentum learning rate η_m, which can be expressed as the lower the symmetric error function, the higher is η_m. Figure 4.21 and table 4.2 show that for the highly elongated error bowl ($\lambda_{\max}/\lambda_{\min} = 3.9/0.1 = 39$), the optimal η_m is about 0.7. Similarly, the results for the symmetric error function ($\lambda_{\max}/\lambda_{\min} = 1$) are presented in figure 4.22 and table 4.3. Here, for given learning rates η, the optimal η_m is about 0.2.

In a real high-dimensional optimization problem, the shape of the error function is usually not known. The calculation of the Hessian matrix that measures the curvature of the error hyperbowl is possible in principle, but in a nonlinear case this curvature is permanently changing, and besides being expensive, it is generally difficult to determine the proper momentum learning rate η_m. Thus, the usual practice is to work with $0.5 < \eta_m < 0.7$. Note that working with the momentum term makes optimization more robust with respect to the choice of the learning rate η.

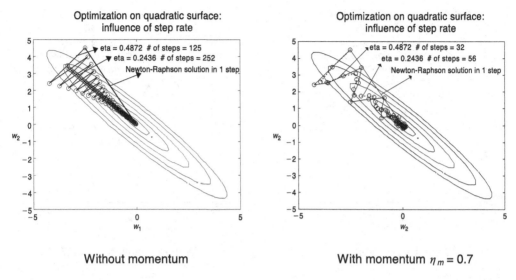

Figure 4.21
Optimization on highly elongated quadratic surface; influence of learning rates.

Table 4.2
Optimization on Highly Elongated Quadratic Surface

	$\eta_m = 0.8$	$\eta_m = 0.9$
$\eta = 0.4872$	41 step	93 steps
$\eta = 0.2436$	44 steps	94 steps

The utilization of the momentum term is a step toward a second-order method at less cost. In the standard EBP algorithm, the information obtained in the preceding iterations is not used at all. Unlike the gradient method of the EBP algorithm, the method using the momentum term takes into account the "prehistory" of the optimization process. In this way, it improves convergence without additional computation. (There is no need to calculate the Hessian, for example.) Polyak (1987) showed that both the gradient procedure and the heavy ball method (gradient with a momentum) for an optimal choice of learning rates η and η_m, have a geometric rate of convergence, but the progression ratios without momentum (r_G) and with momentum (r_{HB}) are different; they are given as

$$
r_G = \frac{\lambda_{\max} - \lambda_{\min}}{\lambda_{\max} + \lambda_{\min}} \quad \text{and} \quad r_{HB} = \frac{\sqrt{\lambda_{\max}} - \sqrt{\lambda_{\min}}}{\sqrt{\lambda_{\max}} + \sqrt{\lambda_{\min}}}, \tag{4.57}
$$

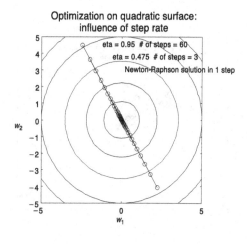
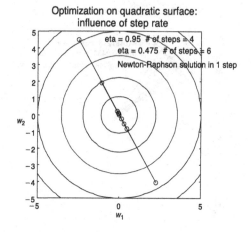

Without momentum   With momentum $\eta_m = 0.7$

Figure 4.22
Optimization on symmetric quadratic surface; influence of learning rates.

Table 4.3
Optimization on Symmetric Quadratic Surface

	$\eta_m = 0.5$	$\eta_m = 0.8$
$\eta = 0.95$	14 steps	41 step
$\eta = 0.475$	17 steps	39 steps

where $\lambda_{\max}$ and $\lambda_{\min}$ represent the maximal and minimal eigenvalue of the Hessian matrix, respectively. The progression ratios are equal for a symmetric error function with equal eigenvalues, and the minimum will be reached in one step only by using optimal learning rates. The less symmetric the hyperbowl, the higher is the ratio $r_\lambda = \lambda_{\max}/\lambda_{\min}$, and for such ill-posed problems the heavy ball method yields a roughly $\sqrt{r_\lambda}$-fold payoff versus the standard gradient-based EBP algorithm. A very strong point for the heavy ball method is that it represents a kind of on-line version of the powerful batch *conjugate gradient* method (see chapter 8).

As in the case of learning rate η, there have been many proposals on how to improve learning by calculating and using the adaptive momentum rate η_m, which varies for each iteration step. In other words, the momentum rate follows and adjusts to changes in the nonlinear error surface. One of the most popular algorithms for the calculation of an adaptive or dynamic momentum rate is the *quickprop method* (Fahlman 1988). This heuristic learning algorithm is loosely based on the Newton-Raphson method; its simplified version is presented here. More details can be found in Fahlman (1988) or Cichocki and Unbehauen (1993). The adaptive momentum rate $\eta_m(n)$ is given by

$$\eta_m(n) = \frac{\nabla E_{\mathbf{w}(n)}}{\nabla E_{\mathbf{w}(n-1)} - \nabla E_{\mathbf{w}(n)}}. \tag{4.58}$$

The quickprop method can miss direction and start climbing up to the maximum because it originates from the second-order approach. Thus, bounds, constraints, and several other measures are needed to assure appropriate learning in real situations.

The error function $E(\mathbf{w})$ is a nonlinear function of weights, and the whole optimization procedure is much more complex in the case of more common and standard learning problems when hidden layer weights are the subjects of optimization. This is discussed at length in chapter 8. Here only a few typical phenomena with nonlinear optimization are presented. In figure 4.23 the nonlinear error function $E(\mathbf{w}) = -w_1 \cos(w_1) + \sin(w_2)$, depending on two weights only, is shown. There are two minima $\mathbf{m}_1 = [0.863 \quad -\pi/2]^T$, $\mathbf{m}_2 = [-3.426 \quad -\pi/2]^T$, two maxima, and a few saddle points in the given domain of $\mathbf{w}$. The optimization procedure can have many different outcomes, all of them depending on the method applied, starting point (or initialization), learning rate η, and momentum learning rate η_m.

There are four trajectories shown in figure 4.23. Two of them use gradient learning without momentum, and they end in two different minima. The two others use the Newton-Raphson method; the first one ends in the closest maximum $\mathbf{M}$, while the other trajectory ends in the saddle point $\mathbf{SP}$. The solid line ending in the closest minimum $\mathbf{m}_1$ represents the trajectory for small η ($\eta = 0.05$) without the momentum term (or with $\eta_m = 0$). The dotted trajectory that ends in minimum $\mathbf{m}_2$ is obtained with $\eta = 0.9$, $\eta_m = 0$. It is interesting to note that the second-order Newton-Raphson procedure using learning rate $\eta_H = 0.2$ ends in the closest maximum $\mathbf{M}$ (arrow). The standard Newton-Raphson procedure, with learning rate $\eta_H = 1$, starting from E_0, ends at the saddle point $\mathbf{SP}$ (black dot). Thus, this second-order Newton-Raphson procedure reaches the closest minimum only when the starting point is very close to it (the Hessian matrix at starting point E_0 is positive definite). Otherwise it may end in the closest maximum or the closest saddle point.

This nonlinear optimization example gives an idea of the variety of possible optimization outcomes. Chapter 8 is devoted to such problems, and the important issues of nonlinear optimization in the field of soft models is discussed in much more detail there.

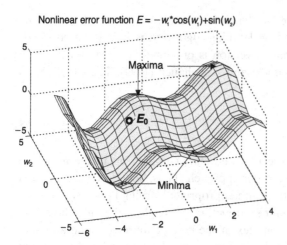

Nonlinear error function $E = -w_1*\cos(w_1)+\sin(w_2)$

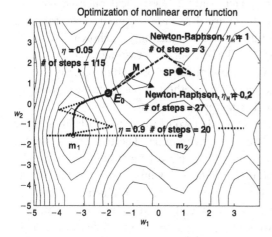

Optimization of nonlinear error function

Figure 4.23
Optimization on a nonlinear surface; influence of learning rates.

Problems

4.1. a. Find the outputs o from the two networks shown in figures P4.1a and P4.1b. The hidden layer activation function is a bipolar sigmoidal function given by (4.12).

b. For the network in figure P4.1b, find outputs for different activation functions $o = f(u)$ when $f(u)$ is a linear AF; $f(u)$ is a bipolar sigmoidal function given by (4.12); and $f(u)$ is a logistic function given by (4.11).

4.2. Find the updating equations Δw_{ij} for the weights w_{41}, w_{53}, and w_{54} in figure P4.2a, for the weights w_{41}, w_{32}, w_{54}, and w_{63} in figure P4.2b, and for the weights w_{41}, w_{32}, w_{63}, w_{76}, and w_{85} in figure P4.2c. Inputs i and desired values d are known. All neurons have the same AF, $o = f(u)$. (*Hint:* First express the delta error signals for the output layer neurons and then find the equations for the HL deltas. With the deltas known, a calculation of the weight changes is straightforward.)

4.3. The NN consisting of a single neuron with a sine as an activation function, $o = \sin(w_1 x + w_2)$ is given in figure P4.3. Using the gradient procedure, find the weights in the next step after the input vector $y = [\pi/8 \quad 1]^T$ is provided at the input. Learning rate $\eta = 0.5$. Desired value $d = 1$.

4.4. Calculate the new weights for the neuron in figure P4.4. Cost function is not a sum of error squares but L_1 norm, i.e., $J = |d - o|$. Input $\mathbf{x} = [1 \quad 1 \quad 1]^T$, desired

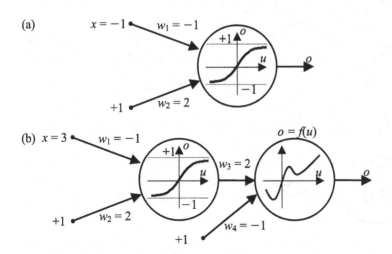

Figure P4.1
Graph for problem 4.1.

(a)

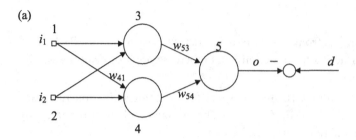

(b)

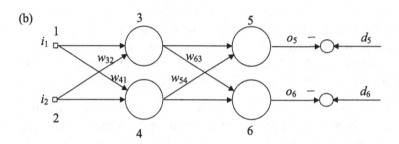

(c)

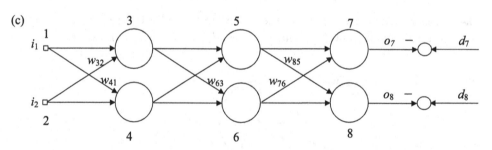

Figure P4.2
Graph for problem 4.2.

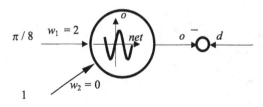

Figure P4.3
Graph for problem 4.3.

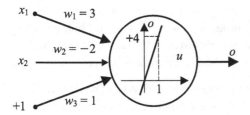

Figure P4.4
Graph for problem 4.4.

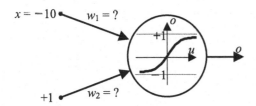

Figure P4.5
Graph for problem 4.6.

output $d = 5$, and the learning rate $\eta = 1$. (*Hint:* When $y = |f(x)|$), then

$$\frac{\partial y}{\partial x} = \frac{|f(x)| \frac{df(x)}{dx}}{f(x)}.$$

4.5. Derive equations (4.28) and (4.29). Find the values of $f'(u)$ at the origin. Find the slopes $f'(x)$ at the origin when $w_1 = 10$.

4.6. A processing unit with a one-dimensional input in figure P4.5 has a shift $x^* = 5$ along the x-axis, and at that point the output is declining at the rate 0.5. What are the values of w_1 and w_2?

4.7. A two-dimensional bipolar sigmoidal function has a shift $x^* = 5$ along the x-axis and $y^* = -1$ along the y-axis. $w_1 = -1$. What is its weight w_2?

4.8. What is the number of weights in the fully connected feedforward NN with one hidden layer having J neurons? There are K neurons in the output layer. Input vector is n-dimensional. Both the input vector **x** and the HL output vector **y** are augmented with a bias term. What is the dimension of the error function $E(\mathbf{w})$ space? (All unknown weights are collected in a weights vector **w**.)

4.9. Consider the feedforward NN in figure P4.6. Justify the statement that this network is equivalent to an NN with only input and output layers (no hidden layer) as long as $|x| < 5$ and for any output layer weights matrix $\mathbf{W}$. (*Hint:* See figure 4.10 and find out what is the operational region of the HL neurons when $|x| < 5$.)

4.10. The NN shown in figure P4.7 uses the bipolar sigmoidal AFs. The outputs have been observed as $o_1 = 0.28$ and $o_2 = -0.73$. Find the input vector $\mathbf{x}$ that has been applied to the network. Find also the slope values of the AFs at the activations u_1 and u_2.

4.11. Perform two training steps for a single neuron with a bipolar sigmoidal activation function. Input $\mathbf{x}_1 = [2 \quad 0 \quad -1]^T$, $d_1 = -1$, $\mathbf{x}_2 = [1 \quad -2 \quad -1]^T$, $d_2 = 1$, initial weight $\mathbf{w}_0 = [1 \quad 0 \quad 1]^T$, and the learning rate $\eta = 0.25$.

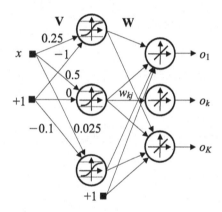

Figure P4.6
Graph for problem 4.9.

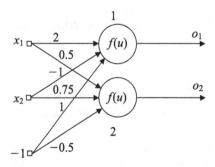

Figure P4.7
Graph for problem 4.10.

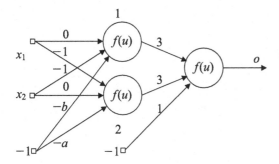

Figure P4.8
Graph for problem 4.13.

4.12. The error function to be minimized is given by $E(\mathbf{w}) = w_1^2 - w_1 - w_1 w_2 + 0.5 w_2^2 + 0.5$. Find analytically the gradient vector $\nabla E(\mathbf{w})$ and the optimal weights vector $\mathbf{w}^*$ that minimizes the error function.

4.13. The NN in figure P4.8 is trained to classify (dichotomize) a number of two-dimensional, two-class inputs.

a. Draw the separation lines between the two classes in the (x_1, x_2) plane, assuming that both the HL and the OL activation functions are discrete bipolar functions, that is, threshold functions between -1 and $+1$.

b. Assume now that all the AFs are bipolar sigmoidal functions. Find the region of uncertainty in the (x_1, x_2) plane using the following thresholding criteria: if $o > 0.9$, then the input pattern belongs to class 1, and if $o < -0.9$, then the input pattern belongs to class 2. For the sake of simplicity, assume $a = b = 0$.

4.14. Show analytically that the decision boundary in the input space $\Re^n$ implemented by a single neuron with a logistic function (depicted in figure P4.9) is a hyperplane.

4.15. Show analytically that the output from the perfectly trained neuron in figure P4.9 represents the posterior probability of a Gaussian distribution in the case of a binary classification. Work with the one-dimensional input x. Assume same prior probabilities, that is, the data from both classes are equally likely. (*Hint:* Data from both classes are produced according to Gaussian normal distributions. Express likelihood functions for each class. Assume different means and the same variance. Use Bayes' rule and show that the posterior probability is a logistic function.)

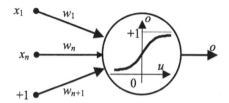

Figure P4.9
Graph for problems 4.14 and 4.15.

4.16. In the case of a multiclass classification, instead of the logistic function we use the softmax function (also known as the Pott's distribution), given as

$$y_i = \frac{e^{x_i}}{\sum\limits_{j=1}^{n} e^{x_j}},$$

where $i = 1, \ldots, n$, and n is a number of classes. Find the derivatives $(\partial y_i / \partial x_j)$. Express your result in terms of y_i and y_j. Sketch the graph y_i in the two-dimensional case.

4.17. An important issue in neural networks learning is the relation between the error (cost) function E and the OL activation functions for various tasks. A lot of experimental evidence shows that learning improves when the delta signal is linear with respect to the output signal y from the OL neuron. Find the delta signals in regression tasks (when the error function is a sum of error squares) for

a. a linear OL activation function,

b. a logistic OL activation function.

(*Hint:* Start with the instantaneous sum-of-error-squares cost function $E = \frac{1}{2}(d - y)^2$, and find the delta signals for the two AFs. The notation y is used instead of the usual notation for the output signal o, for your convenience. The use of y may be more familiar and should ease the solution of this and the following problem.)

Discuss which of the two proposed OL activation functions is better in terms of the preceding comments about experimental evidence.

4.18. Find the delta signals in a classification task when the appropriate error function is a *cross-entropy* given for stochastic, or on-line, learning as $E = -[d \log y + (1 - d) \log(1 - y)]$, where d denotes a desired value and y is the OL neuron output. Find the delta signals for

(a) a linear OL activation function,

(b) a logistic OL activation function,

(c) a tangent hyperbolic activation function.

Discuss which of the three AFs is best in terms of the comments in problem 4.17.

4.19. Derive the cross-entropy error function E given in problem 4.18. (*Hint:* For the two-class classification, data are generated by the Bernoulli distribution. Find the likelihood of P independent identically distributed data pairs, take its logarithm (find the log-likelihood l), and the error (cost) function for the whole data set is $E = -l$.)

4.20. Show that using a pair of softmax output neurons is mathematically equivalent to using a single OL neuron with a logistic function. Express the connections between the weights vectors and biases in the softmax model and the weights vector and bias in the logistic model.

Simulation Experiments

The simulation experiments in chapter 4 have the purpose of familiarizing the reader with EBP learning in multilayer perceptrons aimed at solving one-dimensional regression problems. However, the learning algorithm is written in matrix form, i.e., it is a batch algorithm, and it works for any number of inputs and outputs. The examples in the ebp.m routine are one-dimensional for the sake of visualization. Three examples are supplied. See the description of all input variables in the program ebp.m.

The experiments are aimed at reviewing many basic facets of EBP learning (notably the learning dynamic in the dependence of the learning rate η, the smoothing effects obtained by decreasing the number of HL neurons, the influence of noise, and the smoothing effects of early stopping). It is important to analyze the geometry of learning, that is, how the HL activation functions change during the course of learning. Be aware of the following facts about the program ebp.m:

1. It is developed for one-dimensional nonlinear regression problems.

2. However, the learning part is in matrix form, and it can be used for more complex learning tasks.

3. The learning is the gradient descent with momentum.

4. The program is user-friendly, even for beginners in using MATLAB, but you must cooperate. Read carefully the description part of the ebp.m routine first. Giving the input data will be easier. The ebp.m routine prompts you to select, to define, or to choose different things during the learning.

5. Analyze carefully the graphic windows presented. There are answers to many issues of learning in them.

Experiment with the program ebp.m as follows:

1. Launch MATLAB.

2. Connect to directory learnsc (at the matlab prompt, type cd learnsc ⟨RETURN⟩). learnsc is a subdirectory of matlab, as bin, toolbox, and uitools are. While typing cd learnsc, make sure that your working directory is matlab, not matlab/bin, for example).

3. Type start ⟨RETURN⟩.

4. Input data for three different functions are given. You will be able to define any other function, too. You will also have to make several choices.

5. Take care about the magnitudes of your output training data. It is clear that if they are larger than 1, you cannot use tgh or the logistic function. However, try using them, and analyze the results obtained.

6. After learning, five figures will be displayed. Analyze them carefully.

Now perform various experiments by changing a few design parameters. Start with the prepared examples. Run the same example repeatedly and try out different parameters.

1. Analyze the learning dynamics in the dependence of the learning rate η. Start with very low one (say, $\eta = 0.001$) and increase it gradually up to the point of instability.

2. Analyze the smoothing effects obtained by increasing the number of HL neurons. Start with a single HL neuron and train it with a small learning rate, say, 5,000 iteration steps. Repeat the simulations, increasing the number of neurons and keeping all other training parameters fixed (learning rate and number of iteration steps).

3. Analyze the smoothing effects of early stopping. Take the number of neurons to be $(P - 1)$, or approximately $(0.75 - 0.9)^*P$, where P stands for the number of training data points. Start modeling your data by performing 500 simulation runs. Repeat simulations by increasing the number of iterations and keeping all other training parameters fixed (learning rate and number of HL neurons).

In all the preceding simulational experiments, there must not be the influence of random initialization and noise. Therefore, run all simulations with the same *random number generator seed*; that is, select a fixed seed that ensures the same initial conditions and starting points.

1. Now, disable the random number generator seed. Run the experiments without noise and analyze the effects of different random initializations of the weights. Keep all other parameters unchanged.

2. Look at the effects of different noise levels on various approximators. Note that defining noise = 0.2 means that there is 20% noise. For many practical situations, this is too high a noise level. Repeat some of the experiments with a different noise level.

3. Analyze the influence of the momentum term on learning dynamics.

Generally, in performing simulations you should try to change only *one* parameter at a time. Meticulously analyze all resulting graphs after each simulation run. There are many useful results in those figures.

You are now ready to define your own one-dimensional functions to do nonlinear regression by applying multilayer perceptrons. This is the name given to NNs with sigmoidal activation functions in a hidden layer that learn by applying the first-order gradient (steepest descent) method with momentum. In the neural networks field, this gradient procedure is also known as the error backpropagation learning algorithm.

5 Radial Basis Function Networks

Radial basis function (RBF) networks have gained considerable attention as an alternative to multilayer perceptrons trained by the backpropagation algorithm. Both multilayer perceptrons and RBF networks are the basic constituents of the feedforward neural network. They are structurally equivalent. Both have one hidden layer[1] (HL) with a nonlinear activation function (AF) and an output layer (OL) containing one or more neurons with linear AFs. Hence, figure 4.4 might well represent an RBF network, provided that instead of the S-shaped AF there were RBF functions in the hidden layer's neurons. In the case of an RBF network, also, one does not augment both the n-dimensional input vector $\mathbf{x}$ and the HL outgoing vector $\mathbf{y}$ with a bias term $+1$. (However, sometimes one can find RBF networks having the HL outgoing vector $\mathbf{y}$ augmented with a bias term. And for classification tasks, instead of the linear AF in OL neurons one can use the S-shaped logistic function. But it should be stressed that the AF in the OL neurons of an RBF network derived from regularization theory is strictly linear.)

One important feature of RBF networks is the way the input signal u to a neuron's AF is formed. In the case of a multilayer perceptron, the input signal u is equal to $\mathbf{w}^T\mathbf{x}$. In other words, u is equal to the scalar product of the input vector $\mathbf{x}$ and a weights vector $\mathbf{w}$. The input signal u to the radial basis function is equal to the distance between the input vector $\mathbf{x}$ and a center of the specific AF $\mathbf{c}$, or $u_j = f(\|\mathbf{x} - \mathbf{c}_j\|)$. Note that for an RBF network, centers $\mathbf{c}_j$ of the neuron's AF represent the HL weights.

The advantages of RBF networks, such as linearity in the parameters (true in their most basic applications only) and the availability of fast and efficient training methods, have been noted in many publications. Like a multilayer perceptron, an RBF network has universal approximation ability (Hartman, Keeler, and Kowalski 1990; Park and Sandberg 1991). Unlike the former, an RBF network has the best approximation property (Girosi and Poggio 1990). But the most appealing feature of RBF networks is their theoretical foundation. Unlike multilayer perceptrons, which originated from the more heuristic side of engineering, RBF networks have a sound theoretical foundation in regularization theory, developed by the Russian mathematician Tikhonov and his coworkers (Tikhonov 1963; 1973; Tikhonov and Arsenin 1977; Morozov 1993).

Thus, let us consider first the nature of ill-posed problems and the regularization approach to solving such problems, and then how RBF networks fit naturally into the framework of the regularization of interpolation/approximation tasks. For these problems, *regularization* means the *smoothing* of the interpolation/approximation curve, surface, or hypersurface. This approach to RBF networks, also known as *regularization networks*, was developed by Poggio and Girosi (1989a; 1989b; 1990a;

1990b; 1990c). Their research focused on the problem of learning a multivariate function from sparse data. Poggio and Girosi's group developed a theoretical framework, based on regularization theory, that has roots in the classical theory of function approximation. Subsequently, they showed that regularization networks encompass a much broader range of approximation schemes, including many of the popular general additive models, some tensor product splines, and some neural networks (Girosi, Jones, and Poggio 1996). This result is important because it provides a unified theoretical framework for a broad spectrum of neural network architectures and statistical techniques.

Independently, and not from a regularization approach, RBF networks have been developed and used in many different areas. They were used in the framework of the interpolation of data points in a high-dimensional space (Powell 1987). An RBF type of network developed as a neural network paradigm was presented by Broomhead and Lowe (1988). An early important theoretical result on the nonsingularity of the **G** matrix,[2] which is the core component of an RBF network, was presented by Micchelli (1986).

Here, the presentation of RBF networks in the framework of regularization theory follows Poggio and Girosi (1989a; 1993) and Girosi (1997).

5.1 Ill-Posed Problems and the Regularization Technique

The concept of *ill-posed problems* was originally introduced in the field of partial differential equations by Hadamard (1923). In accordance with his postulates, a problem is *well-posed* when a solution

- Exists
- Is unique
- Depends continuously on the initial data (i.e., is robust against noise)

Otherwise, if the problem fails to satisfy one or more of these criteria, it is ill-posed. Ill-posed problems have been an area of mathematical curiosity for many years because many (especially inverse) practical problems turned out to be ill-posed. Classical problems in mathematical physics are usually well-posed by Hadamard's criteria (e.g., the forward problem for the heat equation, the Dirichlet problem for elliptic equations, and the Cauchy problem for hyperbolic equations). Actually, Hadamard believed that real-life problems are well-posed and that ill-posed problems are merely mathematical oddities. Many other direct problems are well-posed but some are not, for example, differentiation, which is an ill-posed direct problem because

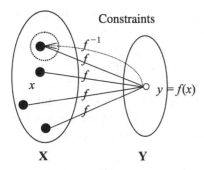

Figure 5.1
Regularization of the ill-posed inverse problem (f = direct map, f^{-1} = regularized inverse map).

its solution does not depend continuously on the data. Inverse problems are typically ill-posed problems. Two examples are in robotics when one needs to calculate the angles given the positions of both the robot's base and the final position of the robot's hand, and in vision when one tries to recover a three-dimensional shape from two-dimensional matrices of light distribution in an image measured by a camera. (The latter problem is the inverse of the standard problem in classical optics when one wants to determine two-dimensional images of three-dimensional physical objects.)

The problems in which one tries to recover an unknown dependency between some input and output variables are typically ill-posed because the solutions are not unique. The only way one can find a solution to an ill-posed problem is to *regularize* such a problem by introducing generic constraints that will restrict the space of solutions in an appropriate way. The character of the constraints depends on a priori knowledge of the solution. The constraints enable the calculation of the desired, or admissible, solution out of other (perhaps an infinite number of) possible solutions. This idea is presented graphically in figure 5.1 for the solution of the inverse problem when there is a one-to-many mapping from the range **Y** to the domain **X**.

An everyday regularized solution results in calculating the distance between two points x_1 and x_2 in a two-dimensional plane when, using the fact that the distance is a positive value (a kind of a priori knowledge in this problem), one takes the positive one only out of the two solutions:

$$d = \sqrt{(x_{11} - x_{12})^2 + (x_{21} - x_{22})^2}.$$

Another classic example of regularized solutions is the solution to the standard overdetermined system of m equations in n unknowns ($m > n$):

$$\mathbf{y} = \mathbf{Ax}, \tag{5.1}$$

where for the given $\mathbf{y}$ and $\mathbf{A}$ one should find $\mathbf{x}$. Out of an infinite number of solutions to this problem the most common *regularized solution* is the one in the least-squares sense, or the one that satisfies the constraint that the sum of squares of the error components e_i is minimal. In other words, the solution $\mathbf{x}$ should minimize $\|\mathbf{e}\|^2 = \mathbf{e}^T\mathbf{e} = (\mathbf{y} - \mathbf{A}\mathbf{x})^T(\mathbf{y} - \mathbf{A}\mathbf{x})$. This least-squares solution is known to be $\mathbf{x} = (\mathbf{A}^T\mathbf{A})^{-1}\mathbf{A}^T\mathbf{y}$.

Standard learning problems, inferring the relationships between some input and output variables, are ill-posed problems because there is typically an infinite number of solutions to these interpolation/approximation tasks. In figure 5.3 only two possible perfect interpolation functions are shown. Note that both interpolation functions strictly interpolate the examples and that the errors on these training points for both interpolants are equal to zero. Despite this fact, one feels that the smooth interpolant is preferable. The idea of smoothness in solving learning (interpolation/approximation) problems is seductive, and the most common a priori knowledge for learning problems is the assumption that the underlying function is smooth in the sense that two close (or similar) inputs correspond to two close (or similar) outputs. Smoothness can also be defined as the absence of oscillations.

Now, the basic problems are how to measure smoothness and how to ensure that the interpolation/approximation function is smooth. There are many ways to measure smoothness; the most common one is to introduce a *smoothness functional*[3] $\Phi(f(\mathbf{x}))$ that will map different functions $f(\mathbf{x})$ onto real and positive numbers. The interpolation/approximation function with the smallest functional value $\Phi_{min}(f)$ will then be the function of choice. This is shown in figure 5.2.

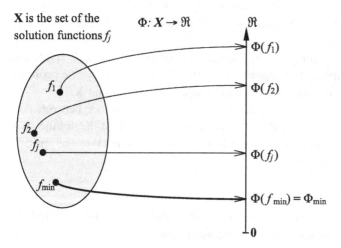

Figure 5.2
The smoothness functional $\Phi(f(\mathbf{x}))$ maps functions onto positive real numbers.

Smoothness functionals should assume large values for nonsmooth functions and small ones for smooth functions. It is well known that taking derivatives of a function amplifies the oscillations, that is, results in less smooth functions. Therefore, natural smoothness functionals that should emphasize a function's nonsmoothness are the ones that use the functions' derivatives. Three smoothness functionals that use different functions' derivatives or their combinations are

$$\Phi_1[f] = \int_R dx \cdot (f'(x))^2 = \int_R ds \cdot s^2 \cdot |\tilde{f}(s)|^2, \tag{5.2a}$$

$$\Phi_2[f] = \int_R dx \cdot (f''(x))^2 = \int_R ds \cdot s^4 \cdot |\tilde{f}(s)|^2, \tag{5.2b}$$

$$\Phi_3[f] = \Phi_1[f] + \Phi_2[f] = \int_R dx \cdot [(f'(x))^2 + (f''(x))^2]$$

$$= \int_R ds \cdot [s^2 + s^4] \cdot |\tilde{f}(s)|^2, \tag{5.2c}$$

where $\tilde{f}(s)$ stands for the Fourier transform of $f(t)$. More generally, the smoothness functional can be given as

$$\Phi[f] = \int_{R^n} ds \cdot \frac{|\tilde{f}(s)|^2}{\tilde{G}(s)}, \tag{5.3}$$

where n represents the dimensionality of the input vector $\mathbf{x}$ and $\tilde{G}(s)$ is a positive symmetric function in the s domain decreasing to zero at infinity. In other words, $1/\tilde{G}(s)$ is a high-pass filter. The smoothness functional $\Phi(f)$ can also be expressed as

$$\Phi[f] = \|\mathbf{P}f(x)\|^2 = \int |\mathbf{P}f(x)|^2 \, dx, \tag{5.4}$$

where the constraints operator $\mathbf{P}$ is (usually) a differential operator $\mathbf{P} = d/dx$, $\mathbf{P} = d^2/dx^2$, or $\mathbf{P} = d^{22}/dx^{22}$, and $\| * \|^2$ is a norm on the function space to which $\mathbf{P}f$ belongs (usually the L_2 norm).

In order to measure their smoothness, the functional $\Phi_1(f)$ from (5.2a) is applied to two different interpolation functions (see figs. 5.3 and 5.4). The procedure is simple. In accordance with (5.2a), one initially calculates the first derivatives of the functions (fig 5.4, top graph), squares them, and finds their integrals (fig 5.4, bottom graph).

Note that the choice of the smoothing functional $\Phi(f)$ (i.e., of the constraints operator $\mathbf{P}$) is a very important step in neural network design because the type of

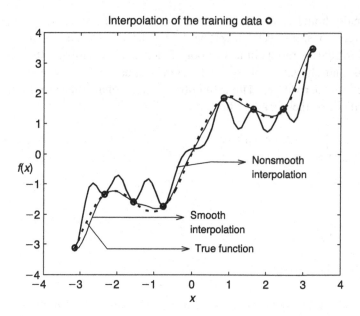

Figure 5.3
Interpolation of the training data (circles) by a smooth interpolant and a nonsmooth interpolant. True function $y = x + \sin(2x)$.

basis (or activation) function in a neuron strictly depends upon the functional $\Phi(f)$ (or **P**) chosen. So, for example, in the case of a one-dimensional input x, the functional $\Phi_1(f)$ from (5.2a) results in a linear spline basis function, and $\Phi_2(f)$ from (5.2b) results in a cubic spline basis function.

The idea underlying regularization theory is simple: among all the functions that interpolate the data, choose the smoothest one (the one that has a minimal measure of smoothness or a minimal value of the functional $\Phi(f)$). In doing this, it is believed, the solution can be obtained from the *variational principle* that contains both data and prior smoothness information.

The regularization approach to solving learning (interpolation/approximation) problems can now be posed as a search for the function $f(\mathbf{x})$ that approximates the training set of measured data (examples) D, consisting of the input vector $\mathbf{x} \in \Re^n$ and the output or system response $d \in \Re$, $D = \{[\mathbf{x}(i), d(i)] \in \Re^n \times \Re, \, i = 1, \dots, \mathbf{P}\}$. This minimizes the functional

$$H[f] = \sum_{i=1}^{P} (d_i - f(\mathbf{x}_i))^2 + \lambda \Phi[f] = \sum_{i=1}^{P} \underbrace{(d_i - f(\mathbf{x}_i))^2}_{\text{Closeness to data}} + \lambda \underbrace{\|\mathbf{P}f\|^2}_{\text{Smoothness}}, \tag{5.5}$$

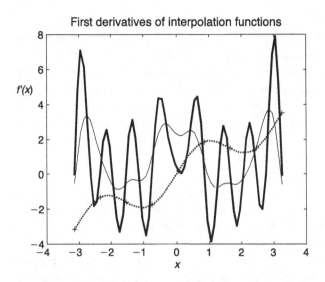

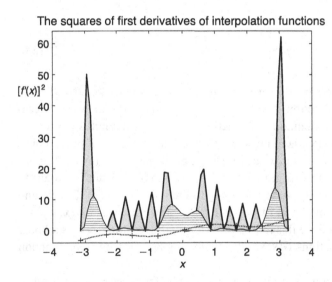

Figure 5.4
Calculation of the smoothness functional $\Phi(f)$. *Top*, first derivatives, smooth interpolant (thin solid curve), nonsmooth interpolant (thick solid curve). *Bottom*, areas below the squares of the first derivatives are equal to the magnitudes of $\Phi(f)$. For smooth interpolant (horizontal stripes), $\Phi_S(f) = 20$; for nonsmooth interpolant (shaded area), $\Phi_{NS}(f) = 56$. True function $y = x + \sin(2x)$ (dotted curve).

where λ is a small, positive number (the Lagrange multiplier), also called the *regularization parameter*. The functional $H[f]$ is composed of two parts. The sum minimizes the *empirical risk*, error or discrepancy between the data d and the approximating function $f(\mathbf{x})$, and the second part enforces the smoothness of this function. The second part of H, $\lambda \|\mathbf{P}f\|^2$, is also called a *stabilizer* that stabilizes the interpolation/ approximation function $f(\mathbf{x})$ by forcing it to become as smooth as possible. The regularization parameter λ, which is usually proportional to the amount of noise in data, determines the influence of this stabilizer and controls the trade-off between these two terms. (The smoothness can be controlled by the number of the neurons, too, although in a different manner). The smaller the regularization parameter λ, the smaller the smoothness of the approximating function $f(\mathbf{x})$ and the closer the approximating function $f(\mathbf{x})$ to the data. Taking $\lambda = 0$ (i.e., no constraints on the solution) results in a perfect interpolation function or in an "approximating" function that passes through the training data points ($f(\mathbf{x}_i) = d_i$).[4]

Before looking at the theoretical derivation, let us consider the general result of this approach. The function that minimizes the functional $H[f]$ has the following general form:

$$f(\mathbf{x}) = \sum_{i=1}^{P} w_i G(\mathbf{x}; \mathbf{x}_i) + p(\mathbf{x}), \qquad p(\mathbf{x}) = \sum_{j=1}^{k} a_j \gamma_j(\mathbf{x}), \qquad (5.6)$$

where G (the Fourier inverse transform of $\tilde{G}$) is the conditionally positive definite function (c.p.d.f.) Green's function of the differential operator $\hat{\mathbf{P}}\mathbf{P}$ of order m centered at $\mathbf{x}_i$, and the linear combination of functions that spans the null space of the operator $\mathbf{P}$, $p(\mathbf{x}) = \sum_{j=1}^{k} a_j \gamma_j(\mathbf{x})$, is in most cases a basis in the space of polynomials of degree $m - 1$. Note that in order to arbitrarily approximate well any continuous function on a compact domain with functions of the type (5.6), it is not necessary to include this second, "polynomial" term belonging to the null space of $\mathbf{P}$ (Poggio and Girosi 1989b). In fact, one of the most popular RBF networks, when $G(\mathbf{x}, \mathbf{x}_i)$ is a Gaussian function, does not have this term at all. Hence, the resulting $f(\mathbf{x})$ is a linear combination of Green's functions $G(\mathbf{x}, \mathbf{x}_i)$ eventually augmented with some function $p(\mathbf{x})$.

The approximating function $f(\mathbf{x})$ given in (5.6) results from the minimization of the functional $H[f]$ by calculating the *functional derivative* as follows.

Assume that the constraints operator $\mathbf{P}$ is linear and that f is the solution that minimizes the functional $H[f]$. Then, the functional $H[f + \alpha g]$ has a (local) minimum at $\alpha = 0$, or

$$\frac{\partial}{\partial \alpha} H[f + \alpha g]|_{\alpha=0} = 0 \tag{5.7}$$

for any continuous function g. Now, it follows that

$$\frac{\partial}{\partial \alpha} H[f + \alpha g] = \frac{\partial}{\partial \alpha}\left[\sum_{i=1}^{P}(d_i - f(\mathbf{x}_i) - \alpha g(\mathbf{x}_i))^2 + \lambda \|\mathbf{P}(f + \alpha g)\|^2\right]$$

$$= \frac{\partial}{\partial \alpha}\left[\sum_{i=1}^{P}(d_i - f(\mathbf{x}_i) - \alpha g(\mathbf{x}_i))^2 + \lambda \int_{R^n}(\mathbf{P}f + \alpha \mathbf{P}g)^2\, d\mathbf{x}\right]$$

$$= \sum_{i=1}^{P}2(d_i - f(\mathbf{x}_i) - \alpha g(\mathbf{x}_i))(-g(\mathbf{x}_i)) + 2\lambda \int_{R^n}(\mathbf{P}f \cdot \mathbf{P}g + \alpha(\mathbf{P}g)^2)\, d\mathbf{x},$$

and with $\alpha = 0$,

$$\sum_{i=1}^{P}2(d_i - f(\mathbf{x}_i))(-g(\mathbf{x}_i)) + 2\lambda \int_{R^n}\mathbf{P}f \cdot \mathbf{P}g\, d\mathbf{x} = 0. \tag{5.8}$$

Now, consider the well-known symbolics for the functional scalar product $\langle f, g \rangle = \int f(\mathbf{x})g(\mathbf{x})\, d\mathbf{x}$ as well as the notion of the *adjoint operator* $\hat{\mathbf{P}}$ such that $\langle \mathbf{P}f, g \rangle = \langle f, \hat{\mathbf{P}}g \rangle$. With this notation it follows from (5.8) that

$$\int_{R^n}\hat{\mathbf{P}}\mathbf{P}f \cdot g\, d\mathbf{x} = \frac{1}{\lambda}\int_{R^n}\sum_{i=1}^{P}(d_i - f(\mathbf{x}))\delta(\mathbf{x} - \mathbf{x}_i)g\, d\mathbf{x},$$

or

$$\hat{\mathbf{P}}\mathbf{P}f(\mathbf{x}) = \frac{1}{\lambda}\sum_{i=1}^{P}(d_i - f(\mathbf{x}_i))\delta(\mathbf{x} - \mathbf{x}_i). \tag{5.9}$$

This is the Euler-Lagrange (partial) differential equation for the functional (5.5), which can be solved by using the Green's function technique. Before solving (5.9), consider the basics of this approach in solving differential equations. Green's function $G(\mathbf{x}; \mathbf{x}_i)$ of an operator $\hat{\mathbf{P}}\mathbf{P} = \mathbf{Q}$ is the function that satisfies the following partial differential equation (in the distribution sense):

$$\mathbf{Q}G(\mathbf{x}; \mathbf{x}_i) = \delta(\mathbf{x} - \mathbf{x}_i) \tag{5.10}$$

where δ denotes a Dirac δ function. Hence, $G(\mathbf{x}; \mathbf{x}_i) = 0$ everywhere except at the point $\mathbf{x} = \mathbf{x}_i$. When the differential operator $\mathbf{Q} = \hat{\mathbf{P}}\mathbf{P}$ is *self-adjoint*, Green's function is symmetric. Note that (5.10) resembles the relationship with the linear algebra $\mathbf{A}\mathbf{A}^{-1} = \mathbf{I}$, or that $G(\mathbf{x}; \mathbf{x}_i)$ represents a kind of inverse of the differential operator $\mathbf{Q}$. Then (like the calculation of the solution to the linear equation $\mathbf{A}\mathbf{x} = \mathbf{y}$, where the solution is given as $\mathbf{x} = \mathbf{A}^{-1}\mathbf{y}$), the solution of $\mathbf{Q}f = h$ has the form $f = G^*h$, where the superscript $*$ stands for the convolution, or

$$f(\mathbf{x}) = G^*h = \int G(\mathbf{x}; \mathbf{v})h(\mathbf{v}) \, d\mathbf{v}.$$

Using (5.10) and the definition of the Dirac δ function, $\int \delta(\mathbf{x} - \mathbf{v})h(\mathbf{v}) = h(\mathbf{u})$,

$$\mathbf{Q}f(\mathbf{x}) = (\mathbf{Q}G)^*h = \delta^*h = h(\mathbf{x}).$$

Now, applying this technique while looking for Green's function of the operator $\hat{\mathbf{P}}\mathbf{P}$ in (5.9), the solution is given as

$$f(\mathbf{x}) = G^*\left[\frac{1}{\lambda}\sum_{i=1}^{P}(d_i - f(\mathbf{x}_i))\delta(\mathbf{x} - \mathbf{x}_i)\right] = \frac{1}{\lambda}\sum_{i=1}^{P}(d_i - f(\mathbf{x}_i))G^*\delta(\mathbf{x} - \mathbf{x}_i),$$

or

$$f(\mathbf{x}) = \sum_{i=1}^{P}\frac{1}{\lambda}(d_i - f(\mathbf{x}_i))G(\mathbf{x}; \mathbf{x}_i), \tag{5.11}$$

where $G(\mathbf{x}; \mathbf{x}_i)$ is the value of Green's function centered at the vector $\mathbf{x}_i$. Defining the first factor on the right-hand side as the weight w_i,

$$w_i = \frac{1}{\lambda}(d_i - f(\mathbf{x}_i)), \tag{5.12}$$

the solution can be rewritten as

$$f(\mathbf{x}) = \sum_{i=1}^{P} w_i G(\mathbf{x}; \mathbf{x}_i). \tag{5.13}$$

Note, however, that (5.13) is not the complete solution (5.6) to this minimization problem. The second term on the right-hand side of (5.6), which lies in the null space[5] of the operator $\mathbf{P}$, is invisible to the smoothing term of the functional $H[f]$.

In order to find the interpolating function in (5.13), both Green's function $G(\mathbf{x}; \mathbf{x}_i)$ and the weights w_i are needed. Green's function $G(\mathbf{x}; \mathbf{x}_i)$ depends only upon the form of the constraint operator $\mathbf{P}$ chosen. For the *translationally invariant* operator $\mathbf{P}$, $G(\mathbf{x}; \mathbf{x}_i) = G(\mathbf{x} - \mathbf{x}_i)$, i.e., Green's function depends only on the difference between $\mathbf{x}$

and $\mathbf{x}_i$. In the case of the *translationally invariant* and *rotationally invariant* operator $\mathbf{P}$, $G(\mathbf{x}; \mathbf{x}_i) = G(\|\mathbf{x} - \mathbf{x}_i\|)$, or Green's function depends only on the Euclidean norm of the difference $\mathbf{x} - \mathbf{x}_i$. In other words, for the translationally and rotationally invariant operator $\mathbf{P}$, Green's function is the RBF and the regularized solution (5.13) takes the form of the linear combination of the RBFs:

$$f(\mathbf{x}) = \sum_{i=1}^{P} w_i G(\|\mathbf{x} - \mathbf{x}_i\|). \tag{5.14}$$

In order to calculate the weights w_j, $j = 1, \ldots, P$, of the regularized solution, assume that the specific Green's function $G(\mathbf{x}; \mathbf{x}_j)$ is known. Note that there are P unknown weights and P examples. Now, from (5.11) and (5.12), two systems of P equations in P unknowns are formed as follows:

$$\mathbf{w} = \frac{1}{\lambda}\mathbf{d} - \frac{1}{\lambda}\mathbf{f} \Rightarrow \begin{bmatrix} w_1 \\ w_2 \\ \vdots \\ w_j \\ \vdots \\ w_P \end{bmatrix} = \frac{1}{\lambda}\begin{bmatrix} d_1 \\ d_2 \\ \vdots \\ d_j \\ \vdots \\ d_P \end{bmatrix} - \frac{1}{\lambda}\begin{bmatrix} f_1 \\ f_2 \\ \vdots \\ f_j \\ \vdots \\ f_P \end{bmatrix}, \tag{5.15a}$$

$$\mathbf{f} = \mathbf{G}\mathbf{w} \Rightarrow \begin{bmatrix} f_1 \\ f_2 \\ \vdots \\ f_j \\ \vdots \\ f_P \end{bmatrix} = \begin{bmatrix} G_{11} & G_{12} & \cdots & G_{1j} & \cdots & G_{1P} \\ G_{21} & G_{22} & \cdots & G_{2j} & \cdots & G_{2P} \\ \vdots & \vdots & \vdots & \vdots & \vdots & \vdots \\ G_{j1} & G_{j2} & \vdots & G_{jj} & \vdots & G_{jP} \\ \vdots & \vdots & \vdots & \vdots & \vdots & \vdots \\ G_{P1} & G_{P2} & \cdots & G_{Pj} & \cdots & G_{PP} \end{bmatrix}\begin{bmatrix} w_1 \\ w_2 \\ \vdots \\ w_j \\ \vdots \\ w_P \end{bmatrix}, \tag{5.15b}$$

where $f_j = f(\mathbf{x}_j)$ is the value of the interpolation/approximation function f from (5.13) at the input vector $\mathbf{x}_j$, and $G_{ji} = G(\mathbf{x}_j; \mathbf{x}_i)$ is the value of Green's function centered at the vector $\mathbf{x}_i$ at the vector $\mathbf{x}_j$. In the case of the one-dimensional input vector $\mathbf{x} = [x]$, figure 5.5 shows how the entries of a matrix $\mathbf{G}$ are formed for the two different basis functions. Substituting $\mathbf{f}$ from (5.15b) into (5.15a) the unknown weights vector $\mathbf{w}$ is found as

$$\mathbf{w} = (\mathbf{G} + \lambda\mathbf{I})^{-1}\mathbf{d}. \tag{5.16}$$

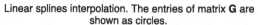

Linear splines interpolation. The entries of matrix **G** are
shown as circles.

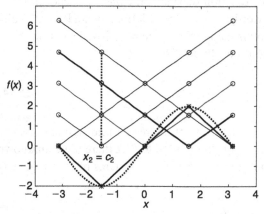

$$\mathbf{G}_{LSP} = \begin{matrix} 0.00 & 1.57 & 3.14 & \mathbf{4.71} & 6.28 \\ 1.57 & \mathbf{0.00} & \mathbf{1.57} & \mathbf{3.14} & \mathbf{3.71} \\ 3.14 & 1.57 & 0.00 & \mathbf{1.57} & 3.14 \\ 4.71 & 3.14 & 1.57 & \mathbf{0.00} & 1.57 \\ 6.28 & 4.71 & 3.14 & \mathbf{1.57} & 0.00 \end{matrix}$$

Gaussian BF interpolation. The entries of matrix **G** are
shown as circles.

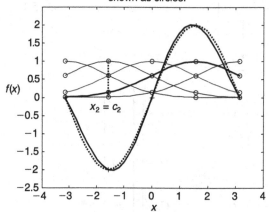

$$\mathbf{G}_{Gauss} = \begin{matrix} 1.00 & 0.61 & 0.14 & \mathbf{0.01} & 0.00 \\ 0.61 & \mathbf{1.00} & \mathbf{0.61} & \mathbf{0.14} & \mathbf{0.01} \\ 0.14 & 0.61 & 1.00 & \mathbf{0.61} & 0.14 \\ 0.01 & 0.14 & 0.61 & \mathbf{1.00} & 0.61 \\ 0.00 & 0.01 & 0.14 & \mathbf{0.61} & 1.00 \end{matrix}$$

Figure 5.5
Forming a matrix **G** for (*top*) linear splines basis functions and (*bottom*) Gaussian basis functions. Underlying function $y = \sin(x)$ (dotted curve). The data set comprises five noiseless data. Second (bold) row of **G** denotes outputs from $G(x_2, c_i)$, $i = 1, 5$; fourth (bold) column of **G** denotes outputs from the fourth basis function (thick solid line) $G(x_i, c_4)$, $i = 1, 5$.

When the operator $\hat{P}P$ is self-adjoint, then because Green's function $G(\mathbf{x}; \mathbf{x}_i)$ is symmetric, so is Green's matrix $\mathbf{G}$ in (5.15b), with the property $\mathbf{G}^T = \mathbf{G}$. Note also that without any constraints ($\lambda = 0$), the function $f(\mathbf{x})$ interpolates the data, or $f(\mathbf{x}_i) = d_i$.

Sometimes, depending upon the operator $\mathbf{P}$ applied, the complete solution as given in (5.6) consists of a linear combination of Green's functions and of the "polynomial" term $p(\mathbf{x})$, i.e., there are two sets of unknown coefficients: $\mathbf{w}$ and $\mathbf{a}$. In this case, weights w_i and a_i satisfy the following linear systems:

$$(\mathbf{G} + \lambda \mathbf{I})\mathbf{w} + \mathbf{\Gamma}^T \mathbf{a} = \mathbf{d},$$

$$\mathbf{\Gamma w} = \mathbf{0}, \tag{5.17}$$

where the entries of the matrices $\mathbf{G}$ and $\mathbf{\Gamma}$ are given as $G(i, j) = G(\mathbf{x}_i; \mathbf{x}_j)$ and $\Gamma(i, j) = \gamma_i(\mathbf{x}_j)$, the weights w_i connect the ith HL neuron with the OL neuron, d_i are the measured system's responses, and a_i are the appropriate parameters of the "polynomial" term $p(\mathbf{x})$. As mentioned earlier, when the RBFs are Gaussians there is no additional term and (5.14) completely describes the regularization (RBF) network.

A graphical representation of (5.14), where a training data set D, consisting of only five examples with one-dimensional inputs $x \in \Re$ and with outputs or system responses $d \in \Re$, $D = \{[x(i), d(i)] \in \Re \times \Re, i = 1, \ldots, 5\}$, is given in figure 5.6. Therefore, (5.14) corresponds to a neural network with one hidden layer and a single linear output layer neuron. The RBF is placed at centers c_i that coincide with the training data inputs x_i, meaning that the basis functions are placed exactly at the inputs x_i. The bias shown in figure 5.6 does not strictly follow from equation (5.14) but can be augmented to the HL output vector $\mathbf{y}$. Thus, the solution to the minimization of the functional (5.5), given as (5.14), can be implemented as a network.

Nothing changes in the graphical representation for a high-dimensional input vector $\mathbf{x}$. The input node represents the input vector $\mathbf{x}$. The hidden layer neurons receive the Euclidean distances ($\|\mathbf{x} - \mathbf{c}_i\|$) and compute the *scalar* values of the basis functions $G(\mathbf{x}; \mathbf{c}_i)$ that form the HL output vector $\mathbf{y}$. Finally, the single linear OL neuron calculates the weighted sum of the basis functions as given by (5.14). There is only a change in notation in the sense that the centers c_i and the width parameter σ (which for the Gaussian basis function is equal to its standard deviation) become the vectors $\mathbf{c}_i$ (of the same dimension as the input vector $\mathbf{x}$) and the ($n \times n$) covariance matrix $\mathbf{\Sigma}$, respectively.

A regularization network (5.14) strictly interpolates the data by summing the weighted basis functions, where the weights are determined by (5.16) or (5.17). The geometry of such a strict interpolation, in the case of a two-dimensional input vector

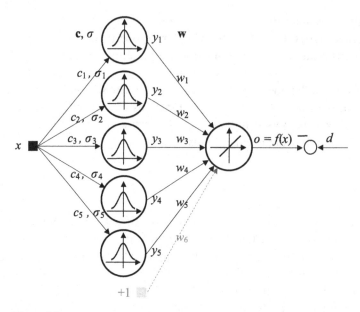

Figure 5.6
A strict interpolating regularization network (5.14) for a one-dimensional input x. The data set comprises five examples. Centers c_i correspond to inputs x_i ($c_i = x_i$), and all variances are equal ($\sigma_i = \sigma$). Bias shown is not mandatory and does not follow from (5.14).

$\mathbf{x} = \begin{bmatrix} x_1 & x_2 \end{bmatrix}^T$ when the basis functions are two-dimensional Gaussians, is shown in figure 5.7. Note that during training or learning, the network was given only data D comprising P training pairs $(\mathbf{x}, d)$. In other words, the surface presented in figure 5.7 is reconstructed by the RBF network as the weighted sum of the Gaussian basis functions shown. During learning, the network saw only measured training data points on this surface. Note that because the HL weights (centers and widths) are known, learning means merely calculating the OL weights vector $\mathbf{w}$. Furthermore, only a part of the Gaussian basis functions and a single training data point are shown in figure 5.7. For the sake of clarity in the graphical presentation, the overlapping of the RBFs is not visible in this figure. Only 10% of the two-dimensional Gaussian basis functions is shown. Typically, the overlapping of the Gaussians is very high. Note also an important characteristic of the RBF model regarding the matrix $\mathbf{G}$. Despite the fact that the input is a vector now (generally an n-dimensional vector), matrix $\mathbf{G}$ remains a two-dimensional array, that is, it is still a (P, P) matrix as in (5.15b) and in figure 5.5.

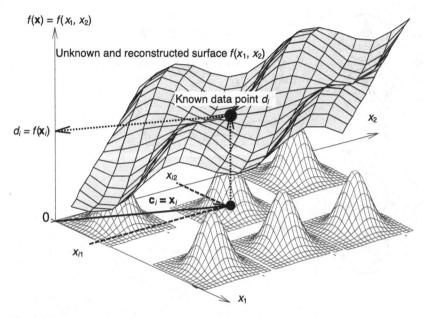

Figure 5.7
A regularization (RBF) network reconstructs the unknown underlying dependency $f(\mathbf{x})$ as the weighted sum of the radial basis functions $G(\mathbf{x}; \mathbf{c}_i)$ by using the training data set $\{\bullet\}$. Only a part of the basis functions and a single training data point are shown.

The neural net architecture given in figure 5.6 can easily be expanded to approximate several functions $\mathbf{f} = [f_1, f_2, \ldots, f_K]^T$ by using the *same set of centers* $\mathbf{c}_i$. In this case, K output layer neurons are needed. Such an $\Re^n \to \Re^K$ mapping can be modeled by the network shown in figure 5.8. The input vector $\mathbf{x}$ is presented in component-wise form. There are two sets of known parameters in the hidden layer: entries of a center matrix $\mathbf{C}$ and elements of a covariance matrix $\mathbf{\Sigma}$. The entries of an output layer weights matrix $\mathbf{W}$ are unknown. The problem is linear again, and the solution is similar to (5.16):

$$\mathbf{W} = (\mathbf{G} + \lambda \mathbf{I})^{-1} \mathbf{D}, \tag{5.18}$$

where $\mathbf{D} = [\mathbf{d}_1^T \quad \mathbf{d}_2^T \quad \ldots \quad \mathbf{d}_K^T]^T$ comprises all the desired output training vectors $\mathbf{d}_k = [d_{1k}, d_{2k}, \ldots, d_{Pk}]^T$, $k = 1, K$. Note that all the OL neurons share the same HL radial basis functions and that the same matrix $(\mathbf{G} + \lambda \mathbf{I})^{-1}$ is used for the calculation of each weights vector $\mathbf{w}_k$, $k = 1, K$. The performance of a regularization (RBF) network is demonstrated in example 5.1.

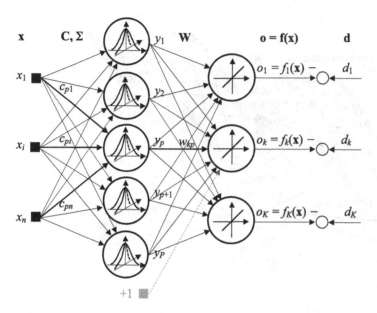

Figure 5.8
Architecture of a regularization (RBF) network for an $\Re^n \to \Re^K$ mapping. The n-dimensional input vector $\mathbf{x}$ is shown componentwise, and the n-dimensional Gaussian basis or activation functions are shown as two-dimensional Gaussian bells.

Example 5.1 Model (reconstruct) the unknown and simple relation $y = f(x) = \sin(x)$ between (just) two variables x and y, using an RBF network with Gaussian basis functions, having a set of ten data pairs from measurements highly corrupted by 50% white noise with zero mean (see fig. 5.9). Examine the smoothing effects achieved by using different parameters λ.

According to (5.5) and (5.6) an RBF network comprises ten neurons with Gaussian basis functions centered at inputs x_i. Without regularization ($\lambda = 0$, or no constraints) the network purely interpolates the data points. As the regularization parameter λ increases, the regularized solution becomes smoother, and with the noise filtered out, it will approximate the data points. If it is too high, the regularization parameter λ acts to disregard the data points as unreliable and results in an approximating function that filters out both the underlying function and the noise. One usually finds the optimal value of the parameter λ by the *cross-validation* technique. ∎

The next section takes up the still unresolved issue of the relation between the stabilizer Φ (i.e., operator $\mathbf{P}$) and Green's function $G(\mathbf{x}; \mathbf{x}_i)$.

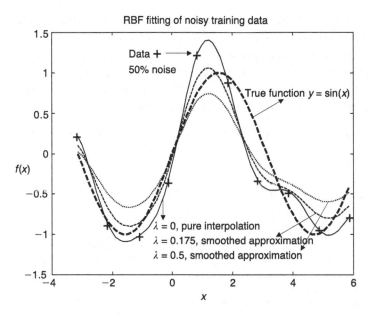

Figure 5.9
RBF network and regularized solutions to an underlying function $y = \sin(x)$ for a data set (crosses) of ten noisy examples using three different regularization parameters λ: $\lambda = 0$, which results in a strict interpolation function, and with error = 0.3364. Smoothed approximation functions achieved with two different lambdas: $\lambda = 0.175$, error = 0.2647; $\lambda = 0.5$, error = 0.3435 (smoothing too high). Number of Gaussian RBFs is equal to the number of examples. Noise filtering is achieved through parameter λ.

5.2 Stabilizers and Basis Functions

First recall that during the derivation of the expressions (5.16) and (5.17) Green's basis function $G(\mathbf{x}; \mathbf{x}_i)$ was assumed known for the calculation of the regularization network's OL weights. It was also mentioned that Green's function is the RBF for the translationally and rotationally invariant operator **P**. Radial stabilizers are the most common ones, and they a priori assume that all variables are of equal concern, or that no directions are more relevant (privileged) than others in n-dimensional examples.

Radial stabilizers are not the only types of smoothing operators. There are other types of smoothing functionals belonging to the class (5.3) that do not lead to radial basis functions. Consequently, the outcomes of such nonradial stabilizers are not RBF networks. Each of these different stabilizers corresponds to different a priori assumptions about smoothness. The two kinds of stabilizers are *tensor product* stabilizers and *additive* stabilizers. Consideration of these is outside the scope of this book; the interested reader is referred to the work of Girosi, Jones and Poggio (1996).

Here, the focus is on stabilizers that have a radial symmetry as well as on the corresponding RBF interpolation/approximation technique. Example 5.2 demonstrates that the classical approximation techniques for an $\Re^1 \rightarrow \Re^1$ mapping, linear and cubic spline interpolations, belong to regularization RBF networks.

Example 5.2   Show that the smoothing functionals $\Phi_1[f] = \int_R dx \cdot (f'(x))^2$ given in (5.2a) and $\Phi_2[f] = \int_R dx \cdot (f''(x))^2$ given in (5.2b) lead to RBF network models for an $\Re^1 \rightarrow \Re^1$ mapping of P data pairs (see fig. 5.10).

In the first case, (5.2a), the smoothing operator $\mathbf{P} = df/dx$ and the functional $\Phi_1[f]$ can be written as

$$\Phi_1[f] = \int_R dx \cdot (f'(x))^2 = \int_R ds \cdot s^2 \cdot |\tilde{f}(s)|^2 = \int_R \frac{|\tilde{f}(s)|^2}{1/s^2}\, ds = \int_R \frac{|\tilde{f}(s)|^2}{\tilde{G}(s)}\, ds.$$

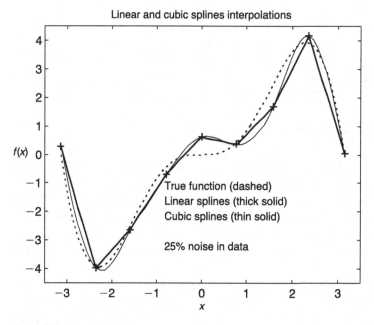

Figure 5.10
Interpolation of noisy examples by two RBF networks having piecewise linear and piecewise cubic polynomial basis functions.

In other words, $\tilde{G}(s) = 1/s^2$, and its inverse corresponds to $G(x, x_i) = |x - x_i|$. Hence, a regularization network (an interpolation function) has the form of a piecewise[6] linear function

$$f(x) = \sum_{i=1}^{P} w_i |x - x_i| + a.$$

Note that a polynomial of zero order $p(x) = a$ is in the null space of the operator $\mathbf{P} = df/dx$. Speaking colloquially, the constant term a is not visible to the operator $\mathbf{P}$.

When the smoothing functional $\Phi_2[f]$, $\mathbf{P} = d^2f/dx^2$, the very same procedure leads to an interpolation function in the form of a piecewise cubic polynomial

$$\Phi_2[f] = \int_R dx \cdot (f''(x))^2 = \int_R ds \cdot s^4 \cdot |\tilde{f}(s)|^2 = \int_R \frac{|\tilde{f}(s)|^2}{1/s^4} \, ds = \int_R \frac{|\tilde{f}(s)|^2}{\tilde{G}(s)} \, ds,$$

or $\tilde{G}(s) = 1/s^4$, and its inverse corresponds to $G(x, x_i) = |x - x_i|^3$, which results in

$$f(x) = \sum_{i=1}^{P} w_i |x - x_i|^3 + (ax + b).$$

As with the case of linear splines, $d^2p(x)/dx^2 = d^2(ax + b)/dx^2 = 0$, that is, the polynomial term is in the null space of the smoothing operator $\mathbf{P} = d^2f/dx^2$. It is clear that a nonsmooth interpolation function will be punished more strongly by using a second instead of a first derivative. In other words, a piecewise cubic polynomial interpolation function will be smoother than a linear one.   ■

Generally, a class of admissible RBFs is a class of conditionally positive definite functions (c.p.d.f.) of any order because for c.p.d.f. the smoothness functional (5.3) is a seminorm and the associated variational problem is well defined (Madych and Nelson 1990). Table 5.1 gives the most important examples of stabilizers and resulting RBFs. Note that for a positive definite n-dimensional Gaussian function, (5.3) defines the norm, and since $\Phi[f]$ is a norm, its null space contains only zero elements. Therefore, when a basis function is a Gaussian function, the additional null space term $p(\mathbf{x})$ is not needed in (5.6). Gaussian basis functions are the most popular ones for at least the following reasons:

· They show much better smoothing properties than other known RBFs. This is clear from the exponentially acting stabilizer $\tilde{G}(s) = 1/e^{\|\mathbf{s}\|^2/\beta}$, which will heavily damp,[7] or punish, any nonsmooth interpolation function $f(\mathbf{x})$ in areas of high frequencies $\mathbf{s}$.

Table 5.1
Stabilizers and Corresponding Radial Basis Function

Stabilizer $\Phi[f] = \int_{R^n} ds \, \dfrac{|\tilde{f}(s)|^2}{\tilde{G}(s)}$	Radial Basis Function	Definiteness	Order of Null Space Terms	Comments
$\tilde{G}(s) = \dfrac{1}{s^2}$	$|x - c|$	c.p.d.f.	0	*x is one-dimensional, x = (1,1):* Linear spline
$\tilde{G}(s) = \dfrac{1}{s^4}$	$|x - c|^3$	c.p.d.f.	1	Cubic spline
$\tilde{G}(s) = \dfrac{1}{\|\mathbf{s}\|^{2m}}$	$\|\mathbf{x} - \mathbf{c}\|^{2m-n} \ln\|\mathbf{x} - \mathbf{c}\|$	c.p.d.f.	Polynomials of degree m in n variables at most, with a dimension	*Duchon multivariate splines,* $\mathbf{x} = (n, 1)$: n is even if $2m > n$
	$\|\mathbf{x} - \mathbf{c}\|^{2m-n}$	c.p.d.f.	$k = \left(\begin{array}{c} n+m-1 \\ n \end{array} \right)$	n is odd otherwise
$\tilde{G}(s) = \dfrac{1}{\|\mathbf{s}\|^4}$	$\|\mathbf{x} - \mathbf{c}\|^2 \ln\|\mathbf{x} - \mathbf{c}\|$	c.p.d.f.	Polynomials of degree 1 in 2 variables	"Thin plate" splines for two-dimensional $\mathbf{x}$
$\tilde{G}(s) = e^{-(\|\mathbf{s}\|^2/\beta)}, \quad \beta = 2\sigma^2$	$e^{-(\|\mathbf{x}-\mathbf{c}\|^2/2\sigma^2)}$	p.d.f.	No null space terms	Gaussian function[a]
Not known yet	$\sqrt{\|\mathbf{x} - \mathbf{c}\|^2 + \beta}$	c.p.d.f.	1	Multiquadric function
Not known yet	$\dfrac{1}{\sqrt{\|\mathbf{x} - \mathbf{c}\|^2 + \beta}}$	p.d.f.	No null space terms	Inverse multiquadric function

Notes: c.p.d.f. = conditionally positive definite function; p.d.f. = positive definite function.

a. A more general representation in an case of an n-dimensional input vector $\mathbf{x}$ for any radial function would be $\|\mathbf{x} - \mathbf{c}\|^2 = (\mathbf{x} - \mathbf{c})^T \Sigma^{-1}(\mathbf{x} - \mathbf{c})$, where Σ^{-1} is the corresponding metric, which for a Gaussian function corresponds to an inverse covariance matrix (see section 5.3.1). In the case of uncorrelated inputs having the same scales, Σ is diagonal $\Sigma = \sigma^2 \mathbf{I}$, and $\|\mathbf{x} - \mathbf{c}\|^2 = (\mathbf{x} - \mathbf{c})^T (\mathbf{x} - \mathbf{c})/\sigma^2$.

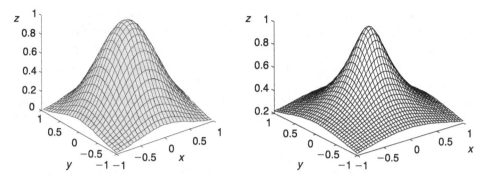

Figure 5.11
Two-dimensional radial basis functions. *Left*, Gaussian *Right*, inverse multiquadric. Both activation functions are normalized here: their maximum is equal to 1.

• They are local in the sense that they model data only in a neighborhood near a center.

• They are more familiar to everyday users than other RBFs.

• There is a sound geometrical understanding even of n-dimensional Gaussian functions.

• They do not require additional null space terms.

• Because of their finite response, it seems as though they may be more plausible biologically.

The disadvantage of Gaussian RBFs is that they require determination of *width parameters* or *shape parameters*: standard deviation σ or covariance matrix Σ in the case of one- and n-dimensional input vectors, respectively. At this point, the very design or learning of appropriate width parameters is an heuristic, basically good approach that results in suboptimal but still reliable solutions. An *inverse multiquadric* function is similar to a Gaussian one, and for the two-dimensional input **x**, these two functions are shown in figure 5.11.

5.3 Generalized Radial Basis Function Networks

Regularization networks have two practical shortcomings. First, there are as many basis functions (neurons) as there are examples in a training data set. Therefore, having a training data set containing several thousands of examples would require the inversion of very large matrices (see (5.16), for example). This operation is far outside the capacity of most computing machines available today. Second, training data are usually imprecise or contaminated by noise. Thus, there is a need to filter contaminated examples and in this way avoid modeling noise. While the problem with noise can be resolved by using an appropriate regularization parameter λ, the only way to escape the problem of modeling a large data set, that is, to have a network with a computationally acceptable number of neurons in an HL, is to design an RBF network with appreciably fewer basis functions (neurons) in an HL than there are examples.

Here, a few different approaches are presented for the selection of the best basis function subset or the design of a network of appropriate size. These involve reducing the number of HL neurons. Recall that the problem of subset selection was successfully solved by applying support vector machines to both classification and regression tasks (see chapter 2). Section 5.3.4 will introduce linear programming for a subset selection, too.

First, a few early and common subset selections are described that are strictly random or semirandom choices, not necessarily the best. Using a strictly random procedure, a random subset of p training data is chosen out of P examples. In the case of semirandom selection, basis functions are placed at each rth (at each third, fifth, twenty-fifth) training data point. Another possibility is to evenly spread the centers of p RBFs over a domain space, in which case they do not correspond to training examples. Yet another selection method is to preprocess training data by some *clustering* algorithm first (k means, for example, where k corresponds to the desired number of RBFs, i.e., HL neurons, p). In the framework of RBF networks, these heuristic approaches are suggested by Broomhead and Lowe (1988) and Moody and Darken (1989).

After choosing the centers, the shape parameters (β, i.e., σ) are determined. The basic idea now is to ensure suitable overlapping of a basis function. For Gaussians a rule of thumb is to take $\sigma = \Delta c$ or some other multiple of Δc that depends upon the character of the modeled surface or hypersurface, where Δc denotes the (average) distance between the centers (for a one-dimensional x). In the case of an n-dimensional input vector $\mathbf{x}$, the diagonal elements of a covariance matrix Σ, that is, the standard deviations σ_i, can be selected as $\sigma_i \sim \Delta c_i$. Note that for the equal units of the components of $\mathbf{x}$, $\Sigma = \mathrm{diag}(\sigma^2)$ and the Gaussian is radial. When the input vector components' dimensions differ (this is the most common situation), the width parameters σ_i will be different and $\Sigma = \mathrm{diag}(\sigma_i^2)$. The corresponding Gaussians will no longer be radial functions. In more complex situations, the components of input vector $\mathbf{x}$ (features) may be correlated, and in this case Σ will no longer be a diagonal matrix either. This is but one part of an overall problem; these points are taken up in more detail later.

Nevertheless, many problems may successfully be solved with the preceding heuristic methods. A basic idea in selecting smaller number of RBFs is to find an approximation to regularized solutions where, instead of using a strict interpolation function

$$f(\mathbf{x}) = \sum_{i=1}^{P} w_i G(\|\mathbf{x} - \mathbf{x}_i\|),$$

to implement a smooth approximation function, the following function is used:

$$f_a(\mathbf{x}) = \sum_{j=1}^{p} w_j G(\|\mathbf{x} - \mathbf{c}_j\|^2), \tag{5.19}$$

where $p \ll P$ and the centers $\mathbf{c}_j$ and the shape parameters (elements of the covariance matrix Σ for Gaussians) are selected by using one of the approaches proposed earlier. The matrix $\mathbf{G}$ is no longer square as in (5.15b) and in figure 5.5 but a rectangular (P, p) matrix. (Note that the notation is slightly changed to explicitly stress the quadratic dependence of f_a on the distance $\| \cdot \|$). Having fixed centers and shape parameters (for fixed HL weights) only p OL weights w_j are calculated. The problem is still linear in parameters ($\mathbf{w}$), and the best solution is the renowned least-squares solution, which results in a *least-squares RBF* that follows from the minimization of the cost function

$$E(\mathbf{w}) = \sum_{i=1}^{p} (d_i - f_a(\mathbf{x}_i))^2.$$

As in solving (5.14), this is a convex and quadratic problem in w_j, and the solution that follows from the requirement that $\partial E / \partial w_j = 0$ is $\mathbf{G}^T \mathbf{G} \mathbf{w} = \mathbf{G}^T \mathbf{d}$, or

$$\mathbf{w} = \mathbf{G}^+ \mathbf{d}, \qquad \lambda = 0, \tag{5.20a}$$

where $\mathbf{G}^+ = (\mathbf{G}^T \mathbf{G})^{-1} \mathbf{G}^T$ is the *pseudoinverse* of $\mathbf{G}$, and

$$\mathbf{w} = (\mathbf{G}^T \mathbf{G} + \lambda \mathbf{g})^{-1} \mathbf{G}^T \mathbf{d}, \qquad \lambda \neq 0, \tag{5.20b}$$

where $g_{jk} = G(\mathbf{c}_j, \mathbf{c}_k)$. Note that there are two smoothing parameters in (5.20b), λ and the number of HL neurons p. The most common approach is to neglect λ and to achieve the smoothing effects by choosing the right number of HL neurons p. As already stated, the smoothing effects of λ and p are different, and it may sometimes be worthwhile to try using both parameters.

A least-squares RBF represents an approximation function that results from previously fixed HL weights. Sometimes, the preceding heuristics result in poor RBF network performance. Generally, the modeling power of RBF networks with fixed HL weights is likely to decrease with an increase in the dimensionality of the input vector **x.** Furthermore, having a basis function with the same shape parameters over the whole input space cannot guarantee proper modeling of multivariate functions, which differ over the input space. This is shown in figure 5.12, where for $x < 0$ the function displays oscillatory behavior and for positive values of x the dependency between y and x is smooth. An RBF network with a fixed and same shape parameter for all the basis functions could not model this function equally over the whole input space.

The poor performance of the RBF in figure 5.12 could be significantly improved with basis functions having different shape parameters. Essentially, having examples but no information about the underlying dependency, these width parameters would also be subjects of training.

Thus, in most real-life problems, during the learning phase it may be practical to simultaneously adapt both the centers and the shape parameters (the HL weights) as well as the OL weights. The difficult part of learning is the optimization of the HL weights, because the cost function depends nonlinearly upon these position and shape parameters. The learning of the OL weights is for RBF models always a linear problem, which can be solved in batch (off-line) mode by using all the examples at once, as given by (5.16) or (5.20), or in on-line mode by iterative implementation.

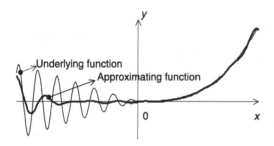

Figure 5.12
Modeling using an RBF network with 20 Gaussian basis functions having the same fixed standard deviation σ. The underlying function (thin curve) behaves differently over the input space, and the approximating function (thick curve) is not able to model the data equally over the whole input space.

As in the case of the selection of centers and shape parameters, the now nonlinear task of learning all the RBF weights can be performed via many different approaches. First, for the learning of the HL weights, the standard error back-propagation (the first-order gradient) algorithm can be applied; this method is usually called *moving centers learning*. Second, the *orthogonal least squares* (OLS) method for finding an optimal subset of p basis functions can be implemented. Another common approach utilizes nondeterministic controlled random search methods such as genetic algorithms or evolutionary computing techniques (see chapter 8). Recall also that the SVM approach can be used to solve quadratic programming problems for optimal subset selection (see chapter 2).

The following sections discuss moving centers learning, regularization with nonradial basis functions, orthogonal least squares, and a linear programming (LP)–based algorithm for subset selection that is a promising approach for NN and SVM training. LP-based learning is computationally more efficient and simpler than the quadratic programming algorithm applied in standard SVM training, and it seems to produce models with a generalization capacity similar to that of quadratic programming–based trained networks or machines.

5.3.1 Moving Centers Learning

Now, in addition to the OL weights w_j, the centers $\mathbf{c}_j$ and the shape parameters (elements of the covariance matrix Σ)[8] are unknown and subjects of the optimization procedure. The problem is nonlinear and, for the standard cost function

$$E(\mathbf{w}, \mathbf{c}, \Sigma) = \sum_{i=1}^{P} (d_i - f_a(\mathbf{x}_i))^2,$$

no longer convex and quadratic. Therefore, many local minima can be expected, and the error backpropagation (EBP) algorithm (with an appropriate learning rate η) merely guarantees convergence to the closest local minimum. The EBP is a first-order gradient procedure, and the solutions must satisfy $\partial E/\partial w_j = 0$, $\partial E/\partial \mathbf{c}_j = 0$, and $\partial E/\partial \Sigma_j = 0$. The EBP algorithms for learning the OL weights w_j and the centers $\mathbf{c}_j$ are presented first. Then the learning algorithm for shape parameters (σ_{jk}) adaptation, which involves departing from the strictly radial basis function, is discussed. A separate section is devoted to nonradial basis functions because of their immense importance. In many practical cases, the radially nonsymmetric basis function will result from learning. Note that for simplicity the regularization parameter is taken as $\lambda = 0$. Thus, smoothing will be achieved using fewer RBFs than in previous examples, although in a different manner than when applying parameter λ.

The cost function that follows from (5.5) is equal to

$$E(\mathbf{w}, \mathbf{c}) = H_{w,c}[f_a] = \sum_{i=1}^{P} (d_i - f_a(\mathbf{x}_i))^2$$

$$= \sum_{i=1}^{P} \underbrace{\left(d_i - \sum_{i=1}^{P} w_j G(\|\mathbf{x} - \mathbf{c}_j\|^2) \right)^2}_{e_i} = \sum_{i=1}^{P} (e_i)^2 \tag{5.21}$$

and the standard EBP learning algorithms for the OL weights and centers that result after the calculations of $\partial E / \partial w_j$ and $\partial E / \partial \mathbf{c}_j$ are given as

$$w_j^{s+1} = w_j^s + 2\eta \sum_{i=1}^{P} e_i^s G(\|\mathbf{x}_i - \mathbf{c}_j^s\|^2), \tag{5.22}$$

$$\mathbf{c}_j^{s+1} = \mathbf{c}_j^s - 4\eta w_j^s \sum_{i=1}^{P} e_i^s G'(\|\mathbf{x}_i - \mathbf{c}_j^s\|^2)(\mathbf{x}_i - \mathbf{c}_j^s), \tag{5.23}$$

where s stands for the iteration step and G' denotes the derivative of $G(\cdot)$. Note, however, that the OL weights w_j do not necessarily need to be calculated using an EBP algorithm as given in (5.22). The weights w_j can, simultaneously with (5.23), be computed by using the iterative second-order recursive least squares (RLS) method (see section 3.2.2). In fact, by combining the second-order RLS method for the adaptation of the weights w_j with a first-order EBP algorithm for the calculation of the centers as given by (5.23), one usually obtains faster convergence. Despite the fact that it is simple to implement an EBP algorithm for RBF network training, this gradient descent method suffers from more difficulties in this application than when applied to multilayer perceptron learning. One of the reasons for such poor performance is that the derivative of the RBF G' (an important part of an EBP learning algorithm) changes sign. This is not the case for sigmoidal functions. Therefore, an EBP approach is rarely used for training an RBF network. Many other deterministic techniques instead of the first-order gradient procedure can be used. In particular, second-order methods (Newton-Raphson or quasi-Newtonian algorithms) can be implemented, though all of them can easily get stuck at some local minimum. There is a standard heuristic in moving centers learning: restart optimization from several different initial points and then select the best model. Despite these standard problems in a nonlinear learning environment, the moving centers technique may produce good models at the expense of higher computational complexity and a longer learning phase.

Next to the QP based algorithms that originate in the framework of SVMs, the most popular and reliable method for RBF network training used to be the OLS technique (see section 5.3.3). However, the LP-based learning (presented in section 5.3.4) seems to produce model with better generalization ability at lower computational costs than the OLS method. Other alternatives are the non-deterministic massive 'random' search techniques such as GA (EC) or, simulated annealing (see chapter 8).

5.3.2 Regularization with Nonradial Basis Functions

It is sometimes useful to relax (or abandon) the concept of strictly radial basis functions. In many practical instances, HL neurons' basis functions will depart from radiality, and such nonradial functions constitute an important class of regularization networks.

Radial basis functions follow from the assumption that all variables have the same relevance and the same dimensions. There are many practical situations when

• There is a different dependence on input variables, $f(x, y) = z = 5 \sin(\pi x) + y^2$ (see fig. 5.13, top graph).

• Variables have different units of measure (dimensions, scales), $f = f(x, x', x'')$.

• Not all the variables are relevant, $f(x, y) \sim f(x)$ (see fig. 5.13, bottom graph).

• Some variables are dependent or only some (linear) combinations of variables are important, $f(v, x, y) = g(v, x, y(v, x))$ or $f(v, x, y) = \sin(v + x + y)$.

In order to overcome the problem of the choice of relevant variables when the components of the input vector $\mathbf{x}$ are of different types, it is usually useful to work with linearly transformed variables $\mathbf{Sx}$ instead of the original variables $\mathbf{x}$. In such cases the natural norm is not the Euclidean one but a *weighted norm* defined as

$$\|\mathbf{x} - \mathbf{c}\|_{\mathbf{S}}^2 = (\mathbf{x} - \mathbf{c})^T \mathbf{S}^T \mathbf{S}(\mathbf{x} - \mathbf{c}). \tag{5.24}$$

Note that in general $\mathbf{S} \neq \mathbf{I}$, and the basis functions are no longer radial. (In strict mathematical terms, the basis functions are radial in the new metric defined by (5.24)).

Nonradial geometry is visible in the level curves of basis functions that are no longer (hyper)circles but rather (hyper)ellipses, whose axes (in the most general case when some of the input components may be correlated) do not have to be aligned with the coordinate axes (see the third Gaussian in fig. 5.14). For uncorrelated inputs, $\mathbf{S}^T \mathbf{S}$ is a diagonal matrix, with generally different diagonal elements. Only for equal diagonal entries of the matrix $\mathbf{S}^T \mathbf{S}$ will the basis functions be radial. For the Gaussian

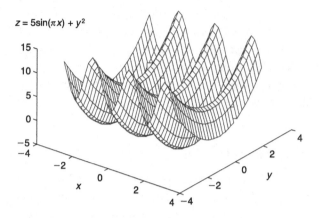

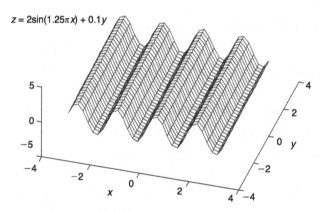

Figure 5.13
Examples of (*top*) different dependence upon input variables and (*bottom*) two-dimensional dependence with a practically irrelevant variable y over a given domain.

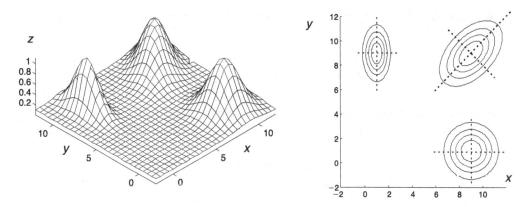

Figure 5.14
Left, three different normalized Gaussian basis functions. *Right*, their corresponding level curves or contours. The first RBF with a covariance matrix $\Sigma = [2.25 \quad 0; 0 \quad 2.25]$, $(\sigma_x = \sigma_y = 1.5)$, is placed at the center $(9, 1)$. The second Gaussian is nonradial, with a covariance matrix $\Sigma = [0.5625 \quad 0; 0 \quad 2.25]$, $(\sigma_x = 0.75 \ \sigma_y = 1.5)$ and with a center at $(1, 9)$. The third one is also nonradial, centered at $(9, 9)$, with correlated inputs $(\rho = 0.5)$ and with a covariance matrix $\Sigma = [2.25 \quad 1.125; 1.125 \quad 2.25]$, $(\sigma_x = \sigma_y = 1.5)$.

basis function, $\mathbf{S}^T\mathbf{S} = \Sigma^{-1}$, that is, the matrix $\mathbf{S}^T\mathbf{S}$ is equal to the inverse covariance matrix, and its diagonal elements correspond to $1/\sigma_j^2$.

When, together with centers $\mathbf{c}$, the elements of $\mathbf{S}$ are known either from some prior knowledge (which is rarely the case) or from assumptions, the solution (OL weights vector) is the same as in the case of the strictly radial basis function given by (5.20).

A more interesting and powerful result may be obtained when the parameters of a matrix $\mathbf{S}$ are unknown and are the subject of learning from training examples. Now the problem can be formulated as in section 5.3.1. In other words, the cost function (5.21) is now $E(\mathbf{w}, \mathbf{c}, \Sigma^{-1}) = H_{w,c,\Sigma^{-1}}[f_a]$, and Σ^{-1} that minimizes it must be found. Note that the matrix $\mathbf{S}$ never appears separately but always in the form $\mathbf{S}^T\mathbf{S}$ (usually set equal to Σ^{-1}). Using the same EBP procedure as for centers, it can be shown that the adaptation of the parameters of the matrix Σ^{-1} can be achieved as,

$$\Sigma_j^{-1\,s+1} = \Sigma_j^{-1\,s} + 2\eta \sum_{j=1}^{p} w_j^s \sum_{i=1}^{P} e_i^s G'(\|\mathbf{x}_i - \mathbf{c}_j^s\|_{\mathbf{S}}^2)(\mathbf{x}_i - \mathbf{c}_j^s)(\mathbf{x}_i - \mathbf{c}_j^s)^T. \tag{5.25}$$

When a covariance matrix differs from an identity matrix, and when it is the subject of an optimization algorithm (5.25), the EBP solution for the centers $\mathbf{c}_j$ given in (5.23) becomes

$$\mathbf{c}_j^{s+1} = \mathbf{c}_j^s - 4\eta w_j^s \sum_{i=1}^{P} e_i^s G'(\|\mathbf{x}_i - \mathbf{c}_j^s\|_{\mathbf{S}}^2)\Sigma^{-1}(\mathbf{x}_i - \mathbf{c}_j^s). \tag{5.26}$$

Note also that (5.25) can be expressed in terms of a transformation matrix $\mathbf{S}$ as follows:

$$\mathbf{S}_j^{s+1} = \mathbf{S}_j^s + 4\mathbf{S}_j^s \eta \sum_{j=1}^{p} w_j^s \sum_{i=1}^{P} e_i^s G'(\|\mathbf{x}_i - \mathbf{c}_j^s\|_{\mathbf{S}}^2)(\mathbf{x}_i - \mathbf{c}_j^s)(\mathbf{x}_i - \mathbf{c}_j^s)^T. \tag{5.27}$$

More on the theoretical aspects of nonradial stabilizers and on the solution to the corresponding regularization problem can be found in Girosi (1992). There is no exact closed form solution now, and from a mathematical point of view, this is a much more difficult problem to study than the standard regularization problem. Nevertheless, usually a good approximate solution of the following form can be found:

$$f_a(\mathbf{x}) = \sum_{j=1}^{p} w_j G(\|\mathbf{x} - \mathbf{c}_j\|_{\mathbf{S}}). \tag{5.28}$$

Parameters $\mathbf{c}$ and $\mathbf{S}$ (i.e., $\boldsymbol{\Sigma}^{-1}$) can now be computed using (5.25)–(5.27). The OL weights $\mathbf{w}$ can be found by applying a second-order RLS method or by using a first-order EBP algorithm (5.22). The solution simplifies a lot if the input variables are mutually independent (when there is no correlation). Then a diagonal matrix $\mathbf{S}$ is chosen that takes into account the possibly different scales of the input variables. A special and important case for uncorrelated input variables is given for Gaussian basis functions placed at a center $\mathbf{c}_j$, when the diagonal entries of matrix $\mathbf{S}$ are the reciprocals of the variances along the input coordinates:

$$\mathbf{G}_j = \mathbf{G}(\|(\mathbf{x} - \mathbf{c}_j)\|_{\mathbf{S}}^2)$$

$$= \exp\left(-\frac{(x_{1j} - c_{1j})^2}{\sigma_{1j}^2}\right) \exp\left(-\frac{(x_{2j} - c_{2j})^2}{\sigma_{2j}^2}\right) \cdots \exp\left(-\frac{(x_{nj} - c_{nj})^2}{\sigma_{nj}^2}\right). \tag{5.29}$$

Note that the Gaussian basis functions are typically normalized, by missing a scaling factor, which in the framework of a probability-density function ensures that the integral over the entire p-dimensional input space $x_1, x_2, \ldots, x_n$ is unity. The output of each particular Gaussian basis function is always multiplied by the corresponding OL weight w_j, and the standard scaling factor of the Gaussian probability-density function $1/|\boldsymbol{\Sigma}^{-1}|^{1/2}(2\pi)^{n/2}$ will be part of the OL weight w_j.

In terms of learning time and computational complexity, the OLS method, starting with a large number of basis functions placed over a domain at different (randomly chosen or preprocessed) centers and having different covariance matrices $\boldsymbol{\Sigma}$, very

Table 5.2
The Character of a Learning Problem in a Regularization (RBF) Network

Fixed[a]	Unknown	Cost Surface
c and Σ	OL weights **w**	Convex. Single minimum. Solution by least squares.
Σ	Centers **c** and OL weights **w**	Not convex. Many local minima. Solution by nonlinear optimization: (1) deterministic—first- or second-order gradients, OLS, SVMs, LP; (2) stochastic—massive random search, genetic algorithms, simulated annealing.
c	OL weights **w** and shape parameters Σ	
None	Centers **c**, OL weights **w**, and shape parameters Σ	

[a] After preprocessing or randomly.

often finds an acceptable suboptimal subset of p basis functions. These basis functions are either radial or nonradial, and the chosen subset is problem-dependent, or in statistics terms, it is data-driven. Table 5.2 shows the character of a learning problem in a regularization network. Learning complexity increases down through the table.

5.3.3 Orthogonal Least Squares

Training data sets in use today can be huge even by modern computing standards. Designing an RBF network by taking as many RBFs as there are data pairs would lead to numerically unsolvable tasks. In addition, one always want to filter the noise from data and to perform smooth approximation. This smoothing is also achieved by reducing the number of the HL neurons. Therefore, the objective is to select the smallest number p of basis functions that can model the training data to the desired degree of accuracy. These are the most relevant RBFs; finding them is a similar task to searching for p support vectors (and $p \ll P$) in designing SVMs.

An interesting and powerful method for choosing the subset p out of P basis functions is the orthogonalization procedure (Chen, Cowan, and Grant 1991). The presentation here follows that paper. However, there are improved versions of this approach (e.g., Orr 1996). An arbitrary selection of centers is clearly unsatisfactory. Orthogonalization avoids many drawbacks of early methods in RBF network training. However, it does not guarantee the optimal selection of p RBFs. It often results in suboptimal solutions (see Sherstinsky and Picard (1996)).

The orthogonal least squares (OLS) method involves sequential selection of RBF centers, which ensures that each new center chosen is orthogonal to the previous selections. This is the well-known Gram-Schmidt orthogonalization method in applied mathematics. In choosing the best RBFs, the contribution of each RBF to the modeling error decrease is measured. Each chosen center maximally decreases the squared error of the network output, and the method stops when this error reaches an acceptable level or when the desired number of centers have been chosen.

It may be useful to present the geometry of the modeling by an RBF network and to consider this modeling as a linear algebra problem. Hence, recall that the original problem was to solve equation (5.13) $\mathbf{y} = \mathbf{G}_0\mathbf{w}$, where $\mathbf{y} = f(\mathbf{x})$ are known values. When there are exactly P RBFs placed at each noncoinciding input vector $\mathbf{x}_i$ (i.e., $\mathbf{c}_i = \mathbf{x}_i$), a design matrix $\mathbf{G}_0$ is a (P, P) nonsingular matrix and the solution vector $\mathbf{w}$ ensures interpolation of the training data points. However, an interpolation, or perfect approximation, of the training data points does not guarantee a good model. Therefore, one wants to design an RBF network having fewer neurons than data points. Now, data cannot be interpolated and the model is given as

$$\mathbf{y} = \mathbf{G}\mathbf{w} = \sum_{i=1}^{p} \mathbf{g}_i w_i, \tag{5.30}$$

where $\mathbf{y}$ is a $(P, 1)$ desired target vector, $\mathbf{G}$ is now a (P, p) matrix, and $\mathbf{w}$ is a $(p, 1)$ weights vector that can be calculated by using the pseudoinverse that guarantees the best solution in L_2 norm, that is, the best sum-of-error-squares solution. We presented this solution in method 1 of section 3.2.2 (see (3.52)). Here, the design matrix $\mathbf{X}$ is $\mathbf{G}^T$. Thus, the best least-squares solution follows from (5.30) after its left multiplication by $\mathbf{G}^T$. The resulting equation is known as the normal equation

$$\mathbf{G}^T\mathbf{G}\mathbf{w} = \mathbf{G}^T\mathbf{y}, \tag{5.31}$$

and its solution is

$$\mathbf{w}^* = (\mathbf{G}^T\mathbf{G})^{-1}\mathbf{G}^T\mathbf{y} = \mathbf{G}^+\mathbf{y}. \tag{5.32}$$

Here $\mathbf{M} = \mathbf{G}^T\mathbf{G}$ is a symmetric (p, p) matrix with elements $m_{ij} = \mathbf{g}_i^T\mathbf{g}_j$, where $\mathbf{G} = [\mathbf{g}_1 \ \mathbf{g}_2 \ \cdots \ \mathbf{g}_p]$, and (5.31) gives p linear equations for the unknown elements in $\mathbf{w}$. The matrix $\mathbf{G}^T\mathbf{G}$ is nonsingular if and only if the columns of $\mathbf{G}$ are linearly independent. In the case of the RBF networks the columns of $\mathbf{G}$ are linearly independent (Micchelli 1986) and (5.31) can always be solved. The optimal solution $\mathbf{w}^*$ approximates the data in the sense that it minimizes the Euclidean length of the error $\mathbf{e}$ (also known as the residual vector $\mathbf{r}$), that is, $\|\mathbf{e}\|_2 = (\mathbf{e}^T\mathbf{e})^{1/2}$ is minimal, where $\mathbf{e} = \mathbf{y} - \mathbf{G}\mathbf{w}^*$.

There is a serious problem in designing the optimal RBF network in the sense that there are a lot of different possible ways to choose p columns from a (P, P) matrix. In fact, there are

$$n_c = \binom{P}{p} = \frac{P!}{p!(P-p)!}$$

possible arrangements of P columns taken p at a time. For practical purposes, calculating all the n_c possible combinations and choosing the one that results in the smallest error e_{min} is not feasible because n_c is a huge number. Even for a very small data set containing only 50 training data pairs ($P = 50$) there are 126,410,606,437,752 (or about 126 trillion) possible ways to form a matrix $\mathbf{G}$ with 25 columns. This number of different $\mathbf{G}$ matrices when there are several thousand training data patterns and the desired selection is only a few hundred basis vectors (columns of a matrix $\mathbf{G}$) is just unthinkingly huge. Thus, the combinatorial solution is not feasible, and the alternative is to try to orthogonalize the columns of $\mathbf{G}_0$ first and then to select the most relevant orthogonal columns.

Figure 5.15 shows the column geometry and the essence of an orthogonalization. Two interpolations of a quadratic function $y = x^2$ are given. Narrow Gaussian basis functions are obtained when the standard deviation of all three Gaussian functions is chosen to be $\sigma = 0.25\Delta c$, where Δc is a distance between the adjacent centers. Such narrow basis functions result in an orthogonal design matrix $\mathbf{G}_0$ and a bad interpolation (top left graph). Gaussian basis functions with high overlapping ($\sigma = 2\Delta c$) produce a good interpolation and a nonorthogonal matrix $\mathbf{G}_0$ (top right graph). The first property is good news but the second is not. Nonorthogonality of matrix $\mathbf{G}_0$ columns makes the selection of $p \ll P$ basis vector a very difficult task.

The interpolated function, interpolating function, and the three Gaussian basis functions are also shown in the figure. Three different normalized Gaussian basis functions are placed at the training data. The column vectors of $\mathbf{G}_0$ span the three-dimensional space. They are mutually orthogonal or nonorthogonal (see the matrix equations that follow). The nonorthogonal matrix $\mathbf{G}_0$ belonging to broad Gaussian basis functions is orthogonalized, and a new orthogonal basis is obtained by selecting as a first basis vector the third column of $\mathbf{G}_0$ (see light dashed curves in fig. 5.15, bottom right graph). Then the second column is orthogonalized with respect to the third one, and finally the first column is orthogonalized with respect to the plane spanned by the orthogonalized third and second vectors. This plane is shown as a shadow plane in the figure. The desired vector $\mathbf{y}$ is shown as an arrow line.

$$\mathbf{G}_{\sigma=0.25\Delta c} = \begin{bmatrix} 1.0000 & 0.0003 & 0.0000 \\ 0.0003 & 1.0000 & 0.0003 \\ 0.0000 & 0.0003 & 1.0000 \end{bmatrix}, \quad \mathbf{G}_{\sigma=2\Delta c} = \begin{bmatrix} 1.0000 & 0.8825 & 0.6065 \\ 0.8825 & 1.0000 & 0.8825 \\ 0.6065 & 0.8825 & 1.0000 \end{bmatrix}$$

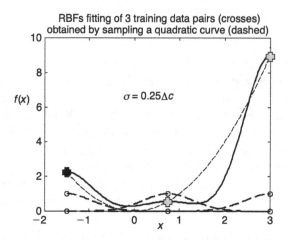

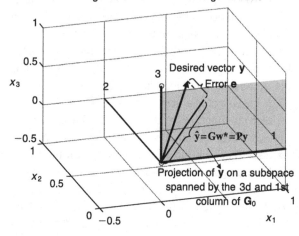

Figure 5.15
Two interpolations of a quadratic function $y = x^2$. *Top left*, narrow Gaussian basis functions result in an orthogonal design matrix $\mathbf{G}_0$ and a bad interpolation. *Top right*, Gaussian basis functions with high overlapping produce both a good interpolation and a nonorthogonal matrix $\mathbf{G}_0$. Interpolated function (thin dashed curve), interpolating function (solid curve), and the three Gaussian basis functions (thick dashed curves). Three different normalized Gaussian basis functions are placed at the training data. Column vectors of $\mathbf{G}_0$ span the three-dimensional space. They are (*bottom left*) mutually orthogonal or (*bottom right*) nonorthogonal. Desired vector $\mathbf{y}$ is shown as an arrow line.

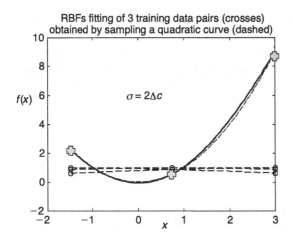

RBFs fitting of 3 training data pairs (crosses)
obtained by sampling a quadratic curve (dashed)

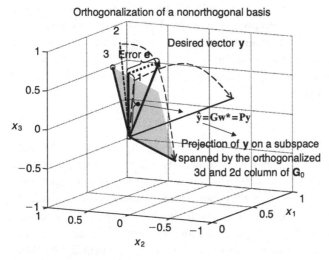

Orthogonalization of a nonorthogonal basis

Figure 5.15 (continued)

Thus, the general design problem is to select p columns of $\mathbf{G}_0$ that span a p-dimensional subspace U in $\Re^P$ in such a way that the orthogonal projection of the P-dimensional desired vector $\mathbf{y}$ onto a subspace U results in the smallest error vector $\mathbf{e}$. The error vector $\mathbf{e}$ is orthogonal to the subspace U, and its magnitude is the value of the error function E. There is a useful matrix related to orthogonal projections called a *projection matrix* that follows from

$$\mathbf{e} = \mathbf{y} - \mathbf{Gw}^* = \mathbf{y} - \mathbf{GG}^+\mathbf{y} = (\mathbf{I} - \mathbf{P})\mathbf{y}. \tag{5.33}$$

The symmetric projection matrix $\mathbf{P}$ is given as

$$\mathbf{P} = \mathbf{GG}^+. \tag{5.34}$$

Note that the matrix $(\mathbf{I} - \mathbf{P})$ in the expression for the error vector $\mathbf{e}$ in (5.33) is also a projection matrix. It projects the desired vector $\mathbf{y}$ onto the orthogonal complement of a subspace U. This projection is the error vector $\mathbf{e} = (\mathbf{I} - \mathbf{P})\mathbf{y}$. Hence, the preceding expressions split a desired vector into two perpendicular components: $\hat{\mathbf{y}} = \mathbf{Py}$ is in the column subspace U, and the other component, $\mathbf{e} = (\mathbf{I} - \mathbf{P})\mathbf{y}$, is in the left null space of $\mathbf{G}^T$, which is orthogonal to the column subspace U. (More details on projection matrices can be found in standard linear algebra books.)

Thus, using a projection matrix, the projection of a desired vector $\mathbf{y}$ onto the subspace U can be expressed as

$$\hat{\mathbf{y}} = \mathbf{Gw}^* = \mathbf{Py}. \tag{5.35}$$

Note that in the case pictured in figure 5.15 ($P = 3$, $p = 2$), there are three different two-dimensional subspaces U_i that can be spanned by taking two columns of a matrix $\mathbf{G}_0$ at time. In the left graph ($\sigma = 0.25\Delta c$, low overlapping, bad interpolation but orthogonal columns) the projection of $\mathbf{y}$ onto a two-dimensional subspace U spanned by the third and first column vectors results in the smallest error $\mathbf{e}$. In the right graph, ($\sigma = 2\Delta c$, high overlapping, good interpolation but nonorthogonal columns) the projection of $\mathbf{y}$ onto a two-dimensional subspace U spanned by the third and second column vectors results in the smallest error $\mathbf{e}$.

Finally, the technical part of the orthogonalization should be discussed. The basic idea is to select the columns according to their contributions to the error of approximation. The following algorithm is based on the classic Gram-Schmidt orthogonalization as given in Chen, Cowan, and Grant (1991). The graphs and pseudocode are from Shah (1998). The method is a sequential selection of RBF centers (columns of a (P,P) matrix $\mathbf{G}_0$), which ensures that each new center chosen is orthogonal to the previous selections and that each selected center maximally decreases the squared error of the network output. After selecting such columns, the desired vector $\mathbf{y}$ can be represented as

$$\mathbf{y} = \mathbf{G}\mathbf{w} + \mathbf{e} \Rightarrow \begin{bmatrix} y_1 \\ y_2 \\ \vdots \\ y_P \end{bmatrix} = \begin{bmatrix} g_{11} & g_{12} & \cdots & g_{1p} \\ g_{21} & g_{22} & \cdots & g_{2p} \\ \vdots & \vdots & \vdots & \vdots \\ g_{P1} & g_{P2} & \cdots & g_{Pp} \end{bmatrix} \begin{bmatrix} w_1 \\ w_2 \\ \vdots \\ w_p \end{bmatrix} + \begin{bmatrix} e_1 \\ e_2 \\ \vdots \\ e_p \end{bmatrix}, \quad 1 \leq i \leq p, \quad (5.36)$$

where $\mathbf{G} = [\mathbf{g}_1 \quad \cdots \quad \mathbf{g}_i \quad \cdots \quad \mathbf{g}_p]$ and $\mathbf{g}_i = [g_{1i} \quad g_{2i} \quad \cdots \quad g_{Pi}]^T$ and the $\mathbf{g}_i$ are the individual, often nonorthogonal column (regressor) vectors. (The use of the name regressor vectors for column vectors of $\mathbf{G}_0$ is borrowed from Chen's paper but it is common.) The least-squares solution of $\mathbf{w}^*$ maps $\mathbf{G}\mathbf{w}^*$ as the projection of $\mathbf{y}$ onto the space spanned by the chosen regressor basis vectors. Since a number of regressor vectors are added to provide the desired output $\mathbf{y}$, the contribution from individual regressor vectors needs to be calculated. Once the relative contributions from individual regressor vectors are found, the vectors with higher contributions are found to be more important in the RBF approximation than the vectors with lower contributions. (This is similar to the search for support vectors in the SVM approach or in the linear programming method that follows in section 5.3.4.)

To find the contributions and the output from different regressor basis vectors, these vectors need to be first orthogonalized relative to each other. Here, the OLS method uses the Gram-Schmidt method to transform the set of $\mathbf{g}_i$ into a set of orthogonal basis vectors by Cholesky decomposition of the regressor matrix $\mathbf{G}$ as follows:

$$\mathbf{G} = \mathbf{S}\mathbf{A}, \tag{5.37}$$

where

$$\mathbf{A} = \begin{bmatrix} 1 & \alpha_{12} & \alpha_{13} & \cdots & \cdots & \alpha_{1p} \\ 0 & 1 & \alpha_{23} & \cdots & \cdots & \alpha_{2p} \\ 0 & 0 & \cdots & & \vdots & \vdots \\ \vdots & \vdots & \vdots & 1 & \vdots & \vdots \\ \vdots & \vdots & \vdots & 0 & 1 & \alpha_{(p-1)p} \\ 0 & \cdots & \cdots & 0 & 0 & 1 \end{bmatrix} \tag{5.38}$$

is a (p, p) upper triangular matrix and

$$\mathbf{S} = [\mathbf{s}_1 \quad \cdots \quad \mathbf{s}_i \quad \cdots \quad \mathbf{s}_p] \tag{5.39}$$

is a (P, p) matrix with orthogonal columns satisfying

$$\mathbf{S}^T\mathbf{S} = \mathbf{H}, \tag{5.40}$$

where $\mathbf{H}$ is a positive diagonal (p, p) matrix. The $\mathbf{S}$ matrix is the orthogonalized $\mathbf{G}$ matrix, where selection of orthogonalized columns from $\mathbf{G}$ depends on the approximation outputs of individual regressor vectors. For example, in figure 5.15, $\mathbf{s}_1 = \mathbf{g}_3$ has the maximum approximation output from the orthogonalized columns of matrix $\mathbf{S}$. The relevance of columns decreases from left to right with the least approximation contribution provided by $\mathbf{s}_p$.

The space spanned by the orthogonal regressor basis vectors $\mathbf{s}_i$ is the same space spanned by the nonorthogonal basis vectors $\mathbf{G}_i$, and consequently (5.36) can now be rewritten as

$$\mathbf{y} = \mathbf{S}\gamma + \mathbf{e}, \tag{5.41}$$

where the least-squares solution $\hat{\gamma}$ is given by

$$\hat{\gamma} = \mathbf{H}^{-1}\mathbf{S}^T\mathbf{y}, \tag{5.42}$$

or

$$\hat{\gamma}_i = \frac{\mathbf{s}_i^T\mathbf{y}}{\mathbf{s}_i^T\mathbf{s}_i}, \qquad i = 1,\ldots,p. \tag{5.43}$$

Therefore, the parameter estimates (weights) are computed from the triangular system

$$\mathbf{A}\hat{\mathbf{w}} = \hat{\gamma}, \tag{5.44}$$

where the Gram-Schmidt procedure calculates $\mathbf{A}$ one column at a time and orthogonalizes $\mathbf{G}$. At the kth step, the kth column is made orthogonal to each of the $k-1$ previously orthogonalized columns, and the operation is repeated for $k = 2,\ldots,p$. This procedure is represented as

$$\left.\begin{aligned} \mathbf{s}_1 &= \mathbf{g}_1, \\[2mm] \alpha_{ik} &= \frac{\mathbf{s}_i^T\mathbf{g}_k}{\mathbf{s}_i^T\mathbf{s}_i}, \qquad 1 \leq i < k \\[2mm] \mathbf{s}_k &= \mathbf{g}_k - \sum_{i=1}^{k-1}\alpha_{ik}\mathbf{s}_i, \end{aligned}\right\} \quad k = 2,\ldots,p. \tag{5.45}$$

The main reason for using the OLS method is to obtain the optimal subset selection from a large number of regressors (columns of a matrix $\mathbf{G}_0$) for adequate modeling.

Thus, the regressors providing the best approximation to the output $\mathbf{y}$ must be found. Since $\mathbf{S}$ is already orthogonalized, the sum of squares of the dependent variable $\mathbf{y}$ is

$$\mathbf{y}^T\mathbf{y} = \sum_{i=1}^{p_s} \gamma_i^2 \mathbf{s}_i^T \mathbf{s}_i + \mathbf{e}^T\mathbf{e}, \tag{5.46}$$

where p_s is the number of significant regressors in the model. The error reduction ratio [err] due to $\mathbf{s}_i$ can now be defined as

$$[\text{err}]_i = \frac{\gamma_i^2 \mathbf{s}_i^T \mathbf{s}_i}{\mathbf{y}^T\mathbf{y}}, \qquad 1 \le i \le p_s. \tag{5.47}$$

The code for regressor selection is summarized in box 5.1, and the geometric interpretation of the OLS procedure is shown in figures 5.16 and 5.17.

Box 5.1
Orthogonal Least Squares Learning Algorithm

```
Step 1. Selection of the First Orthogonal Vector

k=1;
for i=1 to p,
    sₖ(:,i)=G(:,i);
    γₖ=sₖ(:,i)ᵀ*y/(sₖ(:,i)ᵀ*sₖ(:,i));
    errₖ(i)=γₖ²*sₖ(:,i)ᵀ*sₖ(:,i)/(yᵀ*y);
end
[erraₖ,ind]=max(errₖ);
s(:,k)=G(:,ind);
index(1)=ind;

Step 2. General Selection of Orthogonal Vectors

A=eye(p);
for k=2:p,
    for i=1:p-k, (i≠i₁,...,i₁≠iₖ₋₁)
            for j=1:k-1,
                α(j,i)=s(:,j)ᵀ*G(:,i)/(s(:,j)ᵀ*s(:,j));
            end
            sₖ(:,i)=G(:,i)-s*α(:,i);
            γ=sₖ(:,i)ᵀ*y/(sₖ(:,i)ᵀ*sₖ(:,i));
            errₖ(i)=γ²*sₖ(:,I)ᵀ*sₖ(:,i)/(yᵀ*y);
    end
    [erraₖ,ind]=max(err);
    s(:,k)=sₖ(:,ind);
end
A(1:k-1,k)=γ(:,ind);
```

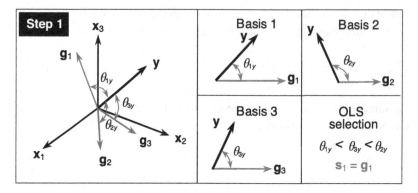

Figure 5.16
Initial regressor selection where three nonorthogonal regressors $\mathbf{g}_1$, $\mathbf{g}_2$, and $\mathbf{g}_3$ are given relative to target $\mathbf{y}$ and the angles θ_{1y}, θ_{2y}, and θ_{3y} are shown. The system of orthogonal basis vectors $\mathbf{x}_i$ represents any orthogonal system and is shown merely to stress the nonorthogonality of the column vectors $\mathbf{g}_i$. First selected is regressor $\mathbf{g}_1$ (angle θ_{1y} is the smallest, i.e., $\mathbf{g}_1$ is the closest to $\mathbf{y}$).

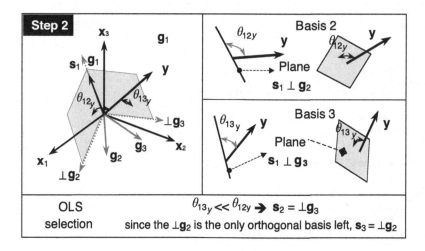

Figure 5.17
Regressors $(\mathbf{g}_2, \mathbf{g}_3)$ are orthogonalized as $\perp\mathbf{g}_2$ and $\perp\mathbf{g}_3$ relative to $\mathbf{g}_1$. The orthogonalized basis vector $\perp\mathbf{g}_3$ and the previously selected regressor $\mathbf{g}_1$ form a plane, as do the orthogonalized basis vector $\perp\mathbf{g}_2$ and the previously selected regressor $\mathbf{g}_1$. These two planes are shown. A third column vector $\mathbf{g}_3$ is chosen as the second orthogonal basis $\mathbf{s}_2 = \perp\mathbf{g}_3$ because the angle θ_{13y} between the desired vector $\mathbf{y}$ and the plane $\mathbf{s}_1\perp\mathbf{g}_3$ is smaller than the angle θ_{12y} formed between the plane $\mathbf{s}_1\perp\mathbf{g}_2$ and the target vector $\mathbf{y}$. The least significant basis vector $\perp\mathbf{g}_2$ is selected last, $\mathbf{s}_3 = \perp\mathbf{g}_2$.

The initial selection of the regressor is illustrated in figure 5.16. The original non-orthogonal regressor basis vectors are represented by $\mathbf{g}_1$, $\mathbf{g}_2$, and $\mathbf{g}_3$. Angles θ_{1y}, θ_{2y}, and θ_{3y} between the basis vector and the desired vector $\mathbf{y}$ are computed, and the regressor whose angle is the smallest is selected as the most significant regressor. Here, θ_{1y} is minimal for the first basis vector, denoting that this is the one closest to the target $\mathbf{y}$, so the first orthogonal basis vector is $\mathbf{s}_1 = \mathbf{g}_1$. Selecting regressor $\mathbf{g}_1$ results in the least squared error and in the maximal output $\hat{\mathbf{y}}$ compared to other available regressors. After the first selection is made, the first chosen column from a (P, P) matrix $\mathbf{G}_0$ (first regressor) and any other previously selected regressors cannot be selected again. Every selection made hereafter would be orthogonal to the subspace spanned by the previously selected regressor basis vectors and would maximally decrease the squared error.

Figure 5.17 shows the sequential orthogonalization of the regressor basis vectors $\mathbf{g}_2$ and $\mathbf{g}_3$. These two basis vectors are orthogonalized to the vector $\mathbf{g}_1$, selected previously, and the angle created between the (hyper)plane formed by the basis vector and the previously selected regressors and the target $\mathbf{y}$ is minimized. This minimization results in the best approximation to the target $\mathbf{y}$ in an L_2 norm.

5.3.4 Optimal Subset Selection by Linear Programming

The previous section discussed the application of the OLS method in choosing a subset p out of P basis functions in the RBF network design. The OLS method provides a good parsimonious model as long as the design matrix $\mathbf{G}$ is not far from being orthogonal. In the case of the Gaussian basis function, this will happen for not-too-wide Gaussian (hyper)bells. Unfortunately, in order to achieve a good model, the $\mathbf{G}$ matrix is typically highly nonorthogonal, and OLS will achieve a suboptimal solution at considerable computational cost for large data sets. Another theoretically sound approach was presented in chapter 2—one that uses quadratic programming (QP) in calculating support vectors. This support vector selection is similar to the choice of columns of $\mathbf{G}$ by orthogonalization, but the QP-based learning in support vector machines (SVMs) controls the capacity of the final model much better: it matches model capacity to data complexity. There is a price to pay for such a nice algorithm, and, as mentioned in section 2.4, QP-based training works almost perfectly for not-too-large training data sets. However, when the number of data points is large (say, $l > 2000$), the QP problem becomes extremely difficult to solve with standard methods.

The application of linear programming (LP) in solving approximation and classification problems is not a novel idea. One of the first implementations of mathematical programming to statistical learning from data was described by Charnes, Cooper, and Ferguson (1955), and many others have independently applied LP to approximation problems (Cheney and Goldstein 1958; Stiefel 1960; Kelley 1958; Rice 1964). These results follow from minimizing the L_1 norm in solving regression problems. A summary and very good presentation of mathematical programming application in statistics are given by Arthanari and Dodge (1993).

Interestingly, the first results on L_1 norm estimators were given as early as 1757 by Yugoslav scientist Bošković (see Eisenhart 1962).

Early work on LP-based classification algorithms was done in the mid-1960s (see Mangasarian 1965). Recently, a lot of work has been done on implementing the LP approach in support vectors selection (Smola, Friess, and Schölkopf 1998; Bennett 1999; Weston et al. 1999; Graepel et al. 1999). All these papers originate from the same stream of ideas for controlling the (maximal) margin. Hence, they are close to the SVM constructive algorithms.

The LP-based approach is demonstrated here using the regression example. However, the same method can also be applied to classification tasks. This is currently under investigation by Hadžić (1999). A slight difference between standard QP-based SVM learning and the LP approach is that instead of minimizing the L_2 norm of the weights vector $\|\mathbf{w}\|_2$, the L_1 norm $\|\mathbf{w}\|_1$ is minimized. This method for optimal subset selection shares many nice properties with SVM methodology. Recall that the minimization of the L_2 norm is equivalent to minimizing $\mathbf{w}^T\mathbf{w} = \sum_{i=1}^{n} w_i^2 = w_1^2 + w_2^2 + \cdots + w_n^2$, and this results in the QP type of problem. In chapter 2, it was shown that the minimization of $\|\mathbf{w}\|_2$ leads to a maximization of a margin M. The geometrical meaning of the minimal L_1 norm is not clear yet, but the application of the LP approach to subset selection of support vectors or basis functions results in very good performance by a neural network or an SVM. At the same time, there is no theoretical evidence that minimization of either the L_1 norm or L_2 norm of the weights vector $\mathbf{w}$ produces superior generalization. The theoretical question of generalization properties is still open. Early comparisons show that the L_1 norm results in more parsimonious models containing fewer neurons (support vectors, basis functions) in a hidden layer. In addition to producing sparser networks, the main advantage of applying the L_1 norm is the possibility of using state-of-the-art linear program solvers that are more robust, more efficient, and capable of solving larger problems than quadratic program solvers. The basic disadvantage of the LP approach is the lack of the theoretical understanding of the results obtained.

Here, the application of the LP method for the best subset selection follows Zhang and Fuchs (1999). They use LP in an initialization stage of the multilayer perceptron network. Interestingly, in order to start with a good initial set of weights, they use a much larger number of basis functions than there are available training data. This means that the initial design matrix (kernel matrix $\mathbf{K}(x_i, x_j)$, denoted here as $\mathbf{G}$) is rectangular. In fact, they use 100 times as many basis functions as training data points, and they mention applications with even 1,000 times as many. In other words, the number of columns of a $\mathbf{G}$ matrix n_c is approximately 100 to 1,000 times larger than the number of its rows n_r. (Note that in an LP approach matrix $\mathbf{G}$ does not strictly have to satisfy the Mercer conditions for kernel functions.) Here, in order to be in accordance with standard procedure in designing SVMs, the number of basis functions (neurons) is taken as equal to the number of the training data P. However, there are no restrictions on the number of $\mathbf{G}$ matrix columns insofar as the LP algorithm is concerned.

The original problem, the same as in the OLS method, is not to interpolate data by solving the equation $\mathbf{y} = \mathbf{Gw}$, where $\mathbf{G}$ is a (P, P) matrix and P is the number of training data, but rather to design a parsimonious neural network containing fewer neurons than data points. The sparseness of a model follows from minimization of the L_1 norm of the weights vector $\mathbf{w}$. In other words, the objective is to solve $\mathbf{y} = \mathbf{Gw}$ such that $\|\mathbf{Gw} - \mathbf{y}\|$ is small for some chosen norm and such that $\|\mathbf{w}\|_1 = \sum_{p=1}^{P} |w_p|$ is as small as possible. In order to perform such a task, reformulate the initial problem as follows.

Find a weights vector

$$\mathbf{w} = \arg \min_{\mathbf{w}} \|\mathbf{w}\|_1 \quad \text{subject to} \quad \|\mathbf{Gw} - \mathbf{y}\|_\infty \leq \varepsilon, \tag{5.48}$$

where ε defines the *maximally* allowed error (that is why the L_∞ norm is used) and corresponds to the ε-insensitivity zone in an SVM. This constrained optimization problem can easily be transformed into standard linear programming form. First, recall that $\|\mathbf{w}\|_1 = \sum_{p=1}^{P} |w_p|$; this is not an LP problem formulation where typically $\mathbf{c}^T \mathbf{w} = \sum_{p=1}^{P} c_p w_p$ is minimized and $\mathbf{c}$ is some known coefficient vector. In order to apply the LP algorithm, replace w_p and $|w_p|$ as follows:

$$w_p = w_p^+ - w_p^-, \tag{5.49a}$$

$$|w_p| = w_p^+ + w_p^-, \tag{5.49b}$$

where w_p^+ and w_p^- are two non-negative variables, that is, $w_p^+ > 0$, $w_p^- > 0$. Note that the substitutions in (5.49) are unique—for a given w_p there is only one pair (w_p^+, w_p^-) that fulfills both equations. Furthermore, both variables cannot be larger than zero at the same time. In fact, there are only three possible solutions for a pair of variables

(w_p^+, w_p^-), namely, $(0,0)$, $(w_p^+, 0)$ or $(0, w_p^-)$. The constraint in (5.48) is not in a standard formulation either, and it should also be reformulated as follows. Note that $\|\mathbf{Gw} - \mathbf{y}\|_\infty \leq \varepsilon$ in (5.48) defines an ε tube inside which the approximating function should reside. Such a constraint can be rewritten as

$$\mathbf{y} - \varepsilon\mathbf{1} \leq \mathbf{Gw} \leq \mathbf{y} + \varepsilon\mathbf{1} \tag{5.50}$$

where $\mathbf{1}$ is a $(P,1)$ column vector filled with 1's. Expression (5.50) represents a standard set of linear constraints, and the LP problem to solve is now the following.

Find a pair

$$(\mathbf{w}^+, \mathbf{w}^-) = \arg\min_{\mathbf{w}^+, \mathbf{w}^-} \sum_{p=1}^{P} (w_p^+ + w_p^-)$$

subject to $\tag{5.51}$

$$\mathbf{y} - \varepsilon\mathbf{1} \leq \mathbf{G}(\mathbf{w}^+ - \mathbf{w}^-) \leq \mathbf{y} + \varepsilon\mathbf{1}, \qquad \mathbf{w}^+ > 0, \quad \mathbf{w}^- > 0,$$

where $\mathbf{w}^+ = [w_1^+ \ w_2^+ \ \ldots \ w_P^+]^T$ and $\mathbf{w}^- = [w_1^- \ w_2^- \ \ldots \ w_P^-]^T$.

LP problem (5.51) can be presented in a matrix-vector formulation suitable for an LP program solver as follows:

$$\min_{\mathbf{w}} \mathbf{c}^T\mathbf{w} \Rightarrow \min_{\mathbf{w}} \begin{bmatrix} 1 & 1 & \cdots & 1 & 1 & 1 & \cdots & 1 \\ & \text{\small P columns} & & & & \text{\small P columns} & & \end{bmatrix} \begin{bmatrix} w_1^+ \\ w_2^+ \\ \vdots \\ w_P^+ \\ w_1^- \\ w_2^- \\ \vdots \\ w_P^- \end{bmatrix}$$

subject to $\tag{5.52}$

$$\begin{bmatrix} \mathbf{G} & -\mathbf{G} \\ -\mathbf{G} & \mathbf{G} \end{bmatrix} \begin{bmatrix} \mathbf{w}^+ \\ \mathbf{w}^- \end{bmatrix} \leq \begin{bmatrix} \mathbf{y} + \varepsilon\mathbf{1} \\ -\mathbf{y} + \varepsilon\mathbf{1} \end{bmatrix}, \qquad \mathbf{w}^+ > 0, \quad \mathbf{w}^- > 0,$$

where both $\mathbf{w}$ and $\mathbf{c}$ are $(2P,1)$-dimensional vectors. The vector $\mathbf{c} = \mathbf{1}(2P,1)$, that is, $\mathbf{c}$ is a $(2P,1)$ vector filled with 1's, and $\mathbf{w} = [\mathbf{w}^{+T} \ \mathbf{w}^{-T}]^T$. Note that in the LP problem formulation the Hessian matrix from the QP learning for SVMs is equal to the matrix of the LP constraints.

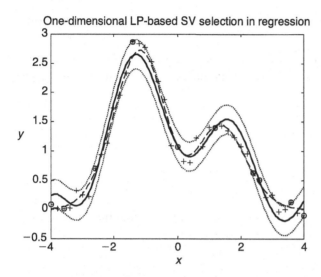

Figure 5.18
The SV selection based on an LP learning algorithm (5.52). Hermitian function $f(x) = 1.1(1 - x + 2x^2) \cdot$ $\exp(-0.5x^2)$ polluted with a 10% Gaussian zero mean noise (dashed curve). The training set contains 41 training data points (crosses). An LP algorithm has selected ten SVs, shown as encircled data points. Resulting approximation curve (solid). Insensitivity zone is bounded by dotted curves.

In figure 5.18, the SV selection based on an LP learning algorithm (5.52) is shown for a Hermitian function $f(x) = 1.1(1 - x + 2x^2) \exp(-0.5x^2)$ polluted with a 10% Gaussian zero mean noise. The training set contains 41 training data pairs, and the LP algorithm has selected ten SVs. The resulting graph is similar to the standard QP-based learning outcomes.

This section on LP-based algorithms is inconclusive in the sense that much more investigation and comparison with QP-based SV selection on both real and artificial data sets are needed. In particular, the benchmarking studies should compare the performances of these two approaches depending upon the complexity of the modeled underlying dependency, noise level, size of the training data set, dimensionality of the problem, and the computation time needed for performing the QP- and LP-based training algorithms. Despite the lack of such an analysis at present, the first simulation results show that LP subset selection may be a good alternative to QP-based algorithms when working with huge training data sets. In sum, the potential benefits of applying LP-based learning algorithms are as follows:

· LP algorithms are faster and more robust than QP algorithms.
· They tend to minimize the number of weights (SVs) chosen.

• They share many good properties with an established statistical technique known as basis pursuit.

• They naturally incorporate the use of kernels for creation of nonlinear separation and regression hypersurfaces in pattern recognition and function approximation problems.

Problems

5.1. Show why differentiation is an ill-posed problem.

5.2. In figure P5.1, why is the mapping of the grip position (x, y) onto links' angles (α, β) of the two-links planar robot an ill-posed problem?

5.3. Find the Euler-Lagrange equation of the following regularized functional for the one-dimensional input x:

$$H[f] = \sum_{i=1}^{P}(d_i - f(x_i))^2 + \lambda \|\mathbf{P}f\|^2 = \sum_{i=1}^{P}(d_i - f(x_i))^2 + \lambda \int (f''(x))^2 \, dx.$$

5.4. Derive equations (5.22) and (5.23).

5.5. It was stated that an advantage in applying Gaussian RBFs is that "they show much better smoothing properties than other known RBFs. This is clear from the exponentially acting stabilizer $\tilde{G}(s) = 1/e^{\|\mathbf{s}\|^2/\beta}$, which will heavily damp, or punish, any nonsmooth interpolation function $f(\mathbf{x})$ in areas of high frequencies $\mathbf{s}$." Prove this statement by analyzing the product of an interpolation/approximation function $f(s)$ and a Gaussian stabilizer $\tilde{G}(s) = 1/e^{\|\mathbf{s}\|^2/\beta}$ in the s domain.

5.6. In figure P5.2, the recorded data (represented by small circles) should be interpolated using an RBF network. The basis (activation) functions of the neurons are triangles (also known as B-splines).

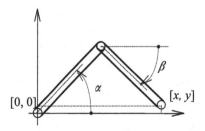

Figure P5.1
Graph for problem 5.2.

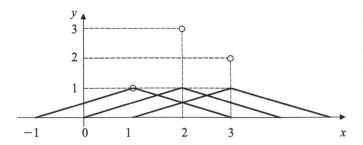

Figure P5.2
Graph for problems 5.6 and 5.7.

a. Find the weights that will solve this interpolation problem. Draw the interpolating function on the given diagram.

b. Draw the RBF network and show the value of each weight on this plot.

c. Select the first and the third triangle as the basis functions, and model the given data pairs with them. Namely, find the corresponding weights and draw basis functions, data pairs, and approximating function in the (x, y) plane.

5.7. Repeat the calculations in problem 5.6 (a), (b), and (c) by augmenting the hidden layer output vector with a bias term, i.e., $y_4 = +1$. Draw networks and the corresponding graphs in the (x, y) plane.

5.8. Model (find the weights of the RBF network for) the training data from problems 5.6 and 5.7 using linear splines, i.e., using the basis functions $g(x, x_i) = |x - x_i|$, where the x_i are the given training inputs.

a. Find the weights by placing the splines at each training data input (no bias).

b. Find the weights by placing the splines at the first and third inputs only (no bias).

c. Repeat the calculation in (b) augmenting the HL output vector with a bias term.

d. Find the weights by placing the splines at the second and third inputs only (no bias).

e. Repeat the calculation in (d) augmenting the HL output vector with a bias term.

Draw the corresponding graphs in the (x, y) plane containing data pairs and interpolation or approximation functions. Comment on the influence of the bias term. (Note that the training data set is chosen deliberately small. There are only three data pairs. Therefore, you do not need a computer for problems 5.6–5.8, and all calculations can be done with pencil and paper only).

5.9. It was stated that a desired vector $\mathbf{y}$ can be split into two perpendicular components by implementation of a projection matrix $\mathbf{P}$: the error vector $\mathbf{e}$ and the projection of $\mathbf{y}$ onto the column subspace $U\hat{\mathbf{y}}$. Prove that $\mathbf{e}$ is orthogonal to $\hat{\mathbf{y}}$.

5.10. The columns of a matrix

$$\mathbf{G} = \begin{bmatrix} 2 & 3 & 1 \\ 0 & 4 & 2 \\ 0 & 0 & 3 \end{bmatrix}$$

span a three-dimensional space. Find three orthonormal systems that span the same space, selecting the new orthonormal basis in this order: $[\mathbf{g}_{1N}\mathbf{g}_{2N}\mathbf{g}_{3N}]$, $[\mathbf{g}_{2N}\mathbf{g}_{1N}\mathbf{g}_{3N}]$, $[\mathbf{g}_{3N}\mathbf{g}_{2N}\mathbf{g}_{1N}]$. The subscript N denotes normalized. Express the unique decompositions of vector $\mathbf{y} = \begin{bmatrix} 3 & 2 & 1 \end{bmatrix}^T$ in these three orthonormal systems.

5.11. Let U be the space spanned by the $\mathbf{u}$'s, and write $\mathbf{y}$ as the sum of a vector in U and a vector orthogonal to U.

a. $\mathbf{y} = \begin{bmatrix} 1 & 3 & 5 \end{bmatrix}^T$, $\mathbf{u}_1 = \begin{bmatrix} 1 & 3 & -2 \end{bmatrix}^T$, $\mathbf{u}_2 = \begin{bmatrix} 5 & 1 & 4 \end{bmatrix}^T$.

b. $\mathbf{y} = \begin{bmatrix} 4 & 3 & 3 & -1 \end{bmatrix}^T$, $\mathbf{u}_1 = \begin{bmatrix} 1 & 1 & 0 & 1 \end{bmatrix}^T$, $\mathbf{u}_2 = \begin{bmatrix} -1 & 3 & 1 & -2 \end{bmatrix}^T$, $\mathbf{u}_3 = \begin{bmatrix} -1 & 0 & 1 & 1 \end{bmatrix}^T$.

5.12. The columns of a matrix

$$\mathbf{G} = \begin{bmatrix} 2 & -2 & 1 \\ 0 & 2 & 1 \\ 0 & 0 & 1 \end{bmatrix}$$

span a three-dimensional space. The desired vector is $\mathbf{y} = \begin{bmatrix} 1 & 1 & 0 \end{bmatrix}^T$. Find the best projection of $\mathbf{y}$ onto a two-dimensional subspace U spanned by two columns of $\mathbf{G}$. Show that the OLS learning algorithm as given by (5.45) or as code in box 5.1 will result in a suboptimal selection of the best regressors (columns of $\mathbf{G}$). (*Hint:* Draw all given vectors, meaning $\mathbf{g}_i$, $i = 1, 3$, and $\mathbf{y}$ in a three-dimensional space, find the best selection of two columns, and follow the given algorithm. If you make a careful drawing, the best selection of two columns will be obvious.)

5.13. Section 4.3.3 mentioned that for normalized inputs, feedforward multilayer perceptrons with sigmoidal activation functions can always approximate arbitrarily well a given Gaussian RBF, but that the converse is true only for a certain range of the bias parameter in the sigmoidal neuron. Prove this statement.

5.14. Consider an RBF network given by (5.13). Derive expressions for the elements of the Jacobian matrix given by $J_{ij} = \partial f_i / \partial x_j$.

5.15. Equation (5.14)

$$f(\mathbf{x}) = \sum_{i=1}^{P} w_i G(\|\mathbf{x} - \mathbf{x}_i\|)$$

represents an RBF interpolation scheme. Show that, on the interval $[1, 3]$, this radial basis function expansion can also be written in the form

$$f(\mathbf{x}) = \sum_{i=1}^{P} y_i \varphi_i(\mathbf{x}),$$

where the y_i are the values to be interpolated. Take the data points given in problem 5.6, i.e., $y_1 = 1$, $y_2 = 3$, $y_3 = 2$. Derive and draw the explicit form for the dual kernels $\varphi_i(\mathbf{x})$.

5.16. Consider the following kernel regression approximation scheme

$$f_\sigma(\mathbf{x}) = \frac{\displaystyle\sum_{i=1}^{P} y_i G_\sigma(\mathbf{x} - \mathbf{x}_i)}{\displaystyle\sum_{i=1}^{P} G_\sigma(\mathbf{x} - \mathbf{x}_i)},$$

where G_σ is the Gaussian

$$G_\sigma = e^{-\|\mathbf{x}\|^2 / \sigma^2}.$$

Derive the behavior of this approximation in the cases $\sigma \to 0$ and $\sigma \to \infty$.

Simulation Experiments

The simulation experiments in chapter 5 have the purpose of familiarizing the reader with the regularization networks, better known as RBF networks. The program rbf1.m is aimed at solving one-dimensional regression problems using Gaussian basis functions. The learning algorithm is a standard RBF network batch algorithm given by (5.16). One-dimensional examples are used for the sake of visualization of all results. A single demo function is supplied but you may make as many different one-dimensional examples as you like. Just follow the pop-up menus and select the inputs you want.

The experiments are aimed at reviewing many basic facets of RBF batch learning (notably the influence of the Gaussian bell shapes on the approximation, the smoothing effects obtained by decreasing the number of HL neurons, the smoothing effects obtained by changing the regularization parameter λ, and the influence of noise). Be aware of the following facts about the program rbf1.m:

1. It is developed for one-dimensional nonlinear regression problems.

2. However, the learning part is in matrix form, and it can be used for more complex learning tasks.

3. The learning takes place in an off-line (batch) algorithm given by (5.16).

4. rbf1.m is a user-friendly program, even for beginners in using MATLAB, but you must cooperate. Read carefully the description part of the rbf1.m routine first. The program prompts you to select, to define, or to choose different things during the learning.

5. Analyze carefully the resulting graphic windows. There are answers to various issues of learning and RBF network modeling in them.

Experiment with the program rbf1.m as follows:

1. Launch MATLAB.

2. Connect to directory learnsc (at the matlab prompt, type cd learnsc ⟨RETURN⟩). learnsc is a subdirectory of matlab, as bin, toolbox, and uitools are. While typing cd learnsc, make sure that your working directory is matlab, not matlab/bin, for example).

3. Type start ⟨RETURN⟩, and pop-up menus will lead you through the design procedure. You should make some design decisions. Do them with understanding and follow all results obtained.

4. After learning, five figures will be displayed. Analyze them carefully.

Now perform various experiments by changing some design parameters. Start with the demo example and then create your own. Run the same example repeatedly, and try out different parameters.

1. Perform the interpolation first ($t = 1$, i.e., you will have P RBFs, where P stands for the number of training data points). Start with overlapping Gaussian basis functions ($ks = 1$ to 3). Repeat simulations with differently shaped Gaussians. Use narrow ($ks \ll 1$) and broad ($ks \gg 1$) ones.

2. Analyze the smoothing effects obtained by decreasing the number of HL neurons (Gaussian basis functions). Pollute the function with more than 25% noise ($n > 0.25$). Start with P RBFs ($t = 1$) and reduce the number of Gaussians by taking $t = 2$, or greater. Repeat the simulations, decreasing the number of neurons and keeping all other training parameters (noise level and shape) fixed. In order to see the effects of smoothing, run an example with 50–100 training data pairs.

3. Analyze the smoothing effects of regularization parameter λ. Take the number of neurons to be P. Choose $ks = 2$ and keep it fixed for all simulations. Start modeling your data without regularization ($\lambda = 0$) and gradually increase the regularization factor. Keep all other training parameters fixed.

In all the preceding simulation experiments, there must not be the influence of random noise. Therefore, run all simulations with the same *random number generator seed fixed*, which ensures the same initial conditions for all simulations. Generally, in performing simulations you should try to change only *one* parameter at time. Meticulously analyze all resulting graphs after each simulation run. There are many useful results in those figures.

6 Fuzzy Logic Systems

Together with neural networks, fuzzy logic models constitute the modeling tools of soft computing, and it seems appropriate to start with a short definition of fuzzy logic: *Fuzzy logic is a tool for embedding structured human knowledge into workable algorithms.*

One can say, paraphrasing Zadeh (1965; 1973), that the concept of fuzzy logic is used in many different senses. In a narrow sense, fuzzy logic (FL) is considered a logical system aimed at providing a model for modes of human reasoning that are approximate rather than exact. In a wider sense, FL is treated as a fuzzy set theory of classes with unsharp or fuzzy boundaries. Fuzzy logic methods can be used to design intelligent systems on the basis of knowledge expressed in a common language. The application areas of intelligent systems are many. There is practically no area of human activity left untouched by these systems today. The main reason for such versatility is that this method permits the processing of both symbolic and numerical information. Systems designed and developed utilizing FL methods have often been shown to be more efficient than those based on conventional approaches.

Here, the interest is chiefly in the role of FL as a technique for mathematical expression of linguistic knowledge and ambiguity. In order to follow the presentation, it is first useful to understand the relation between human knowledge and basic concepts such as sets and functions. A graphical presentation of these relations is given in figure 6.1. It seems natural to introduce FL modeling following the bottom-up approach outlined in the figure: from sets, their operations and their Cartesian products to relations, multivariate functions, and IF-THEN rules as a linguistic form of structured human knowledge.

Consequently, in section 6.1, the basics of fuzzy set theory are explained and compared with classic crisp logic. The important concept of the membership function is discussed. The representation of fuzzy sets by membership functions will serve as an important link with neural networks. Basic set operations (notably intersection and union) are presented and connected with the proper operators (for example, MIN and MAX). Then the concepts of (fuzzy) relations, the relational matrix, and the composition of fuzzy relations are examined. A formal treatment of fuzzy IF-THEN statements, questions of fuzzification and defuzzification, and the compositional rule of fuzzy inference with such statements concludes the section on the basics of fuzzy logic theory.

In earlier chapters it was mentioned that neural networks and fuzzy logic models are based on very similar, sometimes equivalent, underlying mathematical theories. This very important and remarkable result, which has been discovered by different researches independently, is discussed in section 6.2. The development follows a paper by Kecman and Pfeiffer (1994), which shows when and how learning of fuzzy

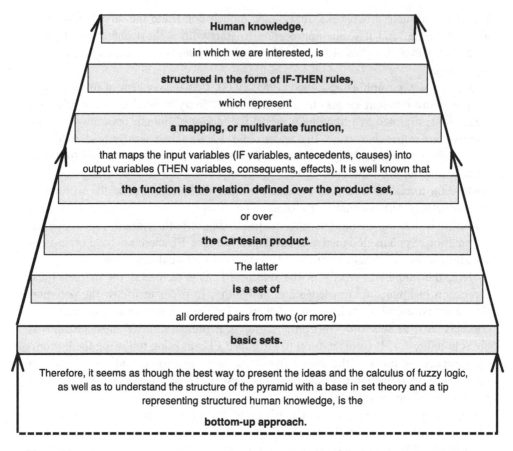

Figure 6.1
Pyramid of structured human knowledge in the world of fuzzy logic.

rules from numerical data is mathematically equivalent to the training of a radial basis function, or regularization, network. Although these approaches originate in different paradigms of intelligent information processing, it is demonstrated that the mathematical structure is the same. The presentation in section 6.2 can be readily extended to other, not necessarily radial, activation functions.

Finally, in section 6.3 fuzzy additive models (FAMs) are introduced. They are naturally connected with, and represent an extension of, the soft-radial basis models from section 6.2. FAMs are universal approximators. They are very powerful fuzzy modeling tools, and unlike early fuzzy models that used the MAX operator, FAMs add the THEN-parts of all active rules, that is, they use the SUM operator.

6.1　Basics of Fuzzy Logic Theory

The theory of fuzzy sets is a theory of graded concepts—"a theory in which every-thing is a matter of degree, or everything has elasticity" (Zadeh 1973). It is aimed at dealing with complex phenomena that "do not lend themselves to analysis by a classical method based on bivalent logic and probability theory." Many systems in real life are too complex or too ill-defined to be susceptible to exact analysis. Even where systems or concepts seem to be unsophisticated, the perception and under-standing of such seemingly unsophisticated systems are not necessarily simple. Using fuzzy sets or classes that allow intermediate grades of membership in them, opens the possibility of analyzing such systems both qualitatively and quantitatively by allow-ing the system variables to range over fuzzy sets.

6.1.1　Crisp (or Classic) and Fuzzy Sets

Sets[1] or *classes* in a *universe of discourse* (universe, domain) U could be variously defined:

1. By a list of elements:

$S_1 = \{Ana,\ John,\ Jovo,\ Mark\}.$　　$S_2 = \{beer,\ wine,\ juice,\ slivovitz\}.$

$S_3 = \{horse,\ deer,\ wolf,\ sheep\}.$　　$S_4 = \{1, 2, 3, 5, 6, 7, 8, 9, 11\}.$

2. By definition of some property:

$S_5 = \{x \in N \,|\, x < 15\}.$　　$S_6 = \{x \in R \,|\, x^2 < 25\}.$

Note that $S_4 \in S_5$.

$S_7 = \{x \in R \,|\, x > 1 \wedge x < 7\}.$　　$S_8 = \{x \in R \,|\, ``x \text{ is much smaller than } 10"\}.$

(The symbol $\wedge$ stands for logical AND, the operation of *intersection*.)

3. By a *membership function* (in crisp set theory also called a *characteristic*). For crisp sets (see fig. 6.2, left graph),

$$\mu_S(x) = \begin{cases} 1 & \text{if } x \in S \\ 0 & \text{if } x \notin S \end{cases}.$$

For fuzzy sets (see fig. 6.2, right graph), $\mu_S(x)$ is a mapping of X on $[0, 1]$, that is, the degree of belonging of some element x to the universe X can be any number $0 \le \mu_S(x) \le 1$.

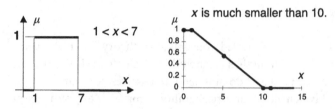

Figure 6.2
Membership functions of (*left*) crisp and (*right*) fuzzy sets.

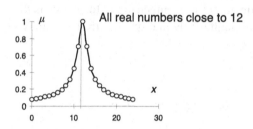

Figure 6.3
Membership function of fuzzy set S "all real numbers close to 12".

In engineering applications, the universe of discourse U stands for the domain of (linguistic) input and output variables, i.e., for antecedent and consequent variables, or for the IF and the THEN variables of the rule. Membership functions (possibility distributions, degrees of belonging) of two typical fuzzy sets are represented in figure 6.2, right graph, and in figure 6.3. The latter shows a fuzzy set S of "all real numbers close to 12":

$$S = \{(x, \mu_S(x)) \mid \mu_S(x) = (1 + (x - 12)^2)^{-1}\}.$$

Note the similarities between the two membership functions and sigmoidal and radial basis activation functions given in previous chapters.

In human thinking, it is somehow natural that the maximal degree of belonging to some set cannot be higher than 1. Related to this is a definition of *normal* and *not-normal* fuzzy sets. Both sets are shown in figure 6.4. Typically, the fuzzy set of input variables (the IF variables of IF-THEN rules) is a normal set, and the fuzzy set of output variables (the THEN variables of IF-THEN rules) is a not-normal fuzzy set.

There is an important difference between crisp sets and fuzzy sets (see table 6.1). Fuzzy logic is a tool for modeling human knowledge, or human understanding and concepts about the world. But the world is not binary: there is an infinite number of numbers between 0 and 1; outside of Hollywood movies, people are not divided into

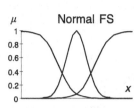 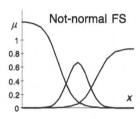

Figure 6.4
Membership functions of normal and not-normal fuzzy sets.

Table 6.1
Differences Between Crisp Sets and Fuzzy Sets

Crisp Sets	Fuzzy Sets
either or	and
bivalent	multivalent
yes or no	more or less

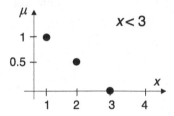

Figure 6.5
Membership functions of the set "x smaller than 3" as discrete pairs μ/x.

only *good* and *bad*; there is a spectrum of colors between *black* and *white*; we are usually not *absolutely healthy* or *terminally ill*; our statements are not *utterly false* or *absolutely true*. Thus, binary concepts like *yes-no* or 0-1, as well as the very wording while dealing with such graded concepts, should be extended to cover a myriad of vague states, concepts, and situations.

In fuzzy logic an *element* can be a member of two or more sets at the same time. Element x belongs to A AND to B, not only to one of these two sets. The very same x is just *more* or *less* a member of A and/or B. See table 6.1

Another notation for *finite* fuzzy sets (sets comprising a finite number of elements) is when a set S is given as a set of pairs μ/x (see fig. 6.5). Note that μ is a function of x

$$\mu = \mu(x): \quad S = \{\mu/x \mid x < 3\}, \quad \text{e.g.,} \quad S = \{(1/1), (0.5/2), (0/3)\}.$$

Usually, human reasoning is very approximate. Our statements depend on the contents, and we describe our physical and spiritual world in a rather vague terms. Imprecisely defined "classes" are an important part of human thinking. Let us illustrate this characteristic feature of human reasoning with two more real-life examples that partly describe the subjectivity with which we conceive the world.

The modeling of the concept "young man" is both imprecise and subjective. Three different membership functions of this fuzzy set, or class, depending on the person using it, are given in figure 6.6. (Clearly, the two dashed membership functions would be defined by persons who are in their late thirties or in their forties. The author personally prefers a slightly broader membership function, centered at age $= 45$.) Similarly, the order given in a pub, "Bring me a cold beer, please,"[2] may have different meanings in different parts of the world. It is highly subjective, too. The author's definition of this fuzzy class is shown in figure 6.7. The membership functions may have different shapes. The choice of a shape for each particular linguistic variable (attribute or fuzzy set) is both subjective and problem-dependent. The most common ones in engineering applications are shown in figure 6.8.

Any function $\mu(x) \rightarrow [0, 1]$ describes a membership function associated with some fuzzy set. Which particular membership function is suitable for fuzzy modeling can

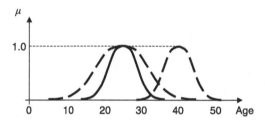

Figure 6.6
Three different membership functions $\mu(x)$ of the class "young man".

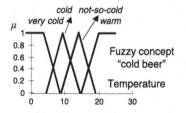

Figure 6.7
Membership functions $\mu(x)$ for S ("cold beer") $= \{very\ cold,\ cold,\ not\text{-}so\text{-}cold,\ warm\}$.

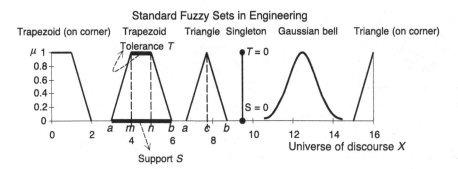

Figure 6.8
The most common fuzzy sets in engineering applications.

be determined in a specific context. Here, the most general triangular and trapezoidal membership functions are defined. Note that all membership functions in figure 6.8 (except the Gaussian one) are specific cases of the following expressions.

Triangular Membership Functions   *Trapezoidal Membership Functions*

$$\mu(x) = \begin{cases} 0 & \text{if } x < a \\ \dfrac{x-a}{c-a} & \text{if } x \in [a,c] \\ \dfrac{b-x}{b-c} & \text{if } x \in [c,b] \\ 0 & \text{if } x > b \end{cases} , \quad (6.1a) \qquad \mu(x) = \begin{cases} 0 & \text{if } x < a \\ \dfrac{x-a}{m-a} & \text{if } x \in [a,m] \\ 1 & \text{if } x \in [m,n] \\ \dfrac{b-x}{b-n} & \text{if } x \in [n,b] \\ 0 & \text{if } x > b \end{cases} , \quad (6.1b)$$

where a and b denote lower and upper bounds (i.e., they are "coordinates" of a support S), c is a "center" of a triangle, and m and n denote "coordinates" of a tolerance (see fig. 6.8).

6.1.2 Basic Set Operations

Out of many set operations the three most common and important are *complement* S^C (or *not-S*), *intersection*, and *union*. Figure 6.9 shows the complement S^C of crisp and fuzzy sets in Venn diagrams and using membership functions. Figure 6.10 shows the intersection, union, and complement operations using membership functions. The graphs in figure 6.10 are obtained by using the MIN operator for an intersection (interpreted as logical AND) and the MAX operator for a *union* (interpreted as

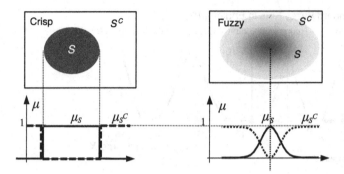

Figure 6.9
Two different ways of representing (*left*) crisp and (*right*) fuzzy sets S and corresponding complement sets S^C. *Top*, Venn diagrams. *Bottom*, membership functions. The brightness of the fuzzy set patch in the right graph denotes the degree of belonging, or membership degree μ, of elements of U to the fuzzy set S (black – $\mu = 1$ and white – $\mu = 0$). For the complement set, the following is true: $\mu_{S^C} = \mu_{not\text{-}S} = 1 - \mu_S$.

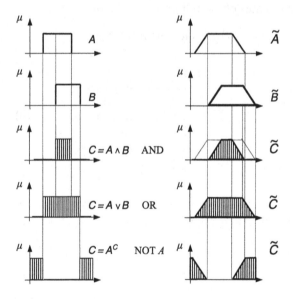

Figure 6.10
Intersection and union as well as complement of A operations for (*left*) crisp and (*right*) fuzzy sets represented by the corresponding membership functions.

logical OR):

$$\mu_{A \wedge B} = \mathrm{MIN}(\mu_A, \mu_B), \tag{6.2}$$

$$\mu_{A \vee B} = \mathrm{MAX}(\mu_A, \mu_B). \tag{6.3}$$

These are not the only operators that can be chosen to model the intersection and union of a fuzzy set, but they are the most commonly used ones in engineering applications. For an intersection, a popular alternative to the MIN operator is the *algebraic product*

$$\mu_{A \wedge B} = \mu_A \cdot \mu_B, \tag{6.4}$$

which typically gives much smoother approximations. In addition to MIN, MAX, and product operators there are many others that can be used. In fuzzy logic theory, intersection operators are called *T-norms*, and union operators are called *T-conorms* or *S-norms*. Table 6.2 lists only some classes of *T-norms* and *S-norms*.

Before closing this section on basic logical operators, it is useful to point out some interesting differences between crisp and fuzzy set calculus. Namely, it is well known that the intersection between a crisp set S and its complement S^C is an empty set, and that the union between these two sets is a universal set. Calculus is different in fuzzy

Table 6.2
T-Norms and *S*-Norms

AND *T*-Norm $T(\mu_A(x), \mu_B(x))$	OR *S*-Norm $S(\mu_A(x), \mu_B(x))$
Minimum $\mathrm{MIN}(\mu_A(x), \mu_B(x))$	Maximum $\mathrm{MAX}(\mu_A(x), \mu_B(x))$
Algebraic product $\mu_A(x)\mu_B(x)$	Algebraic sum $\mu_A(x) + \mu_B(x) - \mu_A(x)\mu_B(x)$
Drastic product $\mathrm{MIN}(\mu_A(x), \mu_B(x))$ if $\mathrm{MAX}(\mu_A(x), \mu_B(x)) = 1$ 0 otherwise	Drastic sum $\mathrm{MAX}(\mu_A(x), \mu_B(x))$ if $\mathrm{MIN}(\mu_A(x), \mu_B(x)) = 0$ 1 otherwise
Lukasiewicz AND (Bounded Difference) $\mathrm{MAX}(0, \mu_A(x) + \mu_B(x) - 1)$	Lukasiewicz OR (Bounded Sum) $\mathrm{MIN}(1, \mu_A(x) + \mu_B(x))$
Einstein product $\mu_A(x)\mu_B(x)/(2 - (\mu_A(x) + \mu_B(x) - \mu_A(x)\mu_B(x)))$	Einstein sum $(\mu_A(x) + \mu_B(x))/(1 + \mu_A(x)\mu_B(x))$
Hamacher product $\mu_A(x)\mu_B(x)/(\mu_A(x) + \mu_B(x) - \mu_A(x)\mu_B(x))$	Hamacher sum $(\mu_A(x) + \mu_B(x) - 2\mu_A(x)\mu_B(x))/(1 - \mu_A(x)\mu_B(x))$
Yager operator $1 - \mathrm{MIN}(1, ((1 - \mu_A(x))^b + (1 - \mu_B(x)^b)^{1/b}))$	Yager operator $\mathrm{MIN}(1, (\mu_A(x)^b + \mu_B(x)^b)^{1/b})$

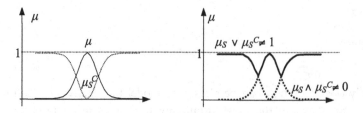

Figure 6.11
Interesting properties of fuzzy set calculus.

logic. Expressed by membership degrees, these facts are as follows:

Crisp Set Calculus   *Fuzzy Set Calculus*

$\mu \wedge \mu^C = 0. \quad \mu \vee \mu^C = 1.$ $\mu \wedge \mu^C \neq 0. \quad \mu \vee \mu^C \neq 1.$

This can be verified readily for fuzzy sets, as shown in figure 6.11.

6.1.3 Fuzzy Relations

Let us consider the notion of an ordered pair. When making pairs of anything, the order of the elements is usually of great importance (e.g., the points $(2, 3)$ and $(3, 2)$ in an (x, y) plane are different). A pair of elements that occur in a specified order is called an *ordered pair*. A *relation* is a *set of ordered pairs*.

Relations express connections between different sets. A crisp relation represents the presence or absence of association, interaction, or interconnectedness between the elements of two or more sets (Klir and Folger 1988).

If this concept is generalized, allowing various degrees or strengths of relations between elements, we get fuzzy relations. Because a *relation itself is a set*, all set operations can be applied to it without any modifications. Relations are also subsets of a Cartesian product, or simply of a product set. In other words, relations are defined over *Cartesian products or product sets*.

The *Cartesian product* of two crisp sets X and Y, denoted by $X \times Y$, is the crisp set of all ordered pairs such that the first element in each pair is a member of X and the second element is a member of Y:

$$X \times Y = \{(x, y) \mid x \in X \text{ and } y \in Y\}.$$

Let $X = \{1, 2\}$ and $Y = \{a, b, c\}$ be two crisp sets. The Cartesian product is given as,

$$X \times Y = \{(1, a), (1, b), (1, c), (2, a), (2, b), (2, c)\}.$$

Now, one can choose some subsets at random, or one can choose those that satisfy specific conditions in two variables. In both cases, these subsets are relations. One typically assumes that variables are somehow connected in one relation, but the random choice of, say, three ordered pairs $\{(1,b),(2,a),(2,c)\}$, being a subset of the product set $X \times Y$, is also a relation.

A Cartesian product can be generalized for n sets, in which case elements of the Cartesian product are n-tuples $(x_1, x_2, \ldots, x_n)$. Here, the focus is on relations between two sets, known as a *binary relation* and denoted $R(X, Y)$, or simply R. Thus the binary relation R is defined over a Cartesian product $X \times Y$.

If the elements of the latter come from discrete universes of discourse, this particular relation R can be presented in the form of a *relational matrix* or graphically as a discrete set of points in a three-dimensional space $(X, Y, \mu_R(x, y))$.

Example 6.1 Let X and Y be two sets given as follows. Present the relation R: "x is smaller than y" graphically and in the form of a relational matrix.

$$X = \{1, 2, 3\}, \qquad Y = \{2, 3, 4\}, \qquad R: x < y.$$

$$R = \{(1, 2), (1, 3), (1, 4), (2, 3), (2, 4), (3, 4)\}.$$

Note that R is a set of pairs and a binary relation. The relational matrix, or membership array, in this crisp case comprises only 1's and 0's. Figure 6.12 shows the discrete membership function $\mu_R(x, y)$ of this relation.

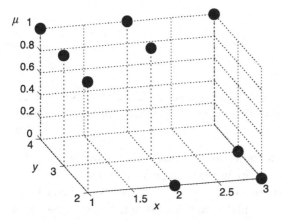

Figure 6.12
The discrete membership function $\mu_R(x, y)$ of the relation R: "x is smaller than y".

$x \setminus y$	2	3	4
1	1	1	1
2	0	1	1
3	0	0	1

∎

The elements of the relational matrix are degrees of membership $\mu_R(x, y)$, that is, possibilities, or degrees of belonging, of a specific pair (x, y) to the given relation R. Thus, for example, the pair $(3, 1)$ belongs with a degree 0 to the relation "x is smaller than y", or the possibility that 3 is smaller than 1 is zero. The preceding relation is a typical example of a crisp relation. The condition involved in this relation is precise and one that is either fulfilled or not fulfilled.

The common mathematical expression "x is approximately equal to y", or the relation R: $x \approx y$, is different. It is a typical example of an imprecise, or fuzzy, relation. Example 6.2 is very similar to example 6.1, the difference being that the degree of belonging of some pairs (x, y) from the Cartesian product to this relation can be any number between 0 and 1.

Example 6.2 Let X and Y be two sets given as follows. Present the relation R: "x is approximately equal to y" in the form of a relational matrix.

$X = \{1, 2, 3\}, Y = \{2, 3, 4\}, \qquad R: x \approx y$

$R = \{(1,2), (1,3), (1,4), (2,2), (2,3), (2,4), (3,2), (3,3), (3,4)\}$

$x \setminus y$	2	3	4
1	0.66	0.33	0
2	1	0.66	0.33
3	0.66	1	0.66

The discrete membership function $\mu_R(x, y)$ is again a set of discrete points in a three-dimensional space $(X, Y, \mu_R(x, y))$ but with membership degrees that can have any value between 0 and 1.

∎

When the universes of discourse (domains) are *continuous sets* comprising an infinite number of elements, the membership function $\mu_R(x, y)$ is *a surface* over the Cartesian product $X \times Y$, not a curve as in the case of one-dimensional fuzzy sets.[3] Thus, the relational matrix is an (∞, ∞) matrix and has no practical meaning. This is a common situation in everyday practice, which is resolved by appropriate discretization of the universes of discourse. Example 6.3 illustrates this.

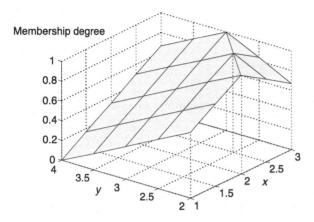

Figure 6.13
Membership function $\mu_R(x, y)$ of the relation R: "x is approximately equal to y" over the Cartesian product of two continuous sets X and Y.

Example 6.3 Let X and Y be two sets given as follows. Show the membership function of the relation R: "x is approximately equal to y" and present the relational matrix after discretization.

$$X = \{x \in R \mid 1 \le x \le 3\}, \qquad Y = \{y \in R \mid 2 \le x \le 4\}, \qquad R: x \approx y.$$

Figure 6.13 shows the membership function, and the relational matrix after discretization by a step of 0.5 is

$x \setminus y$	2	2.5	3	3.5	4
1	0.6667	0.5000	0.3333	0.1667	0.0000
1.5	0.8333	0.6667	0.5000	0.3333	0.1667
2	1.0000	0.8333	0.6667	0.5000	0.3333
2.5	0.8333	1.0000	0.8333	0.6667	0.5000
3	0.6667	0.8333	1.0000	0.8333	0.6667

In the preceding examples, the sets are defined on the same universes of discourse. But relations can be defined in linguistic variables expressing a variety of different associations or interconnections.

Example 6.4 Relation R is given as an association or interconnection between fruit color and state. Present R as a crisp relational matrix.

$$X = \{green, yellow, red\}, \qquad Y = \{unripe, semiripe, ripe\}.$$

R	unripe	semiripe	ripe
green	1	0	0
yellow	0	1	0
red	0	0	1

This relational matrix can be interpreted as a notation, or model, of an existing empirical set of IF-THEN rules:

R_1: IF (the tomato is) *green*,   THEN (it is) *unripe*.

R_2: IF *yellow*,   THEN *semiripe*.

R_3: IF *red*,   THEN *ripe*.

In fact, relations are a convenient tool for modeling IF-THEN rules. However, the relational matrix in example 6.4 is a crisp one and not in total agreement with our experience. A better interconnection between fruit color and state may be given by the following fuzzy relational matrix:

R	unripe	semiripe	ripe
green	1	0.5	0
yellow	0.3	1	0.4
red	0	0.2	1

Example 6.5 Present the fuzzy relational matrix for the relation R that represents the concept "very far" in geography. Two crisp sets are given as

$X = \{$Auckland, Tokyo, Belgrade$\}$.

$Y = \{$Sydney, Athens, Belgrade, Paris, New York$\}$.

R: "very far"	Sydney	Athens	Belgrade	Paris	New York
Auckland	0.2	0.8	0.85	0.90	0.55
Tokyo	0.5	0.5	0.5	0.55	0.4
Belgrade	0.8	0.1	0	0.15	0.5

Hence, the relational matrix does not necessarily have to be square. Many other concepts can be modeled using relations on different universes of discourse. Note that, as for crisp relations, fuzzy relations are fuzzy sets in product spaces. As an example, let us analyze the meaning of the linguistic expression *"a young tall man"* (Kahlert and Frank 1994).

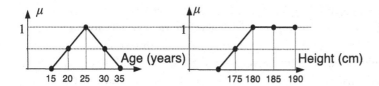

Figure 6.14
The fuzzy sets, or linguistic terms, "young man" and "tall man" given by corresponding membership functions.

Example 6.6 Find the relational matrix of the concept "a young tall man".

Implicitly, the concept "a young tall man" means "young AND tall man". Therefore, two fuzzy sets, "young man" and "tall man", are defined first, and then the intersection operator is applied to these two sets defined on different universes of discourse, age and height. One out of many operators for modeling a fuzzy intersection is the MIN operator. (Another commonly used one is the algebraic product.) Thus,

$$\mu_R(\text{age, height}) = \text{MIN}(\mu_1(\text{age}), \mu_2(\text{height})).$$

After discretization, as in figure 6.14,

$$(S_1 = \{15, 20, 25, 30, 35\}, \qquad S_2 = \{170, 175, 180, 185, 190\},$$

the relational matrix follows from

$$\mu_1 = \begin{bmatrix} 0 \\ 0.5 \\ 1 \\ 0.5 \\ 0 \end{bmatrix}, \quad \mu_2 = \begin{bmatrix} 0 \\ 0.5 \\ 1 \\ 1 \\ 1 \end{bmatrix}, \quad \mathbf{R} = \mu_1 \times \mu_2^T = \begin{bmatrix} 0 \\ 0.5 \\ 1 \\ 0.5 \\ 0 \end{bmatrix} \times [0 \quad 0.5 \quad 1 \quad 1 \quad 1], \quad (6.5)$$

or

R	170	175	180	185	190
15	0	0	0	0	0
20	0	0.5	0.5	0.5	0.5
25	0	0.5	1	1	1
30	0	0.5	0.5	0.5	0.5
35	0	0	0	0	0

■

The relational matrix in example 6.6 is actually a surface over the Cartesian product age $\times$ height, which represents the membership function, or a possibility distribution of a given relation. Generally, one can graphically obtain this surface utilizing the extension principle given the different universes of discourse (cylindrical extension, in particular). However, this part of fuzzy theory is outside the scope of this book.

6.1.4 Composition of Fuzzy Relations

Fuzzy relations in different product spaces can be combined with each other by *composition*. Note that fuzzy sets can also be combined with any fuzzy relation in the same way. A composition is also a fuzzy set because relations are the fuzzy sets. (This is the same attribute as the product of matrices being a matrix.)

Many different versions of the compositional operator are possible. The best known one is a MAX-MIN composition. MAX-PROD and MAX-AVERAGE can also be used. The MAX-PROD composition is often the best alternative. A discussion of these three most important compositions follows.

Let $R_1(x, y), (x, y) \in X \times Y$ and $R_2(y, z), (y, z) \in Y \times Z$ be two fuzzy relations. The MAX-MIN composition is a fuzzy set

$$R_1 \circ R_2(x, z)$$

$$= \left\{ \left[(x, z), \max_y \{ \min\{ \mu_{R_1}(x, y), \mu_{R_2}(y, z) \} \} \right] \middle| x \in X, y \in Y, z \in Z \right\}, \qquad (6.6)$$

and $\mu_{R_1 \circ R_2}$ is a membership function of a fuzzy composition on fuzzy sets.

The MAX-PROD composition is

$$R_1 \underset{\otimes}{\circ} R_2(x, z) = \left\{ \left[(x, z), \max_y \{ \mu_{R_1}(x, y) \cdot \mu_{R_2}(y, z) \} \right] \middle| x \in X, y \in Y, z \in Z \right\}. \qquad (6.7)$$

The MAX-AVE composition is

$$R_1 \underset{\text{ave}}{\circ} R_2(x, z) = \left\{ \left[(x, z), \frac{1}{2} \max\{ \mu_{R_1}(x, y) + \mu_{R_2}(y, z) \} \right] \middle| x \in X, y \in Y, z \in Z \right\}. \qquad (6.8)$$

Later, while making a *fuzzy inference*, a composition of a fuzzy set and a fuzzy relation (and not one between two fuzzy relations) will be of practical importance. Example 6.7 will facilitate the understanding of the three preceding compositions.

Example 6.7 R_1 is a relation that describes an interconnection between color x and ripeness y of a tomato, and R_2 represents an interconnection between ripeness y and taste z of a tomato (Kahlert and Frank 1994). Present relational matrices for the MAX-MIN and MAX-PROD compositions.

The relational matrix $\mathbf{R}_1$ (x–y connection) is given as

$\mathbf{R}_1(x, y)$	unripe	semiripe	ripe
green	1	0.5	0
yellow	0.3	1	0.4
red	0	0.2	1

The relational matrix $\mathbf{R}_2$ (y–z connection) is given as

$\mathbf{R}_2(y, z)$	sour	sweet-sour	sweet
unripe	1	0.2	0
semiripe	0.7	1	0.3
ripe	0	0.7	1

The MAX-MIN composition $\mathbf{R} = \mathbf{R}_1 \circ \mathbf{R}_2$ results in the relational matrix

$\mathbf{R}(x, z)$	sour	sweet-sour	sweet
green	1	0.5	0.3
yellow	0.7	1	0.4
red	0.2	0.7	1

The entries of the relational matrix $\mathbf{R}$ were calculated as follows:

$r_{11} = \mathrm{MAX}(\mathrm{MIN}(1, 1), \mathrm{MIN}(0.5, 0.7), \mathrm{MIN}(0, 0)) = \mathrm{MAX}(1, 0.5, 0) = 1,$

$r_{23} = \mathrm{MAX}(\mathrm{MIN}(0.3, 0), \mathrm{MIN}(1, 0.3), \mathrm{MIN}(0.4, 1)) = \mathrm{MAX}(0, 0.3, 0.4) = 0.4.$

The MAX-PROD composition will give a slightly different relational matrix:

$$\mathbf{R} = \mathbf{R}_1 \underset{\otimes}{\circ} \mathbf{R}_2$$

$$= \mathrm{MAX} \begin{bmatrix} (1 \cdot 1, 0.5 \cdot 0.7, 0 \cdot 0) & (1 \cdot 0.2, 0.5 \cdot 1, 0 \cdot 0.7) & (1 \cdot 0, 0.5 \cdot 0.3, 0 \cdot 1) \\ (0.3 \cdot 1, 1 \cdot 0.7, 0.4 \cdot 0) & (0.3 \cdot 0.2, 1 \cdot 1, 0.4 \cdot 0.7) & (0.3 \cdot 0, 1 \cdot 0.3, 0.4 \cdot 1) \\ (0 \cdot 1, 0.2 \cdot 0.7, 1 \cdot 0) & (0 \cdot 0.2, 0.2 \cdot 1, 1 \cdot 0.7) & (0 \cdot 0, 0.2 \cdot 0.3, 1 \cdot 1) \end{bmatrix}$$

$$= \mathrm{MAX} \begin{bmatrix} (1, 0.35, 0) & (0.2, 0.5, 0) & (0, 0.15, 0) \\ (0.3, 0.7, 0) & (0.06, 1, 0.28) & (0, 0.3, 0.4) \\ (0, 0.14, 0) & (0, 0.2, 0.7) & (0, 0.06, 1) \end{bmatrix} = \begin{bmatrix} 1 & 0.5 & 0.15 \\ 0.7 & 1 & 0.4 \\ 0.14 & 0.7 & 1 \end{bmatrix} \quad (6.9)$$

Note that the resulting MAX-MIN and MAX-PROD relational matrices differ a little only in two elements; r_{13} and r_{31}. It is also interesting to compare the result of the MAX-PROD composition with the classical multiplication of the two matrices $\mathbf{R}_1 \times \mathbf{R}_2$. Recall that in standard matrix multiplication, the SUM operator is used instead of the MAX operator, after the multiplication of the specific elements in corresponding rows and columns. Thus, matrix multiplication would result in

$\mathbf{R}_1 \times \mathbf{R}_2$

$$= \begin{bmatrix} (1\cdot1+0.5\cdot0.7+0\cdot0) & (1\cdot0.2+0.5\cdot1+0\cdot0.7) & (1\cdot0+0.5\cdot0.3+0\cdot1) \\ (0.3\cdot1+1\cdot0.7+0.4\cdot0) & (0.3\cdot0.2+1\cdot1+0.4\cdot0.7) & (0.3\cdot0+1\cdot0.3+0.4\cdot1) \\ (0\cdot1+0.2\cdot0.7+1\cdot0) & (0\cdot0.2+0.2\cdot1+1\cdot0.7) & (0\cdot0+0.2\cdot0.3+1\cdot1) \end{bmatrix}$$

$$= \begin{bmatrix} 1.35 & 0.7 & 0.15 \\ 1 & 1.34 & 0.7 \\ 0.14 & 0.9 & 1.06 \end{bmatrix}$$

The linguistic interpretation of the resulting relational matrix $\mathbf{R}$ is a straightforward one, corresponding to our experience, and can be given in the form of IF-THEN rules. This example clearly shows that fuzzy relations are a suitable means of expressing fuzzy (uncertain, vague) implications. A linguistic interpretation in the form of rules for the relational matrices (6.9) is as follows:

R_1:   IF the tomato is *green*,   THEN it is *sour*, less likely to be *sweet-sour*, and unlikely to be *sweet*.

R_2:   IF the tomato is *yellow*,   THEN it is *sweet-sour*, possibly *sour*, and unlikely to be *sweet*.

R_3:   IF the tomato is *red*,   THEN it is *sweet*, possibly *sweet-sour*, and unlikely to be *sour*.

The fuzzy sets (also known as attributes or linguistic variables) are shown in *italics*. Note the multivalued characteristic of the fuzzy implications. Compare the crisp relational matrix in example 6.4 with the $\mathbf{R}_1$ given here, and compare their corresponding crisp and fuzzy implications.   ∎

6.1.5   Fuzzy Inference

In classical propositional calculus there are two basic inference rules: the *modus ponens* and the *modus tollens*. Modus ponens is associated with the implication "*A* implies B" or "B follows from A", and it is the more important one for engineering applications.

Modus ponens can typically be represented by the following inference scheme:

Fact or premise	"x is A"
Implication	"IF x is A, THEN y is B"
Consequence or conclusion	"y is B"

In modus tollens inference, the roles are interchanged:

Fact or premise	"y is not B"
Implication	"IF x is A, THEN y is B"
Consequence or conclusion	"x is not A"

The modus ponens from standard logical propositional calculus cannot be used in the fuzzy logic environment because such an inference can take place if, and only if, the fact or premise is exactly the same as the antecedent of the IF-THEN rule. In fuzzy logic the *generalized modus ponens* is used. It allows an inference when the antecedent is only partly known or when the fact is only similar but not equal to it. A typical problem in fuzzy approximate reasoning is as follows:

Implication	IF the tomato is *red*, THEN it is *sweet*, possibly *sweet-sour*, and unlikely to be *sour*.
Premise or fact	The tomato is *more* or *less red* ($\mu_{Re\,d} = 0.8$).
Conclusion	Taste = ?

The question now is, Having a state of nature (premise, fact) that is not exactly equal to the antecedent, and the IF-THEN rule (implication), what is the conclusion?

In traditional logic (classical propositional calculus, conditional statements) an expression such as "IF A, THEN B" is written as $A \Rightarrow B$, that is, A implies B, or B follows from A. Such an *implication* is defined by the following truth table:

A	B	$A \Rightarrow B$
T	T	T
T	F	F
F	T	T
F	F	T

The following identity is used in calculating the truth table:

$A \Rightarrow B \equiv A^C \vee B$.

Note the "strangeness" of the last two rows. Conditional statements, or implications, sound paradoxical when the components are not related. In everyday human reasoning, implications are given to combine somehow related statements, but in the use of the conditional in classical two-valued logic, there is no requirement for relatedness. Thus, "unusual" but correct results could be produced using the preceding operator. Example 6.8 illustrates this curious character of standard Boolean logic.

Example 6.8 The statement "IF $2 \times 2 = 5$, THEN cows are horses" is *true* (row 4 in the truth table), but "IF $2 \times 2 = 4$, THEN cows are horses" is *false* (row 2 in the truth table). ∎

In Boolean logic there does not have to be any real causality between the antecedent (IF part) and the consequent (THEN part). It is different in human reasoning. Our rules express cause-effect relations, and fuzzy logic is a tool for transferring such structured knowledge into workable algorithms. Thus, *fuzzy logic cannot be and is not Boolean logic*. It must go beyond crisp logic. This is because in engineering and many other fields, there is no effect (output) without a cause (input).

Therefore, which operator is to be used for fuzzy conditional statements (implications) or for fuzzy IF-THEN rules? In order to find an answer to this question, consider what the result would be of everyday (fuzzy) reasoning if the *crisp implication* algorithm were used. Starting with the crisp implication rule

$$A \Rightarrow B \equiv A^C \vee B, \qquad A^C = 1 - \mu_A(x),$$

and

$$A \vee B = \text{MAX}(\mu_A(x), \mu_B(y)) \quad \text{(fuzzy OR operator)},$$

the *fuzzy implication* would be

$$A \Rightarrow B \equiv A^C \vee B = \text{MAX}(1 - \mu_A(x), \mu_B(y)).$$

This result is definitely not an acceptable one for the related fuzzy sets that are subjects of everyday human reasoning because in the cases when the premise is not fulfilled $(\mu_A(x) = 0)$, the result would be the truth value of the conclusion $\mu_B(y) = 1$. This doesn't make much sense in practice, where a system input (cause) produces a system output (effect). Or, in other words, if there is no cause, there will be no effect. Thus, for $\mu_A(x) = 0$, $\mu_B(y)$ must be equal to zero. For *fuzzy implication*, the implication rule states that *the truth value of the conclusion must not be larger than that of the premise*.

There are many different ways to find the truth value of a premise or to calculate the relational matrix that describes a given implication. The minimum and product implications are the two most widely used today. (They were used by Mamdani and Larsen, respectively).

$$\mu_{A \Rightarrow B}(x, y) = \text{MIN}(\mu_A(x), \mu_B(y)) \quad \text{(Mamdani)}, \tag{6.10}$$

$$\mu_{A \Rightarrow B}(x, y) = \mu_A(x)\mu_B(y) \qquad \text{(Larsen)}. \tag{6.11}$$

6.1.6 Zadeh's Compositional Rule of Inference

If R is a fuzzy relation from the universe of discourse X to the universe of discourse Y, and x is a fuzzy subset of X, then the fuzzy subset y of Y, which is induced by x, is given by the *composition*

$$y = x \circ R.$$

As mentioned earlier, the operator of this composition is MAX-MIN, with alternatives MAX-PROD or MAX-AVE.

Example 6.9 Show a compositional rule of inference using the MAX-MIN operator. R represents the relation between color x and taste z of a tomato, as given in example 6.7, and the state of nature (premise, fact, or input x) is

The tomato is *red.*

First, this premise should be expressed as the input vector $\mathbf{x}$. Note that X has three possible linguistic values: *green, yellow,* and *red.* Thus, the fact that the tomato is red is expressed by the vector $\mathbf{x} = [0 \quad 0 \quad 1]$. This is a *fuzzification step*, which transforms a crisp value into a vector of membership degrees.

Premise or fact: $\mathbf{x} = [0 \quad 0 \quad 1]$.

Implication $\mathbf{R}$:

$x \setminus z$	sour	sweet-sour	sweet
green	1	0.5	0.3
yellow	0.7	1	0.4
red	0.2	0.7	1

The linguistic interpretation of this implication (or of this relational matrix) is given in the form of IF-THEN rules in example 6.7.

The conclusion is a result of the following composition (m denotes a MIN operator):

$$y = \mathbf{x} \circ \mathbf{R} = [0 \quad 0 \quad 1] \circ \begin{bmatrix} 1 & 0.5 & 0.3 \\ 0.7 & 1 & 0.4 \\ 0.2 & 0.7 & 1 \end{bmatrix}$$

$$= \mathrm{MAX}[m(0,1), m(0,0.7), m(1,0.2), m(0,0.5), m(0,1),$$

$$m(1,0.7), m(0,0.3), m(0,0.4), m(1,1)]$$

$$= [0.2 \quad 0.7 \quad 1]. \tag{6.12}$$

∎

Example 6.9 showed a composition between $\mathbf{x}$ and a given relational matrix $\mathbf{R}$. Thus, when modeling structured human knowledge, the IF-THEN rules (in their most common form for expressing this knowledge) *should first be transformed into relational matrices*. Only after the appropriate relational matrix $\mathbf{R}$ of the rules is calculated can a fuzzy inference take place. How to find this relational matrix $\mathbf{R}$ of the IF-THEN rules is shown in example 6.10. In section 6.3, however, the FAMs that are introduced do not use relational matrices in modeling human knowledge at all. They are closer to the ways in which neural networks model data.

Example 6.10   Find the relational matrix $\mathbf{R}$ of the following rule (implication);

R: IF $x = small$,   THEN $y = high$.

First, the fuzzy sets *low* and *high* should be defined. These are shown in figure 6.15 by their membership functions. In order to obtain a matrix $\mathbf{R}$ of finite dimension, each membership function must be discretized. The discrete points shown in figure 6.15 (but not the straight lines of the triangles) now represent the fuzzy sets *low* and

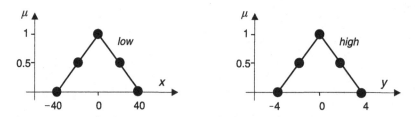

Figure 6.15
Fuzzy sets, or linguistic terms, "low" and "high" given by corresponding membership functions in different universes of discourse.

high (see fig. 6.5). Thus, the universes of discourse X and Y now have five (or a finite number of) elements each:

$$X = \{-40, -20, 0, 20, 40\}, \qquad Y = \{-4, -2, 0, 2, 4\}.$$

In order to calculate the entries of the relational matrix $\mathbf{R}$, recall that *the truth value of the conclusion must be* smaller than, or equal to, *the truth value of the premise*. This is ensured by using the MIN or PROD operator, for example. The result obtained by the MIN operator (the Mamdani implication) is

$$\mu_R(x, y) = \text{MIN}(\mu_L(x), \mu_H(y)). \tag{6.13}$$

The relational matrix $\mathbf{R}$ can be calculated by a vector product, using the same procedure as in example 6.6:

$$\mathbf{R} = \text{MIN}\{\mu_L(x)^T \mu_H(y)\} = \text{MIN}\{[0 \quad 0.5 \quad 1 \quad 0.5 \quad 0]^T [0 \quad 0.5 \quad 1 \quad 0.5 \quad 0]\}.$$

For example, for $x = -20$ and $y = 0$, the membership degree of the relational matrix will be

$$\mu_R(x = -20, y = 0) = \text{MIN}\{\mu_L(-20)\mu_H(0)\} = \text{MIN}\{0.5, 1\} = 0.5.$$

The whole $\mathbf{R}$ is

$\mathbf{R}$	-40	-20	0	20	40
-40	0	0	0	0	0
-20	0	0.5	0.5	0.5	0
0	0	0.5	1	0.5	0
20	0	0.5	0.5	0.5	0
40	0	0	0	0	0

The fuzzy inference for $x' = -20$ (the framed row of $\mathbf{R}$) is the result of the following composition:

$$\mu_{L' \circ R}(y) = \mu_{H'}(y) = \underset{x \in X}{\text{MAX}} \ \text{MIN}(\mu_{L'}(x), \mu_R(x, y)), \tag{6.14}$$

$$\mu_{L' \circ R}(y) = \mu_{H'}(y) = [0 \quad 1 \quad 0 \quad 0 \quad 0] \begin{bmatrix} 0 & 0 & 0 & 0 & 0 \\ 0 & 0.5 & 0.5 & 0.5 & 0 \\ 0 & 0.5 & 1 & 0.5 & 0 \\ 0 & 0.5 & 0.5 & 0.5 & 0 \\ 0 & 0 & 0 & 0 & 0 \end{bmatrix}$$

$$= [0 \quad 0.5 \quad 0.5 \quad 0.5 \quad 0].$$

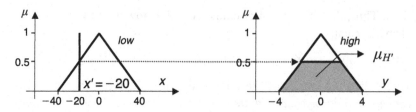

Figure 6.16
MAX-MIN fuzzy inference. The conclusion is not a crisp value but a not-normal fuzzy set.

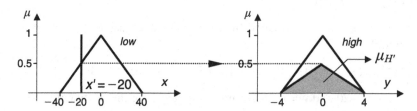

Figure 6.17
MAX-PROD fuzzy inference. The conclusion is not a crisp value but a not-normal fuzzy set.

Note that the crisp value $x' = -20$ was *fuzzified*, or *transformed into a membership vector* $\mu_{L'} = [0 \quad 1 \quad 0 \quad 0 \quad 0]$, first. This is because x is a singleton at x' (see fig. 6.16).

Another popular fuzzy inference scheme employs MAX-PROD (the Larsen implication), which typically results in a smoother model. The graphical result of the MAX-PROD inference is given in figure 6.17, and the relational matrix **R** is as follows:

R	−40	−20	0	20	40
−40	0	0	0	0	0
−20	0	0.25	0.5	0.25	0
0	0	0.5	1	0.5	0
20	0	0.25	0.5	0.25	0
40	0	0	0	0	0

Typical real-life problems have more input variables, and the corresponding rules are given in the form of a rule table:

R_1: IF $x_1 = low$ AND $x_2 = medium$,   THEN $y = high$.

R_2: IF $x_1 = low$ AND $x_2 = high$,   THEN $y = very\ high$.

$\vdots$

Now, the rules R are three-tuple fuzzy relations having membership functions that are hypersurfaces over the three-dimensional space spanned by x_1, x_2, and y. For instance, for rule R_1,

$$\mu_R(x_1, x_2, y) = \text{MIN}(\mu_L(x_1), \mu_M(x_2), \mu_H(y)). \tag{6.15}$$

The relational matrix has a third dimension now. It is a cubic array. This is studied in more detail later but is illustrated in example 6.11 with two inputs and one output.

Example 6.11   Find the consequent of the rule R_1. The membership functions of two fuzzy sets "low" and "medium" are shown in figure 6.18, and rule R_1 is

R_1:   IF $x_1 = low$ AND $x_2 = medium$,   THEN $y = high$.

Figure 6.18 shows the results of a fuzzy inference for the two crisp values $x_1' = 2$ and $x_2' = 600$.[4] The objective is to find the output for the two given input values, or $y(x_1' = 2, x_2' = 600) = ?$ At this point, nothing can be said about the crisp value of y. A part of the tool, the *defuzzification method*, is missing at the moment. It is discussed in section 6.1.7. But the consequent of rule R_1 can be found. First note that the antecedents 1 and 2 (*small* and *medium*) are connected with an AND operator, meaning that the fulfillment degree of rule R_1 will be calculated using a MIN operator, $H = \text{MIN}(\mu_L(2), \mu_M(600)) = 0.5$. Thus, the resulting consequent is a not-normal fuzzy set μ_H', as shown in figure 6.18.

In actual engineering problems there are typically more input variables and fuzzy sets (linguistic terms) for each variable. In such a situation, there are $N_R = n_{\text{FS1}} \times n_{\text{FS2}} \times \cdots \times n_{\text{FS}u}$ rules, where $n_{\text{FS}i}$ represents the number of fuzzy sets for the ith input variable x_i, and u is the number of input variables. For example, when there are three ($u = 3$) inputs with two, three, and five fuzzy sets respectively, there are $N_R = 2 \times 3 \times 5 = 30$ rules. During the operation of the fuzzy model, more rules are generally active simultaneously. It is important to note that all the rules make a *union* of rules. In other words, the rules are implicitly connected by an OR operator.

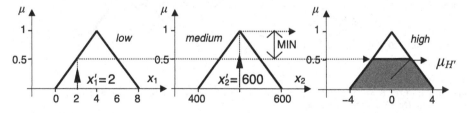

Figure 6.18
Construction of the consequent membership function $\mu_{H'}$ for the rule R_1.

Example 6.12 shows a fuzzy inference in a simple case with one input and one output (an $\Re^1 \to \Re^1$ mapping). A slightly more complex generic situation with two inputs and one output (an $\Re^2 \to \Re^1$ mapping) pertains in example 6.13.

Example 6.12 For $x' = 20$, find the output fuzzy set of the single-input, single-output system described by the two following rules:

R_1:   IF $x = S$,   THEN $y = H$.

R_2:   IF $x = M$,   THEN $y = M$.

Figure 6.19 illustrates the consequent of these rules, and the equations are as follows:

Rule R_1:

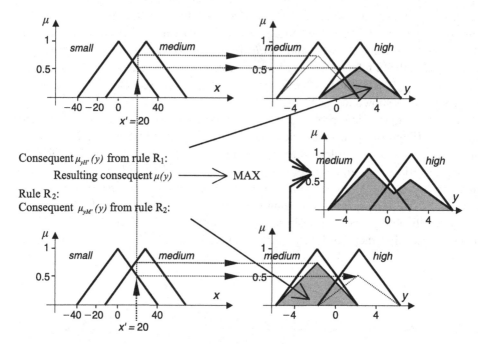

Figure 6.19
Construction of the consequent membership function from the two active rules for a single-input, single-output system (MAX-PROD inference).

$$y(x' = 20) = ? \qquad \mu_x = S(20) = 0.5, \qquad \mu_x = M(20) = 0.75,$$

$$\mu(y) = \text{MAX}(\text{PROD}(0.5, \mu_{y=H}(y), \text{PROD}(0.75, \mu_{y=M}(y))$$

$$= \text{MAX}(\mu_{yH'}(y), \mu_{yM'}(y)). \qquad\qquad\qquad\qquad \blacksquare$$

Note that the result of this fuzzy inference is a *not-normal* fuzzy set. In real-life problems, one is more interested in the single crisp value of the output variable. How to find this crisp value y is discussed in section 6.1.7.

Example 6.13 Find the output fuzzy set for a system with two inputs (having two fuzzy sets for each input) and one output, described by the following four rules:

R_1: IF $x_1 = low$ AND $x_2 = low$,   THEN $y = low$.

R_2: IF $x_1 = low$ OR $x_2 = high$,   THEN $y = medium$.

R_3: IF $x_1 = zero$ AND $x_2 = low$,   THEN $y = medium$.

R_4: IF $x_1 = zero$ OR $x_2 = high$,   THEN $y = high$.

The output fuzzy set is shown in figure 6.20.

Finally, how one finds the crisp output value y from the resulting not-normal sets $\mu(y)$, or how one can *defuzzify* $\mu(y)$, will be introduced below.

6.1.7 Defuzzification

In the last few examples, the conclusions happened to be not-normal fuzzy sets. For practical purposes, a crisp output signal to the actuator or decision maker (classifier) is needed. The procedure for obtaining a crisp output value from the resulting fuzzy set is called *defuzzification*. Note the subtle difference between fuzzification (as in examples 6.9 and 6.10) and defuzzification: *Fuzzification* represents the transformation of a crisp input into a vector of membership degrees, and *defuzzification* transforms a (typically not-normal) fuzzy set into a crisp value.

Which method is to be used to find the crisp output value? Several methods are in use today. Here the four most popular are presented. It may be useful first to get an intuitive insight into defuzzification. What would be a crisp output value for the resulting not-normal fuzzy set in example 6.13? Just by observing the geometry of the resulting fuzzy set (fig. 6.21) one could conclude that the resulting output value y might be between $y = 50$ and 80 and that the right value could be $y = 58$. At this value is actually the *center-of-area* (or *center-of-gravity*) of the resulting consequent from the four rules given in example 6.13. This is one of the many methods of defuzzification. Figure 6.22 shows three of the most common defuzzification methods.

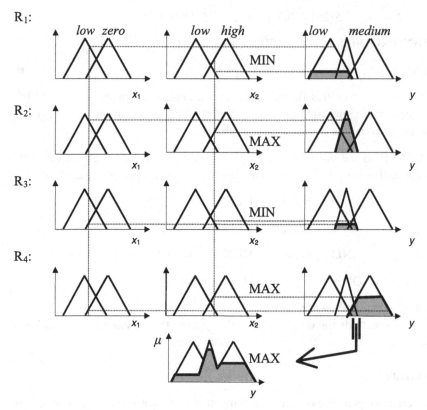

Figure 6.20
Construction of the consequent membership function from four active rules for a system with two inputs and one output.

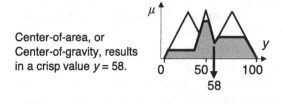

Center-of-area, or
Center-of-gravity, results
in a crisp value $y = 58$.

Figure 6.21
Defuzzification, or obtaining a crisp value from a fuzzy set: center-of-area (or center-of-gravity) method.

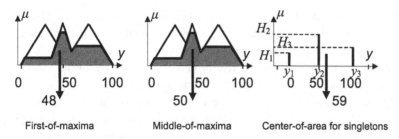

First-of-maxima   Middle-of-maxima   Center-of-area for singletons

Figure 6.22
Graphical representation of three popular defuzzification methods.

Each of these methods possesses some advantages in terms of, for example, complexity, computing speed, and smoothness of the resulting approximating hypersurface. Thus, *the first-of-maxima method* is the fastest one and is of interest for real-time applications, but the resulting surface is rough. The *center-of-area for singletons method* is eventually the most practical because it has similar smoothness properties as the *center-of-area method* but is simpler and faster.

When the membership functions of the output variables are singletons and when the PROD operator is used for inference, it is relatively easy to show the equality of the neural network and fuzzy logic models (see section 6.2). The resulting crisp output in this particular case is calculated as

$$y' = \frac{\sum_{i=1}^{N} y_i H_i}{\sum_{i=1}^{N} H_i},$$ (6.16)

where N is the number of the output membership functions. Equation (6.16) is also valid if the MIN operator is used when singletons are the consequents. Note the important distinction between the relational matrices models used in section 6.1 and the fuzzy additive models (FAMs) used in section 6.3. Here, MAX-PROD or MAX-MIN implication is used, but FAMs use SUM-PROD or SUM-MIN or SUM-any-other-T-norm implication. The practical difference regarding (6.16) is that in the case of FAMs, N stands for the number of rules.

At the beginning of this chapter it was stated that human knowledge structured in the form of IF-THEN rules represents a mapping, or a multivariate function, that maps the input variables (IF variables, antecedents, causes) into the output ones (THEN variables, consequents, effects). Now, this is illustrated by showing how our common knowledge in controlling the distance between our car and the vehicle in front of us while driving is indeed a function. It is a function of which we are usually not aware. To show it graphically, the input variables are restricted to the two most relevant to this control task: the distance between the two vehicles and the speed.

The surfaces shown in figure 6.23 are *surfaces of knowledge* because all the control actions (producing the braking force, in this task) are the results of sliding on this surface. Normally, we are totally unaware of the very existence of this surface, but it is stored in our minds, and all our decisions concerning braking are in accordance with this two-dimensional function. In reality, this surface is a projection of one hypersurface of knowledge onto a three-dimensional space. In other words, additional input variables are involved in this control task in the real world. For example, visibility, wetness, or the state of the road, our mood, and our estimation of the quality of the driver in the car in front. Taking into account all these input variables, there is a mapping of five more input variables besides the two already mentioned into the one output variable (the braking force). Thus, in this real-life situation, the function is a hypersurface of knowledge in eight-dimensional space (it is actually an $\Re^7 \to \Re^1$ mapping). Let us stay in the three-dimensional world and analyze a fuzzy model for controlling the distance between two cars on a road.

Example 6.14 Develop a fuzzy model for controlling the distance between two cars traveling on a road. Show the resulting surface of knowledge graphically.

There are two input variables (distance and the speed) and one output variable (braking force), and five chosen fuzzy subsets (membership functions, attributes) for each linguistic variable. The membership functions for the input (the IF) variables are triangles. The fuzzy subsets (attributes) of the output variable are singletons.

Fuzzy subsets (attributes) of distance	[*very small, small, moderate, large, very large*]
Fuzzy subsets (attributes) of speed	[*very low, low, moderate, high, very high*]
Fuzzy subsets (attributes) of braking force	[*zero, one-fourth, one-half, three-fourths, full*]

Now, the rule basis comprises 25 rules of the following type:

R$_1$:   IF distance *very small*   AND speed *very low*,   THEN braking force *one-half*.

The inference was made using a MAX-MIN operator. Two surfaces of knowledge are shown in figure 6.23. The smooth one (left graph) is obtained by center-of-gravity defuzzification, and the rough one (right graph) is obtained by first-of-maxima defuzzification.   ■

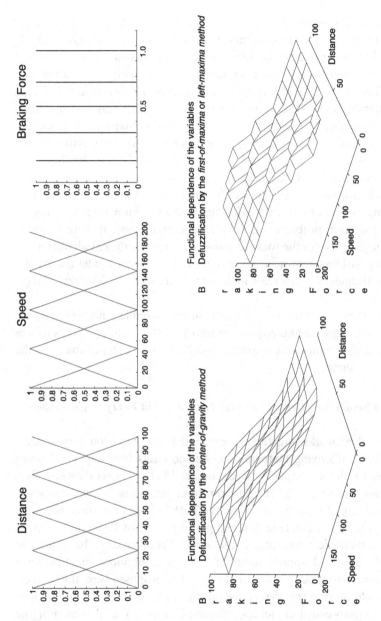

Figure 6.23
Fuzzy model for controlling the distance between two cars. *Top*, the fuzzy subsets of the two input variables (distance and speed) and one output variable (braking force). *Bottom*, the two surfaces of knowledge obtained by different defuzzification methods.

Some comments and conclusions can now be stated. First, using fuzzy logic models, one tries to model structured human knowledge. This knowledge is highly imprecise. We all drive a car differently. Even at the very first step, each of us would differently define the universes of discourse, that is, the domains of the input and output variables. Younger or less cautious drivers would definitely consider distances of 100 meters intolerably large. They would drive *very close*, meaning that the maximal value of the distance's fuzzy subsets (*very large*) would perhaps be 50 m. On the other hand, more cautious drivers would probably never drive at velocities higher than 120 km/h. Second, the choice (shapes and positions) of the membership functions is highly individual. Third, the inference mechanism and the defuzzification method applied will also have an impact on the final result. Despite all these fuzzy factors, the resulting surface of knowledge that represents our knowledge with regard to the solution of the given problem is usually an acceptable one. If there is usable knowledge, fuzzy logic provides the tools to transfer it into an efficient algorithm.

Compare the two surfaces shown in figure 6.23. Both surfaces model the known facts: a decrease in distance or an increase in driving speed, or both, demands a larger braking force.

Note that where there are several input and output variables, nothing changes except required computing time and required memory. If the resulting hypersurfaces reside in four- or higher-dimensional space, visualization is not possible but the algorithms remain the same.

6.2   Mathematical Similarities Between Neural Networks and Fuzzy Logic Models

As mentioned, neural networks and fuzzy logic models are based on very similar, sometimes equivalent, underlying mathematics. To show this very important result the presentation here follows a paper by Kecman and Pfeiffer (1994) showing when and how the *learning of fuzzy rules* (LFR) from numerical data is mathematically equivalent to the training of a *radial basis function* (RBF) or regularization, network. Although these approaches originate in different paradigms of intelligent information processing, their mathematical structure is the same. These models also share the property of being a universal approximator of any real continuous function on a compact set to arbitrary accuracy. In the LFR algorithm proposed here, the subjects of learning are the rule conclusions, that is, the positions of the membership functions of output fuzzy sets (also called attributes) that are in form of singletons. For the fixed number, location, and shape of the input membership functions in the FL model or the basis functions in an RBF network, LFR and RBF training becomes a least-squares optimization problem that is linear in unknown parameters. (These

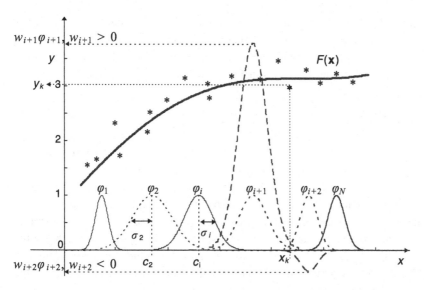

Figure 6.24
Training data set (asterisks), basis functions φ or membership functions μ, and nonlinear approximating function $F(x)$. Note that with fixed φ (or μ) this approximation is linear in parameters.

parameters are the OL weights $\mathbf{w}$ for RBFs or rules $\mathbf{r}$ for LFR). In this case, the solution boils down to the pseudoinversion of a rectangular matrix. The presentation here can be readily extended to the other, not necessarily radial, activation functions.

Using these two approaches, the general problem of approximating or learning mapping f from an n-dimensional input space to an m-dimensional output space, given a finite training set of P examples of $f\{(\mathbf{x}_1,\mathbf{y}_1),(\mathbf{x}_2,\mathbf{y}_2),\ldots,(\mathbf{x}_P,\mathbf{y}_P),\mathbf{y}_p=f(\mathbf{x}_p)\}$, is exemplified by the one-to-one mapping presented in figure 6.24.

For real-world problems with noisy data, one never tries to find the function F that interpolates a training set passing through each point in the set, that is, one does not demand $F(x_p)=y_p, \forall p \in \{1,\ldots,P\}$. The approximating function F of the underlying function f will be obtained on the relaxed condition that F does not have to go through all the training set points but should merely be as close as possible to the data.

Usually, the criterion of such closeness is least squares. It is clear that in the case of noisy free data, interpolation is the better solution. This will be true as long as the size of the data set is not too large. Generally, in the case of large data sets (say, more than 1,000 data patterns) because of numerical problems, one is forced to find an approximation solution.

In RBF approximation techniques (which resulted from the regularization theory of Tikhonov and Arsenin (1977), a good theoretical framework for the treatment of approximation or interpolation problems), after making some mild assumptions the expression for an approximating function $\mathbf{F}$ has the following simple form:

$$\mathbf{y} = \mathbf{F}(\mathbf{x}) = \sum_{i=1}^{N} w_i \varphi_i(\mathbf{x}, \mathbf{c}_i), \qquad (6.17)$$

where w_i are weights to be learned and $\mathbf{c}_i$ are the centers of the radial basis functions φ_i. RBF φ_i can have different explicit forms (e.g., spline, Gaussian, multiquadric).

It is important to realize that when the number N, the positions $\mathbf{c}_i$, and the shapes (defined by the parameter σ and by the covariance matrix $\mathbf{\Sigma}$ for one-dimensional and higher-dimensional Gaussian basis functions, respectively) are fixed before learning, the problem of approximation is linear in the parameters (weights w_i), which are the subject of learning. Thus, the solution boils down to the pseudoinversion of matrix $\Phi(P, N)$. This matrix is obtained using (6.17) for the whole training set. If any of the parameters $\mathbf{c}_i$ or σ_i, which are "hidden" behind the nonlinear function φ_i, become part of the training for any reason, the problem of learning will have to be solved by nonlinear optimization. Certainly then it will be much more involved.

Consider a scalar output variable in order to show the equality of neural networks and fuzzy logic models without loss of generality. The RBF network modeling the data set is given as

$$y = F(\mathbf{x}) = \sum_{i=1}^{N} w_i \varphi_i(\mathbf{x}, \mathbf{c}_i). \qquad (6.18)$$

If φ is a Gaussian function (usually the normalized Gaussian with amplitude $G(\mathbf{c}_i, \mathbf{c}_i) = 1$ is used), one can write

$$y = F(\mathbf{x}) = \sum_{i=1}^{N} w_i G_i(\mathbf{x}, \mathbf{c}_i). \qquad (6.19)$$

Figure 6.24 presents (6.19) graphically. For $N = P$ and $N < P$ an interpolation or an approximation, respectively, will occur.

The same approximation problem can be considered a problem of learning fuzzy rules from examples. Figure 6.24 still represents the problem setup but now the Gaussian bumps are interpreted as membership functions μ_i of the linguistic attributes (fuzzy subsets) of the input variable x (input is now a one-dimensional variable).

For reasons of computational efficiency, the attributes of the linguistic output variable are defuzzified off-line by replacing the fuzzy set of each attribute with a singleton at the center of gravity of the individual fuzzy set (as in fig. 6.23, the braking force graph).

The parameters to be learned are the positions r_i of the singletons describing the linguistic rule conclusions. The corresponding continuous universes of discourse for linguistic input and output variables $\text{Input}_1, \ldots, \text{Input}_n$, and Output, are called $X_1, \ldots, X_n$, Y, respectively. Rule premises are formulated as fuzzy AND relations on the Cartesian product set $X = X_1 \times X_2 \times \cdots \times X_n$, and several rules are connected by logical OR. Fuzzification of a crisp scalar input value x_1 produces a column vector of membership grades to all the attributes of Input_1, and similarly for all other input dimensions, for instance,

$$\mu_1 = \begin{bmatrix} \mu_{1,\text{"attr1"}}(x_1) \\ \mu_{1,\text{"attr2"}}(x_1) \\ \vdots \end{bmatrix}, \qquad \mu_2 = \begin{bmatrix} \mu_{2,\text{"attr1"}}(x_2) \\ \mu_{2,\text{"attr2"}}(x_2) \\ \vdots \end{bmatrix}. \tag{6.20}$$

The degrees of fulfillment of all possible AND combinations of rule premises are calculated and written into a matrix $\mathbf{M}$. For ease of notation, the following considerations are formulated for only two input variables, but they can be extended to higher-dimensional input spaces. If the *algebraic product* is used as an AND operator, this matrix can be directly obtained by the multiplication of a column and a row vector:

$$\mathbf{M}(\mathbf{x}) = \mu_1(x_1)\mu_2^T(x_2). \tag{6.21}$$

Otherwise, the minimum or any other appropriate operator from table 6.2 can be applied to all pairs of membership values. Because the attributes of the linguistic output variable are singletons, they appear as crisp numbers in the fuzzy rule base. The first rule, for example, reads

R_1:   IF Input_1 is *attribute$_1$*   AND Input_2 is *attribute$_2$*,   THEN Output is r_{11}.

and its conclusion is displayed as the element r_{11} in the relational (rule) matrix

$$\mathbf{R} = \begin{bmatrix} r_{11} & r_{12} & \cdots \\ r_{21} & r_{22} & \cdots \\ \vdots & \vdots & \vdots \end{bmatrix}. \tag{6.22}$$

R has the same dimensions as **M**. IF-THEN rules are interpreted as AND relations on $X \times Y$, that is, the degree of membership in the output fuzzy set of a rule is limited to the degree up to which the premise is fulfilled. A crisp output value y is computed by the center-of-area for singletons, or center-of-singletons, algorithm (6.16) as a weighted mean value

$$y = F(x) = \frac{\sum_{jl} \mu_{jl}(x) r_{jl}}{\sum_{jl} \mu_{jl}(x)}, \tag{6.23}$$

where $\mu_{jl} = H_i$ and $r_{jl} = y_i$. The sum covers all elements of the two matrices **M** and **R**. If the membership functions of the input attributes are Gaussians, the μ_{jl} are space bumps $G_i(\mathbf{x}, \mathbf{c}_i)$ representing the joint possibility distribution of each rule. Moreover, if the elements of matrix **R** are collected in a column vector

$$\mathbf{r} = (r_{11}, r_{12}, \ldots r_{21}, r_{22}, \ldots)^T = (r_1, r_2, \ldots, r_N)^T, \tag{6.24}$$

the approximation formula becomes

$$y = F(\mathbf{x}) = \frac{\sum_{i=1}^{N} G(\mathbf{x}, \mathbf{c}_i) r_i}{\sum_{i=1}^{N} G(\mathbf{x}, \mathbf{c}_i)}. \tag{6.25}$$

The structural similarity of (6.19) and (6.25) is clearly visible: the rule conclusions r_i correspond to the trainable weights w_i. These two equations could be given a graphical representation in the form of "neural" networks. For bivariate functions $y = f(x_1, x_2)$ this is done in figure 6.25.

The structures of both networks are the same in the sense that each has just one hidden layer and the connections between the input and the hidden layer are fixed and not the subject of learning. The subjects of learning are the connections w or r between the hidden layer and the output layer. It must be stressed that the seemingly second hidden layer in a fuzzy (or soft RBF) network is not an additional hidden layer but the normalization part of the only hidden layer. Because of this normalization, the sum of the outputs from the hidden layer in a soft RBF network is equal to 1, that is, $\Sigma o_{iF} = 1$. This is not the case in a classic RBF network.

The equivalence of these two approximation schemes is clear if (6.19) and (6.25) are compared. The only difference is that in fuzzy approximation the output value from the hidden layer y is "normalized." The word *normalized* is in quotation marks because y is calculated using the normalized output signals o_{iF} (fig. 6.25) from neurons

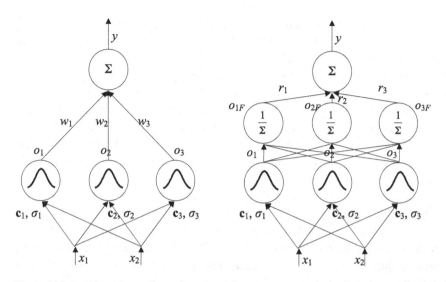

Figure 6.25
Networks for the interpolation $(N = P)$ or approximation $(N < P)$ of a bivariate function $y = f(x_1, x_2)$. *Left*, an RBF. *Right*, a fuzzy network or soft RBF. Here $N = 3$.

whose sum is equal to 1. This is not the case with a standard RBF network. Because of the effect of normalization, fuzzy approximation is a kind of soft approximation, with the approximating function always going through the middle point between the two training data. As an analogy to the softmax function introduced to the neural network community for the sigmoidal type of activation function (Bridle 1990), fuzzy approximation is called a soft RBF approximation scheme.

The mathematical side of the solution is defined as follows: for a fixed number N, positions c_i, and width σ_i of the basis function φ_i or membership function μ_i, the problem of approximation is linear in learned parameters w or r and will be solved by the simple inversion of the matrix $\mathbf{A}$ given in (6.30). (In the case of interpolation, i.e., when the number N of basis or membership functions (attributes) for each input variable is equal to the number P of data pairs, $\mathbf{A}$ is a square matrix. When there are fewer basis or membership functions than data pairs, $\mathbf{A}$ is rectangular. The latter type of approximation is more common in real-life problems.) This property of being linear in parameters is not affected by the choice of the algebraic product as a fuzzy AND operator. This algorithm remains the same for the minimum operator.

It seems as though the soft RBF is more robust with respect to the choice of the width parameter and has better approximation properties in cases when there is no large overlapping of basis functions φ or membership functions μ. In such a situation (for small σ in the case of Gaussian functions) the approximation obtained with the classic RBF given by (6.19) will be much more spiky than the one obtained with fuzzy approximation, or the soft RBF given by (6.25).

There is a significant difference in the physical meaning of the learned (or trained) weights w_i or rules r_i in these two paradigms. Approaching the problem from a fuzzy perspective, the rules have from the very start of problem formulation a clear physical meaning, stating that an output variable must take a certain value under specified conditions of input variables. There is no such analogy in the classic RBF approach to functional approximation. In the latter case, the meaning of weights w_i is more abstract and depends on such small subtleties as whether normalized Gaussians $G(c_i, c_i) = 1$ are used. Generally, in both methods, with increased overlapping of the basis or membership functions, the absolute values of the parameters w or r will increase. But, in the fuzzy case, when the resulting output variables are rules r, we are aware of their physical limits, and these limits will determine the actual overlapping of the membership functions in input space. There are no such caution signs in a classic RBF because that approach is derived from a mathematical domain.

In order to apply a standard least-squares method in the spirit of parameter estimation schemes, the dedicated fuzzy identification algorithm for the center-of-singletons defuzzification method must be slightly reformulated by collecting the elements of $\mathbf{M}$ in a column vector

$$\mu = [\mu_{11} \quad \mu_{12} \quad \cdots \quad \mu_{21} \quad \mu_{22} \quad \cdots]^T, \tag{6.26}$$

and by defining a vector of 1's with the same dimension $\mathbf{1} = (1 \quad 1 \quad \cdots \quad 1)^T$. Using these vectors, (6.23) can be written with the numerator and denominator calculated as scalar products

$$y = \frac{\mu^T \mathbf{r}}{\mu^T \mathbf{1}}, \tag{6.27}$$

which is equivalent to

$$\mu^T \mathbf{r} = \mu^T \mathbf{1} y. \tag{6.28}$$

The input data are fuzzified according to the attributes of the linguistic variables Input$_1$ and Input$_2$. For each sample p, and input data set $\mathbf{x}_p$, a corresponding vector μ_p is obtained by applying formulas (6.20), (6.21), and (6.26) successively, and an equation of the form (6.28) is stated as

$$\mu_p^T \mathbf{r} = \mu^T \mathbf{1} y_p. \tag{6.29}$$

From this equation a system of linear equations is constructed for $p = 1, \ldots, P$

$$\mathbf{Ar} = \mathbf{b} \Rightarrow \begin{bmatrix} \mu_1^T \\ \mu_2^T \\ \vdots \\ \mu_P^T \end{bmatrix} \mathbf{r} = \begin{bmatrix} \mu_1^T \mathbf{1} y_1 \\ \mu_2^T \mathbf{1} y_2 \\ \vdots \\ \mu_P^T \mathbf{1} y_P \end{bmatrix}. \tag{6.30}$$

This system is in linear form, with a known rectangular matrix $\mathbf{A}$ and a known vector $\mathbf{b}$.

$$\mathbf{Ar} = \mathbf{b}. \tag{6.31}$$

Now (6.31) can be solved for the unknown vector $\mathbf{r}$ by any suitable numerical algorithm, for instance, by taking the pseudoinverse as an optimal solution in a least-squares sense:

$$\mathbf{r} = (\mathbf{A}^T\mathbf{A})^{-1}\mathbf{A}^T\mathbf{b} = \mathbf{A}^+\mathbf{b}. \tag{6.32}$$

Finally, the elements of vector $\mathbf{r}$ can be regrouped into the rule matrix $\mathbf{R}$. The matrix $\mathbf{A}$ actually contains degrees of fulfillment of all rules. For a system with N rules, its dimensions are (P, N). Therefore the matrix $\mathbf{A}^T\mathbf{A}$ is of the dimension (N, N) and can be easily inverted, even for very large numbers of data samples. This explains the equivalence of the RBF and FL models and also shows how the weights or rules can be adapted (trained). The final learning rule (the matrix $\mathbf{R}$ in (6.22)) was a relatively simple one because the hidden layer weights were fixed.

The structural equivalence of a certain type of learning fuzzy system with trainable RBF neural networks is of considerable importance to the neural network and fuzzy logic communities.

A regularization (RBF) network can be interpreted in terms of fuzzy rules after learning, providing an insight into the physical nature of the system being modeled that cannot be obtained from a black-box neural network. Moreover, the "linear" training algorithm (6.32) can be transformed to recursive notation according to method 5 in section 3.2.2. This opens the door to recursive training of RBF networks in real time with much better convergence properties than error backpropagation networks. From an RBF perspective, a recursive formulation will avoid the problems of pseudoinversion of large matrices when dealing with a large number of basis functions. Also, in using soft RBFs there is no requirement for basis functions to be radial. Experiments by the author and colleagues used logistic and tangent hyperbolic functions with an approximation quality comparable to radial Gaussian functions.

The relevance of this result for the fuzzy logic community is of another nature. It suggests preference for a certain type of membership function (e.g., Gaussian); fuzzy operator (e.g., algebraic product); and a specific kind of inference and defuzzification scheme (e.g., the center-of-singletons algorithm) for modeling tasks. Namely, for fuzzy models, good approximation qualities are guaranteed by the equivalence to regularization networks, whose mathematical properties are firmly established. Moreover, this equivalence provides new insight into the interpolation/approximation aspects of fuzzy models and into such questions as the selection of a suitable number of membership functions and degrees of overlapping. If the nonlinear learning techniques known from neural networks are applied to such fuzzy systems, they allow the learning of input membership functions as well.

6.3 Fuzzy Additive Models

A fuzzy model given by (6.23) or (6.25) is equivalent to an RBF model. This means that fuzzy logic models are also universal approximators in the sense that they can model any multivariate function to any desirable degree of accuracy. The higher the required accuracy, the more rules are needed. This expression is valid for any $\Re^n \to \Re^m$ mapping. In the case of an $\Re^n \to \Re^1$ function, (6.25) becomes

$$y = F(\mathbf{x}) = \frac{\sum_{i=1}^{N} \mu(\mathbf{x}, \mathbf{c}_i) r_i}{\sum_{i=1}^{N} \mu(\mathbf{x}, \mathbf{c}_i)}, \tag{6.33}$$

where the notation μ is used for a membership function (degree of belonging) instead of G. N denotes the number of rules, and r_i stands for the center of area (center of gravity, centroid) of the ith output singleton. When modeling an $\Re^1 \to \Re^1$ relation, equation (6.33) describes a standard fuzzy IF-THEN rule: IF $x = S_{xi}$, THEN $y = S_{yi}$, where S_{xi} and S_{yi} are the antecedent and consequent membership functions, respectively.

This is the simplest form of a *fuzzy additive model* (FAM), also known as a *standard additive model* (SAM).[5] The adjective *additive* refers to the summations that take place in (6.33). Hence, this model can also be called a SUM-PROD or SUM-MIN implication model. All the models in section 6.1 are based either on the Mamdani implication (MAX-MIN) or the Larsen inference method (MAX-PROD). Consequently, they are not additive models. It is important to realize that so far only additive models are proven universal approximators for fuzzy membership functions of any shape.

The simplest FAM model as given by (6.33) is valid when the output membership functions are singletons. A more general model for an $\Re^n \to \Re^1$ mapping (when the output fuzzy subsets, i.e., attributes or membership functions, are fuzzy subsets of any shape) is given by

$$y = F(\mathbf{x}) = \frac{\sum\limits_{i=1}^{N} w_i \mu(\mathbf{x}, \mathbf{c}_i) A_i m_i}{\sum\limits_{i=1}^{N} w_i \mu(\mathbf{x}, \mathbf{c}_i) A_i}. \tag{6.34}$$

where N denotes the number of rules, w_i stands for the relative rule weight (if the ith rule is more relevant than the jth rule, $w_i > w_j$), A_i is the area of the corresponding ith output fuzzy subset (membership function), and m_i stands for the mode, that is, the center of area (center of gravity, centroid) of the ith output fuzzy subset.

In the case of an $\Re^n \to \Re^m$ mapping, a FAM given by (6.34) becomes

$$\mathbf{y} = F(\mathbf{x}) = \frac{\sum\limits_{i=1}^{N} w_i \mu(\mathbf{x}, \mathbf{c}_i) V_i \mathbf{m}_i}{\sum\limits_{i=1}^{N} w_i \mu(\mathbf{x}, \mathbf{c}_i) V_i}, \tag{6.35}$$

where V_i is the volume of the corresponding ith output fuzzy subset (membership function). When all rules are equally relevant, $w_i = w_j$, $i = 1, N, j = 1, N$, and when the output fuzzy subsets have equal volumes (or areas in the case of an $\Re^m = \Re^1$ mapping), (6.35) reduces to (6.33).

The basic description of how this additive model achieves the desired accuracy is given in example 6.15 for an $\Re^1 \to \Re^1$ mapping. The design steps in fuzzy modeling are shown in box 6.1.

Box 6.1
Design Steps in Fuzzy Modeling

Step 1. Define the universes of discourse (domains and ranges, i.e., input and output variables).

Step 2. Specify the fuzzy membership functions (fuzzy subsets or attributes) for the chosen input and output variables.

Step 3. Define the fuzzy rules (i.e., the rule base).

Step 4. Perform the numerical part (SUM-PROD, SUM-MIN, MAX-MIN, or some other) inference algorithm.

Step 5. Defuzzify the resulting (usually not-normal) fuzzy subsets.

Example 6.15   Design a fuzzy controller for controlling a distance between two cars traveling on a road.

Example 6.14 demonstrated how the braking force B depends upon the distance D and the velocity v, but it did not give details. Here, in order to get a geometrical impression of a FAM works and to enable visualization, it is assumed that the distance D is constant, and only the mapping, $B = f(v)$, is modeled. Figure 6.26 shows the scheme for this model.

In the case of a mapping $B = f(v)$, a very simple (rough) model can be obtained by having three rules only. Both the fuzzy subsets and the rule base are shown in figure 6.27. The rule base is linguistically expressed everyday driving expertise on how to brake depending upon the velocity of the car.

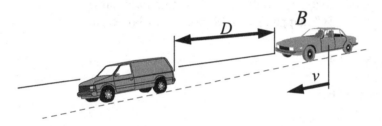

Figure 6.26
Scheme for modeling a fuzzy braking force controller.

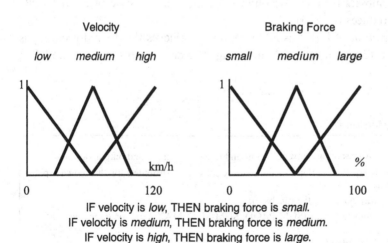

IF velocity is *low*, THEN braking force is *small*.
IF velocity is *medium*, THEN braking force is *medium*.
IF velocity is *high*, THEN braking force is *large*.

Figure 6.27
Fuzzy subsets (membership functions) and a rule base for a fuzzy braking force controller.

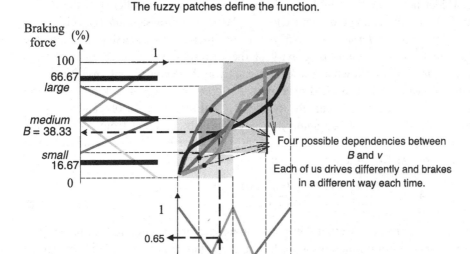

Figure 6.28
Fuzzy rules define the fuzzy patches. More rules result in smaller patches. This means finer granulation, i.e., more precise knowledge.

Figure 6.28 shows the four possible mapping curves that may result from a FAM's having three rules only. A much finer (more accurate) model could have been obtained with finer discretization (more membership functions and rules). The rules and the fuzzy subsets with high overlapping produce the three square patches in a (B, v) plane inside which must lie the function $B = f(v)$, the desired $\Re^1 \to \Re^1$ mapping. The very shape of a function $B = f(v)$ depends on the shapes of the membership functions applied, on the implication mechanism, and (heavily) on the defuzzification method used. Figure 6.28 shows four possible solutions. This is the soft part of the fuzzy modeling that models the basic dependency stating that with an increase in velocity there must be an increase in braking force. Patch size generally defines the vagueness or uncertainty in the rule. It is related to the number of rules: more rules, smaller patches. There is no unique or prescribed way to brake. We all drive differently, and the way each of us applies the force to the brakes is different each time. Hence, many possible functions result from different experiences, and the fuzzy models that are based on expertise will also be different. Some of the possible variety can be seen in figure 6.28.

Consider now how the FAM models the braking force controller. For the output fuzzy subsets, three singletons are chosen, placed as follows: *small* ($r_1 = 16.67\%$), *medium* ($r_2 = 50\%$), *large* ($r_3 = 66.67\%$). These singleton membership functions are chosen to be at the centers of gravity of the corresponding triangle fuzzy subsets (i.e., $r_i = m_i$) and are shown as thick lines exactly at these given locations. (Note they are not shown in the fig. 6.27.) For a particular crisp input $v = 49.5$ km/h, shown in figure 6.28, only two rules, namely R_1 and R_2, will be active. In other words, their corresponding degrees of belonging μ_i, $i = 1, 2$, will be different from zero, or only these two rules will "fire." The output—a braking force B—for this particular input $v = 49.5$, follows from the FAM model (6.33) as

$$B = f(v = 49.5) = \frac{(0.35 \cdot 16.67) + (0.65 \cdot 50) + (0 \cdot 66.7)}{0.35 + 0.65} = 38.33\%. \qquad \blacksquare$$

It is important to realize that the FAMs do not perform very complex calculations. After the membership functions are selected, the volumes V_i and centroids m_i can be computed in advance. Now, the N membership degrees $\mu_i(\mathbf{x})$, $i = 1, N$, are calculated for each specific input $\mathbf{x}$. Finally, having defined the rule weights w_i, the corresponding output value y is found using (6.35) and (6.34) for an $\mathfrak{R}^n \to \mathfrak{R}^m$ mapping and for an $\mathfrak{R}^n \to \mathfrak{R}^1$ mapping, respectively. Note that only a part of the corresponding degrees μ_i will be different from zero, meaning that only a part of rules will be active.

The most serious problem in applying FAMs is a *rule explosion* phenomenon. The number of rules increases exponentially with the dimensions of the input and output spaces. Thus, for example, if there are four input variables ($\mathbf{x}$ is a four-dimensional vector) and a single output y, and if one chooses five fuzzy subsets for each input variable, one has to define $5^4 = 625$ rules. In other words, according to figure 6.25, this represents a network with 625 hidden layer neuron. Another serious problem is the learning part in fuzzy models. Theoretically, because of the equivalence of RBF networks and FL models, one can apply any learning approach from the neural field, including the gradient descent method. However, the standard membership functions are not smooth differentiable functions, and error backpropagation is not as popular in the fuzzy logic field as it is in the neural field. Genetic algorithms may be viable techniques, as may other methods for RBF networks training. In particular, a linear programming approach, as given in section 5.3.4, seems promising for selecting the most relevant rules in FAM.

The single important computational step in applying FAMs is the calculation of membership degrees $\mu_i(\mathbf{x})$, $i = 1, N$. In performing this task the most popular operators are MIN and PROD. A standard fuzzy rule is expressed separately for each input variable, for instance,

R: IF x_1 is *small* AND x_2 is *large* AND, ..., x_n is *medium*, THEN y is *positive*.

In other words, a typical IF-THEN rule operation is a *conjunction* (interpreted as logical AND), and any T-norm operator can be used in the calculation of membership degrees $\mu_i(\mathbf{x})$, $i = 1$, N. The two most popular operators (shown here for an n-dimensional input vector $\mathbf{x}$) are the MIN operator $\mu_{x_1 \wedge x_2 \wedge \cdots \wedge x_n} = \mathrm{MIN}(\mu_{x_1}, \mu_{x_2}, \ldots, \mu_{x_n})$ and the PROD (algebraic product) operator $\mu_{x_1 \wedge x_2 \wedge \cdots \wedge x_n} = \mu_{x_1} \mu_{x_2} \cdots \mu_{x_n}$. If the IF part contains an OR connection, the MIN operator must be replaced with a MAX operator or some other S-norm. However, an application of the OR in an IF part rarely happens in practice.

The algebraic product gives much smoother approximations because it does not ignore information contained in the IF part as the MIN operator does. How the two operators use the information contained in an input vector is shown by a simple example here.

Suppose that an input vector results in following membership degrees (activations) $\boldsymbol{\mu}_1 = [\mu_1 \quad \mu_2 \quad \mu_3 \quad \mu_4 \quad \mu_5]^T = [0.7 \quad 0.4 \quad 0.4 \quad 0.5 \quad 0.5]^T$ and that another input vector gives $\boldsymbol{\mu}_2 = [0.7 \quad 0.4 \quad 0.9 \quad 0.9 \quad 1.0]^T$. The MIN operator results in $\boldsymbol{\mu}_1(\mathbf{x}) = \boldsymbol{\mu}_2(\mathbf{x}) = 0.4$, while the PROD operator gives $\boldsymbol{\mu}_1(\mathbf{x}) = 0.028$ and $\boldsymbol{\mu}_2(\mathbf{x}) = 0.2268$. Hence, the MIN operator does not differentiate the joint strength of the inputs and in both cases results in the same activation despite the obvious fact that $\boldsymbol{\mu}_2$ contains much stronger activations.

The product $\mu(\mathbf{x}) = \mu_1(x_1)\mu_2(x_2) \cdots \mu_n(x_n)$ gets smaller for larger input dimension n, but this does not affect the FAM output because $\mu(\mathbf{x})$ is a part of both the numerator and denominator in (6.33)–(6.35). Note an important fact that by using the product of n scalar membership functions $\mu(\mathbf{x}) = \prod_{i=1}^{n} \mu_i(x_i)$, the possible correlations among the input components x_i were ignored.

The relational matrix approach as given in section 6.1 does not add the resulting output (typically) not-normal fuzzy sets, and instead of the SUM operator it uses MAX. Figure 6.19 shows the resulting consequent not-normal fuzzy membership function after the MAX operator has been applied. This MAX-PROD resulting consequent fuzzy subset is shown in figure 6.29 together with the resulting consequent not-normal fuzzy membership function after applying the SUM operator.

There are two distinct advantages in using FAMs (SUM-MIN or SUM-PROD or SUM-any-other-T-norm model) with respect to an application of the relational

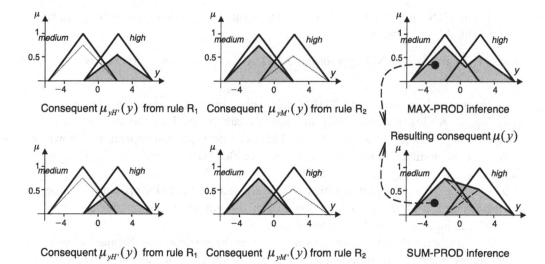

Figure 6.29
Construction of the consequent membership functions from example 6.12 for a single-input, single-output system. *Top*, MAX-PROD inference. *Bottom*, SUM-PROD inference.

models presented in section 6.1 (MAX-MIN or MAX-PROD models). First, on theoretical level, FAMs are universal approximators, and there is no proof of this capacity for the relational models yet. Second, the computational part of a reasoning scheme is simplified through bypassing the relational matrix calculus.

Problems

6.1. On a cold winter morning, your mother tells you, "The temperature is about $-10\,°C$ today." Represent this piece of information by

a. a crisp set (a crisp membership function),

b. a fuzzy set.

6.2. Human linguistic expressions depend upon both the context and individual perceptions. Represent the following expressions by membership functions:

a. "large stone" (while you are in the mountains)

b. "large stone" (while you are in a jewelry store)

c. "high temperature today" (winter in Russia)

d. "high temperature today" (summer in Greece)

e. "high temperature today" (summer in Sweden)

6.3. Given is the fuzzy set S for a power plant boiler pressure P (bar) with the following membership function:

$$S(P) = \begin{cases} \frac{1}{25}(P - 200) & \text{if } 200 \le P \le 225 \\ -\frac{1}{25}(P - 200) & \text{if } 225 < P \le 250 \\ 0 & \text{otherwise} \end{cases}$$

a. Sketch the graph of this membership function, and comment on its type.

b. Give the linguistic description for the concept conveyed by S.

6.4. Let three fuzzy sets be defined by an ordered set of pairs, where the first number denotes the degree of belonging (the membership degree) and the second number is the element:

$A = \{1/3, 0.2/4, 0.3/5, 0.4/6, 0.6/7, 0.8/8, 1/10, 0.8/12, 0.6/14\}.$

$B = \{0.4/2, 0.6/3, 0.8/4, 1/5, 0.8/6, 0.6/7, 0.4/8\}.$

$C = \{0.4/2, 0.8/4, 1/5, 0.6/7\}.$

Determine the intersections and unions of

a. the fuzzy sets A, B, and C,

b. the complements of fuzzy sets B and C if both sets are defined on the universe of discourse $X = \{1, 2, 3, 4, 5, 6, 7, 8, 9, 10\}$. (*Hint:* First express the complements B^C and C^C, taking into account X.)

6.5. Let the two fuzzy sets $A = \{x \text{ is considerably larger than } 10\}$ and $B = \{x \text{ is approximately } 11\}$ be defined by the following membership functions:

$$\mu_A(x) = \begin{cases} 0 & \text{for } x \le 10 \\ [1 + (x - 10)^{-2}]^{-1} & \text{for } x > 10 \end{cases}.$$

$\mu_B(x) = [1 + (x - 11)^4]^{-1}.$

a. Sketch the graphs of these fuzzy sets, and draw the graphs of a fuzzy set $C = \{x \text{ is considerably larger than } 10 \text{ AND } x \text{ is approximately } 11\}$; and a fuzzy set $D = \{x \text{ is considerably larger than } 10 \text{ OR } x \text{ is approximately } 11\}$.

b. Express analytically the membership functions μ_C and μ_D.

6.6. Let two fuzzy sets be defined as follows:

$A = \{0.4/2, 0.6/3, 0.8/4, 1/5, 0.8/6, 0.6/7, 0.4/8\}.$

$B = \{0.4/2, 0.8/4, 1/5, 0.6/7\}.$

Determine the intersections of A and B by applying three different T-norms:

a. minimum,

b. product,

c. Lukasiewicz AND (bounded difference).

6.7. Determine the unions of A and B from problem 6.6 by applying three different T-conorms (S-norms):

a. maximum,

b. algebraic sum,

c. Lukasiewicz OR (bounded sum).

6.8. Prove that the following properties are satisfied by Yager's S-norm:

a. $\mu_{A \vee B}(x) = \mu_A(x)$ for $\mu_B(x) = 0$.

b. $\mu_{A \vee B}(x) = 1$ for $\mu_B(x) = 1$.

c. $\mu_{A \vee B}(x) \geq \mu_A(x)$ for $\mu_A(x) = \mu_B(x)$.

d. For $b \to 0$, the Yager's union operator (S-norm) reduces to a drastic sum.

6.9. Show that the drastic sum and drastic product satisfy the law of excluded middle and the law of contradiction. (*Hint:* The law of excluded middle states that $A \cup A^C = X$, and the law of contradiction says that $A \cap A^C = \emptyset$).

6.10. Prove that De Morgan's laws are satisfied if we take the union MAX operator and the intersection MIN operator, with the negation defined as

a. $N(x) = \dfrac{1 - x}{1 + \lambda x}$, $\lambda \in (-1, \infty)$.

b. $N(x) = \sqrt[r]{1 - x^r}$, $r \in (0, \infty)$.

(*Hint:* De Morgan's laws state that $\overline{A \cup B} = \bar{A} \cap \bar{B}$ and $\overline{A \cap B} = \bar{A} \cup \bar{B}$).

6.11. Let $X = \{8, 3, 10\}$ and $Y = \{2, 1, 7, 6\}$. Define the relational matrices for the following two relations: R_1: "x is considerably larger than y" and R_2: "y is very close to x". Now find the relational matrices for these two relations:

a. "x is considerably larger OR is very close to y"

b. "x is considerably larger AND is very close to y"

6.12. Consider a fuzzy rule: IF x is A, THEN y is B. The two fuzzy sets are given as follows:

$A = \{0/1, 0.1/2, 0.4/3, 0.8/4, 1/5\}, \qquad B = \{0/-2, 0.6/-1, 1/0, 0.6/1, 0/2\}.$

Find the relational matrices representing this rule by applying

a. MIN (Mamdani) implication (R_m),

b. Lukasiewicz implication (R_L),

c. Fuzzy implication MIN($1, 1 - \mu_A(x) + \mu_B(x)$) ($R_F$).

6.13. Consider the input fuzzy set for the rule in problem 6.12. $A' = \{0/1, 0.2/2,$ $0.8/3, 1/4, 0.1/5\}$. Apply the three compositional rules of inference, and find the output fuzzy set (consequent) for a

a. MAX-MIN composition by using R_m from problem 6.12,

b. MAX-Lukasiewicz T-norm by using R_L from problem 6.12,

c. MAX-Lukasiewicz T-norm by using R_F from problem 6.12.

6.14. Two fuzzy relations are given as

$$\mathbf{R}_1 = \begin{bmatrix} 0.3 & 0 & 0.7 & 0.3 \\ 0 & 1 & 0.2 & 0 \end{bmatrix} \quad \text{and} \quad \mathbf{R}_2 = \begin{bmatrix} 1 & 0 & 1 \\ 0 & 0.5 & 0.4 \\ 0.7 & 0.9 & 0.6 \\ 0 & 0 & 0 \end{bmatrix}.$$

Find the composition of these two relations using

a. MAX-MIN composition,

b. MAX-PROD composition,

c. MAX-AVERAGE composition.

6.15. Find and present graphically the output fuzzy set for the system in figure P6.1 with two inputs (having two fuzzy sets per each input) and one output described by

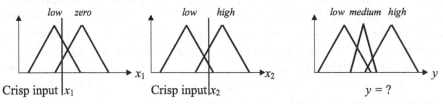

Figure P6.1
Graphs for problem 6.15.

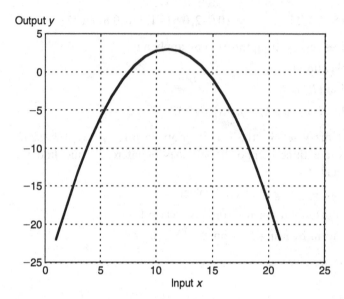

Figure P6.2
Graph for problem 6.16.

following four rules:

R_1: IF $x_1 = low$ AND $x_2 = low$,   THEN $y = low$.

R_2: IF $x_1 = low$ AND $x_2 = high$, THEN $y = medium$.

R_3: IF $x_1 = zero$ AND $x_2 = low$,   THEN $y = medium$.

R_4: IF $x_1 = zero$ OR $x_2 = high$,   THEN $y = high$.

6.16. Figure P6.2 shows the functional dependency between two variables: $y = y(x)$. Make a fuzzy model of this function by using proper fuzzy tools and algorithms. In particular, use three membership functions for the Input x and three membership functions for the Output y. Choose the shapes and positions of the membership functions that you think can solve the problem. Make the corresponding rule base, find the relational matrices if needed, and for $x = 10$, using your fuzzy model, find the crisp value of y. Use any operator, inference rule, or defuzzification method you think is proper for modeling the given function.

6.17. The fuzzy controller is acting according to the following rule basis ($N = negative$, $M = medium$, $P = positive$):

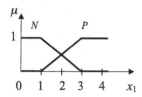 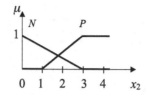

Figure P6.3
Input (antecedent) membership functions for problems 6.17 and 6.18.

R_1:   IF x_1 is N AND x_2 is N,   THEN u is N.

R_2:   IF x_1 is N OR x_2 is P,   THEN u is M.

R_3:   IF x_1 is P OR x_2 is N,   THEN u is M.

R_4:   IF x_1 is P AND x_2 is P,   THEN u is P.

The membership functions (possibility distributions) of the input variables are given in figure P6.3, and the membership functions of the output variable (which is a controller action) u are singletons placed at u is equal to 1, 2, and 3 for N, M, and P, respectively. Actual inputs are $x_1 = 2.5$ and $x_2 = 4$. Which rules are active, and what will be the controller action u? Find u by applying both the relational models (MAX-MIN or MAX-PROD) and the FAM. Comment whether there is any difference between the MAX-MIN and MAX-PROD here?

6.18. Consider a fuzzy controller acting according to the following rule basis ($N = $ negative, $M = medium$, $P = positive$):

R_1:   IF x_1 is N OR x_2 is N,   THEN u is N.

R_2:   IF x_1 is N AND x_2 is P,   THEN u is P.

R_3:   IF x_1 is P AND x_2 is N,   THEN u is P.

R_4:   IF x_1 is P OR x_2 is P,   THEN u is N.

The membership functions of the input variables are same as in problem 6.17 and are shown in figure P6.3. The membership functions of the output variable (which is a controller action) u are singletons placed at u is equal to 2 and 4 for N and P, respectively. Actual inputs are $x_1 = 2$ and $x_2 = 4$. Which rules are active, and what will be the controller action u? Find u by applying both the relational models (MAX-MIN or MAX-PROD) and the FAM.

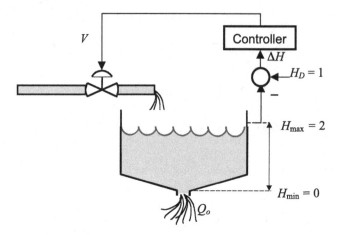

Figure P6.4
Plant scheme for problem 6.19.

6.19. Design the fuzzy controller for a water level control shown in figure P6.4 using three rules only. The input value to the controller is an actual water level perturbation ΔH (meters) $\in [-1, 1]$, and the controller output is the valve opening V (%) $\in [0, 100]$. For $\Delta H = -0.25$, calculate the actual valve opening V by using a FAM. (*Hint:* Follow the design steps in box 6.1.)

6.20. Equation (6.32) can be used for off-line (batch) learning of the output singletons' positions r_i having fixed input fuzzy subsets and data (the "activations" μ_i and the desired outputs y_{di}, namely, a matrix $\mathbf{A}$ and a vector $\mathbf{b}$, are known). Derive the on-line gradient descent error backpropagation adapting algorithm for the output singletons' positions r_i given by (6.33) when the error function is a sum of error squares $E = 1/2(y_d - y)^2$. (*Hint:* Start with $r_{iNew} = r_{iOld} - \eta \nabla_r E$, and find the gradient $\nabla_r E$.)

6.21. A Cauchy bell-shaped function may be a good candidate for an input membership function. In the case of an $\Re^1 \rightarrow \Re^1$ mapping, this function is given by

$$\mu_i(x) = \frac{1}{1 + \left(\dfrac{x - m_i}{d_i}\right)^2}.$$

It is placed at m_i and acts locally, and the area of activation is controlled by the width parameter d_i, which corresponds to the standard deviation at the Gaussian function.

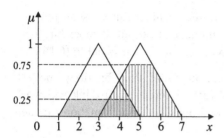

Figure P6.5
Graph for problem 6.23.

In addition, it is differentiable, and both the centers m_i and the width parameter d_i can be adapted by applying the error backpropagation (EBP) algorithm. (Note that m_i and d_i correspond to the hidden layer weights of neural networks). Derive the EBP learning laws for adapting m_i and d_i in a FAM with Cauchy membership functions. The error function is a sum of error squares $E = 1/2(y_d - y)^2$. (*Hint:* Start with the learning algorithm, e.g., for m_i with $m_{i(p+1)} = m_{ip} - \eta \nabla_{m_i} E$, and use the FAM model (6.33). This means that the output membership functions are singletons.)

6.22. Derive the gradient descent EBP learning laws for a FAM to adapt both the centers m_i and the width parameter d_i of the sinc membership function defined as

$$\mu_i(x) = \frac{\sin\left(\dfrac{x - m_i}{d_i}\right)}{\dfrac{x - m_i}{d_i}}.$$

The error function is a sum of error squares $E = 1/2(y_d - y)^2$. Use the FAM model (6.33).

6.23. Consequents (output membership functions) are given in figure P6.5. Find the crisp output y' by applying

a. center-of-gravity defuzzification method for a MAX-MIN inference,

b. FAM method,

c. height method for a MAX-MIN inference that calculates the crisp output as

$$y' = \frac{\displaystyle\sum_{i=1}^{N} c_i H_i}{\displaystyle\sum_{i=1}^{N} H_i},$$

where the c_i are the centers of gravity or means of the resulting rule consequents, and H_i are their maximal heights. N stands for the number of output membership functions. If the consequents are singletons, the preceding equation is equal to (6.16).

6.24. Approximate the two functions presented in figure P6.6 by fuzzy models. Choose the membership functions and type of fuzzy inference you think will work best. Make one rough (small number of rules) and one finer approximation for each function.

6.25. Design a fuzzy logic pattern recognition model for a classification of two letters V and U, shown in figure P6.7. First, make a class description and define only two features based on this description. These two features will be your two inputs to the fuzzy classifier. Then define the membership functions. Choose two membership functions for each input. Define the rules.

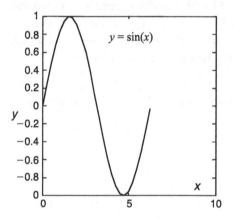
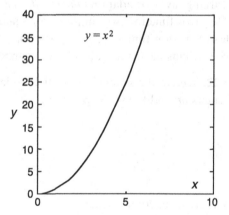

Figure P6.6
Graphs for problem 6.24.

Figure P6.7
Graphs for problem 6.25.

Simulation Experiments

The simulation experiments in chapter 6 have the purpose of familiarizing the reader with the fuzzy logic modeling tools. There are two programs for performing a variety of fuzzy modeling tasks. They can be found in two directories: `fuzzy1` and `fuzzy2`. In addition, there is a program `fuzfam` in `aproxim` file. Both programs were developed as the final-year projects at the University of Auckland under the supervision, guidance, and gentle cooperation of the author. (It is interesting to mention that the students had only a half-semester's introduction to fuzzy logic before commencing the final-year thesis.)

The `fuzzy1` program was created by D. Simunic and G. Taylor, and it was aimed at the application of fuzzy logic to a vehicle turning problem. The `fuzzy2` program was developed by W. M. Chen and G. Chua for guidance of mobile robots using fuzzy logic theory.

`Fuzzy1` can be used to develop other fuzzy logic models, whereas `fuzzy2` is merely a demo program for simulation of a given problem and cannot be used by the reader to create models. However, `fuzzy2` can be used to explore various aspects of FL modeling. Both programs have a nice graphic interface, and they are user-friendly. The user need only follow the pop-up menus and graphic windows.

You can perform various experiments aimed at reviewing many basic facets of fuzzy logic modeling, notably the influence of the membership functions' shape and overlap on the accuracy of model, the influence of the rule basis on model performance, and the effect of inference and defuzzification operators on the final modeling results.

Experiment with the programs `fuzzy1` and `fuzzy2` as follows:

1. Launch MATLAB.

2. Connect to directory `learnSC` (at the `matlab` prompt, type `cd learnsc` ⟨RETURN⟩). `learnSC` is a subdirectory of `matlab` as `bin`, `toolbox`, and `uitools` are. While typing `cd learnsc`, make sure that your working directory is `matlab`, and not `matlab/bin`, for example).

To start the program type `start` ⟨RETURN⟩. Pop-up menus will lead you through a design procedure. There are several options. You can either design your own fuzzy model or run one of several demo programs. It may be best to begin with the simplest *heating* demo. This is a model of how one controls the temperature in a room by changing the heat supplied.

Click to `file — open — heating.mat`. The input and output membership functions will be displayed. Click on `model — inference`, and you will see surface of knowledge, or in the case of a one-dimensional input, curve of knowledge. By activating the slide bar, you can follow the fuzzy calculations. Active rules are shown by red bars over the corresponding output membership functions.

To see the effects of applying various inference and defuzzification mechanisms, go to options and select any of the given operators. Choose merely one change at time, that is, do not change both inference and defuzzification operators at the same time (unless you really want to). Analyze the change in the resulting curve of knowledge.

Note that all changes during the simulation should go through the pop-up menu. Hence, if you want to run another example, do not kill the existing window by clicking the x-corner button. Rather, click options — main menu, and begin a new simulation.

When you are done with the one-dimensional example, you may run the application of fuzzy logic to a vehicle turning problem. Select one of the demos starting with car**.mat, e.g., click file — open — cartes55.mat. Click model — animation for 2-D car, and drive the car around the corner from various initial positions. You can trace the car paths and keep the traces. Just try out various options of the program. Choose various operators, and keep the traces to compare them. Note that the car is not allowed to go backward, and this makes some initial positions impossible to solve, even for humans.

You can also repeat example 6.14 by selecting one of the two prepared demos, namely brake55.mat or brake35.mat. Choose some operators from options and analyze the surfaces of knowledge obtained.

Program fuzzy2 controls the movement of several mobile robots in a workshop. They service several machines and must avoid collision with each other.

Run several simulations, trying out different numbers of robots on the floor and different numbers of machines. Repeat the simulations with various inference and defuzzification operators. Carefully analyze the three-dimensional graphs of the surfaces of knowledge obtained.

There are small programming bugs in both routines. None is of crucial importance, but some do influence the performance of the fuzzy model created. This will be readily visible in following the trajectories of the mobile robots. Note that all robots have different, constant, and randomly chosen velocities. There will be odd solutions in the situations when the faster robot is closing the distance to the slower one. The very overtaking will be unusual because all robots are programmed to turn to the right only in order to avoid collision.

7 Case Studies

7.1 Neural Networks–Based Adaptive Control

This section focuses on neural networks–based adaptive control and also addresses the class of fuzzy logic models that are equivalent to neural networks (see section 6.2). In particular, after a review of the basic ideas of NN-based control, the *adaptive backthrough control* (ABC) scheme is introduced. ABC is one of the most serious candidates for the future control of the large class of nonlinear, partially known, time-varying systems. Recently, the area of NN-based control has been exhaustively investigated, and there are many different NN-based control methods. Rigorous comparisons show that NN-based controllers perform far better than well-established conventional alternatives when plant characteristics are poorly known (Bošković and Narendra 1995). A systematic classification of the different NN-based control structures is a formidable task (Agarwal 1997). Here, the focus is on an approach based on feedforward networks having static neurons, as given in figures 4.4 and 5.6. This section follows the presentation in Kecman (1997).

A standard control task and basic problem in controlling an unknown dynamic plant is to find the proper, or desired, control (actuation) value u_d as an input to the plant that would ensure

$$y(t) = y_d(t), \qquad \forall t, \tag{7.1}$$

where the subscript d stands for desired. $y(t)$ and $y_d(t)$ denote the plant output and desired (reference) plant output, respectively. The best controller would be one that could produce the value u_d that ensures (7.1), when the output of the plant exactly follows the desired trajectory y_d. In linear control, (7.1) will be ensured when

$$G_{ci}(s) = G_p^{-1}(s). \tag{7.2}$$

Hence, the ideal controller transfer function $G_{ci}(s)$ should be the inverse of the plant transfer function $G_p(s)$. Because of many practical constraints, this is an idealized control structure (Kecman 1988). However, one can try to get as close as possible to this ideal controller solution, $G_{ci}(s)$. The ABC approach, which is presented in section 7.1.4, can achieve a great deal (sometimes even nearly all) of this ideal controller. The block diagram of the ideal control of any nonlinear system is given in figure 7.1. $\mathbf{f}(\mathbf{u}, \mathbf{y})$ in the figure stands for any nonlinear mapping between an input $\mathbf{u}(t)$ and an output $\mathbf{y}(t)$. In the general case of a dynamic system, $\mathbf{f}(\mathbf{u}, \mathbf{y})$ represents a system of nonlinear differential equations. Here, the focus is primarily on discrete-time systems, and the model of the plant in the discrete-time domain is in the form of a nonlinear discrete equation $\mathbf{y}(k+1) = \mathbf{f}(\mathbf{u}(k), \mathbf{y}(k))$. Now, the basic problem is how to learn, or obtain, the inverse model of the unknown dynamic plant by using an NN.

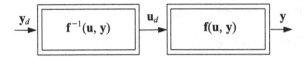

Figure 7.1
The ideal (feedforward) control structure for any plant.

The wide application of NN in control is based on the universal approximation capacity of neural networks and fuzzy logic models (FLMs). Thus, the learning (identification, adaptation, training) of plant dynamics and inverse plant dynamics represents both the mathematical tool and the problem to be solved. Therefore, the analysis presented here assumes a complete controllability and observability of the plant. To represent a dynamic system, a NARMAX model is used.[1] In the extensive literature on modeling dynamic plants, it has been proved, after making some moderate assumptions, that any nonlinear, discrete, time-invariant system can always be represented by a NARMAX model,

$$y(k+1) = f\{y(k), \ldots, y(k-n); u(k), \ldots, u(k-m)\},$$

or

$$y_{k+1} = f(y_k, y_{k-1}, y_{k-2}, \ldots, y_{k-n}, u_k, u_{k-1}, u_{k-2}, \ldots, u_{k-m}), \tag{7.3}$$

where y_k and u_k are the input and the output signals at instant k, and y_{k-i} and u_{k-j}, $i = 1, \ldots, n$, $j = 1, \ldots, m$, represent the past values of these signals. Typically, one can work with $n = m$. Equation (7.3) is a simplified deterministic version of the NARMAX model (there are no noise terms in it), and it is valid for dynamic systems with K outputs and L inputs. For $K = L = 1$, one obtains the SISO (single-input, single-output) system, which is studied here.

In reality, the nonlinear function f from (7.3) is very complex and generally unknown. The whole idea in the application of NNs is to try to approximate f by using some known and simple functions, which in the case of the application of NNs or FLMs are their activation or membership functions.

This identification phase of the mathematical model (7.3) can be given a graphical representation (fig. 7.2). Note that two different identification schemes are presented in the figure: *series-parallel* and *parallel*. (The names are due to Landau (1979).) Identification can be achieved by using either of the two schemes:

$$\hat{y}(k+1) = f\{y(k), \ldots, y(k-n); u(k), \ldots, u(k-n)\} \quad \text{(series-parallel)}, \tag{7.4}$$

$$\hat{y}(k+1) = f\{\hat{y}(k), \ldots, \hat{y}(k-n); u(k), \ldots, u(k-n)\} \quad \text{(parallel)}. \tag{7.5}$$

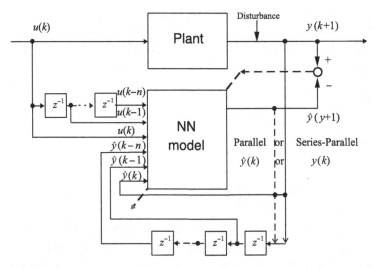

Figure 7.2
Identification scheme using neural networks.

It is hard to say which scheme is a better one. Narendra and Annaswamy (1989) showed (for linear systems) the series-parallel method to be globally stable, but similar results are not available for the parallel model yet. The parallel method has the advantage of avoiding noise existing in real-plant output signals. On the other hand, the series-parallel scheme uses actual (meaning correct) plant outputs, and this generally enforces identification. It should be said that questions of performance, advantages, and shortcomings of the series-parallel model (as advanced and used by Narendra and Parthasarathy (1990), for example) and the parallel model are still open.

Seemingly the strongest stream of NN-based control strategies is *feedforward control*, where a few relatively independent and partly dissimilar directions were followed in the search for a good control strategy. The main idea was the same in all these otherwise different control schemes: to determine a good inverse model of plant dynamics $\mathbf{f}^{-1}(\mathbf{u}, \mathbf{y})$, as required in the ideal feedforward control structure in figure 7.1.

7.1.1 General Learning Architecture, or Direct Inverse Modeling

Figure 7.3 shows how the inverse plant model of a *stable* plant can be trained using the *general learning architecture*, introduced by Psaltis, Sideris, and Yamamura (1988). Another name for the same approach, independently developed by Jordan

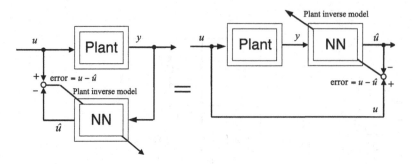

Figure 7.3
General learning architecture, or direct inverse modeling.

and Rumelhart (1992), is *direct inverse modeling*. This is basically an off-line procedure, and for nonlinear plants it will usually precede the on-line phase. (If the plant is
unstable, stabilization with a feedback loop must be done first. This can be done with
any standard control algorithm.) To learn the inverse plant model, an input signal u
is chosen and applied to the input of the plant to obtain a corresponding output y.
In the following step, the neural model is trained to reproduce this value u at its
output.

After this training phase, the structure for an on-line operation looks like the one
shown in figure 7.1, that is, the NN representing the inverse of the plant precedes the
plant. The trained neural network should be able to take a desired input value y_d
and produce the appropriate $u = u_d$ as an input to the plant. This architecture is
unfortunately not goal-directed. Note that one normally does not know which output
u_d of the controller corresponds to the desired output y_d of the plant. Therefore, this
learning scheme should cover a large operational regime of the plant, with a limitation that a control system cannot be selectively trained to respond accurately in a
region of interest. Thus, one important part of learning with the general learning
architecture is the selection of adequate training signals u, which should cover the
whole input range. Because this is an off-line approach unsuitable for on-line applications, the controller cannot operate during this learning phase. Besides, because
of the use of the error backpropagation (EBP) algorithm (which minimizes the sum-
of-error-squares cost function), this structure may be unable to find a correct inverse
if the plant is characterized by many-to-one mappings from the control inputs u
to the plant outputs y. Despite these drawbacks, in a number of domains (stable systems and one-to-one mapping plants), this general learning architecture is a viable
technique.

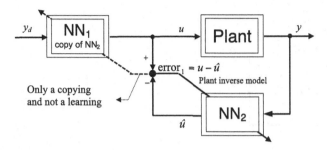

Figure 7.4
Indirect learning architecture.

7.1.2 Indirect Learning Architecture

Psaltis, Sideris, and Yamamura (1988) introduced an *indirect learning architecture* as a second concept. In this adaptive control structure, the controller or network NN_1 (which is a copy of the trained inverse plant model NN_2) produces, from the desired output y_d, a control signal u_d that drives the plant to the desired output $y = y_d$ (see fig. 7.4). The aim of learning is to produce a set of NN_2 weights, which will be copied into network NN_1 in order to ensure a correct mapping $y_d \rightarrow u$ over the range of the desired operation.

The positive feature of this arrangement is that the network can be trained in a region of interest, that is, it is goal-directed. Furthermore, an advantage of the indirect learning architecture is that it is an on-line learning procedure. However, Psaltis et al. unfortunately conclude that this method is not a valid training procedure because minimizing the controller error $e_1 = u - \hat{u}$ does not necessarily minimize the performance error $e_3 = y_d - y$. (Actually, the name of this architecture highlights the fact that the subject of minimization is not *directly* the performance error e_3 between the desired and actual plant output but rather the controller error e_1). This structure also uses the EBP algorithm, and it has problems similar to the general learning architecture if the plant performs many-to-one mappings from control inputs u to plant outputs y.

7.1.3 Specialized Learning Architecture

A third approach presented by Psaltis et al. (1988) is a *specialized learning architecture* (see fig. 7.5). This structure operates in an on-line mode, and it trains a neural network to act as a controller in the region of interest, that is, it is goal-directed. In this way, the scheme avoids some of drawbacks of the two previous structures. Here, in a specialized

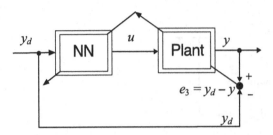

Figure 7.5
Specialized learning architecture.

learning architecture, the controller no longer learns from *its* input-output relation but from a *direct* evaluation of the *system's* performance error $e_3 = y_d - y$. The network is trained to find the best control value u that drives the plant to an output $y = y_d$. This is accomplished by using a steepest descent EBP learning procedure. Despite the fact that a specialized architecture operates in an on-line mode, a pretraining or off-line phase in the case of a nonlinear plant is usually be useful and highly recommended.

A critical point in specialized learning architecture is that the EBP learning algorithm requires knowledge of the Jacobian matrix of the plant. (For SISO systems the Jacobian matrix becomes a scalar that represents the plant's gain.) The emergence of the Jacobian is clear. The subjects of learning are NN weights, and in order to correct the weights in the right direction, a learning algorithm should contain information of errors caused by wrong weights. But there is no such direct information available because the plant intervenes between the unknown NN outputs, or control signals u, and the desired plant outputs y. The teacher in the EBP algorithm is typically an error (here the performance error $e_3 = y_d - y$), and this teacher is now a distal one (Jordan and Rumelhart 1992).

Let us consider the EBP algorithm for a general *distal teacher* learning situation. In order to apply the EBP algorithm, the NN and the plant are treated as a single neural network in which the plant represents a fixed (unmodifiable) output layer (OL). In this way, the real OL of the NN becomes the hidden layer (HL). EBP learning is now concerned with the calculation of proper deltas, or error signals δ, associated with each neuron (see box 4.1 and example 4.1). In order to find these signals, the delta signals δ_{ok} for true OL neurons of the NN should be determined first. For the sake of simplicity (avoiding matrix notation), it is demonstrated how this can be done for a SISO plant. Having δ_{ok} enables a relatively straightforward calculation of all other deltas and specific weight changes (see (4.24)–(4.26)).

Assume that an NN is a network operating in parallel mode having $2n$ inputs (where n represents the model order), or that an NN is given by the nonlinear discrete model

$$u(k+1) = f\{y_d(k), \ldots, y_d(k-n); u(k), \ldots, u(k-n)\}.$$

There are enough HL neurons that can provide a good approximation, and there is one *linear* OL neuron with an output u. The plant is given as $y = g(u, y)$. An EBP algorithm for learning NN weights, as given in box 4.1, is a steepest descent procedure, and the cost (error) function to be optimized is

$$E = \tfrac{1}{2}e^2 = \tfrac{1}{2}(y_d - y)^2 = E(w_{ij}). \tag{7.6}$$

Note that $y = g(u, y)$ and $u = f_{OL}(u_{OL})$, so that $y = g[f_{OL}(u_{OL}), y]$, where f_{OL} and u_{OL} stand for the activation function of, and the input signal to, the OL neuron, respectively. (For a linear OL neuron, f_{OL} represents an identity, $u = u_{OL}$.)

In order to calculate the OL neuron's error signal δ_o, apply the chain rule to calculate the cost function's gradient:

$$\frac{\partial E}{\partial w_i} = \frac{\partial E}{\partial e}\frac{\partial e}{\partial y}\frac{\partial y}{\partial u}\frac{\partial u}{\partial u_{OL}}\frac{\partial u_{OL}}{\partial w_i} = \underbrace{(y_d - y)(-1)\frac{\partial g(u, y)}{\partial u}f'_{OL}}_{-\delta_o}\frac{\partial u_{OL}}{\partial w_i}$$

$$= -\delta_o\frac{\partial u_{OL}}{\partial w_i}. \tag{7.7}$$

The error signal of the OL neuron δ_o is determined in accordance with (4.9). f'_{OL} stands for the derivative of the OL neuron activation function, and here for a linear neuron, $f'_{OL} = 1$. For a multilayer perceptron (MLP) network, where the input signal to the neuron is obtained as a scalar product $u_{OL} = \mathbf{w}^T\mathbf{x}$, the derivative $\partial u_{OL}/\partial w_i = x_i$. (Note that in RBF networks this expression for the OL error signal δ_o is identical. However, there will be a difference between the MLP and RBF networks in the expressions for HL neuron weights learning.

It is important to realize that the derivative $\partial g(u, y)/\partial u$ represents the Jacobian of the plant. Here, for a SISO plant, this is a scalar or, more precisely, a $(1, 1)$ vector. Generally, plant dynamics and the Jacobian are unknown, which is a serious shortcoming of this final result that is otherwise useful. There are two basic approaches to overcome this difficulty.

First, some final comments concerning weights adaptation in a specialized learning architecture with the following assumptions: the Jacobian is known, the OL neuron is linear, and the input to the neuron is calculated as a scalar product. With these assumptions, box 4.1a can be used directly. Note that the calculation of δ_o in (7.7) means that step 6 in this box is completed. Knowing the structure of an NN and following box 4.1a, steps 7–11, results in HL deltas and in new weights adapted by their corresponding weight changes $\Delta w_i = \eta\delta x_i$. Hence, in this *backpropagation through a plant* algorithm, the determination of the networks' OL delta signal is the most important step. In order to do this, the Jacobian of the plant must be known.

Generally the preceding assumptions do not hold, and two alternative approaches for handling a plant with an unknown Jacobian are *approximation of the plant Jacobian by its sign* and the *distal teacher approach*.

Approximation of the Plant Jacobian by Its Sign   Specialized learning with EBP through a plant can be achieved by approximating the partial derivatives of the Jacobian by their signs (Saerens and Soquet 1991). In principle, the same basic equations for the calculation of deltas are used, with the difference that sensitivity derivatives in a Jacobian matrix are approximated by their signs, which are generally known when qualitative knowledge about the plant is available. In practice, this means that the entries in a Jacobian matrix are $+1$ or -1. The main disadvantage of this approach is slower training. This is a consequence of the fact that this approach does not use all of the available information.

The Distal Teacher Approach   The structure and concept presented by Jordan and Rumelhart (1992)[2] differ significantly from the preceding method, using a *Jacobian of the plant forward model* instead of a real plant's Jacobian or instead of the signs of Jacobian derivatives of real plants. The whole feedforward control system now comprises two neural networks. One is a model of the plant; the second, an NN trained with the help of the first network, acts as a controller. This structure is practically the same as that of ABC (see fig. 7.6).

Learning or modeling proceeds in two phases. In the first phase, a *forward model* of a plant mapping from inputs u to outputs y is learned by using the standard supervised learning algorithm, EBP. In the second phase, the inverse model and the forward model are combined, and identity mapping is learned across the composed network. Note that the whole learning procedure is based on the performance errors e_3 between the desired plant outputs y_d and the actual outputs y.

The learner or controller (NN_1) is assumed to be able to observe states, inputs, and outputs, and can therefore model the inverse plant dynamics. If the plant is characterized by a many-to-one mapping from the input to the output, then there may be a number of possible inverse models. In their paper, Jordan and Rumelhart discuss how the distal teacher approach resolves this problem of finding a particular solution. (Unfortunately, they don't give details.) An important feature of this approach is that the feedforward model of a plant (NN_2) can be an approximate model. It is the use of the performance error e_3 that ensures that NN_1 can learn an exact inverse model of the plant even though the forward model is only approximate. Before closing this survey of the basic approaches to NN or FLM control, a few comments concerning the practical aspects of NN implementation may be in order.

In the case where the plant is nonlinear, the standard approach is to combine the general and the specialized learning architectures. This method combines the advantages of both procedures. A possible way to combine these two approaches is to first learn (with a general architecture) the approximated behavior of the plant. After that, the fine-tuning of the network in the operating region of the system should be done by specialized training (Psaltis, Sideris, and Yamamura 1988). The advantage is that a general learning architecture will produce a better set of initial weights for specialized learning. In this way, one will be able to cover a spacious range of input space as well as make specialized learning faster. The same approach is used in the ABC scheme, discussed in the next section. In the case of nonlinear plants, pretraining both the controller (NN_1) and the plant model (NN_2) is essential. After this pretraining step the on-line ABC adaptation can be started with these previously learned weights. In the case of a linear plant, this pretraining is not essential.

Sometimes it may be useful to introduce a reference model, too. This step is not crucial for an ABC approach, but an important result with a reference model could be that fine-tuning of the control effort is possible. This will be necessary for many real systems because the actuators usually operate only within a specific range, and leaving this range is either not possible or can harm a system's performance.

7.1.4 Adaptive Backthrough Control

NN-based control typically uses two neural networks, as shown in figure 7.6. The depiction of the ABC structure with two networks is in the line with the previous approaches, but it is suggested later in this section that ABC can perform even better with only one NN and that there is no need for NN_1, which acts as an inverse of plant dynamics.

The control loop structure pictured in figure 7.6 comprises NN_2, which represents the (approximate) model of the plant, and NN_1, which acts as a controller. NN_1 represents an approximate inverse of NN_2, that is, of the plant model and not of the plant itself. The structure shown in figure 7.6 is a standard one in the field of neuro-fuzzy control. In this respect, the ABC structure shown in the figure is in line with the basic results and approaches of Psaltis, Sideris, and Yamamura (1988), Saerens and Soquet (1991), Garcia and Morari (1982), Jordan (1993), Jordan and Rumelhart (1992), Hunt and Sbarbaro (1991), Narendra and Parthasarathy (1990), Saerens, Renders, and Bersini (1996), and Widrow and Walach (1996).

While it is similar in appearance to other NN-based control methods, the ABC approach has a few distinctive features that differentiate it from them. The principal

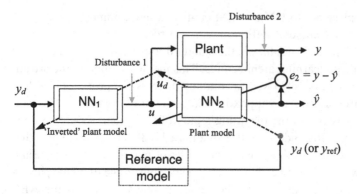

Figure 7.6
Neural networks–based adaptive backthrough control (ABC) scheme.

feature of the ABC method is that, unlike other approaches, it does not use standard training errors (e.g., e_3) as learning signals for adapting controller (NN$_1$) weights. Rather, the true desired value y_d (the signal that should be tracked, the reference signal) is used for the training of NN$_1$. In this manner, the desired but unknown control signal u_d results from the *backward* transformation of the y_d *through* NN$_2$. The origin of the name for this approach as a *backthrough* method lies in this backward step for the calculation of u_d. Thus, ABC basically represents a younger (and apparently more direct and powerful) relative of the distal teacher idea of Jordan and Rumelhart (1992) and Jordan (1993) or of the approach of Saerens and Soquet (1991) and Saerens, Renders, and Bersini (1996). Besides using different error signals for training, they use the steepest descent for optimization.

With ABC, as long as the control problem is linear in parameters (linear dependence of the cost function upon NN weights), the recursive least squares (RLS) learning algorithm is strictly used. This is a second interesting feature of the ABC approach. Note that in many cases, for both an NN-based and a fuzzy logic model–based controller, this assumption about the linear in parameters model is a realistic and acceptable one. This is typically the case when the hidden layer weights (positions and shapes of basis functions or membership functions in NNs or FLMs) are fixed (Kecman and Pfeiffer 1994). However, the ABC algorithm does not strictly depend on the use of the RLS technique. The standard gradient EBP or any other learning procedure can also be used. RLS-based learning in the ABC method does behave much better on a quadratic error surface than any gradient-based search procedure. This is another reason why the ABC algorithm seems more promising than the first-order EBP approach.

Similar to adaptive inverse control (AIC), devised by Widrow (1996), the ABC scheme is effective as long as the plant is a stable one. It solves the problems of tracking and disturbance rejection for any stable plant. The same will be true in the case of unstable plants as long as the unstable plant is stabilized by some classic control method first. It seems as though the ABC algorithm can handle nonminimum phase systems more easily than the AIC. The ABC is an adaptive control system design algorithm in a discrete domain, and as long as a suitable (not too small) sampling rate is used, there are no difficulties with discrete zeros outside the unit circle. The control structure in figure 7.6 has some of the good characteristics of an idealized control system design with a positive internal feedback that does not require the plant model NN_2 to be a perfect model of the plant (Tsypkin 1972). The latter control scheme is structurally equivalent to the internal model control (IMC) approach. Recall that besides a structural resemblance there is the learning (feedback) part that will cause the ABC system to behave differently (better). In addition, it seems as if the ABC method uses fewer weights than either the AIC or IMC approach. Also, there is no need for the explicit design of first-order filters that is the typical design practice in IMC. (The reference block shown in figure 7.6 is not required, unless some control of the actuator signal variable u is needed. All the results that follow were obtained by using $G_{ref}(s) = 1$).

The basic idea of ABC is to design an adaptive controller that acts as the inverse of the plant. In order to learn the characteristics of the plant and to adapt the controller to the plant's changes, the neural network that works as a controller must be told what the desired control value should be. In general, this value u_d is not available, but using the ABC approach, desired control values u_d can be found that will usually be very close to the ideal ones.

During the operation of the whole system (the adaptation or learning of both the plant model and the controller parameters) there are several error signals that may be used for adjusting these parameters. As in Jordan and Rumelhart (1992), several errors are defined in table 7.1. (If the reference model is used, the value y_d should be replaced with the output value of the reference model y_{ref}.)

Table 7.1
Definition of Errors

Controller error	$e_1 = \hat{u}_d - \hat{u}$
Prediction error	$e_2 = y - \hat{y}$
Performance error	$e_3 = y_d - y$
Predicted performance error	$e_4 = y_d - \hat{y}$

Other researchers (Psaltis, Sideris, and Yamamura 1988; Widrow and Walach 1996; Saerens and Soquet 1991; Jordan and Rumelhart 1992) use different approaches in order to find the error signal term that can be used to train the controller. Psaltis et al. (1988) make use of the performance error e_3 modified by the plant Jacobian to train the controller. Saerens and Soquet (1991) use a similar approach when using the performance error e_3, but unlike Psaltis et al., they multiply e_3 by the sign of the plant Jacobian only. Jordan and Rumelhart (1992), in their distal teacher method, differ appreciably from the preceding two approaches in using the Jacobian of the plant model and not the one of the real plant. They discuss the application of three errors in training of the plant model and controller. For plant forward model learning, they use the prediction error e_2 (which is the usual practice in identification of unknown systems), and for controller learning, they propose either the use of performance error e_3 or predicted performance error e_4.

In the approaches proposed by Widrow and his colleagues (Widrow and Walach 1996; performance error e_3 for controller training is used. As far as the structure of the whole control system is concerned, they use different structures depending upon whether the plant is a nonminimum phase and whether there is a need for noise canceling. The adaptive neural networks in Widrow's approach are primarily of the FIR (finite impulse response) filter structure. In the ABC approach sented here, the IIR (infinite impulse response) structure is typically used.

The ABC structure originated from the preceding structures with a few basic and important differences. The estimate of the desired control signal u_d can be calculated, and an error (delta) signal, as found in the distal teacher approach, is not needed. For ABC of linear systems, the calculation of u_d is straightforward. The forward model NN$_2$ is given as

$$\hat{y}(k+1) = \sum_{i=1}^{N} w_{2,i} \cdot x_{2,i} = \mathbf{w}_2^T \cdot \mathbf{x}_2, \tag{7.8}$$

where n is the order of the model, $N = 2n$, and x_2 is an input vector to NN$_2$ composed of present and previous values of u and y. For the calculation of the desired value $\hat{u}_d$, this equation should be rearranged with respect to the input of the neural network NN$_2$:

$$\hat{u}_d(k)$$
$$= \left(\frac{y_d(k+1) - w_{2,1}y_d(k) - , \ldots, - w_{2,n}y_d(k-n+1) - w_{2,n+2}\hat{u}(k-1) - , \ldots, - w_{2,2n}\hat{u}(k-n+1)}{w_{2,n+1}} \right). \tag{7.9}$$

Therefore, when applied to the control of linear systems, the calculation of the control signal u_d using (7.9) is similar to the predictive (deadbeat) controller approach. In the calculation of the best estimates of the desired control signal $\hat{u}_d(k)$ to the plant and to NN_2, the desired output values of the system $y_d(k + 1), y_d(k), \ldots, y_d(k - n)$ are used. It is interesting to note that instead of using the present and previous *desired* values, one can use the present and previous *actual plant outputs* $y(k), \ldots, y(k - n)$. This second choice of variables is a better one. (Kecman, Vlačić, and Salman (1999) give a detailed analysis of various controller algorithms.)

In the case of nonlinear systems control, the calculation of the desired control signal u_d that corresponds to the desired output from the plant y_d is a much more involved task. For *monotonic* nonlinearities (for one-to-one-mapping of plant inputs u into its outputs y), the control signal u_d can be calculated by an *iterative algorithm* that guarantees the finding of the proper u_d for any desired y_d.

This iterative (on-line) algorithm is the most important result in the ABC algorithm. Two other alternative approaches to the calculation of the desired u_d were investigated by Rommel (1997).

Iterative Calculation of u_d with Steepest Descent Gradient Method for Nonlinear Plants   Given y_d, the desired value u_d can be calculated by using a standard (iterative) steepest descent method, which basically represents a gradient search algorithm. Note that NN_2 is a NARMAX model as given in (7.4) or (7.5). The *series-parallel* model is rewritten as

$$\hat{y}(k + 1) = f\{y(k), \ldots, y(k - n); u(k), \ldots, u(k - n)\}. \tag{7.10}$$

If the function f of an identified plant model is a monotone increasing or decreasing one, then this NARMAX model represents a one-to-one mapping of the desired control signal u_d (and corresponding previous values of u and y) into the desired y_d.

Now, the basic idea of an adaptive backthrough calculation of u_d for any given y_d is the same as in the linear case. But unlike the linear example, where the solution is given by (7.9), in the case of a *general nonlinear model*, which is represented by NN_2, it is no longer possible to express u_d explicitly. Therefore, the solution should be obtained by some numerical iterative procedure. Here, the use of a standard gradient algorithm is proposed.

PROPOSITION   In the case of monotonic nonlinearity, it is always possible to find the desired control signal u_d to any desired degree of accuracy by using a *sufficiently small* optimization step of the gradient optimization method.

Proof   A proof follows from the standard properties of gradient optimization algorithms. Having NN_2 as a NARMAX model (7.10), define the function

$$e(k) = y(k+1) - f = 0, \tag{7.11}$$

and the problem to solve is to find $u_d(k)$ for known $y_d(k+1)$. Note that all past values of y and u that appear in f are known, and the objective is to find the root $u_d(k)$ of (7.11). This one-dimensional search problem is solved by finding the minimum of the function

$$E = e(k)^2. \tag{7.12}$$

Thus, the problem of finding the root of the nonlinear equation (7.11) is transformed into the minimization problem of equation (7.12). In this specific case of monotonic mapping f, the "hypersurface" E is a convex function having a known minimum $E(u_d) = 0$. For a given $y_d(k+1)$ and known past values of y and u, the root u_d represents the mapping f^{-1} of the known point from a $2n$-dimensional space into a one-dimensional space $\Re^{2n} \to \Re$. For a monotonic nonlinear mapping

$$f\{y(k), \ldots, y(k-n); u(k), \ldots, u(k-n)\},$$

the solution u_d is unique and can be obtained by any one-dimensional search technique. Here, a massive random search is combined with a gradient method. (The solution in the case of nonmonotonic functions is the subject of current research.) ∎

Figure 7.7 demonstrates the geometry of the procedure for the simplest case of an NN representing an $\Re \to \Re$ mapping and having two neurons with Gaussian activation function only. The graphs on the left of the figure show a convex function

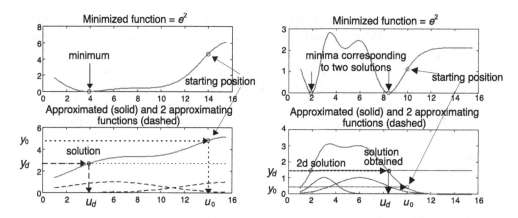

Figure 7.7
Iterative calculation of u_d with a gradient method. *Top*, graphs show the shapes of the cost function. *Bottom left*, monotonic nonlinear function. *Bottom right*, nonmonotonic nonlinear function.

$E = e^2$ for a monotonic nonlinear function f, and the graphs on the right show the solutions for a nonmonotonic nonlinear mapping f. The mathematics in the case of nonlinear dynamic systems is much more involved and without great hope for graphical presentation. In the case of the lowest (first)-order dynamic system, graphical representation is possible, but only the numerical part of the backthrough calculation of u_d is given here.

For a first-order dynamic nonlinear discrete system, the output $\hat{y}$ from a neural network NN_2 can be calculated as follows:

$$\hat{y} = \sum_{k=1}^{K} w_k \cdot \exp\left(-\frac{1}{2}\left(\left[\frac{(\hat{u} - c_{\hat{u},k})^2}{\sigma_{\hat{u},k}^2}\right]\left[\frac{\hat{y}^{\text{old}} - c_{\hat{y},k})^2}{\sigma_{\hat{y},k}^2}\right]\right)\right), \tag{7.13}$$

where K denotes the number of HL neurons and the use of the circumflex denotes that all variables of NN_2 are estimates. c and σ denote the centers and standard deviations of the Gaussian activation function.

To find the estimate of the desired control signal $\hat{u}_d$ for a given desired NN output y_d, solve the following nonlinear equation:

$$e = y_d - \sum_{k=1}^{K} w_k \cdot \exp\left(-\frac{1}{2}\left(\left[\frac{(\hat{u} - c_{\hat{u},k})^2}{\sigma_{\hat{u},k}^2}\right]\left[\frac{(\hat{y}^{\text{old}} - c_{\hat{y},k})^2}{\sigma_{\hat{y},k}^2}\right]\right)\right) = 0. \tag{7.14}$$

The solution will be found by minimizing the function $E = e(k)^2$. A minimum $E = 0$ will be achieved by the following gradient optimization rule

$$\hat{u} = \hat{u} - \eta \frac{\partial E}{\partial \hat{u}}. \tag{7.15}$$

From the chain rule for the expression $\dfrac{\partial E}{\partial \hat{u}}$ there follows

$$\frac{\partial E}{\partial \hat{u}} = \frac{\partial E}{\partial e}\frac{\partial e}{\partial \hat{y}}\frac{\partial \hat{y}}{\partial \hat{u}} = -2(y_d - \hat{y})\frac{\partial \hat{y}}{\partial \hat{u}}. \tag{7.16}$$

The derivative $\dfrac{\partial \hat{y}}{\partial \hat{u}}$ follows as

$$\frac{\partial \hat{y}}{\partial \hat{u}} = \sum_{k=1}^{K} w_k \cdot \exp\left(-\frac{1}{2}\left(\left[\frac{(\hat{u} - c_{\hat{u},k})^2}{\sigma_{\hat{u},k}^2}\right]\left[\frac{(\hat{y}^{\text{old}} - c_{\hat{y},k})^2}{\sigma_{\hat{y},k}^2}\right]\right)\right)\left(-\frac{(\hat{u} - c_{\hat{u},k})}{\sigma_{\hat{u},k}^2}\right). \tag{7.17}$$

Before starting the calculation of the root u_d using this gradient procedure, a massive search for u that is closest to the desired u_d is usually useful. Then the iterative calculation of u is continued until the error is below some prescribed limit $E_{\min}$. If this error limit is reached, the calculated value $\hat{u}$ is equal to the estimate of the desired control signal $\hat{u}_d$.

This iterative method works very well for monotonic nonlinearities. If the function is not monotonic, the inverse function is ambiguous for every y_d, and for a single desired output y_d several solutions for the desired control signal u_d can be obtained. In such a case this method will always find one out of -many possible solutions, which may not be the best solution. Some additional assumptions, or some constraints on the character of the solution for u_d, can ensure the calculation of the best control signal u_d. One possible limitation for very fast processes may be the calculations of u_d in real time. (The method may be a time-consuming one, and this may be critical because the value $\hat{u}_d$ has to be calculated within each iteration step.) Note, however, that there is no danger of getting trapped at a local minimum in the case of the nonmonotonic nonlinear function f, because it is known that for the correct solution u_d the error E must be equal to zero. (Because of lack of space, no specifics details are given here. Instead, the performance of ABC will be demonstrated in a number of examples.)

One of the additional important features of ABC is that output layer weights adaptation is strictly based on the RLS algorithm, though any other established NN learning algorithm, for example, first-order gradient EBP, may be used.

ABC uses different error signals for forward plant model (NN_2) learning and for controller adaptation (NN_1). A prediction error e_2 is used for the training of NN_2, and the controller error e_1 is used for the adaptation of the controller NN_1. *All previous methods do not use e_1 in combination with a forward plant model during learning at all.* This is an interesting advantage, and it seems a powerful novelty, because there is *no direct* influence of plant output disturbance on the learning of controller weights as in the distal teacher procedure from Jordan and Rumelhart (1992). Theoretically, it is clear that in linear systems, for any Gaussian disturbance at the output (provided that one has an infinitely long learning time, the orders of the plant model and of the real plant are equal, and the training signal u is rich enough and uncorrelated with noise), there will be no influence from noise at all, and the controller will perfectly produce the desired u_d.

Let us consider the performance of ABC for a number of different systems. First, in a *linear third-order nonminimum phase* oscillatory system it is demonstrated that ABC, in the linear case, when the orders of the plant and plant model (or emulator NN_2) are the same and without noise, results in perfect *adaptive poles-zeros canceling* (example 7.1). In the presence of uncorrelated noise, perfect canceling will be

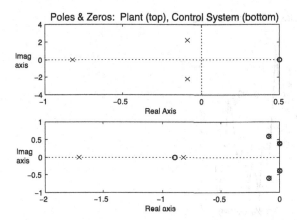

Figure 7.8
Perfect poles-zeros canceling by ABC. Sampling rate was $2.25s$. Plant model (emulator NN_2) was of third order, too. The resulting controller (NN_1) perfectly cancels the poles of the system.

achieved after a longer training time. The larger the noise, the longer the learning should take. Example 7.2 presents the capabilities of ABC with *mismatched model orders* of a plant and of an emulator NN_2. Here, the plant is a seventh-order linear system, and both NNs are second-order IIR filters. Example 7.3 shows the results of ABC in a *monotonic nonlinear first-order plant* (one-to-one mapping of the plant).

Example 7.1 Consider the ABC of a third-order nonminimum phase linear system given by the transfer function

$$G(s) = \frac{s - 0.5}{s^3 + s^2 + 5s + 4}.$$

The results are shown in figure 7.8. Thus, when the order of plant and NN model are equal, the ABC ensures perfect canceling of the system's poles. ∎

Example 7.2 Consider the ABC of a seventh-order plant using a second-order model (NN_2) and a controller (NN_1). Both networks are IIR filters.

The plant is a stable linear system without zeros and with poles at $[-1, -2, -5, -8, -10, -12, -15]$. Plant gain $K_{plant} = 0.5$. Additive output measurement noise during training $n_2 = 5\%$. Note the extremely large errors at the beginning of learning and very good performance at the end of learning (fig. 7.9). After only 750 learning steps, ABC performs well. It tracks desired y_d with a settling time $\sim 2s$ (fig. 7.9, bottom graph). The settling time of a seventh-order plant is $\sim 7s$. Sampling rate is $1.75s$.

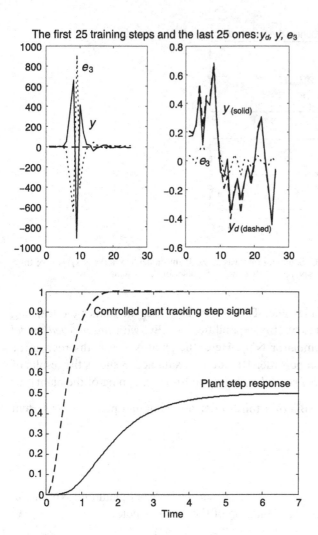

Figure 7.9
Top, desired output y_d, actual plant output y, and error $e_3 = y_d - y$ in the first 25 and the last 25 learning steps. *Bottom*, tracking of the unit step input signal without a controller (solid) and with a controller (dashed). Noise $n_2 = 5\%$.

At the beginning of training, and because learning indeed started from the scratch, there are large discrepancies between the NN model and the real plant output (fig. 7.9, top graph). But after only a few hundred steps, the whole system has adjusted, and shows acceptable behavior. Thus, when the order of the emulator is lower than the one of the actual plant (typical real-life situation) the ABC scheme performs well. It is robust with respect to unmodeled plant dynamics as well as additive measurement noise. ∎

Example 7.3 A nonlinear first-order dynamic plant given by the following difference equation is to be controlled by an ABC structure:

$$y(k + 1) = 0.1y(k) + \tan(u(k))$$

Both neural networks were RBF networks with 100, HL neurons having two-dimensional Gaussian activation functions each. (It should be mentioned that ABC worked well with networks having fewer HL neurons after optimization by the orthogonal least squares method; see section 5.3.3). All Gaussians were symmetrically placed and had fixed centers and width. In other words, HL weights were not subjects of learning.

During learning only the output layer weights were changed. Pretraining was done using 1,000 random uniformly distributed input signals y_d. After this off-line learning phase, two tests by previously unseen ramp signals were done. In both simulations, the hidden layer weights were not subjects of learning. In the first simulation (fig. 7.10, left graph) the OL weights were fixed, and in the second both networks operated in a learning mode by adapting the OL weights (fig. 7.10, right graph). The graphs in figure 7.10 show that the whole ABC structure can be successfully trained in on-line mode as long as the plant surface is monotonic.

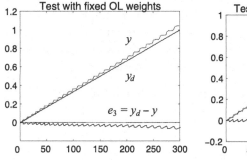 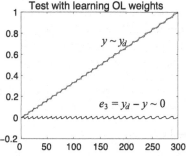

Figure 7.10
Test results with previously unseen ramp y_d (*left*) without on-line training and (*right*) with on-line training.

The top graph of figure 7.11 shows that an NN is a good model of this nonlinear plant. There is no big difference between the actual plant surface and the one modeled by NN_2. Note that all the trajectories of the controlled plant lie on this surface. The graphs in figure 7.11 are obtained by implementing off-line learning first. For nonlinear systems this pretraining of both networks is necessary. The ABC scheme with two networks performs well when faced with monotonic nonlinear plants.   ■

All former results were obtained using an ABC structure comprising two networks, as shown in figure 7.6. This structure is inherited from previous approaches, and it is directly related to classical EBP learning. The task of a network NN_1, which acts as a controller, is to learn the inverse dynamics of the controlled plant. Having been properly trained and after receiving the desired plant output signal y_d, NN_1 should be able to produce the best control signal u_d that would drive the plant to output this desired y_d. However, ABC learning is different from an EBP algorithm. Note that in an ABC algorithm the best control signal u_d is calculated in each operating step and is used for the adaptation of an NN_1's weights so that this controller can produce an output signal u, which should be equal or very close to the u_d. Thus, there is a great deal of redundancy, and it seems as though both the structure of the whole control system and the learning can be halved.

Having calculated the signal u_d, the controller network NN_1 is not needed any longer. An ABC structure with only one NN that simultaneously acts as a plant model and as a controller (inverse plant model) is shown in figure 7.12.

The performance of an ABC scheme with one NN is superior to the structure comprising two networks as given in figure 7.6. The redundant part of the training and of the utilization of NN_1 is avoided here, and this contributes to overall efficiency. This is demonstrated in the following examples.

Example 7.4 shows that for time-invariant plants an ABC perfectly tracks any desired signal, and that ABC can cope with nonlinear time-variant plants as well, which is one of the toughest problems in the control field. Example 7.5 shows a series of simulation results of ABC performance while controlling nonlinear plants described by nonmonotonic mappings. Both examples use first-order systems only, for the sake of the graphical visualization of the results obtained.

Example 7.4   A nonlinear first-order dynamic plant is to be controlled by an ABC scheme comprising one network only:

$$y(k) = \frac{y(k-1)}{1 + y^2(k-1)} + u^3(k-1).$$

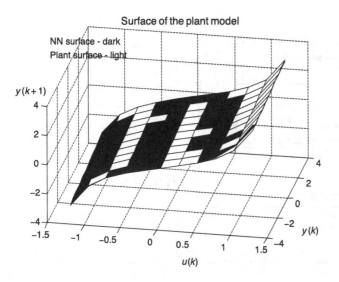

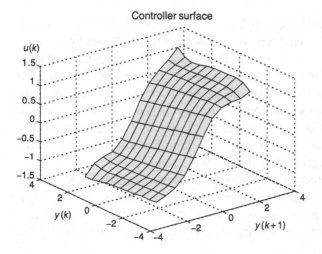

Figure 7.11
Top, modeling of a nonlinear plant by NN_2. *Bottom*, modeling of its inverse by NN_1, or controller.

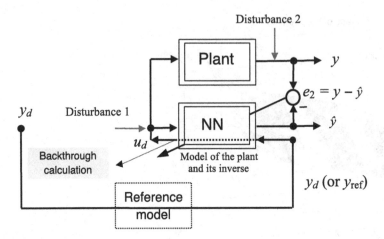

Figure 7.12
Neural (or fuzzy) network–based ABC scheme with one network that simultaneously acts as a plant model and as a controller (inverse plant model).

A neural network that simultaneously acts as a plant model and as its controller comprises 39 neurons in a hidden layer. Basis functions in all HL neurons are two-dimensional Gaussians with the same covariance matrix $\Sigma = \mathrm{diag}(0.2750, 0.0833)$, with positions determined by an orthogonal least squares selection procedure (Orr 1996). The NN was pretrained using 1,000 data pairs. The training input signal was a uniformly distributed random signal. (Note that the ABC control structure is much simpler than the one found in Narendra and Parthasarathy (1990). They used two NNs for identification and one as a controller. Each of their networks had 200 neurons. In the off-line training phase they used 25,000 training pairs.)

After the training, a number of simulation runs showed very good performance of the ABC scheme while controlling this *time-invariant nonlinear* system. Figure 7.13 (left graph) shows the plant response while tracking input $y_d = \sin(2\pi k/25) + \sin(2\pi k/10)$. The plant response is indistinguishable from the desired trajectory. One can say that the tracking is perfect.

A much more complex task is controlling a *time-variant nonlinear* plant. There is no general theory or method for the adaptive control of nonlinear time-variant plants. These are very tough control problems. Here, the author presents initial results on how an ABC scheme copes with such plants without claiming to answer open questions in this field. In particular, problems of convergence or the stability of ABC with respect to a nonlinear time-variant plant are not discussed. Rather some light is cast on the performance of ABC under these conditions. (Note that the

Performance of the ABC scheme. No on-line learning.

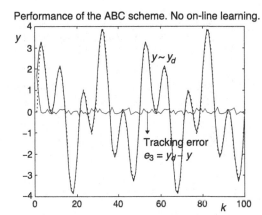
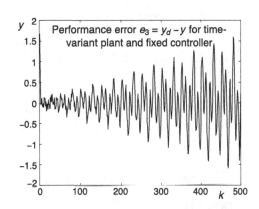

Figure 7.13
ABC. *Left*, perfect tracking in the case of a nonlinear monotonic time-invariant plant. *Right*, performance error for fixed pretrained NN controlling a time-variant plant. (The time-variant plant is halving its gain every 500 steps.)

problems of NN-based control of a time-variant plant are rarely discussed in the literature.)

Figure 7.13 (right graph) shows the error when a pretrained but fixed NN tries to control a fast-changing plant as given by

$$y(k) = \frac{y(k-1)}{1 + y^2(k-1)} + (1 - 0.001k)(u^3(k-1)).$$

This is a model of a plant which halves plant gain in 500 steps. Without any adaptation the performance error $e_3 = y_d - y$ increases rapidly (fig. 7.13, right graph).

Figure 7.14 shows e_3 in the case of the on-line adaptation of a neural network. Results are obtained by using a forgetting factor $\lambda = 0.985$. The adaptation and control process is a stable one, and in comparison to the error in figure 7.13, the final error in figure 7.14 is three times smaller. The process is a "hairy" one, and this problem of smoothing the adaptation procedure should be investigated more in the future. (Readers who are familiar with the identification of linear systems are well acquainted with the wild character of identification procedures. In the case of nonlinear system identification, one can only expect even rougher transients.)   ■

There are many open questions in the adaptive control of nonlinear time-variant processes. All important questions from linear domains are present here (dual character of adaptive controller, identifiability, persistency of excitation, and so on). One

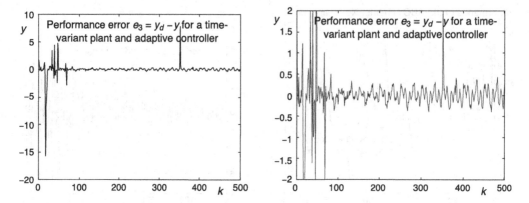

Figure 7.14
ABC. Performance error while controlling a time-variant plant with an on-line adaptation of output layer weights. Forgetting factor $\lambda = 0.985$. The scale in the right graph is the same as in figure 7.13, right graph.

specific question in nonlinear domains is the choice of the input signals for the pre-training phase. The standard binary signals used in linear systems identification are not good enough. During pretraining the entire region of a plant operation should be covered, and the best choice would be the use of uniformly distributed random signals. (Figures 7.15–7.17 (bottom graphs) show what parts of a plant dynamic surface are properly covered by using three different desired signals y_d.) Lack of space prevents detailed presentation of these important details here. Instead, a few more simulated results are shown of ABC controlling a nonmonotonic nonlinear plant. In this way, the reader will be able to understand at least a part of the important properties and specific features of an NN-based ABC of nonlinear dynamic systems.

Example 7.5 Consider the ABC of the nonlinear dynamic plant given by

$$y_{k+1} = \sin(y_k)\sin(u_k) - u_k/\pi. \tag{7.18}$$

The characteristic feature of this plant is that there is a one-to-many mapping of its inverse, that is, $u_k = f^{-1}(y_k, y_{k+1})$ is a nonmonotonic function. At the same time, the function $y_{k+1} = f(u_k, y_k)$ represents a one-to-one mapping. The NN is optimized by using a feedforward orthogonal least squares method. The basis functions in all neurons are two-dimensional Gaussians with the same covariance matrix $\Sigma = \text{diag}(0.0735, 0.1815)$. At the beginning of the RBF selection, there were 169 symmetrically placed neurons in a hidden layer (stars in fig. 7.18, top graph), and at the end 47 centers were chosen (dots in fig. 7.18, top graph). Such a network models

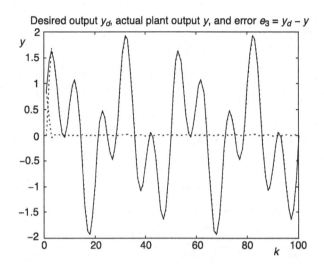

Desired output y_d, actual plant output y, and error $e_3 = y_d - y$

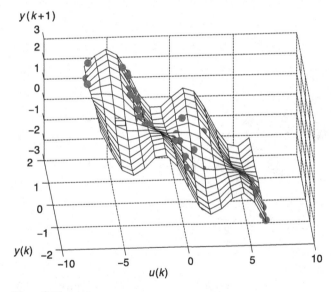

Figure 7.15

ABC. *Top*, perfect tracking of the desired signal $y_d = \sin(2\pi k/25) + \sin(2\pi k/10)$ for a time-invariant plant given in (7.18). Pretrained NN weights are fixed. No adaptation. *Bottom*, trajectory shown by dots lies on the surface described by (7.18).

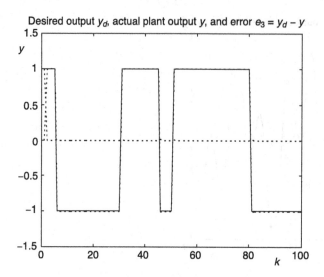

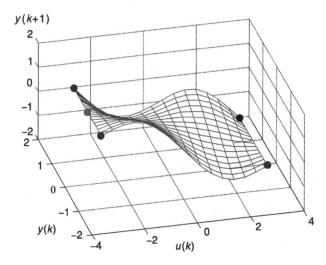

Figure 7.16

ABC. *Top*, perfect tracking of the desired rectangular signal for a time-invariant plant given in (7.18). Pretrained NN weights are fixed. No adaptation. *Bottom*, Trajectory shown by dots lies on the surface described by (7.18).

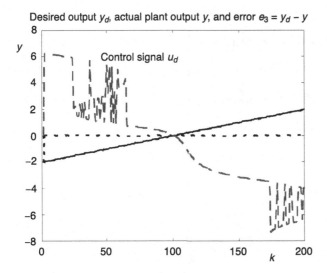

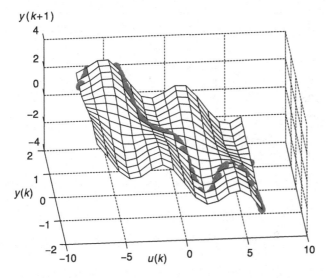

Figure 7.17
ABC. *Top*, perfect tracking of a desired ramp signal $[-2, 2]$ for a time-invariant plant given in (7.18). Pre-trained NN weights are fixed. No adaptation. Control signal (dashed curve). *Bottom*, trajectory shown by dots lies on, or "sneaks through," the surface described by (7.18).

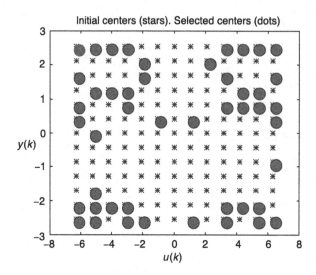

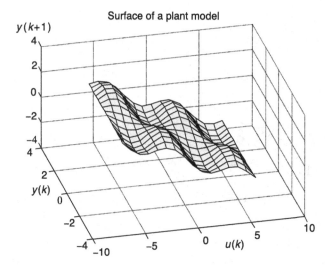

Figure 7.18
Top, initial choice (stars) and final choice (dots) of the centers of radial basis functions. *Bottom*, the non-monotonic surface of a first-order dynamic plant.

the plant very well (fig. 7.18, bottom graph). Note that this structure corresponds to the fuzzy logic model with a rule basis comprising 47 rules.   ∎

Note the wild dynamics of the control signal u_d in the nonmonotonic part of a nonlinear surface. This is a consequence of the unconstrained iterative design algorithm, as given by (7.13)–(7.17) and shown in figure 7.7 (right graph). Simply, without any constraint, the algorithm uses one out of the two possible control signals u_d. This results in perfect tracking but with a wild actuator signal u_d. It is relatively easy to smooth this control signal u_d by imposing constraints on its behavior. Out of the two or more solution control signals u_d, the simplest to choose is the one that is closest to the previous actuator signal u.

7.2   Financial Time Series Analysis

The objective of this section is to give a brief introduction to the application of NNs in forecasting share market or any other (weather, biomedical, engineering, financial) time series. Basic concepts are discussed, and a (more or less) successful application involving prediction of New Zealand stock exchange (NZSE) indices is presented. One of the strengths of NNs, SVMs, FLMs that has been identified is that they can approximate any nonlinear dependency to any desired degree of accuracy. However, the basic question when applying these modeling tools to financial time series is whether there is any dependency at all. The share market behaves wildly; it cycles from coherence to chaotic activity in an unpredictable manner. Experts disagree about the fundamental phenomena in the share market. Some economists say there are no dependencies at all because the financial market has random behavior. Others say the financial market shows definite patterns and these patterns can be exploited to generate excess profits, although this may take considerable experience to achieve.

Such questions are not considered here. Rather, the objective is to use recorded stock market data to find whether there are any functional relations in a financial market. Although this approach may seem to be a "brute force" methodology, there has been an upsurge of interest in new promising techniques for forecasting in recent years. This was made possible by the arrival of fast powerful computers as well as new nonlinear techniques of learning from data. With NNs and SVMs many professionals have tried to extract nonlinear relations from financial market indices to develop profitable strategies. If these were truly possible, it would mean a challenge to the weak efficient market hypothesis held true by economists. What follows relies entirely on the results of an application of RBF networks to New Zealand share market prediction as given by Shah (1998).

Table 7.2
Some Factors Affecting the Performance of the Share Market

Economic Factors	Seasonal Factors	Miscellaneous Factors
Population growth	Tax payments	Market sentiment
Balance of trade	Budget time	Industry trading
Government policy	Annual reports	Company expectations
Budget policy		Take-overs
Credit policy		New flotations
Import controls		Company failures
Wage settlements		Mineral discoveries
Interest rates		Financial advisers
International conditions		Media

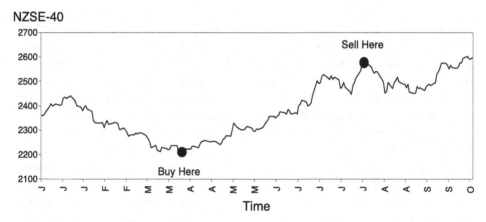

Figure 7.19
Optimal buy and sell times for NZSE-40 from January to October 1997.

The seemingly random character of share market time series is due to many factors that influence share prices. Some relevant factors are shown in table 7.2. Financial market modeling is a difficult task because of the ever-changing dynamics of the fundamental driving factors. Because of many different and partly uncontrollable factors, a typical financial time series has a noisy appearance (see fig. 7.19). There is evidence to suggest that financial markets behave like complex systems in the sense that they are partly *random* and partly *ordered*. Random systems are chaotic and unpredictable, whereas ordered mathematical rules and models are capable of capturing ordered systems. The discussion here exploits this ordered part of a share market.

There is a simple idea and a law of survival for all participants in share market trades that can be reduced to "Buy low and sell high." These two significant trading points for NZSE-40 are given in figure 7.19. However, the basic problem for any stockbroker in achieving the goal of buying low and selling high is to predict or forecast these significant points. Stockbrokers are faced with the problem of investing funds for clients so that the return from the investment is maximized while the risk is kept to a minimum. Usually an increase in risk means higher returns, and often clients are only prepared to gamble with a risk that they can afford to lose.

There are two basic approaches to share market prediction, to the forecasting of the two significant points: fundamental analysis and experimentation. Fundamental analysis is the basic tool for economists in valuing assets. In this approach, the market is assumed to be an ordered system, and each company is characterized by its fundamental factors, such as the company's strategic plan, new products, anticipated gain, long- and short-term optimism, to determine share value compared to its market price. Accounting ratios and the latest measures of earnings to show the company's value have become fundamental factors in this analysis. However, this approach often leads to different conclusions by different economists, pointing up the uncertainties in the arbitrary measures used as the basis of this approach.

A more complex and arguably more powerful approach in valuing assets is the experimental (technical) one, in which statistical and other expert systems such as NNs, SVMs, and fuzzy logic inference systems are involved. This approach uses historical data or expert knowledge to make predictions.

To represent a dynamic system (and time series belong to this class), a NARMAX model is used (see section 7.1). A financial time series is represented by the following NARMAX model:

$$y(k + 1) = f\{y(k), \ldots, y(k - n); u(k), \ldots, u(k - m)\}, \tag{7.19}$$

or,

$$y_{k+1} = f(y_k, y_{k-1}, y_{k-2}, \ldots, y_{k-n}, u_k, u_{k-1}, u_{k-2}, \ldots, u_{k-m}), \tag{7.20}$$

where y_k and u_k are the input and the output signals at instant k, and y_{k-i} and u_{k-j}, $i = 1, \ldots, n$, $j = 1, \ldots, m$, represent the past values of these signals. The basic input and output signals are used here to model NZSE-40.

The nonlinear function f from (7.20) is very complex and generally unknown. The whole idea in the application of the RBF NNs is to try to approximate f by using known Gaussian functions. The graphical representation of any time series identification is given in figure 7.2. Here the series-parallel scheme (7.19), or (7.20) is applied.

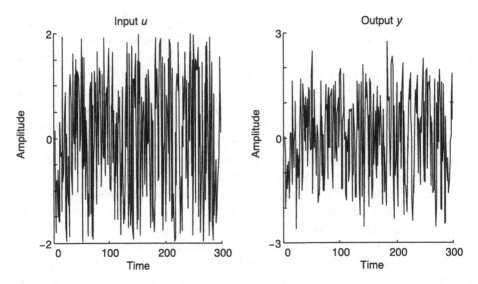

Figure 7.20
White noise input signal u and second-order linear plant output response y with 5% noise.

Before a nonlinear NZSE-40 time series is modeled, let us consider the performance of an RBF network in modeling and predicting the behavior of a linear second-order system that is known to us but not to the RBF network. The unknown dependency between the input and the output is given by the transfer function

$$G(s) = \frac{2s + 1}{3s^2 + 2s + 1}.$$

This transfer function can be represented in a discrete-time domain (sampling time is $2s$) as

$$G(z) = \frac{0.9921z^{-1} - 0.3318z^{-2}}{1 - 0.6033z^{-1} + 0.2636z^{-2}}.$$

This z-transfer function can be rewritten as the *difference* equation (ARMA model)[3]

$$y_k = 0.9921u_{k-1} - 0.3318u_{k-2} + 0.6033y_{k-1} - 0.2636y_{k-2}.$$

The input signal to this plant is a white noise and output response is polluted with 5% noise. Both signals are shown in figure 7.20. They are the only information for the RBF network about the process. Using these two data sets, the RBF network is to model the unknown system dynamics and predict the response to the previously

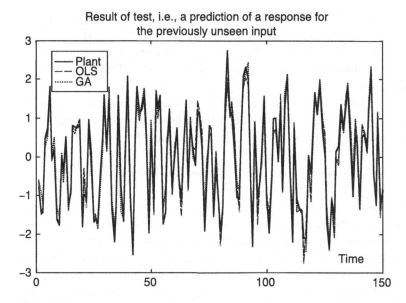

Figure 7.21
Identification and prediction of a second-order linear plant response by using an RBF model with an orthogonal least squares selection method and genetic algorithm parameter optimization.

unseen input. During learning, the HL weights were fixed, and two techniques for RBF subset selection were used: orthogonal least squares (OLS) and a genetic algorithm (GA). Note that the difference equation represents an $\Re^4 \to \Re^1$ mapping. This means that the Gaussian basis functions are four-dimensional bells.

The result of a prediction is shown in figure 7.21, and it illustrates the good identification capabilities of an RBF network trained by both OLS and GA. Here, the GA optimization resulted from only 25 Gaussian basis functions for a test error of 0.2035, whereas the OLS method used 60 Gaussian basis functions for a test error of 0.1992. Computing time on a Pentium 233 MHz PC for a GA optimization was 421 seconds, and the OLS method took 334 seconds.

Figure 7.21 shows that both the OLS and GA subset selections almost perfectly model the unknown plant. Having fewer RBF bells in the network decreases both the complexity of the network and the training time. However, the computing time may still cause difficulties in modeling real-time series that typically contain large data sets. This is always the case when modeling financial time series.

Note that an RBF network (which is a nonlinear modeling tool) was used for modeling a linear system here. Had a single linear neuron like the one shown in figure

3.18 been applied for modeling this linear second-order plant, the training would have been much faster and a better model would have been obtained. However, the RBF network did not know that the actual plant dynamics were linear, and figure 7.21 shows that the nonlinear RBF network can also successfully model linear dynamic dependencies.

Let us go back to the world of NNs and SVMs—to the modeling and forecasting of nonlinear dependencies. Here, in modeling a financial time series, it seems likely that there is an underlying (nonlinear) function and that the RBF network can grasp this dependency.

To provide a comprehensive measurement of price trends for all equity securities listed on the market, the NZSE gross and capital indices were developed in 1986. The indices had a base value of 1000 on July 1, 1986, and included all New Zealand listed and quoted ordinary shares. NZSE-40, which covers 40 of the largest and most liquid stocks listed and quoted, weighted by the number of securities on issue, is the main public market index. (The NZSE-10 index comprises selected securities of the top ten companies and is used as the basis for the NZSE-10 Capital Share Price Index Futures Contract offered by the New Zealand Futures and Options Exchange. This index reflects the movement of prices in the selected securities and accounts for the majority of the turnover. Other indices monitored by the NZSE are the NZSE-30 and the NZSE-SCI for smaller companies. Here the objective is to model and predict the NZSE-40 index.)

The share market index is a good example of a time series system that is difficult to predict. The factors affecting the market are many (see table 7.2), and modeling all these factors at once is well out of reach for even today's supercomputers. Hence there is a need to select the most relevant factors for a given time series. This is (possibly) the most important preprocessing part and relies heavily on expert knowledge. In this section, the most influential factors that affect the New Zealand share market are used to create a model of the capital NZSE-40 indices.

MLPs and RBF networks are capable of creating models of a system from the given inputs and outputs. However, the network model is only as good as the training it goes through. Therefore, it is extremely important to select suitable training data carefully. Ideally, the greater the number of inputs or share market factors included, the more complete the model becomes. However, an increase in the number of inputs leads to an exponential increase in model complexity. Since it is impossible to do the required complex computations even with the most powerful computers, the number of inputs relative to the number of training data is very much restricted. Only the essential factors are used as training inputs and the final share market indices as outputs during training of the share market models.

The factors thought by fund managers at Merrill Lynch and BZW Investment Bank to be most influential to the New Zealand share market, including the NZSE-40 indices, in order of merit are

1. Historical NZSE-40 data
2. Overseas financial markets
3. Currency movements
4. Economic activity

The past performance, or the history, of the NZSE-40 index is important in understanding and predicting future indices. This is the autoregressive part in (7.20). Because of the size of the NZSE relative to other leading financial markets of the world, the NZSE is very much dependent on overseas share market movements. The overseas markets modeled by Shah (1998) are the U.S. S&P 500 and the Australian All-Ords. Their relationships to the NZSE-40 are illustrated in figure 7.22. Fig 7.22b, for example, shows the strongest correlation between NZSE-40 and Australian All-Ords.

To maintain external economic stability the currency movement in New Zealand is controlled by the Reserve Bank. The exchange rate influences the trading range of the New Zealand dollar, which is adjusted to match increasing or decreasing interest rates. The Trade Weighted Index (TWI) and the New Zealand to United States (NZ-US) exchange rate are also used as inputs for modeling and representing the currency movements within and outside of New Zealand. Past relationships between the NZSE-40 and TWI and NZ-US exchange rates are also presented in figure 7.22.

Economic activity is measured by Gross Domestic Product (GDP), which is the value of all products produced in the country during a year, as well as the 90-Day Bill Rate and 10-Year Bond Rate. A short-term view of interest rates is given by the 90-Day Rate, whereas the 10-Year Rate gives a longer-term view. The model for the NZSE-40 indices here uses the 90-Day Rate and the 10-Year Rate because the GDP is released only every three months. The relationships between the NZSE-40 and the 90-Day Rate and 10-Year Rates are also shown in figure 7.22.

The network model inputs are some more or less astute selection and combination of the factors discussed, because modeling of the NZSE-40 indices is experimental, that is, from the recorded data. It is not known in advance which factor is actually the most influential, and it is merely the performance of different models that can provide evidence of any existing level of dependency. Predictions obtained by models with different network structures or complexity are used to explore this unknown domain bridging the gap between reality and speculation.

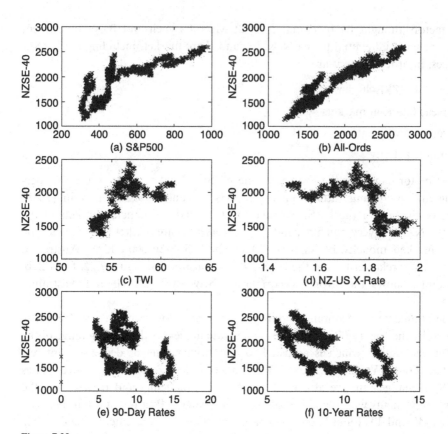

Figure 7.22
Relationships between NZSE-40 stock indices and other factors affecting the New Zealand share market.

A general structure of an RBF network for an NZSE-40 prediction is shown in figure 7.23. Both data preprocessing and features extraction are important parts of any NN modeling. To improve the success and enhance the RBF network model of the share market, preprocessing is employed on the raw data. Leaving aside a detailed description of this preprocessing stage, one can state that the best results are obtained when a good compromise is made between

1. The number of factors as inputs to the model (order of the model)

2. The size of the training data

3. The number of basis functions for approximation

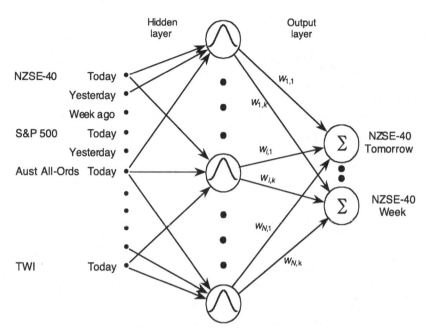

Figure 7.23
A typical RBF network for forecasting NZSE-40 indices with multiple inputs, N Gaussian bells in the hidden layer, and k outputs. Hidden layer weights are centers and covariance matrices that are fixed. Output layer weights w are subjects of learning. Not all connections are shown.

All these factors are used in simple autoregressive models and more complex, higher-order ARMA models by Shah (1998); only some of the results are shown here. The first simulation attempts were performed by applying the simplest second- and third-order autoregression models. These models assume that the system is dependent only on itself; in other words, they use only the autoregressive part of the input vector. The models are given as

$$y_k = f(y_{k-1}, y_{k-2}, y_{k-3}, \ldots, y_{k-n}),$$

where y in this case is the NZSE-40 index. The order of the system n is the number of previous NZSE-40 values used as inputs for the RBF network.

The two stages of modeling, namely, the training and the testing phase, are shown in figure 7.24. In the training stage, the recorded previous values of NZSE-40 and the selected inputs form the input vector to the RBF model. In the test or prediction phase, the input vector is formed of the previous values of selected inputs and the previous values of the actual NN predicted output $\hat{y}$.

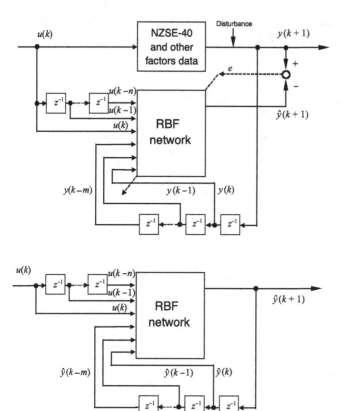

Figure 7.24
Typical RBF network structures for NZSE-40 index forecasting in a (*top*) training phase and (*bottom*) a
test or prediction phase.

It is hard to believe that simple, low-order autoregressive models can satisfactorily predict the NZSE-40 index. Indeed, the autoregressive modeling of only NZSE-40 capital indices did not give good results but at least provided a starting point for the many models and simulations performed by Shah (1998). The results from the second- and third-order autoregression models show that the RBF network is incomplete and needs other share market factors to be included in the model in order to satisfactorily model the NZSE-40 indices. However, there is enough correlation, even though the test results were poor, to encourage continuation of the search for an NZSE-40 model that can predict future indices more accurately or at least indicate any major trends that may lie ahead.

Results from two of Shah's reasonably good models follow.

Procedure and Results from Two Models of NZSE-40   Many complex higher-order models were designed. As mentioned, share market indices such as the S&P 500, the Australian All-Ords, TWI, NZ-US exchange rates, 90-Day Rate, and 10-Year Rate were considered to be the factors influencing share prices and share market indices. The fundamental and statistical analysis of these relationships is difficult, but RBF network modeling has the capability to extract relevant information in creating a model of the NZSE-40 indices using these factors.

Because of the experimental nature of these models, a structured search was performed, with the overseas share market indices modeled first and the New Zealand currency movements next. Past economic trends were also modeled using the 90-Day Rate and 10-Year Rate to find any dependencies between economic stability and the NZSE-40 index. Although these basic models may seem trivial, the extraction of relevant information from individual share market factors is the key to a successful final model. As emphasized earlier, it is always difficult to calculate how much and in what way a factor affects the final share market index, but NNs, including RBF networks, have the capability to solve this formidable task.

The objective of modeling different share market factors is to find the main factors in some order of merit based on model performance. A number of simulations were carried out, and the models presented here performed the best.

The TWI values were modeled in relation to the NZSE-40 index. Two previous TWI values, together with two previous values of the NZSE-40 index formed the network's input vector. Thus, the model is of the fourth order and is given as the following NARMA model:

$$y_k = f(y_{k-1}, y_{k-2}, u_{k-1}, u_{k-2}).$$

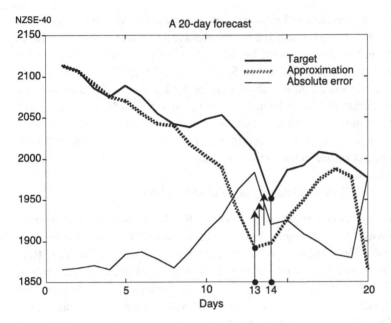

Figure 7.25
Fourth-order NARMA RBF network model of NZSE-40 indices using delayed values of NZSE-40 index and TWI. Graph shows a 20-day forecast.

Six hundred training data pairs containing 600 days' records

$$([y_{k-1}, y_{k-2}, u_{k-1}, u_{k-2}]^T, y_k)$$

were used during the training. Initially, at each second training data pair, five four-dimensional Gaussian bells with different covariance matrices were placed. This means that the OLS selection procedure started with 1,500 Gaussian bells. At the end of the OLS learning, 50 Gaussian bells were selected. The learning stage took 1 hour and 423 minutes on a Pentium 233 PC.

After training, 50 selected Gaussian bells produced an approximation to NZSE-40 with an error of 0.0587, which compared to previous models is small. However, the test on training data gave an error of 1114.5 and this is regarded as poor. This significant difference can be attributed to the length of the test as well as to overfitting of training data. Close fitting of training data during learning can cause small variances from the actual values to lead to an inaccurate result. On the other hand, this model gave a much better forecast than other models. The forecast for the next 20 days, including the actual NZSE-40 capital indices, is shown in figure 7.25. As marked by the arrows, the upward trend on day 14 was predicted a day earlier, exhibiting the good prediction ability of an RBF network.

In the previous model, the modeling or mapping is incomplete because only one factor (TWI) was used as a delayed input together with the autoregressive inputs of the NZSE-40 capital index. As mentioned earlier, the NZSE-40 index is affected by a number of factors, but modeling all these factors in one model is almost impossible. Not all the factors are known, and most cannot be measured, such as market sentiment and political unrest. The next RBF network combines more factors to model the NZSE-40 capital index.

A higher-dimensional model with five factors as inputs and the NZSE-40 index as an output was created using a sixth-order RBF model. In this model, u^{ov}, which is the average overseas share market index of the S&P 500 and All-Ords, plus the NZ-US exchange rate and the 90-Day Rate and 10-Year Rate were used to model the NZSE-40 capital index. As with the average overseas share market index, the 90-Day Bill Rate and the 10-Year Bond Rate formed a single input into the network by taking the average of the two rates:

$$u^{rt} = \frac{90\text{daybill} + 10\text{yearbond}}{2}.$$

The model used two delayed inputs each of the NZSE-40 index and u^{ov} and one input each of the NZ-US exchange rate u^{nzus} and u^{rt} to form the six-dimensional input vector to the RBF network that should represent the following nonlinear function:

$$y_k = f\left(y_{k-1}, y_{k-2}, u^{ov}_{k-1}, u^{ov}_{k-2}, u^{nzus}_{k-1}, u^{rt}_{k-1}\right).$$

Training of this model was carried out with 725 sets of input and output data representing the period between beginning of 1992 to middle of April 1995. Test data are for the period just after training to mid-May 1995. Thus, 725 training data pairs containing the records

$$\left(\left[y_{k-1}, y_{k-2}, u^{ov}_{k-1}, u^{ov}_{k-2}, u^{nzus}_{k-1}, u^{rt}_{k-1}\right]^{T}, y_k\right)$$

were used during learning. Seven six-dimensional Gaussian basis functions were initially placed at every third training data pair, giving a total of 1,687 bases for OLS selection. All Gaussian basis functions had standard shape factors in the range from 0.5 to 30 Δc_i, where Δc_i denotes the average distance between the data in each direction. This defines the covariance matrices. Therefore, standard covariances that use factor 30 give very wide Gaussian bells with a high degree of overlapping. This ensures adequate covering of any hyperspace or high-dimensional input space, such

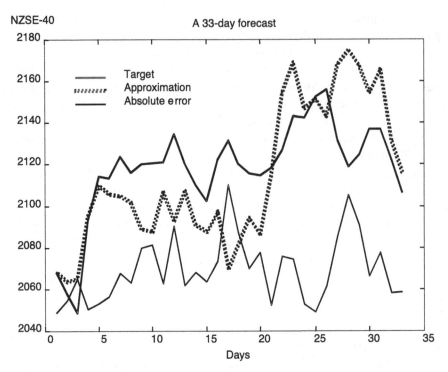

Figure 7.26
Forecasting results of NZSE-40 indices. The RBF network is a sixth-order NARMA model that uses two delayed NZSE-40 indices, two delayed average overseas share market indices, the NZ-US exchange rate, and the average of the 90-Day Rate and 10-Year Rates as inputs. Graph shows a 33-day forecast.

as in this six-input model. Wide Gaussian bells are required to provide satisfactorily smooth output mapping. At the end of the OLS learning, 100 Gaussian bells were selected. The learning took 9 hours and 21 minutes on a Pentium 233 MHz PC. Note the huge increase in computing time with respect to the previous case.

This model gave a much better forecast than other models. The forecast for the next 33 days, including the actual NZSE-40 capital indices, is shown in figure 7.26. The dotted line shows good trend anticipation even though the extent of appreciation or depreciation of the NZSE-40 index was not always perfectly modeled. Most of the trends are captured here, but any improvement in the model during training would enhance the performance of this forecast. Utilizing this forecast, an investor should buy in the first few days and sell after 20 days to extract reasonable returns in a short time.

Many other models did not perform very well. Such weaknesses are mainly attributable to the lack of training data. Only 765 data sets were available for the modeling. A lot more data are required for mapping such a high-dimensional hypersurface.

While the findings in this section are promising, it cannot be claimed that this approach would be successful in general. For simplicity, the models focused on NZSE-40 and its factors between 1990 and 1997, using OLS and GA for basis selection. Given enough computer capacity and time, a host of other strategies can be applied to these models to improve their performance, such as other identifiers in extraction of features from share market factors used by fund managers.

However, there is still reason to be cautiously optimistic about the heuristic adapted here, with a number of promising findings and directions for future research. Perhaps the most attractive result from the models is trend anticipation. Most models demonstrated reliable anticipation of upward and downward trend movement, even though the magnitude of these changes was not well emphasized. Therefore, the predictions must be looked at qualitatively rather than quantitatively.

7.3   Computer Graphics

Fundamental advances in computational power and new techniques of learning from examples have made possible the wide application of NNs' approximation power in the computer graphics domain. NNs can be applied successfully in the fields of computer graphics, vision, and animation. The basic idea in utilizing NN models for these tasks is to replace the tedious drawing of many similar pictures with approximations between training frames. Such an application in graphics is also known as *in-betweening* (Poggio and Girosi 1993). This section presents part of the results from Wang (1998). In particular, it describes how an RBF network can perform morphing tasks (between the human, horse, tiger, and monkey facial masks) as well as human figure animation and human facial expression and pose synthesis.[4] In addition, the application of RBF networks for synthesizing technical (e.g., mechanical and architectural) drawings is described.

Let us consider a simple example of in-betweening to clarify the whole procedure for motion synthesis using an RBF neural network. In figure 7.27 one triangle is placed between two rectangles, and the three shapes are taken as training pictures. The NN should draw as many pictures as needed between these three training frames. This is a classical approximation task. Each shape is defined by four feature points that define the shapes marked with circles. For the computational

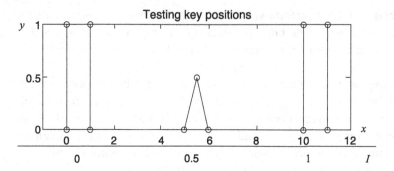

Figure 7.27
Training and test feature points for a simple one-dimensional in-betweening.

implementation, the first point is repeated as the last one, which results in five feature points.

The one-dimensional input learning domain is set to be $I = [0, 1]$, and the three shapes are placed at $I = [0, 0.5, 1]$, as shown in figure 7.27. The RBF network has one input I, three HL neurons placed at the three training data vectors, and ten output neurons corresponding to the (x, y) coordinates of the five feature points.

Training patterns $\mathbf{D}$ in matrix form and the design matrix $\mathbf{G}$ are as follows:

$$
\mathbf{D} = \begin{array}{cccccccccc} x_1 & y_1 & x_2 & y_2 & x_3 & y_3 & x_4 & y_4 & x_5 & y_5 \end{array}
$$

$$
\mathbf{D} = \begin{bmatrix} 0 & 0 & 1 & 0 & 1 & 1 & 0 & 1 & 0 & 0 \\ 5 & 0 & 6 & 0 & 5.5 & 0.5 & 5.5 & 0.5 & 5 & 0 \\ 10 & 0 & 11 & 0 & 11 & 1 & 10 & 1 & 10 & 0 \end{bmatrix} \begin{array}{l} \text{left rectangle} \\ \text{triangle} \\ \text{right rectangle} \end{array}
$$

$$
\mathbf{G} = \begin{bmatrix} 1.0000 & 0.9460 & 0.8007 \\ 0.9460 & 1.0000 & 0.9460 \\ 0.8007 & 0.9460 & 1.0000 \end{bmatrix}.
$$

At the learning stage, the RBF network weights are learned (calculated) from these three examples in the data matrix. Thus, the weights matrix $\mathbf{W}$ is obtained by multiplying $\mathbf{D}$ by the pseudoinverse of $\mathbf{G}$ (here, the matrix $\mathbf{G}$ is square, i.e., $\mathbf{G}^+ = \mathbf{G}^{-1}$) and

$$\mathbf{W} = \mathbf{G}^+\mathbf{D}$$

$$
= \begin{bmatrix} -0.66 & 0 & 4.23 & 0 & 46.99 & 47.66 & -43.43 & 47.66 & -0.66 & 0 \\ -41.23 & 0 & -49.47 & 0 & -130.89 & -89.66 & 40.19 & -89.66 & -41.23 & 0 \\ 49.53 & 0 & 54.41 & 0 & 97.18 & 47.66 & 6.76 & 47.66 & 49.53 & 0 \end{bmatrix}.
$$

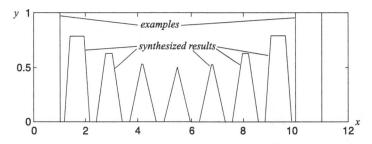

Figure 7.28
RBF network–generated results with three training and six in-between pictures.

At the synthesis stage, this weights matrix is used to generate as many as needed in-betweens from a newly assigned input vector. Thus, for example, if a new input vector is

$$\mathbf{I}_{new} = [0 \quad 0.1250 \quad 0.2500 \quad 0.3750 \quad 0.5000 \quad 0.6250 \quad 0.7500 \quad 0.8750 \quad 1.0000]$$

nine figures are obtained. Note that three out of these nine graphs should be the training frames because 0, 0.5, and 1 are part of the new input vector. This new input vector results in the RBF network output vector **o**, which contains the coordinates of the nine in-between shapes as follows:

$$\mathbf{o} = \begin{bmatrix} 0.0000 & 0 & 1.0000 & 0 & 1.0000 & 1.0000 & 0.0000 & 1.0000 & 0.0000 & 0 \\ 1.1630 & 0 & 2.1634 & 0 & 1.9512 & 0.7882 & 1.3752 & 0.7882 & 1.1630 & 0 \\ 2.3991 & 0 & 3.3993 & 0 & 3.0294 & 0.6304 & 2.7690 & 0.6304 & 2.3991 & 0 \\ 3.6861 & 0 & 4.6862 & 0 & 4.2191 & 0.5329 & 4.1533 & 0.5329 & 3.6861 & 0 \\ 5.0000 & 0 & 6.0000 & 0 & 5.5000 & 0.5000 & 5.5000 & 0.5000 & 5.0000 & 0 \\ 6.3147 & 0 & 7.3148 & 0 & 6.8477 & 0.5329 & 6.7819 & 0.5329 & 6.3147 & 0 \\ 7.6038 & 0 & 8.6040 & 0 & 8.2341 & 0.6304 & 7.9737 & 0.6304 & 7.6038 & 0 \\ 8.8406 & 0 & 9.8410 & 0 & 9.6289 & 0.7882 & 9.0528 & 0.7882 & 8.8406 & 0 \\ 10.0000 & 0 & 11.0000 & 0 & 11.0000 & 1.0000 & 10.0000 & 1.0000 & 10.0000 & 0 \end{bmatrix}.$$

The resulting graphs are shown in figure 7.28.

Next, consider the application of NNs to morphing tasks. Here, also, the inputs to the NN are the vectorized image representation. With this technique, information about the shape of an object is represented as a set of feature points that are identified in each training picture. This identification can be done manually or automatically. The vectorized representation is an ordered vector of image measurements, that is, the feature points have been enumerated $o_1, o_2, \ldots, o_N$ and the vector representation

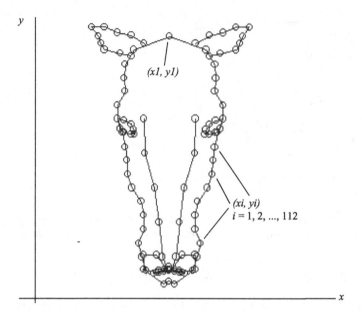

Figure 7.29
Feature detection of horse facial mask. The circles denote feature points.

first contains measurements from o_1, then o_2, and so on. The measurements of a feature include its (x, y) location, which defines the shape. The key part of this vectorized representation is that the features $o_1, o_2, \ldots, o_N$ are effectively identified across all training pictures being vectorized.

Figure 7.29 shows a horse facial mask, where 112 points are taken as feature points to represent the horse facial shape. These feature points are the important points in the mask, including eye, nose, mouth, ear, and base shape. Given the locations of features $o_1, o_2, \ldots, o_N$, the shape is represented by the vector $\mathbf{o}$ of length $2N$ consisting of the concatenation of x and y coordinate values as follows: $\mathbf{o} = \begin{bmatrix} x_1 & y_1 & x_2 & y_2 & \ldots & x_N & y_N \end{bmatrix}^T$.

7.3.1 One-Dimensional Morphing

The simplest use of the technique is to morph between two pictures or shapes. This is one-dimensional approximation in the sense that there is only one input—which can be thought of as degree of morph—that controls the relative contribution of merely two training pictures. Thus, the approximation network has in this case only one input and is trained using only two examples.

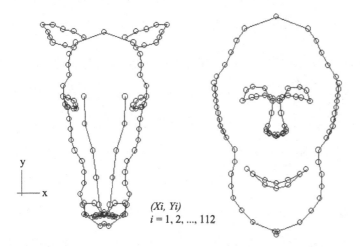

(X_i, Y_i)
$i = 1, 2, ..., 112$

Figure 7.30
Manually detected feature points (circles) in horse and monkey masks.

Figure 7.30 is an example of manually detected feature points from horse and monkey facial masks. Both pictures contain 112 related feature points. The RBF network is structured with only one input I (degree of morph), two Gaussian bells in HL, and 224 OL neurons (x and y coordinates of the 112 feature points), as shown in figure 7.31. The degree of morph is set to be between 0 and 1. At the learning stage, the RBFs network maps from input $I = [0, 1]$ to corresponding training picture feature points. At the second stage, the trained RBF network generates in-between pictures according to a given new input vector $\mathbf{I}_{new} = [0 \quad 0.333 \quad 0.667 \quad 1]$. These in-betweens are shown in figure 7.32. The two framed pictures of the horse and monkey are originally given as training pictures, and the two in-betweens are generated by the RBF network. The second picture, obtained by a degree of morph 33.3%, can be described as 33.3% monkey and 66.7% horse.

Figure 7.33 shows the moving paths of all training feature points in morphing from horse to monkey. It can be seen that morphing here is not simply traditional linear interpolation. Instead, the paths are smooth transients between examples, which may contribute to the final more realistic effect.

Five other one-dimensional morphing results are depicted in figure 7.34 (horse–tiger, horse–man, monkey–tiger, monkey–man, and tiger–man). The RBF networks have the same structure as in figure 7.31. The framed pictures are the training examples, and the RBF network generated the in-betweens.

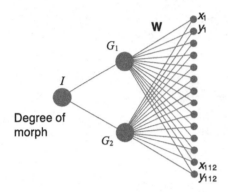

Figure 7.31
One-dimensional morphing RBF network structure with one input, two hidden layer neurons, and 224 outputs.

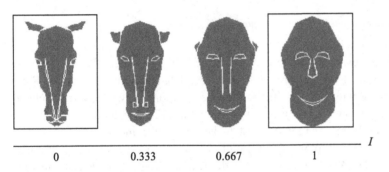

Figure 7.32
One-dimensional morphing from horse mask to monkey mask.

7.3.2 Multidimensional Morphing

The approximation/interpolation ability of an RBF network can be used to synthesize images in a multidimensional input space, too. Figure 7.35 shows the four training example frames of the facial masks and their position parameters in a two-dimensional input space. Here, $I_{\text{monkey}} = [0, 0]$, $I_{\text{tiger}} = [1, 0]$, $I_{\text{horse}} = [0, 1]$, $I_{\text{human}} = [1, 1]$. The learning stage is again a calculation of the weights that should ensure mapping from these input states I to RBF network output feature points. The trained RBF network is then used to generate novel in-between pictures for the new desired inputs. These inputs are the two-dimensional vectors. The network structure comprises two input neurons, four HL neurons, and 224 OL neurons.

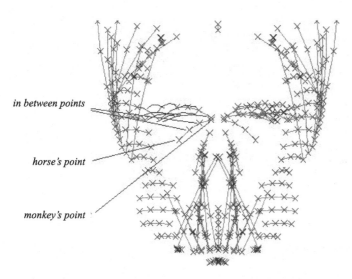

Figure 7.33
Morphing paths from horse to monkey. The crosses denote feature points.

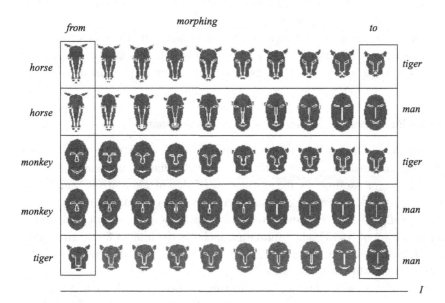

Figure 7.34
Several different one-dimensional morphing examples (horse–tiger, horse–man, monkey–tiger, monkey–man, and tiger–man). The framed pictures are the training examples.

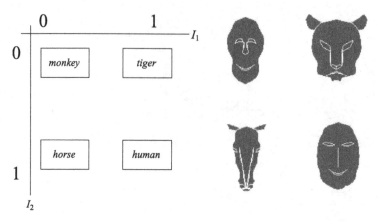

Figure 7.35
Training picture positioning in a two-dimensional morphing example.

Figure 7.36 shows the result of a two-dimensional morphing. The four training pictures, which are framed, have been placed at the corners of the unit square in an (I_1, I_2) plane. All the other pictures are generated by the RBF network, which can produce as many pictures as needed.

The multidimensional interpolation/approximation capability of an NN has made possible the creation of new pictures in the morphing world. As shown in figure 7.36, the newly synthesized in-between pictures have some similarity to all the training examples.

7.3.3 Radial Basis Function Networks for Human Animation

Human animation is becoming increasingly important for the purpose of design evaluation, occupational biomechanics tasks, motion simulation, choreography, and the understanding of motion. In the evaluation of design alternatives, animation provides a noninvasive means of evaluating human-environment interaction. This will result in a final design with improved safety features, greater acceptance, and higher comfort level of use. Human animation includes the human figure animation and human facial animation. Here, some results from Wang (1998) about these two parts of human animation are described.

The realistic animation of a human figure has always been a challenge that requires an in-depth understanding of physical laws. Animated characters are usually modeled as articulated figures, comprising rigid rods connected by flexible joints. This is the kind of physical model used for human walking, running, and jumping animation.

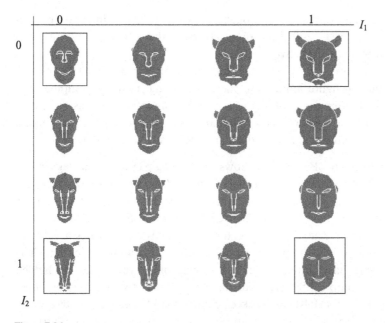

Figure 7.36
A two-dimensional morphing synthesis with an RBF network having two inputs, four hidden units, and 224 outputs. The four training examples are framed. The others are in-betweens.

Animators generally use one of the two techniques for generating realistic and natural-looking human motion: key framing and dynamic simulation. These techniques vary in the control given to the animator, in the realism of the generated motion, and in the ease of generalizing from one motion to another. Key frame animation allows greater flexibility in designing the motion but is unable to generate highly coordinated motions such as walking and grasping. This is because the method is based on geometrically interpolating the parameters of motion (e.g., position, velocity) between the key postures. Geometric interpolation methods such as splines, quaternions, and Bezier curves, although producing smooth motion, do not produce animation that has the features of realistic motion.

Methods using the law of dynamics suffer two serious drawbacks. First, solution of the dynamic equations of the human figure consumes significant computation time. Second, the user is required to specify the external forces that produce the desired motion. Most solutions to this problem are adopted from control theory applied to robotics. Thus, the same requirements as in robotics apply. This means that the user would still need to supply information such as optimization function, control energy function, and desired end effect trajectory.

Both the kinematics and dynamic approaches lack the ability to integrate parameters other than geometrical and force data, correlate them to key postures, and
consequently interpolate the in-between values.

The approach here used the preceding RBF network for motion synthesis to
produce realistic human figure animation, such as walking, running, jumping, and
vaulting. This method offers the flexibility of key frame animation and has the ability
to accommodate more parameters, such as dynamic strength, when the need arises.
An example of running animation created using an RBF network follows.

Human Running Animation   Figure 7.37 shows six training pictures of the legs in one
running cycle. The broken lines represent the left leg, and the solid lines represent the
right leg. Each joint point in the figure is denoted by a circle numbered 1–7, and has
an (x, y) coordinate that forms the 14 desired outputs for the RBF neural network training. The input vector is set to be the running history and has a value of
$I = [0 \quad 0.2 \quad 0.4 \quad 0.6 \quad 0.8 \quad 1]$ corresponding to the six training pictures. The
resulting RBF network has a single input (I is a phase of the run cycle), six hidden
neurons, and fourteen outputs. Six HL Gaussians are placed at six training pictures.

At the learning stage, the RBF network calculates the OL weights matrix **W** by
using the frames coordinates and given input vector that defines the design matrix **G**.
At the second stage, a new input vector is given to generate 30 in-between pictures.
The resulting outputs are the 30 pictures shown in figure 7.38 of an entire running
cycle.

The moving path of the seven joint points in this running cycle is given in figure
7.39, which shows the smooth and realistic trajectories of the mapping. This is particularly visible for the left and right heels (points 2 and 6, respectively). Such smooth
mappings cannot be realized by standard animation based on straight-line con-

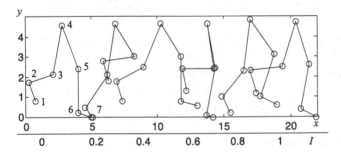

Figure 7.37
Human running training pictures. Broken lines represent the left leg, and solid lines represent the right leg.
The circles denote feature points.

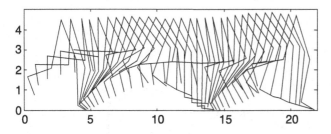

Figure 7.38
Human running animation with 30 generated in-between pictures.

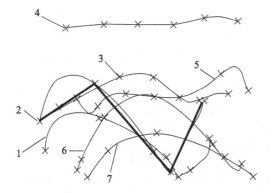

Figure 7.39
Moving paths of joint points in human running. The crosses denote leg joints in training pictures. The thick straight line depicts the conventional (rigid and unnatural) path of the left heel obtained by linear approximations between training points. The RBF path is a naturally smooth movement of the left heel (path 2).

nections of training points. The thick straight line depicts the conventional (rigid and unnatural) path obtained by linear approximations between training points for the left heel. The RBF path represents the naturally smooth movement of joint 2.

Human Facial Animation   Facial animation is an essential part of human animation. Much research has been done on methods for generating facial animation. Current standard methods can be classified as a mixture of three separate categories: key framing, parameterization, and muscle-based modeling. These and other interesting approaches to facial animation are extensively treated in the specialized literature. Our approach for human facial animation again takes advantage of a multivariate mapping technique by an RBF neural network. The conventional method for human facial animation usually cannot work well with both face shape and expression of

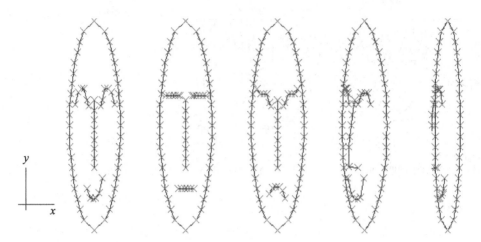

Figure 7.40
Human facial animation. The crosses denote feature points.

feelings at the same time, which leads to difficulties in real-time animation. The solution to this problem is very important for the cartoon industry.

Here, a simplified example of human facial expression (from happy to angry) and a rotation angle (which reflects the shape changes) serve as the two inputs to the RBF network. The x and y coordinates of the characteristic feature points in the human face drawings are taken to be the network outputs. Figure 7.40 shows 67 feature points for five training examples. These examples are located in a two-dimensional input plane. The first input I_1 corresponds to facial expression and varies from -1 (happy), through 0 (moderate or neutral feeling) to $+1$ (anger). (The choice of signs is not related to the author's nature.) The another input, I_2, corresponds to the rotation angle, from 0^0 through 45^0 to 90^0 (see fig. 7.41). Figure 7.42 shows the result of animation of human expressions of feelings. Twenty-five faces are generated. The framed pictures are reproduced originals that were used as training examples.

7.3.4   Radial Basis Function Networks for Engineering Drawings

Drawings of engineering and architectural designs are usually presented as orthographic projections, that is, as parallel projections in directions that will present an object in top (or plan), front (or front elevation), side, bottom, and back views. Because most items are designed in rectangular shapes, orthographic projections often show features in true length that can be readily dimensioned.

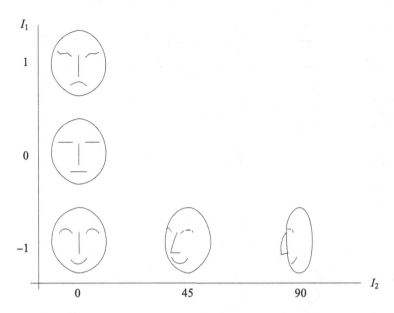

Figure 7.41
Training pictures for human facial animation.

Orthographic views may be drawn as separate two-dimensional drawings, or they may be displayed as special views of a three-dimensional CAD object. Because they may be hard to visualize from orthographic projections, complex objects are often presented in projections that provide a three-dimensional representation, such as an isometric projection, an oblique projection, or the more general axonometric projection. The different projections can be calculated from algebraic formulas that represent transformations from the three-dimensional space of the object to the two-dimensional projection plane of the computer screen or plotter paper.

Here, the previously introduced RBF network synthesis method is used to generate the axonometric projection from normally available engineering drawings. The presentation here follows the work of Wang (1998). For comparison, a brief introduction to the conventional way of solving this problem by geometrical rotation and transformation is given first.

Conventional Approach for Axonometric Projection   For an axonometric projection, the viewpoint or camera-coordinate system shown in figure 7.43 is used. This (x_c, y_c, z_c) coordinate system is left-handed, with its z-axis pointing toward the origin of the world-coordinate system. The transformation from the world-coordinate

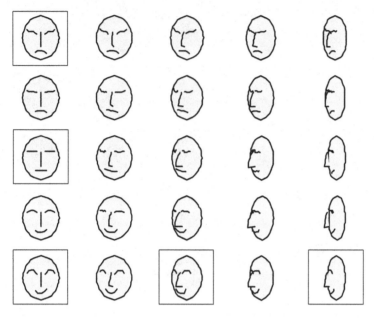

Figure 7.42
Animation of human expressions of feelings. All pictures are produced by an RBF model that was trained using the five framed faces.

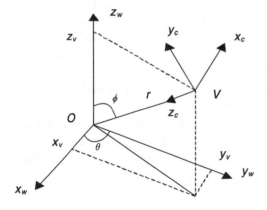

Figure 7.43
Camera-coordinate system (x_c, y_c, z_c) based at viewpoint V.

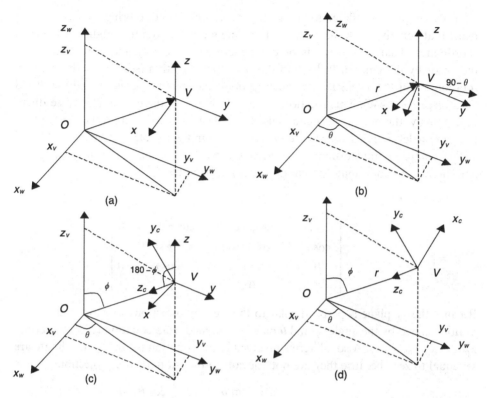

Figure 7.44
Transformation from world coordinates to camera coordinates.

system to the camera-coordinate system may be achieved by combining a translation, two rotations, and a reflection. These transformations are illustrated in figure 7.44. First, a translation of the origin from $(x_w, y_w, z_w) = (0, 0, 0)$ to $(x_w, y_w, z_w) = (x_v, y_v, z_v)$ is achieved by the matrix operator $[T(-x_v, -y_v, -z_v)]$. Here x_v, y_v, and z_v are the coordinates of the viewpoint V in the world-coordinate system. Negative signs are used in the translation matrix because moving the coordinate system from $(0, 0, 0)$ to (x_v, y_v, z_v) is equivalent to moving the objects from $(0, 0, 0)$ to $(-x_v, -y_v, -z_v)$.

From the geometry shown in figure 7.43, the following expressions may be derived between the Cartesian coordinates (x_v, y_v, z_v) and the spherical coordinates (r, θ, ϕ) of the viewpoint V:

$$x_v = r \sin \phi \cos \theta, \qquad y_v = r \sin \phi \sin \theta, \qquad z_v = r \cos \phi. \qquad (7.21)$$

After the origin is translated to (x_v, y_v, z_v), a rotation is used to bring the y-axis into a plane that contains both the z-axis and the line joining V and the origin of the world coordinates. That is, the y-axis of the camera-coordinate system is rotated about the z-axis by the amount $90^0 - \theta$ in the clockwise direction (see fig. 7.44b). Next, a rotation about the x-axis is performed to point the camera z-axis toward the world origin (see fig. 7.44c). This rotation angle is $180^0 - \phi$ in the counterclockwise direction. Finally, the mirror reflection is used to reflect the x-axis across the $x = 0$ plane to form the left-handed coordinate system shown in figure 7.43 and figure 7.44d.

The complete transformation between the world-coordinate system (x_w, y_w, z_w) and the camera-coordinate system (x_c, y_c, z_c) is given by

$$[x_c \quad y_c \quad z_c \quad 1]$$

$$= [x_w \quad y_w \quad z_w \quad 1] \begin{bmatrix} -\sin\theta & -\cos\phi\cos\theta & -\sin\phi\cos\theta & 0 \\ \cos\theta & -\cos\phi\sin\theta & -\sin\phi\sin\theta & 0 \\ 0 & \sin\phi & -\cos\phi & 0 \\ 0 & 0 & r & 1 \end{bmatrix}. \tag{7.22}$$

Because the xy plane is perpendicular to the viewing direction, an axonometric projection defined by the angles ϕ and θ may be obtained from equation (7.22) by setting $x_{\text{plot}} = x_c$, $y_{\text{plot}} = y_c$. Also, all terms involved in the equation for the z_c coordinate are set equal to zero because they are not relevant to the axonometric projection.

$$[x_{\text{plot}} \quad y_{\text{plot}} \quad 0 \quad 1] = [x_w \quad y_w \quad z_w \quad 1] \begin{bmatrix} -\sin\theta & -\cos\phi\cos\theta & 0 & 0 \\ \cos\theta & -\cos\phi\sin\theta & 0 & 0 \\ 0 & \sin\phi & 0 & 0 \\ 0 & 0 & 0 & 1 \end{bmatrix} \tag{7.23}$$

RBF Network Approach for Axonometric Projection   In practice, users of such projection formation should not be pressed into mastering the complexities behind the mechanism of producing such transformations.

As an application of the neural network motion synthesis method, an RBF network is used to generate the axonometric projections from some orthographic pictures, which are normally available from standard engineering drawings. Here only a simple example of a beveled cube is presented to explain the novel approach.

Four orthographic drawings are taken as training pictures, as shown in figure 7.45. The RBF network has two inputs, four hidden neurons, and 18 outputs. The 18 outputs correspond to the (x, y) coordinates of the nine feature points. After training the RBF network can create as many three-dimensional projections of the beveled cube as needed. Figure 7.46 shows 25 projections; the four training pictures are

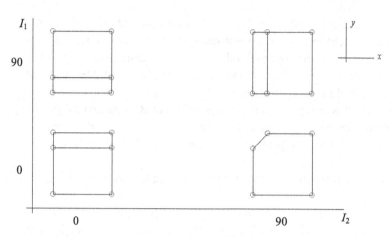

Figure 7.45
Training pictures of a beveled cube. The circled vertices are the feature points.

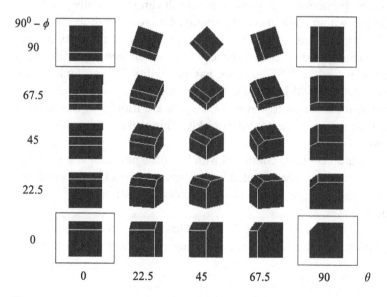

Figure 7.46
Axonometric projections of a beveled cube generated by an RBF neural network.

framed. The results are identical with those from conventional geometrical transformations, so the conventional ones are not need repeated here. This method provides a short-cut to the conventional method. Because the same principle applies to
more complicated structures in real situations, this methodology could be extended to
actual mechanical or architectural structures.

This last case studies section presented the capabilities of RBF networks in solving
various problems in computer graphics. The RBF network solves these problems
in the same fashion as it solves problems in other areas. It learns from training
examples.

All the human animation results show that the resulting human motion is smooth
and realistic. The advantage over conventional key frame animation is apparent. In
conventional key frame animation, key postures are recalled and in-between values
are interpolated. In the neural network approach, only the set of weights corresponding to the desired behavior is retrieved. This means that after the training
phase, the computation of the output pictures is not very difficult.

In the case of facial animation, the network approach can successfully synthesize
the in-between pictures within a specified input parameter space (both facial expression and pose). To some extent, this can solve the problems in the conventional
method when the facial position cannot be changed simultaneously with facial
expression. In fact, because the RBF network has the ability for any multivariate
mapping, more parameters could be included in the model, and the NN can guarantee the best approximation results. Once the weights are trained in the learning
stage, the new desired pictures come out very quickly. This enables the realization of
real-time animation.

Human facial animation could be combined with human figure animation. All the
necessary state parameters could be included in one network model to deal with the
whole human body, and a more comprehensive human animation RBF network
model could be built.

The last example shows that the same principle of learning from examples can be
used for solving various graphics problems, including two- and three-dimensional
transformations.

8 Basic Nonlinear Optimization Methods

Optimization theory and its different techniques are used to find the values of a set of parameters (here called the weights) that minimize or maximize some error or cost function of interest. The name *error* or *cost function*, stands for a measure of how good the solution is for a given problem. This measure is also called *merit* or *objective function* and *performance index* or *risk*. In the genetic algorithms and evolutionary computing community, a well-established name for the error or cost function is *fitness function*. One can also loosely use the word *norm*. The problem of learning some underlying function (mapping, dependency, or degree of relatedness between input and output variables) boils down to the nonlinear search (estimation, identification) of the weights of NNs, SVMs, and FLMs. Therefore, the theory of nonlinear optimization is of crucial importance for understanding the overall learning process of soft models.

The problem of finding an optimal (best) or suboptimal (close to best) set of weights in soft models may be approached in various ways. The fact that in a mathematical workshop there are many different nonlinear optimization tools is of help. However, as with any other tool, unless we understand its purpose and how to apply it, not too much use will be made of it. This chapter gives a brief and solid introduction to nonlinear optimization algorithms that at present stand behind learning from experimental data. It does not pretend to provide a comprehensive review of such a broad field, but the material will prove to be a useful and sound basis for better understanding and further improvement of the learning process in soft models.

This chapter actually began in section 1.3, which placed the nonlinear optimization problem into the framework of training (learning) of soft model weights. The highly nonlinear character of the cost or error function $E(\mathbf{w})$ was illustrated in examples 1.5 and 1.6, where $\mathbf{w}$ was the weights vector and E was a scalar cost function. There, the simplest one-dimensional input neural networks with sine and bipolar sigmoidal activation functions were used. Such choices of low-dimensional input activation functions enabled graphical representation of the nonlinear error surfaces. Recall, however, that in real-life applications, the error function E is a hypersurface representing the mapping of a high-dimensional weights matrix into the measure of goodness. Thus, E is typically a nonlinear hypersurface that cannot be visualized.

The fact that there are no general theories or theorems for analyzing nonlinear optimization methods leads to the introduction of a local quadratic approximation to a nonlinear error function. There are two basic reasons and justifications for introducing such a quadratic function. First, quadratic approximations result in relatively simple theorems concerning the general properties of various optimization methods.

Second, in the neighborhood of local minima (or maxima), quadratic approximations behave like the original nonlinear functions. Therefore, the theory developed for quadratics might be applicable to the original problem, too.

This chapter continues the presentation of a gradient (steepest descent) method given in section 1.3 and discusses second-order iterative methods for finding the minima of general high-dimensional nonlinear and nonquadratic error surfaces. It presents the two most important variable metric methods and two conjugate gradient algorithms that are widely used in soft computing. Two special methods (Gauss-Newton and Levenberg-Marquardt) for finding the sum-of-error-squares error function are discussed in detail. These methods have much better performance on the sum-of-error-squares hypersurface than very good general nonlinear optimization algorithms. Finally, an overview is given of the direct-search and massive-search methods called genetic algorithms (GAs) or evolutionary computing (EC), which have proved to be useful for training soft models.

8.1 Classical Methods

The concept of an error function $E(\mathbf{w})$ is basic in an optimization of soft models. After choosing the structure and activation (membership) functions of such models, the network is characterized by the $(N, 1)$ weights vector $\mathbf{w}$. The weights w_i can be arranged in a matrix also. We usually differentiate between two groups of weights, the hidden layer (HL) and the output layer (OL) weights. The difficult part is learning the HL weights that describe the positions and shapes of the HL activation function because $E(\mathbf{w})$ depends nonlinearly upon this set of weights. An error function $E(\mathbf{w})$ represents the transformation from the vector space spanned by the elements of the weights vector into the space of a real scalar $E(\mathbf{w})$. Geometrically, this mapping $\Re^N \to \Re^1$ represents an error hypersurface over the weight space. $E(\mathbf{w})$ was shown in figures 1.15, 1.17, and 1.18 for $N = 1$ or 2 as a nonlinear curve or surface, respectively. This error surface is typically nonlinear and nonquadratic, meaning that it does not look like a paraboloidal bowl with a guaranteed minimum. At the same time, near a minimal point, a quadratic approximation might be a good one (see fig. 1.17).

Only in very special cases will the error hypersurface be quadratic (convex) with a guaranteed single minimum (or possibly a continuum of degenerate minima lying on the principal hyperplane). In the case of the quadratics, the point of minimal error, or the optimal point, can be calculated as discussed in section 3.2.2. This particular quadratic hypersurface will occur only in two cases:

• When all the activation functions in neurons are linear and the error function is expressed as the sum of error squares

• When the activation functions in the HL neurons are nonlinear but fixed (not the subjects of learning), the OL neurons are linear, and the error function is expressed as the sum of error squares

Generally, the error function of the soft models having hidden and output layer neurons with nonlinear activation functions (at least in the hidden layer) will be a highly nonlinear hypersurface that may have many local minima, saddle points, and eventually one global minimum. Figure 8.1 shows the kind of rough error terrain that results from the mapping of just two weights to the error function E (an $\Re^2 \to \Re^1$ mapping from the weight space to the error). In the general case, which is of greater importance in the world of soft computing, there will be an $\Re^N \to \Re^1$ mapping. Neural networks will have hundreds (or thousands) of weights, or in fuzzy logic systems there will be as many rules, and the dimension of the weight space N will be of the same order. However, the basic task to solve remains the same: finding the optimal set of weights $\mathbf{w}_{opt}$ that guarantees the model's making the best approximation f_a of the desired underlying function f.

Typical learning in a neural network starts with some random initial weight (see points E_1 or E_2 in fig. 8.1). If this first $\mathbf{w}_0$ lies on the slope leading to the global minimum, as point E_1 does, a global minimum will definitely be attained using established methods from the neural networks learning tools. This is a lucky case. A less fortunate case is if one starts to descend the slope of some local minima (there are a few of them in fig. 8.1). It will be even worse if the optimization starts from point E_2, in which case one might stay on a plateau high over the global minimum. However, even in such a situation, one is not lost. If this happens, there is a simple solution. The learning sequence should be started again with a different initial random weight. This may have to be repeated many times at the cost of more computation time. Recall that in the case of a high-dimensional error hypersurface very little is known. But if the underlying function to be approximated were known, there would be no need for neural networks or fuzzy logic models. One would simply write the program containing the known function and that would solve the problem.

Therefore, it is clear that a good understanding of following issues is of crucial importance: what the error surface is like, can it be approximated by quadratics, and if so, what algorithms are the most convenient and promising for finding the general quadratic error function.

By now the reader should be familiar with the answer to the first question: the error hypersurface $E(\mathbf{w})$ is nonlinear and nonquadratic. There are no good algo-

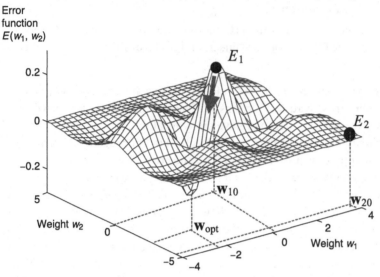

Figure 8.1
Two-dimensional error function $E(w_1, w_2)$ having many different stationary points.

rithms for such a general nonlinear nonquadratic $E(\mathbf{w})$. At the same time, an abundance of nonlinear optimization methods have been developed for quadratic hypersurfaces. All of them can be applied to optimization of the nonquadratic error function $E(\mathbf{w})$ after its quadratic approximation about some local point is obtained.

This leads to the introduction of a local quadratic approximation to the nonlinear error function $E(\mathbf{w})$. Quadratic approximations result in relatively simple theorems and algorithms concerning the general properties of various optimization methods. In addition, in the neighborhood of local minima, they behave like the original nonlinear function. Therefore, the theory developed for quadratics might also be applicable to the original problem.

In order to get a quadratic approximation to the nonquadratic error function $E(\mathbf{w})$, expand $E(\mathbf{w})$ about some point $\mathbf{w}_0$ in a Taylor series, retaining only first- and second-order terms. Starting with a simple two-dimensional weights vector $\mathbf{w} = [w_1, w_2]^T$, for the sake of simplicity, yields

$$E_{qa}(w_{10} + \Delta w_{10}, w_{20} + \Delta w_{20})$$

$$= E(w_{10}, w_{20}) + \Delta w_{10} E_{w_1}(w_{10}, w_{20}) + \Delta w_{20} E_{w_2}(w_{10}, w_{20}) + \tfrac{1}{2} \Delta w_{10}^2 E_{w_1 w_1}(w_{10}, w_{20})$$

$$+ \Delta w_{10} \Delta w_{20} E_{w_1 w_2}(w_{10}, w_{20}) + \tfrac{1}{2} \Delta w_{20}^2 E_{w_2 w_2}(w_{10}, w_{20}) + O(\Delta w_{10}^3, \Delta w_{20}^3), \qquad (8.1)$$

where

$$E_{w_i} = \frac{\partial E}{\partial w_i} \quad \text{and} \quad E_{w_{ij}} = \frac{\partial^2 E}{\partial w_i \partial w_j}, \qquad i, j = 1, 2.$$

Equation (8.1) can be rewritten in matrix notation for an N-dimensional vector $\mathbf{w}$ as follows:

$$E_{qa}(\mathbf{w}) = E_0 + \mathbf{g}^T(\mathbf{w} - \mathbf{w}_0) + \tfrac{1}{2}(\mathbf{w} - \mathbf{w}_0)^T \mathbf{H}(\mathbf{w} - \mathbf{w}_0), \tag{8.2}$$

where $E_0 = E(\mathbf{w}_0)$ is scalar, $\mathbf{g}$ is an $(N, 1)$ gradient vector, and $\mathbf{H}$ is an (N, N) Hessian matrix of $E(\mathbf{w})$ defined by (1.41) and (1.46), respectively, and both are evaluated at $\mathbf{w} = \mathbf{w}_0$. It is easy to find a stationary point of a quadratic approximation $E_{qa}(\mathbf{w})$ to the original nonquadratic error function $E(\mathbf{w})$. This is done by equating the derivative of $E_{qa}(\mathbf{w})$ with respect to $\mathbf{w}$ to the null vector. Suppose that $E_{qa}(\mathbf{w})$ takes its minimum value at $\mathbf{w} = \mathbf{w}^*$. Then $\nabla E_{aq}(\mathbf{w}^*) = \mathbf{H}(\mathbf{w}^* - \mathbf{w}_0) + \mathbf{g} = 0$, which yields

$$\mathbf{w}_a^* = \mathbf{w}_0 - \mathbf{H}^{-1}\mathbf{g}. \tag{8.3}$$

8.1.1 Newton-Raphson Method

The Newton-Raphson method uses $\mathbf{w}^*$, which is a minimum of the quadratic approximation $E_{qa}(\mathbf{w})$ and not of the original nonquadratic error function $E(\mathbf{w})$, as the next current point, giving the iterative formula

$$\mathbf{w}_{k+1} = \mathbf{w}_k - \mathbf{H}_k^{-1}\mathbf{g}_k. \tag{8.4}$$

A better variant of (8.4) that is often used is

$$\mathbf{w}_{k+1} = \mathbf{w}_k - \eta\mathbf{H}_k^{-1}\mathbf{g}_k, \tag{8.5}$$

where the learning rate is determined by a line search from $\mathbf{w}_k$ in the direction $\mathbf{H}_k^{-1}\mathbf{g}_k$. (The line search can be a quadratic one, as in section 1.3.2.) The convergence of the Newton-Raphson algorithm is rapid when $\mathbf{w}_k$ is near the optimal point $\mathbf{w}_0$. However, the convergence to a minimum is not guaranteed, and if $\mathbf{H}_k$ is not positive definite, the method can fail to converge (see fig. 8.2).

Figure 8.2 shows a quadratic approximation and the first five Newton-Raphson steps. The first three steps converge to the minimum, but the fourth step resulted in a negative definite Hessian matrix $\mathbf{H}$. This leads to a backward divergent step. This does not necessarily mean that the fifth step will not again be in a direction of a global minimum. However, it can also diverge again, as shown in figure 8.2.

The method of steepest descent presented in section 1.3.2 and the Newton-Raphson algorithm are identical when $\mathbf{H}_k^{-1}$ is a unit matrix ($\mathbf{H}_k^{-1} = \mathbf{I}$). This fact and the desire

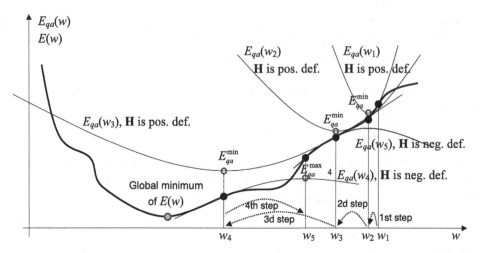

Figure 8.2
Quadratic approximation of a nonquadratic error function and the first five Newton-Raphson steps.

to avoid calculation of the Hessian matrix in every step leads to a large class of gradient methods known as quasi-Newton or variable metric methods.

8.1.2 Variable Metric or Quasi-Newton Methods

Note that the Newton-Raphson stationary points computed at each iteration step can be minimum, maximum, or saddle point depending on the character of the Hessian matrix. For negative definite $\mathbf{H}$, the maximum is like the one obtained in the fourth iteration step in figure 8.2. If this happens, iteration diverges and the method can fail. In addition, a calculation of the Hessian matrix in every step can be high computational burden. Many methods have been proposed to replace $\mathbf{H}_k^{-1}$ by a positive definite symmetric matrix $\mathbf{H}_k$ that is updated in each iteration step without the need for matrix inversion. The resulting (variable metric) iterative formula is

$$\mathbf{w}_{k+1} = \mathbf{w}_k - \eta \mathbf{H}_k \mathbf{g}_k, \tag{8.6}$$

with randomly chosen initial $\mathbf{w}_0$ and $\mathbf{H}_0$. Many choices are available for construction of $\mathbf{H}_k$. The two best known are the Davidon-Fletcher-Powell method (DFP, also known as Fletcher-Powell) and a related algorithm that goes by the name Broyden-Fletcher-Goldfarb-Shano (BFGS). All the variable metric methods are batch algorithms that use all available data.

8.1.3 Davidon-Fletcher-Powell Method

The DFP method starts with $\mathbf{H}_0 = \mathbf{I}$, that is, it begins as steepest descent and changes over to the Newton-Raphson method during the course of a number of iterations by continually updating an approximation to the inverse of the Hessian matrix (matrix of second derivatives) at the minimum. DFP does it in such a way as to ensure that the matrices $\mathbf{H}_k$ are positive definite. For a quadratic error surface $E(\mathbf{w})$, where $\mathbf{w}$ is an $(N, 1)$ vector, DFP converges to the minimum after N iterations.

The steps of the DFP method are as follows:

1. Start with the matrix $\mathbf{I}$ as the initial guess $\mathbf{H}_0$. For the kth step proceed as follows.

2. Compute the gradient $\mathbf{g}_k$.

3. Compute the new direction $\mathbf{v}_k = -\mathbf{H}_k \mathbf{g}_k$.

4. Find the variable learning rate η_k that minimizes $E(\mathbf{w}_k + \eta_k \mathbf{v}_k)$.

5. Compute the new weight $\mathbf{w}_{k+1} = \mathbf{w}_k + \eta_k \mathbf{v}_k$.

6. Let $\mathbf{u}_k = \eta_k \mathbf{v}_k$ and $\mathbf{y}_k = \mathbf{g}_{k+1} - \mathbf{g}_k$.

7. Compute the matrix for the next iteration $\mathbf{H}_{k+1} = \mathbf{H}_k + \mathbf{A}_k + \mathbf{B}_k$, where the matrices $\mathbf{A}_k$ and $\mathbf{B}_k$ are given as

$$\mathbf{A}_k = \frac{\mathbf{u}_k \mathbf{u}_k^T}{\mathbf{u}_k^T \mathbf{y}_k} \quad \text{and} \quad \mathbf{B}_k = -\frac{\mathbf{H}_k \mathbf{y}_k (\mathbf{H}_k \mathbf{y}_k)^T}{\mathbf{y}_k^T (\mathbf{H}_k \mathbf{y}_k)}.$$

8. Check the stopping criterion, and if it is not satisfied, go to step 2 for the next iteration.

The most important formula in the DFP method is given in step 7 for the updating of the matrix $\mathbf{H}$. Note that all quasi-Newton methods avoid the calculation of the Hessian matrix, and this leads to huge savings in computing time, particularly for large networks. Updating of the $\mathbf{H}$ matrix looks complicated but, apart from the computation of the gradient vector $\mathbf{g}$, merely $2N^2$ multiplications are needed in each iteration step, while a classic Newton-Raphson algorithm requires $N^3/6$ multiplications plus the computation of the gradient and the Hessian.

Example 8.1 Find the minimum point of a positive definite quadratic error function $E(\mathbf{w}) = 0.5\mathbf{w}^T \mathbf{A}\mathbf{w}$, where $\mathbf{A} = [3 \quad -1; -1 \quad 1]$, using the DFP method. $E(\mathbf{w})$ is quadratic, and you must be at a minimum in two steps only. Check whether $\mathbf{H}_2 = \mathbf{A}^{-1}$.

At the start, $k = 0$.

1. We start with $\mathbf{w}_0 = [10 \quad 10]^T$ as the initial estimate of the minimum point and with $\mathbf{H}_0 = \mathbf{I}$.

2. The gradient vector is $\mathbf{g}_0 = \mathbf{Aw} = [3w_1 - w_2 \quad -w_1 + w_2]^T = [20 \quad 0]^T$.

3. $\mathbf{v}_0 = -\mathbf{H}_0\mathbf{g}_0 = -[20 \quad 0]^T$.

4. The variable learning rate η_0 that minimizes $E(\mathbf{w}_0 + \eta_0\mathbf{v}_0)$ follows from

$$E(\mathbf{w}_0 + \eta_0\mathbf{v}_0) = \frac{1}{2}[10 - 20\eta \quad 10]\begin{bmatrix} 3 & -1 \\ -1 & 1 \end{bmatrix}\begin{bmatrix} 10 - 20\eta \\ 10 \end{bmatrix} = 100 - 400\eta + 600\eta^2,$$

which attains a minimum with respect to η at $\eta_0 = 0.33$.

5. A new weight $\mathbf{w}_1 = \mathbf{w}_0 + \eta_0\mathbf{v}_0 = [3.34 \quad 10]^T$.

6. $\mathbf{u}_0 = \eta_0\mathbf{v}_0 = -[6.6 \quad 0]^T$, $\mathbf{g}_1 = [0.02 \quad 6.66]^T$, and $\mathbf{y}_0 = \mathbf{g}_1 - \mathbf{g}_0 = -[20 \quad -6.66]^T$.

7. $\mathbf{A}_0 = \dfrac{\mathbf{u}_0\mathbf{u}_0^T}{\mathbf{u}_0^T\mathbf{y}_0} = \begin{bmatrix} 0.33 & 0 \\ 0 & 0 \end{bmatrix}$ and $\mathbf{B}_0 = -\dfrac{\mathbf{H}_0\mathbf{y}_0(\mathbf{H}_0\mathbf{y}_0)^T}{\mathbf{y}_0^T(\mathbf{H}_0\mathbf{y}_0)} = -\begin{bmatrix} 0.9 & -0.3 \\ -0.3 & 0.01 \end{bmatrix}$.

The matrix for the next iteration $\mathbf{H}_1 = \mathbf{H}_0 + \mathbf{A}_0 + \mathbf{B}_0 = \begin{bmatrix} 0.43 & 0.3 \\ 0.3 & 0.99 \end{bmatrix}$.

8. Go to step 2 for the next iteration.

Now, $k = 1$.

2. The gradient vector $\mathbf{g}_1$ is given in step 2 of the preceding list.

3. $\mathbf{v}_1 = -\mathbf{H}_1\mathbf{g}_1 = -[2.22 \quad 6.65]^T$.

4. The variable learning rate η_1 that minimizes $E(\mathbf{w}_1 + \eta_1\mathbf{v}_1) = E([3.34 - 2.22\eta_1 \quad 10 - 6.65\eta_1]^T)$ and $\eta_1 = 1.5$.

5. A new weight $\mathbf{w}_2 = \mathbf{w}_1 + \eta_1\mathbf{v}_1 = [-0.01 \quad 0.15]^T$. Note that in theory we should have $\mathbf{w}_2 = [0 \quad 0]^T$. Here, $\mathbf{w}_2 \neq \mathbf{0}$ because of computational roundoff errors. Check whether the final matrix $\mathbf{H}_2$ is equal to the exact inverse of $\mathbf{A}$, which is a Hessian matrix. If not, Continue with step 6.

6. $\mathbf{u}_1 = \eta_1\mathbf{v}_1 = -[3.33 \quad 9.85]^T$, $\mathbf{g}_2 = [-0.18 \quad 0.16]^T$, and $\mathbf{y}_1 = \mathbf{g}_2 - \mathbf{g}_1 = -[0.2 \quad 6.5]^T$.

7. $\mathbf{A}_1 = \begin{bmatrix} 0.17 & 0.51 \\ 0.51 & 1.5 \end{bmatrix}$ and $\mathbf{B}_1 = -\begin{bmatrix} 0.1 & 0.31 \\ 0.31 & 0.99 \end{bmatrix}$.

Finally, the matrix $\mathbf{H}_2 = \begin{bmatrix} 0.5 & 0.5 \\ 0.5 & 1.5 \end{bmatrix}$, and this is exactly the inverse $\mathbf{A}^{-1}$. ∎

8.1.4 Broyden-Fletcher-Goldfarb-Shano Method

The key step in a DFP algorithm is step 7, where the new direction matrix $\mathbf{H}_k$ is calculated. An alternative formula for updating $\mathbf{H}_k$, which seems to be superior to the

DFP approach, is the improvement proposed independently in the BFGS method. The BFGS iteration steps are same as in DFP, but there is a change in step 7:

7. Compute the matrix for the next iteration $\mathbf{H}_{k+1} = \mathbf{H}_k + \mathbf{A}_k + \mathbf{B}_k + \mathbf{C}_k$, where the matrices $\mathbf{A}_k$ and $\mathbf{B}_k$ are given as

$$\mathbf{A}_k = \frac{\mathbf{u}_k \mathbf{u}_k^T}{\mathbf{u}_k^T \mathbf{y}_k}, \qquad \mathbf{B}_k = -\frac{\mathbf{H}_y \mathbf{y}_k (\mathbf{H}_k \mathbf{y}_k)^T}{\mathbf{y}_k^T (\mathbf{H}_k \mathbf{y}_k)}, \qquad \mathbf{C}_k = \mathbf{y}_k^T (\mathbf{H}_k \mathbf{y}_k)^T \mathbf{z}_k \mathbf{z}_k^T,$$

where

$$\mathbf{z}_k = \frac{\mathbf{u}_k}{\mathbf{u}_k^T \mathbf{y}_k} - \frac{\mathbf{H}_k \mathbf{y}_k}{\mathbf{y}_k^T (\mathbf{H}_k \mathbf{y}_k)}.$$

The updating in the BFGS method avoids the tendency that is present in the DFP method for the matrices $\mathbf{H}_k$ to become singular. There are variants of the BFGS method that do not require line search provided that suitable step lengths are chosen. This is an important property because of savings in computing time by dispensing with linear search. The most important requirement fulfilled here is that the matrices $\mathbf{H}_k$ remain positive definite. This is ensured for quadratic error surfaces. For non-quadratic functions, the property is ensured by imposing some mild extra conditions (see the specialized literature on nonlinear optimization).

A possible disadvantage of the quasi-Newton methods is that they require the storage and updating of (N, N) matrices $\mathbf{H}_k$, where N is the number of unknown weights (i.e., they are $O(N^2)$ methods). This may become a serious problem for large networks having a few thousand weights. The BFGS method is the best out of many variable metric algorithms. It possesses the same basic numerical features as the others: it iteratively computes an estimate of the inverse Hessian, it usually requires line search, it works in batch mode only, and it is an $O(N^2)$ method.

Another group of algorithms with smaller computational requirements ($O(N)$ order only) are the conjugate gradient methods.

8.1.5 Conjugate Gradient Methods

The main disadvantage of the standard gradient method (i.e., of an EBP algorithm) is that it does not perform well on hypersurfaces that have different curvatures along different weight directions. The error function is no longer radially symmetric; it has the shape of an elongated bowl. Therefore, section 4.3.6 introduced a close relative of the class of conjugate gradient (CG) algorithms in order to avoid highly oscillatory paths on such bowls. This was the momentum method, which can be considered an on-line variant of the CG method. Another reason for applying conjugate gradients can be seen in figure 1.22: after line search is applied, the iterative steps are orthogonal to each other, and this necessarily leads to the unwanted sharp changes in descent directions.

At the same time, all variable metric methods show another kind of difficulty. They must calculate some approximation to the Hessian matrix $\mathbf{H}$, which for large networks with several thousand weights, is computationally not welcome.

CG methods are popular in the soft computing community for a few important reasons:

• They attempt to find descent directions that minimally disturb the result of the previous iterations.

• They do not use the Hessian matrix directly.

• They are $O(N)$ methods.

Some common features in variable metric methods are as follows:

• CG methods also need line search (i.e., they rely on calculation of the optimal step length).

• CG methods also use all the training data at once, meaning that they operate only in batch mode.

With the CG method, one can modify well-known descent methods, such as the gradient method, to take advantage of mutually conjugate directions of descent. To do that, one must generate mutually conjugate gradients. Algorithms that use only error function values $E(\mathbf{w})$ and gradient vectors $\mathbf{g}$ in calculation of CG directions of search are desirable because these quantities can usually be readily computed. In particular, such algorithms should avoid computation of the matrix of second derivatives $\mathbf{H}$ in order to generate mutually conjugate vectors with respect to $\mathbf{H}$. Fletcher and Reeves (1964) proposed such a method of minimization, and there is also a Polak-Ribiere algorithm that seems to perform better on nonquadratic error hypersurfaces (see following sections). The presentation of conjugate gradients here follows Walsh (1975).

Consider finding the minimum value of a quadratic function

$$E(\mathbf{w}) = E_0 + \mathbf{g}^T \mathbf{w} + \tfrac{1}{2} \mathbf{w}^T \mathbf{H} \mathbf{w}, \tag{8.7}$$

where $\mathbf{H}$ is positive definite and symmetric. The contours $E(\mathbf{w}) = c$ are for different values of c concentric ellipses (see fig. 8.3).

Suppose that the search for a minimum begins at point A in the direction AD, that this minimum occurs at B, and that C is the minimal (optimal) point. Then the direction BC is *conjugate* to the direction AD since, for any ellipse $E(\mathbf{w}) = c$, the diameter

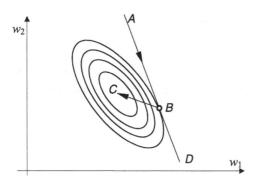

Figure 8.3
Conjugate directions.

through B is conjugate (in the geometrical sense) to the diameter parallel to AD. The idea of conjugate directions can be extended to n dimensions.

Let $\mathbf{u}$ and $\mathbf{v}$ denote two vectors in $\Re^N$. As noted earlier, $\mathbf{u}$ and $\mathbf{v}$ are said to be *mutually orthogonal* if their scalar product is equal to zero ($\mathbf{u}^T\mathbf{v} = 0$). Now, for an (N, N) symmetric positive definite matrix $\mathbf{H}$, the vectors $\mathbf{u}$ and $\mathbf{v}$ are said to be *mutually conjugate* with respect to $\mathbf{H}$ if $\mathbf{u}$ and $\mathbf{Hv}$ are *mutually orthogonal*, that is, if

$$\mathbf{u}^T\mathbf{Hv} = 0. \tag{8.8}$$

Clearly, if $\mathbf{u}$ and $\mathbf{v}$ are mutually conjugate with respect to the identity matrix, they are mutually orthogonal. Hence, the concept of mutual orthogonality can be thought of as a special case of the mutual conjugacy of vectors. It is clear, for example, that the eigenvectors $\mathbf{x}$ and $\mathbf{y}$ of a square symmetric positive definite matrix $\mathbf{A}$ are mutually conjugate with respect to $\mathbf{A}$, since $\mathbf{y}^T\mathbf{Ax} = \mathbf{y}^T\lambda\mathbf{x} = \lambda\mathbf{y}^T\mathbf{x} = 0$. Hence, given a positive definite matrix $\mathbf{H}$, one can be sure of the existence of at least one set of vectors mutually conjugate with respect to given matrix $\mathbf{H}$.

Several methods are available for generating sets of mutually conjugate directions. The DFP method also produces a set of mutually conjugate directions. Fletcher and Reeves (1964) derived a simple recurrence formula that generates a sequence of mutually conjugate directions. This method locates the minimum of a given function. Note that if a set of mutually conjugate vectors in $\Re^N$ does not span $\Re^N$, then one could be searching in a proper subspace of $\Re^N$ not containing the minimum. However, it is easy to show that this is not the case, since a set of mutually conjugate vectors in $\Re^N$ constitutes a basis and therefore spans $\Re^N$. In designing CG methods the basic approach is similar to the variable metric methods in the sense that the crucial computing step is calculation of new directions. The basic formula is always the same, or very similar, and it calculates the new search direction as follows:

$$\mathbf{v}_k = -\mathbf{g}_k + c_{k-1}\mathbf{v}_{k-1}, \tag{8.9}$$

where $\mathbf{g}_k$ is a current gradient, c_{k-1} is a previous coefficient of conjugacy, and v_{k-1} is a previous search direction. Various CG methods differ in how one calculates the coefficient of conjugacy c.

8.1.6 Fletcher-Reeves Method

The iterative steps for the Fletcher-Reeves method are as follows:

1. Let $\mathbf{w}_0$ denote the first approximation to optimal $\mathbf{w}_{\text{opt}}$. This can be a randomly chosen vector. Compute the gradient $\mathbf{g}_0$ and define $\mathbf{v}_0 = -\mathbf{g}_0$.

2. For the $k = 1, \ldots, N - 1$ step, proceed as follows:

a. Set $\mathbf{w}_k = \mathbf{w}_{k-1} + \eta_{k-1}\mathbf{v}_{k-1}$, where η_{k-1} minimizes $E(\mathbf{w}_{k-1} + \eta\mathbf{v}_{k-1})$ with respect to η. (This is the line search part of a CG algorithm.)

b. Compute the gradient $\mathbf{g}_k = \nabla E(\mathbf{w}_k)$.

c. When $k < N$, define

$$\mathbf{v}_k = -\mathbf{g}_k + \frac{\|\mathbf{g}_k\|^2}{\|\mathbf{g}_{k-1}\|^2}\mathbf{v}_{k-1}, \quad \text{where} \quad \mathbf{g}_k = \nabla E(\mathbf{w}_k). \tag{8.10}$$

3. Replace $\mathbf{w}_0$ by $\mathbf{w}_N$ and go to step 1 unless the stopping rule is satisfied.

Thus, the most relevant difference with respect to a standard gradient descent procedure (where one moves from $\mathbf{w}_k$ to $\mathbf{w}_{k+1}$ along $\mathbf{v}_k = -\mathbf{g}_k = -\nabla E(\mathbf{w}_k)$, i.e., along the negative gradient) is that in a CG method the gradient is modified by adding

$$\frac{\|\mathbf{g}_k\|^2}{\|\mathbf{g}_{k-1}\|^2}\mathbf{v}_{k-1}.$$

When $E(\mathbf{w})$ is a positive definite quadratic function, this modification results in a set of mutually conjugate vectors $\mathbf{v}_k$, $k = 1, \ldots, N$. When used with nonquadratic error functions, the preceding CG method is iterative. Fletcher and Reeves suggest that the direction of search should revert periodically to the direction of steepest descent, all previous directions being discarded. With this procedure, the algorithm retains the property of quadratic termination provided that such restarts are not made more often than every Nth iteration. Thus, satisfactory results are obtained if the direction of steepest descent is used for $\mathbf{v}_0, \mathbf{v}_{N+1}, \mathbf{v}_{2N+1}, \ldots$. For line search, quadratic or cubic methods can be used.

Example 8.2 Consider a positive definite quadratic form $E(\mathbf{w}) = 0.5\mathbf{w}^T\mathbf{H}\mathbf{w}$, where $\mathbf{H} = [1 \quad 1; 1 \quad 2]$. Find the minimum point of this function by the Fletcher-Reeves CG method.

It is clear that the minimum of $E(\mathbf{w})$ is located at $[0 \quad 0]^T$. The reader may check whether the optimal gradient method can locate this minimum point starting from any random weight $\mathbf{w}_0$.

The convergence of the CG method is not affected by the choice of initial point, so $\mathbf{w}_0 = [10 \quad -5]^T$ can be chosen arbitrarily. First, find the analytical expression for a gradient $\mathbf{g} = \nabla E(\mathbf{w}) = \mathbf{H}\mathbf{w} = [w_1 + w_2 \quad w_1 + 2w_2]^T$.

In step 1, $\mathbf{v}_0 = -\mathbf{g}_0 = -\nabla E(\mathbf{w}_0) = -[5 \quad 0]^T$ is defined and a line search is performed with respect to a learning rate η for

$$E(\mathbf{w}_0 + \eta\mathbf{v}_0) = \frac{1}{2}[10 - 5\eta \quad -5]\begin{bmatrix} 1 & 1 \\ 1 & 2 \end{bmatrix}\begin{bmatrix} 10 - 5\eta \\ -5 \end{bmatrix} = \frac{1}{2}[50 - 75\eta + 50\eta^2].$$

This function attains a minimum at $\eta_0 = 0.75$.

Therefore, $\mathbf{w}_1 = \mathbf{w}_0 + \eta_0\mathbf{v}_0 = [6.25 \quad -5]^T$, and the gradient $\mathbf{g}_1 = \nabla E(\mathbf{w}_1) = [1.25 \quad -3.75]^T$. Now, in order to use (8.10), find $\|\nabla E(\mathbf{w}_1)\|^2/\|\nabla E(\mathbf{w}_0)\|^2$. Here, $\|\nabla E(\mathbf{w}_0)\|^2 = 5^2 + 0^2 = 25$, and $\|\nabla E(\mathbf{w}_1)\|^2 = 1.25^2 + (-3.75)^2 = 15.55$. Now, according to (8.10),

$$\mathbf{v}_1 = -[1.25 \quad -3.75]^T + (15.55/25)[-5 \quad 0]^T = [-4.36 \quad 3.75]^T.$$

Now compute $E(\mathbf{w}_1 + \eta\mathbf{v}_1) = \frac{1}{2}[26.55 - 38.95\eta + 14.45\eta^2]$, which attains a minimum at $\eta_1 = 1.34$. Then $\mathbf{w}_2 = \mathbf{w}_1 + \eta_1\mathbf{v}_1 = [0.4 \quad 0.01]^T$. Note that a genuine minimum point $\mathbf{w}_{opt} = [0 \quad 0]^T$ should have been obtained. This was not accomplished, because of computational roundoff errors. However, this CG descent can be continued by replacing $\mathbf{w}_0$ by $\mathbf{w}_2$ and repeating the computation. ∎

8.1.7 Polak-Ribiere Method

The Polak-Ribiere method differs with respect to the Fletcher-Reeves method merely in how one calculates the coefficient of conjugacy c in (8.9), or in (8.10). Thus, iteration step 2c in the Polak-Ribiere method is

When $k < N$, define

$$\mathbf{v}_k = -\mathbf{g}_k + \frac{\mathbf{g}_k^T(\mathbf{g}_k - \mathbf{g}_{k-1})}{\|\mathbf{g}_{k-1}\|^2}\mathbf{v}_{k-1}, \quad \text{where} \quad \mathbf{g}_k = \nabla E(\mathbf{w}_k). \tag{8.11}$$

For quadratic error surfaces, both methods perform the same. For (more realistically) nonquadratic error hypersurfaces, equations (8.10) and (8.11) show different numerical properties. Many experimental studies have found the Polak-Ribiere method to give slightly better results than the Fletcher-Reeves algorithm.

CG methods require the computation of a gradient $\nabla E(\mathbf{w}_k)$ at each iteration to generate the direction of descent. This amounts to computing $N + 1$ function values at each step. Powell (1964) has developed an alternative method, generating CG directions by one-dimensional searches at each iteration. The interested reader can find more on Powell's and other variants of the CG method in the specialized litera-ture on nonlinear optimization (e.g., Fletcher 1987 or Wismer and Chattergy 1976.)

8.1.8 Two Specialized Algorithms for a Sum-of-Error-Squares Error Function

All the preceding methods are developed for the general form of the error function $E(\mathbf{w})$. However, one of the most used norms or error functions in the soft computing field is a sum-of-error-squares function, given as

$$E(\mathbf{w}) = \mathbf{e}(\mathbf{w})^T \mathbf{e}(\mathbf{w}). \tag{8.12}$$

Several minimization algorithms exploit the special properties of the error function (8.12). Because $\mathbf{e}(\mathbf{w})$ is usually a differentiable function of the weights $\mathbf{w}$, the matrix of the first derivatives can be expressed as

$$\mathbf{J}(w_{ij}) = \left(\frac{\partial e_i}{\partial w_j}\right), \tag{8.13}$$

which is known as the Jacobian matrix, or the Jacobian. A matrix of second deriva-tives is the Hessian matrix $\mathbf{H}$. It is interesting to express both the gradient and the Hessian of $E(\mathbf{w}) = \mathbf{e}(\mathbf{w})^T \mathbf{e}(\mathbf{w})$ in vector notation. Thus, differentiating (8.12), one obtains

$$\mathbf{g} = \nabla E(\mathbf{w}) = E_\mathbf{w} = 2\mathbf{J}^T \mathbf{e}, \tag{8.14}$$

$$\mathbf{H} = E_{\mathbf{ww}} = 2\mathbf{J}^T \mathbf{J} + 2\frac{\partial \mathbf{J}^T}{\partial \mathbf{w}} \mathbf{e}. \tag{8.15}$$

The specific error function (8.12) is minimized during the iteration, and one usually assumes that the errors e_i are small numbers. With such an assumption the second term on the right-hand side of (8.15) can be neglected, meaning that the Hessian can be approximated as

$$\mathbf{H}_a \approx 2\mathbf{J}^T \mathbf{J}. \tag{8.16}$$

The last expression is equivalent to making a linear approximation to the errors. It exploits in this way the structure of the sum-of-error-squares function (8.12). Note an important feature of this expression. It uses a matrix of first derivatives $\mathbf{J}$ to calculate a matrix of second derivatives $\mathbf{H}$. Recall that all quasi-Newton methods might take N iteration steps to estimate $\mathbf{H}$ satisfactorily. The straight calculation of $\mathbf{H}_a$ given by (8.16) will result in faster convergence of the Gauss-Newton method.

Gauss-Newton Method   Plugging the expressions for a gradient $\mathbf{g}$ (8.14) and a Hessian matrix $\mathbf{H}_a$ (8.16) into the iterative Newton-Raphson algorithm (8.4), one obtains the Gauss-Newton algorithm for optimizing the sum-of-error-squares cost function as follows:

$$\mathbf{w}_{k+1} = \mathbf{w}_k - \mathbf{H}_{ak}^{-1}\mathbf{g}_k = \mathbf{w}_k - (2\mathbf{J}^T\mathbf{J})^{-1}2\mathbf{J}^T\mathbf{e} = \mathbf{w}_k - (\mathbf{J}^T\mathbf{J})^{-1}\mathbf{J}^T\mathbf{e}. \tag{8.17}$$

The Gauss-Newton updating method (8.17) is also known as a *generalized least-squares method.* It is particularly good when one is close to the minimum, for two reasons: the errors e_i are small and the error surface $E(\mathbf{w})$ is almost linear. The iterative procedure can be improved if a line search (as shown in the previous methods) is performed. Such an algorithm is superior to the best quasi-Newton methods that use the same information.

The Gauss-Newton method can also diverge if the Jacobian $\mathbf{J}$ loses rank during the iterations, and because of possible problems a further modification is proposed. One of the best modifications is the Levenberg-Marquardt method.

Levenberg-Marquardt Method   Very often the neglected errors e_i are not small and the second-order term on the right-hand side of (8.15) cannot be ignored. In this case, the Gauss-Newton method converges very slowly or diverges. Hence, it may be better to use the full Hessian matrix $\mathbf{H}$. The Levenberg-Marquardt method avoids the calculation of the Hessian matrix $\mathbf{H}$ and uses the regularization approach when the matrix $\mathbf{J}^T\mathbf{J}$ is rank-deficient. Instead of using (8.17), Levenberg (1944) and Marquardt (1963) proposed the following iteration scheme:

$$\mathbf{w}_{k+1} = \mathbf{w}_k - (\mathbf{J}^T\mathbf{J} + \lambda_k\mathbf{I})^{-1}\mathbf{J}^T\mathbf{e}, \tag{8.18}$$

where λ_k is a scalar that may be adjusted to control the sequence of iterations, and $\mathbf{I}$ is an (N, N) identity matrix. Note that (8.18) approaches the steepest descent as λ_k is increased because $(\mathbf{J}^T\mathbf{J} + \lambda_k\mathbf{I}) \approx \lambda_k\mathbf{I}$; thus $\mathbf{w}_{k+1} = \mathbf{w}_k - (1/\lambda_k)\mathbf{J}^T\mathbf{e} = \mathbf{w}_k - (1/2\lambda_k)\mathbf{g}_k$ in virtue of (8.14). The last expression is a steepest descent where the learning rate $\eta_k = (1/2\lambda_k)$. When $\lambda_k \to 0$, the Levenberg-Marquardt algorithm tends to the Gauss-Newton method. For a nonquadratic error surface, this is shown in figure 8.4.

By changing λ_k at each iteration one can control the convergence properties. Using λ_k to control the iterative procedure enables the method to take advantage of the reliable improvement in the error function $E(\mathbf{w})$ given by steepest descent when still

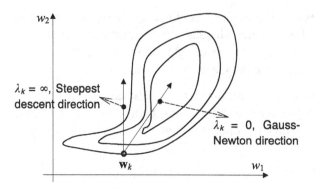

Figure 8.4
Levenberg-Marquardt descent directions fall between steepest descent and Gauss-Newton directions.

far from the minimum and the rapid convergence of the Gauss-Newton method when close to the minimum. Marquardt (1963) describes a scheme for selecting λ_k at each iteration, which seems to be very efficient, although Fletcher (1987) has pointed out possible difficulties.

The following strategy has been proposed specifically for neural network training (Hagan, Demuth, and Beale 1996). At the beginning of training the regularization parameter λ_k is set to some small value, say, $\lambda_k = 0.01$. If the iteration does not decrease the value of the error function $E(\mathbf{w})$, the step is repeated with a larger λ_k value, say, $\lambda_k^{\text{new}} = 10\lambda_k$. The larger values of λ_k move in the direction of steepest descent and $E(\mathbf{w})$ may decrease. Once an iteration step produces a smaller error function value, the value of λ_k is decreased, so the algorithm would approach Gauss-Newton directions for faster convergence. Because the Levenberg-Marquardt algorithm was specifically designed for the sum-of-error-squares cost function it can be expected to converge faster than general methods.

8.2   Genetic Algorithms and Evolutionary Computing

Genetic algorithms (GAs) are optimization algorithms based on the mechanics of natural selection and natural genetics. They combine the idea of survival of the fittest (in classical optimization terms, survival of the best set of weights) with a structured yet randomized information exchange to form a search algorithm with some of the talent of human search. GAs efficiently exploit historical information to speculate on new search points with expected improved performance. The GA techniques are subdivided into evolutionary strategy (ES) and genetic algorithms (GenA). The interest in heuristic search algorithms with underpinnings in natural and physical processes arose in the 1970s, when Holland first proposed GenA. This technique of optimization is very similar to ES, which was developed by Rechenberg and Schwefel about the same time. ES encodes the strings with real number values, and GenA encodes the strings with binary values.

8.2.1 Basic Structure of Genetic Algorithms

As mentioned, GAs are another nonlinear optimization tool used to find the best solution (set of network parameters) for a given data set and network structure. They can also be used to optimize the structure of the network. The GA algorithm begins with the random initialization of a set of possible solutions (see fig. 8.5). Each solution (or *gene string*) with its parameters (e.g., shape parameters of membership functions in FL models, or centers and standard deviations of Gaussian bells in RBF networks) produces a special point of the error, cost, or fitness function in the search space (weights space). This set of different weights in each iteration is called a *population*. Further, from a part (say, one half or one quarter) of the best solutions of one population, *children* (new weights parameters) will be produced. It is expected that these new weights (children) will be better than the old ones (their parents). (We all know that this is not necessarily the case in biology or in humankind, but that is how the algorithm is set up.)

A simple GA consists of three operations: *selection, genetic operation*, and *replacement* (see fig. 8.6). The population $P(t) = \{\mathbf{w}_1, \mathbf{w}_2, \ldots, \mathbf{w}_n\}$ comprises a group of gene strings (weights) $\mathbf{w}_i$, each being a candidate to be selected as a solution of the problem, at the iteration t. Here, $\mathbf{w}$ is a vector that contains network parameters (the centers and standard deviations of Gaussian bells in a RBF network, or the HL and OL weights of an MLP). The fitness values for all the gene strings are the corresponding values of the error (cost) function. Thus, to each gene string $\mathbf{w}_i$ a corresponding fitness $J_i(\mathbf{w})$ is assigned. Further, a new population (the next set of network parameters at iteration $t + 1$) is produced through the mechanisms of selection, genetic operation, and replacement. After a certain number of iterations (generations), the GA should be able to find a gene string (weights vector) that is a solution close to the global minimum of the multidimensional error function.

8.2.2 Mechanism of Genetic Algorithms

As mentioned, the simple GA passes through the loop of three operations:

1. Selection of the best gene strings (by, for example, using a so-called roulette wheel)
2. Genetic operation (crossover or resemblance, mutation)

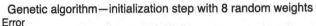

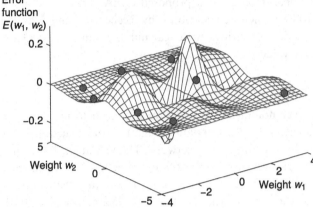

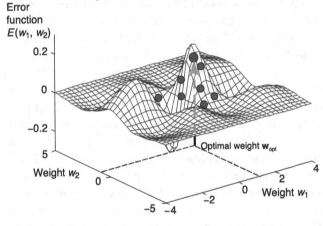

Figure 8.5
Maximization by genetic algorithm. Initial population comprises a set with eight randomly produced two-dimensional weights. At each iteration step, the four best weights produce four "children." The generation obtained in this way (four parents and four children) calculates the four best weights again, which act as parents for the next generation. The whole procedure repeats until the stopping criterion is met.

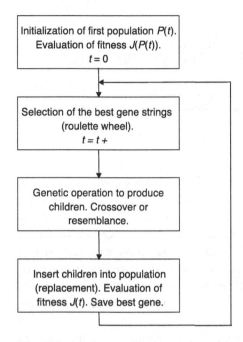

Initialization of first population $P(t)$.
Evaluation of fitness $J(P(t))$.
$t = 0$

Selection of the best gene strings
(roulette wheel).
$t = t +$

Genetic operation to produce
children. Crossover or
resemblance.

Insert children into population
(replacement). Evaluation of
fitness $J(t)$. Save best gene.

Figure 8.6
Simple genetic algorithm structure.

3. Replacement of bad gene strings of the old population with new gene strings (children)

Before the optimization loop begins, the parameters that should be optimized have to be transformed into a corresponding form. This is called encoding. The encoding is an important issue in any GA because it can severely limit the window of information that is observed from the system. The gene string stores the problem-specific information. Usually it is expressed as a string of variables, each element of which is called a gene. The variable can be represented by a binary or a real number, or by other forms (e.g., embedded list for factory scheduling problems), and its range is usually defined by the specified problem. The two most common ways for encoding the parameters are binary or real number forms (see fig. 8.7).

The principal difference between ES and GenA is that ES encodes the strings with real numbers, whereas GenA encodes the string with binary numbers. This difference has significant consequences for the mutation.

The GA works with an aggregation of gene strings, called a population. Initially, a population is generated randomly. However, this randomness is controlled. The

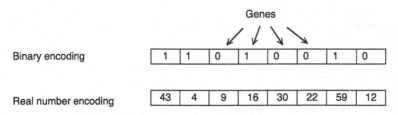

Figure 8.7
Encoding of parameters in gene strings.

fitness values of all the gene strings are evaluated by calculating error functions for each set of parameters (gene string). Some of the gene strings with the highest fitness values are selected from the population to generate the children. The standard genetic algorithm uses a roulette wheel method for selection, which is a stochastic version of the survival-of-the-fittest mechanism. In this method of selection, candidate strings from the current generation $P(t)$ are selected for the next generation $P(t+1)$ by using a roulette wheel where each string in the population is represented on the wheel in proportion to its fitness value. (Here, one string is one column vector containing one set of HL weights.)

Thus, the strings (HL weights) that have a high fitness, meaning that make a good approximation, are given a large share of the wheel, while the strings with low fitness are given a relatively small portion of the roulette wheel. Finally, selections are made by spinning the roulette wheel m times and accepting as candidates those strings that are indicated at the completion of the spin (m may be one half of a population or any other chosen ratio).

The reason that the stochastic version is used rather than just deterministically always choosing the best strings to survive, gets at the crux of the underlying theory and assumptions of genetic search. This theory is based on the notion that even strings with very low fitness may contain some useful partial information to guide the search. For this reason, the survival probability of low-quality weights is small, but they are not altogether excluded from the search.

The selected gene strings have to pass through the genetic operations of either crossover or resemblance and mutation to create the children for the next generation.

Crossover is a recombination operator that combines subparts of two parents gene strings, which were chosen by the selection, to produce children with some parts of both parents' genetic material. The simplest form is the single-point crossover. Both the parents from $P(t)$ and the so-called crossover point are randomly selected. The portions of the two gene strings beyond the crossover point are exchanged to form

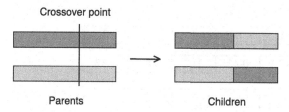

Figure 8.8
A simple one-point crossover.

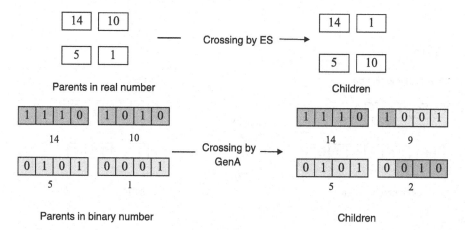

Figure 8.9
Crossover in ES and GenA.

the children (see fig. 8.8). Multipoint crossover is similar to single-point crossover except that several crossover points are randomly chosen. Figure 8.9 shows an example of the crossover in GenA and ES.

It can be seen that ES does not change the real number of the next generation because the crossover point is always between the real numbers. This means that both parents and children contain the same numbers (1, 5, 10, and 14). With GenA the crossover point can be at any place, and the newly produced real value is typically different. In figure 8.9, one can see that the parents' numbers (1, 5, 10, and 14) are different from the children's weights (2, 5, 9, and 14).

The *resemblance* operator seems to be a part of nature, and it can be applied to data encoded by real numbers. Typically the resemblance operator recomputes (changes) the parents' values, applying a normal distribution operator in the sense

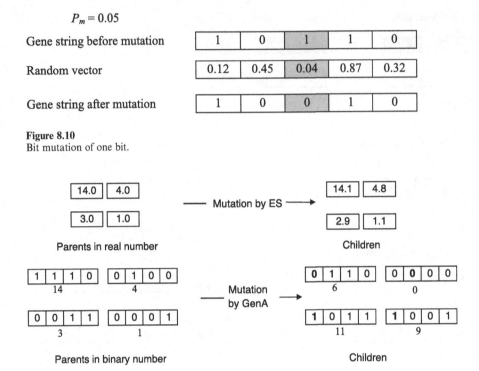

Figure 8.10
Bit mutation of one bit.

Figure 8.11
Mutation in ES and GenA.

that the parents' values are treated as a mean of some normal distribution and the children's values are calculated as $w_{children} = N(w_{parents}, \sigma_i)$, where i denotes the generation (iteration step) and σ_i is decreasing toward the end of the calculation. The smaller σ_i is, the higher the degree of resemblance between parents and children will be. Applying the resemblance operator on parents (see fig. 8.9) [14 10] and [5 1], one obtains children [11.3 10.5] and [6.2 1.1].

Mutation is an operator that introduces variations into the gene string. The operation occurs occasionally, usually with a small probability P_m. Each bit in a gene string will be tested and, if necessary, inverted. An easy way to test the bits in a gene string is as follows. A vector of the same size as the gene string is created, which consists of random numbers between 0 and 1. This vector is compared bit for bit with the mutation probability P_m. If a value of the generated random vector is smaller than P_m, the bit in the same place in the gene string is inverted. An example is shown in figure 8.10. As crossover does, mutation has different effects in ES and GenA. In

Table 8.1
Summary of Properties of the Genetic Algorithm and Orthogonal Least Squares Optimization

Genetic Algorithm	Orthogonal Least Squares
Description Searches globally using a probabilistic random search technique analogous to the natural evolution for optimum solution.	*Description* Searches locally, selecting from the given or offered set of basis functions (regressors) to find an optimal subset of basis functions.
Search Strategy Employs a multipoint search strategy to continuously select the set of solutions with higher fitness. This approach is similar to natural reproduction from two parents in creating children, which are expected to be better than their parents. The fittest survive whereas the rest are "disqualified." The whole selection procedure, from choosing parents for reproduction to disqualification of unfit solutions, is carried out in a probabilistic random manner.	*Search Strategy* A set of basis functions is selected for a network from a previously defined set of basis functions (regressors) that have varying shapes and locations, usually evenly scattered inside the input training space. The selection of basis functions depends on the associated approximation levels of the basis function. The selection procedure maximally selects the basis functions with higher approximation levels to form a subset of bases.
Search Space Since this is a random probabilistic method that searches globally, there are no restrictions on the search space. If an optimal solution exists, GA is capable of finding it.	*Search Space* OLS is a structured search technique that only searches locally, i.e., inside a predefined set of basis functions, to find an optimal solution. Unless the global optimal solution is contained in the set of basis functions, OLS is not capable of finding it.
Efficiency Although GA is powerful in finding the optimal solution, the path it takes to get to this solution is complicated and may not be repeatable because of the random nature of this technique. There are often several paths the optimization algorithm could take to arrive at the same solution, making this a very time-consuming, inefficient, but effective procedure.	*Efficiency* Unlike GA, OLS does not guarantee an optimal solution but a solution close to it if the initial set of basis functions covers the input space adequately. However, the optimization is a lot faster than GA, and the solution is more practical in the given time. This optimization procedure is easily repeatable because of the nature of the search.

ES mutation can be understood as a fine adjustment in the sense that the values of the gene strings will be modified through adding a small normally distributed random number. In GenA an inversion of a bit can have a large effect (see fig. 8.11). The imitation of biological mutation can be understood as an attempt to jump out of a local minimum at the beginning of the optimization and later make a fine adjustment.

After the selection and the genetic operations by which the new children are produced, they will replace a bad part of the parents' generation and become a component of the following generation $P(t+1)$. Each sequence produces the new set of weights (gene strings), and one must check whether the new weights are better than the ones in last generation. If so, this new set should be kept in case a better one is not found. These weights would be the result of the optimization and thus the solution of the problem. Each sequence can also calculate the average fitness of the whole generation, which can be used to measure the quality of the generation. This shows also the trends of the optimization.

To finish the optimization, various criteria can be used. A common way is to stop the algorithm after a certain number of generations. Another criterion could be a predefined fitness value that the algorithm has to reach. Yet another possibility is that the algorithm finishes after the fitness value has not changed for a certain number of generations.

GAs have been applied to a diverse range of problems. The author and his students have been using GA to optimize RBF networks and FL models. In particular, GA was used for learning the HL weights (parameters that define positions and shapes of activation or membership functions). All these parameters are encoded as real numbers, as in evolutionary algorithms. Once the HL weights have been calculated, the OL weights are computed by a simple pseudoinverse operation in each iteration step.

There are various ways of using GA-based optimization in neural networks. The most obvious way is to search the weights space of a neural network with a predefined architecture. GA is capable of global search and is not easily fooled by local minima. GAs do not use the derivative of the fitness function. Therefore, they are possibly the best tool when the activation functions are not differentiable (e.g., for hard limiting threshold functions, triangles, and trapezoidals).

A comparison of the GA (actually, ES because all computation was done with real numbers) and the OLS optimization techniques is presented in table 8.1 (Shah 1998). GA was applied for finding optimal centers and standard deviations of the HL Gaussian basis functions. The output layer weights for an RBF network were obtained by a pseudoinverse operation. As discussed, GA and OLS each have their own strengths and weaknesses but in Shah (1998), the OLS method of optimization was preferred for share market forecasting because of the large amount of data and the highly complex nature of the RBF network. However, recall that there is no guarantee that OLS will find the best subset at all and that it can take an unrealistically huge processing time for GA to find the best solution.

9 Mathematical Tools of Soft Computing

In this chapter, the focus is on specific topics that might be helpful for understanding the mathematical parts of soft models. Since each of these concepts and tools is a broad subject, they cannot be covered in detail. However, a summary of the basic and important mathematical techniques is necessary not only for understanding the material in the previous chapters but also for further study and research in learning and soft computing. It is supposed that the reader has some knowledge of probability theory, linear algebra, and vector calculus. This chapter is designed only for easy reference of properties and notation. Its contents are used freely in this text without further reference.

We start with a classic problem: the task of solving a system of linear equations. It is an very important concept and set of techniques because it is eventually the most commonly encountered problem in modern applications.

9.1 Systems of Linear Equations

Insight into the geometry of systems of linear equations helps a lot in understanding the (matrix) algebra and concepts involved. Recall that $x + y = 3$ is a straight line, $x + y + z = 3$ is a plane, and for more than three variables, $x + y + z + w + u + \cdots = 3$ is a hyperplane. In solving systems of linear equations, we seek an n-dimensional solution vector $\mathbf{x}$ that satisfies all the m equations.

Clearly, an infinite number of vectors exist that satisfy a single ($m = 1$) equation $ax + by = c$, in two unknowns ($n = 2$), where a, b, and c are known. With two equations in two unknowns (meaning two straight lines), the variety of solutions is larger—two lines can intersect (*unique* solution), can be parallel (*no* solution), or can lie one over the other (an *infinity* of the points, i.e., vectors, satisfies both equations). If there are more lines, there are still only the three kinds of solutions (unique, none, or an infinity of solutions).

The same reasoning applies for three unknowns, but now instead of straight lines in a two-dimensional space, there are planes in a three-dimensional space. These planes can intersect at a single point (but there must be at least three of them to do that), can be parallel, can intersect along a single line (imagine the pages of your opened book as, say, 325 planes intersecting along the single binding axis), or can mutually intersect each other along different straight lines. Two planes can never intersect at a single point, just as $n - 1$ hyperplanes can never intersect at a single n-dimensional point (vector). The algebra describing all these different kinds of solutions is simple, and the geometry just described may help in understanding the language of matrices. Consider now the system

$$a_{11}x_1 + a_{12}x_2 + \cdots + a_{1n}x_n = y_1$$

$$a_{21}x_1 + a_{22}x_2 + \cdots + a_{2n}x_n = y_2$$

$$\vdots$$

$$a_{m1}x_1 + a_{m2}x_2 + \cdots + a_{mn}x_n = y_m$$

which in matrix notation is simply $\mathbf{Ax} = \mathbf{y}$.[1] Entries a_{ij} of the (m, n) matrix $\mathbf{A}$ are known, as are the elements y_i of the $(m, 1)$ vector $\mathbf{y}$. When $\mathbf{y} = \mathbf{0}$, the system is *homogeneous*; otherwise it is *nonhomogeneous*. Any system of m linear equations in n unknowns (x_j) may

1. Have *no* solution, in which case it is an *inconsistent* system

2. Have *exactly one* solution (a *unique* solution)

3. Have an *infinite number of* solutions

In the last two cases, the system is *consistent*. (See fig. 9.1.)

Two Unknowns   Consider the following systems, corresponding matrices, ranks, solutions, and geometries.

$$\begin{array}{|l|} \hline x + y = 2, \\ x - y = 0. \\ \hline \end{array}$$

$$\mathbf{A} = \begin{bmatrix} 1 & 1 \\ 1 & -1 \end{bmatrix}, \qquad \mathbf{y} = \begin{bmatrix} 2 \\ 0 \end{bmatrix}, \qquad \mathbf{A_y} = \begin{bmatrix} 1 & 1 & 2 \\ 1 & -1 & 0 \end{bmatrix}.$$

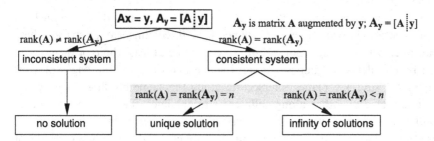

Figure 9.1
Conditions for the existence of solutions to a system of linear equations.

$r(\mathbf{A}) = r(\mathbf{A_y}) = n = 2$. There is unique solution $[x \quad y] = [1 \quad 1]$. It is a section of the two lines.

$$\boxed{\begin{aligned} x - y &= 2, \\ x - y &= 0. \end{aligned}}$$

The first equation changes to $x - y = 2$, and matrices $\mathbf{A}$, $\mathbf{y}$, and $\mathbf{A_y}$ change, too. $r(\mathbf{A}) = 1$ and $r(\mathbf{A_y}) = 2$. Inconsistent system. No solution. Two lines are parallel.

$$\boxed{\begin{aligned} x - y &= 2, \\ x - y &= 0, \\ x + y &= 1. \end{aligned}}$$

This is an *overdetermined* system ($m = 3 > n = 2$). $r(\mathbf{A}) = 2$ and $r(\mathbf{A_y}) = 3$. Inconsistent system. No solution. Two out of three lines are parallel.

$$\boxed{\begin{aligned} x + y &= 2, \\ x - y &= 0, \\ 2x - y &= 1. \end{aligned}}$$

This is an *overdetermined* system ($m = 3 > n = 2$). But now $r(\mathbf{A}) = r(\mathbf{A_y}) = 2$. Consistent system. Unique solution $[x \quad y] = [1 \quad 1]$.

$$\boxed{\begin{aligned} x + y &= 2, \\ 2x + 2y &= 4, \\ 3x + 3y &= 6. \end{aligned}}$$

This is an *overdetermined* system ($m = 3 > n = 2$). Now $r(\mathbf{A}) = r(\mathbf{A_y}) = 1$. Consistent system but an infinity of solutions. All three lines lie over each other. There is a single specific *minimal length* solution $\mathbf{x} = [x \quad y] = [1 \quad 1]$, which can be obtained using the *pseudoinverse* A^+ of the matrix A, $x = A^+y$. Note that out of all (out of an infinite number of) solutions, there is one having the minimal length (or the one closest to the origin) $x = A^+y$.

$$\boxed{x + y = 2.}$$

This is an *underdetermined* system ($m = 1 < n = 2$). $r(A) = r(A_y) = 1$. Consistent system but an infinity of solutions. There is a specific minimal length solution $x = [x \quad y] = [1 \quad 1]$, which can be obtained using the pseudoinverse A^+ of the matrix A, $x = A^+y$. This minimal length solution (or the one closest to the origin) is the same as the preceding $x = A^+y = [1 \quad 1]$.

More Than Two Unknowns   Nothing changes when there are more unknowns except that when $n > 3$, visualization of the solutions is no longer possible. Figure 9.2 depicts a few different cases for $n = 3$.

$$\boxed{\begin{aligned} x + y + \ z &= 3, \\ 2y + \ z &= 2, \\ y + 2z &= 2. \end{aligned}}$$

This is a consistent system with a unique solution: $[5/3 \quad 2/3 \quad 2/3]$. $r(A) = r(A_y) = 3$ (see fig. 9.2, top graph).

$$\boxed{\begin{aligned} x + y + \ z &= 3, \\ -x \quad\ \ + \ z &= -1, \\ y + 2z &= 2. \end{aligned}}$$

This is a consistent system ($r(A) = r(A_y) = 2 < n$) with an infinite number of solutions. Note that the matrix A is a *rank-deficient* matrix, $\det(A) = 0$. All three planes intersect along a single line (see fig. 9.2, bottom graph). However, it is possible to calculate the minimal length solution: $[-1.667 \quad 0.333 \quad 0.867]$.

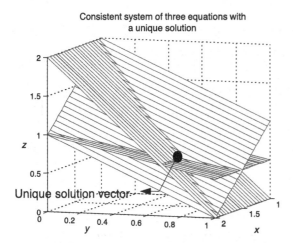

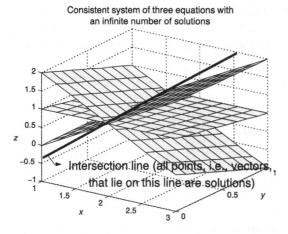

Figure 9.2
Two solutions to the system of three linear equations in three unknowns. Other cases are possible, too.

9.2   Vectors and Matrices

A vector defined as a column $(n, 1)$ vector and an (m, n) *matrix* **A** that has m rows and n columns are given as follows:

$$\mathbf{x} = \begin{bmatrix} x_1 \\ x_2 \\ \vdots \\ x_n \end{bmatrix}, \mathbf{x} = [x_1 \quad x_2 \quad \cdots \quad x_n]^T. \quad \mathbf{A} = \begin{bmatrix} a_{11} & a_{12} & \cdots & a_{1j} & \cdots & a_{1n} \\ a_{21} & a_{22} & \cdots & a_{2j} & \cdots & a_{2n} \\ \vdots & \vdots & \vdots & \vdots & \vdots & \vdots \\ a_{i1} & a_{i2} & \vdots & a_{ij} & \vdots & a_{in} \\ \vdots & \vdots & \vdots & \vdots & \vdots & \vdots \\ a_{m1} & a_{m2} & \cdots & a_{mj} & \cdots & a_{mn} \end{bmatrix}.$$

Matrix **A** is called *square* if $m = n$, or **A** is an (n, n) matrix. An (m, n) matrix is a *rectangular* matrix. Vectors may also be viewed as particular rectangular matrices $(m = 1)$. $[a_{ij}]_{m,n}$ is an entry (element) from the ith row and jth column of the matrix **A**. When the entries of a matrix are real, $\mathbf{A} \in \mathfrak{R}^{m,n}$, the columns of **A** are denoted by $\mathbf{a}_i = \in \mathfrak{R}^{m,1} = \mathfrak{R}^m$, $i = 1, 2, \ldots, n$, and **A** can be expressed in terms of its columns by $\mathbf{A} = [\mathbf{a}_1 \quad \mathbf{a}_2 \quad \ldots \quad \mathbf{a}_n]$.

The *transpose* $\mathbf{A}^T$ of the (m, n) matrix **A** is an (n, m) matrix. Its (i,j)th entry is a_{ji} element of **A**.

$$(\mathbf{A}^T)^T = \mathbf{A}. \quad (\mathbf{AB})^T = \mathbf{B}^T\mathbf{A}^T \quad (\mathbf{ABCD})^T = \mathbf{D}^T\mathbf{C}^T\mathbf{B}^T\mathbf{A}^T.$$
$$\mathbf{A}^T = [a_{ji}]. \quad [\mathbf{A} + \mathbf{B}]^T = \mathbf{A}^T + \mathbf{B}^T.$$

A matrix is *symmetric* if $\mathbf{A} = \mathbf{A}^T$. This property is defined for square matrices only.

If $\mathbf{A}^T = \mathbf{A}$, then **A** is symmetric.
If $\mathbf{A}^T\mathbf{A} = \mathbf{AA}^T = \mathbf{I}$, then **A** is orthogonal.
If $\mathbf{A}^T = -\mathbf{A}$, then **A** is skewsymmetric.
If $\mathbf{A}^T\mathbf{A} = \mathbf{A}$, then **A** is idempotent.
I is an identity, or unit, matrix.

A matrix is *diagonal* if $a_{ij} = 0$ for $i \neq j$, that is, $\mathbf{A} = \text{diag}(a_{11}\, a_{22} \ldots a_{nn})$. If $a_{ii} = 1$, the matrix is an identity (unit) matrix.

Addition, Subtraction, and Multiplication of Matrices

$\mathbf{C} = \mathbf{A} \pm \mathbf{B}$,   or $c_{ij} = a_{ij} \pm b_{ij}$.

$\mathbf{A} \pm \mathbf{B} = \mathbf{B} \pm \mathbf{A}$. $\mathbf{A} \pm (\mathbf{B} \pm \mathbf{C}) = (\mathbf{A} \pm \mathbf{B}) \pm \mathbf{C}$.

$k\mathbf{A} = \mathbf{A}k = [ka_{ij}]$. $k\mathbf{A} + k\mathbf{B} = k(\mathbf{A} + \mathbf{B})$.

The *product* $\mathbf{AB}$ of an (m, n) matrix $\mathbf{A}$ by an (n, p) matrix $\mathbf{B}$ is an (m, p) matrix $\mathbf{C}$:

$$\mathbf{C} = \mathbf{AB}, \quad \text{or} \quad c_{ij} = \sum_{r=1}^{n} a_{ir}b_{rj}, \quad i = 1, \ldots, m, j = 1, \ldots, p.$$

$\mathbf{AB} \neq \mathbf{BA}$. $(\mathbf{AB})\mathbf{C} = \mathbf{A}(\mathbf{BC})$. $(\mathbf{A} + \mathbf{B})\mathbf{C} = \mathbf{AC} + \mathbf{BC}$.

For symmetric and diagonal matrices,

$\mathbf{AD} = \mathbf{DA}$ and $\mathbf{ABC} = \mathbf{BAC} = \mathbf{CAB} = \mathbf{CBA}$.

Inner and Outer Product   The *inner (scalar, dot)* product of two n-dimensional vectors $\mathbf{x}$ and $\mathbf{w}$ is a *scalar* a: $a = \mathbf{x}^T\mathbf{w} = \mathbf{w}^T\mathbf{x}$. The *outer* product of $\mathbf{x}$ and $\mathbf{w}$ is a matrix $\mathbf{A}$. ($\mathbf{x} \in \Re^m$ and $\mathbf{w} \in \Re^n$.)

$$\mathbf{A} = \mathbf{x}\mathbf{w}^T = \begin{bmatrix} x_1w_1 & x_1w_2 & \cdots & x_1w_j & \cdots & x_1w_n \\ x_2w_1 & x_2w_2 & \cdots & x_2w_j & \cdots & x_2w_n \\ \vdots & \vdots & \vdots & \vdots & \vdots & \vdots \\ x_iw_1 & x_iw_2 & \vdots & x_iw_j & \vdots & x_iw_n \\ \vdots & \vdots & \vdots & \vdots & \vdots & \vdots \\ x_mw_1 & x_mw_2 & \cdots & x_mw_j & \cdots & x_mw_n \end{bmatrix}.$$

The **results of matrix multiplication** are as follows:

• An expression ending with a column vector is a column vector: $\mathbf{ABx} = \mathbf{c}$.

• An expression beginning with a row vector is a row vector: $\mathbf{y}^T\mathbf{BCD} = \mathbf{r}^T$.

• An expression beginning with a row vector and ending with a column vector is a scalar: $\mathbf{x}^T\mathbf{Ay} = s$.

Linear Independence of Vectors $\mathbf{a}_1, \mathbf{a}_2, \ldots, \mathbf{a}_n$ are vectors in $\Re^m$, and $\alpha_1, \alpha_2, \ldots, \alpha_n$ are scalars. The vectors $\mathbf{a}$ are linearly independent if

$$\sum_{i=1}^{n} \alpha_i\mathbf{a}_i = \mathbf{0} \Leftrightarrow \alpha_1 = \alpha_2 = \cdots = \alpha_n = 0.$$

The columns (rows) of $\mathbf{A} \in \Re^{m,n}$ are linearly independent if and only if $\mathbf{A}^T\mathbf{A}$ is a *nonsingular* matrix, $\det(\mathbf{A}^T\mathbf{A}) = |\mathbf{A}^T\mathbf{A}| \neq 0$.

The *rank* of an (m,n) matrix is equal to the maximal number of linearly independent columns or, equivalently, the maximal number of linearly independent rows. Apparently, the rank can be at most equal to the smaller of the two integers m and n. If $\text{rank}(\mathbf{A}) = \min(m,n)$, $\mathbf{A}$ is of *full rank*.

$$\text{rank}(\mathbf{A}) = \text{rank}(\mathbf{A}^T) = \text{rank}(\mathbf{A}^T\mathbf{A}) = \text{rank}(\mathbf{A}\mathbf{A}^T).$$

Vector Norms Norms are (positive) scalars and are used as measures of length, size, distance, and so on, depending on context. An L_p norm is a *p*-norm of an $(n,1)$ vector $\mathbf{x}$:

$$\|\mathbf{x}\|_p = \left(\sum_{i=1}^{n} |x_i|^p \right)^{1/p}.$$

Mostly, $p = 1, 2$, or ∞, and these norms are called *one-*, *two-*, or *infinity norms*.

$$\|\mathbf{x}\|_1 = \sum_{i=1}^{n} |x_i|. \qquad \qquad \text{(absolute value, one-norm, } L_1 \text{ norm)}$$

$$\|\mathbf{x}\|_2 = \sqrt{\mathbf{x}^T\mathbf{x}} = \sqrt{x_1^2 + x_2^2 + \cdots + x_n^2} = \left(\sum_{i=1}^{n} x_i^2 \right)^{1/2}. \qquad \text{(two-norm, modul, Euclidean, } L_2 \text{ norm)}$$

$$\|\mathbf{x}\|_\mathbf{W} = \sqrt{\mathbf{x}^T\mathbf{W}\mathbf{x}}, \ \mathbf{W} \text{ symmetric positive.} \qquad \text{(weighted Euclidean norm)}$$

$$\|\mathbf{x}\|_\infty = \max|x_i|. \qquad \qquad \text{(infinity, Chebyshev, } L_\infty \text{ norm)}$$

$$\|\mathbf{x}\| \geq 0 \quad \text{if} \quad \mathbf{x} \neq 0, \qquad \|\alpha\mathbf{x}\| = |\alpha|\, \|\mathbf{x}\| \quad \text{for any } \alpha. \qquad \text{(any norm)}$$

$$\|\mathbf{x} + \mathbf{y}\| \leq \|\mathbf{x}\| + \|\mathbf{y}\|. \qquad \qquad \text{(triangular inequality)}$$

A symmetric matrix $\mathbf{A}$ is *positive* (or *negative*) *definite* if the quadratic form $\mathbf{x}^T\mathbf{A}\mathbf{x}$ satisfies $\mathbf{x}^T\mathbf{A}\mathbf{x} > 0$ (or <0) for $\mathbf{x} \neq 0$, *positive semidefinite* if $\mathbf{x}^T\mathbf{A}\mathbf{x} \geq 0$, and *negative semidefinite* if $\mathbf{x}^T\mathbf{A}\mathbf{x} \leq 0$.

Inverse and Pseudoinverse Matrices $\mathbf{A}, \mathbf{B} \in \Re^{n,n}$ (square matrices). If $\mathbf{A}\mathbf{B} = \mathbf{B}\mathbf{A} = \mathbf{I}$, $\mathbf{B}$ is the inverse of $\mathbf{A}$, denoted as $\mathbf{A}^{-1}$. If $\mathbf{A}^{-1}$ exists, $\mathbf{A}$ is nonsingular. $\mathbf{A}$ is singular if its determinant $|\mathbf{A}| = 0$, that is, if $\text{rank}(\mathbf{A}) < n$.

For every rectangular matrix $\mathbf{A} \in \Re^{m,n}$, a unique $\mathbf{A}^+$ exists that is called the *pseudoinverse* of $\mathbf{A}$ (or the Moore-Penrose *generalized inverse*):

$$\mathbf{A}\mathbf{A}^+\mathbf{A} = \mathbf{A}, \qquad \mathbf{A}^+\mathbf{A}\mathbf{A}^+ = \mathbf{A}^+, \qquad (\mathbf{A}\mathbf{A}^+)^T = \mathbf{A}\mathbf{A}^+, \qquad (\mathbf{A}^+\mathbf{A})^T = \mathbf{A}^+\mathbf{A},$$

that is, $\mathbf{A}\mathbf{A}^+$ and $\mathbf{A}^+\mathbf{A}$ are symmetric.

For a square nonsingular matrix, $\mathbf{A}^+ = \mathbf{A}^{-1}$. If $\mathbf{A}^T\mathbf{A}$ or $\mathbf{A}\mathbf{A}^T$ is nonsingular, $\mathbf{A}^+ = (\mathbf{A}^T\mathbf{A})^{-1}\mathbf{A}^T = \mathbf{A}^T(\mathbf{A}\mathbf{A}^T)^{-1}$.

$\mathbf{A}^+$ could be interpreted by a set of linear equations

$$\mathbf{A}\mathbf{x} = \mathbf{y}, \qquad \mathbf{A} \in \mathfrak{R}^{m,n}, \mathbf{x} \in \mathfrak{R}^n, \mathbf{y} \in \mathfrak{R}^m, m > n.$$

$m > n$ denotes the overdetermined system, that is, there are more equations than unknowns x_j, $j = 1, \dots, n$. rank$(\mathbf{A}) = n$ (see "singular value decomposition" following). Recall that in examples in earlier chapters, a typical linear equation was connected with the calculation of the output layer weights, and it was given as $\mathbf{G}\mathbf{w} = \mathbf{d}$. An unknown vector $\mathbf{x}^* = \mathbf{A}^+\mathbf{y}$ solves this system in the sense that the scalar error (cost, objective, or merit) function $J(\mathbf{x})$ becomes a minimum for $\mathbf{x}^*$:

$$J(\mathbf{x}) = \frac{1}{2}\sum_{i=1}^{m} e(\mathbf{x})_i^2 = \frac{1}{2}(\mathbf{A}\mathbf{x} - \mathbf{y})^T(\mathbf{A}\mathbf{x} - \mathbf{y}).$$

The minimal sum of quadratic errors is equal to $J_{\min}(\mathbf{x}^*) = \mathbf{y}^T(\mathbf{I} - \mathbf{A}(\mathbf{A}^T\mathbf{A})^{-1}\mathbf{A}^T)\mathbf{y}$. For scalar α, $\alpha^+ = \alpha^{-1}$ if $\alpha \neq 0$, $\alpha^+ = 0$ otherwise. More properties follow:

$$(\mathbf{A}^+)^+ = \mathbf{A}, \qquad (\alpha\mathbf{A})^+ = \alpha^{-1}\mathbf{A}^+, \alpha \neq 0, \qquad (\mathbf{A}^+)^T = (\mathbf{A}^T)^+.$$

$$\mathbf{A}\mathbf{A}^T(\mathbf{A}^+)^T = \mathbf{A}, \qquad \mathbf{A}^+\mathbf{A}\mathbf{A}^T = \mathbf{A}^T, \qquad (\mathbf{A}^+)^T\mathbf{A}^T\mathbf{A} = \mathbf{A}, \qquad \mathbf{A}^T\mathbf{A}\mathbf{A}^+ = \mathbf{A}^T.$$

A set $\{\mathbf{x}_i\} \in \mathfrak{R}^n$ is *orthogonal* if $\mathbf{x}_i^T\mathbf{x}_j = 0$, $i \neq j$. A set is *orthonormal* if $\mathbf{x}_i^T\mathbf{x}_j = \delta_{ij}$. $\delta_{ij} = 1$ for $i = j$ and zero otherwise. A real matrix $\mathbf{A}$ is orthogonal if $\mathbf{A}^T\mathbf{A} = \mathbf{A}\mathbf{A}^T = \mathbf{I}$. This implies that $\det(\mathbf{A}) = 1$, that is, $\mathbf{A}$ is nonsingular.

Eigenvalues and Eigenvectors $\mathbf{A} \in \mathfrak{R}^{n \times n}$. If λ exists such that $\mathbf{A}\mathbf{v} = \lambda\mathbf{v}$, $\mathbf{v} \neq \mathbf{0}$, λ is an eigenvalue of $\mathbf{A}$, and $\mathbf{v}$ is the corresponding eigenvector. λ_i are solutions of $\det(\mathbf{A} - \lambda\mathbf{I}) = 0$. If $\mathbf{A}$ is normal, that is, if $\mathbf{A}\mathbf{A}^T = \mathbf{A}^T\mathbf{A}$, then $\mathbf{A}$ can be factorized into $\mathbf{A} = \mathbf{V}\mathbf{\Lambda}\mathbf{V}^T$. $\mathbf{\Lambda}$ is a diagonal matrix with $\lambda - s$ on the diagonal. $\mathbf{\Lambda} = \mathbf{V}^T\mathbf{A}\mathbf{V}$.

Singular Value Decomposition A set of linear equations is given by $\mathbf{A}\mathbf{x} = \mathbf{y}$, $\mathbf{A} \in \mathfrak{R}^{m \times n}$, $\mathbf{x} \in \mathfrak{R}^n$, $\mathbf{y} \in \mathfrak{R}^n$. When $\mathbf{A}$ is very close to singular, that is, when $\det(\mathbf{A}) \approx 0$, Gaussian elimination (or LU decomposition) will fail, and singular value decomposition techniques will solve the problem. Any (m, n) matrix $\mathbf{A}(m \geq n)$ can be written as a product

$$\mathbf{A} = {}_m[\mathbf{A}]^n = {}_m[\mathbf{U}]^n \begin{bmatrix} \sigma_1 & & \\ & \sigma_2 & \\ & & \sigma_n \end{bmatrix} {}_n[\mathbf{V}^T]^n = \mathbf{U}\mathbf{S}\mathbf{V}^T.$$

$\mathbf{U}$ is an (m,n) column-orthogonal matrix, and $\mathbf{S}$ is an (n,n) diagonal matrix with $\sigma_{ii} \geq 0$. $\mathbf{V}^T$ is a transpose of an (n,n) orthogonal matrix. $\mathbf{U}$ and $\mathbf{V}$ are orthonormal matrices,

$$\mathbf{U}^T\mathbf{U} = \mathbf{V}^T\mathbf{V} = \mathbf{I} = [\mathbf{U}^T][\mathbf{U}] = [\mathbf{V}^T][\mathbf{V}] = \begin{bmatrix} 1 & & \\ & 1 & \\ & & 1 \end{bmatrix}.$$

For a square matrix $\mathbf{A} = (n,n)$,

$$\mathbf{A}^{-1} = \mathbf{V}\left[\text{diag}\frac{1}{\sigma_i}\right]\mathbf{U}^T.$$

The σ_i are singular values, which are square roots of the nonzero eigenvalues of $\mathbf{A}^T\mathbf{A}$ or $\mathbf{A}\mathbf{A}^T$. For an (m,n) matrix $\mathbf{A}$, $\mathbf{A}^+$ (pseudoinverse) is related to the singular value decomposition of $\mathbf{A}$ by the formula

$$\mathbf{A}^+ = \mathbf{V}\mathbf{S}^+\mathbf{U}^T, \qquad \left[\mathbf{S}^+ = \mathbf{S}^{-1}, \text{ i.e., } \mathbf{S}^+ = \text{diag}\frac{1}{\sigma_i}\right].$$

An important use of singular value decomposition is the solution of a system of linear equations (in the sense of the minimum L_2 norm). This is particularly reliable for badly conditioned matrices

$$\mathbf{x}^* = \sum_{i=1}^{r} \sigma_i^{-1}\mathbf{v}_i\mathbf{u}_i^T\mathbf{y} = \mathbf{V}\mathbf{S}^+\mathbf{U}^T\mathbf{y}.$$

Linear Least-Squares Problem   The last result solves the minimization problem called the linear least-squares problem. Find $\mathbf{x}$ that minimizes $\|\mathbf{A}\mathbf{x} - \mathbf{y}\|_2^2$, that is, $\mathbf{x}$ should minimize the error function

$$E(\mathbf{x}) = \tfrac{1}{2}(\mathbf{A}\mathbf{x} - \mathbf{y})^T(\mathbf{A}\mathbf{x} - \mathbf{y}).$$

$$\frac{\partial E}{\partial \mathbf{x}} = \mathbf{0} = \frac{\partial(\mathbf{A}\mathbf{x} - \mathbf{y})^T(\mathbf{A}\mathbf{x} - \mathbf{y})}{\partial \mathbf{x}} = \frac{\partial(\mathbf{y} - \mathbf{A}\mathbf{x})(\mathbf{y} - \mathbf{A}\mathbf{x})^T}{\partial \mathbf{x}}$$

$$= \frac{\partial(\mathbf{y}\mathbf{y}^T + \mathbf{A}\mathbf{x}\mathbf{x}^T\mathbf{A}^T - \mathbf{A}\mathbf{x}\mathbf{y}^T - \mathbf{y}\mathbf{x}^T\mathbf{A}^T)}{\partial \mathbf{x}}$$

$$= 0 + 2\mathbf{A}^T\mathbf{A}\mathbf{x} - \mathbf{A}^T\mathbf{y} - \mathbf{A}^T\mathbf{y} = \mathbf{0}.$$

$$2(\mathbf{A}^T\mathbf{A}\mathbf{x} - \mathbf{A}^T\mathbf{y}) = \mathbf{0}.$$

$$\mathbf{x}^* = (\mathbf{A}^T\mathbf{A})^{-1}\mathbf{A}^T\mathbf{y}.$$

Curve (Surface) Fitting—Regression, Estimation, Identification   The approximating function

$$f_a(\mathbf{x}, \mathbf{w}) = \sum_{i=1}^{N} w_i \varphi_i(\mathbf{x})$$

is shown in figure 9.3. We form an *error, cost, objective, merit, fitness* function or a *performance index* of approximation $J(\mathbf{w})$, or $E(\mathbf{w})$. Note that different names are used in different fields for the same $J(\mathbf{w})$. Measurement errors or source errors are usually called *noise*.

$$J(\mathbf{w}) = \frac{1}{2}\sum_{i=1}^{P} e_i^2 = \frac{1}{2}\sum_{i=1}^{P}\left(y_i - \sum_{i=1}^{N} w_i\varphi_i\right)^2,$$

$$y_1 = y(x_1) = w_1\varphi_1(x_1) + w_2\varphi_2(x_1) + \cdots + w_{n-1}\varphi_{n-1}(x_1) + w_N\varphi_N(x_1)$$

$$y_2 = y(x_2) = w_1\varphi_1(x_2) + w_2\varphi_2(x_2) + \cdots + w_{n-1}\varphi_{n-1}(x_2) + w_N\varphi_N(x_2)$$

$$\vdots$$

$$y_P = y(x_P) = w_1\varphi_1(x_P) + w_2\varphi_2(x_P) + \cdots + w_{n-1}\varphi_{n-1}(x_P) + w_N\varphi_N(x_P)$$

$$\mathbf{y} = \mathbf{G}\mathbf{w}.$$

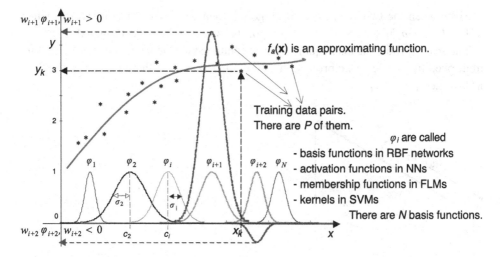

Figure 9.3
Nonlinear regression (interpolation or approximation) with linear combination of nonlinear basis functions (one-dimensional case).

The subject of optimization is **w**. Find **w** in order that $J(\mathbf{w}) = \min$, by pseudo-inversion of **G**,

$$\mathbf{w} = (\mathbf{G}^T\mathbf{G})^{-1}\mathbf{G}^T\mathbf{y} = \mathbf{G}^+\mathbf{y}.$$

The solution is a one-step procedure. (Note that this is valid for linear in parameters regression). A few different cases follow:

$P = N$ as many basis functions as data (interpolation); no filtering of noise.

$P > N$ one least-squares solution for **w**; filtering of noise.

$P < N$ infinite number of solutions or no solution.

9.3   Linear Algebra and Analytic Geometry

Consider two $(n, 1)$ vectors **a** and **b**. The scalar (inner or dot) product is given as

$$\mathbf{a}^T\mathbf{b} = \mathbf{b}^T\mathbf{a} = a_1b_1 + a_2b_2 + \cdots + a_nb_n.$$

The length of vector **a** is given as $\|\mathbf{a}\| = \sqrt{\mathbf{a}^T\mathbf{a}} = \sqrt{a_1^2 + a_2^2 + \cdots + a_n^2}$. The angle α between the two vectors **a** and **b** can be obtained from $\mathbf{a}^T\mathbf{b} = \|\mathbf{a}\|\,\|\mathbf{b}\|\cos\alpha$ as

$$\cos\alpha = \frac{\mathbf{a}^T\mathbf{b}}{\|\mathbf{a}\|\,\|\mathbf{b}\|} = \frac{a_1b_1 + a_2b_2 + \cdots + a_nb_n}{\sqrt{a_1^2 + a_2^2 + \cdots + a_n^2}\,\sqrt{b_1^2 + b_2^2 + \cdots + b_n^2}}.$$

Clearly, when the two vectors are orthogonal, then $\cos\alpha = 0$. In other words, when $\mathbf{a}^T\mathbf{b} = \mathbf{b}^T\mathbf{a} = a_1b_1 + a_2b_2 + \cdots + a_nb_n = 0$, the two vectors are orthogonal.

The scalar product is also equal to the absolute value (the length) of one of vectors multiplied by the algebraic projection of the other vector on the direction of the first: $\mathbf{a}^T\mathbf{b} = \|\mathbf{a}\|b_\mathbf{a} = \|\mathbf{b}\|a_\mathbf{b}$.

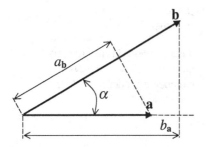

Hyperplane   The set of points $(x_1, x_2, \ldots, x_n) \in \mathfrak{R}^n$ satisfying the equation

$$w_1 x_1 + w_2 x_2 + \cdots + w_n x_n + w_{n+1} = 0, \tag{HP}$$

where the w_i are not all zero, form a hyperplane (a linear manifold of dimension $n - 1$). Conversely, any plane in $\mathfrak{R}^n$ can be defined by the preceding equation.

The equation of the plane through the point $(x_{10}, x_{20}, \ldots, x_{n0})$ normal to a vector $\mathbf{n}$ given with coordinates $[w_1, w_2, \ldots, w_n]^T$ is

$$w_1(x_1 - x_{10}) + w_2(x_2 - x_{20}) + \cdots + w_n(x_n - x_{n0}) = 0$$

Conversely, given (HP) we can determine a vector orthogonal to the plane as $\mathbf{n} = [w_1, w_2, \ldots, w_n]^T$. Thus, for example, in a two-dimensional classification problem, a decision plane

$$4x + (-2y) + 4z - 6 = 0$$

defines the separation line in the feature plane (x, y) with a unit normal vector

$$\mathbf{n}_u = \begin{bmatrix} -\dfrac{w_1}{w_3} & -\dfrac{w_2}{w_3} \\ \|\mathbf{n}\| & \|\mathbf{n}\| \end{bmatrix}^T, \quad \text{where} \quad \|\mathbf{n}\| = \sqrt{\left(-\dfrac{w_1}{w_3}\right)^2 + \left(-\dfrac{w_2}{w_3}\right)^2}.$$

The vector $\mathbf{n}_u = [0.89 \quad -0.45]^T$ points to the feature (x, y) half-plane for which $z > 0$. For the decision plane $4x + (-2y) + (-4z) - 6 = 0$, $\mathbf{n}_u = [-0.89 \quad 0.45]^T$.

Quadratic Form   A quadratic form is a quadratic function of the form

$$\mathbf{Q} = \mathbf{x}^T \mathbf{A} \mathbf{x} = \sum_{i=1}^{n} \sum_{j=1}^{n} a_{ij} x_i x_j$$

$$= a_{11} x_1^2 + (a_{12} + a_{21}) x_1 x_2 + (a_{13} + a_{31}) x_1 x_3 + \cdots + a_{22} x_2^2 + \cdots),$$

where $\mathbf{x}$ is an $(n, 1)$ vector and $\mathbf{A}$ is a symmetric matrix of order n. The (real) quadratic form is said to be *positive definite* if $\mathbf{x}^T \mathbf{A} \mathbf{x} > 0$ for all nonzero vectors $\mathbf{x}$. It is said to be *negative definite* if $\mathbf{x}^T \mathbf{A} \mathbf{x} < 0$ for all nonzero vectors $\mathbf{x}$, and it is said to be *positive semidefinite* if $\mathbf{x}^T \mathbf{A} \mathbf{x} \geq 0$ for all nonzero vectors $\mathbf{x}$. The definiteness of the matrix $\mathbf{A}$ is the same as the definiteness of the quadratic form. Both can be determined by analyzing the eigenvalues of $\mathbf{A}$:

Eigenvalues λ_i

Positive	Zero	Negative	Type of Form	Matrix A of Form
•			Positive definite	Nonsingular
•	•		Positive semidefinite	Singular
•		•	Indefinite	Nonsingular
•	•	•	Indefinite	Singular
		•	Negative definite	Nonsingular
	•	•	Negative semidefinite	Singular
	•		Null	Singular

Every quadratic form has a diagonal representation, that is, it can be reduced to a sum of squares. There exists a nonsingular matrix $\mathbf{M}$ such that $\mathbf{M}^T\mathbf{A}\mathbf{M} = \mathbf{\Lambda}$, where $\mathbf{\Lambda}$ is a diagonal matrix of order n. Letting $\mathbf{y} = \mathbf{M}\mathbf{x}$ quadratic forms becomes

$$\mathbf{y}^T\mathbf{A}\mathbf{y} = \mathbf{x}^T\mathbf{M}^T\mathbf{A}\mathbf{M}\mathbf{x} = \mathbf{x}^T\mathbf{\Lambda}\mathbf{x} = \sum_{i=1}^{n} \lambda_i x_i^2.$$

9.4 Basics of Multivariable Analysis

Functions Set of real-valued functions $F_1(\mathbf{x}), F_2(\mathbf{x}), \ldots, F_m(\mathbf{x})$ on $\mathfrak{R}^n$ can be regarded as a single vector function $\mathbf{F}(\mathbf{x}) = [F_1 \quad F_2 \quad \cdots \quad F_m]^T$, $\mathbf{F}: \mathfrak{R}^n \to \mathfrak{R}^m$.

Gradient $F(\mathbf{x}) = F(x_1 x_2 \ldots x_n)$, $F: \mathfrak{R}^n \to \mathfrak{R}$. Note that F is *scalar* function of a real vector $\mathbf{x} \in \mathfrak{R}^n$.

$$\nabla_{\mathbf{x}} F(\mathbf{x}) = \frac{\partial F(\mathbf{x})}{\partial \mathbf{x}} = \left[\left[\frac{\partial F}{\partial x_1}\right] \left[\frac{\partial F}{\partial x_2}\right] \cdots \left[\frac{\partial F}{\partial x_n}\right] \right]^T.$$

The gradient is a column vector.

Jacobian $\mathbf{F}$ is now a vector function $\mathbf{F}: \mathfrak{R}^n \to \mathfrak{R}^m$.

$$\mathbf{F}(\mathbf{x}) = [F_1 \quad F_2 \quad \cdots \quad F_m]^T, \quad J = \left[\frac{\partial F_i}{\partial x_j}\right] = \begin{bmatrix} \dfrac{\partial F_1}{\partial x_1} & \cdots & \cdots & \dfrac{\partial F_1}{\partial x_n} \\ \vdots & & & \vdots \\ \vdots & & & \vdots \\ \dfrac{\partial F_m}{\partial x_1} & \cdots & \cdots & \dfrac{\partial F_m}{\partial x_n} \end{bmatrix}.$$

Hessian $F(\mathbf{x}) = F(x_1 \, x_2 \ldots x_n)$, F: $\mathfrak{R}^n \to \mathfrak{R}$. F is *scalar* function again. The Hessian matrix of $F(\mathbf{x})$ is defined as the symmetric matrix with the (i,j)th element $\dfrac{\partial^2 F(\mathbf{x})}{\partial x_i \partial x_j}$:

$$\mathbf{H}(\mathbf{w}) = \nabla_{\mathbf{x}}^2 F(\mathbf{x}) = \begin{bmatrix} \dfrac{\partial}{\partial x_1}\left(\dfrac{\partial F}{\partial \mathbf{x}}\right)^T \\ \vdots \\ \dfrac{\partial}{\partial x_n}\left(\dfrac{\partial F}{\partial \mathbf{x}}\right)^T \end{bmatrix} = \begin{bmatrix} \dfrac{\partial^2 F(\mathbf{x})}{\partial x_1^2} & \dfrac{\partial^2 F(\mathbf{x})}{\partial x_1 \partial x_2} & \cdots & \dfrac{\partial^2 F(\mathbf{x})}{\partial x_1 \partial x_n} \\ \dfrac{\partial^2 F(\mathbf{x})}{\partial x_2 \partial x_1} & \dfrac{\partial^2 F(\mathbf{x})}{\partial x_2^2} & \cdots & \dfrac{\partial^2 F(\mathbf{x})}{\partial x_2 \partial x_n} \\ \vdots & \vdots & \vdots & \vdots \\ \dfrac{\partial^2 F(\mathbf{x})}{\partial x_n \partial x_1} & \dfrac{\partial^2 F(\mathbf{x})}{\partial x_n \partial x_2} & \cdots & \dfrac{\partial^2 F(\mathbf{x})}{\partial x_n^2} \end{bmatrix}.$$

The Hessian of $F(\mathbf{x})$ is the Jacobian of the gradient $\nabla F(\mathbf{x})$. A typical application of the Hessian matrix is in nonlinear optimization (minimization or maximization) tasks, when the Hessian of cost function $J(\mathbf{w})$ is used.

Differentiation of a Scalar Function with Respect to a Vector

1. $\dfrac{\partial (\mathbf{a}^T(\mathbf{x})\mathbf{b}(\mathbf{x}))}{\partial \mathbf{x}} = \left[\dfrac{\partial(\mathbf{a}(\mathbf{x}))}{\partial \mathbf{x}}\right]^T \mathbf{b}(\mathbf{x}) + \left[\dfrac{\partial(\mathbf{b}(\mathbf{x}))}{\partial \mathbf{x}}\right] \mathbf{a}(\mathbf{x}) = [\nabla_{\mathbf{x}}\mathbf{a}^T(\mathbf{x})]\mathbf{b}(\mathbf{x}) + [\nabla_{\mathbf{x}}\mathbf{b}^T(\mathbf{x})]\mathbf{a}(\mathbf{x}).$

2. $\dfrac{\partial(\mathbf{x}^T\mathbf{y})}{\partial \mathbf{x}} = \mathbf{y}.$

3. $\dfrac{\partial(\mathbf{x}^T\mathbf{x})}{\partial \mathbf{x}} = 2\mathbf{x}.$

4. $\dfrac{\partial(\mathbf{x}^T\mathbf{A}\mathbf{y})}{\partial \mathbf{x}} = \mathbf{A}\mathbf{y}.$

5. $\dfrac{\partial(\mathbf{y}^T\mathbf{A}\mathbf{x})}{\partial \mathbf{x}} = (\mathbf{y}^T\mathbf{A})^T = \mathbf{A}^T\mathbf{y}.$

6. $\dfrac{\partial(\mathbf{x}^T\mathbf{A}\mathbf{x})}{\partial \mathbf{x}} = (\mathbf{A} + \mathbf{A}^T)\mathbf{x}$ if $\mathbf{A}$ is not symmetric.

7. $\dfrac{\partial(\mathbf{x}^T\mathbf{A}\mathbf{x})}{\partial \mathbf{x}} = 2\mathbf{x}^T\mathbf{A} = 2\mathbf{A}\mathbf{x}$ if $\mathbf{A}$ is symmetric.

8. $\dfrac{\partial[\mathbf{a}^T(\mathbf{x})\mathbf{Q}\mathbf{a}(\mathbf{x})]}{\partial \mathbf{x}} = 2[\nabla_{\mathbf{x}}\mathbf{a}^T(\mathbf{x})]\mathbf{Q}\mathbf{a}(\mathbf{x}).$

In the preceding expressions, $\mathbf{a}(\mathbf{x})$ and $\mathbf{b}(\mathbf{x})$ are $(m, 1)$ vector functions of $\mathbf{x}$.

Chain Rule   Let $F(\mathbf{x}) = h(g(\mathbf{x}))$, $x \in \Re^n$, and F, h, and g are scalar functions.

$$\frac{\partial F}{\partial x_i} = \frac{\partial h}{\partial g} \frac{\partial g}{\partial x_i}.$$

In the general case, $\mathbf{h}$: $\Re^r \to \Re^m$, and $\mathbf{g}$: $\Re^n \to \Re^r$. Thus, $\boldsymbol{F}$: $\Re^n \to \Re^m$. The chain rule now looks like this: $\nabla F(\mathbf{x}) = \nabla_{\mathbf{g}} \mathbf{h}(\mathbf{g}(\mathbf{x})) \nabla_{\mathbf{x}} \mathbf{g}(\mathbf{x})$.

9.5   Basics from Probability Theory

Sets   A set theory describes the relations between events. There are sets, subsets, elements, empty sets.

Set Operations

$\bar{A}$	Complement of A
$A \cup B$	Union of A and B
$A \cap B$	Intersection of A and B

Properties

Commutative	Associative	Distributive
$A \cup B = B \cup A$	$(A \cup B) \cup C = A \cup (B \cup C)$	$A \cap (B \cup C) = (A \cap B) \cup (A \cap C)$
$A \cap B = B \cap A$	$(A \cap B) \cap C = A \cap (B \cap C)$	$A \cup (B \cap C) = (A \cup B) \cap (A \cup C)$

Probability   To each event A of a class of possible events in a simple experiment, a number $P[A]$ is assigned. This number is called probability if it satisfies

1. $P[A] \geq 0$.
2. $P[\Omega] = 1$ if Ω is a certain event.
   $P[\phi] = 0$ if ϕ is an impossible event.
3. $P[A \cup B] = P[A] + P[B]$ if $A \cap B = 0$ (if the events are mutually exclusive),

and when there is an infinite number of events,

4. $P[A_1 \cup A_2 \cup A_3 \cup \cdots] = \sum_{i=1}^{\infty} P[A_i]$ if $A_i \cap A_j = 0$ for each $i \neq j$.

Combined Experiments   The outcomes of two simple experiments, A_i and B_j, are considered a (combined) event $[A_i, B_j]$.[2]

$$0 \leq P[A_i, B_j] \leq 1. \qquad \sum_{i,j} P[A_i, B_j] = 1.$$

$$P[A_i] = \sum_j P[A_i, B_j] \quad \text{if } B_k \cap B_j = \phi \text{ for each } k \neq j.$$

$$P[B_i] = \sum_j P[A_i, B_j] \quad \text{if } A_k \cap A_i = \phi \text{ for each } k \neq i.$$

Conditional Probability   Defined as

$$P[A_i \mid B_j] = \frac{P[A_i, B_j]}{P[B_j]} \quad \text{if } P[B_j] \neq 0;$$

consequently,

$$P[A_i \mid B_j]P[B_j] = P[A_i, B_j] = P[B_j \mid A_i]P[A_i].$$

For independent events,

$$P[A_i \mid B_j] = P[A_i]. \qquad P[A_i, B_j] = P[A_i]P[B_j].$$

A *random variable x* is a quantity that can have different values in such a way that for each given real number X the probability $P[x \leq X]$ is defined. The random variable x can be *discrete*, that is, it can have a finite set of distinct values, or it can be *continuous*. The basic probability functions and parameters for both discrete and continuous variables are given in tables 9.1 and 9.2. In many cases, it is useful to work with probability parameters instead of probability functions (see table 9.2).

Table 9.1
Probability Functions for a Random Variable x

	Discrete	Continuous
One-Dimensional Case		
Distribution function	$F(X) = P[x \leq X]$	$F(X) = P[x \leq X]$
Probability-density function (PDF)	$P_i = P[x = X_i]$	$P(x) = \dfrac{dF(x)}{dx}$
Probability	$\displaystyle\sum_{some\ i} P_i$	$P(X)\Delta X \approx P[X < x \leq X + \Delta X]$
		$\displaystyle\int_a^b P(\xi)\,d\xi = P[a < x \leq b]$
Properties	$0 \leq P_i \leq 1$	$0 \leq P(x)$
	$\displaystyle\sum_1 P_i = 1$	$\displaystyle\int_{\infty}^{+\infty} P(\xi)\,d\xi = 1$
	$F(x) = \displaystyle\sum_{all\ x_i \leq x} P_i$	$F(x) = \displaystyle\int_{-\infty}^{x} P(\xi)\,d\xi$
		$F(-\infty) = 0, \quad F(x) = 1$

Table 9.1 (continued)

	Discrete	Continuous
Examples of density functions	Binomial	Normal

$$P[x] = \binom{n}{x} p^x (1-p)^{n-x},$$
$$x = 0, 1, \ldots, n$$

$$P(x) = \frac{1}{\sigma\sqrt{2\pi}} \exp\left[-\frac{1}{2}\left(\frac{x-\mu}{\sigma}\right)^2\right],$$
$$-\infty \leq x \leq \infty$$

Poisson

Exponential

$$P[x] = \frac{\lambda^x \varepsilon^{-\lambda}}{x!}, \quad x = 0, 1, 2, \ldots$$

$$P(x) = \begin{cases} \lambda \varepsilon^{-\lambda x} & 0 \leq x \leq \infty \\ 0 & -\infty < x < 0 \end{cases}$$

Two-Dimensional Case

(Joint) distribution function

$$F(X, Y) = P[x \leq X, y \leq Y]$$

$$F(X, Y) = P[x \leq X, y \leq Y]$$

(Joint) probability-density function

$$P_{ij} = P[x = X_i, y = Y_j]$$

$$P(x, y) = \frac{\partial^2 F(x, y)}{\partial x \partial y}$$

(Joint) probability

$$\sum_{\substack{\text{some } i \\ \text{some } j}} P_{ij}$$

$$P(X, Y)\Delta X \Delta Y \approx P[X < x \leq X + \Delta X, Y < y \leq Y + \Delta Y]$$

Properties

$$0 \leq P_{ij} \leq 1$$

$$0 \leq P(x, y)$$

$$\sum_{i,j} P_{ij} = 1$$

$$\int_{-\infty}^{+\infty} \int_{-\infty}^{+\infty} P(\xi, \eta)\, d\xi\, d\eta = 1$$

$$F(x, y) = \sum_{\text{all } x_i \leq x,\, \text{all } y_i \leq y} P_{ij}$$

$$F(x, y) = \int_{-\infty}^{+\infty} \int_{-\infty}^{+\infty} P(\xi, \eta)\, d\xi\, d\eta$$

$$F(-\infty, y) = 0, \quad F(x, -\infty) = 0,$$
$$F(\infty, \infty) = 0$$

Marginal distribution function

$$F(X, \infty) = P[x \leq X, y \leq \infty]$$
$$= P[x \leq X]$$
$$F(\infty, Y) = P[x \leq \infty, y \leq Y]$$
$$= P[y \leq Y]$$

$$F(X, \infty) = P[x \leq X, y \leq \infty]$$
$$= P[x \leq X]$$
$$F(\infty, Y) = P[x \leq \infty, y \leq Y]$$
$$= P[y \leq Y]$$

Marginal probability-density function

$$P_i = \sum_j P_{ij}$$

$$P(x) = \frac{dF(x, \infty)}{dx} = \int_{-\infty}^{+\infty} P(x, \eta)\, d\eta$$

$$P_j = \sum_i P_{ij}$$

$$P(y) = \frac{dF(\infty, y)}{dy} = \int_{-\infty}^{+\infty} P(\xi, y)\, d\xi$$

Conditional distribution function

$$F(X|Y) = P[x \leq X \mid y = Y]$$
$$F(Y|X) = P[y \leq Y \mid x = X]$$

$$F(X|Y) = P[x \leq X \mid y = Y]$$
$$F(Y|X) = P[y \leq Y \mid x = X]$$

Conditional probability-density function

$$P(x = X_i \mid y = Y_j) = \frac{P_{ij}}{P_j}$$

$$P(x|y) = \frac{P(x, y)}{P(y)}$$

$$P(y = Y_j \mid x = X_i) = \frac{P_{ij}}{P_i}$$

$$P(y|x) = \frac{P(x, y)}{P(x)}$$

$$P(x|y)P(y) = P(x, y) = P(y|x)P(x)$$

Independence of X and Y

$$F(x, y) = F(x)F(y)$$
$$P_{ij} = P_i P_j$$

$$F(x, y) = F(x)F(y)$$
$$P(x, y) = P(x)P(y)$$

An important example of a continuous PDF is a bivariate normal (Gaussian) PDF:

$$P(x, y) = \frac{1}{2\pi\sigma_x\sigma_y(1-\rho^2)^{1/2}} \exp\left[-\frac{1}{2}D\right]$$

$$D = \frac{1}{1-\rho^2}\left\{\left(\frac{x-\mu_x}{\sigma_x}\right)^2 - 2\rho\left(\frac{x-\mu_x}{\sigma_x}\right) \times \left(\frac{y-\mu_y}{\sigma_y}\right) + \left(\frac{y-\mu_y}{\sigma_y}\right)^2\right\}$$

Table 9.2
Probability Parameters for a Random Variable x

	Discrete	Continuous
One-Dimensional Case		
Expectation	$\mathbb{E}[\ldots] = \sum \ldots P_i$	$\mathbb{E}[\ldots] = \int_{-\infty}^{+\infty} \ldots P(x)\,dx$
	$\mathbb{E}[f(x)] = \sum_i f(x_i) P_i$	$\mathbb{E}[f(x)] = \int_{-\infty}^{+\infty} f(x) P(x)\,dx$
Linearity of the expectation operator	$\mathbb{E}[\alpha x + \beta y] = \alpha \mathbb{E}[x] + \beta \mathbb{E}[y]$	$\mathbb{E}[\alpha x + \beta y] = \alpha \mathbb{E}[x] + \beta \mathbb{E}[y]$
nth moment	$\mathbb{E}[x^n] = \sum_i x_i^n P_i$	$\mathbb{E}[x^n] = \int_{-\infty}^{+\infty} x^n P(x)\,dx$
First moment (mean, expectation)	$\mu = \mathbb{E}[x]$	$\mu = \mathbb{E}[x]$
	$\mu = \sum_i x_i P_i$	$\mu = \int_{-\infty}^{+\infty} x P(x)\,dx$
nth central moment	$\mathbb{E}[(x-\mu)^n]$	$\mathbb{E}[(x-\mu)^n]$
First central moment	$\mathbb{E}[(x-\mu)]$	$\mathbb{E}[(x-\mu)]$
Second central moment	$\sigma^2 = \mathbb{E}[(x-\mu)^2] = \mathbb{E}[x^2] - \{\mathbb{E}[x]\}^2$	$\sigma^2 = \mathbb{E}[(x-\mu)^2] = \mathbb{E}[x^2] - \{\mathbb{E}[x]\}^2$
Variance	$\sigma^2 = \sum_i x_i^2 P_i - \mu^2$	$\sigma^2 = \int_{-\infty}^{+\infty} x^2 P(x)\,dx - \mu^2$
Standard deviation or spread		σ
Two-Dimensional Case		
	$\mathbb{E}[\ldots] = \sum_{i,j} \ldots P_{ij}$	$\mathbb{E}[\ldots] = \int_{-\infty}^{+\infty} \int_{-\infty}^{+\infty} \ldots p(x,y)\,dx\,dy$
	$\mathbb{E}[f(x,y)] = \sum_{i,j} f(x_i, y_i) P_{ij}$	$\mathbb{E}[f(x,y)] = \iint f(x,y) p(x,y)\,dx\,dy$
Mean	$\mu_x = \mathbb{E}(x)$	$\mu_x = \mathbb{E}(x)$
	$\mu_x = \sum_{i,j} x_i P_{ij}$	$\mu_x = \iint x p(x,y)\,dx\,dy$
Variance	$\sigma_x^2 = \mathbb{E}[(x-\mu_x)^2]$	$\sigma_x^2 = \mathbb{E}[(x-\mu_x)^2]$
	$\sigma_x^2 = \sum_{i,j} x_i^2 P_{i,j} - \mu_x^2$	$\sigma_x^2 = \iint x^2 p(x,y)\,dx\,dy - \mu_x^2$
Covariance	$\sigma_{xy}^2 = \operatorname{cov}[xy] = \mathbb{E}[(x-\mu_x)(y-\mu_y)]$ $= \mathbb{E}[xy] - \mu_x \mu_y$	$\sigma_{xy}^2 = \operatorname{cov}[xy] = \mathbb{E}[(x-\mu_x)(y-\mu_y)]$ $= \mathbb{E}[xy] - \mu_x \mu_y$
Correlation coefficient	$\rho_{xy} = \dfrac{\sigma_{xy}^2}{\sigma_x \sigma_y}$	$\rho_{xy} = \dfrac{\sigma_{xy}^2}{\sigma_x \sigma_y}$

Table 9.2 (continued)

	Discrete	Continuous
Conditional expectation	$\mathbb{E}[x\lvert y=y_j]=\dfrac{\sum_i x_i P_{ij}}{P_j}$	$\mathbb{E}[x\lvert y]=\dfrac{\int xp(x,y)\,dx}{p(y)}$
Property	$\mathbb{E}[\mathbb{E}[x\lvert y]]=\mathbb{E}[x]$	$\mathbb{E}[\mathbb{E}[x\lvert y]]=\mathbb{E}[x]$
Independence of x and y	$\mathbb{E}[xy]=\mathbb{E}[x]\mathbb{E}[y]$ $\rho_{xy}=0$	$\mathbb{E}[xy]=\mathbb{E}[x]\mathbb{E}[y]$ $\rho_{xy}=0$
	$\sum_{i,j} x_i y_j P_{ij}=\left\{\sum_i x_i P_i\right\}\left\{\sum_j y_j P_j\right\}$ $=\mu_x\mu_y$	$\iint xy\,p(x,y)\,dx\,dy$ $=\left\{\int xp(x)\,dx\right\}\left\{\int yp(y)\,dy\right\}$ $=\mu_x\mu_y$

Selected Abbreviations

ABC	adaptive backthrough control
AF	activation function
AIC	adaptive inverse control
ARMA	auto-regressive moving average
BF	basis function
CG	conjugate gradient
EBP	error backpropagation
EC	evolutionary computing
ERM	empirical risk minimization
FAM	fuzzy additive model
FIR	finite impulse response
FLM	fuzzy logic model
GA	genetic algorithm
GRBF	generalized radial basis function
HL	hidden layer
IIR	infinite impulse response
IMC	internal model control
LFR	learning of fuzzy rules
LMS	least mean square
LP	linear programming
MAP	maximum-a-posteriori (decision criterion)
MLP	multilayer perceptron
MSE	mean squared error
NARMAX	nonlinear auto-regressive moving average (with) exogenous variable
NN	neural network
NZSE	New Zealand stock exchange
OCR	optical character recognition
OCSH	optimal canonical separating hyperplane
OL	output layer
OLS	orthogonal least squares
PDF	probability-density function

QP   quadratic programming
RBF   radial basis function
RLS   recursive least squares
SLT   statistical learning theory
SRM   structural risk minimization
SVM   support vector machine
VC   Vapnik-Chervonenkis

Notes

Preface

1. This language is sometimes called Serbocroatian or Croatian. Soon, unfortunately, there may be some more recently created names for the unique Serbian language.

Chapter 1

1. In different references in the literature, one may find examples of confusion in presenting novel computing techniques. A typical one is equating the genetic algorithm (GA) or evolutionary computing (EC) techniques with NNs and FL models. NNs and FL models are modeling tools, whereas GA and EC are two out of many optimization algorithms that can be applied for parameter adjustment during the learning (training, adaptation) phase of neural or fuzzy models.

2. Note the simplicity of this notation. The use of the summation sign is avoided. Product $\mathbf{V}\mathbf{x}$ is a column vector of the inputs to the HL neurons. After these inputs have been transformed through the HL activation functions (here sigmoidals), the NN output is obtained as a scalar product $\mathbf{w}^T\boldsymbol{\sigma}$ between the OL weights $\mathbf{w}$ and the HL neurons output vector $\boldsymbol{\sigma}$, where $\boldsymbol{\sigma} = \mathbf{y}$.

3. The prefix *hyper* is used whenever the space dimensionality is higher than 3. In these cases, nothing can be visualized. But the math works in any space, and this makes the problems solvable.

4. The difference between interpolation and approximation is discussed later. In short, interpolation is just a special case of approximation when $F(x, \mathbf{w})$ passes through the given training data points.

5. Instead of "measure of goodness," "closeness of approximation" or simply "error" is also in use.

6. Throughout this book the black square marks the end of an example.

7. Equations (1.27) and (1.28) represent the two most popular feedforward neural networks used today—the multilayer perceptron and the radial basis function NN. Their graphical representations are given later. A multilayer perceptron is an NN with one or more hidden layers comprising neurons with sigmoidal activation functions. A typical representative of such functions is a tangent hyperbolic function. The structure of RBF networks is the same, but the HL activation functions are radially symmetric.

8. Optimization implies either maximizing or minimizing. Because the maximum of a function $f(x)$ occurs at the same place as does the minimum of $-f(x)$, it is convenient to discuss only the minimization.

9. The Hessian matrix is formally introduced by (1.46) and used in chapter 8.

10. *Learning machine* means all the different models one can use (neural networks, fuzzy logic models, any mathematical function with unknown parameters, RBF networks and the like) in trying to find the regularities between the input and the output variables.

11. Note that in presenting the theoretical regression curve, the basic assumption, which will hardly ever be met in real applications while learning from a finite data set, is that the joint probability-density function $P(x, y)$ is known.

12. It is supposed that readers has some knowledge of probability theory. If not, they should consult chapter 9, which is designed for easy reference of properties and notation. The contents of chapter 9 are used freely in this text without further remark.

13. Note that the form of the expression for expected (average, mean) profit is a sum of the products between the corresponding loss functions and probabilities. This may be useful in understanding more complex expressions for risk that follow.

14. Figure 1.31 shows a three-class classification in a two-dimensional feature space for classes having the same covariance matrices $\Sigma_1 = \Sigma_2 = \Sigma_3$ but different means.

Chapter 2

1. The theory of SLT, structural risk minimization, and support vector machines has been developed since the late 1960s by V. Vapnik and A. Y. Chervonenkis (see the references at the end of the book).

2. In many practical problems, inputs x_i are usually selected before the experiment is conducted, and the training data consist of predetermined input values X and measured output values Y conditioned on X. The model (2.1) is general and covers this situation as a special case.

3. More on this issue, including when and why these models are linear or nonlinear, as well as on the similarity of RBF networks and FL models, can be found in chapter 6.

4. The presentation that follows is also valid for classification problems using the corresponding norm, and in that case, the target (regression) function is the Bayes' discriminant function.

5. In this book, the number of training data pairs or patterns are generally denoted by P. However, in the literature on SLT and SVMs, the usual notation for sample size is l. In order to accord with the standard notation in those fields, l is used as the notation for sample size (the number of training data pairs or patterns) in this section.

6. Terminology in the field of learning machines, which has roots in both approximation theory and statistics, is exceptionally diverse, and very often the same or similar concepts are variously named. Different terms are deliberately used in this section to equip the reader with terminology and skills to readily associate similar concepts with different names. The most notoriously inconsistent terminology here concerns the terms *risk* and *error*. They describe different mathematical objects, but in spirit minimizing generalization error is very like minimizing true (expected, guaranteed) risk. On the other hand, both minimization procedures also minimize the bound on test error.

7. Confidence level $1 - \eta$ should not be confused with the confidence term Ω.

8. Actually, for $\mathbf{x} \in \Re^2$, the separation is performed by planes $w_1 x_1 + w_2 x_2 + b = 0$. In other words, the decision boundary (separation line in input space) is defined by the equation $w_1 x_1 + w_2 x_2 + b = 0$.

9. In the rest of this book the following alternative notation is used for a scalar or dot product: $\mathbf{w}^T \mathbf{x} = \mathbf{x}^T \mathbf{w} = (\mathbf{w}\mathbf{x}) = (\mathbf{x}\mathbf{w})$. This use is mostly contextual and will, one hopes, not be confusing.

10. In forming the Lagrangian for constraints of the form $f_i > 0$, the inequality constraints equations are multiplied by *non-negative* Lagrange multipliers $\alpha_i \geq 0$ and *subtracted* from the objective function.

Chapter 3

1. This should be read as "planes or hyperplanes."

2. The parity problem is one in which the output required is 1 if the input pattern contains an odd number of 1's, and is 0 otherwise. This problem is a difficult one because the similar patterns that differ by a single bit have different outputs. This is pronounced with an increase in the dimension of feature space (Rumelhart Hinton, and Williams 1986).

3. Very often, particularly in the literature on identification, signal processing, and estimation, the appearance of this optimal solution vector $\mathbf{w}^*$ may be slightly different than shown in (3.25). One can come across such an expression as $\mathbf{w}_e^* = (\mathbf{X}_e^T \mathbf{X}_e)^{-1} \mathbf{X}_e^T \mathbf{D} = \mathbf{X}_e^+ \mathbf{D}$, where subscript $_e$ is used only to differentiate expressions for $\mathbf{w}_e^*$ and $\mathbf{w}^*$. This is merely a consequence of a differently arranged input data matrix $\mathbf{X}_e$. In fact, changing notation such that $\mathbf{X}_e = \mathbf{X}^T$, the notations for $\mathbf{w}^*$ and $\mathbf{w}_e^*$ are equivalent.

4. Quadratic surfaces are described by equations that combine quadratic terms only with linear terms and constants.

5. The adjective *ideal* with regard to this method is used to mean that the gradient is calculated after all the data pairs from the training data set have been presented. Thus, the gradient is calculated in an off-line, or batch, mode.

Chapter 4

1. Just for curiosity, what might "sufficient" be? Cybenko (1989) felt "quite strongly that the overwhelming majority of approximation problems would require astronomical numbers of terms." Fortunately, it turns out that this feeling was just a cautious sign of scientific concern and that in many applications the practical problems can be solved with a technically acceptable number of neurons.

2. Most heuristics presented in this section are related to another important class of multilayer neural networks—radial basis function (RBF) neural networks. The RBF network is a network with a single hidden layer, comprising neurons having radial basis activation functions. The input to these neurons u is not the scalar product of the input and the weights vector but rather the distance between the center of the radial basis function (which now represents the HL weight) and the given input vector.

3. With the RBF and FL models, the use of the bias term is optional, but with the multilayer perceptron it is mandatory.

Chapter 5

1. Multilayer perceptrons can have two or more HLs, but RBF networks typically have only one HL.

2. See the $\mathbf{G}$ matrix in (5.15) and figure 5.5.

3. A functional is an operator that maps a function onto a number.

4. The constraints that one finds in classical optimal control theory are similar: while minimizing the quadratic performance criterion given as $J = 0.5 \int_0^\infty (\mathbf{x}^T \mathbf{Q} \mathbf{x} + \mathbf{u}^T \mathbf{R} \mathbf{u})\, dt$, $\mathbf{Q} \geq 0, \mathbf{R} \geq 0$, one tries to minimize both the deviations of the state vector $\mathbf{x}$ and the control effort $\mathbf{u}$. Taking $\mathbf{Q} = \mathbf{I}$, the only design parameter left is the weighting matrix $\mathbf{R}$, which corresponds to the regularization parameter λ here. The influence of the regularization parameter λ (or of matrix $\mathbf{R}$) on the overall solution of these two different problems is the same: an increase in λ (or in $\mathbf{R}$) results in an increase of the error term $(d - f(\mathbf{x}))^2$ or of the deviations of the state vector $\mathbf{x}$ in optimal control problems.

5. The null space of the operator $\mathbf{P}$ comprises all functions $n(\mathbf{x})$ for which $\mathbf{P}n(\mathbf{x})$ is equal to zero.

6. In the case of piecewise functions, the domain is broken up into a finite number of (here P) subregions via the use of centers or knots, and the same number of (here P) piecewise functions are placed at these centers.

7. For a one-dimensional input x, compare the exponential damping $\tilde{G}(s) = e^{-\|\mathbf{s}\|^2/\beta}$ with a polynomial one $\tilde{G}(s) = s^{-4}$, which corresponds to a piecewise cubic splines approximation.

8. For two-dimensional input the covariance matrix of the Gaussian basis function $\Sigma = [\sigma_x^2 \ \sigma_x\sigma_y\rho; \sigma_x\sigma_y\rho \ \sigma_y^2]$, where ρ denotes the correlation coefficient between the input variables. For independent input variables $\rho = 0$.

Chapter 6

1. Notation: Sets are denoted by uppercase letters and their members (elements) by lowercase letters. Thus, A denotes the universe of discourse, or a collection of objects, that contains all the possible elements a of concern in each particular context. A is assumed to contain a *finite number* of elements a unless otherwise stated.

2. The author would rather order *hot slivovitz* as a nice *rememorari a patria mea*.

3. Note also that if there are n independent universes of discourse (n linguistic or input variables) the membership function is a hypersurface over an n-dimensional Cartesian product.

4. Note the unlike units of x_1 and x_2 intentionally defined on different universes of discourse.

5. Kosko (1997) has written a whole book based on SAMs. Interestingly, there is not a single line in it commenting on or describing relational matrices.

Chapter 7

1. NARMAX stands for nonlinear auto-regressive moving average with exogenous variable.

2. Similar approaches and structures have been proposed and used in many publications by Widrow and his co-workers under the global name of *adaptive inverse control*.

3. ARMA stands for auto-regressive moving average.

4. Only running animation is described. Details on walking, jumping, and vaulting animation can be found in Wang (1998).

Chapter 9

1. In the neural networks and fuzzy logic fields, this equation is typically $\mathbf{Gw} = \mathbf{d}$, where the elements of $\mathbf{G}$ are the hidden layer outputs (for neural networks) or the membership function degrees (for fuzzy logic models), $\mathbf{d}$ is a vector of the desired values, and $\mathbf{w}$ denotes the unknown output layer weights (or the rule conclusions $\mathbf{r}$ for fuzzy logic models).

2. The symbols Σ_i and $\Sigma_{i,j}$ mean summation over all i, that is, all combinations i, j.

References

Agarwal, M. 1997. A systematic classification of neural network–based control. *IEEE Control Systems* 17 (2): 75–93.

Aizerman, M. A., E. M. Braverman, and L. I. Rozonoer. 1964. Theoretical foundations of the potential function method in pattern recognition learning. *Automation and Remote Control* 25: 821–837.

Anderson, J. A., and E. Rosenfeld, eds. 1988. *Neurocomputing: Foundations of research*. Cambridge, MA: MIT Press.

Anderson, T. W. 1958. *An introduction to multivariate statistical analysis*. New York: Wiley.

Arthanari, T. S., and Y. Dodge. 1993. *Mathematical programming in statistics*. New York: Wiley.

Bello, M. G. 1992. Enhanced training algorithms, and integrated training/architecture selection for multi-layer perceptron networks. *IEEE Trans. on Neural Networks* 3 (6): 864–875.

Bennett, K. 1999. Combining support vector and mathematical programming methods for induction. In *Advances in kernel methods—SV learning*, ed. B. Schölkopf, C.J.C. Burges, and A. Smola, 307–326. Cambridge, MA: MIT Press.

Bialasiewicz, J. T., and D. I. Soloway. 1990. Neural network modeling of dynamical systems. In *Proc. IEEE Int. Symposium on Intelligent Control*, Philadelphia, 500–505.

Bishop, C. M. 1995. *Neural networks for pattern recognition*. Oxford: Clarendon Press.

Boser, B., I. Guyon, and V. N. Vapnik. 1992. A training algorithm for optimal margin classifiers. In *Proc. Fifth Annual Workshop on Computational Learning Theory*. Pittsburgh, PA: ACM Press.

Bošković, J. D., and K. S. Narendra. 1995. Comparison of linear, nonlinear and neural network–Based adaptive controllers for a class of fed-batch fermentation processes. *Automatica* 31 (6): 817–840.

Bridle, J. S. 1990. Probabilistic interpretation of feedforward classification network outputs, with relationships to statistical pattern recognition. In *Neurocomputing: Algorithms, architectures, and applications*, ed. F. Fogelman Soulie and J. Herault, 227–236. New York: Springer-Verlag.

Brogan, W. L. 1991. *Modern control theory*. 3d ed. Englewood Cliffs, NJ: Prentice Hall.

Broomhead, D. S., and D. Lowe. 1988. Multivariable functional interpolation and adaptive networks. *Complex Systems* 2: 321–355.

Bryson, A. E., and Y. C. Ho. 1969. *Applied optimal control*. New York: Blaisdell.

———. 1975. *Applied optimal control: Optimization, estimation, and control*. New York: Wiley.

Burges, C.J.C. 1998. A tutorial on support vector machines for pattern recognition. *Data Mining and Knowledge Discovery* 2 (2).

Charnes, A., W. W. Cooper, and R. O. Ferguson. 1955. Optimal estimation of executive compensation by linear programming. *Management Science* 1: 138.

Chen, S., C.F.N. Cowan, and P. M. Grant. 1991. Orthogonal least squares learning algorithm for radial basis function networks. *IEEE Trans. on Neural Networks* 2 (2): 302–309.

Chen, W. M. 1998. *Automobile robots guidance simulation by using fuzzy logic basics*. Project Report No. PME 98-19. University of Auckland, Auckland, NZ.

Cheney, E. W., and A. A. Goldstein. 1958. Note on a paper by Zuhovickii concerning the Chebyshev problem for linear equations. *Journal of the Society for Industrial and Applied Mathematics* 6: 233–239.

Cherkassky, V. 1997. An introduction to statistical learning theory. Tutorial T2A. ICONIP-97 Conference, Dunedin, NZ.

Cherkassky, V., and F. Mulier. 1998. *Learning from data: Concepts, theory, and methods*. New York: Wiley.

Chester, D. 1990. Why two hidden layers are better than one. In *Proc. IEEE Int. Joint Conference on Neural Networks*, Washington DC, 265–268.

Chua, G. 1998. *Automobile robots guidance simulation by using basic fuzzy logic*. Project Report No. PME 98-22. University of Auckland, Auckland, NZ.

Cichocki, A., and R. Unbehauen. 1993. *Neural networks for optimization and signal processing*. Chichester, UK: Wiley.

Cios, K. J., W. Pedrycz, and R. M. Swiniarski. 1998. *Data mining methods for knowledge discovery*. Boston: Kluwer.

Cortes, C. 1995. Prediction of generalization ability in learning machines. PhD thesis, Department of Computer Science, University of Rochester, Rochester NY 14627.

Cortes, C., and V. N. Vapnik. 1995. Support vector networks. *Machine Learning* 20: 273–297.

Cybenko, G. 1989. Approximation by superpositions of a sigmoidal function. *Mathematics of Control, Signals, and Systems* 2: 304–314.

Dahlquist, G., and A. Björck. 1974. *Numerical methods*. Englewood Cliffs, NJ: Prentice Hall.

Drucker, H., C.J.C. Burges, L. Kaufman, A. Smola, and V. N. Vapnik. 1997. Support vector regression machines. In *Advances in neural information processing systems*. Vol. 9, 155–161. Cambridge, MA: MIT Press.

Duda, R. O., and P. E. Hart. 1973. *Pattern classification and scene analysis*. New York: Wiley.

Eisenhart, C. 1962. Roger Joseph Boscovich and the combination of observations. In *Proc. Int. Symposium on R. J. Boskovic*, Belgrade-Zagreb-Ljubljana, 19–25.

Eykhoff, P. 1974. *System identification*. London: Wiley.

Fahlman, S. E. 1988. Fast learning variations on back-propagation: an empirical study. In *Proc. 1988 Connectionist Models Summer School*, ed. D. Touretzky, G. E. Hinton, and T. J. Sejnowski, 38–51. San Mateo, CA: Morgan Kaufmann.

Fletcher, R. 1987. *Practical methods of optimization*. 2d ed. New York: Wiley.

Fletcher, R., and C. M. Reeves. 1964. Function minimization by conjugate gradients. *Computer Journal* 7: 149–154.

Funahashi, K. 1989. On the approximate realization of continuous mappings by neural networks. *Neural Networks* 2 (3): 183–192.

Gajić, Z., and M. Lelić. 1996. *Modern control system engineering*. London: Prentice Hall Europe.

Gallant, S. I. 1993. *Neural network learning and expert systems*. Cambridge, MA: MIT Press.

Garcia, C. E., and M. Morari. 1982. Internal model control: 1. Unifying review and some new results. *Ind. Eng. Chem. Proc. Des. Dev.* 21: 308.

Geman, S., E. Bienenstock, and R. Doursat. 1992. Neural networks and the bias/variance dilemma. *Neural Computation* 4 (1): 1–58.

Girosi, F. 1992. Some extensions of radial basis functions and their applications in artificial intelligence. *Computers and Mathematics with Applications* 24 (12): 61–80.

———. 1997a. Introduction to regularization networks. http://www.ai.mit.edu/projects/cbcl/computational/rbf/rbf.html.

———. 1997b. An equivalence between sparse approximation and support vector machines. A.I. Memo No. 1606. MIT, Cambridge, MA 02139.

Girosi, F., M. Jones, and T. Poggio. 1996. Regularization theory and neural networks architectures. *Neural Computation* 7: 219–269.

Girosi, F., and T. Poggio. 1989. Representation properties of networks: Kolmogorov's theorem is irrelevant. *Neural Computation* 1 (4): 465–469.

———. 1990. Networks and the best approximation property. *Biological Cybernetics* 63: 169–176.

Gorman, R. P., and T. J. Sejnowski. 1988. Learned classification of sonar targets using a massively parallel network. *IEEE Trans. on Acoustics, Speech, and Signal Processing* 36: 1135–1140.

Graepel, T., R. Herbrich, B. Schölkopf, A. Smola, P. Bartlett, K.-R. Müller, K. Obermayer, and R. Williamson. 1999. Classification on proximity data with LP-machines. In *Proc. Ninth Int. Conference on Artificial Neural Networks*, Edinburgh.

Gunn, S. 1997. *Support vector machines for classification and regression*. ISIS Technical Report. University of Southampton, UK.

Hadamard, J. 1923. *Lectures on the Cauchy problem in linear partial differential equations*. New Haven, CT: Yale University Press.

Hadžić, I. 1999. SVMs by linear programming. PhD thesis (work in progress), University of Auckland, Auckland, NZ.

Hagan, M. T., H. B. Demuth, and M. Beale. 1996. *Neural network design*. Boston: PWS.

Hartman, E. J., J. D. Keeler, and J. M. Kowalski. 1990. Layered neural networks with Gaussian hidden units as universal approximations. *Neural Computation* 2 (2): 210–215.

Hassibi, B., and D. G. Stork. 1993. Second-order derivatives for network pruning: Optimal brain surgeon. In *Advances in neural information processing systems*, ed. S. J. Hanson, J. D. Cowan, and C. L. Giles. Vol. 5, 164–171. San Mateo, CA: Morgan Kaufmann.

Hayashi, Y., M. Sakata, and S. I. Gallant. 1990. Multi-layer versus single-layer neural networks and an application to reading hand-stamped characters. In *Proc. Int. Conference on Neural Networks*, Paris. 781–784.

Haykin, S. 1991. *Adaptive filter theory*. 2d ed. Englewood Cliffs, NJ: Prentice Hall.

———. 1994. *Neural networks: A comprehensive foundation*. New York: Macmillan.

Hertz, J., A. Krogh, and R. G. Palmer. 1991. *Introduction to the theory of neural computation*. Redwood City, CA: Addison-Wesley.

Ho, Y. C. 1999. The no-free-lunch theorem and the human-machine interface. *IEEE Control Systems Magazine* (June): 8–11.

Hornik, K., M. Stinchcombe, and H. White. 1989. Multilayer feedforward networks are universal approximators. *Neural Networks* 2 (5): 359–366.

Huang, W. Y., and R. P. Lipmann. 1988. Neural net and traditional classifiers. In *Neural information processing systems*, ed. D. Z. Anderson, 387–396. New York: American Institute of Physics.

Hunt, K. J., and D. Sbarbaro. 1991. Neural networks for nonlinear internal model control, *IEE Proc.-D* 138 (5): 431–438.

Hush, D. R., and B. G. Horne. 1993. Progress in supervised neural networks: What's new since Lippmann? *IEEE Signal Processing Magazine* 10: 8–39.

Jacobs, R. A., and M. I. Jordan. 1991. A modular connectionist architecture for learning piecewise control strategies. *Proc. American Control Conference*. TP1, 1597–1602.

Jacobs, R. A., M. I. Jordan, S. J. Nowlan, and G. E. Hinton. 1991. Adaptive mixtures of local experts. *Neural Computation* 3: 79–87.

Johnson, R. A., and D. W. Wichern. 1982. *Applied multivariate statistical analysis*. Englewood Cliffs, NJ: Prentice Hall.

Jordan, M. I. 1993. Connectionist models of cognitive processes. Lectures, Course 9.641, MIT, Cambridge, MA, 02139.

Jordan, M. I., and R. A. Jacobs. 1994. Hierarchical mixtures of experts and the EM algorithm. *Neural Computation* 6: 181–214.

Jordan M. I., and D. E. Rumelhart. 1992. Forward models: Supervised learning with a distal teacher. *Journal of Cognitive Science* 16: 307–354.

Jordan, M. I., and L. Xu. 1993. Convergence results for the EM approach to mixtures of experts architectures. A.I. Memo No. 1458. MIT, Cambridge, MA 02139.

Kahlert, J., and H. Frank. 1994. *Fuzzy-logik und fuzzy-control*. Wiesbaden: Vieweg Verlag (in German).

Karush, W. 1939. Minima of functions of several variables with inequalities as side constraints. Master's thesis, Department of Mathematics, University of Chicago, Chicago, IL 60637.

Kecman, V. 1988. *Foundations of automatic control*. Zagreb: Školska knjiga (in Serbocroatian).

———. 1993a. *Application of artificial neural networks for identification of system dynamics*. Technical Report No. TR 93-YUSA-01. Department of Mechanical Engineering, MIT, Cambridge, MA 02139.

———. 1993b. On the relation between the cost function and the output-layer neurons activation function. In *Proc. Fifteenth Salzhausen's Kolloquium der Automatisierungstechnik*, Institut für Automatisierung, Universität Bremen, Germany.

———. 1993c. EBP can work with hard limiters. In *Proc. Int. Conference on Artificial Neural Networks*, Amsterdam.

———. 1997. *Neural networks and fuzzy logic systems–based control*. Report No. 575. University of Auckland, Auckland, NZ.

Kecman, V., and B.-M. Pfeiffer. 1994. Exploiting the structural equivalence of learning fuzzy systems and radial basis function neural networks. In *Proc. Second European Congress on Intelligent Techniques and Soft Computing* (EUFIT-94), Aachen. Vol. 1, 58–66.

Kecman V., L. Vlačić, and R. Salman. 1999. Learning in and performance of the new neural network–based adaptive backthrough control structure. In *Proc. Fourteenth IFAC Triennial World Congress*, Beijing. Vol. K, 133–140. New York: Pergamon Press.

Kelley, E. J., Jr. 1958. An application of linear programming to curve fitting. *Journal of the Society for Industrial and Applied Mathematics* 6: 15–22.

Klir, G. J., and T. A. Folger. 1988. *Fuzzy sets, uncertainty, and information*. Englewood Cliffs, NJ: Prentice Hall.

Kolmogorov, A. N. 1957. On the representation of continuous functions of several variables by superposition of continuous functions of one variable and addition. *Doklady Akademiia Nauk SSSR* 114 (5): 953–956 (in Russian).

Kosko, B. 1997. *Fuzzy engineering*. Upper Saddle River, NJ: Prentice Hall.

Kuhn, H. W., and A. W. Tucker. 1951. Nonlinear programming. In *Proc. Second Berkeley Symposium on Mathematical Statistics and Probabilities*, 481–492. Berkeley: University of California Press.

Kurepa, S. 1990. *Finite dimensional vector spaces and applications*. 5th ed. Zagreb: Tehnička knjiga (in Serbocroatian).

Kurkova, V. 1991. Kolmogorov's theorem is relevant. *Neural Computation* 3 (4): 617–622.

———. 1992. Kolmogorov's theorem and multilayer neural networks. *Neural Networks* 5: 501–506.

Landau I. D. 1979. *Adaptive control*. New York: Marcel Dekker.

Le Cun, Y. 1985. Une procedure d'apprentissage pour reseau a seuil assymetrique. *Cognitiva* 85: 599–604.

Le Cun, Y., B. Boser, J. S. Denker, D. Henderson, R. E. Howard, W. Hubbard, and L. D. Jackel. 1989. Backpropagation applied to handwritten zip code recognition. *Neural Computation* 1 (4): 541–551.

Le Cun, Y., J. S. Denker, and S. A. Solla. 1990. Optimal brain damage. In *Advances in neural information processing systems*, ed. D. S. Touretzky. Vol. 2, 598–605. San Mateo, CA: Morgan Kaufmann.

Levenberg, K. 1944. A method for the solution of certain non-linear problems in least squares. *Quarterly Journal of Applied Mathematics* 2 (2): 164–168.

Löchner, J. 1997. *Identification of dynamic systems using neural networks and their optimisation through genetic algorithms*. Report No. 96-30. Department of Mechanical Engineering, University of Auckland, Auckland, NZ.

Madych, W. R., and S. A. Nelson. 1990. Multivariate interpolation and conditionally positive definite functions, *II Mathematics of Computation* 54 (189): 211–230.

Majetic D., and V. Kecman. 1991. Synthesis of PID controller by neural network. In *Proc. JUREMA 36*, Zagreb. Vol. 2, 1.55–1.57 (in Serbocroatian).

Mangasarian, O. L. 1965. Linear and nonlinear separation of patterns by linear programming. *Operations Research* 13: 444–452.

Marquardt, D. W. 1963. An algorithm for least-squares estimation of nonlinear parameters. *Journal of the Society of Industrial and Applied Mathematics* 11 (2): 431–441.

Maruyama, M., F. Girosi, and T. Poggio. 1992. A connection between GRBF and MLP. A.I. Memo No. 1291. MIT, Cambridge, MA 02139.

Mason, J. C., and P. C. Parks. 1995. Selection of neural network structures: Some approximation theory guidelines. In *Neural network applications in control*, ed. G. W. Irwin et al. Ch. 4. IEE Control Engineering Series 53. London.

Melsa, J. L., and D. L. Cohn. 1978. *Decision and estimation theory*. Tokyo: McGraw-Hill Kogakusha.

Mercer, J. 1909. Functions of positive and negative type and their connection with the theory of integral equations. *Philosophical Trans. Royal Society, London* A 209: 415–446.

Micchelli, C. A. 1986. Interpolation of scattered data: Distance matrices and conditionally positive definite functions. *Constructive Approximation* 2: 11–22.

Minsky, M. L., and S. A. Papert. 1969. *Perceptrons*. Cambridge, MA: MIT Press.

———. 1988. *Perceptrons*. Expanded ed. Cambridge, MA: MIT Press.

Moody, J., and C. J. Darken. 1989. Fast learning in networks of locally tuned processing units. *Neural Computation* 1 (2): 281–294.

Morozov, V. A. 1993. *Regularization methods for ill-posed problems*. Boca Raton, FL: CRC Press.

Müller, V. 1996. *Optimisation of a neural network with different genetic algorithms*. Report No. 95-30. Department of Mechanical Engineering, University of Auckland, Auckland, NZ.

Narendra K. S., and A. M. Annaswamy. 1989. *Stable adaptive systems*. Engelwood Cliffs, NJ: Prentice Hall.

Narendra, K. S., and K. Parthasarathy. 1990. Identification and control of dynamical systems using neural networks. *IEEE Trans. on Neural Networks* 1: 4–27.

Niyogi, P., and F. Girosi. 1994. On the relationship between generalization error, hypothesis complexity, and sample complexity for radial basis functions. A.I. Memo No. 1467. MIT, Cambridge, MA 02139. See also *Neural Computation* 8 (1996): 819–842.

Orr, M.J.L. 1996. *Regularization in the selection of radial basis function centers*. Report. Center of Cognitive Science, University of Edinburgh, Edinburgh, UK.

Osuna, E., R. Freund, and F. Girosi. 1997. Support vector machines: Training and applications. A.I. Memo No. 1602. MIT, Cambridge, MA 02139.

Park, J., and I. W. Sandberg. 1991. Universal approximation using radial basis function networks. *Neural Computation* 3 (2): 246–257.

Parker, D. B. 1985. *Learning logic*. Technical Report No. TR-47. MIT Center for Research in Computational Economics and Management Science, Cambridge, MA 02139.

Platt, J. C. 1998. *Sequential minimal optimization: A fast algorithm for training support vector machines*. Technical Report No. MSR-TR-98-14. Seattle, WA: Microsoft Research.

Plaut, D., S. Nowlan, and G. E. Hinton. 1986. *Experiments on learning by back propagation*. Technical Report CMU-CS-86-126. Department of Computer Science, Carnegie Mellon University, Pittsburgh, PA 15213.

Poggio, T., and F. Girosi. 1989a. A theory of networks for approximation and learning. A.I. Memo No. 1140. MIT, Cambridge, MA 02139.

———. 1989b. Networks and the best approximation property. A.I. Memo No. 1164. MIT, Cambridge, MA 02139.

———. 1990a. Regularization algorithms for learning that are equivalent to multilayer networks. *Science* 247: 978–982.

———. 1990b. Networks for approximation and learning. *Proc. IEEE* 78: 1481–1497.

———. 1990c. Extensions of a theory of networks for approximation and learning: Dimensionality reduction and clustering. A.I. Memo No. 1167. MIT, Cambridge, MA 02139.

———. 1993. Learning, approximation and networks. Lectures, Course 9.520, MIT, Cambridge, MA, 02139.

———. 1998. Learning, approximation, and networks. Lectures, Course 9.520 (Spring), MIT, Cambridge, MA 02139. http://www.ai.mit.edu/projects/cbcl/course9.520/.

Polyak, B. T. 1987. *Introduction to optimization.* New York: Optimization Software.

Pomerlau, D. A. 1989. ALVINN: An autonomous land vehicle in a neural network. In *Advances in neural information processing systems,* ed. D. Touretzky. Vol. 1. San Mateo, CA: Morgan Kaufmann.

Popčanovski, K., and O. Wohlfarth. 1995. Parameteroptimierung in neuronalen netzen (RBF-Netzen) mit hilfe von genetischen algorithmen. Studienarbeit Bericht. FH Heilbronn.

Powell, M.J.D. 1964. An efficient method for finding the minimum of a function of several variables without calculating derivatives. *Computer Journal* 7: 152–162.

———. 1987. Radial basis functions for multivariable interpolation: a review. In *Algorithms for approximation,* ed. J. C. Mason and M. G. Cox, 143–167. Oxford: Clarendon Press.

Psaltis, D., A. Sideris, and A. A. Yamamura. 1988. A multilayered neural network controller. *IEEE Control System Magazine* 8 (April): 17–21.

Rao, C. R., and S. K. Mitra. 1971. *Generalized inverse of matrices and its applications.* New York: Wiley.

Rice, J. R. 1964. *The approximation of functions.* Vol. 1. Reading, MA: Addison-Wesley.

Rommel, T. 1997. *Neural networks–based adaptive control.* Report No. 97-30. University of Auckland, Auckland, NZ.

Rosenblatt, F. 1962. *Principles of neurodynamics: Perceptrons and the theory of brain mechanisms.* Washington DC: Spartan.

Rumelhart, D. E., and J. L. McClelland, eds. 1986. *Parallel distributed processing: Explorations in the microstructure of cognition.* Vol. 1. Cambridge, MA: MIT Press.

Rumelhart, D. E., G. E. Hinton, and R. J. Williams. 1986. Learning internal representations by error propagation. In *Parallel distributed processing: Explorations in the microstructure of cognition,* ed. D. E. Rumelhart, J. L. McClelland, and the PDP Research Group. Vol. 1, *Foundations,* 318–362. Cambridge, MA: MIT Press. Reprinted in Anderson and Rosenfeld (1988).

Russo, A. P. 1991. Neural networks for sonar signal processing. Tutorial No. 8, IEEE Conference on Neural Networks for Ocean Engineering, Washington, DC.

Saerens, M., J.-M. Renders, and H. Bersini. 1996. Neurocontrollers based on backpropagation algorithm. In *IEEE press book on intelligent control systems,* ed. M. Gupta and N. Sinha. IEEE Computer Society Press.

Saerens, M., and A. Soquet. 1991. Neural controllers based on backpropagation algorithm. *IEE Proc.-F* 138 (1): 55–62.

Salman, R., and V. Kecman. 1998. Feedforward action based on adaptive backthrough control. In *Proc. IPENZ '98,* Auckland, NZ.

Sarapa, N. 1989. *Probability theory.* Zagreb: Školska knjiga (in Serbocroatian).

Schölkopf, B. 1996. Künstliches lernen. *Forum für Interdisziplinäre Forschung* 15: 93–117. (See also *Komplexe adaptive systeme,* ed. S. Bornholdt and P. H. Feindt. Dettelbach: Verlag Röll.

———. 1998. Support vector learning. Tutorial. http://www.first.gmd.de/~bs

Schölkopf B., C.J.C. Burges, and A. Smola, eds. 1999. *Advances in kernel methods—Support vector learning.* Cambridge, MA: MIT Press.

Schürmann, J. 1996. *Pattern classification.* New York: Wiley.

Sejnowski, T. J., and C. R. Rosenberg. 1987. Parallel networks that learn to pronounce English text. *Complex Systems* 1: 145–168.

Shah, F. F. 1998. Radial basis function approach to financial time series modelling. Master's thesis, University of Auckland, Auckland, NZ.

Sherstinsky, A. and R. W. Picard. 1996. On the efficiency of the orthogonal least squares training method for radial basis function networks. *IEEE Trans. on Neural Networks* 7 (1): 195–200.

Shynk, J. J. 1990. Analysis of the momentum LMS algorithm. *IEEE Trans. on Acoustics, Speech, and Signal Processing* ASSP-38: 2088–2098.

Simunic, D. 1996. *Application of fuzzy logic to a vehicle turning problem*. Project Report No. PME 96-66. University of Auckland, Auckland, NZ.

Smith, M. 1993. *Neural networks for statistical modeling*. New York: Van Nostrand Reinhold.

Smola A., T. T. Friess, and B. Schölkopf. 1998. *Semiparametric support vector and linear programming machines*. NeuroCOLT2 Technical Report Series, NC2-TR-1998-024.

Smola, A., and B. Schölkopf. 1997. *On a kernel-based method for pattern recognition, regression, approximation and operator inversion*. GMD Technical Report No. 1064. Berlin.

Soloway, D. I., and J. T. Bialasiewicz. 1992. Neural network modeling of nonlinear systems based on volterra series extension of a linear model. In *Proc. IEEE Int. Symposium on Intelligent Control*, Glasgow, UK, 7 12.

Stiefel, E. 1960. Note on Jordan elimination, linear programming, and Chebyshev approximation. *Numerische Mathematik* 2 (1).

Support Vector Machines Web Sites: http://svm.first.gmd.de/ and http://www.isis.ecs.soton.ac.uk/research/svm/.

Sveshnikov, A. A. 1965. *Problems in probability theory, mathematical statistics and theory of random functions*. Moscow: Nauka (in Russian).

Taylor, G. 1996. *Application of fuzzy logic to a vehicle turning problem*. Project Report No. PME 96-73. University of Auckland, Auckland, NZ.

Therrien, C. W. 1989. *Decision estimation and classification*. New York: Wiley.

Tikhonov, A. N. 1963. On solving incorrectly posed problems and method of regularization. *Doklady Akademii Nauk USSR* 151: 501–504 (in Russian).

———. 1973. On regularization of ill-posed problems. *Doklady Akademii Nauk USSR* 153: 49–52 (in Russian).

Tikhonov, A. N., and V. Y. Arsenin. 1977. *Solutions of ill-posed problems*. Washington, DC: V. H. Winston.

Tsypkin, J. Z. 1972. *Fundamentals of automatic control theory*. Moscow: Nauka (in Russian).

Vapnik, V. N. 1979. *Estimation of dependences based on empirical data*. Moscow: Nauka (in Russian). (English translation, New York: Springer-Verlag, 1982.)

———. 1995. *The nature of statistical learning theory*. New York: Springer-Verlag.

———. 1998. *Statistical learning theory*. New York: Wiley.

Vapnik, V. N., and A. Y. Chervonenkis. 1968. On the uniform convergence of relative frequencies of events to their probabilities. *Doklady Akademii Nauk USSR* 181 (4) (in Russian).

———. 1971. On the uniform convergence of relative frequencies of events to their probabilities. *Theory of probability and its applications* 16 (2): 264–280.

———. 1974. *Theory of pattern recognition*. Moscow: Nauka (in Russian), (German translation: W. Wapnik and A. Tscherwonenkis. *Theorie der Zeichenerkennung*. Berlin: Akademie-Verlag, 1979.)

———. 1989. The necessary and sufficient conditions for the consistency of the method of empirical minimization. In *Yearbook of the Academy of Sciences of the USSR on recognition, classification, and forecasting*. Vol. 2, 217–249. Moscow: Nauka (in Russian). (English translation: *Pattern Recognition and Image Analysis* 1 (1991): 284–305).

Vapnik, V. N., S. Golowich, and A. Smola. 1997. Support vector method for function approximation, regression estimation, and signal processing. In *Advances in neural information processing systems*. Vol. 9. Cambridge, MA: MIT Press.

Walsh, G. R. 1975. *Methods of optimization.* London: Wiley.

Wang, C. B. 1998. Radial basis function networks for motion synthesis in computer graphics. Master's thesis, University of Auckland, Auckland, NZ.

Werbos, P. J. 1974. Beyond regression: New tools for prediction and analysis in the behavioral sciences. Ph.D. thesis, Harvard University, Cambridge, MA 02138.

Weston, J., A. Gammerman, M. O. Stitson, V. N. Vapnik, V. Vovk, and C. Watkins. 1999. Support vector density estimation. In *Advances in kernel methods—Support vector learning*, ed. B. Schölkopf, C.J.C. Burges, and A. Smola, 307–326. Cambridge, MA: MIT Press.

White, H. 1990. Connectionist nonparametric regression: Multilayer feedforward networks can learn arbitrary mappings. *Neural Networks* 3 (5): 535–549.

Widrow, B., and M. E. Hoff. Jr. 1960. Adaptive switching circuits. In *IRE Western Electric Show and Convention Record*. Pt. 4, 96–104. Reprinted in Anderson and Rosenfeld (1988).

Widrow, B., and M. A. Lehr. 1990. Thirty years of adaptive neural networks: Perceptron, madaline, and backpropagation. *Proc. IEEE* 78 (9): 1415–1442.

Widrow, B., and S. D. Stearns. 1985. *Adaptive signal processing.* Englewood Cliffs, NJ: Prentice Hall.

Widrow, B., and E., Walach. 1996. *Adaptive inverse control.* Upper Saddle River, NJ: Prentice Hall.

Wismer, D. A., and R. Chattergy. 1976. *Introduction to nonlinear optimization.* New York: North-Holland.

Zadeh, L. A. 1965. Fuzzy sets. *Information and Control* 8: 338–353.

———. 1973. Outline of a new approach to the analysis of complex systems and decision processes. *IEEE Trans. on Systems, Man, and Cybernetics* SMC-3: 28–44.

———. 1994. Soft computing and fuzzy logic. *IEEE Software* (November): 48–56.

Zhang, Q. H., and J.-J. Fuchs. 1999. Building neural networks through linear programming. In *Proc. Fourteenth IFAC Triennial World Congress*, Beijing. Vol K, 127–132. New York: Pergamon Press.

Zimmermann, H. J. 1991. *Fuzzy set theory and its applications.* 2d ed. Boston: Kluwer.

Zurada, J. M. 1992. *Introduction to artificial neural systems.* St. Paul, MN: West Publishing.

Index

Printed in the United States
By Bookmasters